THE
WORLD DISPLAYED

IN ITS

HISTORY AND GEOGRAPHY

THE
WORLD DISPLAYED

IN ITS

HISTORY AND GEOGRAPHY

EMBRACING

A HISTORY OF THE WORLD

FROM THE

CREATION TO THE PRESENT DAY

ROYAL ROBBINS

GYAN

Published by

GYAN

Gyan Publishing House
5, Ansari Road
Daryaganj, New Delhi-110002
Phone: 011-47034999, 9811692060
E-mail: books@gyanbooks.com

Distribution Network
gyanbooks.com
India, USA, Canada, UK, Australia

ISBN: 978-93-7097-192-9 (PB)

First Published, 1833

2nd Impression 2025

Printed at: Gyan Press, Delhi.

THE WORLD DISPLAYED IN ITS HISTORY AND GEOGRAPHY
Author ROYAL ROBBINS

THE

WORLD DISPLAYED,

IN ITS

HISTORY AND GEOGRAPHY;

EMBRACING

A HISTORY OF THE WORLD,

FROM THE

CREATION TO THE PRESENT DAY.

WITH GENERAL VIEWS OF THE POLITICS, RELIGION, MILITARY AND NAVAL AFFAIRS, ARTS, LITERATURE, MANNERS, CUSTOMS, AND SOCIETY, OF ANCIENT AS WELL AS MODERN NATIONS.

BY THE REV. ROYAL ROBBINS.

TO WHICH IS ADDED,

AN OUTLINE OF MODERN GEOGRAPHY

TWO VOLUMES IN ONE.

VOL. I.

New-York:
PUBLISHED BY H. SAVAGE.

1833.

PUBLISHERS' NOTICE.

THE Volume here offered to the public, had its origin in the belief, that a Historical and Geographical View of the World, united in one work, and constructed on the plan here adopted, would be an acceptable addition to the already multiplied stock of books for general reading. The plan of the work is original, and is believed to offer many advantages. It divides Ancient and Modern History into twenty distinct periods, and then gives a detail of the events during each of them. At the end of every period is a detailed biography of many eminent individuals who flourished during the same, and a sketch is given of the progress of the arts, of science, and of literature. Hence a clear delineation of the advancement of human society, and its various revolutions, is exhibited; and the reader can easily trace not only the particular history of each country and people, but can keep in view, at the same time, the grand movements of the nations, regarded as one common family.

In order to perfect the plan originally contemplated by the author, the volume has been increased far beyond what was at first anticipated—nearly one hundred pages have been added; an advance which, it is believed, will be gratifying to the patrons of the work, and sufficiently attest the wish of the publishers to make it in every way satisfactory to them.

The System of Modern Geography is of course a condensed one—but it will be found fully adequate to the purposes for which it is attached to the volume.

On the whole, as no expense has been spared, and as the Author, whose reputation as a historical writer is of the first order, has bestowed unwearied pains upon the work, we commit the volume to the public, with much confidence that it will be received with favour.

CONTENTS.

Period VII.

Period VIII.

Period IX.

Period X.

GENERAL VIEWS.

INTRODUCTION.

1. The term History comprehends a record of all the remarkable transactions which have taken place among the human family. It is the collected result of individual experience in every age and nation; and is, consequently, a source of practical wisdom to legislators and rulers, and of profitable reflection to private persons.

The benefits to be expected from history deserve a few remarks in detail. When it is written with a proper spirit, and in strict agreement with facts, there is scarcely any branch of letters so well calculated to furnish an agreeable relaxation to the student; to improve his understanding and enlarge his stores of useful knowledge; or, in general, to subserve the cause of morality and religion in human society.

From the infinite variety of aspects in which history presents the dealings of Providence, and from the immense number of characters and incidents which it brings into view, it becomes a source of perpetual interest and enjoyment. The novelist, with all the license he possesses to imagine such physical and moral combinations as he pleases, cannot clothe his subject with half the attractions which a reflecting mind attaches to true narrative.

The view of past ages fills the mind with a sublime and pleasing melancholy. We dwell with deep and tender emotion on the actions, sufferings, and changes of those who were "bone of our bones, and flesh of our flesh"—we regret that some of them should ever have lived to disorder the world with their crimes, and that others should have died, to leave it without the benefit of their continued active labours.

History improves our understanding, and enlarges our stores of useful knowledge, by bringing to our assistance the experience of others—the experience of all time; by making us acquainted with human nature; by delivering the mind from bigotry and prejudice—from narrow and sectional feelings; by opening to us the springs of human affairs, and the causes of the rise, greatness, decline, and fall of empires.

There is something in the picture of the generations before us, of their achievements and projects; of their manners, pursuits, and attainments; of their mode of thinking and acting; of their religion, government, and literature; which, going beyond the gratification of curiosity, or storing the mind with mere ideas, teaches us wisdom, by the comparison of their situation with our own, and by a great variety of interesting reflections naturally suggested to our thoughts.

From the whole that history presents us, we deduce conclusions that have an important bearing on human happiness and virtue. This we consider as the most signal benefit derivable from the record of past ages. It gives us, in connexion with revelation, which furnishes a most interesting portion of the world's history, a correct estimate of life and of human nature in all its variety. It shows us how man has acted according to his own pleasure, whether uprightly or wickedly, and, at the same time, how God has conducted the train of events to bring about the purposes of His wisdom and grace.

Speaking in the way of aphorism, history is a record of what God has done, and of what he has either enabled or suffered man to do, on the stage of the world. Even, therefore, without the direct comments of the writer, which nevertheless are due, we can derive important instruction from it; and can hardly help being impressed with the grandeur or solemnity of the movements of Providence, in the destiny of nations.

In short, it is here that we are supplied with the most rational entertainment, and our faculties of imagination, memory, reason, and judgment, are put to a most agreeable and salutary exercise. It is here we learn political science and philosophy; we ascertain the necessity of government, the blessings of civilization, the progress of reason and society; and especially it is here we see

"a God employed
In all the good and ill that chequer life,"

and in all the events that have a bearing on the interests of true religion.

2. History is derived to us from various sources, differing in degrees of authenticity, but in general illustrating and confirming one another. The principal sources are the narratives of writers, whose knowledge of the events they describe may have been acquired by personal observation; inspection of public documents; poetic legends; and oral tradition. In addition to these, there are several other sources that are highly valuable, supplying the want of direct and regular narrative, such as monuments, ruins, coins, &c.

Monuments on the surface of the ground, such as pillars and heaps of stone or earth, since they are intended to perpetuate the knowledge of important events, throw some light on the proper subjects of history.

Ruins indicate the existence of arts and wisdom in ancient times, which are still astonishing to the civilized world. They afford a knowledge of antiquity, which description, in many cases, could never supply. Such are the ruins that exist in Egypt, the Holy Land, Greece, and Italy, in their cities, temples, aqueducts, columns, &c.

Coins and medals offer very valuable means of historical information. They have often been examined and studied for that purpose, are abundant, and some of them possess considerable antiquity. The oldest known, belong to the 5th century B. C.

Inscriptions on marble may be mentioned as another source of history. The Arundelian marbles, so called from the earl of Arundel, who brought them from Greece into England, are the most celebrated collection of marbles bearing inscriptions, and thus communicating knowledge of antiquity. The Chronicle of Paros is the most important of these inscriptions, as it contains the chronology of Athens, from the time of Cecrops 1582, commonly put 1556 B. C., to 264 B. C.

ANCIENT HISTORY.

GENERAL DIVISION.

History may be divided into two great parts, viz. Ancient and Modern. Ancient History includes a period of 4004 years, and extends from the Creation of the World to the Nativity of Jesus Christ. Modern History includes a period of 1829 years, and extends from the Nativity of Jesus Christ, to the present time.

Observations. Ancient History, which is the subject of this volume, comprehending an account of the Creation, and the grand events connected with it; of the fall of man; of the deluge; of the origin of nations; and of the principles, achievements, manners, habits, religion, learning, &c. of the early race of mortals, is equally curious and instructive.

Period I. will extend from the Creation of the World, 4004 years, B. C., to the Deluge, 2348 years B. C. This is the Antediluvian Period.

Period II. will extend from the Deluge, 2348 years B. C., to the Calling of Abraham, 1921 years B. C. This is the period of the Confusion of Languages.

Period III. will extend from the Calling of Abraham, 1921 years B. C., to the Departure of the Israelites from Egypt, 1491 years B. C. This is the period of Egyptian Bondage.

Period IV. will extend from the Departure of the Israelites from Egypt, 1491 years B. C., to the Dedication of Solomon's Temple, 1004 years B. C. This is the period of the Trojan War.

Period V. will extend from the Dedication of Solomon's Temple, 1004 years B. C., to the Founding of Rome, 752 years B. C. This is the period of Homer.

Period VI. will extend from the Founding of Rome, 752 years B. C., to the Battle of Marathon, 490 years B. C. This is the period of Roman Kings.

Period VII. will extend from the Battle of Marathon, 490 years B. C., to the Birth of Alexander, 356 years B. C. This is the period of Grecian Glory.

Period VIII. will extend from the Birth of Alexander, 356 years B. C., to the Destruction of Carthage, 146 years B. C. This is the period of Roman Military Renown.

Period IX. will extend from the Destruction of Carthage, 146 years B. C., to the First Campaign of Julius Cæsar, 80 years B. C. This is the period of the Civil War between Marius and Sylla.

Period X. will extend from the First Campaign of Julius Cæsar, 80 years B. C., to the Nativity of Jesus Christ, and the Commencement of the Christian Era. This is the period of Roman Literature.

Observations. The characteristic, or title of each of these periods, is derived from some prominent event, or striking peculiarity by which it is marked. Thus, for instance, during the last period but one, Rome, which was beginning to be mistress of the world, was for a long time disturbed by the contentions of rival chiefs. The period, therefore, is denominated that of the Civil War between Marius and Sylla, as marking the most important event in the history of the world during that time. Thus, also, during the last, or 10th period, literature greatly flourished among the Romans, under the auspices of Augustus. It is, therefore, designated as the period of Roman literature, as being the most striking peculiarity of that era, among the nations. In the same manner, also, the characteristics of all the others are derived.

PERIOD I.

The Antediluvian Period, extending from the Creation of the World, 4004 *years B. C. to the deluge,* 2348 *years B. C.*

The Bible affords the only authentic history of the first ages of the world. The events which it relates of those ages, are confirmed by the *appearances of nature*, and by *legendary tradition.*

Section 1. All human records agree that men and empires first appeared in the East. There, those demigods and heroes, who are the subjects of heathen fable, are represented as having lived and acted. When, therefore, the Bible points to that quarter of the globe, as the cradle of nations and of the arts, and as the theatre of the most wonderful events, it only coincides with the general belief of mankind on this subject.

The account contained in that sacred book respecting the creation of the world, or the beginning of time, is equally worthy of credit. This, of course, is the first grand event which history presents to us. The cosmogonies of nations, that is, the schemes they have adopted respecting the formation of the world, vary very much from one another, and most of them are manifestly absurd and incredible. That of the Hebrews, which constitutes the scriptural account, is the only one that deserves implicit belief.

2. According to this account, it appears that about 5829 years ago, God called the visible universe into being, by the word of his power; that a determinate length of time was occupied in the work, the various portions of the world being produced on six successive days; that man was created on the last day of those six, and constituted the head of all the animal tribes; that his happiness and increase were provided for by the institution of marriage, which was soon announced; that God saw that all his work was good; and that he rested on the seventh day, hallowing it, as a day to be devoted to religious solemnittes.

§ The earth, immediately subsequent to its creation, was a fluid, dark, and shapeless mass of matter. The first thing done to bring it into a perfect state, was the creation of light. Then the firmament expanded, to divide the upper from the lower waters.

Succeeding this, the assembled waters retired to their destined bed; and, at length, the dry land was seen, crowned with a rich profusion of herbage, fruits, and flowers. These great occurrences occupied the first three days.

The following day was devoted to an illumination of the earth. The heavens were accordingly adorned with myriads of stars; and the greater luminaries were so disposed, as to distinguish between day and night, and to divide the seasons of the year.

On the fifth and sixth days, the waters were replenished with fish, the air was filled with birds, the meadows were stocked with cattle, and every part of the earth's surface was inhabited by its appropriate tribes.

The last work of the sixth day was the creation of man. This was the crowning work of the whole. God formed him of the dust of the ground, breathed into his body the breath of life, or immortality, and hence man became a living soul. Woman was also formed, out of the side of the man, who was cast into a deep sleep for that purpose.

After the creation of this helper for man, she was given to the latter, and the sacred institution of marriage was ordained by the Creator himself. From this pair sprang all the various nations of mankind.

As a matter of curiosity, and forming a perfect contrast to the rational account of the Scriptures, we will mention a few theories of philosophers and others, on the formation of the universe.

It was the opinion of Zenophanes, Strabo, and others, that the earth, and the whole system of the universe, was the Deity himself Pythagoras inculcated the famous numerical system of the monad dyad, and triad; and, by means of his sacred quaternary, elucidated the formation of the world, and the secrets of nature.

Other philosophers adhered to the mathematical system of squares and triangles; the cube, the pyramid, and the sphere, &c. While others maintained the great elementary theory, which refers the construction of our globe, and all it contains, to the combinations of the four material elements, air, earth, fire, and water, with the assistance of a fifth, an immaterial and vivifying principle.

It is recorded by the Brahmins, in the pages of their inspired Shastah, that the angel Bistnoo, transforming himself into a great boar, plunged into the watery abyss, and brought up the earth on his tusks. Then issued from him a mighty tortoise and snake; and Bistnoo placed the snake erect upon the back of the tortoise, and he placed the earth upon the head of the snake.

The negroes of Congo affirm that the world was made by the hands of angels, excepting their own country, which the Supreme Being constructed himself; that he took great pains with the inhabitants, and made them very black and beautiful; and when he had finished the first man, he was well pleased with him, and smoothed him over the face; and hence his nose, and the noses of all his descendants, became flat.

Buffon, a modern infidel philosopher, conjectures that this earth was originally a globe of liquid fire, struck from the body of the sun, by means of a comet, as a spark is produced by the collision of flint and steel; that at first it was surrounded by gross vapors, which, cooling and condensing in process of time, constituted, according to their densities, earth, water, and air; which gradually arranged themselves according to their respective gravities, round the burning mass that formed their centre.

Darwin, an infidel also, in accounting for the origin of the world, supposes that the mass of chaos suddenly exploded, like a barrel of gunpowder, and in that act exploded the sun, which, in its flight, by a similar convulsion, exploded the earth, which in like manner exploded the moon; and thus, by a chain of explosions, the whole solar system was produced, and set in regular motion.

3. Adam and Eve, the names of the first human pair, were placed by the Deity, immediately subsequent to their creation, in the garden of Eden, with instructions to keep and dress it. They were allowed the free use of all the fruit of the garden, with a single reservation, which was designed as a trial of their obedience. The penalty of death was threatened if they should transgress the command of their Maker. Created pure and innocent, and placed in a state of unalloyed happiness, they had every inducement to do well.

§ Adam and Eve seem to have been created without the garden, and immediately afterwards brought into it. It is evident that Eden was east of Canaan, or of the wilderness where Moses wrote the sacred history. But the precise spot cannot now be ascertained.

The most extravagant opinions have been entertained on this subject; and not only the four quarters of the globe, but even the air and the moon, have been conjectured to include this delightful abode. Following the Bible as nearly as we are able, and judging from the well known names of the Hiddekel, or Tigris, and the Euphrates, we may determine, with some probability, that the Garden of Eden was situated in or near Mesopotamia, probably Diarbec, a part of that country.

It is clear that Moses intended to give an intelligible description of the situation of Eden to his countrymen, who might know it exactly, though we cannot; and it is clear, also, that, though the face of the country may have been greatly changed by means of the deluge, the Tigris and Euphrates continued nearly the same course after that event as before.

The tree, the fruit of which Adam was forbidden to eat, is called the tree of the knowledge of good and evil, which intimates that, by abstaining from this fruit, the knowledge of good would be enjoyed, but, by eating it, the knowledge of evil would be fatally introduced.

4. The innocence and felicity of the first pair were of very short duration. They violated, with daring impiety, the sole command of their Maker. The precise time of this transaction cannot be determined; but it was probably only a few days after their creation.

The woman, being deceived by the subtlety of Satan, in the form of a serpent, was the first in transgression; and, by her means, Adam also sinned. A sense of guilt and misery unknown before, then pervaded their bosoms; though they were preserved from despair by the promise of a Saviour.

§ The greatness of the sin of our first parents is no less evident than the subtlety of the Tempter. In their sin was involved almost every crime—ingratitude, sensuality, ambition, unbelief, distrust, malignity, pride, insubordination.

The effect was decisive. The face of creation was altered. "Nature ...... gave signs that all was lost." Death was introduced into the system, and our first parents, from that moment, became liable to dissolution, with all their posterity. The seeds of death were then planted in their frame, and the moral qualities of their souls became wholly corrupt and sinful.

The disclosure of their crime was in the highest degree distressing to the guilty pair. God called them to account, and his awful frown and displeasure, chilled and penetrated their souls. The ground was cursed for their sakes, and a great variety of evils was entailed upon them.

The serpent, who was the instrument of the crime, received his doom, in connexion with the promise of a deliverer on the part of man, who had been so fatally beset and overcome. The seed of the woman was eventually to bruise the Serpent's head—a declaration referable, in its full extent, only to Jesus Christ, the Saviour of mankind. The immediate expulsion of Adam and Eve from paradise, was the natural conclusion of this dreadful and calamitous scene, after their Maker had first mercifully provided them with coats of skin, to cover their nakedness. Cherubims, and a flaming sword, which turned every way, placed at the east of the garden, prevented all access to the once happy abode, particularly to the tree of life.

5. In the first year of the world, 4004 years B. C. was born Cain, the first begotten of the human family. The succeeding year. Abel was born. These brothers not only followed different occupations, but possessed very different characters. The bitter fruits of the apostacy appeared at length in the murder of the one by the other.

On an occasion of presenting an offering unto God, Cain, who was a husbandman, brought of the fruit of the ground; Abel, who was a shepherd, brought of the firstlings of his flock. The offerers, being dissimilar in character, and their offerings having a dissimilar significancy, were not alike accepted of Jehovah. Cain and his offering were rejected. This circumstance excited the indignation of Cain, who, taking his opportunity when they were alone in the field, rose up against his brother and slew him.

On account of his crime, Cain was forthwith punished by Jehovah. He was called to a solemn reckoning, and, hearing with anguish his doom pronounced, "a fugitive and a vagabond shalt thou be in the earth," he went out from the presence of the Lord, and dwelt in the land of Nod, on the east of Eden.

He, however, built a city, at length, and his family and descendants became famous as inventors of useful and ingenious arts, though it does not appear that any of them were pious, and enjoyed the divine favour.

§ The murder of Abel occurred, it is generally supposed, but a short time before the birth of Seth, or about 130 years after the creation. As Adam and Eve, in the mean time, must have had other children, the human family was no doubt considerably multiplied during 130 years. Hence the events that are recorded by Moses, in connexion with the murder of Abel, are easily accounted for, without supposing more than one human pair, from whom all the inhabitants then on the earth were descended.

After the death of Abel, Adam and Eve had many other children, the eldest of the sons was named Seth, and his descendants, from their piety, were styled "the children of God," in opposition to the descendants of Cain, who were styled "the children of men." These at length mingled together, and thus prepared the way for the universal wickedness that afterwards prevailed.

6. After a short account of Cain and his family, the sacred historian informs us respecting "the generations of Adam;" and recording the births of **Enos**, Cainan, Mahalaleel, and Jared, he presents us with a brief but interesting history of Enoch. Being eminently pious, he is said to have walked with God, for the space of 300 years, and at the expiration of that time, to have been taken up to heaven, without passing through the scene of death.

The sacred genealogy is carried on to the time of Noah and his sons, and the date of the life of each one of the patriarchs is minutely given.

§ As Adam lived 930 years, he must have beheld a numerous posterity, and been conversant with many who survived till near the time of the deluge. Doubtless he must have been greatly affected, in view of the wickedness which so soon began to spread over the earth, and which he had been the instrument of introducing.

The place of his sepulchre is not mentioned in scripture; yet various conjectures (and they are mere conjectures) have been formed on the subject. St. Jerome stations his remains in the cave of Machpelah; and the generality of the primitive fathers suppose him to have been buried on Mount Calvary, in the very spot whereon Christ, the second Adam, shed his blood for mankind.

The descendants of Seth, at first continuing pure and uncorrupted, at length, by intermarriages with the family of Cain, became, with the rest of mankind, exceedingly degenerate. From these intermarriages sprang the giants of those times, men of extraordinary strength and stature, and, perhaps, of more extraordinary wickedness. These became "men of renown," heroes, conquerors, and chieftains.

7. The Deity, justly provoked by the enormous degeneracy of his creatures, determined to destroy, by a universal deluge, the race of man, together with the whole animal creation, except a very small remnant who were to restock the earth after that catastrophe.

One hundred and twenty years, however, did he mercifully afford to the children of men, as a space for repentance, during which time, Noah, "a preacher of righteousness," endeavoured to reclaim them from their wickedness, and warned them of their doom. His zeal and labours seem to have produced no effect. The earth became at length filled with violence.

From the tremendous sentence which God had pronounced Noah and his family were excepted, he having "found grace in the eyes of the Lord." Connected with the intimation which Noah had received concerning the approaching deluge, were several particular instructions, relative to his deliverance.

This was to be accomplished by means of a large vessel called the ark, which he built during the intervening period, agreeably to the divine directions.

§ The ark was built of gopher wood, which some suppose to be the cypress tree. Its form was that of an oblong square, with a flat bottom and a sloping roof, elevated one cubit in the middle. It consisted of three stories, each of which, excluding the thickness of the floors, might be eighteen feet high, and was divided into separate apartments. It was pitched within and without, to keep it tight, and lighted from the upper part. It was, probably, well supplied with air; and, though it had neither sails nor rudder it was well contrived for lying steadily on the surface of the water

With this means of safety, Noah awaited the destruction which was fast coming upon the world.

Distinguished characters in Period I.

1. Adam, the first of the human race.
2. Eve, the first woman.
3. Cain, the earliest born of mankind, and first murderer.
4. Jubal, the first musician.
5. Tubal-cain, the earliest instructer in the mechanic arts
6. Enoch, translated to heaven on account of his piety.
7. Methuselah, the oldest man that has ever lived, being 969 years old when he died.

§ 1. Adam was created by the Almighty from the dust of the earth, on the 6th day of the creation. His Maker, it is said in Scripture, "breathed into his nostrils the breath of life; and man became a living soul." He was thus endued with an immortal principle, and being placed in a probationary state, not only his own character, but the character of his posterity, was to be affected by his conduct.

As he came from the hands of his Maker, he was pure, holy, and happy; and he had every motive to persuade him to continued rectitude of conduct. His outward circumstances also were favourable for this end. He was placed in a delightful garden, the easy tillage of which constituted his employment. God imposed upon him but one test of obedience, and that was abstinence in regard to eating the fruit of a certain tree in the garden.

Persuaded by Eve, who, having been tempted by Satan, had previously transgressed, he partook of the forbidden food, and thus death entered into the world, and "all our wo." His conduct involved the greatest impiety, and the consequences have been dreadful in time, and will be so throughout eternity, in regard to multitudes of his offspring, who have imitated him in his disobedience, and repented not.

It is highly probable that he, together with the woman, embraced an offered Saviour, immediately made known, both having repented of their sin. He lived many years afterwards, having begot sons and daughters, and died at the advanced age of 930 years. For further particulars, see Genesis, 2d, 3d, and 4th chapters.

2. Eve was created "an help meet" for Adam, having been formed, by the Creator, from one of the ribs of Adam, which was taken from him in a deep sleep. Thus she became "bone of his bones, and flesh of his flesh," and was given to him as his wife.

She proved to be first "in the transgression." Satan, a fallen spirit, assuming the form of a serpent, and, through the organs of that animal, exerting the powers of speech, accosted her when alone, and interrogated her respecting the forbidden tree. Taking her by surprise, and securing her attention and good will, he at length persuaded her to disobey the express command of God.

she partook of the fruit; "and gave also unto her husband with her, and he did eat." This event, in regard to the first human pair, is supposed to have taken place very soon, if not immediately after they were placed in the garden. Eve, as a particular punishment to be inflicted upon her, was doomed in sorrow to bring forth children, and to be subject to her husband.

3. Cain rendered himself famous by his wickedness. In an unprovoked manner he murdered his brother Abel, and thus was the first who committed a crime which has ever been considered as the most atrocious that man commits.

God directly punished him by an awful malediction; and by causing him to become a fugitive and a vagabond in the earth. Going out "from the presence of the Lord," he dwelt in the land of Nod, on the east of Eden. He at length built a city, and called it Enoch, after the name of his son.

Nothing is recorded of the time and manner of his death. He was most probably a person of great energy and enterprise, as has often been the fact with the wicked ones of the earth.

4. Jubal is spoken of in Scripture as "the father of all such as handle the harp and organ," as his brother Jabal is mentioned as "the father of such as dwell in tents." From all accounts, both sacred and profane, music must have been early known among mankind, and its performers must have been among the earliest civilizers of the world.

5. Tubal-Cain is called "an instructer of every artificer in brass and iron." Probably he was so called from his having discovered the art of working in these metals; the most useful of the mechanic arts, and lying at the foundation of all of them.

6. Enoch lived 65 years before he begat Methuselah. He "walked with God after he begat Methuselah 300 years, and begat sons and daughters. And all the days of Enoch were 365 years. And Enoch walked with God, and he was not, for God took him." Such is the simple and sublime record of scripture respecting a good man. It is an infinitely more precious memorial than the splendid marble monument, or the ever-during pyramid.

7. Methuselah is not known to have been remarkable for any thing except his age. He must have lived to the very year of the flood. The circumstance of the longevity of the antediluvians, was extremely favourable to the communication of knowledge, by tradition.

PERIOD II.

The Period of the Confusion of Languages, extending from the Deluge, 2348 *years* B. C. *to the calling of Abraham,* 1921 *years* B. C.

§ It may be observed here, that this period, in profane history, and even two or three others succeeding it, are what is termed *fabulous.* The events recorded are to be admitted with a great degree of caution, except so far as Scripture incidentally throws its light upon them. And it is well known, also, that there is a portion of the early history of almost every nation. which is but little entitled to credit. We shall adduce the common accounts, and when necessary, shall endeavour to distinguish between the probable and improbable events.

SECTION 1. At the appointed time, God brought the waters of the flood upon all the earth. For this purpose, he broke up the fountains of the great deep, and opened the windows of heaven. During forty days and forty nights, without intermission, the waters were thus poured upon the surface of the globe.

As the ark was completed, Noah, being 600 years old, went into it, together with his wife, his three sons, and their wives, taking with him all kinds of beasts, birds, and reptiles, by pairs, and by sevens, agreeably to the divine direction.

According to the antediluvian computation, Noah remained in the ark one year and ten days; and on coming out, he built an altar, and offered a sacrifice to the Lord, who blessed Noah and his sons. They settled in the vicinity of mount Ararat, in Armenia.

§ The waters increased gradually during the space of five months, when they rose to the elevation of 27 feet above the summits of the highest mountains. Men, beasts, birds, and reptiles, thus being deprived of the means of safety, all perished.

The purpose of God being effected, he caused a wind to pass over the earth, in consequence of which the waters began to subside. The ark rested on the mountains of Ararat, on the 17th day of the 7th month, or the 6th of May.

The waters continuing several months afterwards, it was not until the 27th of the 2d month, or the 18th of December, that the inmates of the ark came forth in pursuance of the divine command.

2. The truth of the Bible respecting the deluge, is strikingly confirmed by the general voice of mankind, and by the physical structure and appearance of the earth's surface.

§ The Chaldeans, Egyptians, Syrians, Indians, Chinese, Greeks, and other nations, all had some traditions respecting the deluge. Not to mention any that have been yet published, the author of this outline would state a fact once delivered to him by an intelligent adventurer, his countryman.

Residing some time among the natives of the North West Coast of America, he fell into conversation with one of them around the fire of his wigwam, on various topics. Among other things, the Indian inquired of him, whether his people knew any thing concerning a great flood that had once taken place.

The stranger resident affecting surprise, with a view to learn what notion the natives had on the subject, asked his inquirer, how long ago it happened. The Indian immediately scooping up a handful of ashes that lay before him, promptly replied, "as many moons as there are ashes here."

In agreement with the universal voice of tradition, the surface of the earth, in various respects, indicates the occurrence of such a catastrophe. Its broken state, the disposition of its strata, and the remains of marine productions on the tops of the highest mountains, are no doubtful evidence on this subject.

3. After the deliverance of Noah and his family from the flood, God established a gracious covenant with him, which is recorded at length in the 9th chapter of Genesis. Among other things, he made a grant of flesh as food for mankind, and he engaged no more to destroy the earth with a flood, in confirmation of which he set his bow in the cloud.

4. Not long after this period, Noah, who had engaged in the pursuits of husbandry, having been intoxicated by the juice of the grape, was discovered in this disgraceful situation by his youngest son Ham, who, with indecent levity, informed his brethren of the circumstance. The latter, however, treated their father with the highest degree of filial decorum.

This conduct procured for them the blessing of Noah, while that of Ham subjected him, in his son Canaan, to a dreadful curse.

§ Noah, we are informed by the sacred historian, lived 350 years after the deluge, so that his entire age was 950 years. The Orientals have a tradition that he was buried in Mesopotamia, where they show his sepulchre, in a castle near Dair Abunah, or the "monastery of our father."

5. The three sons of Noah were, of course, the first founders of nations. They peopled the several quarters of the globe, Shem, the east and south of Asia; Ham, Syria, Arabia, and Africa; Japheth, the north and west of Asia, and also Europe.

§ From the immediate descendants of Shem were derived the Elamites or Persians, the Assyrians, and the Lydians. By Joktan, the fourth in descent from Shem, the uttermost parts of the east were peopled, and perhaps America also, where, it is said, some traces of his name yet remain.

Joktan had 13 sons, and scripture says that the dwelling of Joktan's posterity "was from Mesha, as thou goest up to Sephar, a mount in the East."

From the sons of Ham, who is supposed to be the Chronos of the Greeks, were descended the Ethiopians, the Babylonians, the Egyptians, the Colchians, the Philistines, the Lybians, the Canaanites, Sidonians, and the Phœnicians.

From the sons of Japheth were descended the Cimbri, the Gauls, the Germans, the Scythians, the Tartars, the Medes, the Ionians, the Iberians, the Muscovites, and the Thracians. From their sons were derived other particular tribes, whose names need not here be rehearsed.

6. During 101 years after the flood, i. e. till the year 2247 B. C. all the descendants of Noah spoke but one language. The occasion of a diversity of tongues in the world, and of the origin of distinct communities, was the following.

At the time above referred to, the human family, in journeying from the vicinity of mount Ararat, arrived at length at a plain in the land of Shinar. On this spot they began to erect a city and a tower, whose top might aspire to heaven, for the purpose of avoiding the dispersion of their households, and of acquiring a name.

Such a purpose, and perhaps others still worse, being offensive to the Deity, he confounded their language, and thus the workmen, not being able to understand one another, desisted from their undertaking. The consequence was the dispersion of mankind into different nations.

The name given to the city was Babel, which signifies confusion.

§ In erecting the tower they made use of brick instead of stone, and the want of mortar was supplied by slime, or bitumen, of which the region afforded an abundance. The identical materials of this fabric have been supposed, at different times, to have been discovered; but this is uncertain.

7. Mankind having become separated into different communities or nations, their history must thenceforth be given accordingly. We shall commence with the Assyrian nation, and briefly trace the outline of its history, as also the history of other sovereignties that existed during this period.

ASSYRIA.

8. Assyria, considered as afterwards including Babylonia, is the oldest of nations, and founded on the spot where the tower of Babel was erected. We may date the commencement of this empire not many years after the dispersion took place, or about 2229 years B. C. Its founder was Ashur, the son of Shem, who built Nineveh, its capital. It continued alone about 120 years, and then being united to Babylonia, became a mighty empire.

§ In the order of time, there were two empires of the Assyrians. The first is here spoken of, which lasted till the year 767 B. C.

It is supposed by some that Babylon, which was built by Nimrod, the grandson of Ham, the Belus of profane history, was, from the beginning, the capital of Assyria. But we rather follow those authorities that suppose Babylonia and Assyria to have been originally two distinct kingdoms, both founded about the same time, the former by Nimrod, the latter by Ashur.

The Babylonians became, at length, tributary; and Ninus, king of Assyria, having deposed Nabonius, united the two states into one. After his death, Semiramis, his widow, transferred the seat of government from Nineveh to Babylon.

9. Under Semiramis the Assyrian empire was greatly enlarged. She assumed the government during the nonage of Ninias, son of her husband, Ninus. She signalized her name by enlarging and embellishing Babylon, and by her numerous military exploits.

§ It is said, that, in completing Babylon, she employed the labours of 2,000,000 men. This woman, after having enlarged her dominions, conquered a great part of Ethiopia, and invaded India, though without success, was murdered, as is supposed, at the instigation of Ninias.

10. Ninias, her successor, was a very insignificant sovereign; and the history of his successors, for more than 30 generations, is unknown. They must have been an indolent and effeminate race.

§ Ninias, unlike his predecessors, being wholly intent on his pleasures, kept himself secluded in his palace, and seldom appeared before his people. But, to retain them in their duty, he kept a certain number of regular troops, whom he renewed every year, commanded by an officer on whose fidelity he could depend. This method he seems to have adopted, that the officers might have no time to gain the affections of the soldiers, or to form conspiracies against him.

Not only are his successors unknown, as to their conduct or exploits, but even their names, till the time of Sardanapalus, the last of them, (who will be noticed in the proper place,) are a matter of controversy among historians.

During this unrecorded period of the Assyrian history, Sesostris, king of Egypt, if his name may be here anticipated, who carried on his conquests into the East, must have overrun Assyria; but, as his power was not supported by his successors, the Assyrians must have soon regained their former state.

CHINA

11. China, it is not to be doubted, is among the most ancient empires of the world. Its records extend to more than 2200 years B. C. According to the most current or-

nion, it was founded by one of the colonies formed at the dispersion of Noah's posterity, under the conduct of Yao, who took for his colleague Chun, afterwards his successor.

Other accounts state Fo-hi to have been the founder of this monarchy, and many writers consider Fo-hi to have been Noah himself. The Chinese pretend a much higher antiquity than is here assigned to them, but their pretensions are merely the effect of national vanity.

§ The sovereigns of China, from Chun to the present time, are divided into 22 dynasties, the first of which, that of Hia, began 2207 years B. C. Four, and a part of the fifth, of these dynasties, preceded the Christian era.

The first dynasty was founded by Yu, surnamed Ta, or the Great, whom Chun adopted in preference to his own children. It lasted 441 years, under 17 emperors.

Yu-ta was a great proficient in agriculture, astronomy, and the kindred studies. On the subject of the first, he wrote an excellent treatise. He died much regretted, after a reign of 17 years.

Kya, the last monarch of this dynasty, was greatly detested by his subjects. He was driven from the throne, and died after an ignominious exile of three years.

EGYPT.

12. Egypt claims, and certainly possesses, a high antiquity. Its early annals, however, are so obscure, that scarcely any thing can be ascertained respecting its first kings, after Menes.*

Menes is generally acknowledged as the founder of the Egyptian empire, and is supposed to be the same as Misraim, mentioned in scripture among Ham's sons, 2188 years B. C. His children divided the land; whence arose four kingdoms, which subsisted separately during several centuries, and were successively united under one yoke.

These four kingdoms are known by the names of Thebes, Thin, Memphis, and Tanais. The people had attained to considerable civilization, but a period of barbarism soon after-

* Some late writers, adopting the Samaritan text of the Bible, which places the deluge several hundred years beyond the common era, compute the reign of Menes at about 2800 years B. C. With this they cause the other events of the early period of the world to correspond. We mention this circumstance, because the computation which is thus made may possibly be correct, and it seems to derive some little confirmation from the history of the Egyptians, both as touched upon in the Bible, and as gathered from their hieroglyphic records. Still, however, we incline to the common accounts.

wards succeeded, supposed about 2084 years B. C., under the shepherd kings,* which lasted more than two centuries.

§ In the time of Menes, the greatest part of the country was a morass, till he diverted the course of the Nile, and founded the city of Memphis within the ancient bed of that river. He instructed the Egyptians in theology, introduced domestic luxury, and instituted magnificent feasts.

It was under Timaus, one of his successors, that the government was subverted, and the country subdued by a multitude of ignoble persons, who came from the East, and treated in the most inhuman manner the ancient inhabitants.

These invaders were called Hycsos, or shepherd kings, and, according to Manetho, held all Lower Egypt 259 years.

In the kingdom of Thebes, a king by the name of Athothes I. is said to have reigned at a very early period. He was the same as was worshipped under the name of Mercury. After his death his two sons divided the kingdom; but nothing is known of their successors for a long period. In the kingdom of Thin, Venephes is said to have built some pyramids, and to have had his reign distinguished by a great famine, as that also of one of his successors was distinguished by a dreadful plague.

In the kingdom of Memphis, Tosorthros reigned, not long after Menes. From the knowledge he had of physic, he is styled Esculapius. He is said to have invented the arts of building and writing.

Of the last kingdom of Egypt, during this period, there seem to be no records, or none worth naming. Indeed, in regard to those of the others that have come down to us, there is extreme uncertainty.

Distinguished characters in Period II.

1. Noah, from whom the earth was a second time peopled.
2. Ashur, who built Nineveh.
3. Nimrod, a warrior, and supposed to be the first king.
4. Menes, first king of Egypt, and civilizer of the East.
5. Ninus, an Assyrian monarch, who conquered a large portion of Asia.
6. Semiramis, a female conqueror, and able sovereign.

§ 1. Noah is by some considered the Chronos of the Greeks, and is properly the second father of mankind. Little needs to be said of him, besides what has already appeared. His eminent piety procured for him and his family an honourable exemption from the awfully destructive effects of the deluge.

* These kings, who were detested by the Egyptians, held the government when Abraham visited it; but were expelled before the time of Joseph. This circumstance explains the remarkable fact, that Abraham, a shepherd, was very kindly entertained in Egypt; while, in a subsequent age, Joseph's brethren, because they were shepherds, were held in abhorrence by the inhabitants. We have here a pleasing confirmation of the truth of the scriptural narrative.

Having built the ark agreeably to the divine direction, he entered it at the age of 600 years, taking with him seven members of his family, together with the animals that were intended to restock the earth. Under the special care of God, he, and the various inmates of the ark, survived the desolations of a world, and leaving the ark in safety, at a little more than the expiration of a year, he built an altar, and offered sacrifice unto the Lord.

Noah lived 350 years after the flood, was engaged in the tillage of the earth, and saw his descendants increasing around him. For an important incident in his life, which has already been mentioned, we refer to Gen. ix. 20—28.

2. Ashur was one of the sons of Shem, and supposed to be the founder of the Assyrians. Scarcely any thing is recorded of him. The scripture asserts that he went out of the land of Shinar, and builded Nineveh, and the city of Rehoboth, and Calah.

3. Nimrod "seems at first to have exceedingly distinguished himself by hunting, which was then not so much a diversion, as a useful method of preventing the hurtful increase of wild beasts. This employment required great courage and address, and thus afforded a field for ambition to aspire after pre-eminence, and gradually attached a number of valiant men to one leader."

"From such a beginning, Nimrod began to claim authority, and enforce subjection; and, in fact, is the first king we read of in authentic history; and afterwards he took occasion to wage war, to extend his conquests, and to enlarge his acquisitions by violence and blood. Thus, casting off the fear of God, and acting in defiance of the divine prohibition of shedding human blood, he rendered himself notorious, and his name became a proverb."

"The beginning of his kingdom," says scripture, "was Babel, and Erech, and Accad, and Calneh, in the land of Shinar."

4. Menes, the founder of the Egyptian monarchy, was worshipped as a god after death. He appears to have been deservedly popular, by his abilities and wisdom. He built the town of Memphis, as is generally supposed. If he was the same as Misraim, mentioned in scripture, as some assert, he was one of the sons of Ham. He is said to have reigned 62 years over Upper Egypt, and 35 over Lower Egypt.

5. Ninus was a son of Belus. He was very warlike, and extended his conquests from Egypt to the extremities of India and Bactriana. He became enamoured of Semiramis, the wife of one of his officers, and married her, after her husband had destroyed himself, through fear of his powerful rival, or from jealousy. He reigned 52 years, and at his death, left his kingdom to the care of his wife, Semiramis.

6. Semiramis possessed exquisite beauty, and an heroic soul. It was on these accounts that the Assyrian monarch fell in love with her. In her infancy, it is fabulously said, she was exposed in a desert, but her life was preserved by doves one whole year. She was at length found by one of the shepherds of Ninus, and brought up by him as one of his own children.

She was so tenderly beloved by her husband, Menones, that he could not survive his expected loss of her, and the knowledge that she was demanded by his sovereign. After the death of Ninus, whom she had married, assuming the reins of government in her hands, she immortalized her name by enriching Babylon with new works and embellishments.

Of these, the principal were the walls of the city, the quays and the bridge; the lake, banks, and canals, made for draining the river; the palace, the hanging gardens, and the temple of Belus She also enlarged her dominions by the conquest of a large part of Ethiopia.

Her greatest and last expedition was directed against India. She advanced towards the river Indus, and having prepared boats, attempted to pass it with her army. The passage was for a long time disputed, but, after a bloody battle, she put her enemies to flight. Upon this she advanced directly into the country, leaving 60,000 men to guard the bridge of boats built over the river.

As soon as the Indian king thought her far enough advanced, he faced about; a second engagement ensued, more bloody than the first. The Assyrians were routed, and Semiramis, after being twice wounded, was obliged to fly, and return to her country with scarcely one third of her army.

Some time after, discovering that her son was plotting against her, she voluntarily abdicated the throne, put the government into his hands, and withdrew from public life. She lived 62 years, of which she reigned 42. Her character, in respect to those qualities that adorn a woman, seems not to have been highly esteemed.

PERIOD III.

The Period of Egyptian Bondage, extending from the calling of Abraham, 1921 *years* B. C. *to the departure of the Israelites from Egypt,* 1491 *years* B. C.

HEBREWS.

SECTION 1. The HEBREWS or ISRAELITES, commonly called the People of God, are derived from Abraham, the ninth in lineal descent from Shem. His calling of God is a remarkable event in history, and was designed for purposes altogether religious. This took place 1921 years B. C.

The nation of which he was the founder, though neither powerful nor refined, is one of the most interesting that ever existed. Their history instructs us in a way different from that of all others, because it brings directly into view the Divine dealings with them.

Abraham's family increased very slowly at first; but Jacob, his grandson, left a numerous offspring. Twelve sons became the heads of as many separate tribes in the nation.

§ Abraham, according to the Lord's command, left the land of the Chaldees, his native country, and dwelt with his father Terah, in Haran. By the same command, after Terah's death, he went into the land of Canaan, which God promised to his posterity. They were at length to be included within the boundaries of that country.

The divine design in thus setting apart one family from the rest of mankind, was to preserve the true religion in the world, and to prepare the way for the great work of redemption by Jesus Christ. The earth had now begun to be overrun with idolatry.

Abraham having acquired a name by his wealth and piety, and having passed through various trials, died at an advanced age, leaving behind him several sons, of whom only Isaac was the child of promise. Ishmael, by the maid of Abraham's wife, became the progenitor of a distinct tribe or nation.

Two sons were the progeny of Isaac, viz. Esau and Jacob, the former of whom sold his birthright to Jacob, who also by artifice obtained his father's blessing. In the line of Jacob, whose name was afterwards changed to Israel, were the Israelites descended. His twelve sons gave the names to the several tribes of which the nation was composed.

Esau was the father of the Edomites, or Idumeans.

2. Jacob closed an eventful life, 1689 years B. C., in making a prophetic declaration of the future state of his descendants, and the period of the coming of the Messiah. He had previously been brought out of Canaan, into Egypt, by means of his son Joseph, whom his brethren, through envy and malice, sold into that country.

The different occurrences by which Joseph became minister to the king of Egypt, speak the immediate interposition of Divine Providence, which was preparing for the accomplishment of the promises made to the patriarch Abraham.

The history of Joseph, as recorded in Scripture, is unparalleled in beauty and interest. Some of the principal incidents are the following.

Joseph, who was much loved by his father and hated by his brethren, upon a certain occasion which was presented, fell into the power of the latter, who sought to slay him. This horrid design, however, being providentially prevented, they availed themselves of the opportunity of selling him to some Ishmaelite slave merchants, who carried him into Egypt, where he was bought by Potiphar, an officer of the court.

Here, at length, he was wrongfully thrown into prison, by a false accusation of Potiphar's wife; but, being proved to be an interpreter of dreams, he was introduced to the notice of Pharaoh, who, on a certain occasion, wanted his services in this capacity.

His success in interpreting the king's dreams, and his subsequent conduct, procured for him the highest distinction; and he became the administrator of the government. During the famine, which he predicted, and which reached the land of Canaan, all his brethren, except Benjamin, came to him to buy corn.

Joseph knew them, although they did not know him; and by an innocent contrivance, having brought them into Egypt the second time, with their brother Benjamin, he declared to them that he was Joseph whom they had persecuted and sold.

Their surprise, mortification, and terror, were at first overwhelming; but their distressing apprehensions were at length alleviated by his assurances of pardon and kindness; and inviting his father and family into Egypt, he allotted them a portion of the territory. Here they grew and multiplied exceedingly.

3. Joseph continued to rule over Egypt, after the death of Jacob. His own decease, which occurred 1635 years B. C. left the Israelites without a protector. In less than 40 years from this event, they found a cruel tyrant and oppressor in another king, who knew not Joseph.

This king, whose name was Pharaoh,* seeing the Hebrews to be too numerous and mighty, resolved to enfeeble them; and, therefore, condemned them to slavery, and ordered his people to cast every new-born son among them into the river.

The object in view was defeated: for the people increased in an unexampled manner. God was with them, and, in the wonderful preservation of Moses, and his education in the court of Pharaoh, was preparing for them a deliverer from their cruel bondage.

§ For the particulars of this persecution of God's people, we refer to the beginning of the book of Exodus.

CANAANITES.

Section 4. The Canaanites were an ancient people. The country which they inhabited was called the land of Canaan, the name of Ham's youngest son, who settled it immediately after the dispersion at Babel. He divided it among his eleven sons. The general denomination of Canaanites included seven nations, which are frequently mentioned in scripture.

§ The Canaanites seem to have laboured, in a particular manner, under the evil influence of the curse denounced against their proge-

* A name common to the kings of Egypt.

nitor; being doomed, in the end, to subjection, expulsion, or extirpation, and being subdivided into so many little kingdoms.

The beginning of their history is extremely dark. They are supposed, however, upon the increase of their families, to have possessed themselves of the Arabian side of Egypt, and there to have erected a kingdom coeval with that of Misraim. But they seem at length to have been expelled from that region.

5. The first authentic account of this people applies to the inhabitants of the vale of Siddim, who, 1912 years B. C., were invaded by Chedorlaomer, king of Elam, and obliged to pay an annual tribute. When they afterwards revolted, they were punished with great severity.

Fifteen years after this, a most terrific judgment was inflicted on the inhabitants of Siddim, in consequence of their gross wickedness. Four cities in this delightful vale, Sodom, Gomorrah, Admah, and Zeboim, were at once destroyed by fire from heaven. The whole tract of country in their vicinity became a sea, called the Dead Sea.

§ The 18th and 19th chapters of Genesis contain an account of this catastrophe, and of its causes; to these we refer the reader.

At the present time, from the accounts of travellers, it appears that the sea and adjacent region are marked by several peculiarities worthy of notice.

In a journal of one of our American missionaries in Palestine, of recent date, we find the following account. "The water looks remarkably clear and pure; but, on taking it into my mouth, I found it nauseous and bitter, I think beyond any thing I ever tasted.

"It has been said, that these waters are so heavy, that the most impetuous winds can scarcely ruffle their surface. Nothing could be more entirely without foundation. The waves ran so high, that I found difficulty in filling some bottles with water. My clothes were wet by the waves, and, as they dried, I found them covered with salt."

Quantities of bitumen are gathered in the vicinity, which, in appearance, resembles pitch, but may be distinguished from it by its sulphureous smell and taste. Pebbles are also found here which burn when held in a blaze, producing a very disagreeable scent, but they lose nothing of their size.

6. During this period, nothing more of much importance is recorded concerning the Canaanites. The compact of the Hittites with Abraham, respecting the cave of Machpelah, the selling of a piece of ground to Jacob, by Hamor, king of Shechem, and the massacre of his subjects by some of the sons of Jacob, on account of an insult which the patriarch's family had received, are the only events transmitted to us.

GREECE.

7. The GREEKS are an ancient people, whose origin is clouded with fable. All that we know, during the present or preceding period, of the descendants of Japhet, who peopled Europe, is comprised in the history of this nation.

We date the commencement of the Greeks, as a community, from the founding of Argos by Inachus, who arrived in Greece, from Phœnicia, 1856 years B. C. Sicyon is by some thought to have been founded before; but we incline to the opinion that Egialtes, a son of Inachus, was the founder of Sicyon.

§ As much has been written concerning the fabulous times in the history of Greece, we will here present a very brief account of that portion of its history. These fables, however, are supposed to be founded on facts, and the greater part of the deities worshipped by the Greeks, were princes by whom their progenitors had been governed.

Uranus, afterwards worshipped as the heavens, appears to have been one of the earliest of their princes. He married his sister Tithea, and migrated from Asia into Greece, where he founded a kingdom. He had many children, called Titans, who rebelled against their father and dethroned him.

Saturn, or Chronos, succeeded his father Uranus, whom, with the help of his brethren, he dethroned; and dreading lest he should be treated in the same manner by his own children, he ordered them to be shut up, or put to death, immediately after their birth; but Jupiter was concealed by his mother, and sent to Crete, where he was educated.

Jupiter began to reign in Thessaly, after having dethroned Saturn. The Titans, jealous of him, declared war against him, but were vanquished, and expelled Greece. He soon divided his dominions with his two brothers, Pluto and Neptune.

The countries which he reserved to himself, he governed with great wisdom; he had his palace, and held his court, on Mount Olympus, whence the poets gave this name to heaven, when Jupiter was worshipped as a god.

8. The ancient inhabitants of Greece were extremely rude and savage, scarcely one degree superior to brutes. They lived on herbs and roots, and lay either in the open fields, or, at best, sheltered themselves in dens, clefts, and hollow trees.

An improvement of their condition occasionally took place; but Greece, for some ages, was in a continual state of fluctuation. They were unacquainted with letters till the time of Cadmus, who is hereafter to be mentioned.

§ The general names by which the natives of Greece were known to old historians, were Graioi, Hellenists, Achæi, Pelasgi. But the most ancient name of all applied to this country, is generally admitted to be that of Ionia, which the Greeks derive from Ion; but Josephus derives it from Javan, son of Japheth.

9. The several states, except Argos and Sicyon, which at length constituted Greece, had, at this time, no separate existence. They sprang up afterwards, during the latter part of the present period, as there will now be occasion to mention.

In Argos, the descendants of Inachus, having retained possession of the throne for more than 300 years, were deposed, 1511 years B. C., by Danaus, an Egyptian fugitive, who became the founder of a second dynasty, denominated Belidæ, from his father, Belus.

§ At a much later period, Perseus, a sovereign of Argos, having built Mycenæ, transferred the kingdom thither. It was at length conquered by the Heraclidæ, and united to Lacedæmon.

It may be here noticed, that only two of the Grecian states, viz. Lacedæmon and Messenia, appear to have been founded by native Greeks; the rest were established by the various branches of the Celtic family of Uranus, with the exception of Athens, which owed its origin to an Egyptian.

Prior to these establishments, and even long after them, almost every village had its petty tyrant, who bore the title of king. A name has occasionally escaped oblivion. Laws we do not find among them, before the times of the Athenian archons.

Until that period, all depended on the will of the sovereigns; only in perplexed cases, they consulted some oracle, of which the two most celebrated, were that of Jupiter at Dodona, and that of Apollo at Delphi.

10. Cecrops, a native of Egypt, is universally allowed to have founded Athens, 1556 years B. C. At this time he arrived in Attica, with a colony of his countrymen, and built twelve small villages or cities, of which Athens was one.

He gave laws to the wild inhabitants, whom he divided into twelve tribes, and instituted marriage among them. The first altar in Greece was raised by him to Jupiter.

§ The history of Greece is carried on for a time in this event. Athens became the most illustrious of the Grecian states. The province of Attica having been destroyed by the deluge of Ogyges, remained desolate for more than two centuries, previous to the time of Cecrops.

Athens, from its founder, first received the name of Cecropia, but afterwards that of Athenæ, in honour of Minerva, its tutelary deity. The Arundelian marbles, which were brought from Greece by the

Earl of Arundel, and are now kept in England, begin their chronology with the founding of Athens, but place that event 26 years earlier, viz. 1582 B. C.

11. The successor of Cecrops was Cranaus. In his time happened the famous deluge of Deucalion, in Thessaly. The third king of Athens was Amphictyon, who founded the celebrated Amphictyonic council.*

§ The deluge of Deucalion owed much of its importance to the imaginations of the poets. It was probably only a partial inundation.

In the reign of Amphictyon, a famine occurred, during which Ericthonius, said to be the son of Vulcan, arrived from Egypt with a supply of corn, and taught the natives the art of Agriculture, for which he was raised to the throne in the room of Amphictyon.

12. Corinth, another of the Grecian states, was founded 1520 years B. C., but did not receive the name of Corinth till it was rebuilt, 1410 years B. C. It originally formed a part of the kingdom of Sicyon, and was afterwards included in that of Argos, till Sysyphus, some time in the following period, seized it for his possession.

13. Thebes, a state of Greece also, was founded by Cadmus. The city, though begun by him, was finished by Amphion and Zethus. He introduced letters into Greece, 1519 years B. C. Thebes he built a few years afterwards.

§ Cadmus is supposed to have been of Phœnician extraction. To him are ascribed 16 letters of the Greek alphabet. He thus essentially contributed to the literary distinction which Greece afterwards attained.

14. Lacedæmon, or Sparta, another distinguished state of Greece, was founded by Lelex, 1516 years B. C., but received its name from Lacedæmon, its fourth king. The government continued in the family of Lelex till the return of the Heraclidæ to the Peloponnesus, an event to be noticed in the coming period.

§ Sparta was called after the name of the wife of Lacedæmon, the great grand-daughter of Lelex. Sparta properly belongs to the metropolis—Lacedæmon to the kingdom at large. The Peloponnesus, in which Lacedæmon was situated, was the southern part of Greece.

EGYPT.

15. The events in Egyptian history, during the present epoch, refer chiefly to Nitocris and Sesostris, the one a fe-

* See General Views.

male, the other a male sovereign. Nitocris began to reign over Egypt, 1678 years B. C., at Memphis. She afterwards united some other sovereignties to her dominions.

The period when Sesostris began to reign cannot be easily fixed; some place it before that of Nitocris, but others place it after her reign.

The names of a few other kings appear, but little is known concerning their reigns. The successor of Sesostris is said to have been Pheron, and some think that Rameses-Tubaete was the king whose dreams Joseph interpreted.

Nitocris succeeded her brother, an Ethiopian, who was murdered by the Egyptians, and meditating revenge for his untimely fate, put many of her subjects to death privately, and afterwards contrived a building under ground whither she deluded the chief objects of her vengeance to a feast, and, in the midst of their mirth, overwhelmed them with destruction, by turning a river upon them through a secret passage. She then eluded the rage of the populace by taking refuge in a place well fortified with ashes. Her person is said to have been extremely beautiful, but her disposition was cruel.

Sesostris was the most distinguished of all the Egyptian kings, and almost the only conqueror among them. Historians relate that his father was warned by Vulcan, in a dream, concerning the future conquests of his son, and that, in consequence of this dream, he got together all the males born in Egypt on the same day with the prince, and had them nursed and brought up with him, upon the presumption that, being the companions of his youth, they would prove the most devoted warriors and faithful counsellors.

Sesostris forming the design of conquering the world, set out with an army of 600,000 foot, 24,000 horse, and 27,000 armed chariots. His conquests were extensive, and he returned home laden with the spoils of various subjugated nations, and followed by a surprising number of captives. He rendered his power highly advantageous to his subjects, by enriching their country with useful works, and magnificent edifices.

His behaviour, however, was grossly insolent to the kings and chiefs of the conquered nations, who waited upon him to present their tribute. He is said to have caused those princes, four abreast, to be harnessed to his car, instead of horses, that they might draw him to the temple.

In his old age he lost his sight, and then was so weak and wicked as to lay violent hands on himself.

CHINA.

16. The second dynasty of the Chinese emperors commenced during this period, 1766 years B. C. It lasted 656 years, under 30 emperors. Like the first dynasty, it was terminated by the vices of the last of them.

§ Ching-tang was the founder of this dynasty. He is said to have had the most excellent qualities. His modesty was almost unparalleled: he was the only person in the empire who thought he was unfit for so important a trust. He was often on the point of resigning his crown, but his nobles would not consent to it.

Tayvre, one of his successors, being once terrified by a prodigy, which made him apprehensive of a revolution, received the following impressive lesson from his minister. "Virtue has the power of triumphing over presages. If you govern your subjects with equity, you will be beyond the reach of misfortune."

Vuthing, another prince of this dynasty, after having for three years implored heaven to bless him with such virtues as were suitable to his station, is said to have seen, in a dream, a man represented by heaven to be his prime minister, whose features he well recollected when he awoke.

Causing the man to be sought for, such a person was found in the condition of an obscure mason, working in a village, whence he was brought to court. Being questioned on a variety of points concerning government, he returned answers marked with so much wisdom as excited the highest surprise.

The king, addressing him in a very proper manner, immediately appointed him his prime minister, and received the greatest benefit from his prudent and skilful administration of government.

Distinguished characters in Period III.

1. Abraham, the immediate progenitor of the Hebrew nation.
2. Melchisedec, king of Salem, and "priest of the Most High God."
3. Sesostris, an Egyptian hero and conqueror.
4. Joseph, the chief ruler of Egypt under Pharaoh.
5. Cecrops, the founder of Athens.
6. Cadmus, a Phœnician, who built Thebes, and introduced letters into Greece.

1. Abraham was the son of Terah, and born in Chaldea. He was 75 years of age when his father died. After this event he was commanded by God to enter upon the land of Canaan, which God promised to give unto his posterity. In the year following, a famine in the land of Canaan forced Abraham with his family to go into Egypt.

In the same year, Abraham, with his nephew Lot, returned unto Canaan. They however parted at length, because the land was insufficient for both of their flocks. Lot went to Sodom—Abraham removed to Hebron. God blessed Abraham, and the promise of a posterity was confirmed to him again and again.

In the 100th year of his age, Isaac, his son, was born to him, after expectation had been long delayed. Passing through various scenes of life, he was at length called to the severe trial of offering up his son Isaac at the command of the Deity. All his lofty hopes were reposed in that son, yet he hesitated not to execute the divine behest.

Just at the moment, however, in which he stretched forth his hand, to take the life of his son, God interposed, and satisfied with Abraham's intention, accepted that in room of the deed, rescuing Isaac and commending the faith of the patriarch. Abraham died at the age of 175 years.

2. Little is known of Melchisedec. When Abraham was returning from the destruction of Chedorlaomer and his confederates, Melchisedec met and blessed him. The scriptural account is the following: "And Melchisedec, king of Salem, brought forth bread and wine; and he was the priest of the Most High God. And he blessed him, and said, Blessed be Abram of the Most High God, possessor of heaven and earth. And he (Abraham) gave him tithes of all."

The apostle says, in his epistle to the Hebrews, "Now consider how great this man was, unto whom even the patriarch Abraham gave the tenth of the spoils."

3. Sesostris was a king of Egypt. His age is so remote from every authentic record, that many have supposed that the actions and conquests ascribed to this monarch are wholly uncertain and fabulous. The amount of what has come down respecting him, as has already appeared in part, is the following. When he ascended the throne, he became ambitious of military fame, and accordingly, at the head of a numerous army, he proceeded to make the conquest of the world.

He subdued the most of Asia, and even invaded Europe, bringing the Thracians into subjection; and, that the fame of his conquests might long survive him, he placed columns in the subjugated provinces; and, many ages after, this pompous inscription was read in several parts of Asia: "Sesostris, the king of kings, has conquered this territory by his arms."

At his return home, the monarch employed his time in encouraging the fine arts, improving the revenues of his kingdom, erecting temples, building cities, and digging canals. He committed suicide when he had become old and infirm, after reigning 44 years. His era was 1722 years B. C.

4. Joseph is celebrated in sacred history, and no one's life was more eventful in itself, or has been described with greater felicity than his has been, in scripture. It is unnecessary to say over again what has been said respecting this eminent person, especially since the reference to scripture is so easy, and the reader who once begins the story of Joseph, can seldom feel disposed to leave it until it be finished. The triumph of innocence, and the success of piety, in this instance, show the care of God over good men, and may well lead them to put their confidence more and more in him.

5. Cecrops was a native of Egypt. He led a colony to At-

tica, and reigned over part of the country. He married the daughter of a Grecian prince, and was deemed the first founder of Athens. He taught his subjects to cultivate the olive, and was the first who raised an altar to Jupiter, in Greece, and offered him sacrifices.

After a reign of 50 years, spent in regulating his newly formed kingdom, and in polishing the minds of his subjects, Cecrops died, and was succeeded by Cranaus, a native of the country.

6. Cadmus was a Phœnician. He laid the foundation of Thebes. This fact is very much invested with fable, which needs not to be detailed. If Thebes, according to some, sprang up at the sound of Amphion's lyre, i. e. by encouraging the workmen, still Cadmus built a citadel which he called Cadmea, and thus formed the commencement of a city.

Cadmus was the first who introduced the use of letters into Greece, though some maintain that the same alphabet was in existence among the native inhabitants. This alphabet consisted only of 16 letters, to which 8 were afterwards added. The worship of several of the Egyptian and Phœnician deities was also introduced by Cadmus. His era is reckoned to be 1519 years B. C.

PERIOD IV.

The Period of the Trojan War, extending from the departure of the Israelites from Egypt, 1491 *years* B. C. *to the dedication of Solomon's temple,* 1004 *years* B. C.

ISRAELITES.

SECTION 1. The history of the ISRAELITES at this era assumes a very marked character. Oppressed by the Egyptian monarch, they cried unto God for deliverance, and a divine deliverance they experienced.

Moses, selected as the instrument of saving his countrymen, was in due time called to his work; and, after a series of miracles, which he performed by the divine assistance, he led the people out from before Pharaoh, into the borders of the promised land.

The consequence to many of the Egyptians was their destruction; for Pharaoh and his army pursuing the Israelites through the Red Sea, were overwhelmed with its waters.

After wandering in the wilderness 40 years, and frequently rebelling against God, the Israelites were conducted by the hand of Moses in sight of Canaan, when he died, without entering it himself, 1447 years B. C.

§ The story of Moses, and of his agency in delivering the Israelites, is very interesting and instructive; but we have no room for its particulars. We will, however, mention some incidents, subsequent to the retreat of the Israelites from Egypt.

The Israelites were no sooner delivered from the Egyptians, than they murmured against Moses, on account of the want of food; to satisfy them, God sent first a great quantity of quails, and the next morning manna, which fell regularly every day, except on sabbath days, during the 40 years they remained in the wilderness.

Again the people murmured for water, and Moses, by the Lord's command, made a supply to issue from a rock. At this juncture, the Amalekites attacked Israel, and were defeated by Joshua. The people soon after arriving at Mount Sinai, God gave them his law. During, however, the absence of Moses in the mount, they fell into idolatry, in consequence of which 3000 of them were put to death.

In the course of the second year after the retreat from Egypt, Moses numbered the children of Israel from 20 years old and upwards, and there were found 603,550 men able to go to war, besides the Levites.

About this time, 12 men were sent to spy the land of Canaan, who, with the exception of Joshua and Caleb, reported unfavourably which caused the people to murmur. Upon this offence, God condemned all those who were twenty years old and upwards when they came out of Egypt, to die in the wilderness, except Joshua and Caleb.

As a punishment for their murmurs, the Israelites began to travel in the wilderness 1489 years B. C. At this time Korah, Dathan, and Abiram, revolting against Moses, were swallowed by the earth, with 250 of their associates. In 1452 years B. C., the Israelites began their conquests, by the defeat of the kings of the Amorites, Bashan, Moab, &c.

At the age of 120 years Moses died on Mount Nebo, in the land of Moab, having first taken a view of the promised land.

2. The successor of Moses was Joshua, who conducted the people into the promised land, having, by the divine command, mostly destroyed the wicked nations that inhabited it.

After this event, the Israelites, with some intermission, were directed by leaders, called Judges, for the space of 356 years. They paid a high respect to these officers, and also to the priests, but they acknowledged no other king than God.

As the people at length became weary with this state of things, and desired a king, so as to be like the nations around them, a king was, in the divine displeasure, granted to them.

§ Joshua having led the Israelites to the banks of the Jordan, whose waters divided to afford them a passage, conducted them safely over it. He conquered 31 cities in the course of six years. He died 1426 years B. C.

The people were perpetually inclined to forsake the worship of Jehovah, and to pollute themselves with the abominations of the heathen. For this they were repeatedly brought into bondage, and consequent distress. Their Judges were the instruments of delivering them on these occasions.

One occasion was as follows. The Israelites, being brought into the power of the Midianites, after seven years of suffering, they cried unto the Lord, who sent an angel to Gideon to announce to him that he was chosen to deliver Israel from their oppressors.

By divine direction, Gideon retained of 32,000 men whom he had collected, only 300 men, and with them, each carrying a lamp concealed in an earthen vessel, to be broken at a proper opportunity, he so terrified the Midianites, that they fled in confusion, and turned their swords against one another.

Samson also, on another occasion, delivered his countrymen by a series of extraordinary efforts of strength and courage which we cannot particularly recount. It may be only mentioned, that, at the conclusion of his course, having been betrayed by his wife, and deprived of his strength—upon its return, he pulled down, by a single exertion of his muscular energy, the temple of Dagon on the heads of his enemies, the Philistines, with whom he perished in the general ruin.

Samuel, the last and most eminent of these leaders, and a prophet also, rendered signal service to his countrymen, especially by the moral influence which he exercised over them. When old, however, he took for his assistants in the government, his two sons, whose mismanagement occasioned murmurs among the people, and a desire to have a king.

3. Saul, the son of Kish, was the first king of Israel. Having been privately anointed by Samuel, he was afterwards publicly proclaimed, 1079 years B. C. His reign was prosperous at first, but at length was characterized by crime and ill success. He perished miserably.

He was succeeded by David, who, though he erred in several instances, was a man of distinguished talents, bravery, and piety; he raised his people to the highest pitch of national prosperity and happiness. The wise and rich Solomon was his son and successor. He laid the foundation of a magnificent temple, 1011 years B. C.

§ Saul, having spent an unhappy life, and being at war with the Philistines, had his army routed, and three of his sons slain, and he himself, having received a wound, and fearing to fall into the hands of his enemies, took a sword and fell upon it.

David had been previously anointed king, but he at first reigned only over the tribe of Judah. But after the death of Ishbosheth, a son of Saul, who had assumed the government of the tribes, he reigned over the whole of Israel.

He spent a very active and perilous life, and among the conquests he made were the Philistines, the Moabites, the Ammonites, and the Syrians. He had at length some domestic troubles, and was in danger from an insurrection of his subjects, but he lived to see his enemies destroyed, and he left a rich and flourishing realm to his son.

CANAANITES.

4. The history of the CANAANITES, and some of the neighbouring nations or tribes, is involved in that of the Jews during this period. They were mostly subdued by Joshua, but seemed to revive at different times, to the great annoyance of the Israelites. From the time of Solomon, they can scarcely be said to have had a national existence. The remnants of them, except the Canaanites, properly so called, who afterwards went under the appellation of Phœnicians, were swallowed up in the great monarchies that successively existed in Asia.

PHŒNICIANS.

5. The PHŒNICIANS are known in history principally as a navigating and commercial people, among whom the arts were early cultivated. Their country was divided into several small kingdoms; but the most considerable of their sovereignties were the cities of Sidon and Tyre. We know nothing of the kings of Sidon till the present and succeeding periods. Hiram was king of Tyre, and contemporaneous with David and Solomon.

§ Sidon, according to Josephus, was built by Sidon, the eldest son of Canaan. Tyre was founded by the posterity of Sidon. Herodotus gives to the older Tyre a great antiquity. The new city, reared opposite to the ancient, on an island, is said, by Josephus, to have been built in the year B. C. 1255.

The Phœnicians are regarded as the earliest navigators, merchants, and workmen, of the world. We learn from ancient records, that they carried on trade, not only over all the coasts of the Mediterranean, but even over the ocean, as far as England, whence they exported tin.

The early kings are not known, except those who had some commerce with the Jews. To Hiram, king of Tyre, both David and Solomon applied when proposing to build a temple to the Lord. He helped them by furnishing, not only precious materials, but also a great number of workmen. After a glorious reign, Baleazar, his son, succeeded him.

GREECE.

6. The history of GREECE during this period is pursued first in a few details, respecting some of its different sovereignties.

The kings already named, who had governed Athens, had raised it to a considerable degree of civilization. But the king who laid the principal foundation of Athenian greatness, was Theseus. He united the 12 cities of Attica into one confederacy.

§ Theseus is said to have founded a more perfect equality among the citizens, in consequence of which, the state rather resembled a republic than a monarchy. Owing to the inconstancy of the people, he was banished from the country, notwithstanding his many virtues.

7. Codrus, the last Athenian king, devoted himself to the good of his subjects. With him royalty was abolished, since the people thought no man worthy of succeeding him. This change occurred towards the close of the present period, viz. 1069 years B. C.

§ Codrus being engaged in a war with the Heraclidæ, was told by the oracle that the army would be victorious whose chief should perish. He, therefore, with a chosen band, threw himself into the hottest of the battle, and turned the fortune of the day in favour of his countrymen, at the expense of his own life.

A dispute for the succession arose between two of his sons, and before they could accommodate their difference, the Athenians abolished royalty altogether, but placed Medon, one of the claimants, at the head of the state, with the title of Archon. This office was for life during more than 3 centuries; afterwards it was reduced to 10 years, and finally to one year.

8. Corinth, having been seized by Sysyphus, was governed in his family 250 years. The last king of this race was deposed by the Heraclidæ, 1099 years B. C.

9. The first great enterprise of the Greeks was the Argonautic expedition, 1263 years B. C. It was led by Jason, and is supposed to have been both a military and a mercantile adventure. Its destination was to Colchis, the modern Mingrelia, in Asia Minor.

§ According to some, the object was to open the commerce of the Euxine sea, and to secure some establishment on its coast. According to others, Jason wished to avenge the death of his kinsman Phryxus, and to recover his treasures, which had been seized by the king of Colchis. Hence, in the language of fiction or figure, it was the "Golden Fleece" that was the object to be recovered.

This expedition was thought to be of so much importance, that all the heroes of the age were anxious to engage in it. Among the 54 renowned captains who were in the single ship of Argo alone, in which Jason embarked, were Hercules, Theseus, Castor and Pollux, Pirithous, Laertes, Peleus, Oileus, &c.

In the course of their voyage, they attempted to land for refreshment in a part of Phrygia, but were prevented by Laomedon, king of Troy, for which they took ample revenge on their return, by pillaging that city.

On their arrival in Colchis, Medea, the daughter of the king, fell in love with Jason, and, through her assistance, the Argonauts effected the object of their voyage. On their arrival in Greece, Hercules celebrated or instituted the Olympic Games.

10. A dispute for the divided sovereignty of Thebes, between the brothers Eteocles and Polynices, gave rise to a war that was terminated by single combat, in which both were killed. This is called the war of the seven captains, and occurred 1225 years B. C.

The sons of the commanders slain in this war renewed the quarrel of their fathers, about ten years afterwards. This is called the war of the Epigonoi, a subject celebrated by Homer in a poem now lost.

11. But the most celebrated event of this period, in the annals of Greece, is the Trojan war. It commenced 1193 years B. C., and terminated in ten years. Troy was taken and burnt to the ground. This war was undertaken by the princes of Greece to avenge the wrongs sustained by Menelaus, king of Lacedæmon, whose wife, Helen, had been seduced away by Paris, a Trojan prince. The details of this war are derived from Homer; but he is reasonably supposed to have related facts, for the most part.

§ Troy, the capital of Phrygia Minor, was founded 1546 years B. C. by Scamander, who led thither a colony from Crete. Troas, the fifth in succession from Scamander, either built a new city, or enlarged the old one, and named it after himself, Troy. The Trojans were a brave and warlike people.

The number of the Grecian warriors is supposed to have been about 100,000. Nearly all Asia Minor was leagued with Priam, king of Troy. The Greeks, on landing at Troas, were warmly opposed, and they spent the first 8 or 9 years in reducing such cities and islands as favoured the cause of Troy. At length the siege of that capital began, and the most heroic deeds were performed on both sides. At this juncture, the camp of the Greeks was visited by a pestilence, and a quarrel ensued between Agamemnon and Achilles, the Grecian leaders.

The death of Patroclus, slain by Hector, impelled Achilles to return into the Grecian camp. Hector was killed by Achilles, and Achilles fell by the hand of Paris, who was himself slain by an arrow At last the Greeks gained possession of the city by stratagem, and utterly destroyed it. No vestige of its ruins now remains.

Such of the Trojans as survived sought new settlements in distant regions. Antenor established himself in Italy, where he founded the nation of the Heneti. Æneas settled also in Italy, where he founded the kingdom of Alba.

12. The war of the Heraclidæ, among the Greeks, began about 80 years after the destruction of Troy. Hercules, the son of Amphitryon, sovereign of Mycenæ, was banished from his country, with all his family, while the crown was possessed by an usurper. After a period of a century, his descendants, called Heraclidæ, returned to Peloponnesus, and subduing all their enemies, took possession of the states of Mycenæ, Argos, and Lacedæmon. This return of the Heraclidæ is an event often spoken of in history.

13. A long period of civil war succeeded, and Greece, divided among a number of petty tyrants, became a prey to oppression or anarchy. The difficulties of the times drove many of the Greeks from home, who founded important colonies, as we shall hereafter learn.

EGYPT.

14. Concerning the EGYPTIANS, during this period, very little is known with certainty. Apophis is thought to have been the Pharaoh who, together with his army, was drowned in the Red Sea. Amosis, Amenophis II., and one or two others, were warriors and conquerors.

§ A few things may be subjoined respecting some of the Egyptian kings during this period. Mœris caused the celebrated lake, called by his name, to be dug, to receive the waters of the Nile, when the inundation was too abundant, and to water the country when it proved deficient.

Hermes Trismegistes is celebrated for his philosophical writings. He added 5 days to the year, which before consisted only of 360. Amosis abolished the practice of human sacrifices, and conquered Heliopolis, the ancient capital of Lower Egypt.

Actisanes, king of Ethiopia, united Egypt and Ethiopia under his government. He bore his prosperity with great prudence, and behaved himself in a most affectionate manner towards his new subjects.

Having caused a general search to be made after the Egyptian robbers who infested the country, he commanded their noses to be cut off, and then banished them to the remotest part of the desert, between Syria and Egypt, where he built them a town, which, from the mutilation of its inhabitants, was called Rhinocolura.

A Memphite of ignoble extraction was exalted to the throne. The priests characterised him as a magician, and pretended that he could assume whatever form he pleased. His Egyptian name was Cetes, which the Greeks rendered Proteus.

It was during his reign, that Paris and Helen were driven on the coasts of Egypt, in their passage to Troy, but when the Egyptian monarch understood the shameful breach of hospitality which the young stranger had committed, he ordered him to quit his dominions.

LYDIA.

15. The history of the kings of LYDIA is very obscure. They were divided into three dynasties. 1. The Atydæ. 2. The Heraclidæ. 3. The Mermnadæ. The history of Atydæ is altogether fabulous. Argon was the first of the Heraclidæ, and Candaules the last. Argon reigned about 1223 years B. C. The Lydians are celebrated as merchants and traffickers.

§ Lydia is supposed to have been founded by Lud, son of Shem. It was, however, called Lydia, from Lydus, one of its kings. It was previously called Mæonia, from Mæon, also one of its kings. It was conquered at length by the descendants of Hercules.

Lydia Proper was, strictly speaking, at first only that part of Mæonia which was seated on the Ægean Sea; but when the Greeks or Ionians settled there, the ancient inhabitants were driven to the interior. The invaders named the sea coasts where they settled Ionia, after the country whence they had emigrated, or rather, whence they had been driven by the Heraclidæ; while the Lydians gave their name to the new countries in which they settled.

Long before the invasion of the Ionians, the natives of Lydia were devoted to commerce. The earliest instance on record of a gold and silver coinage is found in their history. They were also the first people who exhibited public sports.

ITALY.

16. ITALY appears to have been inhabited at a remote era. So early as 1289 years B. C. we read of a king named Janus, who, having arrived from Thessaly, planted a colony on the river Tiber. Four sovereigns succeeded him in Latium; during the reign of the last of whom, viz. Latinus, arrived Æneas, the Trojan prince, in Italy. Æneas married Lavinia, the daughter of Latinus, and succeeded him in the sovereignty. After Æneas there was a succession of kings to the time of Numitor, the grandfather of Romulus and Remus, the founders of Rome.

The history of these kings is, however, very obscure and confused, and very little dependence can be placed upon it. Of the numerous petty kingdoms of which Italy was composed, those of Etruria and Latium alone deserve attention. The Etruscans are thought to have been a very polished people. The inhabitants of Latium were the immediate ancestors of the Romans. A considerable part of Italy was doubtless peopled by the Greeks.

§ Italy, afterwards the seat of the Roman power, was peopled at an early era, though we cannot determine the particular point of time, with certainty as to the country at large. The colony on the Tiber, as we have seen, was settled nearly 13 centuries before Christ. There is every reason to believe that a part of Italy was inhabited by a refined and cultivated nation, many ages before the Roman name was known.

The Etruscans are justly considered as such a nation; a fact which is indicated by the monuments in the fine arts which they have left, and some of which exist to this day. Their alphabet, resembling the Phœnician, disposes us to believe them to have been of eastern origin.

Though many of the inhabitants of Italy originated from Greece and the east, yet a portion of them, it is believed, must have originated from the Celtic or Gomerian tribes of the north, who entered Italy from that quarter.*

The story of Latinus and Æneas is briefly as follows. At the time of the arrival of the latter in Italy, Latinus was engaged in a war with the Rutuli; and, on hearing of this arrival, he immediately marched towards the strangers, expecting to find an unprincipled banditti.

But Æneas, though commanding a body of hardy veterans, held out the olive of peace. Latinus listened to his melancholy tale, and pitying the misfortunes of the Trojan exiles, assigned them a portion of land, on condition of their joining against the Rutuli.

Æneas eagerly embraced the offer, and performed such essential service in the cause of the Latins, that this monarch bestowed on him his only daughter, Lavinia, in marriage, with the right of succession to the crown.

Distinguished characters in Period IV.

1. Moses, the first Hebrew lawgiver and leader.
2. Joshua, a conqueror of Canaan, and pious military chieftain.
3. Orpheus, the father of poetry.
4. Musæus, a Greek poet.
5. Samson, a judge of Israel, and endowed with extraordinary strength.

* See Edin. Rev. No. 80. Art. V.

6. Sanconiathon, a Phœnician, one of the earliest writers of history.

7. David, a king of Israel, a warrior and poet.

§ 1. Moses, when an infant, having been exposed on the brink of the river Nile, in an ark of bulrushes, the daughter of Pharaoh found the ark, saved the child, and had him educated as her own son. At forty years of age, having renounced the honours of Pharaoh's court, he endeavoured to join his oppressed countrymen, but they would not receive him. After this, circumstances induced him to flee to the land of Midian, where he married, and enjoyed a retirement of 40 years.

At the end of this period, God appeared to him in the mount of Horeb, and ordered him to return to Egypt, with a commission to Pharaoh, respecting his release of the Israelites from bondage. He accomplished this object only after the infliction of ten severe and awful plagues upon that monarch and his people. At length God saw fit, through Moses, to destroy Pharaoh and the flower of his military force in the Red Sea.

From this period, Moses was employed in receiving the moral law from mount Sinai, in prescribing the form of the ceremonial worship of the Hebrews, in regulating their civil polity, in conducting their military operations, and in leading them through the wilderness of Sinai, in which they were doomed to wander during 40 years.

At the age of 120 he died on mount Nebo, in the land of Moab, having first taken a view of the promised land. This occurred 1451 years B. C. Moses was a man of eminent piety and wisdom.

2. Joshua was the successor of Moses, and led the Israelites into the promised land, over the river Jordan, whose waters divided to afford them a passage. The first city which he conquered was Jericho; this was followed by the speedy reduction of 30 others.

Having divided the land of Canaan among the ten tribes, Joshua died, aged 110, 1426 years B. C.

3. Orpheus was the son of Œager, or, as some say, of Apollo, by Calliope. The fictions of poetry have put into his hands a lyre, whose entrancing sounds stayed the courses of rivers, moved mountains, and subdued the ferocity of wild beasts. Doubtless the effects of his song, though not of such a nature, were considerable, in that rude and early age, on the minds of untutored barbarians.

By the power of his music, as fiction reports, he regained his wife, Eurydice, from the infernal regions, but lost her again in consequence of failing to comply with a certain condition, on which she was restored. The condition was, that he should not look behind to see her till he had come to the extremest borders of hell. Contrary to promise he did this, through the impatience of love, or by reason of forgetfulness, and she vanished from before his eyes.

Orpheus, according to story, was one of the Argonauts; of which celebrated expedition he wrote a poetical account. This, however, is doubted; and the poems that pass under his name, are, with reason, ascribed to other and later writers. There is little cause to doubt that such a person as Orpheus existed, and that he was a great poet and musician. The period assigned for him is 1284 years B. C.

4. Musæus is supposed to have been a son or disciple of Linus or Orpheus, and to have lived about 1253 years before the christian era. None of his poems remain. A Musæus, who flourished in the 4th century, according to the judgment of most critics, wrote "The loves of Leander and Hero."

5. Samson was the son of Manoah, of the tribe of Dan. As he was raised up to avenge the Israelites of their oppressors, he was endowed with extraordinary strength. On one occasion, he slew 1000 Philistines with the jaw-bone of an ass. At various other times, he severely molested and distressed them.

At length he was, through stratagem, betrayed by Delilah, and deprived of his strength. It, however, soon returned; and he pulled down the temple of Dagon on the heads of his enemies, the Philistines, with whom he perished in the general ruin. Some parts of his character are very far from deserving imitation. His various exploits and follies are recorded, Judges xiv. xv. xvi.

6. Sanconiathon was born at Berytus, or, according to others, at Tyre. He flourished about 1040 years B. C. He wrote, in the language of his country, a history, in 9 books, in which he amply treated of the theology and antiquities of Phœnicia and the neighbouring places.

This history was translated into Greek by Philo, a native of Byblus, who lived in the reign of the emperor Adrian. Some few fragments of this Greek translation are extant. Some, however, suppose them to be spurious, while others maintain their authenticity.

7. David was the son of Jesse, and anointed king of Israel, while keeping his father's flocks, by Samuel, the prophet. He was a valiant, prosperous, and warlike prince, and raised himself and people to great eminence and renown. His name began to be known and celebrated, from the time that he slew Goliath, the giant. His military operations were planned with wisdom, and executed with vigour.

He was distinguished as a sacred poet and writer of psalms; no one in this department has ever equalled him. These inspired productions are marked by loftiness, vigour, and felicity of expression —abounding in the sublimest strains of devotion, and conveying the most important truths and instructions to the mind.

This pious prince was left to fall into scandalous sins, in a few instances, particularly in the seduction of Bathsheba, and the murder of Uriah, her husband; but he bitterly repented of them, and was restored to the divine favour. He died, 1015 years B. C., after a reign of 40 years.

PERIOD V.

The Period of Homer, extending from the dedication of Solomon's temple, 1004 *years* B. C., *to the founding of Rome,* 752 *years* B. C.

ISRAELITES.

Section 1. From the accession of Solomon to the throne of the Israelites, a period of profound peace and prosperity was enjoyed by that people throughout his reign. The most important undertaking of this monarch, was the building and dedication of the temple of the Lord at Jerusalem.

This magnificent structure was completed in seven years. The dedication was performed by the king, with the most solemn religious rites, in presence of all the elders of Israel, and the heads of the various tribes.

This prince exceeded in wisdom all who went before him; but, in his old age, he took many wives and concubines out of the idolatrous nations around him, who corrupted his heart. The Lord therefore declared, by the prophet Abijah, that he would divide the kingdom after his death, and give ten tribes to Jeroboam; which accordingly took place.

§ The temple at Jerusalem was a most sumptuous and costly edifice. The value of the materials, and the perfection of the workmanship, rank it among the most celebrated structures of antiquity. It was not very large, being little more than 90 feet in length, 30 in breadth, and 45 in height; but was finely proportioned, and, together with a grand porch, was splendidly ornamented.

Towards the close of his reign, as a punishment of his effeminacy and idolatry, the Lord stirred up certain adversaries against him; and, though the principal evil threatened against Israel, was not to occur during *his* day, yet he had the mortification of knowing that it would be inflicted under the administration of his son; and that his own conduct would be the procuring cause.

We cannot help believing that he repented of his awful defection from duty, though nothing in the Bible is recorded concerning this point; and all ought to be profited by the memorials which he has left of his wisdom, and general piety.

2. Rehoboam, the son of Solomon, began to reign over the Israelites 975 years B. C. Having refused to lighten the yoke his father had imposed on his subjects, ten tribes revolted. and followed Jeroboam, an enterprising domestic of the king. The tribes of Judah and Benjamin alone remained

faithful to Rehoboam. From this time Judah and Israel are separate kingdoms.

3. The kingdom of the Ten Tribes, or the Israelites, during this period, was governed by a succession of vicious and idolatrous monarchs; and wars and feuds, treachery and murder, mark their history in a shocking manner. Jeroboam was their first king.

§ A few incidents in the lives of these kings may be noticed. Jeroboam, to prevent his subjects from going to Jerusalem to sacrifice, made two golden calves, which the people worshipped; for which conduct, God declared that his whole house should be cut off.

Zimri, the fourth after Jeroboam, enjoyed the crown only seven days. The city Tirzah, in which he was besieged by Omri, being taken, he burnt himself to death in his palace.

Ahab, the sixth after Jeroboam, was the most impious king who reigned over Israel. He married Jezebel, a daughter of a king of the Sidonians, who excited him to commit all manner of wickedness. Among other things, he wantonly murdered Naboth, for refusing to give up his vineyard to Ahab.

Jehu, a captain under Jehoram, was anointed king by the prophet Elisha; and, though a wicked man, was the instrument of executing the Lord's vengeance upon his impious contemporaries. He killed Jehoram, and the 70 sons of Ahab; and after having slain all the priests of Baal, he destroyed the images, and the house of their god.

Jehoash was successful as a warrior. He defeated Benhadad, king of Syria, in three battles. In a war against Amaziah, king of Judah, he took him prisoner, broke down the wall of Jerusalem, and plundered the temple and the king's palace.

Pekah, the last king during this period, made war against Judah, with Rezin, king of Syria. Under his reign, part of the ten tribes were carried captive to Assyria, by Tiglath Pileser.

4. Several of the kings of Judah, during the present period, were pious men, and adhered to the worship of God. Others of them imitated the profligate kings of Israel. The people whom they governed, and who have survived to the present time, are called Jews, in distinction from Israelites, the name once applied to the whole twelve tribes.

§ We will notice some of the transactions of their reigns. During the reign of Rehoboam, Sesac, king of Egypt, took Jerusalem, and carried off the treasures of the temple, and of the palace.

Jehoshaphat carefully enforced the worship of God. The Moabites and Ammonites declared war against him; but the Lord threw them into confusion in such a manner, that they destroyed one another.

Ahaziah, directed by the councils of Athaliah, his mother, acted wickedly. He went, with the vicious Jehoram, king of Israel, to war against Hazael, king of Syria. When Jehu destroyed the house of Ahab, he sought Ahaziah, who was hid in Samaria, and slew him.

Joash reigned with justice as long as Jehoiada, the high priest, lived. After his death, having fallen into idolatry, Zechariah, the son of Jehoiada, reproved him for this sin, and was stoned by the king's order. God then raised against him the king of Syria, who plundered Jerusalem. His own servants also conspired against him, and slew him in his bed.

Uzziah made successful wars against the Philistines and Arabians Intoxicated with prosperity, he went into the temple to burn incens upon the altar, and the Lord struck him with leprosy for his presumption.

Jotham, a pious prince, fought and overcame the Ammonites, and rendered them tributary.

GREECE.

5. GREECE, at the commencement of the present period, was in an unsettled state. By the emigration of many of its inhabitants, colonies had been formed, particularly in Lesser Asia. Afterwards colonies were sent to Italy and Sicily. These, owing to the freedom of their governments, soon rivalled their parent states; a circumstance which induced the latter to put an end to despotism, and to adopt popular constitutions. In this work of reformation, Lycurgus, the legislator of Sparta, was distinguished.

6. It may be mentioned, in connexion with this subject and previously to an account of the reformation of Sparta, that the poems of Homer were introduced from Asia into Greece by Lycurgus. He met with them in his travels in that region, carefully preserved them, and brought them home on his return, 886 years B. C. Their effect on the national spirit and literature of the Greeks, was at length highly propitious.

§ Homer flourished about 900 years B. C. He was a poor blind man, and used to travel from place to place, singing his verses. But his genius was transcendant. All succeeding ages have bowed to it; and his poems have been taken as the model of all epic productions of any note written since his day.

The present form of his poems is supposed not to have been the ancient form. They were probably produced in separate pieces and ballads; and were united into continuous poems, it is said, by certain learned men, under the direction of Pisistratus, king of Athens.

The era of Grecian splendour was several centuries after the time of Homer; but by the preservation of his poems, the progress of the Greeks in arts and literature was effectually secured.

7. Lycurgus, by his peculiar institutions, raised Sparta

from a weak and distracted state, to superiority in arms over the other republics of Greece. Sparta became truly republican in its government, though the form of royalty was retained. Its kings were merely the first citizens in the state, and acknowledged the superior authority of the Ephori and the people, to whom they were accountable. Their privileges, however, sufficiently distinguished them from the mass of the citizens.

With many things in his institutions that were commendable, there was much that was pernicious. His sole object seems to have been, to render the Spartans fit only for war. The chronological date of the commencement of this reformation, is 884 years B. C.

§ After the return of the Heraclidæ, Sparta was divided between the two sons of Aristodemus, Eurysthenes and Procles, who reigned jointly. The occasion of this was, that Aristodemus having been killed while his children were infants, their mother was unable to tell which of them was the first born, since they were twins. The Spartans consequently agreed that they should be joint kings.

This double monarchy continued in the one line under 30 kings, and in the other line under 27 kings, during a period of about 880 years. Polydectes and Lycurgus were the sons of one of these kings. Upon the death of his brother, the crown devolved on Lycurgus; but his sister-in-law being with child, he resigned it.

She however intimated to Lycurgus that if he would marry her, the child should be destroyed immediately upon its birth. Lycurgus, with a view to save it, desired that she would send it to him, and he would dispose of it. Accordingly, the boy, as soon as he was born, was sent to his uncle.

Lycurgus was at supper with a large party when the royal infant arrived, but he instantly took it into his arms, and holding it to the view of the company, exclaimed, "Spartans! behold your king." The people were delighted, and the boy was called Charilaus.

Lycurgus, with a view to suppress the calumnies published against him by the faction of the queen, determined upon a voluntary exile. In his travels, he made it an object to acquire knowledge, and especially to ascertain the best means of government. It was during this journey that he discovered the poems of Homer, as above mentioned.

Upon his recall to Sparta, he found things in so bad a condition, that he set about a reformation of the manners of the people. He began his labours by instituting a senate to make laws, and see that they were executed; this senate was composed of 30 members, the kings being of the number.

He next made an equal division of the lands, so that all the Spartans shared it fairly between them. When he endeavoured to do the same with the furniture, clothes, &c. he found the rich very averse to his proposals. He therefore took another course. He substituted iron for gold and silver, as the medium of exchange.

As this iron money was of no account among the neighbouring countries, the Spartans could no longer indulge in luxury, by purchasing foreign costly articles. The necessary arts of life he allowed to be practised only by slaves.

He then commanded that all persons, even the kings themselves, should eat at public tables, and that these tables should be served only with plain food. This regulation, more than any other, offended the rich citizens. They rose in a body and assaulted Lycurgus; and one of them, pursuing him to a sanctuary, struck out his eye with a stick.

Lycurgus no otherwise punished this offender, than by making him his page and attendant. In time, these dinners, at which they served up a kind of soup, called black broth, came to be much relished, and very pleasant discourse often enlivened them.

An admirable part of the ceremony at these public meals was the following. When the company were assembled, the oldest man present, pointing to the door, said, "Not one word spoken here, goes out there." This wise rule produced mutual confidence, and prevented all scandal and misrepresentation.

The children were taught in large public schools, and were made brave and hardy. All the people were accustomed to speak in short pithy sentences, so that this style of speaking is even now called after them, *laconic ;* Laconia being one of the names of Lacedæmon.

When Lycurgus had firmly established his new laws, he ensured their observance by the following contrivance. He left Sparta, after having made the people swear, that they would abide by his laws, until he should return. As he intended not to return at all, this was to swear that they would keep his laws for ever.

Lycurgus died in a foreign land. By some it is asserted, that he starved himself to death. His laws continued in force 500 years, during which time the Spartans became a powerful and conquering people.

The institutions of this legislator were impaired by many blemishes. The manners of the Lacedæmonian women were suffered to be shamefully loose. The youth were taught to subdue the feelings of humanity. The slaves were treated with the greatest barbarity. Even theft was a part of Spartan education.

The object of this was to prepare their minds for the stratagems of war. Detection exposed them to punishment. Plutarch tells us of a boy, who had stolen a fox and hidden it under his coat, and who rather chose to let the animal tear out his bowels, than to discover the theft.

SECT. 8. The first of the *Olympiads*, an era by which the events in Grecian history are reckoned, occurred 776 years B. C. The Olympic games were first instituted about 1150 years B. C., but having fallen into disuse, were restored at different times, and from the period above mentioned, form a certain epoch in history.

§ The nature of these games will be described under the "General Views," at the close of this work.

MACEDON.

SECT. 9. MACEDON, a kingdom in Greece, and sometimes considered distinct from it in its history, was founded by Caranus, an Argive and descendant of Hercules, about 795 years B. C. The government continued in his line 647 years, i. e. till the death of Alexander Ægus, the posthumous son of Alexander the Great.

§ The history of Macedon under its first kings is obscure, and presents only some wars with the Illyrians, Thracians, and other neighbouring nations. It became, as we shall hereafter learn, very powerful, and under Philip overturned the liberties of the other states of Greece.

ASSYRIA.

SECT. 10. After a chasm of 800 years in the history of the first kingdom of ASSYRIA, we find a few particulars respecting one or two of its last sovereigns. *Pul*, who is mentioned in scripture, subdued Israel in the reign of Menahem, who became his tributary. This Pul is supposed to be the king of Nineveh, who, with his people, repented at the preaching of Jonah. If this be the fact, he flourished about 800 years B. C.*

§ The object of Jonah's preaching was to denounce the divine judgements against this people on account of their wickedness. The prophet after great reluctance to obey the command of God, and a signal chastisement for his disobedience, repaired at length to Nineveh, and executed his commission.

The Ninevites took the alarm, and humbled themselves before Jehovah, in consequence of which they were delivered at that time from destruction. The Assyrian empire, of which Nineveh was the capital, ended, however, soon afterwards, as we shall now learn.

Sect. 11. *Sardanapalus* was the last and the most vicious of the Assyrian monarchs. In his reign a conspiracy broke out, by which the kingdom was destroyed, 767 years B. C. Three monarchies rose from its ruins, viz. Nineveh, which

* We have here followed Usher, and not the authors of the Universal History. Usher, as we think, more consistently, supposes Pul to be the father of Sardanapalus.

preserved the name of *Assyria*, *Babylon*, and the *kingdom of the Medes*.

§ Sardanapalus was the most effeminate of mankind. He never left his palace, but spent all his time with his women and his eunuchs. He imitated them in dress and painting, and spun with them at the distaff. Being besieged in his city, by Arbaces, governor of the Medes, he at length set fire to his palace, and consumed himself, with his women, eunuchs, and treasures.

EGYPT.

SECT. 12. EGYPT continued to be governed by a race of kings, concerning whom the common accounts seem not to be very satisfactory. The most considerable or the best known of them were Shishak, Rhamses, Amenophis IV. and Thuoris. Shishak is mentioned in scripture, and he is by some authors considered the same as Sesostris. But we are disposed to consider Sesostris as much more ancient, and have accordingly spoken of him in a former period.

§ Concerning *Shishak*, it appears that he built many temples and cities, dug canals, and among other conquests, took Jerusalem and spoilt the temple.

Rhamses possessed a very avaricious disposition. Diodorus informs us, that he was never at any expense either for the honour of the gods, or the welfare of his people; but that his sole delight was in the augmentation of his private treasure, which, at his decease, amounted to no less than 400,000 talents.

Amenophis IV. is thought to be the same with Memnon, whose famous statue was said to utter a sound at the rising of the sun. The monument in which he was buried, is much celebrated for its magnificence. He acquired great renown by his expedition against the Bactrians.

Thuoris lost the Egyptian possessions in the East; and after his death, Egypt, reduced within its natural boundaries, was divided among several little kingdoms for about 44 years.

PHŒNICIANS.

SECT. 13. The PHŒNICIANS, during this period, were governed by the successors of Hiram, of whom the first was *Baleazar*, his son; and the seventh from him was *Pygmalion*, the brother of the celebrated Dido. The cruelties of Pygmalion obliged her to flee to Africa, where she founded a mighty sovereignty, as will now be mentioned.

CARTHAGE.

SECT. 14. According to the most probable accounts, it was 869 years B. C. when Dido arrived at Africa. The history of the CARTHAGINIANS is dated from this event. She fixed her habitation at the bottom of a gulf, on a peninsula, near the spot where Tunis now stands.

From this, Carthage arose, a city which afterwards became famous for its wealth and power, and from its connexion with the Roman wars. The early history of the people, who were called after the name of their principal city, is but little known. Its later history is involved in that of Rome.

It is probable Dido might have found a few inhabitants in this place, whom its local advantages had induced to settle there; but to her and her attendants, Carthage is doubtless indebted for a regular foundation.

The colony had the same language, and national character, and nearly the same laws, with the parent state. In the height of its splendour, it possessed a population of 700,000 inhabitants, and had under its dominion 300 small cities, bordering on the Mediterranean sea.

§ Pygmalion, wishing to possess himself of the immense riches of Sichæus, the husband of Dido, took an opportunity, while they were engaged in a chase, to run him through the body with a spear. The suspicion of his sister was awakened; but, concealing her design, she requested Pygmalion to furnish her with men and ships, to convey her effects to a small city between Tyre and Sidon, that she might live there with her brother Barca.

The king granted her request; but Dido had no sooner embarked her property on board, than her brother and others, who favoured her real design, set sail for Cyprus, whence they carried off a great number of young women, and then steered their course to Africa.

The Tyrian monarch, thus defeated in his schemes, was about to send a fleet after the fugitives; but the tears of his mother, and the threatening predictions of the oracle, prevented his intended revenge.

ITALY.

SECT. 15. In ITALY, at the time of Numitor, about 775 B. C., there was a turn in events deserving our notice. *Amulius*, the brother of *Numitor*, being ambitious of the throne, usurped the government, and connected this act with the murder of the king's only son, and with compelling Rhea Sylvia, his only daughter, to become a vestal. He thus meant to prevent any from becoming claimants to the throne.

The event, however, frustrated the hopes of Amulius; for from Sylvia sprung Remus and Romulus, twin brothers, who, at length overcoming Amulius, replaced their grandfather, Numitor, on the throne.

§ Amulius, hearing of the birth of Remus and Romulus, so contrary to his expectations, ordered the mother to be buried alive, the punishment of incontinent vestals, and the children to be thrown into the river Tiber. The latter sentence was executed, but the former was prevented by the intercession of a daughter of Amulius.

The infants, though put into the Tiber, were saved, since the basket in which they were covered, floated on the surface. It was borne to the foot of the Aventine mount, and there stranded. According to some accounts, a she-wolf suckled them, which is incredible.

According to other accounts, the woman who preserved and nursed them, was called *Lupa*, and as Lupa is the Latin word for she-wolf, this circumstance caused the mistake.

The two brothers became shepherds, were fond of hunting wild beasts, and at length turned their arms against the robbers that infested the country. Having been informed of their high birth, they collected their friends, and fought against Amulius, their uncle, and killed him.

Numitor, after an exile of 42 years, was then called to the throne again, and was happy to owe his restoration to the bravery of his grandsons. Such were the youths who were destined by Providence to lay the foundation of a city, which became the mistress of the world.

Distinguished characters in Period V.

1. *Solomon*, endowed with extraordinary wisdom.
2. *Homer*, the greatest of the Grecian poets.
3. *Hesiod*, an eminent Greek poet.
4. *Lycurgus*, a reformer of the Spartan republic, and wise legislator.
5. *Dido*, a Tyrian princess, who founded Carthage.
6. *Isaiah*, the greatest of the prophetical writers.

§ 1. *Solomon* was the son of David by Bathsheba. He succeeded David in the kingdom of Israel. He was the wisest of mankind. In early life he appeared to be exemplary in piety, but was afterwards guilty of great defection from the strictness of religion. It is believed, however, that he did not die an apostate. The temple which he erected at Jerusalem in honour of the God of Israel, has also rendered his name immortal.

He wrote the books of Proverbs, and Ecclesiastes, and the Canticles, all inspired by the Spirit of God. He died 975 years B. C. aged 58 years, and having reigned 40 years.

2. *Homer* was not only the greatest of the Greek poets, but the earliest whose works have survived the devastations of time. On these accounts he is styled the father of poetry, and indeed, so far as we can know with certainty, he is the most ancient of all profane *classical* writers.

The place of his nativity is unknown. Seven illustrious cities contended for the honour of having given him birth. His parentage and the circumstances of his life are also unknown, except in regard to the latter, it was agreed that he was a *wandering* poet, and that he was *blind.*

His greatest poems, (and they are among the greatest of uninspired books,) are the *Iliad* and *Odyssey*. Other works have been ascribed to him, but without having been sufficiently substantiated. His poetry is characterized by sublimity, fire, sweetness, elegance, and universal knowledge.

The poems of Homer are the compositions of a man, who travelled and examined, with the most critical accuracy, whatever he met in his way. Modern travellers are astonished to see the different scenes which his pen described, almost 3000 years ago, still appearing the same; and the sailor who steers his course along the Ægean, beholds all the promontories and rocks which presented themselves to Nestor and Menelaus, when they returned victorious from the Trojan war.

The first appearance of Homer's poems in Greece, was about 200 years after the supposed time of the bard. Pisistratus, tyrant of Athens, was the first who arranged the Iliad and Odyssey in the form in which they now appear to us. The Arundelian marbles fix the period in which he flourished, at 907 years B. C.

3. *Hesiod* is generally considered as having been a contemporary of Homer. He was born at Ascra in Bœotia. His greatest production was a poem on *Agriculture*, which contains refined moral reflections, mingled with instructions for cultivating fields.

His *Theogony*, another poem, gives a faithful account of the gods of antiquity. Hesiod is admired for elegance and sweetness. Cicero highly commends him, and the Greeks were so partial to his moral poetical instructions, that they required their children to learn them all by heart.

4. *Lycurgus* flourished about 884 years B. C. He was regent of Sparta, until Charilaus, his nephew, had attained to mature years. Then leaving Sparta, he travelled in Asia and Egypt, for the purpose of improving his mind, and observing the manners, customs, and political institutions of different nations.

Upon his return, he reformed the abuses of the state, banished luxury, and produced a system which gave rise to all the magnanimity, fortitude, and intrepidity which distinguished the Lacedæmonians.

Having established his laws, and engaged the citizens not to alter them until his return, he left his country, and, by a voluntary death, rendered that event impossible; thus securing, as far as in his power, he perpetuity of his institutions.

5. *Dido*, also called *Elissa*, was a daughter of Belus, king of Tyre, and married her uncle Sichæus. Her husband having been murdered by Pygmalion, the successor of Belus, the disconsolate princess, with a number of Tyrians, set sail in quest of a settlement. A storm drove her fleet on the African coast, and there she founded, or enlarged a city, that became much celebrated in the annals of history.

Her beauty, as well as the fame of her enterprise, gained her many admirers; and her subjects wished to compel her to marry

Iarbas, king of Mauritania, by whom they were threatened with war. Dido requested three months for consideration; and, during that time, she erected a funeral pile, as if wishing, by a solemn sacrifice, to appease the manes of Sichæus, to whom she had vowed eternal fidelity.

When her preparation was completed, she stabbed herself on the pile, in presence of her people, and by this desperate feat, obtained the name of Dido, *valiant woman.* The poets have made Æneas and Dido contemporaneous, but this is only a fiction, allowed perhaps by the rules of their art.

6. Isaiah was the son of Amos, and of the lineage of David. He prophesied from 735 to 681 B. C. during the reigns of several kings of Judah. He is the greatest and the sublimest of the prophets. He reproved the sinners of his day with boldness, and exposed the many vices that prevailed in the nation. He is called the evangelical prophet, from his frequent allusion to, and prediction of Gospel times. He is said to have been cut in two with a wooden saw, by the cruel king Manasseh.

PERIOD VI.

The period of the Roman kings, extending from the founding of Rome, 752 years B. C., to the battle of Marathon, 490 years B. C.

ROMANS.

SECT. 1. Romulus began the building of ROME 752 B. C. His brother Remus was indeed concerned in the projected undertaking, but a dispute arising between the brothers respecting the place where the city should stand, they had recourse to arms; in consequence of which, Remus lost his life.

Romulus, only 18 years of age, was thus left to pursue the enterprise alone. On the Palatine hill he fixed as the spot, and enclosing about a mile of territory in compass, with a wall, he filled it with 1000 houses, or rather huts. To this collection he gave the name of Rome; and he peopled it with the tumultuous and vicious rabble, which he found in the neighbourhood. At first it was nearly destitute of laws; but it soon became a well regulated community.

§ The liberty of building a city on those hills, where the two brothers had fed their flocks, was granted to them by Numitor, the king. He assigned to them a certain territory, and permitted such of his subjects as chose, to resort thither in aid of the work.

A division taking place, in regard to the particular spot where the city should stand, Numitor advised them to watch the flight of birds, a custom common in that age, when any contested point was to be settled. They took their stations on different hills. Remus saw six vultures; Romulus twice as many; so that each one thought himself victorious—the one having the first omen, the other the most complete.

A contest was the result; and it is asserted that Remus was killed by the hand of his brother. Jumping contemptuously over the city wall, he was struck dead upon the spot by Romulus, who declared that no one should insult his rising walls with impunity.

2. Romulus, having been elected king, introduced order and discipline among his subjects, which gradually improved under his successors.

He adopted many important regulations respecting the government and policy of his newly acquired territory, the wisdom of which has been sanctioned by time. As some of these, and other institutions that were afterwards added, are to be presented under the General Views in this work, they need not here be given.

3. Under the salutary regulations of Romulus, great numbers of men, from the small towns around Rome, flocked to the city, and every day it increased in power and extent. The most important event under the administration of Romulus, was the Rape of the Sabine virgins, by which the Romans were supplied with wives, and which caused the war that thence ensued between the Romans and Sabines.

After conquering some of the neighbouring kings, Romulus was killed (it is supposed) by the Senators, having reigned 37 years, and was succeeded, at the expiration of one year, by Numa Pompilius, a Sabine, the wisest and best of the Roman kings, 715 years B. C.

§ In the want of women, Romulus proposed intermarriages with the Sabines, his neighbours. His proposal, however, was rejected with scorn. He then tried the effect of intrigue and force. Inviting the neighbouring tribes to witness some magnificent spectacle in the city, he had the pleasure of finding that the Sabines, with their wives and daughters, were among the foremost to be present.

At the proper time, the Roman youth rushed in among them with drawn swords, seized the youngest and most beautiful of the women, and carried them off by violence. The virgins, at first offended by the boldness of the intrusion, at length became reconciled to their lot.

The Sabines, as might be expected, resented the affront, and flew to arms. After several unfortunate attempts at revenge, the Sabines, with Tatius, their king, at their head, entered the Roman territories, 25,000 men strong. Having by stratagem passed into the city, they continued the war at pleasure. At length the Romans and Sabines prepared for a general engagement.

In the midst of the fight, however, the Sabine women who had been carried off by the Romans, rushed in between the combatants. "If," cried they, "any must die, let it be us, who are the cause of your animosity; since, if our parents or our husbands fall, we must, in either case, be miserable in surviving them."

This moving spectacle produced an effect. An accommodation ensued. It was agreed that Tatius and Romulus should reign jointly in Rome; that 100 Sabines should be admitted into the senate; and that the privileges of Roman citizens, should be extended to such of the Sabines as chose to enjoy them.

Tatius lived but five years after this; and Romulus, taking advantage of this event, and elated by prosperity, invaded the liberty of his people. The senators opposed his encroachments, and at length, it is said, tore him to pieces in the senate house.

When the throne was offered to Numa, he wished to decline it; and it was not until his friends repeatedly urged him to accept it, that he gave up his own wishes to theirs, and for the good of his country consented to become king of Rome.

He was a wise and virtuous man, and, before his elevation to the throne, lived contentedly in privacy. He proved excellent as a monarch, and reigned 43 years in profound peace, inspiring his subjects with the love of wisdom and virtue.

He multiplied the national gods, built temples, and instituted different classes of priests, and a great variety of religious ceremonies. The Flamines officiated each in the service of a peculiar deity; the Salii guarded the sacred bucklers; the Vestals cherished the sacred fire; the Augurs and Aruspices divined future events from the flight of birds, and the entrails of victims.

4. The third king of Rome was Tullius Hostilius, who was elected, and began to reign, 672 B. C. His disposition was warlike. He subdued the Albans, Fidenates, and other neighbouring states. The Sabines, now disunited from the Romans, became their most powerful enemy. Tullius reigned 33 years, and, according to some accounts, he was killed by lightning. The most remarkable event during the reign of Tullius, was the combat between the Horatii and Curiatii.

In the war between the Romans and Albans, as their armies were about to engage, the Alban general proposed that the dispute should be decided by single combat, and that the side whose champion was overcome, should submit to the conqueror. To this the Roman king acceded.

It happened that there were three twin brothers in each army; those of the Romans were called Horatii, those of the Albans, Curiatii; all remarkable for their prowess. To these the combat was assigned. The armies were drawn up in due order, and the brothers took to their arms.

The signal being given, the youths rushed forward to the encounter. They were soon engaged hand to hand, each regardless of his own safety, seeking only the destruction of his opponent. The three Albans were severely wounded, and loud shouts ran along the Roman army. In a few seconds, two of the Romans fell and expired. The acclamations were heard amid the Albans.

The surviving Roman now saw that all depended on him; it was an awful moment. But he did not despair; he manfully roused his spirits to meet the exigence of the occasion. Knowing that force alone could not avail, he had recourse to art.

He drew back, as if flying from his enemies. Immediately were heard the hisses of the Romans. But Horatius had the felicity to witness what he wished. The wounded Curiatii, pursuing him at unequal distances, were divided. Turning upon the nearest pursuer, he laid him dead at his feet. The second brother advancing, soon shared the same fate.

Only one now remained on each side. The hisses of the Romans were turned into cheerings. But what was their exultation when they saw the last of the Curiatii stretched lifeless on the ground!

What followed, it is painful to relate. When Horatius reached Rome, he saw his sister bitterly lamenting the death of the Curiatii, one of whom she was engaged to marry. In the dreadful moment of ungoverned rage, he killed her on the spot.

Horatius was condemned to die for his crime, but making his appeal to the people, he was pardoned, though his laurels and his character were forever tarnished.

5. Rome was governed by four other kings, in succession, viz. Ancius Martius, Tarquinius Priscus, Servius Tullius, and Tarquinius Superbus.

Ancus inherited the virtues of his grandfather, Numa, and was, besides, a warrior; Tarquin enriched Rome with magnificent works; Servius ruled with political wisdom; but Tarquin the Proud pursued a course of systematic tyranny. With him ended the monarchical form of government at Rome, 509 years B. C.

§ Servius married his two daughters to the two sons of Tarquin, and then having established good government, was preparing to quit the throne and live in peace and retirement. But these intentions were frustrated.

Tullia, one of his daughters, preferred her sister's husband to her own, and he was disposed to reciprocate so vile an attachment. To answer their base purposes, they both killed their respective partners. As one wickedness too surely paves the way for another, these flagitious wretches next plotted the death of Servius.

It will be read with horror, that not only did the cruel Tullia rejoice, when she heard that Tarquinius had murdered her father, but that when she rode forth in her chariot, to congratulate the base murderer, she would not permit her coachman to indulge even his humanity, who seeing the bleeding body of Servius lying in the street, was about to turn down another road, thinking, very rationally, that his mistress would be shocked to behold the mangled corpse of her old father.

Tullia had expelled from her heart all natural feeling, and perceiving the hesitation of the coachman, angrily bade the man drive on; he did so, and the chariot-wheels of the daughter's car wer stained with the blood of her gray-haired father.

Tarquin, surnamed the proud, upon this event, was made king; but though at first he ingratiated himself with the lower classes of the people, yet by his oppressive and tyrannical conduct, he at length became an object of universal detestation. His son Sextus having greatly indulged in detestable vices, became the occasion of his own and the king's ruin.

This prince, and Collatinus a noble Roman, and some officers, when with the army besieging Ardea, a small town not far from Rome, in the height of a debauch, were boasting what excellent wives each possessed. Collatinus was certain that his was the best; in their merriment, the young men mounted their horses, and set off for Rome, to discover whose wife was most properly employed in the absence of her husband.

The ladies were all found visiting and passing the time in amusement and mirth, except Lucretia, the wife of Collatinus. She was industriously spinning wool among her maidens at home. Sextus was so taken with the good sense and right behaviour of Lucretia, that he fell in love with her, and wished her to quit her husband, indulging at the same time the most unwarrantable designs.

Lucretia, shocked at his vile proposals, and unable to survive her dishonour, killed herself for grief, which so distracted Collatinus, that with Junius Brutus, and other friends, he raised an army, and drove Sextus and his infamous father from Rome. The people had suffered so much under the tyranny of this king, that they resolved that he should never come back, and that they would have no more kings.

The cause of the interest which Brutus took in the death of Lucretia, was the following. His father and eldest brother had been slain by Tarquin, and unable to avenge their death, he pretended to be insane. The artifice saved his life; he was called Brutus for his stupidity. When the infamous deed of the Tarquins was done, and the catastrophe which ensued was known, he seized the occasion of revenge.

Snatching the dagger from the wound of the bleeding Lucretia, he swore upon the reeking blade, immortal hatred to the royal family. "Be witness, ye gods," he cried, "that from this moment I proclaim myself the avenger of the chaste Lucretia's cause," &c. This energy of speech and action, in one who had been reputed a fool, astonished Rome, and every patriot's arm was nerved against Tarquin and his adherents—against Tarquin and royalty.

6. From a monarchy, Rome now became a republic, with a gradual increase of the power of the people from time to time. At first the nobles had much the largest share in the government. The supreme authority was committed to two magistrates, chosen from the patrician order every year, who were named consuls. Their power was nearly or quite equal to that of the kings, only it was temporary. Brutus and Collatinus were the first consuls, who, with several of their successors, were engaged in hostility with the banished king.

§ Tarquin, after his expulsion, took refuge in Etruria, where he enlisted two of the most powerful cities, Venii and Tarquinii, to espouse his cause. At Rome also he had adherents. A conspiracy having been formed to open the gates of the city to him, the republic was on the eve of ruin.

It was however discovered in season, and the two sons of Brutus having been concerned in it, he sternly ordered them to be beheaded in his presence. He put off the father, and acted only the consul—a dreadful necessity.

Some time after, in a combat between the Romans and Tarquins, Brutus engaged with Aruns, son of Tarquin, and so fierce was the attack, that they both fell dead together. Brutus was honoured as the father of the republic.

Tarquin now fled for aid to Porsenna, king of Clusium, who advanced with a large army to Rome, and had nearly entered it. The valour of one man saved the city. Horatius Cocles, seeing the enemy approach the bridge where he stood sentinel, and observing the retreat of the Romans, besought them to assist him. He told them to burn or break down the bridge behind him, whilst he went forward to keep back the enemy.

He then remained alone fighting in the midst of his enemies, and when he heard the crash of the bridge and the shouts of the Romans, knowing that no way of entrance was left for the foe, he jumped into the river and swam over to his friends in safety.

In the war with Porsenna occurred another remarkable incident.

Mutius Scævola, a noble young Roman, upon leave obtained of the senate, disguised himself, and entered the tent of Porsenna. There he saw a man so richly drest that he thought he was the king, whom he contrived to kill, but it was only the king's secretary.

While endeavouring to quit the camp, Mutius was seized and carried before Porsenna, who told him he would severely torture him if he did not betray the schemes of the Romans. Mutius only answered by putting his hand into one of the fires lighted near him, and holding it steadily there.

The king, seeing the courage and fortitude of this youth, leaped from his throne, and drawing the hand of Mutius from the flame, highly praised him, and dismissed him without farther harm. Peace was soon concluded upon this incident.

7. The Latins, excited by Mamilius, Tarquin's son-in-law, declared war against the Romans, 501 years B. C. The common people, oppressed by the patrician order, had become disaffected, and refused to enlist into the service. In this crisis, the Romans resorted to the desperate measure of having a dictator, a magistrate with unlimited authority, for the period of six months. This was an effectual resort in times of danger.

A few years after, the people, supposing their grievances not sufficiently redressed, rose in general insurrection, when the senate consented to create five new magistrates, called tribunes, who were to be annually selected by the people.

These were to be sacred; their office was to defend the oppressed, pardon offenders, arraign the enemies of the people, and, if necessary, stop the whole machine of government. They were afterwards increased to ten. The popular or democratic constitution of Rome may be dated from this period, 490 years B. C.

About this time, Coriolanus, a patrician and able warrior, being banished from Rome, for proposing the abolition of the tribunate, retired to the Volsci, among whom he raised an army, and advanced to besiege Rome. Attacking the city, he would probably have conquered it, but he was turned from his purpose by the prayers and tears of his mother, wife, and children.

§ A few particulars respecting Coriolanus must here be related. Passing over the circumstances of his banishment, we find that upon his entrance into the territory of the Volsci, he met a most friendly reception from Tullus Aufidius, a mortal enemy to Rome.

Having advised this prince to make war against the Romans, he marched at the head of the Volsci, as general. The approach of Coriolanus, at the head of so powerful an enemy, greatly alarmed the Romans, who sent him several embassies to reconcile him to his country, and to solicit his return. He was deaf to all proposals; and though each successive embassy was made more and more solemn and urgent, he bade them prepare for war.

At Rome, all was now confusion and consternation. The republic was nearly given up for lost. Coriolanus had pitched his camp at only a very short distance from the city. As a last resort, it was suggested, that possibly his wife or mother might effect what the senate and the ministers of religion could not.

Accordingly his mother, Veturia, and his wife, Vergilia, with his children, and the principal matrons of the city, undertook the last embassy. The meeting of Coriolanus and this train, was in the highest degree tender and affecting. In the sternness of his soul he had resolved to give them a denial; but the authority of a mother, and the entreaties of a wife and of children, must be listened to.

"My son," cried his mother, "how am I to consider this meeting? Do I embrace my son or my enemy? Am I your mother or your captive? How have I lived to see this day—to see my son a banished man—and still more distressful, to see him the enemy of his country? how has he been able to turn his arms against the place that gave him life—how direct his rage against those walls that protect his wife, his children, and his gods? But it is to me only that my country owes her oppressor. Had I never been a mother, Rome had still been free."

With these and similar words, and with the tears and entreaties of his wife and children, his stern and obstinate resolutions were overcome. He was melted under them, and the feelings of a man rose superior to the honour of a soldier and the vengeance of a foe. The Volsci were marched from the neighbourhood of Rome, but the event fulfilled the sad prediction which he addressed to his mother, in reply—a prediction which only a Roman mother could hear—"O my mother, thou hast saved Rome, but lost thy son."

The act of Coriolanus, of course, displeased the Volsci. He was summoned to appear before the people of Antium: but the clamours which his enemies raised were so prevalent, that he was murdered on the spot appointed for his trial. His body was honoured, nevertheless, with a magnificent funeral by the Volsci, and the Roman matrons put on mourning for his loss.

To show their sense of Veturia's merit and patriotism, the Romans dedicated a temple to Female Fortune.

GREECE.

8. Greece, during this period, underwent several changes. After the institutions of Lycurgus had been a number of years in successful operation, those of Athens began to receive attention from some of their wise men. The office of archon had become decennial, at the beginning of this period.

In 648 B. C. the archons were elected annually, were nine in number, and all had equal authority. Under these changes the people became miserable, and a reform was attempted, first by Draco, and 150 years afterwards by the illustrious Solon, 594 years B. C. At the request of the citizens, they each furnished, during his archonship, a written code for the regulation of the state.

§ Draco was a wise and honest, but a very stern man. His laws were characterized by extreme severity. Very trifling offences were punished with death, "because," said Draco, "small crimes deserve death, and I have no greater punishment for the greatest sins,"—a plan ill adapted to the state of human society.

Solon was one of the seven wise men of Greece. He established excellent rules of justice, order, and discipline. But, though possessed of extensive knowledge, he wanted a firm and intrepid mind; and he rather accommodated his system to the habits and passions of his countrymen, than attempted to reform their manners.

He cancelled the bloody code of Draco, except the laws which related to murder; and he abolished the debts of the poor by an act of insolvency. He divided the Athenians into four classes, of which the three first consisted of persons possessing property, and the fourth of those who were poor.

All the offices of the state were committed to the care of the rich; but those who possessed no property, were allowed to vote in the general assembly of the people, in whose hands he lodged the supreme power.

He instituted a senate, composed of 400 persons, (afterwards increased to 500 and 600,) who had cognisance of all appeals from the court of Areopagus, and with whom it was necessary that every measure should originate before it was discussed in the assembly of the people. In this way he sought to balance the weight of the popular interest.

Solon committed the supreme administration of justice to the court of Areopagus. This court had fallen into disrepute, but Solon, by confining its numbers to those who had been archons, greatly raised the reputation of the body.

The following anecdote of Solon and Thespis is worthy of remembrance. Thespis was an actor of plays. Solon having at one time attended those shows, which were then very rude, called Thespis, who had been acting various characters, and asked him if he was not ashamed to speak so many lies?

Thespis replied, "It was all in jest." Solon, striking his staff on the ground, violently exclaimed, "If we encourage ourselves to speak falsely in jest, we shall run the chance of acquiring a habit of speaking falsely in serious matters." Such a sentiment is worthy of the wisdom of Solon.

9. Scarcely had Athens begun to enjoy the benefit of these new regulations, when Pisistratus, a rich and ambitious citizen, usurped the supreme power, (B. C. 560,) which act Solon was unable to prevent. He and his posterity exercised it during 50 years.

Hippias and Hipparchus, his sons, who succeeded him, enjoyed a peaceable crown for a time, but were at length dethroned, and democracy was restored.

§ Pisistratus secured the favour of the people by the following expedient. Wounding himself, he ran into the market place, and proclaimed that his enemies had inflicted the injury. Solon, with contempt, said to him, "Son of Hippocrates, you act Ulysses badly; he hurt himself to deceive his enemies; you have done so to cheat your friends."

The populace, as is generally the case, being deaf to the voice of reason, Pisistratus became tyrant, or king of Athens. He secured the affections of the people by his splendour and munificence. He was eminent for his love of learning, and the fine arts. He adorned Athens with many magnificent buildings.

The restoration of democracy was undertaken by Harmodius and Aristogiton, who were citizens in middle life. They succeeded eventually, though they both lost their lives in the attempt. Aristogiton was previously tortured, having fallen into the hands of Hippias. By the aid of the Lacedæmonians the object was accomplished, and Hippias, who at first escaped the fate of his brother, was at length dethroned.

Passing into Asia, he solicited foreign aid to place him in the sovereignty. Darius at this time meditated the conquest of Greece. Hippias took advantage of the views of an enemy against his native country, and Greece soon became involved in a war with Persia.

10. Under the institutions of Lycurgus the Spartans had become a race of warriors. Being in the neighbourhood of Messenia, they were almost constantly at war with that state. The first Messenian war began 743 years B. C. and lasted 19 years. There were two other periods of contention between Sparta and Messenia, but the latter was finally subdued. The territory was seized and its inhabitants were enslaved.

§ During one of these wars, the Lacedæmonians, it is said, bound themselves by oath not to return home till they had conquered the Messenians. Despairing, however, of ever returning, they sent orders to the women of Sparta to recruit the population, by promiscuous intercourse with the young men, who being children when the war began, had not taken the oath.

The offspring of this singular and improper order were denominated Partheniæ, or Sons of Virgins.

ISRAELITES.

11. The kingdom of Israel, towards the beginning of the present period, (721 B. C.) was subverted by Salmanazar king of Assyria, or Nineveh. The Israelites were carried captive to Assyria, whence they never returned. This event occurred during the reign of Hosea, their last king.

§ Hosea had reigned nine years, when Salmanazar made him tributary. But Hosea having revolted, the Assyrian king besieged Samaria, the capital of the ten tribes, and after three years took and plundered it.

Except a few, who remained in Canaan, the Israelites were dispersed throughout Assyria, and lost their distinctive character. Those who remained in their native country became intermixed with strangers. The descendants of these mingled races were afterwards known by the name of Samaritans.

Thus, in a little more than two centuries after the separation of the ten tribes from those of Judah and Benjamin, were they destroyed as a nation, having, on account of their great sins, previouslv suffered an awful series of calamities.

JEWS.

12. The kingdom of JUDAH from the commencement of this period enjoyed but a doubtful existence. It was invaded at different times by the Babylonians, rendered tributary, and finally subdued.

Nebuchadnezzar, within 115 years after the destruction of Samaria, took Jerusalem, and razed the city and its temple to its foundations.

§ During the latter part of the kingdom of Judah, the greater portion of its kings were impious. Two or three of them, however, were eminently religious. Such were Hezekiah and Josiah. They were both of them reformers, and destroyed the altars of idolatry.

The idolatry of Ahaz was punished by the captivity of 200,000 of his subjects, though they were afterwards sent back upon the remonstrance of the prophet Obed. Manasseh, an impious and cruel prince, was carried to Babylon, bound with fetters. This affliction, becoming the means of his repentance, God heard his supplications, and brought him again into his kingdom.

13. Under Jehoiachin, who was carried captive to Babylon, together with his people, commenced the Seventy years Captivity of the Jews, 606 B. C. The king was afterwards released, but remained tributary to the king of Babylon.

§ In the reign of Zedekiah, the next but one in succession after Jehoiachin, Jerusalem was taken by the Babylonians, and entirely demolished. Zedekiah, after seeing all his children slain, had his eyes put out, and was brought in fetters to Babylon.

14. The Jews having been in captivity to the Babylonians just 70 years, were permitted, by Cyrus, king of Persia, to return to their native land, 536 years B. C. This was accomplished under the direction of Zerubbabel and Joshua, their leaders.

They soon began the rebuilding of the temple, but their enemies prevented them from making any progress. Several years afterwards they commenced the work anew, and completed it in the space of four years, 516 B. C. Upon this event they celebrated the first passover.

§ The return of the Jews from their captivity happened the first year of Cyrus, who, as we shall soon learn, had conquered Babylon, and terminated the Babylonian empire.

The influence of adversity on many of the Jews, seems to have been very favorable on this occasion. It brought them to repentance, and engaged them in the worship and ordinances of their religion. The vessels of the temple, which Nebuchadnezzar had brought with him from Jerusalem, were all restored by the Persian monarch.

NINEVEH.

15. Of the three kingdoms into which the ancient Assyrian empire was divided upon the death of Sardanapalus, NINEVEH or Assyria comes first in order. Its first king is supposed to have been Tiglath Pileser, 747 B. C. A few of his successors, during this period, were Salmanazar, Sennacherib, Esarhaddon, Nebuchadnezzar, and Belshazzar.

Under the last of these kings the kingdom of Nineveh ended. Babylon, its capital, was taken by Cyaxares II. aided by Cyrus, and Belshazzar was killed, 538 years B. C.

§ Salmanazar was the sovereign mentioned above, in the history of the Israelites. He destroyed the kingdom of the Ten Tribes.

Of Sennacherib it is recorded in his war with the Jews, that having written a letter to Hezekiah full of blasphemy against the God of Israel, God, in order to punish him, when he was just ready to take Jerusalem, sent an angel, who in one night smote 185,000 men of his army.

Covered with shame, he returned to his own country, and there his two eldest sons conspired against and killed him in the temple of Nisroch.

About 108 years after this prince, Nebuchadnezzar began to reign over the kingdom of Nineveh. He signalized his reign by many conquests, particularly of Syria, Palestine, and Egypt.

His heart being elated with success, God, to punish him for his pride, reduced him to such a state of insanity, that, wandering in the forests, he lived upon grass, like a wild beast. He recovered twelve months before his death, and, by a solemn edict, published throughout the whole of his dominions the astonishing things that God had wrought in him.

Labynit, or the scripture Belshazzar, became peculiarly infamous, by profanely using the holy vessels which Nebuchadnezzar had brought out of the spoils of the temple. He was at length besieged by Cyaxares II. king of the Medes, in conjunction with Cyrus.

During the siege he made a great entertainment for his whole court on a certain night; but their joy was greatly disturbed by a vision, and still more by the explanation which Daniel, the prophet, a Jewish captive, gave of it to the king, that his kingdom was taken from him, and delivered to the Medes and Persians. That very night Babylon was taken and Belshazzar killed.

BABYLON.

16. BABYLON, the next kingdom in order of the second em-

pire of Assyria, continued separate not quite 70 years. Nabonassar was its first king. After a few successive reigns, and interregnums, it was subdued by Esarhaddon, one of the kings of Nineveh, and annexed to his dominions, 680 B. C.

§ The famous astronomical epocha at Babylon, called the era of Nabonassar, commenced from the reign of this prince. We are unacquainted with the history of his successors, only Merodach seems to be the same prince who sent ambassadors to Hezekiah, to congratulate him on the recovery of his health.

MEDES.

17. The last in order of the kingdoms that constituted the second empire of Assyria was that of the MEDES. After the destruction of the first Assyrian empire, the Medes enjoyed for some time the liberty they had acquired by their valour. They formed a republic; but anarchy having prevailed, they elected a king after 37 years.

Dejoces, the first king, was elected 690 years B. C. The fourth king after him, viz. Cyaxares II. or Darius the Mede, having with his nephew, Cyrus, conquered Babylon, reigned over it two years in conjunction with Cyrus; after which the kingdom of the Medes, and indeed the whole Assyrian empire, was united to that of Persia, 536 years B. C.

§ The Medes are supposed to be the descendants of Madai, the third son of Japhet, from whom they derived their name. They seem to have been independent tribes at first, and not to have been united under one monarchy till the time of Dejoces.

They were governed by petty princes, and some are of opinion, that one of the four kings, who in the time of Abraham, invaded the southern coast of Canaan, reigned in Media. They were first brought into subjection to the Assyrian yoke by Ninus.

Some time after they had shaken off this yoke, they were governed by kings of their own, who became absolute, and were controlled by no law. Of Dejoces it is recorded, that he no sooner ascended the throne, than he endeavoured to civilize and polish his subjects. He built the beautiful city of Ecbatana, and made it the capital of his empire.

He then contrived a code of laws for the good of the state, and caused them to be strictly obeyed. In a war with Nebuchadnezzar I. his capital was plundered, and stripped of all its ornaments, and falling into the conqueror's hands, he was cruelly shot to death with arrows.

Phraortes, his successor, was much more fortunate, and conquered almost all upper Asia. Cyaxares I. a brave prince, made war upon the kingdom of Nineveh, to avenge the wrongs inflicted by Nebuchadnezzar. A battle ensued, in which the Ninevites or Assyrians were defeated; but a formidable army of the Scythians having invaded Media, Cyaxares marched with all his forces against them.

The Medes, however, were vanquished, and obliged to make an alliance with the Scythians, who settled in Media, where they remained for 28 years. Finding that they could not get rid of their troublesome guests by force, they effected it by stratagem. The Scythians being invited to a general feast, which was given in every family, each landlord made his guest drunk, and in that condition massacred him.

After this event, Cyaxares entered into a war with the Lydians. This war continued five years. The battle fought in the fifth year, was remarkable on account of a total eclipse of the sun, which happened during the engagement, and which was foretold by Thales, the philosopher.

The Medes and Lydians, equally terrified, immediately retreated, and soon after concluded a peace. Two more princes succeeded, viz. Astyages and Cyaxares II. Astyages married his daughter to Cambyses, king of Persia, of which marriage Cyrus was the issue. After the death of Cyaxares, Cyrus united the kingdoms of the Medes and Persians.

PERSIA.

18. From the days of Cyrus the Great, 536 years B. C. the PERSIAN empire holds a distinguished place in ancient history. It was originally of small extent, and almost unknown; but after being founded by Cyrus, it included all India, Assyria, Media, and Persia, and the parts adjoining to the Euxine and Caspian Seas. It is sometimes called the Medo-Persian empire.

Cyrus is represented as a prince of an excellent character, and he obtained the surname of Great, from his heroic actions and splendid achievements. Having undertaken an expedition against the Scythians, he was surprised and slain by means of an ambuscade from the enemy, 529 years B.C.

He was succeeded by his son Cambyses, who is called in scripture Artaxerxes, and who added Egypt to his empire. Cambyses was succeeded by Darius, 522 years B. C., the son of Hystaspes, who by a stratagem obtained the sovereignty.

§ The first inhabitants of Persia were called Elamites, and descended from Elam the eldest son of Shem. During, however, more than 16 centuries we have little information relative to their history. Chederlaomer, the only king of Elam recorded in history, conquered the king of Sodom, but was defeated by Abraham. This incident is mentioned in Scripture.

Cyrus was born but one year after his uncle Cyaxares. The manners of the Persians were admirable in those days, great simplicity of dress, and food, and behaviour, universally prevailed, so that Cyrus was plainly and wisely educated, as he was treated like other children of his own age. But he surpassed them all, not only in aptness to learn, but in courage and in address.

When he was yet a boy, his mother took him to visit his grandfather, but the pride and luxury of the court of Media quite surprised and disgusted him. Astyages was so charmed with the sensible conversation and artless manners of the prince, that he loaded him with presents. Cyrus, however, gave them all away to the courtiers, according to their merits, or their services rendered to himself.

Sacas, the cup-bearer, he neglected, because he did not let him visit Astyages when he pleased; and when Astyages lamented his neglect of so good an officer, "Oh," said the young prince, "there is not much merit in being a good cup-bearer; I can do as well myself." He then took the cup, and handed it to his mother with great modesty and gracefulness.

Astyages admired his skill, but laughingly observed, "the young waiter had forgotten one thing." "What have I forgotten?" asked Cyrus. "To taste the wine before you handed it to me and your mother." "I did not forget that, but I did not choose to swallow poison."

"Poison!" exclaimed the king. "Yes, there must be poison in the cup, for they who drink of it sometimes grow giddy and sick, and fall down." "Then do you never drink in your country?" inquired Astyages. "Yes, but we only drink to satisfy thirst, and then a little water suffices."

Many similar anecdotes are recorded of this prince, which may be learnt from larger histories. Having reduced all the nations from the Ægean sea to the Euphrates, he advanced towards Babylon, and at length entered it by stratagem. Having caused deep and large ditches to be dug all around it, he, on a certain night, when all the Babylonians were engaged in feasting and merriment, ordered the dams of the ditches to be thrown open, that the waters of the Euphrates might run into them.

By this means, the channel of the river, which ran through the city, was left dry, so that the troops entered it without opposition. The guards were surprised and slain, together with the king and all his family. The kingdom of Babylon was thus destroyed for ever.

Two years after this, Cyrus reigned over his vast empire alone during seven years, in the first of which he published the famous edict for the return of the Jews.

Of Cambyses, the son of Cyrus, it is recorded that he conquered Egypt, which remained under the Persian yoke 112 years. He made himself master of Pelusium, the key of Egypt, by the following stratagem. He placed in front of his army a great number of those animals considered sacred by the Egyptians, who not daring to injure them, made no opposition to the Persian army.

After an impostor named Smerdis, who reigned 7 months, Darius, a descendant of Cyrus on the mother's side, ascended the throne. In his time it was that the Jews were permitted to rebuild their temple. After a war against the Scythians, he turned his arms, as we shall soon see, against the Greeks.

LYDIANS.

19. In the history of the LYDIANS, the last of its dynasties, was that of the Mermnadæ. Gyges, one of the chief officers of Candaules the king, having murdered the latter, became possessed of his queen and throne, 718 years B. C. He was the first of the Mermnadæ race. The fourth prince after him was Crœsus, so celebrated for his riches. His kingdom was conquered by Cyrus.

§ A circumstance worthy of record occurred in the contest between Cyrus and Crœsus. After Crœsus was taken prisoner, he was condemned by the conqueror to be burnt alive. When the unhappy prince was led to the funeral pile, he exclaimed aloud three times, Solon! Solon! Solon!

Cyrus immediately demanded, why he pronounced that celebrated philosopher's name with so much vehemence in that extremity. Crœsus answered, that the observation of Solon, "That no mortal could be esteemed happy till the end of life," had forcibly recurred to his recollection.

Cyrus was struck with the remark, and, as if in anticipation of his own tragical end, ordered the unhappy king to be taken from the pile, and treated him ever after with honour and respect.

EGYPT.

20. EGYPT, during the present period, was governed by the following kings—Sabbacon, Tharaca, Pharaoh-Necho, Psammenitus, and a few others. Under the last of these, 525 B. C. Egypt was conquered by Cambyses, king of Persia, to which power it was subject more than a century.

§ Sabbacon, a king of Ethiopia, it seems, conquered Egypt. He killed Nechus, king of Sais; burnt Bocchoris, another king, to death, and forced Anysis the blind to retire into the morasses. During his continuance in Egypt, he acquired a high reputation for wisdom and integrity. He finally relinquished the sceptre, and returned into Ethiopia, because he would not massacre the priests, agreeably to a suggestion said to have been imparted unto him by the tutelar god of Thebes.

Tharaca, called in scripture Tirhakah, made war against Sennacherib, king of Assyria. After him there was an anarchy of two years, and an aristocracy of twelve governors for fifteen years.

Pharaoh-Necho waged war against the Assyrians and Jews, killed Josiah king of Judah, captured Jerusalem, imprisoned Jehoahaz, and appointed Jehoiachim king.

Psammenitus reigned only six months before the invasion of Cambyses, and the subjection of his kingdom. He was kindly treated at first by the conquerer, but thirsting for an opportunity to revenge himself, he was condemned to drink bull's blood, and died wretchedly.

Distinguished Characters in Period VI.

1. Romulus, founder and first king of Rome.
2. Sappho, a Greek poetess, inventor of the Sapphic verse.
3. Æsop, a Phrygian philosopher and fabulist.
4. Solon, a legislator of Athens, and one of the wisest men of Greece.
5. Thales, founder of the Ionic philosophy.
6. Cyrus, a wise and successful prince, who conquered most of the East.
7. Anacreon, a Greek poet, and father of the Anacreontic verse.
8. Pythagoras, a Grecian philosopher.

§ 1. Romulus was a son of Rhea Sylvia, and grandson of Numitor, king of Alba, and born at the same birth with Remus. His story has already been told. As the founder of Rome his name is immortal. His virtues were those of a military chieftain and adventurer in a rude age. He is not undistinguished as a legislator, though his institutions had almost exclusively a warlike tendency.

After a reign of 37 or 39 years, he was killed, as is supposed, by the senators. The fable, however, on this subject is, that as he was giving instructions to the senators, he disappeared from their sight—an eclipse of the sun, which happened at that time, being favourable to the rumor that he was taken up to heaven. The Romans paid him divine honours under the name of Quirinus, and ranked him among the twelve great gods.

2. Sappho was born in the island of Lesbos, about 600 years B. C. She is celebrated for her poetical talents and beauty. Her tender attachments were extremely violent, and the conduct into which they betrayed her must be reprobated by every virtuous mind. She conceived such a passion for Phaon, a youth of Mytilene, that upon his refusal to reciprocate it, she threw herself into the sea from Mount Leucas.

She composed nine books in lyric verses, besides epigrams, elegies, &c. Of all these compositions nothing now remains but two fragments, one of which is preserved by Longinus; though they were all extant in the age of Horace. Her poems were admired for their sublimity, sweetness, and elegance; yet they were highly objectionable, it is said, on account of their licentiousness.

3. Æsop flourished about 580 years B. C. Those entertaining and instructive fables which he composed, have acquired for him a high reputation, and he is generally supposed to have been the inventor of that kind of writing. He was originally a slave, and had several masters, but procured his liberty by the charms of his genius. Falling into the hands of an Athenian philosopher, he was enfranchised.

He travelled over the greatest part of Greece and Egypt, but resided much at the court of Crœsus, king of Lydia, by whom he was sent to consult the oracle of Delphi. In this commission Æsop behaved himself with great severity, and sarcastically compared the Delphians to floating sticks which appear large at a distance, but are nothing when brought near.

The Delphians, offended with his caustic remarks, accused him of some act of sacrilege, and pretending to have proved it against him, threw him down from a rock. He is said to have been short and deformed in his person.

4. Solon was born at Salamis and educated at Athens. After devoting the early part of his life to philosophical and political studies, he travelled over the greatest portion of Greece; but was distressed with the dissentions that prevailed among his countrymen.

Having, however, been elected archon and legislator of Athens, he made a reform in every department of the government. He instituted the Areopagus, regulated the Prytaneum, and his laws flourished in full vigour above 400 years. He died, as some report, in Cyprus, at the court of king Philocyprus, in his 80th year, about 558 B. C.

5. Thales was born at Miletus, in Ionia. Like the rest of the ancients, he travelled in quest of knowledge, and for some time resided in Crete, Phœnicia, and Egypt. Under the priests of Memphis he was taught geometry, astronomy, and philosophy, and enabled to measure with exactness, the height and extent of a pyramid, by its shadow.

His discoveries in astronomy were great, and he was the first who calculated accurately a solar eclipse. Like Homer, he looked upon water as the principle of every thing. In founding the Ionic sect of philosophy, which distinguished itself for deep and abstruse speculations, his name is memorable.

He died in the 96th year of his age, about 548 years B. C. His compositions are lost.

6. Cyrus subdued the eastern parts of Asia, and made war against Crœsus, king of Lydia, whom he conquered, B. C. 548. He invaded the kingdom of Assyria, and took the city of Babylon, by drying the channels of the Euphrates, and marching his troops through the bed of this river, while the people were celebrating a grand festival.

He afterwards marched against Tomyris, the queen of the Massagetæ, a Scythian nation, and was defeated in a bloody battle, B. C. 530. The victorious queen, who had lost her son in the previous encounter, was so incensed against Cyrus, that she cut off his head, and threw it into a vessel filled with human blood, exclaiming, "Satisfy thyself with blood, which thou hast so eagerly desired."

According to Xenophon, Cyrus possessed many excellent traits of character.

7. Anacreon had a delicate wit, but he was certainly too fond of pleasure and wine. All that he wrote is not extant; though his odes remain, and their sweetness, gayety, and elegance have been admired in every age. With "flowers, beauties, and perpetual graces," they have a hurtful moral tendency.

He lived to his 85th year, and after every excess of pleasure and debauchery, choked himself with a grape stone, and expired. His statue was placed in the citadel of Athens, representing him as an old drunken man, singing, with every mark of dissipation and intemperance.

8. Pythagoras was born at Samos. In his 18th year he obtained the prize for wrestling at the Olympic games. He afterwards travelled in Egypt, Chaldæa, and the east, and at length, in his 40th year, he retired to Crotona, in Magna Græcia.

Here his universal knowledge gained him friends, admirers, and disciples, and a reformation took place in the morals of the people. The world is indebted to him for the demonstration of the 47th proposition of Euclid, respecting the square of the hypothenuse. By his ingenious discoveries in astronomy he traced the true solar system. The time and place of his death are unknown.

PERIOD VII.

The Period of Grecian Glory, extending from the Battle of Marathon, 490 *years B. C. to the birth of Alexander,* 356 *years B. C.*

GREECE.

1. The GREEKS, soon after the expulsion of Hippias, the king of Athens, became involved in a war with Persia. Under Darius, the Persians invaded Greece, 496 years B. C. His first fleet was wrecked; but a second of 600 sail, containing 500,000 men, ravaged the Grecian islands, and an immense army poured down on Attica.

Miltiades, at the head of the Greeks, met the Persian hosts, and defeated them on the plain of Marathon. The Persians lost 6300 men in that battle, while the Greeks lost but 190. The Grecian force did not exceed 10,000 men. The date of this engagement is 490 years B. C. and one of the most important in its consequences that history records.

§ Ambition and revenge in the breast of Darius, gave rise to his project of invading Greece. The Athenians had rendered assistance to the people of Ionia in attempting to throw off the Persian yoke, and had ravaged Sardis, the capital of Lydia. Darius soon reducing the Ionians to submission, turned his arms against the Greeks; while the exile Hippias, basely seconded the plans of the Persian monarch.

One expedition in a great measure failed; and it was some time before another could be gathered and prepared to act, so that it was six years from the period in which the Persian invasion first commenced, to the battle of Marathon. Previously to the descent on Attica, the Persians, under Mardonius, had attacked Thrace, Macedonia, and the neighbouring provinces.

Marathon, where the Grecian and Persian forces met, was a small town by the sea side. The Greeks were led by ten generals, each of whom was to command for one day by turns, and Miltiades was to take his turn as the others, although he was chief general.

Aristides, (one of the ten,) had sense enough to see the evil of such a plan, and generosity to give up his honours, for the benefit of his country. When it was his day to command he resigned it to Miltiades, because, as he said, "Miltiades is the best general." The other generals saw the propriety of this conduct, and resigned to their commander in like manner.

Miltiades, however, thought it his duty not to act till his proper day came round, but he probably made the necessary preparation. The armies engaged in a fierce and obstinate battle. Themistocles, a brave man, and the compeer of Aristides, fought nobly by his side. From the skill with which Miltiades had placed his troops, as much as from the valour of those troops, the battle of Marathon was won by the Greeks.

A soldier covered with the blood of the enemy ran to Athens with the news, and had just strength enough left to say, "Rejoice! the victory is ours!" and then fell down dead, from his fatigue and wounds.

Not long after this service rendered to his country, Miltiades, who at first was loaded with honours, died in prison, where he was thrust by the Athenians, because he could not pay a fine which they ordered him to pay. On a false pretence of treachery to his country, this great general had been condemned to death, and afterwards the sentence of death was changed to the paying of a fine.

Greece, particularly Athens, abounded with great men about this time. A little tale or two concerning Themistocles may be interesting here. At a time when he was great in power, he laughingly said, that "his son was greater than any man in Greece." "How is that?" said a friend. "Why," replied Themistocles, "the Athenians govern Greece, I command the Athenians, his mother commands me, and this boy commands his mother."

Themistocles was an able general, and saved his country in one instance or more. But he was not an amiable man. Ambition was his god. Plutarch relates that after the battle of Marathon, in which Miltiades gained so glorious a victory, Themistocles was observed to court solitude, and indulge in a profound melancholy.

Upon inquiry made of him respecting the cause of his mental dejection, he replied, that "the trophies of Miltiades would not permit him to sleep." Indeed all his feelings and conduct showed how completely ambition had gotten the mastery over him, and how much, consequently, he wished to be master of Athens and of Greece. Yet under the ungrateful treatment, which he afterwards received from his countrymen, he would not betray the land that gave him birth, though he had an opportunity of doing it.

2. On the death of Darius, his son Xerxes prosecuted the war against Greece. During the early part of this war were fought the celebrated battles of Thermopylæ and Platæa on land, and those of the straights of Salamis and Mycale on water.

The battles of Thermopylæ and Salamis took place 480 years B. C.; and those of Platæa and Mycale, 479. Leonidas, Themistocles, Aristides, Pausanias, and several others, distinguished themselves in the defence of Greece, and acquired lasting renown by their achievements.

Xerxes brought over with him 2,000,000 of fighting men, besides vast numbers of women and domestics—the largest army and assemblage of persons recorded in history. This immense force was effectually resisted, during two days, at the pass of Thermopylæ, by 6000 Greeks.

Their valour, though it could not finally arrest the progress of the Persians, cost the latter the lives of 20,000 warriors. Athens was soon reached, which the Persians pillaged and burnt. The women and children, however, had been previously conveyed to a place of safety, and the men betook themselves to their fleet.

§ Xerxes was a vain mortal. He ordered a passage to be cut through the high mountain of Athos, in Macedonia, and thus a canal was made for his ships. He is said to have written a letter to Mount Athos, in which he "commanded it not to put stones in the way of his workmen, or he would cut it down and throw it into the sea," and he ordered the labourers to be chastised to make them work faster.

When he saw, from a high hill, the plain covered with his soldiers, and the sea with his ships, he at first, in the pride of his heart, called himself the most favoured of mortals; but when he reflected, that in a hundred years, not one of the many thousands whom he beheld would be alive, he burst into tears at the instability of all human things.

Almost all the small cities of Greece submitted to the Persian king when he sent to them, as was the custom, for earth and water; which was the same as to ask them, whether they would receive him as their conqueror. Sparta and Athens, with the small towns of Thespia and Platæa, alone refused to receive the heralds and to send the token of homage.

Every thing gave way before the march of Xerxes, until he came to the pass of Thermopylæ. On this spot Leonidas, one of the two reigning kings of Sparta, with his 6000 of brave soldiers, awaited his coming. Xerxes, after a weak attempt to corrupt him, imperiously summoned him to give up his arms. "Let him come and take them," was the short answer of this true native of Laconia.

The bravest of the Persian troops were ordered out against Leonidas, but they were always driven back with disgrace. At last a wretch went and informed the king of a secret path, by which he could mount an eminence which overlooked the Grecian camp. The Persians gained this advantageous post during the darkness of the night, and the next morning the Greeks discovered that they had been betrayed.

Leonidas knew that it was in vain to expect his small army could conquer the endless forces of Xerxes; he therefore sent away his allies, and kept with him only his 300 Lacedæmonians. He had been told by the oracle that either Sparta or her king must perish, and he longed to die for the good of his country.

Xerxes marched his vast army against this heroic little band. Leonidas fell among the first, bravely fighting, and covered with wounds. Of the 300 heroes, only one escaped to bear to Sparta the news that her valiant warriors had died in her defence.

Xerxes having arrived at Athens, found it desolate and deserted He burnt down its citadel, and sent away its finest pictures and statues to Susa, the capital of Persia. The Athenians having manned their fleet, soon attacked that of the Persians, and put it to flight after a very short, but severe engagement. Themistocles commanded on this occasion.

The Persian king had seated himself on a high mountain, that he might see his Persians overcome the Greeks, but when he saw the issue of the battle, so contrary to his expectations, he hastened with a part of his army across the Hellespont.

A second overthrow awaited his army by land; for Mardonius, his general, at the head of 300,000 Persians, was defeated with immense slaughter, at Platæa, by the combined army of Athenians and Lacedæmonians, amounting to a little over 100,000 men, led by Pausanias and Aristides.

On the same day with this battle, the Greeks engaged and destroyed the remains of the Persian fleet at Mycale. Thus gloriously to the Greeks, ended the celebrated expedition of Xerxes against Greece.

3. From the time of the battles of Platæa and Salamis, the ambitious schemes of Xerxes were at an end. He left Greece suddenly, and his inglorious life was soon after terminated by assassination. The military glory of the Greeks was now at its height. They were for the most part united in opposing the common enemy. Their danger was the cause of their union, and their union was the cause of their prosperity.

4. About 10 years after the return of Xerxes into Asia with a part of his forces, Cimon, son of Miltiades, expelling the Persians from Thrace, destroyed the Persian fleet at the mouth of the river Eurymedon, and landing his troops, signally defeated their army the same day.

Some years afterwards he destroyed a Persian fleet of 300 sail; and landing in Cilicia, completed his triumph by defeating 300,000 Persians under Megabyzes, 460 years B. C. Artaxerxes, who had succeeded his father Xerxes, soon sued for peace. The terms were highly honourable to the Greeks.

§ The prosperity and military glory of the Greeks continued 50 years; after which, upon the return of the peace with Persia, the martial and the patriotic spirit began visibly to decline in Athens. Still, as will soon appear, the following age, called the age of Pericles, was an era of the highest splendour, so far as literature, taste, and the fine arts were concerned.

Cimon was as renowned as his father Miltiades. He was joined with Aristides at one time in the command of the Athenians; yet, notwithstanding the important services which they rendered to their country, they were both punished by the ostracism,* and scarcely with any pretext.

Before Cimon was banished, besides the victories he gained for Athens, he had greatly improved the city; he planted groves and shady walks; he erected fine places for exercise and public speaking. The celebrated tragic poets, Æschylus and Sophocles were wont to recite their pieces before him. Cimon was not less devoted to his ungrateful countrymen after his return from banishment. His victories procured the peace above mentioned. In it, he stipulated for the freedom of all the Grecian cities of Asia.

Of Aristides, who was called "the just," many interesting anecdotes are recorded, but we have room for only two.

Once when he was carrying a prosecution against his enemy, and sentence was about to be pronounced, before the accused had spoken, Aristides entreated that the man might be heard in his defence, and even helped him to make it.

On another occasion, when he was judge, a trial came before him, in which one of the parties thought to irritate him against the other, by declaring that the other had said and done many injurious things against Aristides. "Do not talk about that," said Aristides, "tell me only what harm he has done to thee, it is thy cause I am judging."

5. The authority in Athens became for a time divided between Cimon and Pericles. In a few years, however, Pericles stood at the head of the Athenian republic. His will had almost the force of law. He adorned Athens with the most magnificent structures, and rendered it the seat of learning, taste, and the fine arts. He laboured, however, under the reproach of having corrupted the manners of the people, by his luxuries.

Under his administration commenced the Lacedæmonian war, 431 years B. C., which lasted 28 years. He died three years after its commencement, and was succeeded in the government of Athens by Alcibiades, who ran a similar course, though with less integrity. Alcibiades repeatedly ex

*See "General Views."

perienced the ingratitude of his countrymen—a conduct which he eagerly retaliated.

The Lacedæmonian war ended in the humiliation and submission of Athens. The Athenians agreed to demolish their port, to limit their fleet to 12 ships, and to undertake for the future, no enterprise in war, but under the command of the Spartans, 405 year B. C. Lysander, the Spartan commander, signalized himself in this war.

§ Pericles was remarkable for the dignity of his manners, and the elegance of his speech. For 40 years he secured an unbounded authority. Athens, at this time, was considered as in its highest state of refinement and knowledge, and with Sparta, ranked as the first of the cities of Greece.

When some persons complained that Pericles spent too much of the public money in beautifying the city, he went into the assembly of the people, and asked, "whether, indeed, they thought him extravagant?" The people said, "yes." "Then place the expense at my charge instead of yours," answered Pericles, "only let the new buildings be marked with my name instead of yours."

The people were either so pleased with the spirit of his reply, or were so jealous of the fame which Pericles might acquire, that they cried out, "he might spend as much as he pleased of the public treasures."

At a critical time in the Peloponnesian war, Pericles was taken off in consequence of the ravages of a terrible plague which then afflicted Athens. That plague was one of the most malignant and fatal which history relates to us.

Beginning in Ethiopia, it swept over several countries in its course, and finally rested in Athens. It surpassed the efforts of the medical art to cure it. Few or no constitutions could withstand its attacks. The nature of the disease was such that it threw its victim into a sort of despair, so that he was disabled from seeking or applying relief.

It was dangerous for friends to offer their assistance to the diseased; and the situation of the Athenians was such, in consequence of being shut up by an invading army, that the malignity of the pestilence was greatly increased. They fell down dead upon one another as they passed along the streets, and the dead and the dying were mingled together in the utmost confusion.

In this complication of distress, Pericles displayed a great soul. He was able to inspire courage into the drooping hearts of his countrymen; but after some fresh plans of conquest adopted during a mitigation of the pestilence, he was himself cut off by the plague, which had broken out anew.

On his death bed his friends attempted to console him, by recounting his glorious deeds, particularly his military successes, and the monuments he erected to commemorate them. "Ah," exclaimed the dying statesman and hero, "you have forgotten the most valuable part of my character, and now the most pleasant to my mind—that none of my fellow-citizens have been compelled, through any act of mine, to put on a mourning robe."

The occasion of the Lacedæmonian war was as follows:—Corinth having been included in the last made treaty between Athens and Sparta, the Corinthians in waging war with the people of Corcyra, an ancient colony of their own, solicited the aid of Athens, as did also the people of Corcyra.

The Athenians took the part of the latter—a measure which exceedingly displeased the Corinthians, and was considered as violating their treaty with Sparta. On this ground war was declared between Athens and Lacedæmon, each being supported by its respective allies. This war distracted and enfeebled Greece.

Alcibiades, who bore a conspicuous part in it on the Athenian side, during the interval of a truce with Sparta, persuaded his countrymen to try the conquest of Sicily, and was sent as the general of the troops. When he was gone, his enemies raised an accusation against him, and the fickle people directed him immediately to return.

Alcibiades, fearing to return whilst the Athenians were so incensed against him, fled away secretly, and when he was told that for his disobedience, all his property was confiscated, and that he himself was condemned to death, "I will show them that I am alive," he exclaimed.

He first fled to Argos, and next to Sparta, where he gained all hearts by conforming to their plain dress and simple food. But the king of Sparta perceiving that Alcibiades affected to appear what he was not, was by no means backward to disapprove him, which induced the Athenian to quit Sparta, and seek protection in Persia.

Athens was now governed by a council of 400, and the tyranny of these was so great, that Alcibiades was sent for to assist in restoring the liberty of the people. The Spartans, with some vessels, were watching the city, to take advantage of the confusion that prevailed. Alcibiades, with the small fleet he had collected at Samos, attacked the Spartans, destroyed their ships, and soon after entered Athens in triumph.

The Athenians being again displeased with Alcibiades, he left the city to avoid their displeasure. He at length retired to live in a small village in Phrygia, with a woman called Timandra. The Spartans persuaded the Persians to destroy him.

Accordingly, a party of soldiers went to his house, and fearing his known courage, dared not to enter it, but set fire to the building. Alcibiades rushed out, and the barbarians from a distance (for they feared to approach him) killed him with darts and arrows. Timandra buried the corpse decently, and was the only mourner of this once powerful man.

The defeat of the Athenian fleet at Ægos Potamos, by Lysander, was the means of bringing the tedious Lacedæmonian war to a close. The taking and plundering of Athens were the consequence of it. Having gained possession of the city, Lysander burnt down the houses and demolished the walls. It was said that he was so cruel as to add insult to misfortune, by ordering music to be played whilst the walls were destroyed.

6. Lysander, after the reduction of Athens, abolished the popular form of government in that state, and substituted that of the thirty tyrants, which was absolute. Many of the distinguished citizens fled from their country; but Thrasybulus, aided by a body of patriots, expelled the usurpers, and once more re-established the government of the people, 403 years B. C.

§ The thirty tyrants were as many Lacedæmonian captains, to whom the government of the Athenians was delegated by Lysander. They held their authority but three years. To Lysander, history ascribes the first great breach of his country's constitution, by the introduction of gold into that republic.

7. The persecution and death of Socrates, the philosopher, took place about this time, (401 years B. C.) This transaction has thrown a dark stain on the Athenian character. He was destroyed contrary to every principle of reason and justice.

§ Socrates was the friend and tutor of Alcibiades. The sophists, whose manner of reasoning he turned into ridicule, represented him as an enemy to the religion of his country, because, without conforming to the popular superstitions, he led the mind to a knowledge of the Deity, the Creator of the universe; and to the belief of a future state of rewards and punishments.

He made a noble and manly defence, in all the consciousness of innocence; but in vain. He was condemned to die by his inimical judges. One of his disciples lamenting before him that he should die innocent, "Would you have me die guilty?" replied Socrates, with a smile.

The juice of hemlock, or something resembling hemlock, a liquor which was said to cause death, by its coldness, was administered to the philosopher. He continued calmly conversing with his friends, to the last moment of his life.

8. In the same year with the death of Socrates, occurred the celebrated retreat of 10,000 Greeks, under Xenophon, from Babylon to the banks of the Euxine. This is considered the most remarkable retreat on record. It was accomplished in a few months, the soldiers traversing a hostile country of 1600 miles in extent, amidst incredible hardships and dangers. They lost only 1500 men.

§ The Greeks came into the situation above mentioned, in consequence of assisting Cyrus, a younger brother of Artaxerxes Mnemon, in his attempt to dethrone the latter. Cyrus failed in the attempt, in a battle near Babylon, and lost his life. The Greeks, who amounted to 13,000 at first, were reduced to 10,000, and in this situation were under the necessity either of submitting to the enemy, or of making good their retreat.

The latter they both chose and accomplished. The Greeks were led by Clearchus on this expedition, but he having trusted himself among the Persians, was basely delivered up to the king, by whose order he was beheaded. In this exigency they elected Xenophon, a young Athenian, as their commander, under whom they were to effect their retreat.

They observed the greatest order and discipline; and though in the midst of vindictive enemies, and with deserts, hills, mountains, rivers, and even the sea before them, they arrived with an inconsiderable loss, at the banks of the Euxine. Xenophon himself has written an admirable account of this retreat.

The Greek cities of Asia having taken a part in this enterprise of the Greeks, Sparta was engaged to defend her countrymen, and consequently was involved in a war with Persia. The disunion of the Grecian states, and especially the hostility of Athens against Sparta, rendered the war disastrous to the Spartans; who, to avoid destruction, sued for peace, and obtained it, by the sacrifice of all her Asiatic colonies, 387 years B. C.

9. Among the Grecian states, Thebes became particularly distinguished during the latter part of the present period. It had been comparatively obscure before. The Thebans contending among themselves, the Spartans interfered in the contention, and seized on the Theban fortress. This measure brought on a war between Sparta and Thebes.

Athens at first united with Thebes, but at length Thebes stood alone against Sparta and the league of Greece. Pelopidas and Epaminondas were the Theban leaders, who greatly distinguished themselves in this war. The celebrated battles of Leuctra and Mantinea were gained by the Thebans over their enemies, the one 371 years B. C., and the other 8 years afterwards. In the latter engagement, the great Epaminondas was slain.

The ravages of this contention among the Grecian states, may be said to have paved the way for their entire subjugation by a foreign power.

§ The fortress at Thebes, which the Spartans had seized, was kept by the latter during four years, but the angry and deceived Thebans took their revenge. A party of them, headed by Pelopidas, putting on women's clothes over their armour, entered among the Lacedæmonians, at a feast given to them, and cut their principal officers to pieces.

Archias, the chief Spartan, had that very day received a letter from Athens to inform him of the whole plot, but he had very improperly thrown aside the letter without looking into it, saying, "business to-morrow." He was the first man killed, and thus lost his life for a neglect of his duty, in suffering the pleasure he enjoyed in the company of his friends, to make him forget the interests of his country.

Epaminondas, the friend of Pelopidas, who had acted with the latter, was, upon the expulsion of the Spartans from the citadel, called from a quiet and private life to become the general of the Theban army. He was as much celebrated for his wisdom and virtue, as for his bravery. Of all the excellencies of his character, he gained the most respect for his strict regard to truth, as he was never known to be guilty of a falsehood. In the battle of Leuctra, the Theban army was much smaller than that of Sparta; but the skill of their general, in disposing the force to the best advantage, and the valour of the soldiers and officers, more than made up for the difference in numbers. Besides, the Thebans were fighting for their liberty; the Spartans only for conquest. It is not to be wondered at, therefore, that the Thebans prevailed.

Pelopidas shared the danger and the glory of his friend; yet when these valiant generals returned to Thebes, they were both called before the tribunal of justice for the crime of keeping their command too long. Both were acquitted; yet the enemies of Epaminondas caused him to be elected a city scavenger, on purpose to disgrace and vex him. But what might have been a disgrace to a mean person, was no disgrace to this noble Theban. He accepted the office, saying, "If the office will not give me honour, I will give honour to the office."

Epaminondas fell in the battle of Mantinea, and in the moment of victory. A javelin had pierced his bosom, and becoming disabled, a fierce contest arose between his foes and friends for the possession of his person. The Thebans at length bore him from the field. Epaminondas, though in extreme agony from his wound, thought only of his country; and when informed that the Thebans had conquered, he said, "then all is well."

He drew the weapon from his bosom, as no one around him had the fortitude to do it, it being understood, from the nature of the wound, he would expire as soon as it was extricated. The glory of Thebes rose with this man, and with him it expired.

ROMANS.

10. In the history of Rome, during this period, we may observe an additional change in its constitution of government. It became, in effect, a democracy 471 years B. C. The supreme authority passed from the higher order, into the hands of the people. The popular character of the government had been theoretically established before, but it became now practically democratic.

§ This change was completed by Volero, a Roman tribune, who obtained a law for the election of magistrates, in the comitia held by the tribes. Before this time, the comitia, by centuries and by curiæ, could not be called but in virtue of a decree of the senate, after consulting the auspices, and in those comitia the tribunes had been hitherto elected. In the comitia held by tribes these restraints were unknown

11. Soon afterwards, (456 B. C.) upon the invasion of the Æqui and Volsci, the Romans had recourse to the despotic measure of choosing a dictator. Quinctius Cincinnatus was appointed. He was called from the plough to this office. After having rescued a Roman army from destruction, defeated a powerful enemy, and rendered other signal services to his country, he hastened to resign his power at the end of 16 days, though he might have held it 6 months, the term for which dictators were appointed.

§ Cincinnatus was fixed upon as the wisest and bravest man belonging to the commonwealth. He cultivated a small farm of four acres with his own hands. The deputies of the senate found him following his plough in one of his little fields. They begged him to put on his gown, and hear the message from the senate. Cincinnatus anxiously asked, "if all was well?" and then desired his wife Racilia to fetch his gown from their cottage. After wiping off the dust and dirt with which he was covered, he put on his robe and went to the deputies. They saluted him dictator, and bid him hasten to the city, which was in the greatest peril.

A handsome barge had been sent to carry him over the river, for his farm lay on the opposite side of the Tiber. His three sons, with his friends, and several of the senators, were ready to receive him when he landed at Rome, and to carry him in a pompous procession to the house prepared for him.

The very next morning he began to fortify the city, and marshal the soldiers for battle; and he very soon gained a great victory, and made the officers of the enemy pass under the yoke. His administration was entirely satisfactory to all parties, though the times were extremely turbulent. He most probably saved Rome from destruction, by his wisdom and valour.

He was chosen dictator on another emergency, many years afterwards, in his 80th year, and then also acted with vigour and wisdom.

12. In 451 years B. C. ten persons who were called the Decemviri, were elected to frame a code of laws, and were invested with absolute power for one year, during which all other magistrates were suspended. They afterwards caused their laws to be engraven on 12 tables, and placed in the most conspicuous part of the city.

These laws were long preserved and acted upon, and are to this day respected in some parts of Europe. They however manifested the stern spirit of the people, and like those of Draco, might be said to be written in blood. Nine crimes*

* Parricide was very properly included as one of those crimes. But to the honour of the Romans it should be observed, that this crime was not known to be committed during more than 500 years from the building of the city. L. Ostius was the first parricide.

of very different complexions were punishable with death, one of which was nightly meetings.

§ The Romans had no code of laws until that which was formed and digested by the decemviri. The number of the laws was increased from time to time by the senate and people. Each decemvir, by turn, presided for a day, and had the sovereign authority, with its insignia, the fasces. The nine others acted solely as judges in the determination of law-suits, and the correction of abuses.

Their government lasted only three years. Its dissolution was highly tragical. Appius Claudius, one of the ten, fell in love with the beautiful Virginia; she was engaged to marry Icilius, formerly a tribune of the people, and would not therefore listen to the proposals of Appius.

He therefore, to get possession of the lovely virgin, procured a base dependant to claim her as his slave. The claim was made to Appius himself, who pronounced an infamous decree, by which she was declared to be the property of this profligate minion of his own.

Virginius, her father, who was falsely sworn to have stolen her from the dependant of Appius, was at a distance with the army Intelligence, however, by means of Icilius, was conveyed to him respecting the transactions in the city, and he returned with all imaginable speed.

Finding, notwithstanding his true and simple tale that Virginia was his daughter, that he could not preserve her from the licentious decemvir, he now begged to give her his parting embrace. His request was granted. He clasped his child in his arms, while she clung round his neck, and wet his cheeks with her tears.

As Virginius was tenderly kissing her, before he raised his head, he suddenly plunged a dagger into her bosom, saying, "Oh! my child, by this means only can I give thee freedom." He then held up the bloody instrument to the now pale and frighted Claudius, exclaiming, "By this innocent blood, Appius, I devote thy head to the infernal gods."

All was now horror and confusion. Icilius showed the dead body to the people and roused their fury. Virginius hasted to the camp bearing with him the dagger reeking with his daughter's blood; and instantly the camp was in an uproar. The power of the decemviri and the senators could not still the tumult.

Appius would have been torn to pieces at once, but he found the means of escape and voluntary death. Public tranquillity was at length restored, by the consent of the senate to abolish the decemviri. The consuls were now restored, together with the tribunes of the people, 499 years B. C.

13. A law for the intermarriage of the patricians and plebeians at Rome was passed 445 years B. C. In the same year military tribunes were created. These were in lieu of the consuls: they were six in number, three patricians and three plebeians. The consuls, however, were soon restored.

In 437 years B. C. was established the office of censors, whose duty it was to make the census of the people every five years.

§ The people, in their desire for still more power, endeavoured to break down the only two barriers that separated the patricians from themselves. These were, one, the law which prevented their intermarriage; and the other, the constitutional limitation of all the higher offices to the patrician order.

The first point, after a long contest, was conceded—the other was partially evaded. The senate sought a palliative in the creation of the military tribunes above mentioned. This measure satisfied the people for a time.

The new magistracy of the censors was highly important. In addition to making the census, it was incumbent on the censors to inspect the morals and regulate the duties of the citizens. It became, in after times, the function only of consular persons, and after them, of the emperors.

14. The dissentions between the different orders of the people, raged with violence; but the senate, not long after their concession to the people, adopted for themselves a very wise expedient. This was to give a regular pay to the troops, an expense defrayed by a moderate tax on the citizens. From this period soldiers were to be obtained, and the senate had the army under its control. Roman ambition now became systematic, and irresistible.

15. Veii, the rival of Rome, was besieged by the Romans, and after a siege of ten years, was taken by Camillus, 391 years B. C. Two years after, Falerii, the capital of the Falisci, surrendered to the same general. The dominion of Rome, confined hitherto to a territory of a few miles, was now rapidly extended.

§ The siege of Veii was attended with much expense of blood and treasure to the Romans. They nearly despaired of taking it; but upon the appointment of Camillus dictator, things soon assumed a different aspect. He secretly wrought a mine into the city, which opened into the midst of the capital.

Then giving his men directions how to enter the breach, the city was instantly filled with his legions, to the utter confusion of the besieged. Thus, like a second Troy, was Veii taken after a ten years' siege, and Camillus, according to the manner of the Roman kings, enjoyed the honour of a triumph.

It is related, that during the attack of Falerii, a schoolmaster betrayed into the hands of Camillus all his scholars, expecting to obtain a handsome reward for his treachery. The boys happened to be the sons of the principal Falisci, and the Roman general was given to understand, that they would probably deliver up their city to recover their children.

The noble Roman, shocked at this perfidious action, sent back the boys in safety to their parents, and giving each of them a rod, bade them whip the traitor into town. This generous behaviour of Camillus accomplished more than his arms could have done. The place instantly submitted, leaving to the Roman the conditions of the surrender, which were of course very mild.

The brave Camillus, becoming at length an object of envy or jealousy with the people, he was obliged to quit Rome, and live at Ardea, a town in its neighborhood, but they had reason afterwards to be ashamed of their injustice.

16. Soon after these successes, Rome experienced a terrible calamity. It was taken, devastated, and burnt by the Gauls, under Brennus, 385 years B. C. The capitol, however, was preserved. This the barbarians besieged, but they were soon expelled the city by Camillus.

§ The Gauls were a branch of the great Celtic nation, and inhabited regions beyond the Alps. These they had penetrated at different periods, and a portion of this people had already settled in small towns at the foot of the mountains. This people, it seems, on some occasion, had undertaken the siege of Clusium, a city of Etruria. The Clusians, who were not of a warlike character, immediately entreated the mediation of the Romans.

The latter sent ambassadors to Brennus, but without success. These ambassadors then retired to Clusium, where they appeared at the head of the Clusians in a sally against the besiegers. Upon this, Brennus, in great displeasure, marched directly against Rome.

In this condition, an army was drawn out to save the city; but the numbers and impetuosity of the barbarians were such, that no effectual resistance was made. The greatest part of the citizens fled for protection to the neighbouring cities; the young and brave men entered into the capitol, resolved to hold out to the last against the enemy; and the aged senators assembled in the senate-house, determined patiently to await their fate.

Soon after they entered the city, Brennus, and some of his soldiers, went into the senate-house. The venerable appearance of these noble old men rendered the Gauls afraid or unwilling to harm them. A soldier at last gently shaking the beard of Papyrius, the old Roman was so offended at the act, that he struck the man on his head with an ivory staff he had in his hand: this slight blow instantly aroused the fury of the barbarians; they massacred the senators on the spot, and set fire to the city.

In this season of distress, the Romans did not give up all for lost. The little band, shut up in the capitol, made every possible arrangement for defence. They were assaulted in vain. At this juncture, Camillus, forgetting all his private wrongs, gathered an army, with which he entered Rome, and immediately put the barbarians to flight.

A singular occurrence, showing the providence of God in the government of the world, attended the siege of Rome.

The capitol was at one time nearly taken by surprise: a number of Gauls having climbed up the steep rock on which it stood, were about to kill the sentinels and make themselves masters of the place, when some geese, kept near the spot, being awakened by the noise, began to flutter their wings, and cackle loudly, so as to arouse the soldiers. This little circumstance saved the capitol, and perhaps the Roman name from extinction.

17. The constitution of Rome was still farther altered about this time, 367 years B. C. The plebeians obtained the right of having one of the two consuls chosen from among them. The military tribunes were abolished the next year. From this period the Roman power began rapidly to rise.

§ The vanity and ambition of a young woman produced this change in the government of Rome. Fabius Ambustius, a patrician, had married two daughters, one to a plebeian, and the other to a patrician. The wife of the plebeian, envious of the honours of her sister, pined with discontent.

Her father and brother, learning the cause of her unhappiness promised her the distinction which she desired. By their joint endeavours, after much tumult and contest, they succeeded in obtaining for the plebeians the right of admission into the consulate. Lucius Sextius was the first plebeian consul. The husband of the plebeian lady, viz. Licinius Stolo, was the second.

EGYPT.

18. The kingdom of EGYPT, which had been conquered by Cambyses, king of Persia, was, under Darius Nothus, a distant successor, restored by Amyrthæus, 413 years B. C. It continued independent for 60 years, under eight kings.

At the expiration of this term it was subjected again to the Persian yoke, by Artaxerxes Ochus.

§ No very interesting particulars occur in this portion of the Egyptian history. It is necessary only to observe, that it was by means of aid afforded to them by the Greeks, that the Egyptians, after they had revolted, under Amyrthæus, were enabled to withstand the Persian force which sought to reconquer them. It was under a king called Nectanebis that Egypt again lost her independence.

PERSIA.

19. The history of the PERSIAN empire, during this period, is mostly involved in that of the Greeks, with whom the former was so frequently at war. Darius, Xerxes, and Artaxerxes II. as we have seen, were, during most of their lives, engaged in this war. Concerning the rest of the Persian sovereigns, there is little interesting to be communicated.

§ Artaxerxes I. we are told, killed his brother Darius, being deceived by Artabanus, who imputed the murder of Xerxes to that prince: but upon being acquainted with the truth, he put Artabanus and all his family to death. During his reign the Egyptians attempted to shake off his yoke, but were soon obliged to submit.

Xerxes II. was assassinated by his brother, Sogdianus, 45 days after he ascended to the throne. Sogdianus, who assumed the government, enjoyed the fruits of his fratricide only six months and a half, when he was smothered in ashes, (a mode of torture invented on this occasion, and afterwards inflicted on great criminals,) by order of his brother Ochus, who took the name of Darius Nothus.

Darius Nothus was a weak prince, in whose reign it was that the Egyptians recovered their independence. Artaxerxes II. succeeded him, who was surnamed Mnemon, by the Greeks, on account of his prodigious memory. He killed his brother Cyrus, who had taken arms against him, in single battle. The 10,000 Greeks who retreated under Xenophon, served in the army of this Cyrus.

Ochus succeeded him, who poisoned his brother, and murdered all the princes of the royal family. He invaded Egypt, plundered the temples, and killed the priests. But his chief minister, enraged at the ruin of his country, poisoned him.

MACEDON.

20. The kingdom of Macedon, which was governed, during several hundred years, by the descendants of Caranus, was comparatively unknown till the time of Philip, who was also a descendant of Caranus. Philip soon gave it celebrity. Previously to the birth of his son Alexander, he had conquered Thessaly, Pæonia, and Illyricum. He had also gained a victory over the Athenians, at Mythone, 360 years B. C.

§ Philip ascended the throne by popular choice, in violation of the natural right of the nearer heirs to the crown; he secured his power by the success of his arms against the neighbouring nations. He was brave, artful, and accomplished, and by his intrigues gained over, at an early period of his career, many Greeks to favour his interests.

In his war against the united Pæonians, Illyrians, &c. he met with singularly good fortune. Parmenio, his general, was sent against the Illyrians, and he himself marched an army into Pæonia and Thrace, where he was signally successful. On his return, a messenger arrived with news of Parmenio's victory; and soon after came another, informing him that his horses had been victorious at the Olympic games.

This was a victory that he esteemed preferable to any other. Almost at the same time came a third messenger, who acquainted him that his wife, Olympias, had brought forth a son, at Pella. Philip, terrified at so signal a happiness, which the heathens generally considered as a bad omen, exclaimed, "Great Jupiter, in return for so many blessings, send me a slight misfortune."

Distinguished Characters in Period VII.

1. Confucius, the great Chinese philosopher.
2. Herodotus, a Greek, the father of profane history.
3. Pindar, the chief of the Grecian lyric poets.
4. Phidias, a Greek, the most famous sculptor of antiquity.
5. Euripides, an eminent tragic poet of Greece.
6. Sophocles, an eminent tragic poet of Greece.
7. Socrates, the greatest of heathen moralists.
8. Thucydides, an eminent Greek historian.
9. Hippocrates, the father of medicine.
10. Xenophon, a celebrated general, historian, and philosopher.

§ 1. Confucius was born in the kingdom of Lu, which is now the province of Chan Long, 551 years B. C. He was a man of great knowledge and extensive wisdom, was beloved on account of his virtues—rendered great service to his country by his moral maxims, and possessed much influence even with kings, as well as with his countrymen in general. He died in the 73d year of his age.

2. Herodotus was born at Halicarnassus. His history describes the wars of the Greeks against the Persians, from the age of Cyrus to the battle of Mycale. This he publicly repeated at the Olympic games, when the names of the Muses were given to his nine books.

This celebrated work, which has procured its author the title of father of history, is written in the Ionic dialect. Herodotus is among the historians, what Homer is among the poets. His style abounds with elegance, ease, and sweetness. He also wrote a history of Assyria and Arabia, but this is not extant.

3. Pindar was a native of Thebes. His compositions were courted by statesmen and princes, and his hymns were repeated in the temples, at the celebration of the festivals. Some of his odes are extant, greatly admired for grandeur of expression, magnificence of style, boldness of metaphors, and harmony of numbers.

Horace calls him inimitable; and this eulogium is probably not undeserved. After his death, his statue was erected at Thebes, in the public place where the games were exhibited, and six centuries afterwards it was viewed with pleasure and admiration by the geographer Pausanias. He died B. C. 435, at the age, as some say, of 86.

4. Phidias was an Athenian. He died B. C. 432. His statue of Jupiter Olympius passed for one of the wonders of the world. That of Minerva, in the Pantheon of Athens, measured 39 feet in height, and was made of gold and ivory.

5. Euripides was born at Salamis. He was the rival of Sophocles. The jealousy between these great poets, was made the subject of successful ridicule by the comic poet Aristophanes. It is said that he used to shut himself up in a gloomy cave, near Salamis, in which he composed some of his best tragedies.

During the representation of one of his pieces, the audience, dis pleased with some lines in the composition, desired the writer to strike them off. Euripides heard the reproof with indignation, and advancing forward on the stage, he told the spectators, that he came there to instruct them, and not to receive instruction.

The ridicule and envy to which he was exposed in Athens induced him to retire to the court of Archelaus, king of Macedonia, where he was entertained with the greatest munificence. He was here however destined to meet a terrible end. It is said the hounds of the king attacking him, in one of his solitary walks, tore his body to pieces, 407 B. C. in the 78th year of his age.

As a poet he is peculiarly happy in expressing the passions of love, especially the more tender and animated. He is also sublime, and the most common expressions have received a most perfect polish from his pen. His productions abound with moral reflections, and philosophical aphorisms.

The poet was such an enemy to the fair sex, that some have called him the woman hater. In spite of his antipathy he married twice; but his connexions were so injudicious, that he was compelled to divorce both his wives. From this cause may have arisen his erroneous conceptions of the female character. Of 75 tragedies, only 19 remain.

6. Sophocles was born about 497 B. C. He was distinguished not only as a poet, but as a statesman and general, and filled the office of archon with applause.

Twenty times he obtained the prize of poetry from his competitors. Of one hundred and twenty tragedies which he wrote, seven only are extant, but these prove him to have carried the drama almost to perfection.

Accused of insanity by his children, who wished to obtain his possessions, the poet composed and read his tragedy of Œdipus, at Colonos. Asking his judges whether the author of such a performance could be insane, he was at once acquitted, to the confusion of his ungrateful offspring.

He died in his 91st year, through excess of joy, at hearing of his having obtained a poetical prize at the Olympic Games.

7. Socrates was a native of Athens. He followed the occupation of his father, who was a statuary, for some time; and some have mentioned the statues of the Graces, admired for their simplicity and elegance, as the work of his own hands. He was called away from this meaner employment, for which, however, he never blushed, by a friend; and philosophy soon became his study.

He appeared like the rest of his countrymen in the field of battle, and he fought with boldness and intrepidity. But his character appears more conspicuous as a philosopher and moralist, than as a warrior. He was fond of labour, bore injuries with patience, and acquired that serenity of mind and firmness of countenance which the most alarming dangers could never destroy, or the most sudden calamities alter.

He was attended by a number of illustrious pupils, whom he instructed by his exemplary life, as well as by his doctrines. He spoke with freedom on every subject, religious as well as civil. This independence of spirit, and that visible superiority of mind and genius over the rest of his countrymen, created many enemies to him, and at length they condemned him to death, on the false accusation of corrupting the Athenian youth, of making innovations in the religion of the Greeks, and of ridiculing the gods which the Athenians worshipped. He drank the juice of the hemlock in the 70th year of his age, and died 401 B. C.

Socrates believed the divine origin of dreams and omens, and was a supporter of the doctrine of the immortality of the soul. From his principles, enforced by his example, the celebrated sects of the Platonists, Stoics, Peripatetics, &c. soon after rose.

8. Thucydides was born at Athens. He early appeared in the Athenian armies, but being unsuccessful in some expedition, he was banished Athens, in the 8th year of the Peloponnesian war. He then wrote his history of the important events of that war, to its 21st year.

So deeply was Thucydides inspired by the muse of history, that he shed tears when he heard Herodotus repeat his history of the Persian wars, at the public festivals of Greece; the character of his interesting work is well known. He is considered highly authentic and impartial, and stands unrivalled for the fire, conciseness, and energy of his narrative.

Thucydides died at Athens, where he had been recalled from exile, in his 80th year, 391 B. C.

9. Hippocrates was born in the island of Cos, B. C. 406. He improved himself by reading in the tablets of the temples, the diseases, and means of recovery of individuals. He was skilful, and devoted his whole time to medical applications and professional duties. Some say he delivered Athens from a dreadful plague.

According to Galen, his opinions were respected as oracular. His memory is still venerated, and his writings, few of which remain, procured him the epithet of divine. He died in the 99th year of his age, 361 B. C., free from all disorder of the mind and body, and after death, received the highest honours.

10. Xenophon was an Athenian. He was bred in the school of Socrates, and acquired great literary distinction. He served in the army of Cyrus the younger, and chiefly superintended the retreat of the 10,000, after the battle of the Cunaxa. He afterward followed the fortunes of Agesilaus, and acquired riches in his expeditions.

In his subsequent retirement he composed and wrote for the information of posterity, and died at Corinth, in his 90th year, 359 B. C. He continued the history of Thucydides, wrote a life of Cyrus the Great, and collected Memorabilia of Socrates. The simplicity and elegance of Xenophon's style have procured him the name of the Athenian muse, and the bee of Greece.

PERIOD VIII.

The period of Roman Military Renown, extending from the Birth of Alexander, 356 *years B. C. to the destruction of Carthage,* 146 *years B. C.*

GREECE.

SECT. 1. At the commencement of this period, the GREEKS were greatly embroiled in domestic dissensions, and were fast falling from the enviable height to which their arms and national spirit had formerly raised them. They were no longer the people they had been, and were preparing to receive the yoke of a master. From that time their history is connected with that of the Macedonian monarchy.

An attempt of the Phocians to plunder the temple of Delphos, excited the sacred war, in which almost all the states became involved. The assistance of Philip being solicited by the Thebans and Thessalians, he commenced hostilities by invading Phocis, the key to Attica. The eloquence of Demosthenes roused the Athenians to arms. But their struggle was unsuccessful.

Philip met them at Cheronæa, gained a complete victory, and Greece fell into the hands of the conqueror. This event is dated 338 years B. C. He however chose not to treat them as a conquered people. The separate governments retained their independence, subject only, in their national acts, to the control of Philip. After his death they hoped to recover their liberty, but they only changed masters.

§ The sacrilege of the Phocians in robbing the temple of Delphos, subjected them to a summons to appear before the Amphictyonic council, to answer for their crime. A fine being imposed, disputes arose, which could be settled only by arms. The war continued 10 years.

The interference of Philip at this juncture was, as might have been expected, fatal to the liberties of Greece. He contrived to have the Phocians expelled from the Amphictyonic council, and to be himself chosen in their place.

The eloquence of Demosthenes delayed for a time the fate of Greece. He was ever stirring up the Athenians against Philip and satirizing that king. His speeches were called Philippics, since they were directed against Philip, and hence Philippics has been a term signifying "speeches against any person."

Demosthenes, it is well known, had to contend against many na tural impediments, in attaining the art of addressing a popular assembly. As a proof of his triumphant success, it is recorded, that Æschines, a rival orator, once repeated a speech of his own, and one of Demosthenes. His own was much applauded, but that of Demosthenes applauded much more. "Ah!" said the generous Æschines, "how would you have applauded it, had you heard Demosthenes speak it."

Soon after the battle of Cheronæa, Philip, calling a general council of the states, was appointed commander in chief of the forces of Greece; but on the eve of attempting the conquest of Persia, he was assassinated by Pausanias, a captain of his guards, from private resentment. The hopes inspired by his death proved abortive, as the Greeks soon came under the yoke of his successor.

2. Greece was entered by Alexander, son of Philip, 336 years B. C. He obliged the Athenians to submit, burnt Thebes, and was declared commander in chief of the Grecian forces, in the expedition against Persia, which he began the next year.

§ Alexander was 20 years old, when the death of Philip raised him to the throne. The celebrated Aristotle was his teacher, and under him, the youthful prince early desired to distinguish himself. He read much; Homer's Iliad he especially studied.

When very young, he managed the fiery war-horse Bucephalus, which no one else dared to mount. In honour of this steed, he afterwards built a city which he called Bucephala. When he attended his father to battle, he manifested not only valour, but skill; and once had the happiness to save his parent's life, when it was in great danger from an enemy.

At Corinth he saw Diogenes, named the Cynic, because he affected great dislike to wealth and rank, and lived in a strange, rude manner. Alexander asked him whether he wanted any thing. "Yes," said Diogenes, "I want you to stand out of my sunshine, and not to take from me, what you cannot give me."

Alexander admired this speech, and directly remarked, "Were I not Alexander, I would be Diogenes." As if he had said, "Had I not all things as Alexander, I would desire to scorn all things as Diogenes."

Before his expedition into Asia, which will soon be mentioned, he was resolved to consult the oracle at Delphos; but as he visited the temple on a day on which it was forbidden to ask the oracle, the priestess refused to go into the temple. Alexander, unaccustomed to denial, seized her by the arm and drew her forwards. "Ah, my son, you are irresistible!" exclaimed the priestess. "These words," he observed, "are a sufficient answer."

The Grecian states had revolted after the death of Philip; but Alexander, in a few successful battles, brought them into subjection. In an assembly of the deputies of the nation at Corinth, he communicated to them his resolution of undertaking the conquest of Persia, agreeably to the designs of his father Philip.

3. Alexander, at the head of the Grecian forces, invaded Persia 335 years B. C. He was then not 22 years of age. He took with him only 35,000 men, and with this small force, he conquered not only Persia, but Syria, Egypt, India, and several other countries, and meditated the design of proceeding to the Eastern ocean, which, however, he was obliged to relinquish.

He accomplished his immense undertaking within the short space of six years. On his return home, while he tarried at Babylon, he died suddenly in a fit of debauch, as some have maintained, in the 33d year of his age, and the 13th of his reign. Alexander was not destitute of some traits which we love in human beings; but in a moral point of view, he must be regarded as a mighty murderer, and enemy of human happiness.

§ The first exploit of Alexander in this expedition, was the passage of the Granicus, which he effected notwithstanding the opposition of the Persians, who lost 20,000 men in the conflict. The fruit of this victory was the submission of all Asia Minor.

The next encounter between the Macedonians or Greeks, and the Persians, was in 333 B. C., near the town of Issus, in which the latter lost 100,000 men; and the mother, wife, and children of Darius, the Persian monarch, fell into the hands of Alexander.

After this victory he overrun all Syria, took Damascus, where he found the treasures of Darius, destroyed Tyre, entered Jerusalem, stormed Gaza, subjugated Egypt, and visited the temple of Jupiter Ammon, in the Lybian desert, where he caused himself to be proclaimed the son of that fictitious deity; on his return he built the city of Alexandria.

Returning from Egypt he found Darius with his forces concentrated on the eastern bank of the Tigris; a battle ensued at Arbela, 331 years B. C., in which 300,000 Persians were slain, or as some, with greater probability, say, 40,000, and but 500 Macedonians. Darius betook himself to flight, and was slain by Bessus, one of his lieutenants. Babylon, Suza, and Persepolis, fell into the hands of the conqueror, who set fire to the last, at the instigation of the courtezan Thais.

Having finished the conquest of Assyria, Persia, and Media. Alexander crossed the mountains of Caucasus, entered Hyrcania, and subdued all the nations south of the Oxus. He then, passing into Sogdiana, overtook the perfidious Bessus, and put him to death. While in Sogdiana, he killed the veteran Clitus, his friend, in a fit of intoxication.

In 328 B. C. he projected the conquest of India. Penetrating beyond the Hydaspes, he defeated Porus, a king of that country. He still continued his course to the East; but when he arrived at the banks of the Ganges, his soldiers, seeing no end to their toils, would go no farther. He returned to the Indus, and pursuing his course southward by that river, he arrived at the ocean, whence he despatched his fleet to the Persian Gulf.

After his arrival at Babylon, he gave himself up to much intemperance, but was still projecting new conquests, when death suddenly put an end to his career. Alexander possessed some generosity of nature, but his vicious habits often overpowered it. Intoxication and the love of conquest render his name odious to a good man.

One or two instances of amiable native feeling, will show what h might have been, could he have controlled his violent passions.

He conducted himself very dutifully towards his mother, listened to her reproofs with mildness and patience, and when Antipater, whom he left to govern Macedonia in his absence, wrote a long letter complaining of Olympias, the king said, with a smile, "Antipater does not know that one tear shed by a mother, will obliterate ten such letters as this."

When he conquered Porus, who was seven and a half high, this singularly tall man, as he was introduced to Alexander, was asked by him how he would be treated, "Like a king," replied Porus. Alexander was so much pleased with this answer, that he restored his kingdom to him, and ever afterwards treated him with kindness and respect.

4. The conquests and acquisitions of Alexander were divided, soon after his death, among thirty-three of his principal officers. Four, however, of his generals, at length obtained the whole, 312 years B. C. having partitioned the empire among themselves. It then constituted four considerable monarchies.

The names of these generals were Ptolemy, Lysimachus, Cassander, and Seleucus. Egypt, Lybia, Arabia, and Palestine, were assigned to Ptolemy; Macedonia and Greece to Cassander; Bithynia and Thrace to Lysimachus; but the remaining territories in Asia, as far as the river Indus, which were called the kingdom of Syria, to Seleucus.

The most powerful of these divisions was that of Syria, under Seleucus and his descendants, and that of Egypt under the Ptolemies. Only Ptolemy and Seleucus transmitted their empires to their children.

§ Alexander nominated no successor. He had a son, called Hercules, by one of his wives, named Barsine. He also left a brother, Aridæus. Aridæus, and another son of Alexander, born subsequently to the conqueror's death, and called after his own name, were soon destroyed. Hercules and Barsine, and Cleopatra, the only sister of Alexander, shared the same fate, not long afterwards.

Thus his whole family became extinct. Of this destruction, the contentions of his generals were the cause, and the cause of those contentions was the neglect of appointing a successor. The vanity of human grandeur, in this instance, appears peculiarly striking. Of the wars and intrigues of these generals among themselves, we need give no account, as they are not interesting. Some subsequent events, relating to them or their sovereignties, will be mentioned in the proper place.

5. From the period of Alexander's death, the history of the Grecian states, to the time of their subjugation by the Romans, presents only a series of uninteresting revolutions. This people had lost their political distinction. The last effort made to revive the expiring spirit of liberty, was the formation of the Achæan league, which was a union of 12 of the smaller states, for this object.

This took place 281 years B. C., but it effected little.

§ Immediately after Alexander's death, Demosthenes made one more effort to vindicate the national freedom, and to rouse his countrymen to shake of the yoke of Macedon; but it was too late. The pacific counsels of Phocion, suited far better the timid or languid spirit of the people. Antipater, who governed Greece a short time after Alexander's death, demanded that Demosthenes should be delivered up to him. But Demosthenes prevented this by committing suicide.

Phocion, though he opposed Demosthenes, was one of the most eminent men of Greece. He recommended peace: inasmuch as he was honest himself, he did not suspect the cunning of the enemy of his country. After having been chosen general 45 times, and after having performed the greatest services for his country, he was condemned to die by the ungrateful Athenians.

When about to swallow the dose of hemlock, that was to poison him, he was asked what message he would send to his son. "Tell him," said this virtuous old man, "that I desire he will not remember the injustice of the Athenians."

The government of the Achæan league was committed to Aratus, of Sicyon, with the title of Prætor, a young man of great ambition, who immediately conceived the idea of freeing the whole country from the Macedonian dominion. But this plan was defeated by the jealousy of the greater states.

Sparta refused to follow the guidance of the Prætor of Achaia, and Aratus, forgetful at once of the interests of his country, thought of nothing but to wreak his vengeance against Sparta. For this purpose he solicited the aid even of the Macedonians themselves.

6. Macedonia and Greece were now preparing to follow the fate of all the nations within the grasp of Roman ambition. Their period of conquest was ended; that of their subjugation was at hand. The Romans, as we shall soon learn, had become the most powerful of the contemporary nations.

An occasion was offered for the interference of the Romans in the affairs of Macedonia and Greece—an occasion which was eagerly embraced. Macedonia, with its last king, Perseus, first fell, 167 years B. C. Twenty-one years afterwards, Greece surrendered its independence to Rome, whose legions were led by the consul Mummius. This event was hastened by the dissensions which the Romans fomented between the different states of Greece.

An insult, said to have been received by the deputies of Rome from the Achæans, furnished the pretext for an attack on Greece. From this time, Greece became a province of Rome, under the name of Achaia.

§ The occasion of the introduction of the Romans into Greece, was an invitation from the Ætolians, to assist them in repelling an attack by Macedonia. Nothing could have better suited the wishes of the Romans. Perseus, a successor of Alexander in the part of his empire which fell to Cassander, was then king.

He persuaded the Achæans to join him in his preparations against Rome. After being sometimes the conqueror, and sometimes the conquered, he was at last vanquished by Paulus Æmilius, at Pydna, and himself and all his family taken prisoners. They were carried to Rome, and served to swell the train of the conqueror. Perseus starved himself to death, and Macedonia became a province of Rome.

The Romans had, in effect, conquered Greece, by their arts, before they made use of their arms. They had corrupted many of the principal Greeks; and, on the pretence above mentioned, they marched their legions against this once renowned people. Metellus, the consul, began the war, which Mummius completed.

Corinth, in which the Greeks made a last stand, was razed and burnt to the ground. Diæus, who commanded the Greeks in this city, killed his wife, to prevent her from falling into the hands of the enemy, and then took poison, of which he died. Corinth was destroyed the same year which witnessed the destruction of Carthage, 146 B. C., which latter event we have referred to the beginning of the next period,—having anticipated this item of the Grecian history.

Some time previously to the subjugation of Greece, Philopœmen was selected to command the forces of the Achæan cities. He was an admirable man; but, in one instance, he stained his character by his conduct towards the Spartans, numbers of whom he cruelly butchered, when that city was taken by him.

He was, however, called to suffer in his turn; for, at 70 years of age, he was taken prisoner, when besieging Messena. The Messenians were so delighted to possess this illustrious man in bondage, that they dragged him in chains to the public theatre, for crowds to gaze upon him.

At night, he was put into a dungeon, and the jailor carried to him a dose of poison. He calmly received the cup, and, having heard that most of his friends had escaped by flight, he said, "then I find we are not entirely unfortunate," and, drinking off the fatal draught, without one murmur, laid himself down and expired.

About this same time, Sparta had a king called Nabis, who was notorious for his cruelty and avarice. Most of the wealthy citizens he banished from Sparta, that he might seize their riches, and many he caused to be assassinated. He had received Argos from Philip, in pledge for some money which he had lent that monarch. He there practised the most shocking cruelties.

He had invented a machine, in the form of a statue, resembling his wife, the breast, arms, and hands of which were full of pegs of iron, covered with magnificent garments. If any one refused to give him money, he was introduced to this machine, which, by means of certain springs, caught fast hold of him, and, that he might deliver himself from this exquisite torture, he readily granted whatever Nabis desired.

ROME.

7. Rome, at the commencement of this period, under circumstances more favourable for conquest than it ever had been before, was not long in subduing the petty nations within a moderate distance of its territory. The name of "Gauls" still inspired some terror, but the Romans soon began to despise them, after they had repressed one or two invasions.

8. Having subdued all their neighbours, such as the Hernici, the Æqui, the Volci, &c. the Romans began to look for greater conquests. They soon found an occasion against the Samnites, a numerous and warlike people inhabiting the south of Italy, with whom they were engaged in war 71 years. This war commenced 343 years B. C. A war with the Latins commenced three years afterwards. The Latins were soon subjugated.

§ The Samnites possessed that tract of country, which at this day constitutes a considerable part of the kingdom of Naples. They were a far more formidable enemy, both as to numbers and discipline, than the Romans had hitherto contended with. Two consuls were at first sent against them. The fortune of Rome attended one of them; but the other, Cornelius, was involved in difficulty.

Having been surrounded by the Samnites, his army must have perished had not the tribune Decius, with 400 men, made a diversion in his favour. Decius advanced to seize a hill in the midst of the enemy. This bold attempt cost the life of every one of his soldiers. Decius alone escaped, but he preserved the army of the consul.

In the war with the Latins, at this time a distinct nation, again Titus Manlius, who was consul, gave a most remarkable instance of well meant, but mistaken severity. He had ordered the Roman soldiers not to quit their ranks, without permission, on pain of death.

A son of the consul happened, with his detachment, to meet a troop of Latins, headed by Metius.

Metius scoffingly addressed the Romans, and at last dared their young commander to fight him. The son, forgetful of the orders of his father, or regardless of them, in his indignation, sprang forward to the encounter, and soon conquered the Latin. Then gathering together the arms of the fallen foe, he ran to his father's tent, and throwing them at his feet, told his story.

But tragical was the issue. The consul turned from him, and ordering the troops to be assembled, thus addressed him in their presence.

"Titus Manlius! you this day dared to disobey the command of your consul, and the orders of your father; you have thus done an injury to discipline and military government, and must, by your death, expiate your fault. Your courage has endeared you to me, but I must be just; and if you have a drop of my blood in your veins you will not refuse to die, when justice demands it. Go, lictor, and tie him to the stake."

The astonished young man showed his noble spirit to the last, and as calmly knelt down beneath the axe, as he had bravely wielded his sword against the enemies of his country. The whole Roman armies mourned his early death. How unnatural were even the virtues of the Romans, in many instances!

9. The war with the Samnites continued with occasional suspensions, but was destined to end only with their ruin. The Romans were generally successful in their battles, though, in one instance, a Roman army experienced a signal mortification, in being obliged to pass under the yoke.

The Tarentines, having become the allies of the Samnites, shared their fate. The Samnites were completely subdued, 272 years B. C., although, in the mean time, the Romans had on hand a war with some other states, as will be soon mentioned.

§ During the war with the Samnites, their general, Pontius, decoyed the Romans into a defile, in which they were wholly in the power of their enemies. Rejecting the advice of his father, which was either to put them all to death, or honourably to free them, he chose a middle course, and determined to disgrace them.

For that purpose, he obliged the Roman soldiers, with their officers leading the way, to pass half naked under the yoke—a sort of gallows made of three spears, two being fixed firmly in the ground, and one laid across on the top of the others. This was considered an insufferable disgrace.

The Romans keenly felt the indignity, and not having their power in the least crippled by this means, only became the more impatient to subdue their rivals. They had soon an opportunity of inflicting upon the Samnites a similar odium, and of obliging them at length to sue for peace.

10. The Romans had a short contention with the Tuscans, 312 B. C. During two successive years, they were defeated,—in the last by Fabius. But the most important war, about this time, was that in which they were engaged with Pyrrhus, king of Epirus.

The aid of this celebrated general had been sought by the Tarentines, as allies with the Samnites, in their united contest with Rome. He landed in Italy with 30,000 men, and a train of elephants, and commenced an attack on the Romans.

After various turns of fortune, he was at last totally defeated, with the loss of 26,000 men, and returned with haste to his dominions. From this time, the hostile states, left to bear alone the weight of the Roman power, were no longer formidable, and all Italy submitted to Rome, about 270 years B. C.

§ Pyrrhus was born to be a warrior; but warriors make themselves miserable. When he was preparing to comply with the invitations of the Tarentines, Cineas, a wise and good man, asked him what were his intentions and expectations?

"To conquer Rome," said Pyrrhus.

"And what will you do next, my lord?"

"Next, I will conquer Italy."

"And what after that?"

"We will subdue Carthage, Macedonia, all Africa, and Greece."

"And when we have conquered all we can, what shall we do?"

"Do! then we will sit down, and spend our time in comfort."

"Ah! my lord!" said the reasonable Cineas, "what prevents our being in peace and comfort now?"

Having arrived in Italy, he speedily conquered the Romans under their consul Lævinius. This victory was thought to have been gained by the effect produced by the elephants of Pyrrhus's army, the Roman horses taking fright at the sight of these huge animals. Pyrrhus was surprised at the valiant and skilful conduct of the Romans, for, at that time, all people, except those of one's own nation, were considered barbarians, rude and unknowing.

After the first battle, observing the noble and stern countenances of his enemies, as they lay dead on the field, Pyrrhus, awed into respect, cried out, in the true spirit of military ambition, "O with what ease could I conquer the world, had I the Romans for soldiers, and had they me for their king!" He gained a second victory, but after that he found himself losing ground daily, and was glad to leave Italy before he was entirely conquered. The people of Sicily had sent to him for assistance; thither he went.

In Sicily, he also experienced a change of fortune, at first prosperous, and then adverse. So that he once more returned to Italy, being almost driven from Syracuse by the Carthaginians. The Romans fell before him again; but at last, they terribly defeated him, and he was obliged to return with haste to his own country.

An anecdote, illustrating the generosity of the Romans and of Pyrrhus, and shewing that this was the age of Roman virtue, is worth recording. One of the physicians of Pyrrhus told the Romans, that he would poison his master, if they would give him a large reward. Fabricius, the Roman general, was shocked at this treachery, and directly informed Pyrrhus of it, sending away the physician with scorn; "for," said the general, "we should be honourable even to our enemies." Pyrrhus would not be outdone in generosity, and expressed his gratitude by sending to Rome all his prisoners without ransom, and by desiring to negotiate a peace.

11. The different states of Italy had now lost their independence; but after their conquest, they did not all bear the same relation to Rome. Their privileges were unequal, varying according to the different terms granted to the conquered, and afterwards modified according to their fidelity to the parent state. Some were entirely subjected to the Roman laws; others were allowed to live under the original institutions; and some were tributary, and others allies.

The success of the war with Pyrrhus, gave the Romans reputation abroad. They now seemed to themselves to be equal to any enterprise. They had long been jealous of the growing power of Carthage, and easily found a pretext for declaring war against that republic. It was alleged that Carthage had rendered assistance to the enemies of Rome.

Thus commenced what is commonly called the first Punic War, 264 years B. C. It lasted 23 years. The Romans were in general victorious, though they were once, under Regulus, severely beaten before the gates of Carthage. Their first attempts in naval warfare were made during this contention. They were highly successful in them, although the Carthaginians had been long celebrated for their enterprise and courage on the ocean.

The Romans won several naval battles, and took the strongest of the Sicilian towns, Sicily being the principal scene of the war. The ill success of the Carthaginians, reduced them to the necessity of making peace on very humiliating terms. They were required to quit Sicily, return all the prisoners they had taken, and pay 3,200 talents of silver.

§ The Mamertines, who inhabited a small section of the island of Sicily, had put themselves under the protection of Rome, with a view to ward off impending ruin, with which the Carthaginians threatened them, as allies of Hiero, king of Syracuse. The Romans, too proud to dignify the Mamertines with the name of allies, instead of professing to assist them, boldly declared war against Carthage, alleging as a reason, the assistance not long before rendered by Carthage to the southern parts of Italy, against the Romans.

Such was the frivolous pretext for this sanguinary war. It was the object, both of Carthage and Rome respectively, to reduce Sicily entirely to its sway. The Carthaginians had already possessed themselves of a considerable part of it. The Syracusans at first having confederated with the Carthaginians, at length turned against them.

Agrigentum was taken from the Carthaginians, after a long siege; and a fleet of the Romans, the first they ever possessed, and which they had equipped in a few weeks, defeated that of Carthage, in a most signal manner. A second naval engagement soon followed, attended with like success, the Carthaginians, under Hanno and Hamil car, losing 60 ships of war.

These victories so much encouraged the Romans, that they boldly crossed the Mediterranean sea, and landing in Africa, took the small town of Clypea. Regulus, the leader, was ordered to remain there, and continue, as pro-consul, to command the troops; but he earnestly requested to return home, as he had a small estate of seven acres which required his care.

A person was directed to perform this service, and then Regulus, satisfied that his wife and children would have food, willingly devoted himself to his public duties. The Carthaginians had procured forces from Sparta under Xantippus, and thus supported, defeated the Romans, and took Regulus prisoner.

Regulus having been kept in prison several years, was then sent to Rome to propose peace, and an exchange of prisoners. He was first obliged to take an oath that he would return to Carthage, if he did not succeed in his proposals. When this noble Roman made his appearance among his countrymen, they were all touched by his misfortunes, and were willing to purchase his freedom, by granting the request of his enemies.

But he would not allow his country to suffer for his sake, and, though he knew that torture and death awaited him at Carthage, he besought the Romans to send him back, and to refuse the Carthaginians their prisoners. The senate, with the utmost pain, consented to this disinterested advice; and, in spite of the tears of his wife, the embraces of his children, and the entreaties of his friends, Regulus returned to Carthage.

The sequel may be easily conjectured. As soon as the Carthaginians saw him come back with a denial, they put him to every kind of suffering they could invent—to the most barbarous tortures, all of which he bore with patient silence. He died as heroically as he had lived.

After various successes on both sides, the Romans gained two naval battles, and thus so effectually crippled the strength of the Carthaginians on their own element, that they sought a peace by great sacrifices. The island of Sicily was now declared a Roman province, though Syracuse maintained her independent government.

12. A peace of twenty-three years' continuance subsisted between Rome and Carthage, during which time the Romans had two short contentions—first with the Illyrians, and next with the Gauls. Over both of these nations the Roman arms triumphed. The temple of Janus, which was never shut during a time of war, was now shut for the second time, since the foundation of the city, 235 B. C. The Romans, at this era, began to cultivate the arts of peace, and to acquire a taste for literature.

§ The war with the Illyrians was owing to depredations committed by them, on the trading subjects of Rome. Redress being refused, the consuls marched against them, and most of the Illyrian towns were obliged to surrender. The war with the Gauls was occasioned by the irruption of these barbarians upon Italy. The Romans opposed them, with such success, that they lost two kings, and in one battle alone 40,000 men killed and 10,000 taken prisoners.

13. The peace between the Romans and Carthaginians was rather a matter of policy than of inclination. The Carthaginians particularly had improved the time in preparing for revenge. They began the aggression in the second Punic war, by laying siege to Saguntum, a city of Spain, in alliance with Rome. Their leader in this war was the celebrated Hannibal, son of Hamilcar, under whom the first Punic war was principally conducted. The son inherited the father's enmity to the Romans, and was greatly superior to him in talents.

The war commenced 218 years B. C., and lasted 17 years. It was at first highly favourable to the Carthaginians, and Rome was thrown into imminent danger, and great distress, by the victories of Hannibal, who had carried the war into Italy. But the Roman fortune began at length to prevail, and Hannibal was recalled to save Carthage itself, inasmuch as Scipio the Roman general, who triumphed in Spain, had passed over into Africa, and spread terror to the gates of Carthage.

Hannibal and Scipio met at Zama; the battle of that place decided the fate of the war, and the Carthaginians sued for peace. which they obtained only by abandoning Spain, Sicily, and all the islands—by surrendering all their prisoners, and nearly the whole of their fleet, by paying 10,000 talents, and by engaging to undertake no war without the consent of Rome.

§ Of Hannibal it is recorded, that when only nine years of age, at the instance of his father, he took a solemn oath at the altar, declaring himself the eternal enemy of the Romans; and never had they so terrible a foe. Like most other great soldiers, he was capable of bearing fatigue and hardship, heat and cold, good and bad fortune in the extreme, with entire equanimity, and without shrinking.

He was simple in dress, rigid in self-government—he ate, drank and slept only so much as to support his body, and give him strength to perform the intentions of his great mind. If, however, we are to believe the accounts of his enemies, he was not without striking moral defects—being cruel, negligent of his truth and honour, and a scorner of the religion of his country.

Hannibal crossing the sea from Africa to Europe, and taking Saguntum, in Spain marched through Spain, and over the Pyrennean hills into Gaul, along the coast of that country, and over the lofty Alps crowned with snow, to Italy—a land journey of 1000 miles. Such an exploit had never been done before. The difficulties of the way would have disheartened any other man. In addition to this he passed through various barbarous tribes, with most of whom he was obliged to fight for a passage; the Gauls among the rest attempting to oppose his progress.

He arrived in Italy with only 20,000 foot and 6000 horse. When he began this wonderful enterprise he was only 26 years old. Several Roman generals of approved talent and valour opposed him, yet he was on the point of making himself master of proud Rome. In the first engagement near the Ticinus, the Romans were defeated. and they lost two other important battles at the Trebia and the lake Thrasymenus.

Advancing to Cannæ, the Carthaginians were opposed by the whole force of Rome; but in vain. Their fine army under their consuls was totally routed. Varro gave orders for the battle against the wish of his colleague Paulus Æmilius; but the encounter once begun, Æmilius fought with the utmost skill and bravery, and died covered with wounds.

Just before his death he was found sitting on a stone, faint and streaming with blood. The soldier who discovered him, besought him to mount his horse, and put himself under his protection. "No," said Æmilius with gratitude, "I will not clog you with my sinking frame; go hasten to Rome, and tell the senate of this day's disaster, and bid them fortify the city, for the enemy is approaching it. I will die with my slaughtered soldiers, that I may neither suffer the indignation of Rome myself, nor be called upon to give testimony against my colleague, to prove my own innocence."

It is an opinion generally entertained, though by no means certain, that if Hannibal had marched directly to Rome, after the battle of Cannæ, the fate of the republic would have been inevitable. But this he did not see fit to attempt. The tide of success now began to turn against him. Wintering his troops in the luxurious city of Capua, they lost much of their virtue.

The Romans concentrated all their strength, even the slaves, armed in the common cause; and victory once more attended the stan dards of Rome. Hannibal retreated before the brave Marcellus. The forces of the king of Macedon, who had joined the Carthaginians, were also defeated at this juncture.

While Fabius, who was now opposed to Hannibal, conducted the war prosperously, by always avoiding a general engagement, the younger Scipio accomplished the entire reduction of Spain. Asdrubal was sent into Italy after a long delay, to the assistance of his brother Hannibal, but was defeated by the consul Claudius, and slain in battle.

Scipio, having triumphed in Spain, passed over into Africa, where his path was marked with terror and victory. This policy he had himself suggested to the Roman senate, as the only probable means of driving the Carthaginians from Italy. According to his expectations, when Carthage perceived the danger to which itself was exposed, Hannibal was recalled to protect his native land. He had been absent 16 years.

Scipio was an antagonist worthy of Hannibal. When he was very young, he saved the life of his father in a battle; and after the fatal overthrow at Cannæ, hearing of some young men who thought of abandoning their country, he, with a few other resolute spirits, suddenly entered the room where they were deliberating, and fiercely drew his sword and exclaimed, "whoever is against Rome, this sword is against him." The young men, intimidated by his resolution, or inspired by his spirit, took a vow with him and his companions, to fight for their country whilst a drop of blood remained in their veins.

The meeting at Zama, in Africa, between Hannibal and Scipio, the two greatest warriors in the world, was highly interesting. They gazed on each other with mutual awe and admiration. Hannibal in vain strove to procure honourable terms of peace. The youthful Roman, however, answered him with pride and disdain; and the armies prepared for battle.

The contest was dreadful; but the superior vigour of the Romans, notwithstanding the skill of the Carthaginians, prevailed. The latter lost 40,000 men in killed and in prisoners, and were thus obliged to conclude a fatal peace. Carthage was nearly ruined. As to Hannibal, he survived this battle several years; but being hated and hunted by the Romans from place to place, he committed the unjustifiable act of suicide, so common in ancient times.

"Let us relieve the Romans of their fears," said he, "by closing the existence of a feeble old man." He died at 70 years of age, at the court of Prussias, king of Bythynia. The second Punic war ended with the battle at Zama, B. C. 201.

14. The Roman dominion now rapidly extended. Other victories over other enemies attended the arms of the republic. Philip king of Macedon was defeated by the Romans under Flaminius in Thessaly, 197 years B. C. The Gauls received some signal overthrows.

§ The war with Philip is called the first Macedonian war, and was terminated by the request of Philip for peace, which the senate granted the second year of the contest. The second Macedonian war, which terminated the monarchy, as also that which put a period to Grecian liberty, have already been narrated in the history of Macedonia and Greece.

15. Five years afterwards, or 192 years B. C., commenced the Syrian war, under Antiochus the Great. This ended in his entire defeat, and in the cession to the Romans of all Asia Minor. The pretext of this war was, that Antiochus had made encroachments on the Grecian states, who were then called the allies of Rome. These successes, by pouring wealth into Rome, began to corrupt the simplicity of the ancient manners.

SICILY.

16. The history of SICILY is considerably included in that of Rome and other nations, but a few particulars may deserve a separate notice. In early times the government was a monarchy, but it afterwards became a republic, and continued such, except at Syracuse, the monarchy of which, after 60 years, was re-established in the person of Dionysius the Elder.

The Sicilians were frequently engaged in wars with the Carthaginians, and the latter, in the course of time, possessed themselves of a considerable part of the island. It was the scene and the object of the first Punic war; and in the second, the whole of it was brought under the sway of Rome, by the consul Marcellus, 212 years B. C.

§ This important island in the Mediterranean sea, the granary of Italy, was settled in an early age of the world, though the exact period is unknown. The Phœnicians had sent colonies thither before the Trojan war. The Greeks at later periods made considerable settlements in the island. The Corinthians founded Syracuse, which became the most renowned of the Greek cities of Sicily.

The regal government exercised in the various parts of the island, having become excessively tyrannical, was the cause of its being abolished in all the cities held there by the Greeks. Dionysius, however, a person of mean birth, but great talents, found the means of reviving the monarchy at Syracuse, and though thrice expelled on account of his tyranny, he re-assumed the sceptre, which he transmited to his son, Dionysius the Younger.

This weak and detestable tyrant had been well educated by the great Plato; but he soon forgot all the good that had been taught him. He so provoked his virtuous brother-in-law Dion, (whom the jealousy of the nobles had banished,) by marrying Dion's wife to one of his courtiers, that the latter led an army to Syracuse, drove the tyrant from his throne, and recovered his wife. In the hands of Dion the government was administered with much moderation and ability: but this excellent sovereign was at last cruelly murdered

At his death Dionysius again ascended the throne, and was again driven from it; and after all his various fortunes, it is said he became a school-master at Corinth. The brave and humane Timoleon, a Greek, was the person who accomplished the second banishment of this tyrant. Timoleon was sent for to assist the Syracusans against the Carthaginians, and having defeated them, he entered Syracuse in triumph.

Dionysius, being unfit to rule, surrendered himself and his citadel into his hands, and was sent to Corinth. Timoleon again defeated the Carthaginians under Asdrubal and Amilcar, and at length subdued all the enemies of Syracuse. After having served Syracuse and the whole island to the extent of his power, he gave up his authority, and lived the rest of his days in tranquil retirement.

A few years after the battle of Cannæ, Marcellus the Roman consul, laid siege to Syracuse; and in spite of the wonderful machines constructed and employed by Archimedes, he finally took it. Marcellus, who was acquainted with the extraordinary abilities of this man, when the city had fallen into his hands, gave orders, that Archimedes should be conducted to him in safety.

When the city was taken, this philosopher was so absorbed in study, that he was not aware of the event, until a soldier, rushing into his apartment, bade him rise and follow him. Archimedes desired him to wait a moment until he had solved the problem that he was working. The soldier, not understanding what he was talking about, and provoked at his disobedience, drew his sword and killed him on the spot. Marcellus was greatly disappointed at this event.

SYRIA.

17. During the present period the kingdom of Syria, or Syro-Medio, rose into importance under its founder Seleucus Nicator, or the Conqueror, 312 years B. C. In the first division of Alexander's empire, the country anciently called Syria, fell to the lot of Antigonus. But Seleucus, a distinguished and able officer in the empire, revolted, and made war upon Antigonus, who being slain at the battle of Ipsus, Seleucus remained possessor of his dominions. The sovereigns of this new kingdom, after him, were known under the name of Seleucidæ.

§ Syria was first inhabited by the posterity of Aram, the youngest son of Shem. The kings of this country were little known till the time of Alexander the Great, except what is related of them in the Bible. Hadadezer made an unsuccessful war against David. Benhadad was three times defeated by Ahab and Ahaziah. A few other particulars are related of the Syrian kings, till Syria was made a province of the Assyrian Empire by Tiglath-Pileser, who defeated and slew Rezin, the king of Syria, in battle.

18. The second and last division of Alexander's empire was formerly mentioned. Seleucus who retained Syria to

which other possessions were added, made war upon Lysimachus, who had reduced Macedonia under his sway. Lysimachus was killed, and Seleucus seized on his kingdom. But the conqueror was assassinated the same year, by Ptolemy Ceraunus, who afterwards reigned at Macedon.

§ Of the Seleucidæ, or successors of Seleucus, to the end of this period, the following epitome may be given. Antiochus Soter, or the saviour, succeeded the conqueror. Of this Antiochus it is recorded, that when a young man, he fell in love with one of his father's wives, a young and beautiful woman, to such a degree, as to be nearly reduced to death.

His physician discovering, from the agitation of his pulse at the sight of Stratonice, (the name of the object of his passion,) the true cause of his disease, made it known to Seleucus the father. From affection to the son he renounced Stratonice, and gave her to him in marriage, 280 B. C.

Antiochus Theos, or the God, invaded Egypt. During his absence the provinces of the East were entered by the Parthians, who founded a new kingdom. The Bactrians also became independent. He made peace with Ptolemy Philadelphus, and married his daughter Berenice, after repudiating his wife. The king of Egypt being dead, he took back his former wife, who poisoned him, Berenice, and her son, 261 B. C.

After the reigns of Seleucus Callinicus, and Seleucus Ceraunus, respecting whom nothing remarkable took place, Antiochus the Great ascended the throne. He was at first engaged in subduing some of his revolted governors. Afterwards he invaded Media, Parthia, Hyrcania, Bactria, and even India, 223 B. C.

Having planned the conquest of Asia Minor, and taken some places there, an embassy was sent by the Romans, desiring him to desist. This brought on the war with the Romans which has been particularly detailed. In this attempt he first conquered a part of Greece. Here the Romans defeated him, and being closely pursued by Scipio Asiaticus, he was beaten again in Asia. Among one of the conditions of peace was the delivery of his son Antiochus, as a hostage to the Romans.

Seleucus Philopater, who was left by his father to govern Syria, during his absence, next ascended the throne, 187 years B. C. His general Heliodorus, in attempting to rob the temple of Jerusalem of its treasures, was repulsed by the hand of God, and rigorously chastised. He poisoned Seleucus after his return.

Antiochus Epiphanes, the son who was delivered as a hostage to the Romans, and exchanged, after chastising Heliodorus, gained possession of the throne, 175 years B. C. In attempting to reduce Egypt under his dominion, he was stopped by a Roman ambassador, who obliged him to return.

Incensed at this, he vented his rage against the Jews, took Jerusalem, slaughtered 40,000 persons, and made as many prisoners. The Jews, however, revolted, and under Judas Maccabæus defeated several of his generals. These wars will be detailed in the history of the Jews. Antiochus, in attempting to exterminate the Jews, perished in great torments.

Antiochus Eupator and Demetrius Soter continued the war with the Jews, and Alexander Balas, the last sovereign, during this period, abandoned himself to a life of debauchery.

JEWS.

20. In the history of the Jews at the commencement of this period, we have to notice the favour which was mani fested towards them by Alexander the Great, who granted to them the freedom of their country, laws, and religion, and exempted them from paying tribute every seventh year.

In their dependent state, they had continued to enjoy a degree of prosperity under the sovereigns of Persia, even after the time of Cyrus. His successors, down to the era of Alexander, had, in general, treated them with much kindness. But with the latter expired the prosperous state of Judea, 324 years B. C.

§ Darius, son of Cyrus, favoured the Jews during his long reign. Xerxes confirmed their privileges. Under Artaxerxes they were still more favoured through the influence of his queen Esther, a Jewess. From this prince, Ezra obtained very liberal donations to be applied to the service of the temple, and authority to re-establish the government according to the divine constitution, 480 years B. C.

Several years afterwards, under the same prince, Nehemiah his cup-bearer, obtained leave to go to Jerusalem and rebuild its walls. He and Joiada the high priest reformed many abuses respecting tithes, the observation of the sabbath, and the marrying of strange wives.

In the latter period, to which our accounts more particularly refer, it is recorded that Jaddus, the high priest, in his priestly attire, met Alexander the Great, and shewed him the prophecy of Daniel, in which his conquest was foretold.

21. From this time, 323 years B. C., Judea was succes sively invaded and subdued by the Egyptians and Syrians, and the inhabitants were reduced to bondage. In consequence of an invasion by Antiochus Epiphanes, about 170 years B. C. the sacrifices ceased among the Jews, and there scarcely existed any external signs of their peculiar civil or religious polity.

Such persecutions roused the Jews to drive the Syrians from Judea, which they gloriously achieved under Judas Maccabæus, 166 years B. C.

§ Under the priesthood of Onias I., Ptolemy, governor of Egypt taking advantage of the circumstance that the Jews would not fight on the sabbath, captured Jerusalem on that day, and carried off 100,000 persons, whom, however, he afterwards treated kindly.

When Eleazer was high priest, he sent to Ptolemy Philadelphus six men of every tribe, to translate the sacred scriptures into Greek. This translation is the celebrated one called the Septuagint, 277 B. C.

Jason, 170 B. C., on false reports of Antiochus' death, raised great disturbances in Jerusalem, with a view to recover the high priesthood. Antiochus (Epiphanes) irritated by the frequent revolts of the Jews, marched to Jerusalem, slew 80,000 people, took 40,000 captives, and then entered the temple and plundered the treasures.

Antiochus having commanded the Jews to observe the rites of the heathen, and to eat of the sacrifices, some of the more conscientious among them chose rather the loss of life; among whom were a mother and her seven sons, who expired in dreadful tortures. The same year the king's commissioner, who was entrusted with this iniquitous business, was killed by Mattathias and his five sons, who thereupon fled into the wilderness.

Judas Maccabæus, at the head of those who fled into the wilderness, made war against Antiochus, and defeated several of his generals. The king hearing of the defeat of his troops in Judea, took an oath, that he would destroy the whole nation. As he hastened to Jerusalem, he fell from his chariot, and died miserably.

In a battle with a general of one of his successors, Judas was killed. Jonathan his brother succeeded, and was made high priest, 153 years B. C. A younger brother had been previously killed. The remainder of the history of the Maccabees is to be pursued in the next succeeding period.

EGYPT.

22. Egypt, having been in subjection 30 years since it was last brought under the Persian yoke, was subdued by Alexander the Great, 332 years B. C. He appointed Ptolemy Lagus its governor, who, after the conqueror's death, began a new dynasty of kings, called Ptolemæans or Lagidæ, 323 years B. C.

This dynasty lasted 294 years, and ended in Cleopatra. Of the sovereigns that belong to the period now treated of, we find the names of six of various characters.

Ptolemy Lagus, called also Soter or Saviour, was a man of great bilities, and endeavoured to restore Egypt to its ancient splendour. He erected the famous library at Alexandria. He subdued Syria, Phœnicia, Cyprus, and Jerusalem.

Ptolemy Philadelphus, or Lover of his brother, pursued the steps of his father in a great measure. He protected commerce, arts, and sciences, and erected magnificent buildings. Ptolemy Evergetes, or the Benefactor, was not only a lover of science, but an author. He spared no pains to enrich his library.

Ptolemy Philopater, or Lover of his father, a surname probably given him in derision, being suspected to have put his father to death, was a cruel prince. He slew his brother, murdered his queen, and ordered all the Jews within his dominions to abjure their religion, which however they refused to do.

Ptolemy Epiphanes, or the Illustrious, was famous only for his vices. He suffered every thing to fall into disorder, and was at last poisoned by his subjects.

Ptolemy Philometer, or Lover of his mother, engaged in an unsuccessful war against Syria, in which he was taken prisoner, and the crown given to his brother Physcon; but after Philometer regained his liberty, they reigned jointly.

PARTHIA.

23. The history of PARTHIA begins at this era. Arsaces, a nobleman, descended as some think from Artaxerxes Mnemon, king of Persia, revolted from Antiochus Theos, king of Syria (256 B. C.) and founded the new kingdom of Parthia, which at first consisted only of the province so called. From him his successors are called Arsacidæ.

§ The single province of Parthia was not large; but the Parthian empire included not only Parthia, but Hyrcania, Sogdiana, Bactria, Persia, Media, and several other regions. Parthia was first subject to the Medes, afterwards to the Persians, and lastly to Alexander the Great: upon whose death, it fell to the share of Seleucus Nicator; and his successors held it till the reign of Antiochus Theos.

They were a warlike people, and the best horsemen and archers in the world. For the sake of war, they neglected agriculture, trade, and all other callings.

24. The Arsacidæ were in general conquerors, and greatly extended their dominions from time to time. Mithridates I. the fifth from Arsaces, was a man of uncommon wisdom and courage. He reduced the Bactrians, Persians, Medes, and Elymæans, and extended his dominions into India, beyond the boundaries of Alexander's conquests.

CHINA.

25. The third dynasty of the emperors of CHINA, which commenced 1110 years B. C., ended during this period viz. 246 years B. C. It included 35 emperors. It is called the dynasty of Tcheou.

The fourth dynasty, which began at the latter date, lasted 43 years, terminating 203 years B. C. It included four emperors. It is called the dynasty of Tsin.

§ Chaus the fourth emperor of the third dynasty was excessively fond of hunting. In the pursuit of that sport, he did incalculable damage to the crops of his subjects. Their remonstrances being unheeded, they determined to destroy him. For this purpose, as he was wont to pass a large river, on his return from the chase, in a boat which waited for him, they caused one to be built of such construction as to break in pieces before it reached the opposite shore. Entering his boat, he and his attendants soon went to the bottom.

Ching, the second emperor of the fourth dynasty, left a monument of his power, which still astonishes those that behold it, viz. the famous wall, 500 leagues long, which separates China from its northern neighbours. He suppressed the tributary kingdoms, and reduced them to their former state of provinces.

Elated with his success, he became ambitious of being thought the first sovereign of China. With this view he ordered all the historical writings and public records to be burned, and many of the learned men to be buried alive, that past events might not be transmitted to posterity.

Distinguished Characters in Period VIII.

1. Plato, an eminent Grecian philosopher, called the Divine.
2. Apelles, the greatest of the painters of antiquity.
3. Alexander the Great, conqueror of most of the world known to the ancients.
4. Demosthenes, the prince of orators.
5. Aristotle, the ablest logician and philosopher of antiquity.
6. Euclid, the greatest master of mathematical science.
7. Theocritus, the father of pastoral poetry.
8. Zeno, the founder of the Stoic school of philosophy.
9. Archimedes, a famous geometrician of Syracuse.

1. Plato was born about 429 years B. C. His name, Aristocles, was changed to Plato, from the largeness of his shoulders. He was 8 years the pupil of Socrates, after whose death, he travelled into foreign countries. When he had finished these, he retired to the groves of Academus, where he was attended by a crowd of noble and illustrious pupils.

His learning and virtues were topics of conversation in every part of Greece; he was elegant in his manners, and partook of innocent pleasures and amusements. He died in his 81st year, about 348 B. C.

The works of Plato are numerous; they are all in the form of a dialogue, except twelve letters. The ancients and even the learned moderns have highly respected and admired the writings of this great philosopher. They display unusual depth of thought, and singular elegance, melody, and sweetness of expression. Among other truths, he maintained by many powerful arguments the immortality of the soul.

2. Apelles was born in the island of Cos, and lived contemporary with Alexander, who would suffer no other to draw his picture. His Venus rising out of the sea, was purchased by Augustus, and placed in a temple at Rome. The lower part had sustained some injury which no artist could repair. He wrote some pieces which were extant in the age of Pliny

One of his pictures of Alexander exhibited the conqueror with a thunderbolt in his hand. The piece was finished with so much skill and dexterity, that it used to be said that there were two Alexanders: one invincible, the son of Philip: the other inimitable, the production of Apelles. The date of his death does not appear.

3. Alexander was born at Pella in Macedonia, 355 B. C. At the age of ten years he was delivered to the tuition of Aristotle, and early followed his father to the field. When he came to the throne, he invaded Asia, as has been already described, defeating Darius in three great battles, reducing Egypt, Media, Syria, and Persia, and spreading his conquests over a part of India.

On his return from India he stopped at Babylon, where he died in his 32d year, from excess in drinking, or as some think, from poison. He aspired to be thought a demigod, but was humane, liberal, and a patron of learning. With many valuable qualities, much is it to be regretted that he should have been the scourge, by being the conqueror of the world.

His tender treatment of the wife and mother of Darius, who were taken prisoners, has been greatly praised. The latter, who had survived the death of her son, killed herself when she heard that Alexander was dead. He was guilty of many extravagant and profligate actions; yet amidst them all he was fond of candour and truth, and after any act of wickedness, appeared to be stung with grief and remorse.

When one of his officers read to him as he sailed on the Hydaspes, a history which the officer had composed of his wars with Porus, and in which he had too liberally praised him, Alexander snatched the book from his hand, and threw it into the river saying, "What need is there of such flattery? Are not the exploits of Alexander sufficiently meritorious in themselves, without the colouring of falsehood?"

The death of his friend Clitus, of which he was the author, while it might be in a degree palliated, shewed how capable he was of regret for a wrong action. Clitus had greatly abused Alexander; they were both heated with wine and passion. The monarch after bearing the abuse for some time, ordered Clitus to be carried out of his presence.

The latter, however, soon returned, and renewed his invectives. Alexander giving loose to his indignation, stabbed the veteran; but was so immediately shocked with what he had done, that he was about to kill himself on the spot, and was only prevented by his friends.

4. Demosthenes was only seven years old when his father died, and his guardians, proving unfaithful to their trust, squandered his property, and neglected his education. He was therefore indebted to his own industry and application, for the discipline of his mind.

By unwearied efforts, and by overcoming the greatest obstacles, such as weakness of the lungs, difficulty of pronunciciation, and uncouth habits of body, he became the greatest orator in the world. That he might devote himself the more closely to his studies, he confined himself to a retired cave, and shaved half of his head, so that he could not decently appear in public.

His abilities as an orator soon placed him at the head of the government, and in this capacity he roused and animated his countrymen against the ambitious designs of Philip. He also opposed Alexander, and made every effort to save his country. When the generals of Alexander approached Athens, he fled for safety to the temple of Neptune, and there took poison to prevent himself from falling into their hands, in his 60th year, B. C. 322.

5. Aristotle possessed one of the keenest and most inventive original intellects ever known. His writings treat of almost every branch of knowledge in his time;—moral and natural philosophy, metaphysics, mechanics, grammar, criticism, and politics, all occupied his pen.

His eloquence also was remarkable. He was moderate in his meals, slept little, and was indefatigably industrious. That he might not oversleep himself, Diogenes Laërtius tells us, that he lay always with one hand out of the bed, holding in it a ball of brass, which, by its falling into a basin of the same metal, awaked him.

Though educated in the school of Plato, he differed from his master, and at length formed a new school. He taught in the Lyceum. He had a deformed countenance, but his genius was an ample compensation for all his personal defects. As he expired, he is said to have uttered the following sentiment. "I entered this world in impurity, I have lived in anxiety, I depart in perturbation. Cause of causes, pity me!" If he lived in scepticism, as is affirmed, he hardly died in it. His death occurred in his 63d year.

6. Euclid was a mathematician of Alexandria. He flourished about 300 years B. C. He distinguished himself by his writings on music and geometry, but particularly by 15 books on the elements of mathematics, which consist of problems and theorems, with demonstrations. His elements have gone through innumerable editions. He was greatly respected by antiquity, and his school, which he established at Alexandria, became the most famous in the world, for mathematics.

7. Theocritus flourished at Syracuse in Sicily, 282 years B. C. He distinguished himself by his poetical compositions, of which 30 Idylia, and some epigrams, are extant, written in the Doric dialect, and admired for their beauty, elegance, and simplicity.

He excelled in pastorals. He clothes his peasants with all the rusticity of nature, though sometimes speaking on exalted subjects. It is said he wrote some invectives against Hiero, king of Syracuse, who ordered him to be strangled.

8. Zeno was a native of Cyprus. In early life he followed commercial pursuits; but having been shipwrecked, to divert his melancholy, he took up a book to read. The book was written by Xenophon, and so captivated was he, that from this time he devoted himself to philosophy.

Becoming perfect in every branch of knowledge, he at length opened a school in Athens, and delivered his instructions in a porch, in Greek called *stoa*. He was austere in his manners, but his life was an example of moderation and sobriety. He taught philosophy 48 years, and died in his 98th year, B. C. 264. A stranger to diseases and indisposition, virtue was his chief good.

9. Archimedes was born at Syracuse. At the siege, by Marcellus, he constructed machines which sunk some of the Roman ships, and others he set on fire with burning glasses. These glasses are supposed to have been reflectors made of metal, and capable of producing their effect at the distance of a bow shot.

He was killed at the taking of the place, 208 B. C. by a soldier, who was ignorant of his character, and while the philosopher was engaged in his studies. Some of his works are extant.

PERIOD IX.

The period of the civil war between Marius and Sylla, extending from the destruction of Carthage, 146 *years B. C. to the first campaign of Julius Cæsar,* 80 *years B. C.*

ROME.

SECT. 1. This period, as well as that which follows, properly begins with the affairs of the ROMANS—a people, already possessing vast power and resources, and destined to become in a short time, the conquerors of the whole civilized portion of the human family.

Following the course of their victories, we next light upon their final conquest and destruction of Carthage, the most formidable rival Rome ever possessed. That city fell under the hands of the conquerors 146 years B. C. The war, of which this was the result, had commenced four years before. The Romans were the aggressors, having invaded Africa at a favourable juncture, when the Carthaginians were engaged in a war with another power.

Carthage fell, notwithstanding the desperate efforts of its inhabitants, and was converted into a pile of ruins, with the extinction of the Carthaginian name.

§ When the indications of Roman hostility appeared, the Carthaginians, who had suffered so severely in the last war, recoiled at the idea of another contest with the conquering Romans. They therefore sent a deputation to Rome to settle the matter pacifically, if possible. The Senate gave no decisive answer.

A second deputation followed, but it sought in vain to avert the threatened evil. The demands made upon the Carthaginians were in the highest degree disgraceful to Rome. They were commanded to promise implicit obedience, and to send 300 hostages as a security for their future good conduct. The promise was given, and the Carthaginians yielded up their children, as the required hostages.

They were next ordered to give up all their arms; this order was also obeyed: and to consummate their degradation and the cruelty of the Romans, they were required to quit their beloved city, and allow it to be levelled to the ground. The Carthaginians, as might have been expected, were fired with indignation, and resolved unanimously that if they could not save their capital, they would perish with it.

Despoiled, however, of their arms, they could at first effect but little, although they exerted every nerve, in meeting the foe. Their women cut off their long fine hair to be twisted into cords for bows, they brought out all their gold and silver vessels to be converted into arms, for these were the only metals they had left.

The Romans were astonished at the resistance they experienced, many times were they repulsed from the walls, and many were the soldiers slain in the various attacks. Indeed, it is thought by some, that Carthage would not finally have been taken, had not one of her own officers basely gone over to the enemy. The affairs of the Carthaginians declined from that time.

Scipio Æmilianus cut off their supplies of food, and blocked up the haven. The persevering citizens cut out a new passage into the sea. He next attacked and cut to pieces the army they had stationed without the walls, killing 70,000 men, and taking 10,000 prisoners. After this he broke through the walls, and entered the city, pulling or burning down houses and temples, and public buildings, with indiscriminate fury.

Asdrubal, the Carthaginian general, delivered himself and citadel to the conquerors; but his wife and children, with numbers of the citizens, set fire to the temples, and rushing into them, perished in the flames. So completely was this once beautiful city destroyed, that the place on which it stood cannot be discovered; it was burning 17 days, and was 24 miles in circumference.

All the cities which befriended Carthage, shared her fate; and the Romans gave away the lands to their friends.

2. Soon after the ruin of Carthage, viz. 137 years B. C. the Numantines, a people of Spain, overcame the Romans in battle; but three years after this defeat, Numantia, the finest and largest city in Spain, was taken by the Romans, and he inhabitants, to escape falling into the hands of these cruel conquerors, set fire to their city, and all of them perished in the flames. Thus Spain became a province of Rome 134 years B. C.

§ Previously to the defeat of the Romans by the Numantines, there had been a war between the Romans and Spain, which lasted 9 years. Fabius, who was sent to manage this war, gained a victory over one of the leaders of the Spanish forces, who was obliged to retire into Lusitania.

The reverse which the Romans met with in the contest with Numantia, was highly disgraceful to them. Thirty thousand of their number were conquered by 4000 Numantines. The consul, Mancinus, was recalled, and Scipio was sent into Spain, who restored the discipline of the troops. He soon defeated the Numantines, who, being reduced to the last extremity, perished as above described.

3. Rome at this time, (133 B. C.) was beginning to be greatly disturbed by internal dissensions. Attalus, king of Pergamus, having, by his last will, made the Romans his heirs, Tiberius Gracchus, a tribune of the people, proposed that the money should be divided among the poor. This caused a great disturbance, during which Gracchus was killed.

About twelve years afterwards, Caius Gracchus, brother to Tiberius, having opposed the senate, and become popular and powerful, exposed himself to the resentment of the nobles, who marked him out for destruction. In consequence of some riots, the consul Opimius pursued him so closely, that to avoid falling into his hands, he accomplished his own death, by the assistance of a servant.

§ The Gracchi were sons of Cornelia, the daughter of Scipio Africanus, the conqueror of Hannibal. She was left a widow with twelve children. The following circumstance places her character in a very favourable light. A lady once came to visit her, who prided herself much on her jewels, and after shewing them to Cornelia, asked to see hers in return. Cornelia waited till her sons came home from school, and then presenting them to her guest, said, "Behold, madam, these are my jewels."

The interference of Tiberius, her elder son, in behalf of the poor, had given great offence to the rich. At a public meeting he chanced to put his hand to his head, and those who wished his downfall immediately said that he was desirous of a crown, and in the uproar that ensued, he lost his life.

At his death, the populace placed his younger brother at their head. Caius Gracchus was only 21 at this time, and had lived a life of great retirement, yet he did much good, and caused many useful acts to be passed. He was temperate and simple in his food, and of an active and industrious disposition. His love and respect for his mother were remarkable. At her request he withdrew a law he much desired to have passed: and so much was he esteemed, that a statue was erected to the memory of his mother, with this inscription, "Cornelia, the mother of the Gracchi," a tribute honourable to both parent and children.

The tumults attending the attempts of the Gracchi to remove the corruptions of the higher orders at their expense, were a prelude to those civil disorders, which now rapidly followed to the end of the commonwealth.

4. The Romans, though corrupt at home, still displayed their valour abroad. Besides some small states which they had acquired on the north and east, they defeated Jugurtha, king of Numidia, about this time. The war with him commenced 111 years B. C., and was finished under Marius 108 B. C. The consequence to Jugurtha was the loss of his kingdom and life.

After an engagement in which 90,000 of the Numidian army were slain, he was betrayed and made prisoner, and the senate finally condemned him to be starved to death in a dungeon. Jugurtha's own conduct occasioned his calamity, though the senate of Rome acted with singular cruelty.

In this war Metellus the consul was leader at first, but Marius found means to supplant him, and to succeed in command.

§ Jugurtha, who was grandson of the famous Massinissa, that sided against Hannibal, sought to usurp the crown of Numidia, by destroying his cousins, the sons of the late king. He succeeded in murdering the elder brother; and the younger, applying for aid to Rome, failed of success, since Jugurtha bribed the senate, who decreed to him the sovereignty of half the kingdom.

He then made war upon his cousin, and finally put him also to death. The displeasure of the Roman people being excited by this conduct, the senate were constrained to summon him to Rome, to answer for his perfidy. He accordingly went thither, and pleading his own cause in person, he again, by bribery, secured the favour of the senate.

A repetition of his base conduct in reference to his cousin, drew upon him, however, the vengeance of the Romans. Metellus was sent against him; and in the space of two years, Jugurtha was overthrown in several battles, so that he was forced to negociate a peace. The negociation, however, was soon laid aside.

Metellus had very much broken the strength of the Numidian king, before Marius succeeded to the command. Having by his arts obtained the consulship, Marius enjoyed the reputation of putting an end to the war. This man was the glory and the scourge of Rome. He was born of poor parents, and inured from infancy to penury and toil. His manners were as rude as his countenance was forbidding.

He was thus prepared, however, to become a great general. His stature was extraordinary, his strength incomparable, and his bravery undaunted. When he entered the country of Jugurtha, he quickly made himself master of the cities that yet remained to the latter.

Bocchus, king of Mauritania, at first assisted this prince, but fearing at length for his own crown, and understanding that the Romans would be satisfied with the delivery of Jugurtha into their hands, he resorted to this treacherous measure, and the Numidian, dragged in chains to Rome, experienced the fate above recorded.

5. After a short war with the Teutones and Cimbri, of whom several hundred thousands were slain under Marius, the Romans fell into a contention with the allied states of Italy. This was called the Social War, and was entered into on the part of the states, with a view to obtain the rights of citizenship, 91 years B. C.

This war ended in an allowance of those rights, to such of the allies as should return to their allegiance. It cost the lives of 300,000 of the flower of Italy, and was conducted by the ablest generals, on both sides.

6. Following this was the commencement of the Mithridatic War, 89 years B. C. Sylla, who had distinguished himself in the social war, was appointed to the command of the expedition against Mithridates, to the great disappointment of Marius. This measure was the foundation of those dreadful dissensions by which Rome became soon distracted.

Within the space of three years, Sylla greatly humbled the power of Mithridates, and at the expiration of that time returned to Rome, burning with revenge against his enemies,—Marius and his accomplices.

§ Mithridates was a powerful and warlike monarch, whose dominion at this time extended over Cappadocia, Bithynia, Thrace, Macedon, and all Greece. He was able to bring 250,000 infantry into the field, and 50,000 horse. He had also a vast number of armed chariots, and in his port 400 ships of war.

The Romans desired to attack him, and they wanted no other pretence, than his having invaded some of those states that were under the protection of Rome. Sylla entered with spirit on the war, and soon had an oppotunity to acquire glory by his arms.

This general who now began to take the lead in the commonwealth, belonged to one of the most illustrious families in Rome. His person was elegant, his air noble, his manners easy and apparently sincere, he loved pleasure, but glory still more; and fond of popularity, he desired to please all the world. He rose by degrees into office, and soon eclipsed every other commander. On this account he received the present appointment, in opposition to the claims of Marius.

In the course of the war, which had now commenced in earnest. Mithridates having caused 150,000 Romans, who were in his dominions, to be slain in cold blood, next sent his general Archelaus to oppose Sylla. Archelaus, however, was defeated near Athens, with the loss of an incredible number of his forces.

Another battle followed, by which the Roman general recovered all the countries that had been usurped by Mithridates; so that both parties desired a cessation of arms, Mithridates on account of his losses, and Sylla on account of his designs against Marius.

7. Before much progress was made in the Mithridatic war, the contention between Marius and Sylla had begun, 88 years B. C. Sylla having been recalled from Asia, refused to obey the mandate of the senate, and found his army well disposed to support him. They required their leader to march them to Rome. He accordingly led them on, and they entered the city sword in hand.

Marius and his partisans, after some resistance, fled from the city, and Sylla ruled for a time in triumph. He soon returned, however, into Asia, to finish the war he had undertaken. In the mean time, the party of Marius recovered strength, and he returning to Italy, and joining his forces to those of Cinna, his zealous partizan, laid siege to Rome. The city he compelled to absolute submission.

After putting to death all whom they considered their enemies, they assumed the consulship. But Marius, in a fit of debauch, died a few days after; and Cinna at no great interval followed, having been privately assassinated.

§ After Sylla had entered Rome in arms, his object, with the exception of a few vindictive measures, seemed to be to give peace to the city, and it was not until he had effected this object, as he supposed, that he departed upon his expediton against Mithridates. By confining his efforts solely against Marius, he had, however, overlooked a formidable rising opponent in Cornelius Cinna.

This man, who was of noble extraction, ambitious, bold, and enterprising, had sufficient influence to raise an army with a view to contend against the supporters of Sylla. Just at this juncture, Marius, having escaped a thousand perils during his absence, returned, with his son, to the gates of Rome. An army of veterans and slaves, the latter of whom he had promised liberty, flocked to his standard, and burning with revenge, he entered Rome, having previously received the submission of the senate.

Tragical occurrences followed; for senators of the first rank were butchered in the streets, and every personal enemy which Marius or Cinna had, that could be found, was put to death. In a month Marius died, having satisfied his two prevailing passions of ambition and revenge; and while Cinna was preparing to meet Sylla in arms, he perished in a mutiny of his own soldiers, by an unknown hand.

8. Sylla soon returned to Italy, victorious over his foreign enemy, and joined by Cethegus, Pompey, and other leaders, gave battle to those Romans who had been opposed to him, and entirely defeated them. Rome now for the first time received a native master. A most dreadful massacre and pro-

scription followed, in which Sylla designed to exterminate every enemy he had in Italy.

§ The army opposed to Sylla was headed by young Marius, son of Caius, and although it was more numerous than that of Sylla, it was less united and disciplined. Several misfortunes, however, happening to the forces of Marius, they soon yielded.

A large body of the Samnites, who, at this time, were in the interest of Marius, had carried the war to the gate of Rome. They were on the point of success, when Sylla met them, and a most obstinate contest ensued. Sylla found himself victorious. On the field of battle 50,000 of the vanquished and the victors lay promiscuously in death. Sylla now became undisputed master of his country, and entered Rome at the head of his army.

But he entered it to accomplish the purposes of the direst revenge. A long list of senators, and Roman knights, together with an unnumbered multitude of the citizens, he caused to be put to death. This work of destruction he extended throughout the principal towns of Italy. He permitted his soldiers to revenge their private injuries, and thus almost indiscriminate massacres took place.

9. Such violence, however, could be supported only by an increase of power. Accordingly Sylla invested himself with the Dictatorship, thus designing to give an air of justice to his monstrous oppressions. This dictatorship commenced 82 years B. C., and lasted not quite three years. Rome was now beginning to settle into a despotism, having passed through all the forms of monarchy, aristocracy, and democracy. From this time, though nominally a republic for a number of years, it never freed itself from the yoke of despotism.

Sylla, as perpetual dictator, was without a rival in authority, and absolute master of the government. Every thing was done as he exacted. The least opposition aroused his vengeance. The people saw nothing before them but the prospect of hopeless slavery, for, while they were amused with the show of their former government, Sylla took care that none but his own creatures should be elected to any office.

It was at this crisis, however, that, contrary to all expectation, Sylla laid down the dictatorship. The step was unaccountable, and the reasons of it have ever remained hidden from mankind.

§ He retired in safety. Of all that great multitude which he had so often insulted and terrified, none were found hardy enough to reproach or accuse him, except one young man who pursued him, with bitter invectives, to his own door.

Sylla, without replying to so low an adversary, turning to those who followed, observed, "That this fellow's insolence would, for the future, prevent any man's laying down an office of such supreme authority."

Retiring into the country, in order to enjoy the pleasures of tranquillity and social happiness, if such a wretch could enjoy either, he did not long survive his abdication, dying of a most filthy disease—a loathsome and mortifying object to human ambition.

A little before his death he made his own epitaph, the tenor of which was, "that no man had ever exceeded him in doing good to his friends, or injuries to his enemies."

SYRIA.

10. The affairs of Syria, under the Seleucidæ, or successors of Seleucus, to the end of this period, were in a very unprosperous state. A succession of massacres and usurpations took place, till the time of Tigranes, king of Armenia, whom the Syrians invited to reign over them, 85 years B. C. Indeed Syria existed in independence but a few years after the present period, having been made a province of Rome soon after the commencement of the next succeeding period, viz. 64 years B. C.

§ The following are the names of some of the Seleucidæ of the present era. The first was Demetrius Nicator, or the conqueror, who reigned five years, but was then confined to his palace for a long time. He afterwards recovered his dominions, and reigned four years.

After him Tryphon usurped the sceptre, and reigned four years. He was at length killed by his own soldiers.

Antiochus Sidetes, the second son of Demetrius Sòter, next ascended the throne of his ancestors. He made war against Jerusalem, and obliged it to capitulate, but he granted the Jews a peace upon reasonable conditions.

In attempting to recover all the provinces that belonged to the Syrian empire, of which Parthia was one, he made war against Phraates, king of Parthia, but being obliged to separate his troops and put them into winter quarters, the inhabitants of the country resolved on their destruction, and massacred them all in one day. Including attendants, they amounted to 400,000 persons.

After this prince were Seleucus V. Antiochus Gryphus, who reigned 29 years, Antiochus IX. who was slain by a son of Gryphus; and one or two others whose names need not be mentioned.

The Syrians having suffered so long, and so severely, under the turbulent princes of the race of Seleucus, resolved to exclude them from the throne. This they accomplished by sending an embassy to Tigranes, and inviting him to accept of the sovereignty.

Tigranes complied with their request, and swayed the Syrian sceptre 18 years in perfect peace. Engaging afterwards in a war with the Romans, Lucullus the consul defeated him, and took the city of Tigranocerta, 69 years B. C.

After this, Antiochus Asiaticus, a son of one of the former kings of Syria, was acknowledged as king by Lucullus, and reigned peaceably for the space of four years; but at the expiration of that time he was driven from the throne by Pompey, and Syria was reduced to a Roman province.

JEWS.

11. Pursuing the history of the Jews under the Maccabees it appears, that the brothers of Judas Maccabæus availed themselves of their advantages with perseverance and success. By their exertions they established the independence of their country, and changed its republican government to a vigorous monarchy.

John Hyrcanus, son of Simon Maccabæus, uniting in his person the offices of high priest and generalissimo of the army, subdued the enemies of his country, ceased to pay homage to the kings of Syria, firmly established his government, and is celebrated for his many valuable qualities, 135 B. C. He reigned 28 years.

His sons assumed the title as well as the power of kings; and the high-priesthood remained in his family, though not in the person of the monarch. His descendants are distinguished in the history of the Jewish nation, by the appellation of the Asmonean dynasty, which continued about 126 years. The independence of Judea was, however, drawing near to its close, an event which will be noticed in the succeeding period.

§ Concerning Hrycanus it may be further recorded, that he seized on several of the defenceless cities of Syria, and thus accomplished a complete deliverance of his nation from the oppression of Syria. He also made some conquests, both in Arabia and Phœnicia, turned his victorious arms against the Samaritans, and subdued Idumea. At the time of his death he had raised his nation to a considerable degree of wealth, prosperity, and happiness.

Of Aristobulus, one of the sons that reigned after Hyrcanus, it is recorded that he caused his brother Antigonus to be killed on suspicion of disloyalty; that his mother claiming a right to the sovereignty by virtue of Hyrcanus' will, was barbarously starved to death,—and that her other sons were kept in close confinement.

This tyrannical persecutor assumed the royal diadem, which had not been worn by any of his predecessors, and effected the conquest of Iturea. His successes, however, were soon interrupted by sickness; and the deep remorse he felt on account of the treatment of his mother, produced a vomiting of blood, which speedily closed his wicked life and reign.

EGYPT.

12. Egypt, during this period, continued under the rule of the Ptolemæan dynasty. The nation increased in magnificence and consequence during the reigns of the Ptolemies. Their reigns, however, were disturbed by many plots and insurrections, which arose between the different states over which the princes had dominion.

These states were so numerous, as at one time to include 33,333 well peopled cities.

§ Of the first Ptolemy in this period, viz. Physcon, we remark, that he was so called on account of his corpulency; but the name which he assumed was Evergetes, or the Benefactor. This was changed by his subjects into Kakergetes, or the Evil Doer, for he was the most cruel, wicked, and despicable of the Ptolemies who swayed the Egyptian sceptre.

He murdered the child of his wife Cleopatra in his mother's arms. He caused all persons to be put to death who had lamented the fate of the young prince, and gave free permission to the foreigners who composed his guard, to plunder and massacre the inhabitants of Alexandria. That wealthy city was accordingly stript of its inhabitants, and repeopled by strangers whom he had invited thither.

These, and many other enormities, rank him among the most brutal of mankind. Ptolemy Lathyrus succeeded Physcon. His mother Cleopatra, however, contrived to dethrone him, and to place his brother Alexander on the throne. The latter retained the title of king 18 years. After his death, Lathyrus re-assumed the government.

To Lathyrus a most inhuman action is attributed, in his war with the Jews, on a certain occasion. Having taken up his quarters after a victorious battle, in the neighbouring villages of Judea, he caused all the female and infant inhabitants to be murdered, and their mutilated limbs to be put into boiling caldrons, as if he designed to make a repast for his army. He wished to inspire the Jews with terror by representing their enemies as cannibals.

PARTHIA.

13. Parthia continued, during this period, to be governed by the Arsacidæ, or descendants of Arsaces. This empire, which was greatly extended at one time, and which under Mithridates I. enjoyed the height of its grandeur, was soon afterwards considerably abridged. The principal sovereigns during this peroid, were Phraates II. Artabanus II. and Mithridates II.

§ Phraates II. when preparing to invade Syria at a certain time, found himself under the necessity of fighting the Scythians, whom he had called to his assistance against Antiochus, and to whom he refused to pay the promised sum, on account of their not arriving before the defeat of the Syrians

In order to strengthen his army he enlisted all the Greek mercenaries, who, following Antiochus, were prisoners; but these Greeks having been treated with cruelty during their captivity, resolved to have revenge; and in the first engagement deserted to the Scythians, and in conjunction with them attacked the Parthians, cut their army to pieces, killed the king, and ravaged their country. In this battle the Chinese also assisted the Scythians, which is their first appearance abroad, which history records. They had previously been confined to their own country in their wars and transactions.

Distinguished Characters in Period IX.

1. Polybius, a learned historian, who wrote the history of the Greeks and Romans.
2. Apollodorus, a Greek grammarian.
3. Lucilius, an early Roman poet.
4. Marius, a celebrated Roman general and consul.
5. Sylla, an able general, eminent for his success and cruelty in war.
6. John Hyrcanus, a liberator of the Jews, and father of the Asmonean dynasty.

§ 1. Polybius was a native of Arcadia, in Greece. He was initiated in the duties, and made acquainted with the qualifications of a statesman, by his father, the instructer of Philopœmen. He fought against the Romans in the war of Perseus, but was taken and brought prisoner to Rome, where he was befriended by the younger Scipio.

Polybius acquired an intimacy with the powerful Romans, and was present at the taking of Carthage and Numantia. After the death of Scipio, he retired to Megalopolis, where he died in his 82d year, about 124 years B. C. He wrote a universal history in Greek, divided into 40 books, which began with the first Punic war, and finished with the conquest of Macedonia, by Paulus.

The greatest part of this valuable history is lost. Five books, and numerous fragments, remain. It is highly authentic and accurate.

2. Apollodorus flourished about 115 years B. C. He wrote a history of Athens, besides other works. But of all his compositions nothing is extant, except his Bibliotheca, a valuable work, divided into three books.

3. Lucilius was a Roman knight, born at Aurunca, and distinguished by his virtuous and inoffensive character. He is considered as the first great satirical writer among the Romans, and indeed as the founder of satire. He was superior to his poetical predecessors at Rome; he wrote with great roughness and inelegance, but with much facility, and he gained many admirers.

Blackwell says, that he was "a writer of such keennes of temper and flowing wit, as fitted him to strike out a new road, never trod by poet before." Some, however, admired him beyond his real merits. Of 30 satires which he wrote, nothing but a few verses remains. H died at Naples in the 46th year of his age.

4. Marius was born of obscure and illiterate parents, but became one of the most powerful and cruel tyrants, that Rome ever beheld during her consular government. He became seven times consul. He destroyed the Ambrones, Teutones, and Cimbri, who were preparing to invade Italy, and raised a civil war, to oppose the power of Sylla, as has been narrated in this History. He died B. C. 86, after he had filled all Rome with blood.

Among the instances which are mentioned of his firmness, this may be recorded. A swelling in the leg obliged him to apply to a physician, who urged the necessity of cutting it off. Marius gave it, and saw the operation performed without a distortion of the face, and without a groan. The physician asked the other, and Marius gave it with equal composure.

5. Sylla was the inveterate enemy of Marius, between whom, as we have seen, the most bloody wars were waged. He was descended from a noble family, but was poor in early life. He afterwards became immensely rich. He first entered the army under Marius, as quæstor, in Numidia. He afterwards had the administration of the Mithridatic war.

In his wars with Marius, Sylla acted the tyrant to a terrible extent, and the streets of Rome he filled with devastation and blood. As perpetual dictator, he exercised the most absolute authority; but at length abdicated and died at Puteoli of a most loathsome disease, in his 60th year, 78 B. C. Mankind have never understood the cause of his abdication. He and Marius both sought in their last sickness to drown the stings of conscience by continual intoxication.

6. John Hyrcanus was prince and high-priest of the Jews, after his father. He restored his nation to independence, from the power of Antiochus, king of Syria, and died 106 years B. C. He was illustrious by his virtues, as well as by being the father of a race of princes. He was succeeded on the throne of Judea by a son of the same name.

PERIOD X.

The period of Roman Literature, extending from the first campaign of Julius Cæsar, 80 years B. C. to the nativity of Jesus Christ, or the commencement of the Christian era.

ROME.

Sect. I. Rome, at the commencement of this period, had greatly extended its dominions, and was fast becoming a universal empire. Abroad the Romans triumphed—but at home their affairs were in a melancholy and distracted state. The form of public liberty remained, but the reality had principally departed. The civil dissensions of Marius and Sylla had prostrated many of their most valuable institutions.

Before these dissensions were brought to a close, a man began to appear on the stage, who was destined to destroy the last remnant of the liberties of his country. This man was Julius Cæsar. In his first military enterprise, 80 years B. C., in the siege of Mytilene, under Thermus, the prætor of Asia, his bravery and talents were rewarded with a civic crown.

Soon after this he returned to Rome to prosecute his studies, and for a time refused all interference in the feuds which were then prevailing. Before he had finished his studies, however, he raised troops to repress the incursions of Mithridates, and was successful in saving or rescuing several of the eastern provinces from his grasp.

§ From this time his ambitious views were too apparent, and in seeking office and popularity, he was but too successful. He had escaped with difficulty the proscriptions of Sylla, who was persuaded to let him live, though that tyrant dreaded Cæsar's abilities.

Cæsar was descended from one of the first families in Rome, and had married a daughter of Cinna. His powerful name and connexions he strengthened, by arts of the most consummate policy and address. His powers of mind were of the highest order, and he excelled in whatever branch of pursuit he engaged.

He was in person slender, tall, and delicate, and was reputed to be the handsomest man in Rome. He had a habit of running his finger under the nicely adjusted curls of his head, when he appeared in public assemblies: this led Cicero to remark, "that one would hardly imagine that under such a fine exterior, there was hatching the destruction of the liberties of Rome."

Of his feats in war, and the important part he acted in the commonwealth, we shall have occasion to speak, in following the order of events.

2. After the death of Sylla, contention broke out anew; for the terror of his power had created a short interval of a dreadful repose.

Catulus and Lepidus settled their difficulties only by arms—and the War of Sertorious, and the Servile War ensued. These, however, were safely terminated after a few years. The war of Sertorius commenced 77 years B. C. The Servile War commenced 73 years B. C.

§ Lepidus, who was consul, wishing to annul all the acts of Sylla, was opposed by his colleague Catulus. To carry his point he found it necessary to use force, and accordingly he raised an army in his government of Gaul, with which he approached, in hostile array, towards Rome.

Catulus, to whom Pompey and his forces were joined, met him at the Milvian Bridge, two miles from Rome, and gave him battle. Lepidus was entirely defeated, and escaping into Sardinia, soon died of grief. His party, however, did not expire with him.

A more dangerous enemy still remained in Spain. This was Sertorius, a veteran soldier, who had been bred under Marius, his equal in courage—his superior in virtue. Banished from Rome by Sylla, he had found a refuge in Spain, whither all, who fled from Sylla's cruelty, resorted to him. Having gained the affections of its warlike inhabitants, he resisted, during eight years, the Roman power.

Metellus, and afterwards Pompey, were sent to bring him to submission, but he often came off victorious, and was even threatening to invade Italy, when he was suddenly destroyed by the treachery of one of his lieutenants. The revolted provinces of Spain quickly submitted to Pompey.

The Servile War took its rise from a few gladiators, who broke from their fencing-school at Capua, and having drawn a number of slaves after them, overthrew the force that was sent against them, and from this success, their number soon increased to an army of 40,000 men.

With this strength, and headed by Spartacus, their general, they sustained a vigorous war of three years in the very heart of Italy, and even talked of attacking Rome; but Crassus, having assembled all the forces in the neighbourhood of the capital, destroyed the greatest part of them, and among them Spartacus, fighting bravely to the last.

3. The War which had been carried on against Mithridates, and which Sylla had suspended by means of a peace, was renewed about this time, 72 years B. C. This was one of the most important wars which the Romans ever waged. Mithridates defeated the successor of Sylla, and contracting an alliance with Tigranes, king of Armenia, began to be quite formidable to the power of Rome.

Lucullus, however, an experienced general, was sent against him, and defeated him in several engagements, with immense loss. Tigranes also felt the weight of the Roman arm; and both, doubtless, would have been obliged soon to sue for peace, had not Lucullus, by means of intrigue, been deposed from his command, and Glabrio appointed in his stead.

After this, Mithridates met with success again, till Pompey was appointed to take the command against this powerful enemy of Rome. Under the auspices of this great general, the Roman arms were completely victorious, and the war terminated about 63 years B. C., with the death of Mithridates.

§ Mithridates was the undaunted enemy of Rome during 25 years. His resources in wealth and soldiers were great, and his bravery and talents were equal to his resources. The Roman general with whom he had finally to contend, was an antagonist worthy of him, in every respect. Pompey had already become a favourite hero of the Roman people.

He had generally been successful in his military enterprises, and in the commission which he had recently received of managing the war against the pirates of the Mediterranean, he had shewn equal intrepidity and skill. Pleased with his success, the people had entrusted to him the sole management of the Mithridatic war, with an almost unlimited authority.

His power would have rendered him extremely dangerous to the liberties of his country, had he been an enemy to those liberties. But though highly ambitious, he was desirous rather of glory than of dominion. He wished to be the first man in the state, and for this reason entered into a contest with Crassus for the favour of the people, as he afterwards fought against Cæsar, in behalf of the republic.

In the Mithridatic war he manifested his qualities as a general. He first proposed terms of accommodation to Mithridates. But these were refused; and the king, collecting an army from the wrecks of his former power, was about to carry the war into Armenia. In this project, however, he was disappointed, and was obliged to flee.

Pompey, nevertheless, overtook him before he had time to pass the Euphrates. It was then night, but being compelled to engage, it is said the moon, shining from behind the Roman army, lengthened their shadows so much, that the archers of Mithridates shot their arrows at these, mistaking the shadow for the substance.

He was overthrown with great loss; but he broke through the Roman army with a few hundred horse, and escaped. Here, after wandering through the forests several days, leading his horse, and subsisting on fruits which were found in his way, he met with a few thousand of his troops that had survived the engagement, who conducted him to one of his magazines, containing the treasures deposited to support the war.

After this he sought aid from several princes; but though he failed in this attempt, and though he was betrayed by his unnatural son, he still aimed at great designs, and even in the heart of Asia, he projected the invasion of the Roman empire. Upon being apprized of his intentions, a mutiny ensued, which was promoted by his son.

Being obliged to take refuge in his palace, he sent to his son for leave to depart, with offers of the remnant of his kingdom to him. The monster, however, denied this request, and sternly conveyed a message to the old man, intimating that death was now all that he could expect.

This instance of filial ingratitude aggravated all his other calamities; and he sought for his wives, children, and himself, a voluntary death. They all readily consented to die with their monarch, rather than to undergo the horrors of a Roman captivity.

4. After defeating Mithridates, Pompey made very numerous and extensive conquests, setting up and deposing kings at his pleasure He at length marched against Jerusalem,

and after besieging it three months, took it—12,000 of its defenders having lost their lives. He then returned to Rome, enjoying the most splendid triumph that ever entered its gates, 61 years B. C.

§ Darius, king of Media, and Antiochus, king of Syria, were compelled to submit to the clemency of Pompey, while Phraates, king of Parthia, was obliged to retire, and send to entreat peace. From thence, extending his conquest over the Thuræans and Arabians, he reduced all Syria and Pontus into Roman provinces.

In his conquest of Jerusalem after gratifying his curiosity with the holy things of the place, he restored Hyrcanus to the priesthood and government, and took Aristobulus with him to grace his triumph. This triumph lasted two days. In it were exposed the names of 15 conquered kingdoms, 800 cities taken, 29 cities repeopled, and 1000 castles brought to acknowledge the empire of Rome.

The treasures that were brought home amounted to near 20,000,000 of our money ($;) and the trophies and other splendours of the procession, were such, that the spectators seemed lost in the magnificent profusion. The glory, rather than the real prosperity of Rome, was increased by these victories. While Pompey and the Roman arms were triumphant abroad, the city was near its ruin, by means of a conspiracy in its very bosom.

5. Sergius Catiline, a patrician by birth, at this time, (B. C. 64) plotted the downfall of his country. His object was to rise on its ruins to wealth and power; and accordingly associating with him a number of ambitious, profligate characters like himself, he hoped to throw Rome and all Italy into a state of tumult and insurrection, and to destroy the lives of the most distinguished of the citizens.

But the vigilance of Cicero, who was consul, frustrated this horrible project. Taking the necessary precautions, he secured the conspirators that were in Rome, and ordered them to execution, according to law. Catiline, who had fled, soon raised an army, and coming to battle with the forces of the republic, he was overthrown, and himself and his whole army were given to the sword.

Cicero, by his abilities, patriotism, and zeal for the public good, was raised to the most enviable height of glory and renown.

6. Pompey, after his triumphal entrance into Rome, sought to be the first man in the republic. His contention was more particularly with Crassus, who, on account of his wealth, possessed an influence at this time next to that of Pompey.

Cæsar, who was also aspiring after the same distinction, sought to accomplish his object by uniting these rivals.

This union he brought to pass, and thus he avoided making himself an enemy to either of them, and enjoyed the favour of both. From a regard to their mutual friend, Pompey and Crassus agreed to a partition of power with Cæsar, and thus was formed the First Triumvirate, B. C. 59.

Cæsar was chosen consul. He increased his popularity, by a division of lands among the poorer citizens, and strengthened his interest with Pompey, by giving him his daughter in marriage. The coalition between Pompey, Crassus, and Cæsar, constituted a power distinct from the senate or the people, and yet dependent on both. It was exceedingly detrimental to the public liberties.

7. Having divided the empire between them, these three individuals prepared for their respective destinations. Cæsar, however, previously to his departure, had the address to procure the banishment of Cicero from Rome, and thus removed one of the greatest obstacles to his career of ambition. He accomplished this object by means of his partizans, particularly Clodius, the tribune, 58 years B. C.

The pretext for this base act, was the illegality of certain measures pursued in the suppression of Catiline's conspiracy. Through the interest of Pompey, however, Cicero was at length recalled from exile, with distinguished honour.

§ Cicero continued to be the watchful guardian of the few remaining liberties of his country. He was the greatest man of the Romans, if not of all antiquity. His virtues were as conspicuous as his talents. He appeared, however, to have one foible, and that was vanity. He desired to unite in his character incompatible qualities; and to be thought not only the greatest orator, but the greatest jester in Rome.

In his zeal for the public good, Cæsar had reason to fear him. To procure his banishment from the city, he favoured the designs of Clodius, who was Cicero's inveterate enemy, and in this he was joined by Pompey. Clodius, as tribune, caused a law to be passed, importing that any who had condemned a Roman citizen unheard, should himself be banished. This was designed to have a bearing on Cicero, in regard to his proceedings against Catiline.

Being impeached on this law, Cicero was banished 400 miles from Italy, his houses were ordered to be demolished, and his goods set up for sale. In vain did he protest against the iniquitous sentence; the people had ungratefully forgotten their benefactor, and sixteen months did he spend in solitude and grief. He bore his exile with the greatest impatience.

Pompey, who had concurred in the banishment of Cicero, at length saw his mistake in the growing reputation and power of his rival, Cæsar. To prop his own sinking fortunes, he needed the aid of Cicero, and interceding in his favour, procured his recall to Rome, 57 B. C.

8. Cæsar, who had the government of Transalpine Gaul and Illyria, nobly sustained the military glory of his country, in the wars which he waged on its account. In Gaul, Germany, and Britain, he spread the terror of his arms. His landing on the British isles, and his success in subduing the savage and hardy natives, is a memorable event in history.

His invasion of Britain took place 55 years B. C.; and his subjugation of a considerable part of the country was effected at two different times, in the course of one year, 54 B. C. But the urgency of affairs at home, delayed the progress of his arms in Britain.

§ Cæsar, in the first year of his government, subdued the Helvetii, who had left their own country, and attempted to settle themselves in the more inviting regions of the Roman provinces. Two hundred thousand of their number perished. The Germans, with Ariovistus at their head, were next cut off. The Belgæ, Nervii, the Celtic Gauls, the Suevi, and other warlike nations, were all successively brought under subjection.

At length, urged by the desire of conquest, he invaded Britain. But upon approaching the shores, he found them covered with men to oppose his landing, and it was not without a severe struggle, that the natives were put to flight. Having obtained other advantages over them, and bound them to obedience, he passed over to the continent during winter quarters, meditating a return in the spring.

The absence of the conqueror inspired the Britons, naturally fond of liberty, with a resolution to renounce the Roman power. But in a second expedition, Cæsar so intimidated them with repeated victories, that they no longer resisted in the plains, but fled to the forests. Here, however, they were unsafe, and soon yielded to the necessity of suing for a peace.

In the course of nine years this ambitious general and waster of human life conquered, together with Britain, all that country which extends from the Mediterranean to the German sea. It is said that he took 800 cities; subdued 300 different states; overcame 3,000,000 men, 1,000,000 of whom fell on the field of battle, and the remainder made prisoners of war. Notwithstanding the plaudits of the world, how little glory was there in all this!

9. The death of Crassus, which occurred in an expedition against the Parthians, 53 years B. C., put an end to the Triumvirate. After this event, Cæsar and Pompey, whose union was far from being sincere, began each to entertain the idea of supreme, undivided dominion. Both were extremely

powerful; but Cæsar had superior talents, and an invincible army devoted to his interests. The main body of the people were also in favour of Cæsar who had won them by his liberality.

The strength of Pompey lay in the favour of the consuls, and the good wishes of the Roman senate; and several legions were also at his command. In attitudes so imposing, and with resources so vast, it is not surprising that, in those degenerate times, each should be encouraged to expect the possession of supreme power.

The contest for superiority was not long a contest of plans and feelings merely—it soon became a contest of blows. The result of this terrible civil war was disastrous in the extreme to Pompey and the republic. At Pharsalia, in Thessaly, Cæsar and Pompey met in battle, in which Pompey was entirely defeated, with the loss of 15,000 men killed, and 24,000 taken prisoners, 48 years B. C. Being soon after in the power of Ptolemy, king of Egypt, to whom he had fled for protection, he was basely murdered.

§ Near the expiration of the term of his government, Cæsar applied to the senate to be continued in his authority. This application the senate refused. Cæsar then determined to appeal to arms for what he chose to consider as his right. Having, by the sanction of an oath, engaged the services of his army in his favour, he began to draw towards the confines of Italy, and passing the Alps with his third legion, stopped at Ravenna, from whence he wrote a letter to the consuls, declaring that he was ready to resign all command, if Pompey would show equal submission.

But the senate being devoted to Pompey, was determined to deprive Cæsar of his command, and consequently passed a decree, by which he was to be considered an enemy to the commonwealth, if he did not disband his army within a limited time.

Cæsar, nothing at all intimidated or deterred from his project, marched his army to the Rubicon, a small river which formed the boundary between Italy and Gaul. This boundary the Romans considered as sacred, and not to be passed with impunity, since they had solemnly devoted to the infernal gods, and branded with sacrilege and parricide, any person who should presume to pass it, with an army, a legion, or even a single cohort.

At this spot, he for a moment hesitated, as if profoundly impressed with the fearful consequences which must result from the step he was about to take. His misgivings, however, subsiding, he said to one of his generals, "the die is cast," and putting spurs to his horse, he plunged in, and with his soldiers soon gained the opposite shore.

Terror and indignation seized the citizens of Rome, as the news of this transaction reached their ears. Pompey was not in sufficient force to meet the enemy, and accordingly quitted the city, and led his soldiers to Capua, where he had two legions. From that place he passed over at length into Macedonia, followed by the consuls, and a large body of the senators. At the same time, he caused levies to be raised over both Italy and Greece.

In two months, Cæsar having made himself master of all Italy, entered Rome in triumph, to the great joy of most of the people. He secured to himself the supreme authority and the public treasures and having made profession of respect for the citizens and liberties of Rome, and adjusted the concerns of the city, he left it in a few days, and set out to take the field against his enemies.

The lieutenants of Pompey having possession of Spain, Cæsar marched directly thither, leading his army again over the lofty Alps In the course of 40 days he subdued the whole country, and returned victorious to Rome, where, during his absence, he had been nominated dictator. He was soon after chosen consul also. His dictatorship he relinquished at the expiration of eleven days.

In the meantime, Pompey's preparations were such as became the crisis which was approaching. He had received from the sovereigns of the East very considerable supplies, as well as the assurances of their friendship. He was master of nine Italian legions, and had a fleet of 500 large ships, under the conduct of an experienced commander.

The nobles and most distinguished citizens of Rome, flocked daily around his standard; and he had at one time above 200 senators in his camp, among whom were the great names of Cicero and Cato. Pompey's party glorying in their numbers and strength, were confident of success.

Cæsar, with a courage bordering on rashness, immediately sought his rival, and desired to bring him to an engagement. Near Dyrrachium the opposing armies were so situated that it became necessary to fight. The result was by no means decisive, though it was favourable on the whole to Pompey, who afterwards led his troops to Pharsalia.

Previously to this encounter, a circumstance took place, displaying the lofty spirit of Cæsar. For the purpose of hastening the arrival of a reinforcement, he conceived the design of passing over to Brundusium in the night, by embarking in a fisherman's boat at the mouth of the river Apsus. This he accordingly did with great secrecy, having disguised himself in the habit of a slave.

When they had rowed off a considerable way, the wind suddenly changed against them—the sea began to rise in billows, and the storm increased to an alarming degree. The fisherman, who had rowed all night with extreme labour, was often inclined to put back, but was dissuaded by his passenger. At length, however, he conceived himself unable to proceed, and yet he was too distant from land to hope for making good his return.

In this moment of despair he was about to give up the oar, and commit himself to the mercy of the waves, when Cæsar discovering himself, commanded him to row boldly—"Fear nothing," cried he, "you carry Cæsar and his fortune." The fisherman was encouraged to proceed, but the wind finally forced them to make for land, and return.

Soon after the affair at Dyrrachium, the hostile armies found themselves on the plains of Pharsalia. Cæsar invited and provoked a battle, by all the arts in his power. Pompey had secured an advantageous situation, and it was by the artifice of decamping and inducing the enemy to follow him, that Cæsar drew him from it.

When Cæsar perceived the effect of his stratagem, with joy in his countenance he informed his soldiers that the hour was come which was to crown their glory, and terminate their fatigues. His forces, however, were much exceeded by those of Pompey, who led an army of 45,000 footmen, and 7000 horse, while the troops of Cæsar did not number more than 23,000 men, only 1000 of whom were cavalry. But they were better disciplined than those of Pompey.

Awful was the moment of meeting. The armies were both Roman, mingled indeed with foreigners, and the first in the world—the leaders were consummately brave, and the interest at stake was the dominion of Rome. Every heart was fired and every arm nerved. The generals both addressed their armies previously to the engagement, and urged them to sustain the reputation of their ancient bravery.

The battle commenced on the part of Cæsar. But the cavalry of Pompey were too numerous for their adversaries. Cæsar's men were forced to retire. Their general had foreseen this result, and had made the requisite disposition of his forces. Six cohorts in reserve, who had been ordered to discharge their javelins at the faces of Pompey's cavalry, were, at this crisis, brought up to the engagement. The single circumstance of the manner of their fighting determined the fate of the battle. Pompey's cavalry, who consisted of the younger part of the Roman nobility, valued themselves upon their beauty, and dreaded a scar in the face, more than a wound in the body. They were therefore frightened from the field by the unusual mode of attack, and thus the day was lost to Pompey and the republic.

The loss of Cæsar was inconsiderable, 200 men only being slain. His clemency towards his vanquished enemies deserves to be noticed. Most of the prisoners he incorporated with the rest of his army, and to the senators, and Roman knights, who fell into his hands, he gave liberty to retire whithersoever they pleased. The letters which Pompey had received from several persons who wished to be thought neutral, Cæsar committed to the flames without reading them, as Pompey had done upon a former occasion.

Cæsar followed up his victory with the greatest energy, and after Pompey's flight instantly pursued him. He did not however overtake him alive. Pompey had been destined to suffer the extremity of misery. His fall was from the summit of power to the most abject dependence, and it was as sudden as it was terrible. Escaping from the field of battle, and wandering along the beautiful vale of Tempe, in the greatest agony of mind, he finally found the means of sailing to Lesbos, where he had left his wife Cornelia.

Their meeting was tender and distressing to the last degree. The news of her reverse of fortune had caused Cornelia to faint, and for a considerable time life appeared to be extinguished. At length recovering herself, she ran quite through the city to the sea-side. Pompey received her without speaking a word, and for some time supported her in his arms, with silent anguish. When words found their way, the tenderest expressions of affection and grief were mutually uttered.

But it became necessary to flee, and sailing to the coast of Egypt, they sought the protection of Ptolemy, whose father had formerly found in Pompey a benefactor. The ministers of the king wishing to court the favour of Cæsar, basely proposed to receive and then murder their guest, as he approached the shore. This diabolical counsel prevailing, Achillas, and Septimius, the latter by birth a Roman, were appointed to carry it into execution.

Accordingly, in the very sight of Cornelia, as Pompey arose to go ashore, supporting himself upon his freedman's arm, Septimius stabbed him in the back; when the warrior, perceiving what would be his fate, silently resigned himself to it, at the same time muffling his face with his robe.

The freedman of Pompey, after the people had retired, found the means of burning the body of his master, from which the head had been separated, and over the tomb the following inscription was afterwards placed: "He whose merits deserve a temple, can now scarcely find a grave." Cæsar soon reached Egypt; but the head of Pompey, which was immediately presented to him, and from which he turned his face in horror, informed him, that he had now nothing to fear from a man who had so lately contended with him for the empire of the world.

10. War was Cæsar's element. He found an occasion of gratifying his ruling passion in Egypt. In a contest between Ptolemy and his sister Cleopatra, he interposed in behalf of the latter, and at length brought Egypt under the Roman yoke, 48 B. C. In two years after, he subdued Pharnaces, king of Pontus.

§ Cleopatra, though sister to Ptolemy, was nevertheless married to him, and both jointly held the throne. The ambition of Cleopatra prompted her to aspire after undivided authority. The charms of her person were unequalled, and conquering even the conqueror of the world, they engaged him in a war which was alike easy and desirable. After the reduction of Egypt, Cæsar, forgetful of the respect due to his character, abandoned himself to pleasure in the company of Cleopatra.

From such a course, however, he soon broke off, for hearing of the revolt of Pharnaces, son of Mithridates, who had seized upon Chalcis and Armenia, he bent his way thither. In the battle of Zela, he signally chastised the offending monarch. "I came, I saw, I conquered," is the expressive language in which his report was conveyed to the Roman senate.

11. Leaving the scene of conquest in the East, Cæsar has-

tened to Rome, where his presence was greatly needed. Antony, who acted as his deputy, had created disturbances which Cæsar only could quell. Italy was divided, and the party of Pompey was yet extremely formidable. Cæsar, however, soon restored tranquillity to Rome.

But at this time the two sons of Pompey, with Cato and Scipio, were in arms in Africa, assisted by Juba, king of Mauritania; thither Cæsar hastened, and at Thepsus, meeting them in battle, overthrew them with little or no loss on his side. Scipio, in attempting to escape into Spain, fell among the enemy, and was slain. Cato, confining himself in Utica, at first thought of resisting the victorious Cæsar, but finding his followers irresolute, he deliberately put an end to his own life.

This event finishing the war in Africa, Cæsar returned in triumph to Rome, 45 years B. C. By an unparalleled display of magnificence and by unbounded liberality, he courted and obtained the favour of the great body of the people. Almost every honour and title was conferred upon him. He was styled father of his country, was created perpetual dictator, received the title of emperor, and his person was declared sacred.

§ The story of Cato is deeply tragical. This extraordinary man displayed at once the firmness and the depravity of his nature. When he found it in vain to attempt to animate his soldiers against Cæsar, he resolved to die. After supping cheerfully, he came into his bedchamber, where he laid himself down, and with deep attention, read some time Plato's Dialogue on the immortality of the soul.

Perceiving soon that his sword had been removed from the head of his bed, he made inquiries respecting it of his domestics; but while he was like to obtain no satisfaction from them, his son, who had caused it to be taken away, entered with tears, and besought him, in the most humble and affectionate manner, to change his resolution; but receiving a stern reprimand, he desisted from his persuasions.

His sword being at length handed to him, his tranquillity returned, and he cried out, "Now am I master of myself." He then took up the book again, which he read twice over, and fell into a profound sleep. Upon waking, he made some inquiry of one of his freedmen, respecting his friends, and then shutting himself up in the room alone, he stabbed himself; but the wound not being immediately mortal, with a most ferocious resolution, he tore out his own bowels, and died as he had lived, a stoic. By this deed he has blackened his character, to all futurity.

12. The state of affairs in Spain called Cæsar again into that country, 45 years B. C. Two of the sons of Pompey were in arms, and it was not without severe fighting that

Cæsar subdued the remnant of his enemies in Spain. He returned to Rome to receive new demonstrations of the almost slavish homage of its citizens.

Finding himself in peace, he turned his attention more than ever to the improvement of the empire. He affected great moderation in the enjoyment of his power, though he was evidently eager of its acquisition. He however turned it to a good account. He made no discriminations between his friends and foes: he was liberal alike to both. He adorned the city with magnificent buildings, undertook to level several mountains in Italy, and to drain the Pontine marshes, improved the navigation of the Tiber, reformed the calendar, and meditated distant conquests.

13. His brilliant course, however, was destined shortly to end. He was suspected of aiming at royalty; and though many of the people felt greatly obliged by his clemency and munificence, yet they detested the name of king. This circumstance urged 60 of the senators, who were actuated by the love of liberty, though some of them seem to have been impelled also by private resentment, to league together with a view to deprive him of his life. This they accomplished in the senate house on the ides (15th) of March, in the 56th year of his age, 44 B. C.

§ Cæsar enjoyed all the power of a monarch; and though he might, in the first instance, have ambitiously sought it, yet it was conferred or allowed by the free consent of the people. But the name of king was not to be endured. The particular occasion of envy or alarm among the friends of liberty, was the neglect, on the part of Cæsar, of rising from his seat, when the senate was conferring upon him some special honours.

From that time it began to be rumoured that he was about to take the title of king. Whether such was his purpose cannot now be determined, though it cannot be well conceived why he should desire that empty honour, when he possessed the reality. The conspiracy which was formed against him, was headed by Brutus and Cassius, the one his friend—the other his enemy. Brutus owed his life to the clemency of Cæsar, whom the latter spared at the battle of Pharsalia; and he was not destitute of a strong personal attachment to the dictator.

The conspiracy which had been formed, happened in some way or other to be known by two or three individuals; but the means taken to apprize Cæsar of it, failed. As he proceeded to the senate, on the day agreed upon by the conspirators, a slave hastened to carry him information, but could not come near him for the crowd. Artemidorus, a great philosopher, who had discovered the whole plot, delivered him a memorial, but Cæsar gave it, with other papers, to one of his secretaries, without reading it.

As soon as he had taken his place, the conspirators came near him under pretence of saluting him; and Cimber, who was one of them, pretending to sue for his brother's pardon, approached in a suppliant posture, and so near as to take hold of the bottom of his robe, which prevented Cæsar from rising.

This was the signal agreed on. Casca, who was behind, stabbed him, though slightly, in the shoulder. Cæsar instantly turned round and wounded him in the arm. However, the conspirators were now all in action, and surrounded him. He received a second stab in the breast, while Cassius wounded him in the face. Still he defended himself with great vigour, rushing among them, and throwing down such as opposed him, till seeing Brutus who had struck a dagger in his thigh, he yielded himself to his fate, first exclaiming to his friend, in a subdued and languishing tone, "And you, too, my son!"

He fell, covered with his robe, before him, and pierced with 23 wounds.

The character of a despot and conqueror, as such, is to be detested. Cæsar enslaved his country, and waded to dominion through rivers of blood. His elevation cost the lives of 1,200,000 human beings. We may be permitted to express our abhorrence of such conduct, and to regret that transcendant talents (for such he possessed) should have been perverted to so base a purpose.

The darkness of this picture is however relieved by some lines of light—if it were not so, Cæsar would have been a monster. Besides the splendid endowments of his genius, he was distinguished by liberality, clemency, and modesty. He always spared a vanquished enemy; and perhaps no despot, in his personal feelings and private character, was ever more amiable. How much then is it to be lamented, that such qualities should have been united to an insatiable ambition!

14. The death of Cæsar produced an unheard of crisis in human affairs. There was no longer any tyrant, yet liberty was extinct; for the causes which destroyed it kept it from reviving. The senate and people mutually distrusted each other. There was a very general feeling of sorrow and indignation among the latter at the murder of Cæsar, nor could the senate at all mitigate or repress it.

Mark Antony, a man of consummate military talents, but profligate in the extreme, exposed the bleeding body of Cæsar in the forum. This sight, together with the bloody robe, produced an electric effect on the multitude, which was heighted to an excessive degree, by means of an artful and inflammatory harangue delivered by Antony on the occasion. The conspirators were obliged to flee the city in order to save their lives.

At this juncture, (43 B. C.) a second triumvirate was formed, consisting of Antony, already mentioned, Lepidus, who was immensely rich, and Octavius, afterwards surnamed Augustus, who was Cæsar's grand nephew and adopted heir. This was a most bloody triumvirate. As they divided the supreme authority among themselves, by concert, they stipulated that all their respective enemies should be destroyed, though those might happen to be the best friends of each associate who was required to sacrifice them.

§ Lepidus gave up his brother Paulus to the vengeance of one of his colleagues. Antony permitted the proscription of his uncle Lucius; and Augustus, to his eternal infamy, sacrificed the great Cicero. Three hundred senators, and 2000 Roman knights, besides multitudes of worthy citizens, were included in this horrible proscription.

15. The conspirators were not suffered long to escape the vengeance of the friends of Cæsar. Octavius and Antony now marched against them in Thrace, where they had a formidable army of 100,000 men, commanded by Brutus and Cassius. An engagement took place at Philippi, 42 years B. C., which decided the fate of the empire. It was won by Octavius and Antony, or rather by Antony alone, for Octavius was destitute not only of military talents, but even of personal bravery.

The death-blow was now given to Roman liberty. The republican party was entirely subdued, and Brutus and Cassius, its leaders, escaped the hands of their enemies, only by a voluntary death.

§ The loss of the battle at Philippi by the republicans, was occasioned principally through the hasty despair of Cassius. Brutus, on his part, had been victorious,—Cassius had suffered a severe loss, but would have been relieved by Brutus, had he not ordered himself to be killed in the meantime, in consequence of having mistaken a body of Brutus's cavalry, who was approaching him, for that of the enemy.

When Brutus was informed of the defeat and death of Cassius, he seemed hardly able to restrain the excess of his grief for a man, whom he called "the last of the Romans." He bathed the dead body with his tears. Antony offered him battle on the ensuing day; but it was the policy of Brutus to delay, and even to attempt to starve his enemy; he probably might have done it.

The soldiers of Brutus, however, urged a battle, nor would they submit to a refusal. After a respite of a few days, Brutus took the field. He fought with the resolution to conquer, but some unhappy movement of a part of his troops turned the fortune of the day, and all was lost. He followed the fate of Cassius.

Retiring out of the way of the enemy, with Strato, his master in oratory, he requested the latter to put an end to his life. After much solicitation Strato reluctantly assented, and averting his face, presented the sword's point to Brutus, who threw himself upon it, and immediately expired.

Octavius being sick at this time, took no part in the battle of Philippi. Indeed his presence, had it been afforded, would have been of little service to the combatants, since he possessed neither skill nor courage. He had, however, gained a large share of popularity with the Roman people, partly on account of his name, and his relationship to Cæsar, and partly on account of his personal appearance, and accomplishments. These were in the highest degree prepossessing.

He was destined, as will soon appear, to be much more successful than the other Triumviri, and even at length to place himself at the head of the empire.

16. The power of the Triumviri being established upon the ruins of the commonwealth, they began to think of enjoying the homage to which they had aspired. Lepidus, however, was soon deposed and banished. Antony took his way to the East, where, at Athens, he spent some time in philosophic retirement, and afterwards passed from kingdom to kingdom, attended by a crowd of sovereigns, exacting contributions, and giving away crowns with capricious insolence. While Octavius, with consummate art, was increasing his favour with the people by his munificence, and contriving the means of attaining to supreme power.

§ It may be necessary to observe here, that there were properly four individuals at this period, who were the masters of the Roman empire. Some time after the formation of the second triumvirate, Sextus Pompey, son of Pompey the Great, was admitted to a share of the authority and possessions of the state, in connexion with the triumviri.

An occasion of war soon occurring, Octavius had the good fortune to defeat Pompey in a naval engagement, through the skill and intrepidity of Agrippa, his friend and associate in war. This event occurred 32 years B. C. Augustus had now no competitor for the empire of the world, save Mark Antony.

17. Antony having summoned Cleopatra, queen of Egypt, to answer for her disaffection to the Roman cause, was caught in the toils of love by the artifices of the beautiful queen. In his infatuation he forgot ambition and empire, in devotion to the object of his guilty passion. Octavius saw in this madness the presage of his ruin.

On Cleopatra, her lover had lavished the provinces of the empire for which he was declared a public enemy, and as for her sake he had divorced Octavia, the sister of Octavius, the latter embraced the opportunity, which he had eagerly desired, of declaring war against him.

An immense armament, principally naval, (the land forces being merely spectators,) came to an engagement near Actium, on the coast of Epirus, 31 years B. C. The conflict was decisive. Cleopatra, who attended Antony, deserted him with her galleys, in the midst of the engagement.

Such was his infatuation, that he immediately followed her, leaving his fleet, which after a contest of some hours, yielded to the squadron of Octavius. The conqueror pursued the fugitives to Egypt; and the infamous Cleopatra proffered terms to Octavius, including the surrender of her kingdom and the abandonment of Antony.

After an unsuccessful attempt at resistance, Antony anticipated his doom by falling on his sword. Cleopatra also soon after saw fit to frustrate the design of Octavius, which was to carry her in chains to Rome as an ornament to his triumph, by seeking a voluntary death.

Octavius was now left without a rival, with the government of Rome in his hands. Egypt, which had existed a kingdom from immemorial ages, from this time became a province of Rome, 30 years B. C.

§ The story of Cleopatra will be briefly told under the history of Egypt for this period. Antony, her lover, had few superiors in war, and he was the idol of his army. He was, however, profligate in the extreme, and his infatuated conduct in relation to the Egyptian queen, while it showed the native strength and tenderness of his passions, has imprinted an indelible stain on his character as a hero. His weakness in this respect was the cause of his ruin, and prevented the acquisition of universal empire, which he might perhaps have otherwise obtained.

In the struggle between Antony and Octavius, the strength of the East and of the West were arrayed against each other. Antony's force composed a body of 100,000 foot, and 12,000 horse; while his fleet amounted to 500 ships of war. The army of Octavius mustered but 80,000 foot, but equalled his adversary in the number of his cavalry; while his fleet was only half as large as Antony's; but the ships were better built and better manned.

The fortune of the day in the battle of Actium, was determined by the flight of Cleopatra with 60 galleys. Yet with this diminution of the fleet, and with the abandonment of it by Antony himself, it fought with the utmost obstinacy for several hours, till partly by the conduct of Agrippa, and partly by the promises of Octavius, it submitted to the conqueror. The land forces of Antony soon followed the example of the navy, and yielded to Octavius without striking a blow.

18. The Roman empire had now become the largest which the world had ever seen: and Octavius, now named Augustus, holding the principal offices of the state, was, in effect, the absolute master of the lives and fortunes of the Roman people. During a long administration he almost effaced the memory of his former cruelties, and seemed to consult only the good of his subjects.

His reign constituted the era of Roman taste and genius, under the auspices of Mecænas, his chief minister, who was the most eminent patron of letters recorded in history.

Seventeen years before the close of his life and reign, acaccording to the true computation, (not the vulgar era,) our Lord and Saviour Jesus Christ was born in Judea—an event more important than any other that ever took place in our world.

§ Augustus pursued a pacific course, and restored order to the state During the period of his administration of the government, the temple of Janus, which was shut only at the prevalence of general peace, was closed for the first time since the commencement of the second Punic war, and only the third time from the building of Rome. It was precisely at this happy and singular crisis of human affairs, that the birth of our blessed Saviour happened.

The administration of Augustus was however fatal to liberty; though that circumstance itself tended to general tranquillity, since the corruption of manners required the most absolute restraint. By masterly strokes of policy, he united all interests and reconciled a differences. He disguised his new despotism, under names familiar and allowed by that constitution which he had destroyed.

He claimed to himself the title of emperor, to preserve authority over the army; he caused himself to be created tribune, to manage the people; and prince of the senate, to govern that body. After he had fixed himself in the government, he long hesitated whether he should restore to Rome its liberty, or retain his present situation. The examples, and the differing fortunes of Sylla and Cæsar, were before him, and operated on his hopes and fears.

Disclosing his feelings to Agrippa, who had assisted him in gaining the empire, and to Mecænas, his principal minister and adviser, the former suggested the wisdom of his resigning it—the latter dissuaded him from taking such a step. The opinion of Mecænas, as it was on the whole more agreeable to Augustus, was followed, and perhaps mankind have little reason to regret it, considering what was the awful corruption of the times.

Through the counsels of this great minister, Augustus fostered learning and the arts to the highest degree, and specimens of human intellect then appeared, which have rarely been equalled among mankind. Genius enjoyed all the rewards and all the consideration that it could claim.

The authority which Augustus usurped, he, from policy, accepted only for a limited period, sometimes for ten, and sometimes for only five years; but at the expiration of the term, it was regularly bestowed upon him again.

His situation, which was above all equality, generated virtues to which, in all probability, he was naturally a stranger. He sometimes condescended to plead before the proper tribunals, for those he desired to protect, for he suffered the laws to have their proper course. One of his veteran soldiers entreated his protection in a law-suit. Augustus, taking little notice of his request, desired him apply to an advocate. "Ah!" replied the soldier, "it was not by proxy that I served you at the battle of Actium."

This reply pleased Augustus so much, that he pleaded his cause in person, and gained it for him.

He was so affable, that he returned the salutations of the meanest person. One day a person presented him with a petition, but with so much awe, that Augustus was displeased with his meanness. "What! friend," cried he, "you seem as if you were offering something to an elephant, and not to a man:—be bolder."

A part of his long reign of more than 40 years belongs to modern history, but we may here speak of it as entire. During the whole of it he cultivated the arts of peace. The wars which were carried on in the distant provinces aimed rather at enforcing submission, than at extending dominion. He was however successful in almost all of them. The defeat of his general, Varus, in Germany, was the most serious disaster which he experienced. The choicest troops of the empire constituted the army of Varus, and they were entirely cut off in the forests of that country.

In his domestic life, Augustus was less happy and fortunate, than as master of the Roman people. His wife, Livia, was an imperious woman, and controlled him at her pleasure. Her son, Tiberius, who at length succeeded to the empire, possessed a suspicious and obstinate temper, and gave him so much uneasiness, that he banished him for five years at a distance from Rome. But his daughter, Julia, by his former wife, afflicted him more than all the rest, through her excessive lewdness. The very court where her father presided, was not exempt from her debaucheries.

Augustus lost a favourite son, who, it is supposed, was taken off by poison, lest he should supplant Tiberius. The emperor was often heard to exclaim, "How happy should I have been had I never had a wife or children!" He died during an absence from Rome, at Nola, of a dysentery, in the 76th year of his age, after reigning 41 years, 14 A. C.

19. Little is to be said, separately, of the history of other nations during this period, as they were mostly swallowed up in the Roman empire. We can notice only two or three, and these are very much blended with the Roman history, being included in the number of the Roman provinces before the end of the present period. First, Judea comes under review.

JUDEA.

THE JEWS at this time were ruled by the sacerdotal and royal family of the Maccabees, under the title of the Asmonean dynasty, but they were in the last stages of their independent existence. When Pompey came to Jerusalem to settle the affairs of Judea, he restored Hyrcanus with the title of Prince of the Jews, and conferred the government of the country on Antipater, an Idumean proselyte, 63 years B. C.

§ In the civil wars between Cæsar and Pompey, the former sent Aristobulus, whom Pompey had carried captive to Rome, into Judea, to engage the Jews in his (Cæsar's) cause, but he was poisoned by his enemies. At the same time Pompey ordered his son Alexander to be beheaded.

20. After one other revolution in the person of Hyrcanus, the family of the Herodians was seated on the throne of Judea. Herod, called the Great, son of Antipater, was declared king of that country, by a decree of the Roman senate, 37 years B. C. His reign was splendid, but distinguished by a singular degree of profligacy.

§ Some time after his establishment on the throne, Herod, in order to please Mariamne, the daughter of Hyrcanus, whom he had married, appointed her brother, Aristobulus, High Priest; but perceiving that he was much beloved by the Jews, he caused him to be drowned while bathing. After the battle of Actium he went to Rhodes to meet Augustus, who confirmed his title of king of Judea. Upon his return he condemned to death his wife, Mariamne, and her mother, Alexandra.

From this hour his life was a continual scene of misery and ferocity. At the instigation of his third son, he sentenced to death Aristobulus and Alexander, his children by Mariamne, and the next year Antipater himself experienced the same fate. His last moments also were stained with the blood of the children of Bethlehem and the neighbourhood, whom he ordered to be slain, in the hope that the infant Jesus Christ would fall among them.

EGYPT.

21. The family of the Lagidæ, continued to rule EGYPT Alexander II. was on the throne at the commencement of this period. Cleopatra was the last sovereign. The intermediate sovereigns were Ptolemy Auletes, Berenice, and Ptolemy Dionysius, who reigned for a time jointly with Cleopatra.

With the death of this queen ended the family of the Lagidæ, after having ruled in Egypt about 294 years. Egypt was now reduced to a Roman province, and governed by a Prætor sent thither from Rome, 30 years B. C.

§ Ptolemy Dionysius was 13 years old at the time of his father's death, by whose will he was nominated to the succession, on condition of his marrying his sister Cleopatra, then 17 years of age. The Romans were appointed guardians of these children. Cleopatra married her brother, and they reigned jointly, till, dissatisfied with the Roman ministry, she retired to Syria and Palestine, where she raised an army, and advanced under the walls of Pelusium, to give battle to the ministers of her husband.

At this moment, as we have before learned, Pompey, vanquished at Pharsalia, took refuge in Alexandria, and was assassinated by order of Ptolemy. Julius Cæsar, pursuing his rival, arrived soon afterwards, and endeavoured to compromise the differences between the king and the queen. For a short time they were reconciled; but Ptolemy, renewing the war not long afterwards, was defeated and drowned in the Nile.

Cleopatra then married her youngest brother, a boy of eleven years of age, and already affianced to his sister Arsinoe. Him, however, she soon poisoned, 43 B. C.; and assumed the sole government. After the arrival of Mark Antony in Egypt, and his captivation by Cleopatra, her character became still more remarkable for corruption. The beauties of her person were incomparable; and in polite learning, in brilliancy of wit, and in tunefulness of voice in her conversation, she was as irresistible as in her personal charms. These qualities, joined to an extreme profligacy of manners, rendered her one of the most dangerous foes to virtue that ever lived.

When summoned to present herself before Antony for the first time, her appearance was so splendid and fascinating, that the Roman warrior rather adored than judged her. Every decoration was employed to heighten the most consummate loveliness of features, and gracefulness of motion. Holding Antony in the chains of a base passion, she ruled him at her pleasure.

The profusion of riches displayed at her feasts was astonishing. Antony holding the wealth of plundered provinces, with his utmost efforts could not equal the queen in the sumptuousness of her entertainments. It was at one of these feasts that the incident mentioned by Pliny occurred.

Cleopatra, having laid a considerable wager that she could expend more than 50,000*l*. upon one repast, caused one of the pearls that she wore in her ears, which was valued at the above named sum, to be dissolved in an acid, and then swallowed it. She was then preparing to melt the other in a similar manner, but some one had the address to divert her from her design.

After the battle of Actium, Octavius used every effort to secure the person of the queen, and to effect the death of Antony, by her means. He promised her his protection and friendship if she would kill him This she peremptorily refused to do, but consented to deliver his person and the kingdom of Egypt into the enemy's hand.

Antony, who had before meanly sought his life of Octavius, opening his eyes to his danger, and to the perfidy of Cleopatra, at first made some faint and ineffectual attempt at resistance, and then in his fury attempted to avenge himself of the queen. She, however, eluded his purpose by taking flight to a monument, which she had erected for her safety, and gave out a report that she had killed herself.

Upon this news, Antony forgot his resentment—his former affection rushed into his heart, and his cup of calamity was full. He resolved to follow her example, and die a Roman death. At the moment he had fallen upon his sword, the news of the queen's death was contradicted, and Antony, weltering in his blood, and stil breathing, consented to be carried to see the queen.

After being pulled up to the top of the monument where Cleopatra was, by means of ropes let down and fastened to him, a scene of anguish and affection was presented which can scarcely be conceived. Suffice it to say, he died in her arms, bedewed with her tears, and almost stifled with her caresses.

The queen, though at length taken by Octavius, and apparently secured by the strict guard which he placed over her, found an opportunity of poisoning herself by means of an asp, which she applied to her arm, the sting of which instantly threw her into a fatal lethargy. In such a miserable end were these victims of guilt involved.

PARTHIA.

22. Under the Arsacidæ, PARTHIA continued to enjoy some consequence during this period. Its principal sovereigns were Phraates III. Orodes I. and Phraates IV.

§ Orodes I. was no sooner on the throne, than he was attacked by Crassus, the Roman consul, to whom Syria was allotted in the partition of the provinces of the empire between him, Cæsar, and Pompey, 53 B. C. The Parthian armies were commanded by Surena, a general of extraordinary wisdom and valour. Crassus being led by the king of Edessa into a barren country, his army was completely defeated, and himself taken and killed.

Orodes, jealous of Surena's glory, caused him to be put to death soon after, and entrusted the command of his army to Pacorus, his own son, who made great conquests in several countries, but who was soon after defeated and killed by Ventidias, the Roman general. Orodes, overwhelmed with grief, became insane; but having recovered in some degree, he associated his eldest son Phraates his partner in the throne.

The infamous wretch first attempted to poison his father, but that only curing him of the dropsy, he stifled the old man in bed, and murdered all his brothers. When Augustus came into Asia, he obliged Phraates to restore the ensigns taken from Crassus, and afterwards from Antony, and to deliver four of his sons as hostages. Divine Providence punished him in a remarkable manner, as he was killed by a conspiracy of his concubine and his own son, 13 A. C.

Distinguished Characters in Period X.

1. Lucretius, a Roman didactic poet.

2. Julius Cæsar, a successful warrior and elegant writer.
3. Cicero, the prince of Roman orators and philosophers.
4. Catullus, a Roman epigrammatic poet.
5. Sallust, the first philosophical Roman historian.
6. Varro, the most learned of the Romans.
7. Cornelius Nepos, an eminent Roman historian.
8. Virgil, the prince of Roman poets.
9. Horace, the greatest of the Roman lyric poets.

§ 1. Lucretius was early sent to Athens, where he studied philosophy. He embraced the tenets of Epicurus. In his poem of the Nature of Things, he is the advocate of atheism and impiety, and earnestly endeavours to establish the mortality of the soul. His masterly genius and unaffected elegance are, however, every where conspicuous.

He wrote Latin better than any man ever did before him, and had he lived in the polished age of Augustus, he would have been no mean rival of Virgil. He wrote his poem while he laboured under a delirium, occasioned by a philtre, administered by means of the jealousy of his wife or mistress. He died, some say he destroyed him self, in his 44th year, about 54 B. C.

2. Julius Cæsar was the son of Caius Cæsar, who was descended from Julius, the son of Æneas; in his 16th year he lost his father; and Sylla, aware of his ambition, endeavoured to remove him; his friends, however, interceded, and obtained his life; but Sylla warned them to be upon their guard against that loose-girt boy, alluding to Cæsar's manner of wearing his tunic, or coat, loosely girded; "for in him," said he, "are many Mariuses."

He procured many friends by his eloquence, and obtained the office of high priest; after passing through different dignities, he was sent governor into Spain; and, upon his return, being elected consul, he entered into an agreement with Pompey and Crassus, that nothing should be done in the state without their joint concurrence. After his consulship, he had the province of Gaul assigned him; which, with wonderful conduct and bravery, he subdued in 10 years, carrying the terror of his arms also into Germany and Britain, till then unknown to the Romans.

Pompey now became jealous of his power, and induced the senate to order him to lay down his command; upon which, he crossed the river Rubicon, the boundary of his province, and led his army towards Rome, Pompey and all the friends of liberty fleeing before him.

Having subdued Italy in sixty days, Cæsar entered Rome, and seized upon the money in the public treasury: he then went to Spain, where he conquered the partisans of Pompey under Petreius, Afranius, and Varro; and, at his return, was created dictator, and soon after consul. Leaving Rome, and going in search of Pompey, the two hostile generals engaged on the plains of Pharsalia; the army of Cæsar amounted only to 23,000 men, while that of Pompey amounted to 45,000; but the superior generalship of the former prevailed, and he was victorious.

Making a generous use of his victory, he followed Pompey into Egypt, where he heard of his murder, and making the country tributary to his power, he hastened to suppress the remainder of Pompey's party in Africa and Spain. Triumphing over all his enemies, he was created perpetual dictator, received the names of imperator and father of his country, and governed the people with justice. His engrossing all the powers of the state, and ruling with absolute authority, created general disgust; a conspiracy was therefore formed against him, by more than sixty senators, the chief of whom were Brutus and Cassius. He was stabbed in the senate house, on the 15th of March, B. C. 44, in the 56th year of his age; he at first attempted to make some resistance, but seeing Brutus, his intimate friend, among the conspirators, he submitted to his fate, and covered with 23 wounds, fell at the foot of Pompey's statue.

Cæsar is perhaps the most distinguished character in history. His talents in war and literature were equally great. Amidst his military enterprises he found time to be the author of many works, none of which remain except seven books of commentaries, or memoirs of his wars; these are much admired for their elegance, as well as correctness of style. He spoke in public with the same spirit with which he fought, and had he devoted himself to the bar, would doubtless have rivalled Cicero.

3. Marcus Tullius Cicero was the father of Latin eloquence, and the greatest orator that Rome ever produced. He was the son of a Roman knight, and having displayed promising abilities, his father procured for him the most celebrated masters of his time. He served one campaign under Sylla, and returning to Rome, appeared as a pleader at the bar, where the greatness of his genius, and his superior eloquence, soon raised him to notice.

Having passed through the lower honours of the state, he was made consul in his 43d year. Catiline, a profligate noble, with many dissolute and desperate Romans, conspired against their country; but all their projects were baffled by his extreme vigilance; Catiline was defeated in the field; and Cicero, at Rome, punished the rest of the conspirators with death.

He received the thanks of the people, and was styled the father of his country and the second founder of Rome; but his refusal to agree to the arbitrary measures of Cæsar and Pompey, caused him to be exiled; he did not bear his banishment with fortitude; and was overjoyed when, after 16 month's absence, he was restored with honour to his country. After much hesitation, he espoused the cause of Pompey against Cæsar; and when the latter was victorious at Pharsalia, Cicero was reconciled to him, and treated with great humanity; but as a true republican, he approved of Cæsar's murder, and thus incurred the hatred of Antony, who wished to succeed in power.

Octavius, afterwards called Augustus Cæsar, Antony, and Lepidus, having formed a third triumvirate, agreed on a proscription of their enemies; Octavius struggled two days to preserve Cicero from the vengeance of Antony, but at last gave him up; in his attempt to escape, he was overtaken by a party of soldiers, who cut off his head and right hand, and brought them to Antony; this happened B. C. 43, in the 64th year of his age.

He is to be admired, not only as a great statesman, but as an orator, a man of genius, and a scholar, in which united character, he stands unrivalled; his conduct was not always that of a patriot, and he is frequently accused of timidity.

4. Catullus was a poet of Verona, whose compositions are the offspring of a luxuriant imagination. He directed his satire against Cæsar, whose only revenge was to invite the poet, and hospitably entertain him at his table. Catullus was the first Roman who imitated with success the Greek writers, and introduced their numbers among the Latins.

Though the pages of the poet are occasionally disfigured with indelicate expressions, the whole is written with great purity of style. He died in the 48th year of his age, B. C. 40.

5. Sallust was educated at Rome, and made himself known as a magistrate, in the office of quæstor and consul. He was a man of depraved and licentious manners. He married Terentia, the divorced wife of Cicero, and hence the immortal hatred between the historian and orator.

Of his Roman history little remains; but his narrative of the Catilinarian conspiracy, and the wars of Jugurtha, are extant.

His descriptions, harangues, &c. are animated and correct, and the author is greatly commended for the vigour of his sentences. He died in his 51st year, 35 B. C.

6. Varro wrote 300 volumes, which are all lost, except a treatise, De Re Rustica, and another De Lingua Latina. The latter he wrote in his 80th year, and dedicated to Cicero. In the civil wars, he was taken by Cæsar and proscribed, but escaped. His erudition and extent of information were matter of wonder to Cicero and St. Augustine. He died in his 88th year, B. C. 28.

7. Cornelius Nepos enjoyed the patronage of Augustus. He was the intimate friend of Cicero and Atticus. He possessed a most delicate taste and lively disposition. He composed several works, but his lives of illustrious Greeks are all that remain. He has ever been admired for the clearness and precision of his style, and the delicacy of his expressions. He died 25 years B. C.

8. Virgil was born at Andes, a village near Mantua, about 70 years B. C. Having lost his farms in the distribution of lands to the soldiers of Augustus, after the battle of Philippi, he repaired to Rome, where he obtained an order for the restitution of his property through the interest of Mecænas. When he showed this order to the centurion who was in possession, he nearly killed Virgil, and the latter escaped only by swimming across a river.

Virgil, in his Bucolics, or Pastorals, celebrates the praises of his illustrious patrons. He undertook his Georgics in order to promote the study of agriculture; and the design of the Æneid is thought to have been to reconcile the Romans to a monarchical government.

By his talents and virtues he acquired the friendship of the emperor Augustus, and the most celebrated personages of his time. He died at Brundusium, in the 51st year of his age, B. C. 19, leaving his immense possessions to his friends, and was buried in the neighbourhood of Naples, where his tomb is still to be seen.

9. Horace was born at Venusia; his father, although poor, took him to Rome when a boy, and educated him with great care. At the age of twenty, he went to Athens to study philosophy, and then, with the rank of military tribune, attended Brutus to the civil wars. In the battle of Philippi he saved himself by flight, and returned to Rome.

Finding his father dead, and his fortune ruined, he applied himself to writing verses; and his talents soon recommended him to the protection of Virgil, Mecænas, and Augustus, with whom he afterwards lived on terms of the greatest intimacy and friendship. He died in the 57th year of his age, B. C. 8.

GENERAL VIEWS

OF THE GEOGRAPHY, POPULATION, POLITICS, RELIGION, MILITARY AND NAVAL AFFAIRS, ARTS, LITERATURE, MANNERS, CUSTOMS, SOCIETY, &c. OF ANCIENT NATIONS.

ANTEDILUVIAN WORLD.

The few notices which the Bible has transmitted to us, respecting the Antediluvian world, being mostly confined to the moral history of its inhabitants, leave us greatly in the dark in respect to its physical and geographical facts, the state of the arts, political institutions, and similar subjects. We are here chiefly guided by analogy, and conjecture.

SECT. 1. *Surface of the Earth.*—The earth's surface, there is reason to believe, at that period, differed somewhat from its present state. Concerning this subject, however, there are different opinions. We incline to that which supposes that there were not those inequalities in the surface of the earth which now appear—at least in so great a degree, and that it was thus more uniformly adapted to the purposes of culture, and to the support of its inhabitants.

§ The opinion of Dr. Burnet, that the primitive earth was no more than a crust investing the water contained in the abyss, is somewhat plausible. This crust breaking into innumerable pieces, at the time of the deluge, would naturally sink down amidst the mass of waters, to various depths, and thus cause the mountains and valleys which now exist.

The convulsions occasioned by that terrible event, would be likely to disfigure the earth's surface in a measure, and render it less pleasant as the abode of human beings. Indeed the mountains and hills, the valleys and plains, in many instances, appear as if they had been shaped and fashioned by some " war of the elements." Their form and appearance are precisely such, as we should conjecture would be produced from the force of the retiring waters, in vast eddies and whirlpools.

2. *The Seasons.* The seasons might have been different from what they are at present. Conjecture has assigned to the Antediluvian world but one season, and that an " eternal

spring." This would be the fact, if, as some philosophers suppose, the plane of the earth's orbit was then coincident with that of the equator. They now make a considerable angle with each other, and this alteration is concluded to have taken place at the time of the deluge. Besides, the variety of the seasons is never mentioned in scripture, till after the flood.

§ On this supposition an ingenious, but fanciful French writer,* has accounted for the production of the deluge itself. He imagines, that in consequence of this change, whatever might be its cause, the vast masses of ice which had collected for ages in the cold regions of the globe, being acted upon more immediately by the heat of the sun, suddenly melted, and overflowed the earth.

3. *Population and Longevity.* Nothing can be determined with certainty respecting the extent of population. Some imagine that it was very great, far exceeding what it is at present. This is inferred from the surprising length of men's lives, and from the numerous generations that were then contemporary. But from various circumstances, the probability is, that it was much smaller, and that mankind were not widely diffused over the earth.

§ If any thing on this subject may be ascertained or fairly conjectured, from the discoveries of geology, the opinion of Cuvier, a great adept in that science, is probably correct, viz. that previously to the last considerable convulsion of our globe, the human race inhabited only some narrow districts. It is well known that while shells, fossils, and the bones of animals, have been found in the earth's surface, in great abundance, thus exhibiting the ruins of the deluge, few or no human remains have been discovered, under such circumstances.

If these latter exist, they must be in some circumscribed parts of the earth, such as Asia or Africa, where the labours of the geologist have not been so particularly bestowed, or they may lie buried under some mass of waters. Of course the population of the antediluvian world must have been mostly confined to those quarters of the globe, or to one of them.

The longevity of the antediluvians was remarkable. The contrast, in this respect, of that age of the world and the present times is so great, as to have given rise to many conjectures assigning the cause or causes of their longevity. We need not interest ourselves in these conjectures, as nothing can be known with certainty, except it may be remarked, that the air immediately after the flood was most likely much contaminated and rendered unwholesome.

How far this circumstance should have affected the pristine constitution of the human body, thus shortening the life of man in successive ages, down to the present common standard, is left to the cu-

* St. Pierre.

rious to inquire. If there were no physical causes of this change, God could have effected it without them. It is his own record that the life of man was abridged.

4. *Religion.* In regard to the religious rites of the primeval race of men, it can only be affirmed, that they offered sacrifices, both of animals and of the fruits of the earth. The Sabbath, we know, was instituted immediately after the creation, and it is not likely that its observance was ever wholly discontinued.

§ The descendants of Seth, the son of Adam, were for some time distinguished by their worship of God and observation of religious rites, while those of Cain were notorious for their irreligion and profligacy. These lived separately till intercourses by marriage were formed between them; and then the pure religion and morals of the descendants of Seth were corrupted, and the whole world became alienated from God.

5. *Arts and Sciences.* These must have been cultivated in a degree, and in some of their branches might have been more than we are aware. If we consider that human life was several hundred years in extent, there was space for vast improvements in those arts and sciences that were once discovered. It is much to be doubted, however, whether many of them were known.

The last generation of Cain's line found out the art of working metal; and music seems to have been invented about the same time. A knowledge of agriculture, architecture, and perhaps of astronomy, was possessed.

§ Some suppose that man, in the infancy of the world, was aided by inspiration; but even if left to the ordinary operation of his faculties, he might have been no stranger to knowledge and mental improvement. Still, from the difficulty of originating knowledge, and from the vices of the antediluvians—their probable devotion to gross sensual pleasures, they seem not to have been as extensively acquainted with the more intellectual objects of human pursuit, as their descendants were a few ages after the flood.

We have some accounts, though not from an authentic source, of discoveries made in astronomy by the posterity of Seth. These discoveries, it is said, were engraved on two pillars, the one of brick, and the other of stone. The latter, it is affirmed, existed after the deluge, and remained entire in the time of Josephus, that is, nearly a century after Christ. If this were a fact, it is singular that no other memorial of their intellect should have appeared. It is here given, however, as it is found on historic record.

6. *Government.* On the topic of government, there is hardly a foundation for conjecture. The most probable, is the patriarchal form of government; that is, the government

which was held by the heads of separate families. A number of these might perhaps combine, and place themselves under the direction of some common ancestor. This is the most natural form of government, and indeed no mention is made in the Bible of kingly authority until after the deluge.

§ Still, as some suppose, this form of government might have been set aside by tyranny and oppression; and the change would probably take place, much sooner among the descendants of Cain, than those of Seth. It is thought that after the union of the families of Cain and Seth, all mankind constituted but one nation, divided into several disorderly associations, and living in a state of anarchy, which circumstances would have hastened the progress of wickedness.

7. *Commerce.* The intercourse of the antediluvians might have been easy, because they probably lived contiguous to each other. Yet it is evident that they had no idea of navigation, for had vessels been in use, some families might have escaped the disasters of the flood, besides that of Noah.

§ It is likely that there was not that necessity for commerce, as there has been since. For this opinion, reasons might be given, but the subject is not sufficiently important.

Assyria, (including Babylonia.)

8. *Extent and Cities.* Assyria generally comprehended the territory lying between Armenia, Babylon, Mesopotamia, and Media. The Assyrian dominion, at times, extended over many parts of Asia; its capital was Nineveh, on the Tigris, built by Ashur. The country is now called Curdistan.

§ Nineveh was built on a very spacious plain. It was 15 miles in length, 9 broad, and 47 in circumference, according to Diodorus Siculus and Strabo. On the walls, which were 100 feet high, three chariots could pass together; they were defended by 1500 towers, each 200 feet high. From the number of infants which it contained, as mentioned in the book of Jonah, it is computed that the inhabitants amounted to more than 600,000 at that time.

Its situation is indicated, as some suppose, by vestiges on the Tigris, opposite Mosul, retaining the name of Nino.

Babylonia, which was afterwards united to Assyria, was made up principally of Mesopotamia, the modern Diarbec. Its capital, Babylon, at length the capital of the whole empire, was bisected by the Euphrates, from N. to S., and formed a square, whose sides subtended the four cardinal points. The city stood on a large plain. Its walls were in thickness 87 feet, in height 350 feet, and in compass 60 miles. These were drawn about the city in an exact square.

§ As a more particular description of Babylon, it may be stated, that on each side of this great square were 25 gates of solid brass. Between every two of these gates were three towers; four others were at the corners; and three more between those on the corners and the gate on either side.

The other parts of the city, some of which we will describe, corresponded with the magnitude of the walls. The streets, bridge, quays, the lake, ditches, canals, palaces, and hanging gardens, and above all, the temple of Belus, were so many wonders. From the 25 gates ran as many streets, in straight lines, so that the whole number of streets was 50, crossing each other at right angles. There were also four half streets, round the four sides of the city, next the walls, each of them 200 feet wide; the rest being about 150 feet.

The whole city was thus cut into 676 squares, each of which was two and a quarter miles in circumference. Round these squares, on every side towards the street, stood stately houses three or four stories high, with large spaces between them, and the areas within the squares filled up with yards, gardens, and pleasure grounds.

The celebrated hanging gardens were composed of several large terraces, one above the other. The ascent from terrace to terrace was by stairs ten feet wide, and the whole pile was sustained by vast arches, strengthened by a massy wall of great thickness. On the tops of the arches were first laid prodigiously large flat stones. Over these was a layer of reeds mixed with bitumen, upon which were two tiers of bricks, closely cemented together with plaster. The whole was covered with thick sheets of lead, upon which lay the mould of the garden. This mould was so deep that the largest trees might take root in it, and covered with these and other plants, and every variety of flowers; nothing could be conceived more grand and picturesque.

The temple of Belus, at its foundation, consisted of a square, each side of which was a furlong in length; it consisted of eight towers, built one above another, decreasing gradually to the top, and was a furlong in height.

9. *Government and Laws.* The government both of Assyria and Babylonia was strictly despotic, and its sceptre hereditary. The whole centered in the person of the king; all decrees issued from his mouth; he even affected the power, and claimed the worship which belonged only to the divinity.

§ The great conquerors of the East always courted retirement, as being too glorious to be beheld by vulgar eyes. Thus they contrived to keep in subjection a number of nations of different languages and manners, to a person who must have been a stranger to almost all of them. They adminstered their government by officers of various descriptions, civil and military.

Of the three classes of officers, the first had the charge of the virgins, and were expected to judge of all matters relating to the connubial state; the second took cognizance of theft; and the third of all other crimes.

The laws of the empire were in general vague and uncertain, depending wholly upon the will of the sovereign; but one was fixed and irrevocable, which obliged all, especially the poorer sort of people, to marry.

§ Their punishments were unfixed and arbitrary, according to the disposition of the sovereign. We read of beheading, cutting to pieces, turning the criminal's house into a dunghill, and burning in a fiery furnace.

10. *Religion.* The Chaldeans, properly so called, were both the priests and the literati of the country. They were devoted to the business of religion, and pretended to skill in the prediction of future events. They dealt in charms, incantations, and explánations of dreams, and of the extraordinary phenomena of nature. They built temples to the stars, as being the subordinate agents of the divine power, and by worshipping them, they expected to obtain the good will of the deity. From this they descended, by a natural process, to the worship of objects on earth, as the representatives, or favourites of the stars, or of the deity, through them. Thus idolatry arose not long after the flood, among the earliest of nations —the people left on the plains of Shinar, subsequently to the dispersion at Babel.

§ It is evident that this was the origin of image worship, since the names of the principal gods of the heathen in general, are those of the sun, moon, and five primary planets, Saturn, Jupiter, Mars, Mercury and Venus.

The norrid custom of sacrificing human victims to conciliate their gods, was first practised by the Babylonians, and from them it was communicated to the superstitious of the surrounding nations.

§ There are traces of their ancient cruelty to be discerned in the worship and rites of the Assyrian goddess of Hierapolis, to whom parents, without remorse, sacrificed their children, by throwing them down a precipice in her temple.

11. *Customs.* The principal and most singular of their customs, was the manner in which they disposed of their women in marriage. No man had any power over his own daughters, but as soon as they were marriageable, they were put up to auction; and the price obtained for the more beautiful was assigned as a dowry to the more homely.

§ The consequence of this practice was, that all their young women were disposed of in marriage—the beautiful for their charms, the homely for their wealth.

Another singular custom was their festival called Sacca.

During this festival, which lasted five days, the servants commanded their masters, one of them being, for the time, constituted chief over the house, and wearing a kind of royal garment, called Zogana.

§ They had other extraordinary customs, but some of these are too indecent to be named. In general, they were the most sensual and abandoned people on the face of the earth.

12. *Learning*. The Babylonians were famed for learning, particularly the Chaldeans, who were their priests, philosophers, astronomers, soothsayers, &c. As in many other countries after them, they were divided into several sects, distinguished by their peculiar characteristics.

They were the first who cultivated astronomy, discovered the exact motions of the planets, and pretended to understand the influence these had over things below, and from that to be able to foretel future events. The latter was embodied into a kind of science, called astrology.

§ From this origin of astrology, fortune telling, and similar arts, we perceive at once their opposition to religion and rectitude.

The learning of the Chaldeans was not acquired after the manner of the Greeks, but by tradition from father to son. The only business of the learned was to apply themselves to the instructions they received. They never departed from early principles, and hence made no great advances in the sciences.

13. *The Arts*. The Babylonians, properly so called, applied themselves to the useful arts. Their immense buildings, which could not have been erected without much skill in geometry, prove that they must have been good mathematicians and mechanics.

They never attained to any superior excellence in painting and statuary. Music and poetry were probably but little attended to; and in physic they had no regular science.

§ They exposed their sick in the streets, to be cured by any who, passing by them, saw fit to prescribe for their diseases.

The Babylonians were great architects, ingenious in casting metals and in their manufactures—particularly in their manufactures of embroideries, magnificent carpets, and fine linen. So superb were some of their articles of dress, that we read, in the Roman history, of Cato selling a Babylonian mantle, which had been left him by inheritance, as being what he was ashamed to wear. And it is said that at Rome more than 6000*l*. had been paid for a suit of Babylonian hangings.

China.

14. *Geography*. China, in ancient times, included nearly the same territory that it does at present, so far as we can now

ascertain. The Greeks and Romans, through whom most of our acquaintance with antiquity is derived, had no immediate knowledge of that country; only they mention Serica, and another nation of northern Sinæ, as constituting its westerly provinces.

As, however, the Chinese are not at all given to foreign conquests, and have for many centuries remained the same people in their government and institutions, we may conclud that the ancient territory was the same, or nearly the same, as their modern. It is not our design to state its boundaries or extent, except to say, that it constituted a considerable portion of eastern Asia, and was separated from Tartary, on the north, by its prodigious stone wall of 1500 miles in length.

§ But few general views of this country in other respects can be here given, since we have been presented, in this work, with only a small portion of its civil history; and since from the unchangeable character of the people, these views will answer for an interesting article in modern history.

15. *Government.* The original plan of the Chinese government was patriarchal. Obedience to the father of each family was enforced in the most rigorous manner, and the emperor was considered as the father of the whole. Every father was absolute in his own family, and might inflict any punishment short of death; and every mandarin of a district had the power of life and death over all its members, though the emperor's approbation was requisite to the execution of a capital sentence.

§ Since the invasion of the Tartars, as we shall hereafter learn, the government is called an absolute monarchy, though its great fundamental principles from the beginning have been preserved.

16. *Religion.* The ancient Chinese adored a supreme being, under the name of Changti, or Tien; they also worshipped subaltern spirits, supposed to preside over kingdoms, provinces, cities, rivers, and mountains. Their worship was by prayer and thanksgiving, without any mixture of idolatrous practices.

§ There are now different sects, whose characteristics belong to the details of modern history.

17. *The Sciences and Arts.* The Chinese understood some of the sciences, but seemed to make no progress in them from age to age. Of mathematics, astronomy, and physics, they appear to have been quite ignorant for so civilized a peo-

ple. The knowledge of medicine was very limited among them.

In the arts, at an early age, they attained to a certain point of advancement, which they never exceeded. It is affirmed that they manufactured glass 200 years before the Christian era; that they knew gunpowder from time immemorial, and that they invented printing in the time of Julius Cæsar; but these and other inventions were in a very imperfect state, and have remained so to this day. In agriculture, however, and a few other arts, they seem, from a very early period, to have been highly distinguished.

§ On the whole, considering their ancient state, and knowing the agreement of their present state with it, no people whatever appear to have been so singular and mysterious, and possessed of such a mixture of wisdom and imbecility.

Egypt.

§ A little before the Christian era, Egypt was one of the most distinguished countries of the ancient world, and enjoyed, from the earliest times, a large share of celebrity, on account of its learning and its magnificent public works. In commercial importance, at the time first spoken of, it was much superior to contemporary nations.

18. *Situation, Name, and Division.* Egypt was an extensive country, bounded on the east by Arabia and the Red Sea, and by Lybia on the west, and was properly a long valley, following the course of the Nile from S. to N.

The ancient name was Mitzraim, and is now retained in that of Mesr, under the Turks.

Egypt was divided into three principal parts, distinguished by the appellations of the Upper Egypt, or Thebais; the Middle Egypt, or Heptanomis; and the Lower Egypt, which includes the Delta.

19. *Cities.* There were many cities in this country, whose ruins attest their almost unparalleled magnificence. Among these were Thebes, Memphis, Arsinoe, Heliopolis, and Alexandria, besides many others.

§ Thebes was situated in Upper Egypt, on both sides of the Nile. It was called by the Greeks, Diospolis, and was one of the most illustrious cities in the world. It is distinguished in Homer by the epithet of Hecatompylos, or having a 100 gates. In the time of its splendour, it could send into the field, by each of its gates, 200 chariots, and 2000 fighting men.

Its extent is said to have been 52 miles; and so great was its wealth, that after it had been plundered by the Persians, 300 talents of gold and 2300 of silver, were found among the remains of the pillage.

The ruins of this astonishing city occupy a circumference of 27 miles on either side of the Nile, and contain several villages, the chief of which is Luxor. Habon, on the western side, contains many stupendous monuments. Thebes was severely treated by Cambyses, by Ptolemy Philopater, and under Augustus, for its rebellion. In the adjacent mountains are hewn sepulchres of the ancient kings.

A remarkable feature of these ruins is their size. Every thing is colossal. The smallest pillars of the temples are between 7 and 8 feet in diameter, and some of the largest are 11. Obelisks, Sphinxes, and other monuments of huge dimensions, in different positions, astonish the modern traveller, as he gazes on these wonders of human power and art.

Memphis, supposed to have been founded by Menes, the first Egyptian king, was for several ages the metropolis of the whole kingdom. It contained many beautiful temples, the most splendid of which is said to have been that of the god Apis. This city stood on the western bank of the Nile, 15 miles south of the Delta.

Strabo saw its palaces in ruins. Vestiges of it were apparent in the fifteenth century, but are no longer in being. The Nile may have covered them.

Alexandria was reckoned next to Rome for the grandeur of its buildings, and richness of its materials. It stood on the western side of the Delta, and was built by Alexander the Great, 332 B. C. It was the capital of Lower Egypt, and the metropolis under the Ptolemies. The ancients assert that it was built in the form of a Macedonian cloak, and occupied about 15 miles. The royal palace constituted a fifth part of the city.

Alexandria rose to the first rank in the ancient world, as the great mart for exchange between the east and west. Its commercial advantages continued for a number of ages. It was further distinguished by schools for philosophy, physic, theology, astronomy, and general learning.

20. *Monuments and Works of Art.* Many of these are magnificent beyond conception, and show to what a high state of improvement the inhabitants, at a remote period, had carried the arts. They still excite the admiration of every traveller.

Besides the cities that have been named, the most celebrated of these works of ancient grandeur, are Lake Mœris, the Labyrinth the Catacombs, or Mummy Pits, and the Pyramids.

§ The lake Mœris has been affirmed to be the most wonderful of all the works of the kings of Egypt, the pyramids not excepted. The ancients described it as measuring 3600 stadia in circumference; but modern travellers assure us that its breadth does not exceed half a league; that it is about a day's journey in length, and that its circumference is about 12 or 15 leagues, which will be found sufficiently prodigious, when we consider that it was performed by human labour.

This lake, in the deepest part, has fifty fathoms of water, and is fed from the Nile, by means of a channel cut for that purpose. It was built by a king of the name of Mœris, whose object was to correct the irregularity of supply in the waters of the river, receiving its superabundance, or making up its deficiency.

The Labyrinth was an enormous structure of marble, built partly under the ground. It was designed as a pantheon of all the Egyptian deities, and as a place for the assembly of the magistracy of the whole nation. It contained no less than 3000 chambers, 1500 of which were subterraneous, and set apart for the sepulchre of the kings who built the labyrinth, or for the abodes of the sacred crocodiles.

These were never shewn to strangers; but Herodotus informs us that he viewed every room in the upper part, in which he found sufficient to fill him with astonishment. Innumerable exits by different passages, and infinite returns, afforded him a thousand occasions of wonder. The highest decorations in polished columns and exquisite sculptures, were every where seen.

The Catacombs were subterraneous galleries of prodigious extent, appropriated to the reception of the dead. These sepulchres of the ancient kings are hewn in free-stone rock, and apparently formed upon one general plan, though differing in the construction of their respective parts. These contain the generations that are gone. Some of the embalmed bodies are perfectly preserved, though they have been dead 3000 years.

The Pyramids were deservedly classed by the ancients among the wonders of the world. There are said to be twenty of them in different parts of the country; but there are three superior to the rest in size and magnificence. These are on the western side of the Nile, in the neighbourhood of the ancient Memphis.

The largest of them is 481 feet in height, measured perpendicularly, and the area of its basis comprehends eleven English acres of ground. This is a size which would exceed all belief, had it not been actually and repeatedly measured by modern travellers. It has steps entirely round it, made with polished stones, so large that the breadth and depth of every step is one single stone. The smallest stone is 30 feet in length. The number of steps amounts to 208.

These works are proved, by modern researches, to have been royal sepulchres, but their foundation is lost in antiquity. They are supposed, however, to have been erected between one and two thousand years B. C. It is asserted by Pliny and Diodorus, that no less tnan 360,000 men were employed in erecting the largest pyramid. It is said also that twenty years were spent in the work.

21. *Government and Laws.* The Egyptians were among the earliest nations, if not the very earliest, who had regular established governments and civil regulations. Their government was a despotic, hereditary monarchy, yet so modified by prescribed usages, as to promote the public welfare.

§ Their monarchs were restricted to a certain mode of living, and even their time seems to have been portioned out, and set apart for particular employments, by the sacred Egyptian books. They were confined to exactness, not only in public transactions, but in their private life. They could neither bathe, take the air, nor converse with their queens but at certain times. The choice of their provisions was not left to themselves, but their tables were furnished with the most simple food, (generally veal or goose,) and their allowance of wine was extremely moderate.

These restraints were entirely acceptable to the Egyptian monarchs, and during the period in which they prevailed, the country greatly flourished, and was filled with works of incomparable magnificence

In the administration of public affairs, each nome, or province, had its respective governor, who ordered all things within his jurisdiction. The lands were divided into three parts, of which one was allotted to the maintenance of the priests, and to religious uses; the second was appropriated to the king, for defraying the charges of his wars, &c; and the third part was designed for the soldiers. The husbandmen, taking the lands at an easy rent from the king, priests, and soldiers, devoted the whole of their attention to agriculture; and the son continually succeeded the father in his occupation. They thus became the most famous for tillage of any in the world.

22. *Mythology.* The boasted laws of the Egyptians sink in our estimation, from the influence which a knowledge of their base idolatry and superstitions produces in the reflecting mind. They had a vast number of gods of different ranks, but their two principal ones were Osiris and Isis, supposed to have been the sun and moon. From Egypt the stream of idolatry flowed over the nations.

§ The idolatry of this people was so gross, that exclusive of the worship they paid their pretended gods, they actually bestowed divine honours on animals, insects, birds, and even vegetables, as leeks and onions. Their sacred animals were, during their lives, kept in consecrated enclosures; fed with most delicate food, washed and anointed with frequency, and their burial, after death, attended with the heaviest expense. We are credibly informed that in the reign of Ptolemy, the Apis dying of old age at Memphis, his keeper expended in his funeral, about 13,000*l.* above all his substance.

23. *Education.* In the education of their children, the Egyptians exercised great care, and the children were brought up with the strictest frugality. The priest instructed them in arithmetic, geometry, and other branches of useful literature;

and their fathers, or nearest relations, taught them as early as possible, their paternal art or profession.

24. *Domestic Habits, Manners, and Customs.* The usual drink of the people was the water of the Nile, which was very palatable and fattening. They used also a superior beverage made of barley, so that we are possibly indebted to them for the first invention of beer. Cleanliness was a particular characteristic of this people, who scoured their drinking vessels every day.

§ As great singularities among them, we may notice the inconsistent employments of the men and women; the former being engaged in spinning and domestic concerns, while the latter were employed in trade and business; the kneading of dough with their feet; the tempering of mortar with their hands; and the promiscuous residence of men and beasts in the same apartment

At their principal feasts, it was a very singular custom to bring in the coffin of a friend after supper, with the image of a dead man carved in wood and painted, which was carried to all the company with this strange admonition: "Look upon this, and be merry; for such as this now appears, thou shalt be, when thou art dead."

25. *Literature and Arts.* Egypt was the parent of learning and philosophy. According to the scriptures, Moses was learned in all the wisdom of the Egyptians. Geometry is generally believed to have been found out in Egypt, in consequence of the measurement of those lands that were annually overflowed by the Nile. The science, however, was most probably but little extended by them.

§ Arithmetic, astronomy, and a kind of algebra, were also cultivated in Egypt; and it is certain this nation first adjusted the length of the year to the annual revolution of the sun, by adding to their twelve months of thirty days each, five additional days and six hours. Medicine and the art of embalming were early cultivated among them, particularly the latter. They were very famous also in magic.

In architecture, painting, sculpture, &c. they must have made great proficiency, as is evident from the astonishing works of art which yet remain.

26. *Trade.* Egypt early engaged in commerce, as its situation was peculiarly favourable for that object. We read in scripture that the Midianites and Ishmaelites traded thither, so early as the time of Jacob. It is certain also that Solomon established a very considerable trade in those parts.

27. *Language.* The Egyptian language is one of the most ancient in the world, and probably an original tongue. It is, in some measure, preserved in the Coptic, even to this time, though that language is but little understood.

THE HEBREWS.

28. *Country.* The country in which this ancient and divinely favoured people lived was Palestine. It extended from Cœlo-Syria, to Arabia Petrea; on the west it had the Mediterranean, and on the east Arabia Deserta. Its territory was very limited.

The country of the Hebrews is also called by several other names, as the Land of Canaan, the Holy Land, Judea, &c.; and the people themselves were variously called, as the People of God, Israelites, Jews; the last more commonly in the latter period of their history.

Upon the entrance of the Israelites into Palestine, it was divided into twelve different portions, which were assigned to the twelve several tribes into which they were separated.

29. *Remains of ancient Works.* Among these are Jacob's Well; the Pools of Solomon, Gihon, and Bethesda; and the Sepulchral Monuments.

§ Jacob's well is highly venerated by Christian travellers on account of its antiquity. It is hewn out of the solid rock, about 35 yards in depth, and three in diameter, and is at present covered with a stone vault.

The Pools of Solomon, supposed to have been made by order of that monarch, appear to have been a work of immense cost and labour. They are three in a row, and disposed in such a manner, that the water of the uppermost may fall into the second, and of the second into the third. They are of equal breadth, viz. about 90 paces; their length varies, the longest being 220. They are all walled and plastered, and contain a large quantity of water.

The Pools of Gihon and Bethesda are similar works, and may be ranked among the most stately ruins.

The Sepulchral Monuments are scattered all over the country. The most magnificent pieces of antiquity of this kind are the royal sepulchres without the walls of Jerusalem. They are all hewn out of the solid marble rock, and contain several spacious and elaborate apartments.

30. *Cities.* Of these there were not many that were large. Jerusalem, the metropolis of the country, and the centre of the Jewish worship, was the most celebrated, and indeed no place in the globe has been more celebrated, taking into view its sacred associations. Hebron, Gaza, and Ascalon, were also noted.

Jerusalem was built on several hills, the largest of which was Mount Zion; it formed the southern part of the city. On the east of the second, or lower city, was mount Moriah, on which stood the magnificent temple of king Solomon.

§ Jerusalem, when enlarged by David, Solomon, and other kings, became a most renowned city, and as such is mentioned by the Greek historian, Herodotus, under the name of Cadytis. The city with its temple was destroyed by the Chaldeans, about 600 years B. C. The second temple, which had begun to decay, was rebuilt by Herod the Great.

The destruction of Jerusalem by Titus, was A. D. 70. Under Adrian, a new city, altogether Roman, and called Ælia, was built, but there was an alteration of its site. Zion, the principal quarter of the ancient city, was not comprised within the new city. It subsists at present, but in a deplorable condition, inhabited by a motley group of Turks, Jews, and Christians.

Hebron was a place of high antiquity, and the sepulchre of Abraham and his family. In the time of the crusades, it bore the name of St. Abraham; and the Arabs, who always respect their primitive names, call it Cabr-Ibrahim, or the Tomb of Abraham.

Gaza and Ascalon, on the coast, preserve their names, as also others. Gaza was remarkably strong, and surrounded with walls and towers, after the Philistine manner. It was taken by Caleb, but soon after regained by the ancient inhabitants, who kept possession of it to the time of Samson. It passed into various hands, till finally it was pillaged by Alexander, and a second time destroyed by the Maccabees.

Ascalon was also a maritime town of great strength, but was soon reduced, after the death of Joshua, by the tribe of Judah. It was once adorned with several magnificent edifices; but it is now dwindled into an inconsiderable village.

31. *Religion.* The history of the religion of this people, which was called Judaism, is the history of true religion in the ancient world. It is now eclipsed by the radiance of the Gospel, which has come into its room, abrogated what was ritual in it, and confirmed its great general principles and truths.

§ Religion flourished variously among the people, according to the piety or irreligion of their priests, leading men, or sovereigns. In general, though they had a succession of wise and holy prophets, the nation, as such, was peculiarly obstinate and rebellious, and continually inclined to forsake the worship of God, and to fall into the idolatrous practices of its heathen neighbours.

On this account repeated and severe judgments were sent among them. They were visited, at various times, with all the ministers of divine vengeance—they were conquered, pillaged, and carried into captivity, and soon after the Christian era, ceased to exist independently, and were scattered among all nations.

They are now known, particularly the tribes of Judah and Benjamin, wherever they are dispersed, as the descendants of Abraham, preserving still their national name and peculiarities. Concerning the other ten tribes we have no certain knowledge of their separate existence, at this day. Prophecy has been remarkably fulfilled in the case of this people.

The great general truths of religion were revealed to this people, and to them alone of all the nations of the earth. The being, perfections, and government of God, the moral law, prescribing the duties man owes to God, to his fellow men, and to himself, the awards of eternity, with a thousand particular precepts of a spiritual kind, were explicitly declared t this nation.

The peculiarities of their ritual worship rendered them also a most favoured community. By these they were designed to be preserved a people distinct from all the rest of the world, to be kept from idolatry, and to be prepared for the great salvation, which was to be accomplished not only for them, but for all nations, in "the fulness of the time."

§ The peculiar rites of Judaism were admirably adapted to honour their Creator, and to render themselves completely happy. Its sacrifices were at once calculated to convince them of their sins, and to shadow forth the vicarious sacrifice of the Son of God.

32. *Government.* The government of this people was properly a Theocracy, as being under the immediate direction of God. In this they were distinguished from all other nations. He was considered as the sole dictator of every important transaction, and supreme monarch of the Israelites.

33. *Manners and Customs.* The most interesting of these related to the rite of circumcision, to their diet, diversions, high places, mourning for the dead, and burials.

§ The rite of circumcision has distinguished them as a people, from the beginning. It was always accompanied with great feasting, and other demonstrations of joy. At this time the child was named in the presence of the company assembled, among whom bread and wine were distributed.

Their diet, except on festivals, seems to have been extremely plain. Bread, water, and vinegar, were in common use. Honey was esteemed a peculiar delicacy, and the milk of goats was reckoned excellent for food.

Their diversions seem to have consisted chiefly in social repasts, music, and dancing. The two latter partook of a religious character. Games were never introduced into their commonwealth.

Their high places were of two sorts; those where they burned incense and offered sacrifices to the true God; and those where they committed various abominable idolatries.

Their mourning for the death of friends was expressed by rending their garments tearing their hair, heaping dirt or ashes upon their heads, wearing sackcloth next their skin, and lying upon the bare ground.

As to their burials, it is known that they denied sepulture to none but such as were guilty of suicide, and not even to these, but till after sunset. From the pains which the patriarchs took to provide a place of burial for themselves and their descendants, it is evident they considered it a heavy calamity, to be denied a burial, and a favour to be interred among their ancestors. Their sepulchres were on their own lands, and, where practicable, cut into a rock.

34. *Learning*. The Israelites excelled in the knowledge of theology, and they had places of public instruction called the schools of the prophets. They seem to have had but little knowledge of astronomy.

Their language was the Hebrew, the genius of which is pure, primitive, and natural; and it is highly probable that they had the art of writing very early. The materials on which they wrote were tables of stone; but mention is made also of rolls, which were doubtless more in use. These rolls are supposed to have been made of skin, or some other pliable substance.

35. *Arts*. The arts in which the Israelites made the greatest proficiency were those of war, husbandry, poetry, and music.

§ Their situation made them a warlike people, surrounded as they were by enemies. Their arms of offence were broad crooked swords, javelins, slings, bows and arrows, and two-edged swords. Their arms of defence were shields, helmets, coats of mail, breast plates, and targets.

Their attention was much confined to their lands and domestic avocations, and few trades or manufactures were carried on among them before the reign of Solomon, except such as were absolutely necessary. After Solomon's time, pride and luxury increased with great rapidity. The causes of a change from great economy and simplicity, to their opposites, were laid indeed in the reign of David.

Poetry is said to be the only fine art in which they were peculiarly excellent; and in that they are inimitable. Their inspired productions, in poetry, if not in prose, as to native energy and felicity, are unrivalled.

36. *Commerce*. With respect to commerce, it appears that they received rich stuffs, linen, gold, &c. from Tyre, in exchange for their corn, balm, and other excellent commodities; but they were totally ignorant of navigation. Solomon employed foreign sailors in the ships which he sent to foreign countries.

Canaanites.

§ The country of the Canaanites has been already described, as it was the same with that of the Hebrews, who, some time after they left Egypt, drove out the ancient inhabitants of the Land of Canaan.

37. *Customs, Manners, Arts, and Sciences.* In these, as well as in language, they may be supposed to have differed widely from each other, according to their different situations. It is easy to discern the different classes of merchants, artificers, soldiers, shepherds, and husbandmen.

§ Those who resided on the sea-coasts were merchants, in which capacity they will be considered when spoken of as Phœnicians Those who resided in fixed abodes and walled places, cultivated the land. Shepherds and soldiers led a more wandering life. As to war, they were by no means deficient in courage, craft, or policy.

38. *Religion.* Their religion seems to have been undefiled to the days of Abraham, when Melchisedek among them was a priest of the Most High God; but after this period they must have degenerated apace. They compelled their children to pass through fire to Moloch, and their wickedness became extreme.

Greece.

39. *Appearance and Face of the Country.* This country, rendered illustrious by the intellectual elevation of its inhabitants, was a region of enchanting beauty. Its mountains and valleys, lakes and rivers, sufficiently diversified the surface, while their grandeur or their softness imparted an ineffable charm to every prospect. It enjoyed a delightful climate and exuberant soil.

§ The classical reader need not to be reminded, that among a thousand other spots endeared to association, were Pindus and Parnassus, the seats of the muses; Athens, filled with the monuments of art and genius; woody Arcadia, sacred to Pan, and the haunt of shepherds; and Thessaly with its fields of pleasure, where

> "The smooth Peneus from its glassy flood
> Reflects purpureal Tempe's pleasant scene."

40. *Situation, Extent, and Division.* Greece occupied a large peninsula between the south of Italy and Asia Minor, about 400 miles long and 150 broad. It had Epirus and Macedonia on the north, the Mediterranean on the south, and the Ionian and Ægean seas washed, the one its western, and the other its eastern borders.

§ In subsequent times, Epirus and Macedonia were considered as parts of Greece, and then the northern boundary was constituted by Illyricum, Mœsia, and Thrace.

Greece consisted of two principal divisions—Greece, properly so called, and Peloponnesus.

§ Greece proper included the following states; 1. Attica. 2. Bœotia. 3. Acarnania. 4. Ætolia. 5. Locris. 6. Doris. 7. Phocis. 8. Thessaly. 9. Epirus. 10. Macedonia.

Peloponnesus included the following states; 1. Achaia. 2. Elis. 3. Arcadia. 4. Messenia. 5. Laconia. 6. Argolis.

Connected with Greece were many islands in the seas which surrounded it, the principal of which singly, or in clusters, were Eubœa, Lemnos, the Cyclades, Crete, Cythera, Zacynthus, Cephalonia, Corcyra, Tenedos, Lesbos, Scio, Samos, and Patmos.

41. *Names.* Greece was called Hellas by the natives, and its inhabitants Hellenes. From their different tribes they were denominated by the poets, Achivi, Danai, Argivi, Pelasgi, Iones, Dores, and Æoles.

42. *Interesting Localities.* Almost every considerable place in Greece is marked by some circumstance in its natural features, or by some achievement or event in its history, which connects it in the minds of scholars with the most delightful associations. Several of these localities may be grouped together, as below.

§ Peloponnesus took its name from Pelops, who reigned there. Mycenæ was the city of Agamemnon. At Nemea, games were instituted in honour of Hercules, for killing the Nemean lion. In Epidaurus, Æsculapius was worshipped. Lerna gave name to the Lernæan Hydra, a monster destroyed by Hercules.

Amyclæ abounded in trees, and was honoured with a splendid temple of Apollo. Helos was a place which the Spartans took, reducing the inhabitants to slavery, and hence all their slaves were called Helotes. Near Tænarus, the most southern point of Europe, was a cave through which Hercules is fabled to have dragged Cerberus from the infernal regions. On the mountain Taygetus, the Spartan women celebrated the orgies of Bacchus.

Elis, was famous for its horses. At Olympia, the Olympic games were celebrated in honour of Jupiter—they date from B. C. 776, and form the epoch of Grecian chronology. Corinth was famous for its brass, a mixture of copper with some small quantity of gold and silver.

Arcadia was the country of musicians and shepherds, and sacred to Pan, the rural deity. Mercury was born on mount Cyllene. Hercules destroyed the harpies of the river and lake Stymphalus. At the Isthmus, games were celebrated in honour of Neptune.

Eleusis was famous for the celebration of the mysteries of Ceres, in which secrecy was enjoined to the votaries, and the breach of it punished with death. In Attica were mount Hymettus, celebrated for its honey, and mount Pentelicus, for its quarries of marble. The Bœotians were reckoned characteristically dull, though there were some splendid exceptions.

Chæronea was the birth-place of Plutarch, and remarkable for the defeat of the allied states of Greece, by Philip, which ruined that celebrated nation. Not far from this, was the cave of Trophonius, where oracles were delivered, and which rendered such as entered it melancholy for the rest of their lives. Thespia was sacred to the Muses. Tanagra was infamous for its cock-fighting exhibitions. At Delium stood a temple of Apollo; and the mountain of Helicon, and the fountain Aganippe, were consecrated to the Nine.

Phocis, the Greeks conjectured, was not only the centre of Greece but of the whole earth. Delphi was rendered illustrious for the temple and oracle of Apollo, whose responses were always delivered by a priestess. Parnassus, and the fountain of Castalia at its foot, were the haunts of the Muses. Anticyra was famous for the production of hellebore, once reputed a specific in maniacal cases.

Narix was the native place of Ajax. Thermopylæ was a famous pass, justly reckoned the key of Greece, and is immortalized from the self-devotion of Leonidas. Where narrowest, there was room only for a single carriage, a ridge of impassable mountains being on the west, and the sea on the east, with deep and dangerous morasses.

The Ætolians constituted the best cavalry in Greece. Naupactus was so called from the number of ships built there, but its site is now overflowed by the sea. Acarnania was famous for its horses. On the promontory Leucate, was the rock from which disappointed lovers sought either death or a cure, by leaping into the sea.

Through the lake of Acherusia ran the river Acheron, and into the latter flows the Cocytus, both of which, on account of their muddiness, were feigned by the poets to be rivers of hell. In the interior of Epirus, was the most ancient oracle of Greece, the grove. or vocal oaks of Dodona, sacred to Jupiter.

Chaonia received its name from Chaon, the companion of Helenus, the son of Priam, who was inadvertently killed in hunting. Pindus was holy to Apollo and the Nine. The Acroceraunian mountains were so called from their tops being struck with thunder.

The vale of Tempe was reckoned the most delicious spot on earth, five miles in length, but in general very narrow. It had mount Olympus at the north, and Ossa at the south. These mountains, with Pelion, according to story, were piled one upon another, by the giants in their war with the gods, to scale heaven. The celebrated spear of Achilles, which nône but himself could wield, was cut down on Pelion ; Thessaly was renowned for excellent horses.

Larissa was the city of Achilles. Heraclea was so called from Hercules, who is said to have consumed himself in a burning pile, on the top of Œta, near this place. Othrys was the abode of the Centaurs. On the banks of Amphrysus, Apollo used to feed the flocks of Admetus. Pierus, towards the confines of Macedonia, was sacred to the Muses. The women of Thessaly are said to have possessed remarkable skill in magic.

Athos was a mountain through which Xerxes caused a canal to be cut for the passage of his army. Several towns stood upon it whose inhabitants were remarkable for their longevity. Stagira was the birth place of Aristotle, whence he is called the Stagirite. Apollonia was a place where learning was much cultivated. Strymon was the river along the banks of which Orpheus is imagined to have lamented his lost Eurydice.

In the island Corcyra were the celebrated gardens of Alcinous, which produced fruit twice a year. Ithaca was the residence of Ulysses. Cicero compares it to a nest in a rock. The Strophades were a cluster of islands fabled to be infested by harpies. The inhabitants of Ægina were famed for being the first people that coined money.

Delos was the birth place of Apollo and Diana. It was said to be a floating island. Paros was the birth place of Phidias and Praxiteles, and celebrated, moreover, for the finest marble. Naxos was fruitful in vines, and therefore sacred to Bacchus. Crete was celebrated for its hundred cities, and for the laws of Minos established there. The Cretans were celebrated archers.

Rhodes was famous for its brazen colossus, or image of the sun, about 105 feet high. The metal which composed it loaded 900 camels Patmos was the island to which the apostle John was banished, and where he wrote the book of revelation. Scio was famous for its wine and earthen wares. Lemnos was sacred to Vulcan. In the forum of its principal town was the statue of an ox, made by Myron, the back of which, at the winter solstice, was overshadowed by mount Athos, though 80 miles distant.

43. *Cities*. Of these there were several, the capitals of the different states of which Greece was composed, as Athens, Sparta, Corinth, Thebes, Argos, and others. But of these, Athens and Sparta were by far the most renowned.

Athens, the capital of Attica, was so called from Athenæ, one of the names of the goddess Minerva, the protectress of the city. It was called by the ancients, for its glory in the arts and sciences, the learned city, the eye of Greece, the school of the world.

It was situated in a large plain, about five miles from the sea, having in the midst of it, a mount. In its most flourishing state, according to Dio Chrysostom, it was 25 miles in circumference. It was divided into the upper city or citadel, and the lower city. Both contained 440,000 inhabitants, the far greater part of whom were slaves.

§ The citadel was built on the rocky mount already mentioned. It was called the Acropolis, or the upper city. When from the increase of its inhabitants, the lower grounds were occupied by buildings, these constituted the lower city.

The upper city was 16 miles in circumference, and was surrounded by a strong wall, beautified by 9 gates, to one of which, called the grand entrance, the Athenians ascended by steps, covered with white marble.

The lower city contained all the buildings that surrounded the citadel, and was encompassed with strong walls.

In the citadel were several magnificent edifices, the chief of which were the temple of Neptune, and the beautiful temple of Minerva, called Parthenon. These still continue. The latter is justly esteemed one of the noblest remains of antiquity. It is 229 feet long, 101 broad, and 69 high.

In the lower city, the most magnificent structure of Athens, and scarcely paralleled in the ancient world, was the temple of Jupiter Olympus. It was supported on marble columns, and was half a mile in circuit.

In both portions of Athens there were many other splendid structures, and monuments without number, some of the proudest efforts of art and genius that the world ever beheld.

§ Athens had three harbours on the Saronic gulf, which were joined to the city by two walls, called the long walls. The length of one of these was five miles, that of the other nearly the same.

There were several Gymnasia, or places of exercise, in and near Athens, the principal of which were the Academy, the Lyceum, and the Cynosarges.

A Gymnasium was a large edifice designed to accommodate many thousands of people together, with places for the exercises of the youth, and with apartments for philosophers, rhetoricians, &c. to deliver their lectures. A garden and sacred grove were attached to this edifice.

Sparta, called also Lacedæmon, was built upon the banks of the river Eurotas, and at the foot of mount Taygetus. It was the capital of the province of Laconia. It was of a circular form, and about 6 miles in circumference. The houses were not built close together, but divided into different villages, according to the ancient manner of the Greeks. It was destitute of walls, till it fell under the dominion of tyrants, after the time of Alexander. The bravery of its citizens was its defence.

§ Sparta was divided into different villages, according to the ancient manner of the Greeks. Of these villages there were five, built round an eminence at different distances, each of which was occupied by one of the five tribes of Sparta.

The prevailing manners were hostile to external splendour, and therefore the houses of the Spartans were destitute of ornaments. The great Square, or forum, however, in which several streets terminated, was embellished with temples and statues. It also contained the public edifices, in which the assemblies of the various bodies of magistrates were held.

Sparta was also adorned with a large number of monuments, in honour of the gods and ancient heroes. Religious respect was shown to the memory of Hercules, Tyndarus, Castor, Pollux, Leonidas, &c. In the environs of the city were courses for horse and foot races, and places of exercises for youth shaded by beautiful plane trees. Indeed, Sparta was surrounded, to a great extent, with vineyards, olive and plane trees, gardens, and summer houses.

Corinth, the capital of Achaia, was seated on the Isthmus, which separates Peloponnesus from Attica. It lay between two seas, and had two ports, one on each coast. Its citadel stood on the peak of a hill called Acrocorinthus. This city was one of the best peopled and most wealthy in Greece. It was destroyed by Mummius, the Roman general, during the Achæan league. Corinth was partly rebuilt by Julius Cæsar.

§ The neat order of the pillars which are used at this day, in the decoration of all fine buildings, took from this city the name of Corinthian pillars. Its citizens made high pretensions to politeness, philosophy, and learning.

Corinth enjoyed its liberty, and immense traffic, till B. C. 146, when it was taken and burned by the Romans. It was then deemed the strongest city in the world, and was a distinguished seat of opulence and the fine arts. Since that period it has been often burned, plundered, and subjugated, till of late, under the tyranny of the Turks, it was so decayed, that the population did not exceed 1500 souls, one half Mahometans, and the other half Christians.

Thebes, the capital of Bœotia, was situated on the river Ismenus. It had seven gates, with walls about seven miles in circumference. It was demolished by Alexander, and rebuilt by Cassander. Under Epaminondas, the Thebans became masters of Greece; but in Strabo's time (15 or 20 years A. C.) Thebes was only an inconsiderable village.

§ In the dreadful period of its demolition by Alexander, 6000 of its inhabitants were slain, and 30,000 sold for slaves. The house in which the great lyric poet Pindar was born and educated, was ordered to be spared, and all the rest to be destroyed.

44. *Government.* In general the government of Greece partook of a republican character, though it varied at different periods, and was in fact different in the several states. In some of them it exhibited the features of monarchy or aristocracy. They frequently entered into leagues and confederacies with each other, and in this respect bore some faint resemblance to the present government of the United States of America. But on this article we are under the necessity of speaking of the respective states of Greece, chiefly Athens and Sparta, who were, in general, so superior to the rest.

Government of Athens.

§ The government of Athens was at first monarchical, but after the death of Codrus, it became in a degree democratic.

Classes of the inhabitants. The Athenians were divided into three classes, citizens or freemen, foreigners or sojourners, and slaves. Citizens were the privileged class, who held exclusively the offices of government. The privileges of citizenship were obtained with difficulty, and deemed of great value They were conferred only by an assembly of the people, except where they were inherited by those whose parents were citizens.

§ The citizens of Athens were divided into ten tribes; but they were not limited to the city, a part of them residing in the small boroughs of Attica. These tribes were named after certain ancient heroes; each tribe was again subdivided into three parts, and each of these into 30 families.

Sojourners were persons who came from a foreign country, and settled with their families in Attica. They were permitted to exercise trades in the city, and were protected by the government, but had no vote in the assembly, nor could they be raised to any office.

§ In some instances, when they had rendered important services, they were adopted into the class of citizens.

Slaves or servants were distinguished into two sorts. The first consisted of free born citizens who, through poverty, were forced to serve for wages. These could either change their masters or release themselves when able to procure a subsistence. The second sort were wholly at the disposal of their masters, and in general placed beyond the hope of procuring their own freedom, or leaving it as a legacy to their children.

§ Sometimes slaves obtained their freedom by fighting for the republic, or purchased it by means of their savings.

Magistrates. The Athenian magistrates were divided into three sorts, distinguished by the different methods of their election. These were, 1. the Chirotoneti, chosen by the people in a lawful assembly, in which they voted by holding up their hands. 2. The Cleroti, first approved by the people, and then drawn by lot. 3. The Ereti, extraordinary officers appointed by particular tribes, to take care of any business.

§ The poorer citizens were eligible to office; yet it was seldom that any but the most distinguished persons, were actually appointed as magistrates. The candidates were required to give an account of their past life in the public forum.

Magistrates, while in office, were liable to be tried on an accusation of neglect of duty; and after their term of office had expired, they were obliged to render an account of their conduct. During thirty days, any man who chose might bring a complaint of mal-administration.

The usual government of Athens was carried on by the Archons, the Senate of 500, and assemblies of the people.

The Archons held the supreme executive power. They were elected annually, and by the second method above named, viz. by lot. They wore garlands of myrtle, were protected from violence and insult, and were exempted from certain taxes.

§ The archons were nine in number. The first was called archon, by way of eminence. He decided on causes between married persons, also concerning wills, divorces, and legacies. He was the general guardian of orphans. Some other important concerns were assigned to him.

The second archon was styled Basileus, and wore a crown. The third archon was called Polemarch. The six remaining archons were named Thesmothetæ. Their respective duties need not be described. Suffice it to say, that the concern of the archons, as such, was the execution of laws and the general superintendence of the republic. Subordinate magistrates regulated minor details in the police.

The Senate of five hundred was elected annually by lot, from the different tribes. The business of this body was to consider all proposals intended to come before the people, and to see that nothing improper should be submitted.

§ The power of this senate was considerable. They debated all measures of public interest and welfare, examined the acounts of magistrates, took care of the fleet, and could punish for offences not prohibited by any law.

Assemblies of the people were convened for the purpose of consulting on what was most beneficial to the commonwealth. The right of attending them was enjoyed by all the freemen of Athens. Strangers, slaves, women, and persons who had received an infamous punishment, were excluded. They were held four times every 35 days, and also in cases of peculiar emergency.

§ The smallest number of which an assembly could legally consist was 6000 citizens. The assemblies decided respecting peace or war; received ambassadors; confirmed or abrogated laws; nominated to almost every important office, &c.

Here was the field in which the good or the bad influence of the orators of Athens was exerted; in which their talents were elicited, and their fame acquired; in which Pericles "thundered," Æschines charmed, and Demosthenes ruled the hearts of men.

There were also other bodies of men occasionally concerned

in the government of Athens, as various courts, particularly that celebrated one called Areopagus.

The name of this court was taken from the place where it was held, viz. Mars' Hill. It was in the greatest repute throughout Greece for the wisdom and justice of its proceedings. It took cognizance of crimes, abuses, and innovations either in religion or government. It inspected the laws and public manners.

The strictest propriety of conduct was required of the members. Expulsion followed any act of gross immorality. To laugh during the sitting of the court, was thought a very blameable levity.

There was an absurd peculiarity in the government of Athens, which should not be omitted. It was ostracism, a kind of popular judgment so call from ostrakon, a shell, or tile, on which votes were written.

§ The following was the process in this condemnation. The people being assembled, each citizen writing on a shell the name of the individual most obnoxious to him without the allegation of a crime, carried it to a certain part of the market place fixed for this purpose, and deposited it there. These shells were numbered in gross by the archons. If they did not amount to 6000, the ostracism was void. If they amounted to this number, the archons, laying every name by itself, pronounced him, whose name was written by the major part. banished for ten years, with leave to enjoy his estate. Hence it was that so many eminent citizens suffered from the ingratitude or the spleen of the Athenians.

Government of Sparta.

Classes of the inhabitants. The inhabitants of Sparta consisted of citizens and slaves, or Helots. The citizens were divided into two classes, the Homoii, and the Hypomiones. The privileges of these varied; the former were eligible to office; the latter consisting of the poorer citizens, the freedmen and their sons, were allowed only to vote at the elections.

The slaves, or Helots, were much more numerous than the citizens. Their services were similar to those of servants in general, though less severe than those of servants elsewhere in Greece.

Kings. The republic of Sparta had two magistrates, called kings, but they differed from those of most other nations. They formed a check upon each other, and their power otherwise was very limited.

§ Every month they took an oath that they would rule according to the laws; one of them commanded the army, while the other usually remained at home to administer the laws. As first citizens of the state, they presided in the senate, but their peculiar prerogative was to superintend the religion of the state.

Senate. This body consisted, together with the two kings, of twenty-eight members, who were above sixty years of age, and elected to the office for life, and on account of their virtue. Their duty was to consider all questions respecting peace or war, and other important affairs of the republic.

Ephori. The Ephori were five magistrates, elected annually by the citizens, to inspect the education of the youth, and the administration of justice.

Assemblies. The public assemblies were held to decide on matters laid before them by the Senate. There were two of these bodies; one was called the general assembly, attended by all the freemen of Laconia; the other, the lesser assembly, composed of the Spartans alone, who exceeded thirty years of age.

It is to be noticed, that the kings, as well as the other magistrates, constituted a portion of these bodies.

Government of the other States of Greece.

Like Athens and Sparta, the government of the other sovereignties of Greece was, for the most part, republican. In some of them there was a preponderance of aristocracy, in others of democracy. Thebes was more nearly a monarchy.

§ Many of the sovereigns of Thebes were celebrated for their misfortunes, such as Laius, Œdipus, Polynices, &c.

Pertaining to the government of the Greeks, as a confederated body, was the Amphictyonic Council. This was an assembly composed, at first, of a few states in the northern parts of Greece, but afterwards of twelve states, the object of which was the decision of all differences between cities, and to try such offences as openly violated the laws of nations.

§ The number of deputies usually sent to this council was two from each state. It met twice a year. The vernal assembly was held at Delphi, and the autumnal at Thermopylæ.

45. *Military Affairs.* The armies of the different states of Greece consisted, for the most part, of citizens, whom the laws of their country obliged at a certain age to appear in arms, at the summons of the magistrate.

§ The main body of the Grecian armies was composed of infantry. The rest rode in chariots, upon horseback, or upon elephants.

The Greek arms were at first made of brass, and the boots, and some other parts, of tin. Iron became afterwards the chief material. The defensive arms were a helmet, a breast plate, and a plate for the back, greaves to defend the legs, guards for the hands, a sort of belt which covered a part of the body in front, and a shield.

The offensive arms were the spear, or pike, the sword, the pole axe, a club of wood or iron, the bow and arrow, darts or javelins, and slings.

§ The Greeks, however brave in the field, were very inefficient in undertaking the siege of walled towns. Their armies were generally the militia of the country, called out to temporary service.

The severest punishments were inflicted by the Lacedæmonians on deserters, or cowards, who fled from battle. They forfeited all the privileges and honours of citizens; it was a disgrace to intermarry with them; they might be beaten by any who met them, without the liberty of self-defence; and they wore some distinguishing dress as a mark of infamy.

Archilochus, the poet, was banished Sparta for writing an epigram, in which he jestingly related the loss of his shield.

46. *Naval Affairs.* The Greek ships consisted chiefly of three sorts: ships of war, those of burthen, and those of passage.

§ Ships of passage were used as transports; ships of burthen served as tenders, and were usually of a round form; ships of war contained the men and the weapons by which the naval engagement was carried on, and were distinguished by the several orders or banks of oars which they possessed. These were not fixed in a vertical line over each other, but back of each other, ascending gradually in the form of stairs.

47. *Religion.* The Greeks, who were heathens, worshipped great numbers of gods and demi-gods, whom they divided into three classes:—celestial, marine, and infernal. They were all subject to Jupiter, who was considered the father of gods and men. The above classes are according to their degrees of dignity.

§ The gods of Greece are described by the poets according to tradition, and with such embellishments as poetic genius could invent. As the Greeks had no sacred books, these fictions, sanctioned also by the priests and legislators, were the only authority for the popular belief.

The account we here give of the mythology of the Greeks is to be regarded as a description only of their principal deities, and under the forms in which the poets, sculptors, and painters, represented them. If this article should appear to be somewhat particular, compared with the others respecting Greece, it is because the mythology of this country is the same nearly with that of the whole ancient world, and is necessary to be known in reading the Grecian and Roman classics.

The celestial deities were Jupiter, Apollo, Mars, Mercury

Bacchus, Vulcan, Juno, Minerva, Venus, Diana, Ceres, and Vesta.

Jupiter was the son of Saturn and Cybele; and born at the same birth with Juno, on mount Ida in Crete. He deposed his father, and divided the world between himself and his brethren, Neptune and Pluto. Neptune had the jurisdiction of the sea, and Pluto that of the infernal regions. The sovereignty of heaven and earth he reserved to himself.

One of his great exploits was the conquest of the Titans, or giants, who heaped mountains upon mountains to scale heaven. Jupiter was guilty of indulging the basest lusts, although he is generally represented as the father of men and gods, as shaking heaven with his nod, and governing all things, except the Fates, by his power as supreme. His altars were never defiled with human sacrifices.

He is generally represented as a majestic personage, seated on a throne, with a sceptre in one hand, and thunderbolts in the other, and at his feet an eagle with expanded wings.

Apollo was the son of Jupiter and Latona, and born in the island of Delos. He presided over music, medicine, poetry, divination, the fine arts, and archery. For his offence in killing the Cyclops, he was banished from heaven, and obliged to hire himself as a shepherd to Admetus, king of Thessaly, in which employment he remained nine years.

His adventures on earth are represented as extraordinary. Among others he flayed Marsyas alive for contending with him in music; he caused Midas to receive a pair of ass's ears for preferring Pan's music to his; he turned into a voilet the beautiful boy Hyacinthus, whom he accidentally killed with a quoit; and his mistress Daphne he metamorphosed into a laurel.

He is represented as a tall, beardless youth, with rays round his head; sometimes he holds a lyre in his hand, sometimes he has a bow, with a quiver of arrows at his back.

Mars was the son of Jupiter and Juno. He was the god of war, and patron of all that is bloody, cruel, and furious. The horse, the wolf, the magpie, and the vulture, were offered to him. He had his temples in all nations, as well as among the Greeks and Romans. During the Trojan war Mars was wounded by Diomedes, and hastily retreating to heaven, complained to Jupiter, that Minerva had directed the weapon of his antagonist.

He is represented as an old man, armed and standing in a chariot, drawn by two horses, called Flight and Terror; his sister Bellona, was his charioteer. Discord goes before him in a tattered garment with a torch, and Anger and Clamour follow.

Mercury, the son of Jupiter and Maia, was the messenger of the gods, the patron of travellers, shepherds, orators, merchants, thieves, and dishonest persons. His exploits abundantly support this character. Mercury was doubtless some enlightened person in a remote age, who, on account of his actions or services was worshipped after his death. His Greek name, Hermes, signifies to interpret or explain, and he appears to have taught men the arts of civilization.

He is represented as a naked youth, standing on tiptoe, having a winged cap on his head, and winged sandals on his feet; in one hand he held a rod, and in the other a purse.

Bacchus was the son of Jupiter and Semele, and the god of wine. His festivals were celebrated by persons of both sexes, who dressed themselves in skins, and ran about the hills and country shouting, and accompanying their shouts with drums, fifes, and flutes. These solemnities were attended with disgusting scenes of drunkenness and debauchery. The fir, yew, and fig tree, the ivy and vine, were sacred to him.

Bacchus is depicted as a corpulent and ruddy youth, crowned with ivy and vine leaves; holding in his hand a small javelin bound with vine leaves; his chariot is drawn by lions.

Vulcan, the god of fire, and patron of those who wrought in the metallic arts, was the son of Jupiter and Juno. He was kicked out of heaven by Jupiter, for attempting to deliver his mother from a chain by which she was suspended. He continued to descend nine days and nights, and lighted on the island of Lemnos, but was crippled ever after.

Vulcan was the artificer of heaven; he forged the thunderbolts of Jupiter, also the arms of gods and demi-gods. Though deformed, squalid, and sooty, he is made the husband of Venus and father of Cupid.

Vulcan is represented as working at a forge. One hand raising a hammer ready to strike, the other holding a thunderbolt with pincers on an anvil. An eagle waits to carry it to Jupiter when finished.

Juno, styled the queen of heaven, was both the sister and wife of Jupiter. She was born at Argos, or as some report, in Samos. In her character she was haughty, jealous, and inexorable, though the ancients held her in great veneration, inasmuch as she presided over power, empire, and riches, and was the special protectress of marriage and child birth.

She was lofty, graceful, and magnificent in her face, figure, and motion, and of all the pagan divinities her worship was the most solemn and general.

She is represented seated on a throne, or in a chariot drawn by peacocks, with a diadem or fillet adorned with jewels on her head, and a golden sceptre in her hand. Iris, displaying the rich colours of the rainbow, is her usual attendant.

Minerva, the goddess of wisdom, sprang completely armed from the head of Jupiter. She was the most accomplished of all the goddesses, and the only divinity that seemed equal to Jupiter. She was a benificent goddess, and instructed in ship building, navigation, spinning, and weaving. Her worship was universally established, but Athens claimed her particular attention.

She is represented as a majestic female, of commanding aspect, armed with a helmet, breastplate, shield, and spear. By her side, or on her crest, is an owl, the bird which is sacred to her.

Venus, the goddess of love and beauty, was the daughter of Jupiter and Dione, or as some say, she sprung from the froth of the sea. She was licentious in a high degree, and her worship was celebrated with the most disgraceful ceremonies. The most beautiful of her temples were those of Paphos, Cnidus, Cythera, and Idalia. The island of Cyprus was her favourite residence.

She is represented as a beautiful woman, elegantly attired, and girt about the waist with a cestus, or girdle, that had the power of inspiring love.

Diana was the queen of the woods and the goddess of hunting. She devoted herself to perpetual celibacy, and had for her attendants 80 nymphs, all of whom abjured the rites of marriage. Among plants, the poppy and dittany were sacred to her.

She is represented as a tall, majestic woman, lightly clad, with a crescent on her forehead, a bow in her hand, a quiver on her shoulders, her legs bare, and buskins on her feet.

Ceres, the goddess of corn and harvest, was the daughter of Saturn and Cybele, and the first who taught to cultivate the earth. She was a beneficent goddess, but led a licentious life. To her honour the Eleusinian mysteries were celebrated.

She is represented as a majestic and beautiful woman, crowned with ears of corn; in one hand she held poppies and ears of corn, and in the other a lighted torch.

Vesta was the goddess of fire, and guardian of houses and hearths. She ever remained a virgin, and received the first oblations in sacrifice.

She was represented in a long, flowing robe, a veil on her head, a lamp in one hand, and a javelin in the other.

The marine deities were Neptune, and his wife Amphitrite, Oceanus and his wife Thetys, Triton, Proteus, Nereus, and his sister and consort Doris, &c.

Neptune, the brother of Jupiter, was second in rank among the gods, and reigned over the sea. Conspiring against Jupiter, he was defeated, banished from heaven, and for one year made subject to Laomedon, king of Troy, where he assisted to build the walls of that city.

Neptune is represented seated in a chariot made of a shell and drawn by dolphins and sea horses, surrounded by tritons, nymphs, and sea monsters. On his head he wears a crown, and in his hand holds a trident, or sceptre, with three prongs.

Oceanus, a sea god, was the son of Cœlum and Vesta. He was called the father, not only of rivers, but of animals. He and his wife Thetys are said to have had 3000 sons.

Triton, also a sea god, was the son of Neptune and Amphitrite; he was his father's companion and trumpeter.

Half of him resembles a man; the other part is like a fish; his two feet are like the fore feet of a horse; his tail is cleft and crooked like a half moon; and his hair resembles wild parsley.

Nereus, a sea god, the son of Oceanus, was the father of fifty daughters by his wife Doris, who were called Nereids.

Proteus, the son of Oceanus, a god of the sea, could foretell future events, and change himself into any shape.

The infernal deities were Pluto and his consort Proserpine, Plutus, Charon, the Furies, Fates, and the three judges, Minos, Æacus, and Rhadamanthus.

§ Pluto, who exercised dominion over hell, was the brother of Jupiter. The goddesses all refusing to marry him on account of his deformity and gloomy disposition, he seized Proserpine, the daughter of Ceres, in Sicily, opened a passage through the earth, carried her to his residence, married, and made her queen of hell. No temples were raised to his honour.

He is represented seated on a throne of sulphur, from beneath which flow the rivers Lethe, Phlegethon, Cocytus, and Acheron. His countenance is stern; on his head is a radiated crown; in one hand a sceptre with two teeth, called a bident, and in the other, two keys.

Plutus, an infernal deity, was the god of riches. He was lame, blind, injudicious, and timorous.

Charon was the ferryman of hell, an old man with white hair, a long beard and garments, deformed with filth, in speech morose, and ill-tempered. Every ghost paid a small brass coin for his fare.

None could enter Charon's boat without a regular burial; without this, they wandered a hundred years, amidst the mud and slime of the shore. By him departed souls were ferried over the four rivers of hell, and carried to Pluto's palace.

The Furies were three in number, Alecto, Tisiphone, and Megara. They have the faces of women, their looks are full of terror, they hold lighted torches in their hands, and snakes lash their necks and shoulders. Their office is to observe and punish the crimes of bad men, and torment the consciences of secret offenders.

The Fates were three daughters of Jupiter by Themis. Their names were Clotho, Lachesis, and Atropos. They decided on the fortunes of mankind. Clotho drew the thread of life, Lachesis turned the wheel, and Atropos cut it with her scissors.

Minos, Æacus, and Rhadamanthus, were the three judges of the souls of the dead. They assigned various punishments to the wicked, adapted to their crimes; to the good they gave a place in the delightful realms of Elysium.

There were many other divinities of various characters and descriptions: as, Cupid, the god of love; the Muses, who presided over poetry, music, dancing, and the liberal arts; the Graces, &c.

§ Cupid, representing the passion of love, was a beautiful winged boy, with a bow and arrows, and often with a bandage over his eyes. Sometimes he is bestriding the back of a lion, playing on a lyre; sometimes he appears mounted on a dolphin; at others, breaking the winged thunderbolt of Jove, or amusing himself with childish diversions.

The Muses were the daughters of Jupiter by Mnemosyne. They were nine in number viz.

1st. Calliope, who presides over eloquence and heroic or epic poetry, such as Homer's Iliad.

2d. Clio, who presides over history.

3d. Erato, the muse of elegiac or lyric poetry.

4th. Euterpe, presiding over music.

5th. Melpomene, the inventress and muse of tragedy.

6th. Polyhymnia, the muse of singing and rhetoric.

7th. Terpsichore, who presides over dancing.

8th. Thalia, the muse of pastoral or comic poetry.

9th. Urania, who presides over hymns and sacred subjects, and is the muse of astronomy.

The Graces were the daughters of Bacchus and Venus, and three in number. They were supposed to give to beauty its attractions, and to render even homeliness pleasing.

They are usually represented as young and blooming virgins, lightly clad, and holding each other by the hand, to show the mutual affection that subsisted between them.

Besides these, there were rural deities, as Pan, Sylvanus, Priapus, Aristæus, Terminus, and others. There were also the Sirens, Gorgons, Harpies, Dryads, Naiads, Nereids, Tritons, Lares, Penates, Fauns, Satyrs, Pales, and a vast number of Nymphs.

§ Pan was the principal among the inferior deities, and was the god of hunters, shepherds, and country people generally.

Sylvanus was next to Pan, and presided over woods. Priapus presided over gardens. Aristæus invented the art of extracting oil from olives, and found the use of honey. Terminus was considered as watching over the boundaries of lands.

The Sirens were three fabulous persons, who were said to have the faces of women, and the lower parts of their bodies like fish. They had such melodious voices, that mariners were often allured by them to their own destruction.

The Gorgons, three sisters, had the power of transforming those into stones who looked at them.

The Harpies are said to have been winged monsters which had the face of a woman, the body and wings of a vulture, claws on the hands and feet, and the ears of a bear.

The Dryads were nymphs who presided over the woods.

The Naiads were nymphs of springs and fountains.

The Nereids were nymphs of the sea, and daughters of Nereus and Doris.

The Tritons were sea gods, with their upper parts like a man, and their lower parts resembling a fish.

The Lares and Penates were inferior deities who presided over houses and families.

The Fauns and Satyrs were rural demi-gods, the one attending on Pan, and the other on Bacchus.

Pales was the goddess of shepherds and pastures.

The Nymphs were celestial and terrestrial; the former guided the heavenly bodies, the latter presided over the woods. They are represented as beautiful creatures, inhabiting every forest and glen.

The worship of these divinities was conducted by priests dressed in costly habits, who offered sacrifices of animals, fruits, perfumes, &c. These sacrifices were sometimes accompanied by prayers, music, dancing, &c. Human victims were occasionally sacrificed.

§ The Greeks derived their religion principally from Egypt; but by degrees the legislators, poets, and priests, extended it, till the multitude of gods was almost innumerable. Thirty thousand objects of worship have been enumerated among them. These deities were supposed frequently to mingle in the affairs of men, and are represented as being stained with almost every vice.

Temples were erected, festivals instituted, games celebrated, and sacrifices offered, with more or less pomp to all these gods, as also to the souls of departed heroes.

The religion of the common people consisted chiefly in the external honours paid to their gods, and an attendance upon sacrifices and ceremonies, though these were performed with great reverence. With respect to a future state of existence, the philosophers seem to have been in doubt. The poets inculcated a belief in Tartarus, or Hell, and Elysium, or Paradise. Women were not encouraged with any hope of immortality.

Of Hell they have drawn a picture in the most gloomy and horrific colours, where men who have been remarkable for wickedness are tortured with a variety of miseries adapted to their crimes.

The prospect of Elysium is described by Homer, Hesiod, Pindar, and others, as beautiful and inviting in the highest degree. In that delightful region, there is no inclement weather, but soft winds blow from the ocean to refresh the inhabitants, who live without care or anxiety; there reigns perpetual sunshine and serenity of sky; and the f rtile earth produces thrice in a year delicious fruits for their sustenance.

With the religion of the Greeks were connected their temples, oracles, games, &c.

The principal temples of the Greeks were those of Diana, at Ephesus, of Apollo, in the city of Miletus, of Ceres and Proserpine, at Eleusis, and that of Olympian Jove, at Athens. These were all built of marble, and adorned with the finest ornaments. The most celebrated Grecian temple, however, was that of Apollo at Delphos, which was revered and resorted to by all the surrounding nations.

§ Statues of the gods, to whom these structures were dedicated, were erected in or near the centre of the building, and enclosed by railing. Sacrifices of various kinds were made before these statues the ceremonies of which were generally conducted by the priests.

Temples among the heathen most probably owe their origin to the superstitious reverence paid by the ancients to the memory of their deceased friends and benefactors. As most of their gods were eminent men, who were consecrated after death; so the first heathen temples, we naturally infer, were stately monuments erected in honour of the dead.

Oracles were consulted by the Greeks on all important occasions, and their determinations were held sacred and inviolable. There were certain temples, in which future events were made known to those who devoutly sought to know the will of superior powers. Certain priests or priestesses communicated this supposed will.

§ Well have they been called lying oracles, in comparison with the clear predictions of the prophets of Jehovah in the scriptures The most celebrated oracles were those of Apollo, at Delphi and Delos, the oracle of Jupiter, at Dodona, and that of Trophonius.

The public and solemn games in Greece were the Olympic, Pythian, Nemean, and Isthmian—four in number. The contests at these games were running, leaping, throwing the quoit, boxing, and wrestling. Horse races and chariot races were also in repute. Besides these, there were contests in which musicians, poets, artists, and philosophers, engaged for victory.

These occasions drew together people from all parts of Greece, and even strangers from foreign countries. The utmost emulation obtained to secure the prizes, which were wreaths of various evergreens; and the highest honours and respect were shown towards the victors. Their praises were universally celebrated. The effect of these games on the national spirit was remarkable.

§ The Olympic Games were instituted by Hercules in honour of Jupiter Olympius, 1222 years B. C., and renewed after a long period, first by Lycurgus, 884 B. C., and next by Corœbus, 776 B. C. The last period is the era of the first Olympiad. An Olympiad was the space (which was four years,) intervening between one celebration and another—the Greek method of computing time. The victors were crowned with olive.

The Pythian Games were celebrated every fifth year, in the second year of every Olympiad, near Delphi, in honour of Apollo. The victors were crowned with laurel. The exercises were nearly the same as at the Olympic.

The Nemean Games, which were instituted by Hercules, were celebrated every third year at the town of Nemea, with the usual exercises. The victors were crowned with parsley.

The Isthmian Games were celebrated near the Isthmus of Corinth, whence they derived their name. Their occurrence was every third, and afterwards every fifth year. The victors were crowned with garlands of pine leaves.

48. *Literature.* In literature, Greece was the glory of the whole earth. No nation, ancient or modern, has ever surpassed the Greeks in literary taste and genius. Since their time, great advances have indeed been made in the sciences, strictly so called, and in some branches of polite learning; yet in chaste and beautiful composition, in liveliness of fancy, in sweetness of periods, in the various forms of intellectual effort under the names of poetry, oratory, and history, they are still unrivalled, in mere human productions.

§ The Greeks derived a part of their learning from Egypt and Phœnicia, but they originated much of it, and here consists their peculiar glory. The praise of invention belongs to them, and even of perfection in some departments.

Cadmus taught them the alphabet 1519 years B. C. It then contained but 16 letters, and the method of writing was from left to right, and from right to left alternately. This circumstance essentially contributed to the rapid advances made by the Greeks in civilization and knowledge.

Poetry, in Greece, was extremely ancient. It was cultivated even before the introduction of letters. In the various forms under which it is usually arranged, there are specimens of surpassing excellence, and names that can never be forgotten.

§ In epic poetry, we find the sublime Homer, and the moral Hesiod. In lyric poetry, shine the gay Anacreon, the sweet Sappho, and the fanciful and daring Pindar.

In the drama we meet the names of the wild Æschylus, the pathetic Euripides, the pure and grand Sophocles, and the delicate Menander. In pastoral poetry, we read of the easy Bion and the elegant Moschus; and every classical scholar knows, that Theocritus is only another name for simplicity and nature.

Oratory was greatly cultivated among the Greeks, particularly in Athens, whose institutions were rather more free than was elsewhere the case in Greece. It became an object of attention soon after the Persian invasion, about 480 years B. C. It was cultivated with singular success—was bold and vehement at first, but afterwards more refined and elegant.

§ Here Pericles awed, by the majesty of his expressions; Thucydides, who was an orator, as well as a historian, arrested the thoughts of others, by the force of his own. Here Isocrates soothed the ear by harmony of periods, and Demosthenes flashed conviction and impelled to action, by the united energy of his gesture, voice, and arguments

History, after those earlier ages in which poetry was the vehicle of recorded events, was cultivated with an interest and success demanded by its importance. The Greeks possessed several most distinguished historians.

§ Such were Herodotus, who was characterized by a simple and elegant style and engaging manner; Thucydides, whose reflections were profound, and fidelity unequalled; Xenophon, who combined simplicity of style with sagacity of observation.

Philosophy among the Greeks, was divided into various schools or sects. The professors of philosophy arose from the early Rhapsodists—men who recited the poems of Homer and others at the public games, commenting at the same time upon them, and who, having established schools, were dignified by the name of sophists, or teachers of wisdom. The Grecian philosophy, was, however, merely speculative, and seldom based upon facts.

§ The principal sects of philosophy in Greece were the Ionic, the most ancient, founded by Thales; the Italian, by Pythagoras; the Socratic, by Socrates; the Cynic, by Antisthenes; the Academic, by Plato; the Peripatetic, by Aristotle; the Sceptical, by Pyrrho; the Stoic, by Zeno; the Epicurean, by Epicurus.

These sects were distinguished by certain peculiarities of doctrine, as for instance, the Italian taught the transmigration of souls; the Socratic insisted on the excellence of virtue; the Cynic condemned all knowledge, society, and the arts of life; the Academic dealt in ideal forms, and mystical theogony; the Peripatetic exhibited the model of a perfect logic; the Sceptical inculcated universal doubt; the Stoic decried all weakness, and made insensibility a virtue; and the Epicurean pointed to pleasure as the supreme good.

The Peripatetic sect, or the school of Aristotle, has exerted the greatest influence over the human mind. It reigned in the schools through 1600 years.

The principle of all things was a subject of special research by the philosophers of Greece. It may be curious to know their opinions on this topic.

Anaximenes, taught that this principle consisted of - - Water.
Thales, - - - - - - - - - - Water.
Anaxagoras, - - - - - - - - - Infinite air.
Archelaus, - - - - - - - - - Matter and Spirit.
Heraclitus, - - - - - - - - - - - Fire.
Democritus, - - - - - - - - - - Atoms.
Pythagoras, - - - - - - - - - - Unity.
Plato, - - - - - - - - - God, Idea, and matter.
Aristotle, - - - - - - - Matter, Form, and Privation.
Zeno, - - God and Matter, (the only things without beginning.)
Epicurus, - - - - - - - Matter and empty Space.

The seven wise men of Greece, who are found in the ranks of phi losophy, were Thales, of Miletus; Solon, of Athens; Bias, of Priene; Chilo, of Lacedæmon; Cleobulus, of Lindos; Pittacus, of Mitylene; and Periander, of Corinth.

49. *The arts.* Greece, in the age of Pericles, about 430 B. C., abounded in architects, sculptors, and painters. It was then in the zenith of its glory in literature, as well as the arts. Indeed this was the taste of the public mind, until after the death of Alexander. Even to this day, Greece, particularly Athens, is the instructress of the world in those monuments of its arts and genius that yet remain.

In the useful and necessary arts of life, the Greeks never made any great improvement. Agriculture, manufactures, and commerce, were left for other nations to perfect. But in the fine arts, appropriately so called, Greece was superior to all ancient nations, and probably not excelled by any modern. Indeed, we may say that the Greeks carried architecture, sculpture, and painting, to perfection.

§ This people invented that system of architecture, which is universally considered the most finished and perfect.

The Greek architecture consisted of three distinct orders, the Doric, the Ionic, and the Corinthian. The Doric possessed a masculine grandeur, and sublime plainness. The Ionic was marked with gracefulness and elegance. The Corinthian affected the highest magnificence and ornament, by uniting the characteristics of all the orders.

In sculpture, the Greeks excelled no less than in architecture. Specimens of their art in this respect are perfect models. The Dying Gladiator, the Venus, and the Laocoon, of the Greek sculptors, have an imperishable fame.

In painting, though very few specimens have descended down to us, they are supposed also greatly to have excelled. The works of Zeuxis, Apelles, Parrhasius, Protogens, and Timanthes, which have perished, were highly extolled by the writers of antiquity.

In music, the Greeks appear to have been less conspicuous than several modern nations.

50. *Private and domestic Life.* The dress of the Greeks, as well as of other ancient nations, differed much from that of most modern nations.

The men wore an inner garment called tunic, over which they threw a mantle; their shoes, or sandals, were fastened under the soles of their feet with thongs or ropes.

The women, particularly in Athens, wore a white tunic, which was closely bound with a broad sash, and descended in waving folds down to the heels; also a shorter robe, confined round the waist with a ribbon, bordered at the bottom with stripes of various colours; over this they sometimes put on a robe, which was worn gathered up like a scarf.

In the earlier ages of Greece, its inhabitants used no covering on their heads; but in after times they wore hats, that were tied under the chin. Women, however, always had their heads covered.

§ The Athenians wore in their hair golden grasshoppers, as emblems of the antiquity of their nation, intimating that they were sprung from the earth.

In Sparta, the kings, magistrates, and citizens, were but little distinguished by external appearance. The military costume was of a red colour.

The Greeks, in general, set a high value on scarlet colour, and a still greater on purple.

The meals of the Greeks were usually four in number: Breakfast was taken about the rising of the sun; the next meal at mid-day; then came the afternoon repast; and lastly the supper, which was the principal meal, as it was taken after the business of the day.

§ At Sparta they ate together at public tables, and the chief part of their food consisted of black broth.

In the earliest ages, convivial entertainments were generally acts of public devotion, but afterwards we find them in use in private life

There were also political feasts, in which a whole city, tribe, or other subdivision, met together.

Water and wine were used for drinking. Perfumed wines were introduced at the tables of the rich. Every thing capable of sustaining life was used as food. The Greeks generally were very fond of fish.

Hot baths were very numerous, and bathing in them, and anointing the body, with a change of clean clothes, were usual in preparing for a feast. When guests were invited, men and women were never invited together.

Seats, on which persons sat upright, were employed; but, as luxury prevailed, couches were introduced, on which the guests reclined while feasting.

The marriages among the Greeks were lawful only as the consent of parents or other relatives could be obtained. This institution was greatly encouraged in all parts of Greece. Want of esteem, and sometimes the infliction of punishment, attended the failure of entering into the connubial state.

§ Polygamy was allowed only after times of great calamity, such as war or pestilence. Socrates married a second wife on this account. Violations of the marriage contract, though the punishment was severe, were often committed.

The Grecian women seldom or never appeared in strange company but were confined to the remote parts of the house, into which no male visitants were admitted. When they went abroad, they wore veils to conceal their faces. It was disreputable, however, to appear much abroad.

In some parts of Greece, parents might expose their children, in certain cases. Children were required to maintain their parents in old age; but by the laws of Solon, if a person did not bring up his children to some useful employment, they were to be exempted from such an obligation.

The funerals of the Greeks were attended with many ceremonies, showing that they considered the duties belonging to the dead to be of the highest importance. In their view, it was the most awful of all imprecations, to wish that a person might die without the honours of a funeral.

Phœnicians.

51. *Country.* Phœnicia was little more than a narrow slip of ground situated between mount Libanus and the sea. It had Syria on the north and east, Judea on the south, and the Mediterranean on the west.

52. *Cities and Remains.* Sidon was the capital, and a maritime town of considerable extent, and provided with an excellent harbour. It was distinguished by a high degree of opulence and refinement.

Tyrus, called the daughter of Sidon, was built upon an island south of Sidon, and 25 miles distant. It was ornamented with many magnificent buildings.

§ Sidon is often mentioned by Homer, but Tyrus never. Tyrus was joined by Alexander to the main land, and time has consolidated his work.

The walls of Tyre were 150 feet high, with a proportionate breadth. Old Tyre, on the continent, was destroyed by the Assyrians. It was new Tyre that Alexander took after a siege of seven months. A few fishermen's huts are among its ruins.

Other principal cities were Aradus, Tripoli, Byblus, Sarepta, and Berytus.

Some vestiges of the splendour of this ancient land are still in existence. The ruins of Sidon exhibit many fine columns and other fragments of marble.

§ A double column of granite, consisting of one entire block, 80 feet long, has been noticed among the ruins of Tyre.

53. *Navigation and Colonies.* The Phœnicians, confined between the sea and mountains, acquired power and aggrandizement by navigation. Their navigators were famous for their skill and intrepidity. They engrossed the commerce of the western hemisphere.

They formed establishments on both sides of the Mediterranean, and even on those of the western ocean. In the time of Abraham, they were known to be a commercial and enterprising people.

§ Carthage, Utica, Gades, &c. were colonies founded by the inhabitants of Tyre.

54. *Sciences, Arts, and Manufactures.* From the earliest periods, the Phœnicians were addicted to philosophy. The sciences of arithmetic and astronomy were invented or improved by them, and they are known to have introduced letters into Greece.

§ Before the time of the Trojan war, Moschus, a Sidonian, explained the doctrine of Atoms. In latter ages, we read of some eminent philosophers; among them was Boethius, Antipater, Diodatus, and Apollonius.

In manufactures they were skilled. Glass, purple, and fine linen, were products of their own invention.

In architecture they were so versed, that Solomon sought their aid in erecting his magnificent temple.

55. *Religion.* As the Phœnicians were so nearly connected with the immediate descendants of Noah, they were probably instructed in the worship of the true God; but they became at length immersed in idolatry and superstition.

The principal objects of their mistaken adoration were Beelsmen, or the sun, Baal, Astarte, the "queen of heaven," Hercules, Adonis, and the Patæci, certain small statues, which being venerated as the tutelar gods of sea-faring men, were always carried about in the prows of their vessels.

One of these idolatrous objects Milton describes in mellifluous verse.

> "With these in troop
> Came Ashtoreth, whom the Phœnicians call'd
> Astarte, queen of heaven, with crescent horns;
> To whose bright image, nightly by the moon
> Sidonian virgins paid their vows and songs."

Lydians.

56. *Country.* The country of the Lydians had Mysia on the north, and Caria on the south. It constituted an interesting portion of Asia Minor.

§ The inhabitants on the coast, who were Ionians divided into twelve small states, gave their name to a dialect of the Greek language—Ionic.

57. *Cities.* The principal cities were Ephesus, illustrious in classic and in christian antiquity; Sardis, the ancient me-

tropolis; Philadelphia, in which were celebrated the common feasts of all Asia; and a few others.

§ Ephesus was famous for the temple of Diana, one of the seven wonders of the world, completed 220 years after its foundation. This temple was 425 feet in length, and 200 in breadth. The roof was supported by 127 columns 60 feet high, placed there by so many kings. The rich offerings brought into it were immense.

This temple was burnt on the night that Alexander was born. Erostratus perpetrated this villany merely to eternize his name. It rose, however, from its ruins, with augmented splendour.

Ephesus was famous also as the place where a flourishing christian church was planted by the apostle Paul; and it now stands a monument of the fulfilment of our Saviour's threatening: "Thy candlestick shall be removed out of his place."

The city is now a mass of ruins. The whole contains only 40 or 50 Turkish families, who live in cottages of dirt. Not a single family here exists to invoke the name of Jesus. Says Gibbon, "The desolation is complete. The temple of Diana, or the church of Mary, will equally elude the search of the curious traveller."

58. *Character*. The Lydians, under Crœsus, and some of his predecessors, were a very warlike people; but after the introduction of the Persian luxuries, they became indolent, voluptuous, and effeminate.

59. *Customs*. They are said to be the first people that introduced the coinage of gold and silver to facilitate trade; the first that sold by retail; that kept taverns and eating houses; and invented public games, which were therefore called ludi by the Romans.

Romans.

60. *Country—its name, situation, and division*. The country of this renowned people, from their having ruled over a great part of the civilized world, becomes an interesting object to the scholar or reader. They inhabited that part of Europe which is now called Italy, and their beginning was at Rome, its capital. From the latter they were denominated Romans.

§ Italy had other names, as Hesperia, Ausonia, Œnotria, and Saturnia.

It had the Alps on the north, the Tyrrhene sea on the west, the Adriatic on the east, and the Grecian sea on the south.

The whole territory was divided into Cisalpine Gaul, Italy Proper, and Magna Græcia.

§ Its principal districts were Cisalpine Gaul, Etruria, Umbria, Picenum, Latium, Campania, Samnium, the Hirpini, Apulia, Calabria, Lucania, and the Brutii.

61. *Interesting localities of Italy.* Italy as well as Greece furnishes many recollections of this kind, that are so pleasing to the student of antiquity.

§ Andes, near Mantua, was the birth-place of Virgil, Comum that of the younger Pliny, Verona of Catullus, and Patavium of Livy. Ravenna was the residence of the emperors of the west when driven from Rome. The river Po is famous for the death of Phaeton, who, as the poets mention, was thrown down into it by the thunder-bolts of Jupiter.

Padusa, one of the mouths of the Po, was said to abound in swans. Rubicon was a mountain torrent, which it was forbidden to pass with an armed force, under dreadful imprecations. The inhabitants of Etruria were famous for their skill in augury, early civilization, and resolution, and were conquered by the Romans, only after much bloodshed.

Circeii was the residence of the fabled enchantress Circe. Tusculum was the villa of Cicero. Capua was celebrated for its wealth, voluptuousness, and soft climate. Near the promontory of Cumæ was the residence of the Sibyl. At Nola, east of Naples, bells were first invented. The eruption of Vesuvius, A. C. 79, overwhelmed the cities of Pompeii, Herculaneum, and Stabiæ, and destroyed the life of Pliny.

The city of Arpi was founded by Diomedes. Venusia was the birth-place of Horace. The country of Apulia was celebrated for its wool. Brundusium was the port for passing from Italy to Greece. Rudiæ was the birth-place of Ennius. Tarentum was founded by the Lacedæmonians.

Pæstum in Lucania was famous for its roses. On the coast was Metapontum, the school of Pythagoras. Thurium was also called Sybaris, from the effeminacy of its inhabitants. Petilia was built by Philoctetes, after the Trojan war.

Sicily was famous in antiquity for the birth of Ceres, the rape of Proserpine, the giant Enceladus, mount Ætna, and the Cyclops, with the whirlpool Charybdis, opposite to Scylla on the Italian coast, objects of terror to mariners. Sicily was the storehouse of Italy. Mount Eryx was celebrated for its temple of Venus. The plains of Enna, where Proserpine was carried away by Pluto, abounded in honey.

Lipara was famous for its fruits: its raisins are still in high repute. Vulcan had forges here. Sardinia was called by the Greeks, Ichnusa, from its resemblance to the print of a foot. It was famous for wormwood and bitter herbs, and its air was unwholesome. Corsica was celebrated for its box and yew trees. Urcinium, founded by a son of Ajax, is now Ajaccio, and celebrated in modern times as the birth-place of Napoleon Buonaparte.

62. *Capital of Italy, and Seat of the Roman Empire.* The great city of Italy and the Romans was Rome. Here

was the beginning of this celebrated people. The city was small and mean at first, but in the course of ages became magnificent beyond conception.

The city was built on seven hills, Mount Palatinus, Capitolinus, Quirilinus, Viminalis, Esquilinus, Cœlius, and Aventinus. The Palatine hill was the residence of the kings and emperors. On mount Capitolinus, were the Capitol and Tarpeian rock.

§ The seven hills on which Rome was built are not very distinctly marked, particularly now that the rubbish of so many ruined buildings has, in the course of more than 2500 years, filled up the spaces between them. In any place the ground is about 20 feet deep above the old pavement. The summit of the Capitoline hill is only about 120 feet above the level of the Tiber.

In the times of the republic were built the most magnificent aqueducts, which conveyed water from a vast distance for the service of the city, and some of which supply modern Rome; whilst the vast ruins of others excite wonder and astonishment. The Circus Maximus was of an oval shape, and afforded accommodation for 150,000 people to see the chariot races and other games.

The ruins of the theatres of Pompey and Marcellus still remain. The Coliseum, built by Vespasian and Titus, for shows of gladiators and wild beasts, was capable of containing 100,000 people, and its magnificent remains are still the most remarkable object at Rome.

The Pantheon or Temple of all the gods, was built by Agrippa, in the time of Augustus, and its solid construction promises it a duration for many centuries yet to come.

The columns of Trajan and Antoninus excite the admiration of all beholders. Baths of immense number and extent were made chiefly in the times of the emperors, and the ruins of those of Titus, and Caracalla, still remain. The vast tomb of Adrian is now the castle of St. Angelo. The catacombs are very extensive, but it is uncertain for what purpose they were used. Several vast tombs still remain, one of which was used as a fortress in the middle ages. The triumphal arches of Severus, Titus, and Constantine, still adorn the ancient Forum.

The extent of the walls is stated by Pliny to have been 13 miles 200 paces. A somewhat larger space was enclosed by Aurelian. The modern city encloses also within the walls, the Vatican hill. More than three fourths of the space within the walls are now covered with vineyards, and the modern city is built chiefly in the ancient Campus Martius. Every where are seen magnificent ruins. Egyptian obelisks, blocks of oriental granite, ancient and modern buildings, which still render Rome the most interesting city of the whole earth.

The principal public place in the city was the Forum.—This was a large open space of oblong shape, where the people held their assemblies, justice was administered, and public concerns were transacted. It was surrounded in its whole extent with arched porticoes.

which included spacious halls, where courts of justice sat and decided the affairs of individuals.

The Campus Martius was a large plain without the city, along the river Tiber, where the athletic exercises and sports of the Roman youth were practised. It was adorned with many noble structures, and monuments commemorating the deeds of their ancestors.

63. *Political State.* The political state, or government among the Romans, varied very much during the successive periods of their existence. At first it was a monarchy: next it became a republic with a preponderance of aristrocratic power, which gradually gave way to the influence of the people. A state almost of anarchy followed, which soon settled down into a despotism. That portion of history which we call ancient, includes and ends with the commencement of Roman despotism under Augustus.

The kings of Rome were not absolute or hereditary, but limited and elective. They could neither enact laws, nor make war or peace, without the concurrence of the senate and people.

§ They wore a golden crown, and carried an ivory sceptre. They sat in a curule chair, which was made or adorned with ivory, and they were attended with twelve lictors, carrying fasces, which were bundles of rods with an axe placed in the middle. They convened the senate, assembled the people, conducted the army, and appointed the quæstors or treasurers of the public money.

The Roman people were divided into four classes. 1. The Senate or Patrician order. 2. The Equestrian order or knights. 3. The Plebeians or mass of the people. 4. The Slaves.

The Senate was composed of 100 old men, and afterwards of 200 or more, who were the council of the king. By them most of the business of the state was transacted. They were called Patres, that is, Fathers. The Patrician families were descended from these fathers. They constituted not an hereditary nobility, but were accounted noble, because the members had filled high offices.

§ For some centuries, the senate consisted of 300 members, and in the time of Julius Cæsar, of 900. Augustus reduced the number to 600. They were first chosen by the kings, afterwards by the consuls, and last by the censors. They were distinguished by a particular dress, and had separate seats at the public spectacles.

In their official character, this body was usually assembled three times a month, but was frequently called together on other days for special business. A senatus consultum was a decree passed by a majority of the senate, and approved by the tribunes of the people.

The Knights were not originally a separate order, but consisted of such citizens as could maintain a horse for the wars. They seem to have become a separate order at some period under the kings, but afterwards the knights were chosen by the censors, and presented with a horse and a gold ring, at the public expense.

§ The knights farmed the public revenues. Every year on the 15th July, they went in procession from the Temple of Honour or of Mars, without the city, to the capitol, on horseback, bearing wreaths of olive in their hands. A certain property (3,229 pounds) was required as a qualification to be made a knight.

The Plebeians, or mass of the people, were the remainder of the Roman citizens after the Patricians and Equites or knights. They were called Plebs or Populus. Those who lived in the country were Plebs rustica, and were considered the most respectable. The Plebs urbana consisted chiefly of mechanics, or poorer citizens who followed no trade, and partly maintained themselves from the largesses of corn, &c., distributed among them.

§ The whole body of the people was at first divided into tribes three in number, and each tribe was subdivided in ten curiæ or wards. Other divisions were afterwards made. To the three tribes, Servius Tullius added a fourth. Augustus afterwards divided Rome into 14 wards.

Besides his addition of a fourth tribe, Servius made a division of the people into six classes, and each class into several centuries or portions of citizens, so called, because they were required to furnish, support and equip 100 men in war. These six classes were formed according to their property; the first composed of the richest citizens, and the 6th, which was the most numerous, of the poorest. The centuries amounted to 193.

The slaves constituted a large portion of the population of Rome. Their lives were at the disposal of their masters. They were not only employed in domestic services, but in various trades and manufactures. They were sometimes highly educated, and instructed in the liberal arts and professions, as that of physic.

§ They were considered as mere property, and publicly sold in a market-place—often chained by the leg. If capitally convicted, their punishment was crucifixion.

During the Saturnalia, or Feast of Saturn, slaves were allowed great freedom, and masters at that time would wait upon them at table; the same license was permitted on the Ides of August.

Slaves might be set free by various forms of law. Slaves thus emancipated had the names of Liberti and Libertini. Their children were not equally honourable with other citizens; but their grand-children were reckoned Ingenui, or in every respect on an equality with them.

With a view to connect together the different orders, it was provided by Romulus, that each plebeian should choose a patrician to be his patron, whose client the plebeian was called.

§ The patron was to protect his client, to give him his advice and forward his interest. The client was to be ready to assist his patron on all occasions. In elections, the clients exerted themselves on behalf of their patrons.

The Romans had usually three names, the Prænomen, Nomen, and Cognomen, as in Publius Cornelius Scipio.

§ Publius is the name of the individual, to distinguish him from another of the same family, as Caius Lucius, &c. Cornelius shows that he was of a certain family, the gens Cornelia; and Scipio, that he was of a division of the family, the Scipios being one out of many, into which the whole stock of the gens Cornelia was divided.

The Roman citizens were not merely the inhabitants of Rome and its environs, but the freedom of the city was granted to other parts of Italy, and afterwards to foreign cities and towns in the empire, whose inhabitants, by this means, enjoyed the same rights as the Romans.

The power of the people in Rome was expressed in their public assemblies. The name given to these assemblies, in their transactions, was Comitia. The Comitia were summoned by some magistrate, to pass laws, to elect magistrates, to decide concerning peace and war, and to try persons guilty of certain heinous offences.

§ There were three kinds of Comitia, the Curiata, the Centuriata, and the Tributa. The Comitia Curiata consisted of an assembly of the resident Roman citizens, who were divided into thirty curiæ, a majority of which decided all matters of importance that were laid before them.

The Comitia Centuriata were the principal assembly of the people. They elected Consuls, Prætors, Censors, and sometimes a Proconsul, also the Decemviri, the military Tribunes, and a priest called Rex Sacrorum. They gave their votes, divided into the centuries of their classes, according to the census. The place of their meeting was the Campus Martius, and all Roman citizens, though residing in the country, as well as city, had a right to act, in their several centuries.

The Comitia Tributa were an assembly of the people in which they voted, as they were separated into tribes, according to their wards. At these comitia were created subordinate magistrates, as Ædiles, Tribunes of the people, Quæstors, &c. The laws, called Plebiscita, were passed at these assemblies.

Persons who sought offices and preferment were called candidati, from a white garment which they wore. They canvassed the people and solicited their votes.

After the time of Augustus, the comitia fall into disuse. The formalities were observed, but these were soon after dropped, and the annual magistrates were either chosen by the senate or nominated by the emperors.

The Roman magistrates were elective, and divided into ordinary, extraordinary, and provincial. The ordinary magistrates, who were stated, and always in the republic, were the consuls, censors, tribunes, ædiles, and quæstors. The extraordinary, who were temporary magistrates, were the dictator, the decemvirs, the military tribunes, and the interrex. The provincial magistrates, who were appointed to the government of the provinces, were at first prætors, afterwards pro-consuls and pro-prætors, to whom were joined quæstors and lieutenants.

§ Consuls, after the banishment of the kings, were put in the room of the latter, to perform the duties of royalty. They were two in number, and held their office for one year. At first they had nearly the same badges of authority, except the crown. The eligible age to be made consul was forty-three, but extraordinary circumstances might justify an earlier age.

The Tribunes of the people were officers whose duty it was to guard and protect the plebeians in their rights, when the patricians became oppressive. Their power was contracted at first, but at length became very great. Unprincipled men in this office often converted the public assemblies into scenes of violence and blood.

The censors were appointed to take an account of the number and fortunes of the people. Their power at first was limited, but afterwards, became so great, that it was deemed the most honourable office in the state. There were two censors elected every five years, and they continued in office only one year and a half.

The Prætors, whose rank was next to that of the consuls, and whose place when vacant they supplied, were appointed to administer justice and convoke assemblies of the senate and people. They also presided at certain public games. There was at first but one prætor, but afterwards several.

The Pro-consuls and Pro-prætors usually governed the provinces of the empire. To them were joined quæstors and lieutenants. They had the highest rank within their province. The power of the pro-consuls and pro-prætors was much the same, the former being sent to the larger provinces.

The Ædiles were so named from their having a particular care of the ædes or buildings, as the temples, baths, aqueducts, theatres, &c. They were distinguished into Curule and Plebeian ædiles. The curule ædiles superintended the public games, and occupied a more honourable place in the senate than the plebeian ædiles, who were assistants to the tribunes

The Quæstors were appointed for the management of the public revenues. At first they were two in number, but afterwards, as the empire extended, they amounted to many. Two of them, the city quæstors, remained at Rome, and the rest, who were military and provincial quæstors, accompanied the army and provided for the payment of the soldiers, or attended the consuls or prætors into their provinces, and regulated the tribute.

The Dictators were magistrates, with absolute power, appointed on extraordinary occasions, or in cases of imminent danger. The term of their office was six months.

Their power was supreme in peace and war. They could raise and disband armies, and decide matters, without consulting the senate and people. The consuls submitted to their commands. As a check to their power, they were liable to be called to an account for the abuse of it, after it was resigned.

The Decemviri were ten men appointed, on particular occasions, to collect and promulgate laws, &c. They were chosen for one year, but had interest sufficient to be reappointed for another. They proposed the laws of the twelve tables.

The Military Tribunes had consular power in public affairs; they mediated between the patricians and plebeians, at a time when they could not agree in the election of consuls.

An interrex was appointed to hold the elections at Rome, when the consuls or dictators were absent.

64. *Religion.* The gods of the Romans were nearly the same as those of Greece. The priests of their religion did not form a distinct order of the state; but were selected from the most honourable citizens for that office. They were of two kinds—those that were common to all the gods; and those that were appointed to some one divinity in particular.

Of the former, the principal were the pontifices, the augures, the haruspices, the quindecem-viri, and septem-viri. These were all subordinate to the pontifex maximus, or high priest.

§ The pontifices were judges in sacred things, and prescribed what was to be done in cases where there was no law. The pontifex maximus was the supreme arbiter. The pontifices were 15 in number.

The augures, who were the same in number, were expected to predict future events, and to determine whether any action would be fortunate or not. They divined in various ways,—among others by the flight, chirping, or feeding of birds. They had great authority in the state, as nothing important in peace or war could be determined without them.

The haruspices were required to inspect the beasts offered in sacrifice, and by them to obtain omens with respect to the future.

The quindecem-viri were 15 officers who kept the sibylline books, in which was written the future history of Rome. These were said to have been procured from a woman of extraordinary appearance in the time of Tarquin the Proud, and were kept in a stone chest under the capitol. The quindecem-viri consulted these books in times of great calamity, to provide what should be done, and thus the popular fear was assuaged.

The septem-viri were seven priests who presided at sacred feasts, games, or processions.

As an instance of the kind of priests that were appropriated to particular deities, we may mention the Vestal Virgins. These were consecrated to the worship of Vesta.

§ The Vestal Virgins guarded perpetually the sacred fire of Vesta. They were obliged to observe strict chastity on pain of death. For ten years they learned the sacred rites, for ten years they performed them, and other ten years they spent in teaching others; and after that they might marry, if they could.

65. *Military Affairs.* The Romans were a nation of soldiers, and all their institutions had a tendency towards the encouragement of a military spirit. It was by discipline, skill, and valour, that they conquered the world.

It was the duty of every citizen to be a soldier, should his country call for his services, from the age of 17 to 46. Those affected by disease, or exercising public functions, were exempted. For 350 years from the building of Rome, no pay was allowed to those who served in the army.

§ No man could be appointed to any honourable magistracy, without having been ten years in the army. After Latium and the states of Italy were subdued or admitted into alliance, troops were raised among them in the same manner as at Rome.

About the time of Marius, a very great change took place in the mode of enlisting and supporting the armies. The infantry after that time, consisted of the poorer citizens, and mercenary soldiers from every part of Italy. The cavalry no longer consisted of Roman knights, but of horsemen, raised in Italy and in the provinces, serving for hire.

The Roman legion was a correct display of military arrangement and discipline. Each legion, when full, contained 6000 men divided into 10 cohorts or battalions, with other subdivisions. Each legion had a wing of 300 horse attached. It is to be noticed, however, that the numbers of the legion varied at different periods, from 3000 to 10,000 and 11,000.

The dependence of the Romans was on the strength of their infantry.

§ Their defensive arms consisted of a helmet, a shield four feet long and two broad, a coat of mail, and greaves for the thighs. Their weapons of assault were two long javelins or pila, and a sword.

The pilum was a long heavy spear, and a terrible weapon in the hand of a Roman. No defensive armour or covering could resist its force, when propelled so as to reach its object. Its length was about six feet, and its head consisted of a triangular point of steel 18 inches long. The distance from which it was commonly thrown, varied from ten to six yards. When the pila were discharged, the Roman soldiers rushed upon the enemy with their swords.

The Roman sword was a short two-edged blade of fine temper, adapted to the purpose of striking or thrusting. The latter was deemed the most efficacious.

The legions were usually drawn up in three lines. The first was called hastati, and consisted chiefly of young men. The second line was called principes, consisting of men of middle age; and the third line triarii, consisting of veterans of tried valour.

Besides these heavy armed legionaries, there were light-armed troops, who were chiefly employed in using slings, bows and arrows, and throwing light javelins. They advanced before the rest of the army, and annoyed the enemy as much as possible.

When the army approached the enemy, the light-armed troops discharged their arrows and slings, and as they drew nearer, threw their darts rapidly, and retreated through intervals between the ranks, or by the flanks, and rallied in the rear. The hastati then threw their long javelins, and commenced an attack with their swords.

When repulsed or fatigued, they retired leisurely into the ranks of the principes, or behind them, if necessary. The triarii were a body in reserve. If unable to drive back the enemy, a retreat was all that could be hoped for.

In besieging a town, the method of the Romans, and indeed of all ancient nations, differed much from that of the moderns, since the use of cannons, and was inferior to the latter.

The principal engines of attack among the Romans were the catapultæ, which discharged heavy stones; the balistæ, which discharged arrows, and the aries or battering ram, which was the most effective as applied against the wall.

§ The aries was a long beam, like the mast of a ship, armed at one end, with iron in the form of a ram's head. It was suspended in such a manner, that 100 men, who were frequently changed, by violently thrusting it back and forth, could break almost any wall, that it could be made to reach.

To protect the soldiers in this work, various contrivances were adopted, such as sheds called testudines, or tortoises, from their resemblance to the shell of that fish, and sheds called vineæ, constructed of wood and hurdles, and covered with earth and raw hides, so that they could not be set on fire.

The form of a Roman camp of two legions, was a square of nearly 700 yards on each side, with tents and quarters, laid out in the most regular order. A rampart of 12 feet high surrounded this square, and it was enclosed by a deep and broad ditch.

§ This was the effect of caution, an excellent feature of Roman discipline. No circumstances as to fatigue, or the absence of danger, could induce the legions of Rome to neglect a regular encampment. When their camps were to be left, nothing could exceed the celerity of their movements. Each soldier loading himself with his provisions and utensils, a weight of 60 pounds, besides his very heavy armour, would march by regular step, 20 miles in the space of six hours.

The Roman soldiers were among the best in the world. From the constant practice of athletic exercises, they were inured from infancy to hardiness and fatigue, and bred to that species of life which a soldier leads in actual warfare. Their bravery and knowledge in the art of war were not exceeded, if they were equalled, by any nation of antiquity.

The rewards of soldiers who had distinguished themselves were various kinds of crowns, ornaments of the persons and arms, and donations in money or lands. But the highest object of Roman ambition was the honour of a triumph. This was a grand, solemn procession through the city to the capitol, granted to the victorious general and his army by a decree of the senate, or by the people.

§ The procession which constituted a triumph, marched from the Campus Martius through the most public streets to the capitol. Musicians of various kinds led the way; oxen, with gilt horns and ribbons, intended for sacrifice, followed, with priests in their dresses of ceremony. Then the standards taken from the enemy, the arms, spoils, &c. were carried in procession. The captives followed in chains.

At length came the general in a robe of purple and gold, with a crown of laurel on his head, and other personal brilliant decorations. He stood in a gilded chariot adorned with ivory, drawn by four milk-white horses. His friends and relations accompanied him, and the principal officers were on horseback beside his chariot. His victorious army, crowned with laurel, and singing songs of victory, came last.

An ovation was a triumph also, but accompanied with less splendour.

66. *Fleets.* The Roman ships were extremely small compared with modern vessels. They were quickly constructed and quickly manned. Sailors and rowers were hired to navigate. Soldiers were put on board to fight.

§ The success of the Romans at sea was owing rather to the valour of their men, than to their skill as mariners. Their object in sea-battles, was to approach the enemy as quickly as possible, fasten the ships together, and fight hand to hand.

Until the first Punic war, the Romans were wholly ignorant of the naval military art. A Carthaginian galley was the first model. So little skill was required in building their ships, that we find them on one occasion, fitting out, and sending to sea, a fleet within 45 days after the trees were cut down.

The size of the ships was reckoned by the number of banks of oars, placed in benches on the sides of the ship, called triremes, quadriremes, &c.

67. *Agriculture.* In the earliest and best ages of their existence, the Roman people were much given to agriculture. Except that they were frequently interrupted by war, they might be considered as an agricultural people. They were at once soldiers and farmers.

Many of them residing out of the city, and yet denizens of Rome, were called from the plough to the army. This was the case with several of their most distinguished men and generals, as Q. Cincinnatus, M. Curius, Cato the Censor, and Scipio Africanus.

The pursuits of agriculture were however abandoned, after the acquisition of wealth by foreign conquests and commerce. Menials and slaves tilled the ground, and the people abandoned themselves to every species of luxury and sensuality.

§ The attention of the early Romans to husbandry was partly the effect of necessity. The lands having been divided into equal and minute portions, each one was obliged to labour for a subsistence.

The greater number of the farmers visited the city only on every ninth day, which was the market day. They went there for the purposes of barter, the procuring of necessaries, and the examination of the new laws which were posted on the capitol and in the market-place, some days previously to their adoption by the people.

We may obtain a better conception of the agricultural turn of this people, from knowing a few of their common maxims on this subject, than from any description. Those maxims were such as the following:

1. He is a thriftless farmer that buys any thing which his farm can produce.
2. He is no husbandman who does any work in the day time, that can be done in the night, except in stormy weather.
3. He is worse who does on work days, what he may do on holydays; and
4. He is the worst of all who in a clear sky works within doors, rather than in the field.

68. *Amusements and Public Spectacles.* The drama, though the government was long unfriendly to it, became an amusement of the Roman people. Comedies were the most popular, and very few Roman tragedies remain.

On the stage, pantomimes were much in use, and rope dancers occasionally diversified the entertainment.

§ Rude plays, made up with music, dancing, and buffoonery, were in use in the earlier periods of the republic; but the first regular play was written by Livius Andronicus, in the year of the city 512.

The comic actors wore a low-heeled shoe called soccus; the tragic actors wore a mask, a flowing robe, and a high-heeled shoe called cothurnus. Only temporary theatres were used at first.

The senate correctly judging that theatrical amusements were injurious to the public morals, so late as the year of the city 599, ordered a theatre, building under the direction of the censors, to be pulled down. Pompey the Great, was the first who built a theatre of hewn stone, and the remains of this vast edifice still continue, and are used by the present Romans for the baiting of bulls.

There were various public games, connected however with the religion of the Romans, which were sources of much licentious entertainment. Those of the Circus Maximus were most frequented. The shows exhibited in that place were chariot and horse-races; contests of strength and agility; mock-fights on horseback; combats of wild beasts, and of men with wild beasts; representations of horse and foot battles; and mimic naval fights.

§ The ferocious taste of the Romans was much gratified with the combats of wild beasts, and of men with the latter. Criminals were condemned to fight with wild beasts; others did so for hire, or from native ferocity of character.

For the amusement of the people, lions, leopards, bears, elephants, and all kinds of wild beasts, were sent from Africa and the provinces. Pompey, on one occasion, treated the people with the spectacle of 500 lions, which were despatched in five days.

The gladiatorial shows, however, had superior attractions for the Romans. It is painful to observe this most distinguished people finding their chief pleasure in the combats. wounds, and death of multitudes of their fellow-creatures. Yet not only the populace, but the knights, senators, and Roman ladies of distinction, eagerly crowded to the sight.

§ The first gladiatorial shows were exhibited about the year of the city 490, by two brothers called Bruti, at the funeral of their father. Afterwards they were exhibited by the magistrates at regular periods, and at length they became the chief means of obtaining favour with the people. They were not entirely abolished till the reign of Theodosius the Great.

Incredible numbers of captives, &c. were destroyed on these occasions. Trajan exhibited games for 123 days, when 10,000 wild beasts were killed, and 10,000 gladiators fought. During the reign of Claudius was exhibited the spectacle of 19,000 men slaughtering one another on a certain lake, for the amusement of the Roman populace.

Gladiators consisted chiefly of slaves, captives, and condemned malefactors; but sometimes free-born citizens became gladiators for hire. Even persons of noble birth were induced to display their skill and courage before the people, in these combats.

There were various sorts of armour, and various modes of fighting. One mode was the use of the net. With that a gladiator would entangle his opponent, by casting it over his head; and suddenly drawing it together, could despatch him with his dart. If he missed his aim, he betook himself to flight, preparing his net for a second cast, while his opponent in the pursuit endeavoured to despatch him, before he could have an opportunity.

Amphitheatres were erected for the convenience of the spectators. The most celebrated was the Coliseum already mentioned. Large coverings were drawn over the amphitheatres, as a screen from the heat of the sun, or from rain.

69. *Education.* The system of education among the Romans, when in their most intellectual state, that is, about the time of Cicero, was much to be admired. The utmost attention was bestowed on the early formation of the mind and character.

The Roman matrons themselves nursed their children. Next to the care bestowed upon their morals, a remarkable degree of attention seems to have been given to the language of children. The attainment of a pure and correct expression was a great object. The honours of the state were the prize of eloquence. The politeness which characterized the Romans shewed itself particularly in their speech and gesture.

§ The education of the Romans at first suited their rude state of society and their simple manner of life. But upon their intercourse with the Greeks, a more liberal form of education was adopted. Public schools were opened for the reception of youth of both sexes. In literature and the accomplishments of polished life they were alike instructed.

From the earliest dawn of reason a course of discipline was pursued by some matron of the family; and as children grew towards manhood, they were habituated to all the athletic exercises that could impart agility or grace, and fit them for the profession of arms.

At the age of 17 they were invested with the manly robe, and young men of family were placed under the protection of some senator of distinguished reputation in jurisprudence. Although he was not considered a preceptor, yet under his auspices they were initiated into public business.

Eloquence and the military art were the surest roads to preferment. These accordingly were made commanding objects of pursuit with the Roman youth. Eloquence was taught as a science at public schools.

From the care which the Romans bestowed upon the education of their youth, both male and female, arose the large number of great men and eminent women which Rome has produced, and the virtues with which they were adorned, during the brilliant era of the republic. Happy, could their history be closed at that epoch; but the tide of luxury afterwards swept away the most valuable of their institutions.

70. *Literature.* Previously to their intercourse with Greece, the Romans, though a sensible and energetic, were a rude and illiterate people. Their language for a long tim was in a very imperfect state. The very few fragments of sentences which have come down to us from an early period, such as are found in the "Fratres Arvales," and "Leges Regiæ," show a great difference between the language then in use, and that which was employed during the age of Augustus.

After successive improvements, the Romans became renowned in literature during the last named period. The master-pieces of Greece, kindled the fire of emulation. Roman literature, in the Augustan era, was inferior to that of the Greeks, only because it was necessarily less original and more imitative than theirs. In some respects the Romans improved upon their models. Poetry, history, oratory, philosophy, and the various kinds of fine writing, were cultivated with great success.

§ The dawning of Roman literature appeared in the writings of Livius Andronicus, Plautus, Ennius, Cæcilius, and Terence. These writers improved and polished the language, partly by original compositions, and partly by translations from the Greek.

Poetry among the Romans, as with most other nations, appears to have been the earliest intellectual effort. Of this we have an instance in the Fescennine verses, mentioned by Livy, which are supposed to have been a rude poetical dialogue. This doubtless proved to be the germ of the stage. Other species of poetry naturally followed.

§ The names that adorned the Roman drama were Livius Andronicus; Ennius, who more especially improved it; Plautus, who wrote with strength and spirit; Cæcilius, who is reckoned the best of the Roman dramatists; Terence, who excels in simplicity and purity; Accius, and Pacuvius, who though rough in style shewed strength of genius. All these except the two last were comic writers.

The lyric poetry of the Romans owns the names of Catullus, the earliest in this kind of poetry; and Horace, the greatest among the Romans, if not of antiquity, though he is highly to be censured on account of his occasional indelicacy.

In elegiac poetry, Propertius, and Tibullus poured their tender and elegant strains, and Ovid uttered the language of nature and passion. The two last especially offend on the score of morals.

Of satiric poetry, Lucillius is said to be the inventor: Horace also excelled in this species of poetic composition. Some other names among the Romans, are distinguished as satirists, but they belong to a subsequent era.

In didactic poetry, Lucretius is a great name; and of epic poetry Virgil is prince among the Romans. Homer among the Greeks, and Virgil among the Romans, have come down to us with almost equal renown.

History was cultivated by the Romans with much success, particularly during the Augustan age.

§ The most eminent of their historians were Sallust, who excelled in the philosophy of history; Cæsar, who wrote with purity and simplicity; but especially Livy, whose judgment, perspicuity, copiousness, and eloquence, place him at the head of Roman historical writers.

Oratory was a favourite study at Rome, as it led to the highest honours of the state. The most distinguished senators are said to have exercised their talents in public speaking, in behalf of the poor and oppressed. The characteristics of Roman eloquence were seriousness, copiousness, and majesty.

§ J. Cæsar, Hortensius, and particularly Cicero, distinguished themselves as public speakers. Of Cæsar it is said that "he spoke with the same force with which he fought." Hortensius was eclipsed only by Cicero. And Cicero is the rival of Demosthenes in fame.

Philosophy made its first appearance at Rome, in the interval between the war with Perseus, and the third Punic war. It was derived from Greece. The various systems of the Greek philosophy, had their respective partisans at Rome.

§ A few learned Achæans, banished from their country, and arriving at Italy, diffused a taste for philosophy, polite learning, and the education of youth. Fearing foreign manners with foreign studies, the senate banished the Greek philosophers from Rome. But the Athenian embassy arriving soon after, brought thither Carneades and Critolaus, who revived the taste for the Greek philosophy.

The system of the Stoics was at first more generally received, as this comported with the national character. Among the Roman stoics, were Scipio, Lælius, and the younger Cato.

The philosophy of Aristotle was little known in Rome till the time of Cicero. Cratippus and Tyrannion then taught his system with great reputation.

The Old and New Academy had each its advocates and disciples Marcus Brutus, and Terentius Varro, were ornaments of the former. Of the New Academy, Cicero must be considered as the principal supporter, though his design seems to have been rather to illustrate the Greek philosophy in general. He was the greatest of the Roman philosophers, if not on the whole the greatest man of all antiquity.

With the introduction of luxury, the philosophy of Epicurus became fashionable. The poet Horace was a devotee to this system, as also Lucretius, and many others, who very liberally indulged their appetites, and taught others to indulge them.

Physics, or natural philosophy, seems to have been little cultivated by the Romans or by the Greeks before them. Varro is the only name conspicuous in this department, in the annals of antiquity.

In some instances, splendid libraries were attached to the galleries of some affluent patricians, who patronized learning. These libraries were open to the inspection of the learned and curious, and contributed greatly to the advancement of knowledge at Rome.

§ Among these, the library of Lucullus was remarkable, not only for the number and variety of the books, and specimens of art, but for the liberal use to which it was devoted.

71. *Arts.* The Romans are not to be compared with the Greeks, as to native taste and inventive genius, as the fine arts are concerned. They admired and imitated the master-pieces of Greece. But in execution, for the most part, they fell short of their models. By help derived from Grecian genius, they have, however, left many wonderful specimens in the arts, particularly in architecture.

§ Their conquest of Greece secured to them as spoils the noble productions of Greece in painting and statuary. With these the wealthy Roman citizens adorned the city, its temples, and porticoes, and their own private dwellings.

The names of few Roman artists occur. Vitruvius wrote the only book on architecture that is now extant. He shews that he was a master of his profession. In great and magnificent works, Rome has manifested her unbounded wealth and luxury.

In the mechanic arts some inventions occur, and a degree of perfection was attained among the Romans of ancient history. These however have been greatly extended and improved in more recent ages; and many comforts which we enjoy, derived from a knowledge of mechanism, were unknown to this people.

§ Such conveniences as glass windows and chimneys in houses, not to mention many others, the Romans did not possess; though their ingenuity supplied the want, in part, by various expedients.

72. *Domestic Life and Manners.* The houses and furniture of the early Romans were entirely plain in their con-

struction. When luxury commenced in Rome, this plainness was laid aside, and the decorations of art were assumed in a degree. At this latter period, and before luxury reached its utmost bounds, each house contained one spacious hall, in which the family assembled, and which served all the purposes of society.

§ Towards the close of the republic, however, various apartments were constructed for the reception and entertainment of company, and in the time of the emperors, their embellishment was carried to the highest point of perfection. The eating rooms were remarkable for their grandeur.

The tables were originally made of ordinary wood, square, and on four feet; but the form was afterwards changed to circular, or oval, supported on a single carved pedestal, and they were richly inlaid with ivory, gold, or silver, sometimes with the addition of precious stones.

We read of a single table formed of a kind of wood, called citron wood, with which we are unacquainted, that cost upwards of eight thousand pounds sterling. A canopy was suspended over the table, to guard it, as it is said, from dirt of the ceiling. This, however it may have added to the decoration of the apartments, does not convey a very favourable idea of the cleanliness of the Romans.

Originally, the Roman villa was nothing more than a farm-house of a very humble description; but at length the word lost its original signification, and was used to denote the abode of luxury and opulence. We have fortunately a complete and beautiful description of one, and that his own, in the works of Pliny the younger. They were very numerous about Rome, and very magnificent.

The meals of the earlier Romans were very simple and frugal. The articles of food, and the furniture of the table, were coarse. But afterwards they became costly and luxurious to the highest degree. The epicurism of the later Romans was enormous.

At first they sat upright on benches, but at last adopted the habit of reposing on couches. Their principal meal was their supper, taken a little before four o'clock, P. M. Their breakfast was not a regular meal; it was taken by each one separately and without order; and their dinner was a very slight repast. Their supper was their last regular meal, though it was sometimes followed by a collation, called commissatio.

§ The diet of the earlier Romans consisted of milk and vegetables, with a coarse kind of pudding which served in the room of bread. They rarely indulged in meat, and wine was almost unknown to them. They banished epicures from among them.

The change which took place in the latter days of the republic and in the beginning of the empire, was very striking. Notwithstanding sumptuary laws, epicurism advanced with great rapidity, till finally it reached such a height, that viands were esteemed only in proportion to their cost.

Thus, Maltese cranes, peacocks, and rare singing birds, although hardly eatable, were esteemed great delicacies, and their tongues and brains still greater; oysters from the coast of Britain were more prized than their own, though the former would never have been eaten fresh; and we are told of a singular sur-mullet, which had reached a size somewhat larger than common, having been sold for a sum equivalent to fifty guineas.

The Romans used wine of the most costly kinds at their feasts. The age of it was often very great. We read of some that was 200 years old. The Grecian wines were in greater estimation than even the Italian. They used also mead, metheglin, and other fermented liquors. Such was their depravity, they contrived that even water should contribute to inebriate them.

Gluttony was indulged to such a disgusting excess, that emetics were used to enable the stomach, already gorged with a full meal, to bear a further load. This doubtless was not a universal practice, neither, however, was it confined to a few individual instances.

The services of the tables were at first only of earthen-ware, or wood. The use of plate was then almost unknown. At a later period plate became so general, that it was as common, as it had been previously rare, and in the time of the emperors, it was frequently of gold.

The couches on which they lay down at supper were somewhat similar to the modern sofa. The ladies at first did not adopt this practice, and the indulgence was never extended to young people of either sex.

Each couch could accommodate three or four, but seldom five persons, who laid in a reclining posture, on the left arm, having the shoulders elevated with cushions, and the limbs extended behind whoever was next; so that the head of the one was opposite to the breast of the other, and in serving themselves, they made use only of the right hand. There were many other singular customs observed at their suppers, which we have not time to enumerate.

Daily Bathing was practised by the Roman people, both in warm and cold water. Vast quantities of water were brought to Rome, for this and other purposes, by means of aqueducts. These aqueducts were magnificent works, as also the baths both public and private which were erected.

§ The use of linen, which was unknown to the Romans, has rendered this practice for a long time obsolete in Italy; but in the times of which we speak, it was necessary for the purposes of cleanliness as well as luxury. The remains of some of the baths, are the most astonishing works of Roman grandeur and magnificence.

Bathing commenced with warm and ended with cold water. On

leaving the bath the people were anointed with scented oils, and went immediately to supper.

The Dress of the Romans consisted chiefly of the toga and the tunica. The toga or gown worn by the citizens only, was loose and flowing, and covered the whole body: it was made of wool, had no sleeves, and was disposed in graceful folds, with a view to improve the appearance of the wearer.

The toga virilis, or manly gown, was assumed by young men at the age of seventeen.

The tunica or tunic, was a white woollen vest, which came down a little below the knees before, and to the middle of the leg behind, and was fastened about the waist by a girdle, which also served as a purse.

§ Women wore a tunic as well as the men, but with this difference, at first, that it reached down to the feet of the women, and had sleeves. Afterwards the men wore the tunic in the same manner.

Hats and Caps, though known, were worn only on journeys or at the public games. In the city they usually went bare headed, or covered themselves with the corner of the toga.

Ladies of distinction had many waiting maids, who were appropriated to particular services; and the duties of the toilet, though not perhaps so well understood as in modern times, were as assiduously attended to.

Jewels, bracelets, rings, and various expensive ornaments, were worn in great profusion. The convenience of pins was not known, nor were glass mirrors, though there were substitutes for them. Pure woven silk and linen were little known and used till the time of the emperors, and not at all known during nearly the whole period of the republic.

Marriage was an institution highly countenanced among the Romans. Severe laws were at times enacted to restrain celibacy, though never with much effect. Fathers of large families were particularly respected. Marriages with foreigners were strictly forbidden. The validity of the transaction depended on the legal age of the parties, and the consent of parents.

§ Boys were considered marriageable at fourteen; girls at twelve. A marriage was never solemnized without consulting the auspices, and offering sacrifices to the gods; particularly to Juno; and the animals immolated on the occasion, were deprived of their gall, in allusion to the absence of every thing bitter and malignant in the proposed union. The mode of marriage and the multitude of ceremonies attending it cannot here be described.

Marriage, among the Romans, was not indissoluble. A husband might repudiate his wife for several reasons, besides that of having violated her conjugal faith. But to the honour of the Romans, more than four centuries elapsed without any suit among them for divorce, or complaint of adultery. Afterwards divorces became very frequent, and for the most frivolous causes.

Fathers at Rome were generally invested with the power of life and death over their children. Exposure of infants was at first somewhat frequent, but at length nearly ceased. The adoption of children by married persons who were childless was very common, on account of the privileges connected with having children, whether by issue or adoption.

The funeral rites of the Romans were solemn and impressive. During the greater part of the commonwealth, the dead body was buried. Towards the close, the practice of burning the dead was generally introduced, till it became universal. After the introduction of Christianity into the empire, it fell into disuse.

§ It was a received opinion among the ancients, that the manes of the deceased were propitiated by blood. It was on this account their custom to slaughter, on the tomb of the deceased, those animals to which, while he was living, he was most attached; and in the more barbarous ages, men were the victims of this horrid superstition.

> "Arms, trappings, horses, by the hearse were led
> In long array—the achievements of the dead.
> Then pinion'd, with their hands behind, appear
> The unhappy captives, marching in the rear,
> Appointed offerings in the victor's name,
> To sprinkle with their blood, the funeral flame."
>
> *Dryden's Virgil.*

Many of the Roman sepulchres still exist in the gardens of their villas or by the public roads, (for inhumation was not allowed within the walls,) with their various monumental inscriptions.

72½ *Foreign Commerce.* The foreign commerce of the Romans appears very unimportant, compared with the extensive mercantile transactions of our own times. Their trade, if we except the corn received on account of government from Sicily and the Levant, consisted of little else, than articles of mere luxury. Their purchases were made in bullion, as they had no exportable manufactures of their own. This circumstance necessarily restricted their commercial dealings.

§ They traded, it is true, not only to the ports of the Mediterranean, but to the East Indies, and occasionally even to England; but the interests of commerce were little understood, and less appreciated. Traffic was dishonourable, and they who engaged in it were held in contempt. The consequence was, that it was relinquished to slaves and freemen, who seldom possessed the means to conduct it on an extensive scale.

Their merchant ships were large, if they reached the burthen of fifty tons.

Syria.

73. *Situation and Cities.* Syria lay on the east coast of the Mediterranean below Cilicia. The coast was called Phœnicia, and below it was Palestine. On the south it had Arabia and the Euphrates.

Its towns and noticeable places were Antioch, Daphne, Seleucia, Damascus, Heliopolis, and Palmyra, or Tadmor.

Antioch at one time, was inferior only to Rome and Alexandria in greatness and population. It is now almost depopulated, though its strong walls on both sides of the Orontes, remain.

Daphne was a place consecrated to luxury, and enchanting from its cool fountains and shady groves of laurel, cypress, &c. Milton compares the garden of Eden to it—

—"Nor that sweet grove
"Of Daphne by Orontes."—

Seleucia was on the sea near the mouth of the Orontes.—The bard again speaks of

"The royal towers
Of great Seleucia, built by Grecian kings."

Damascus was the capital of the Phœnicia of Libanus. Its fertile and irriguous valley has ever been famous among the orientals.

Heliopolis, under the name of Baalbeck, has the remains of a magnificent temple dedicated to the sun. The whole edifice, and particularly the roof, glittered with gold.

Palmyra gave the name of Palmyrene to a vast plain, which was united to the desert of Arabia. The bible and Josephus inform us it was founded by Solomon. It maintained a great commerce between two divisions of the ancient hemisphere. The remains of lofty edifices manifest its former magnificence, and attract the curious and astonished traveller.

74. *Character of the ancient Syrians.* The ancient Syrians were miserable idolaters.

An instance of their worship is thus described by the poet before named.

———"Tammuz came next behind,
Whose annual wound in Lebanon allur'd
The Syrian damsels to lament his fate,
In am'rous ditties all a summer's day:
While smooth Adonis from his native rock
Ran purple to the sea, supposed with blood
Of Tammuz yearly wounded."

They were also somewhat of an effeminate race, and remarkable for hiding themselves from the sun, in caves, on the decease of their relatives.

75. *Language.* The Syrian language became a distinct tongue, so early as the time of Jacob. It was spoken not only in Syria, but also in Mesopotamia, Chaldæa, and Assy-

ria. After the Babylonish captivity, it was introduced into Palestine.

§ The Syriac is an easy and elegant, though not a very copious tongue. It abounds in many Greek words.

Carthage.

76. *Extent.* Carthage has been briefly described in the body of this work. It may only be stated here that with its ports, it comprehended an enclosure of 23 miles. It had a cita del named Byrsa, on an eminence.

§ Its military prowess was at its height, under Hamilcar and Hannibal. The city was destroyed by the second Scipio, B. C. 147. It then burned incessantly during 17 days. It was rebuilt by Roman colonies. Its decay may be traced from the seventh century, when it fell into the hands of the Saracens.

77. *Government and Character of the People.* The Carthaginians were governed as a republic, and had two persons yearly chosen among them with regal authority. They were very superstitious as a people, and generally offered human victims to their gods. They also bore the character of being faithless and treacherous, and the proverb, Punic faith, is well known.

Parthia.

78. *Situation, &c.* Parthia had Hyrcania on the north; Aria on the east; Carmania on the south; and Media on the west. It was a healthy country, but sterile. The people were governed by an absolute monarch.

§ The ancient Parthians were originally a tribe of Scythians, who being expelled from their native land, took up their abode in this part of Asia. They were a strong and warlike people, and accustomed from their infancy to the exercises of horsemanship and archery.

The peculiar custom of discharging their arrows while they were retiring full speed, has been greatly celebrated by the ancients. Their flight was more formidable than their attack.

They totally neglected agriculture, trade and navigation, and their morals were dreadfully depraved. Their religious principles were much the same as those of the Persians. Their sovereigns affected to be gods.

Persia.

79. *Extent and Situation.* Ancient Persia extended about 2800 miles in length from the Hellespont to the mouth of the river Indus; and about 2000 miles in breadth, from Pontus to the mouth of the Arabian gulf.

80. *Government.* The government of Persia was an ab-

solute monarchy. The crown was hereditary, and generally bestowed on the eldest of the deceased king's legitimate children.

§ The kings of Persia received almost divine honours from their subjects. No one could approach the seat of majesty without prostrating himself, or remain in the presence, without holding his hands within his sleeves. Death was the consequence of violating this ceremony.

Herodotus mentions that Xerxes being once in great danger by sea, many of his attendants strove who should first leap overboard to lighten the vessel, and sacrifice themselves for the preservation of their prince.

The royal palace at Persepolis was extremely magnificent. The roofs and sides of the apartments were entirely covered with ivory, silver, gold, or amber. The throne was of fine gold and adorned with precious stones. The royal bed was also of gold, and two coffers were placed by it, both containing 8,000 talents.

The Persian monarchs, for the most part, lived only to gratify their sensual appetites. All the delicacies and rarities of the world were sought for their table. Cicero informs us, that the revenues of whole provinces were lavished on the attire of their favorite concubines, one city being compelled to supply them with ornaments for their hair, another for their necks, &c.

81. *Education.* The Persians are said to have paid more particular regard to the education of their children, than any other nation. A son was never admitted into the presence of his father, till he had arrived at the age of five years, lest, if he should die before that period, his parents might be too heavily afflicted by his loss.

§ At the age of five, learned masters taught the children of the better families, in learning and moral virtues, taking with them the utmost pains, and bestowing upon them the greatest care.

82. *Punishments.* The punishments in general were severe, as cutting off the right hand, decapitation, pressing to death between two large stones, &c.

§ The most severe punishment known in Persia, was the inhuman one of fastening the culprit between two boats, in such a manner that he was unable to move, though his head, hands and feet were left uncovered. His face, exposed to the rays of the sun, was smeared with honey, which invited innumerable swarms of flies and wasps to torment him, while the worms that bred in his excrements devoured his bowels; and the executioners compelled him, by thrusting sharp iron instrument into his eyes, to receive nourishment for the express purpose of prolonging his excruciating agonies. One victim is recorded to have lived 17 days under this complication of torments.

83. *Military Art.* The Persians were all trained to military exercise, but more particularly to the use of the bow.

They never fought in the night, nor used any stratagem independent of their own valour.

§ When they designed to make war upon any nation, they had the singular custom of sending heralds to demand of them earth and water, thereby commanding them to acknowledge the king of Persia, as sovereign lord of their country.

84. *Religion.* Their religion was in a degree idolatrous, though less so than that of the nations around them. They professed to worship the one all-wise and omnipotent God though they held fire to be holy, and the purest symbol of the divine nature. In connexion with this, they had a superstitious regard of the sun. They honoured also other elements, as the earth, the air, and water.

§ The Persians are supposed to have been originally instructed in the worship of the true God by their progenitor Elam, but soon to have fallen into the heresy of Zabiism. From this they are thought to have been recovered, and to have afterwards engaged in superstitious acts of reverence to the celestial bodies.

In ancient times, they were destitute of temples, but erected altars for the preservation of their sacred fires, on the tops of mountains. At length Zoroaster persuaded them, for the sake of convenience, to build over each, a pyreum or fire-temple. This Zoroaster is supposed by some to have been a native of Persia, and a restorer of the religion of the Magi.

MYTHOLOGY OF ANCIENT NATIONS.

1. All the nations of antiquity, except the Jews, were heathens and idolaters. Their system of religion was called Polytheism, as acknowledging a plurality of gods. They worshipped divinities by various representations, called idols. Forsaking the service of the only living and true God, as made known at first by traditionary, and afterwards by written revelation, they paid that homage which is due to him, to those that are by nature no God.

2. Besides angels, as presiding over particular kingdoms,—the heavenly bodies, men, beasts, birds, fishes, virtues, vices, diseases, and evil demons, were esteemed deities, and had temples built for their worship.

Among the Egyptians, the principal deities were Osiris and Isis, supposed to be the sun and moon. The people however bestowed divine honours on animals, birds, insects, and even vegetables, as leeks and onions. The poet Juvenal intimates that their religious exercises were not greatly esteemed by the Romans. In fact, they exceeded all the other ancients in these absurdities, and were extremely debased by their vile superstitions.

The Babylonians and Arabians adored the heavenly bodies. They supposed that the angels resided in the stars, and governed the world under the supreme deity. Among the later Babylonians, Belus became their Jupiter, to whom a magnificent temple was erected in Babylon.

The Canaanites and Syrians worshipped Baal, Tammuz, Magog, and Astarte. Moloch was the Saturn of the Phœnicians and Carthaginians. To him, human victims, particularly children, were immolated. Baal-peor was the idol of the Moabites—his rights were detestable and cruel. Dagon was the chief god of the Philistines; his figure was compounded of a man and a fish.

In the mythology of the Scythians, the god of war was their favourite divinity, and to him were consecrated groves of oaks of extraordinary size. Horses were sacrificed, and every hundredth man taken in battle.

In the mythology of the Celts, the Druids had the direction of theological concerns. Their rites were performed in groves, and they paid superstitious reverence to the misletoe. Human victims were often offered; colossal images of wicker-work, filled with human criminals, were consumed by fire.

The Persians in their religion rejected, for the most part, the complicated popular system of polytheism. They believed in one supreme God who formed and governed all things. They, however, preserved the sacred fire, as it was called, which was kindled by con secrated sun-beams. Their rites at first were plain and simple, and their priests were called magi. These tenets of their primitive reli gion gradually degenerated into Zabiism, or the adoration of celestial bodies.

The mythology of the ancient Hindoos resembles, in some of its features, that of the Egyptians, Persians, and Scythians. It is a strange mixture of a few truths with many wild fables. It divides the world into ten parts, setting over each a guardian spirit. The deity Brahma is made the creating power, Vishnu is the preserver and pervader, and Narayda, the mover on the waters.

3. The multitude of gods as an object of faith, is preposterous and wicked; but the elegant forms and agreeable fictions that mythology furnishes, are admirably adapted to the purposes of poetry, statuary, and painting. The imagination revels in a region fairy and enchanting.

§ The theology of Pagan antiquity, according to Scævola and Varro, was of three sorts. The first of these may well be called fabulous, as treating of the theology and genealogy of their deities, in which they relate such things as are infinitely unworthy of the divinity, ascribing to them, thefts, murders, adulteries, and all manner of crimes.

This kind of theology is condemned by the wiser sort of heathens as trifling and scandalous. The writers of this sort of theology were Sanchoniathon the Phœnician; and Orpheus, Hesiod, Pherecydes, &c., among the Greeks.

The second kind called physic or natural, was studied and taught by the philosophers, who rejecting the multiplicity of gods introduced by the poets, brought their theology to a more natural and rational form. They supposed that there was but one supreme God, which they commonly make to be the sun, at least an emblem of him; but at too great a distance to mind the affairs of the world, and therefore devised certain demons, which they considered as mediators between the supreme God and man.

The speculations of the philosophers related to the doctrines of these demons, to their nature, their office, and regard to men. Writers of this class were Thales, Pythagoras, Plato, and the Stoics.

The third kind of theology called politic or civil, was instituted by legislators, statesmen, and politicians. The first among the Romans was Numa Pompilius. This part of the Pagan system chiefly respected their gods, temples, altars, sacrifices, and rites of worship, and was properly their idolatry, the care of which belonged to the priests. The whole was enjoined on the common people, to keep them in obedience to the civil state.

4. In the fictions of mythology, particularly those of Greece and Rome, many things are allegorical and mystical, the true sense of which, though not accommodated to the vulgar apprehension, the refined and liberal may explain. This suggests one use to be derived from the study of the Pagan systems of religion. We learn the religious views of antiquity.

Another use of it is, that the classic authors cannot be read with advantage without a knowledge of mythology; and the classic authors, it is not to be doubted, are the best models of fine writing extant, and are necessary to improve the taste. Connected with this also is the fact, that a knowledge of mythology can alone enable us to understand and become acquainted with antique statues, medals, paintings, &c.

§ The gods of ancient paganism were some mundane, and others supermundane. The mundane are those who were supposed to fabricate the world, and the supermundane are those who produce essences, intellects, and souls. Hence they are distinguished into three orders. Of the mundane gods likewise, some are the causes of the existence of the world; others animate it; others again harmonize it, thus composed of different natures; and lastly, others guard and preserve it when harmoniously arranged.

Since also these orders are four, and each consists of things first, middle, and last, it is necessary that the governors of these should be twelve. Hence Jupiter, Neptune and Vulcan fabricate the world. Ceres, Juno and Diana animate it; Mercury, Venus and Apollo harmonize it; and lastly, Vesta, Minerva and Mars preside over it with a guardian power.

But the truth of this may be seen in statues as in enigmas. For Apollo in marble holds in his hands a lyre; Minerva is invested with arms; and Venus is naked, since harmony produces beauty, and beauty is not concealed in subjects of sensible perception.

As these gods primarily possess the world, it is necessary to consider the other mundane gods as subsisting in them, as Bacchus in Jupiter, Æsculapius in Apollo, and the Graces in Venus. We may also behold the spheres with which they are connected, viz. Vesta with the earth, Neptune with water, Juno with air, and Vulcan with fire. But Apollo and Diana are assumed for the sun and moon; the sphere of Saturn is attributed to Ceres; ether to Minerva; and heaven is common to them all.

The above are a few instances of the real sense of the fictions of mythology. Many of the philosophers in these fictions concealed their better knowledge, often conveying lessons of wisdom under the veil of allegory. The genuine Pagan creed, as given by a heathen philosopher, Maximus Tyrius, is the following:

"There is one God, the king and father of all things, and many gods, sons of God, ruling together with him. This the Greek says, and the barbarian says, the inhabitant of the continent, and he that dwells near the sea; and if you even proceed to the utmost shores of the ocean, there too there are gods, rising very near to some, and setting very near to others." By the rising and setting gods he means the stars, which according to the Pagan theology, are divine animals, co-operating with the first cause in the government of the world.

5. A survey of the heathen mythology presents little to view but absurdity, and the various forms in which human corruption is exhibited. The people at large, whatever the philosophers understood by these "phantasms and monsters," received them as literal truths, till it became dangerous to shake the faith of communities, or disturb the public religion.

§ In this state of things continued the gentile world, until the light of the gospel was sent among them. Those were times of ignorance. The people were unacquainted with the true God and the worship of him—with the Messiah and salvation by him.

The moral world at present is gloriously illuminated. The Bible has scattered the dark shades of spiritual and intellectual night. We behold "one God and one Mediator between God and men," seated upon the throne of the universe; possessed of boundless wisdom, power, purity, goodness; the Creator, the Preserver, the Ruler, and the Redeemer of his creatures; ever present in all parts of his creation; ever providing for its general happiness.

Discoveries, Inventions, and Improvements of Early Ages.

SECT. 1. The little that can be gathered concerning the state of society, and the progress in inventions and improvements before the flood, has already been exhibited. In the account of individual nations, something also has been said concerning their intellectual culture and useful works of art. A few particulars may be added on these topics, with a view to illustrate more fully the advancement of society in the states of antiquity. Special reference will here be had to mechanic inventions, respecting which, less has been said hitherto, than on the subject of the fine arts and general literature.

Sufficient evidence exists, that mankind at a remote period of antiquity, must have made considerable progress in the arts of life. The circumstances under which Egypt is presented to us by Moses, in the book of Genesis, indicate that its inhabitants were at that time a cultivated people. No doubt, the progress of invention in their very favourable situation was quite rapid. From them, even the Israelites, at the early period in which Moses wrote, must have learned much in respect to the useful arts. The same was the case with the Babylonians, Phœnicians, and other nations. Still, though some arts have been lost during the lapse of ages, antiquity cannot compare with modern times in the necessaries, comforts, and luxuries of life.

2. At first, necessity, and afterwards convenience, urged the cultivation of the arts. The useful arts are the product of necessity. The higher branches of knowledge are the fruit of comparative ease and leisure.

Among, the earliest arts, is the construction of huts, and of weapons, adapted to war and hunting.

Astronomy is among the earliest of the sciences, and is said to have originated with the Chaldeans, probably, through the influence of superstition. The occupation of the Chaldeans, many of whom were shepherds, watching their flocks by night, was favourable for the observation of the heavenly bodies.

Geometry was found out by the Egyptians. They were led to the cultivation of this science, by having occasion to measure the lands annually disturbed by the overflowing of the Nile.

Medicine was among the early sciences. The simplest means of cure answer for rude nations. More complex means are required for cultivated nations, who have more complex diseases.

Agriculture is not practised till the tribes of men become stationary, and hold property in the soil. The acquirement, protection, and recognition of property, generally, is the first step from a savage towards a civilized life. The first property consisted of sheep, goats, and oxen; and the care of these was the earliest and simplest occupation of husbandmen. In this stage of husbandry, all the country was open and common to any occupier; but as soon as any man could call a spot his own, and could secure to his family the produce of it, its cultivation would be a great object. Hence, arose the art and science of agriculture, properly so called.

§ Agriculture flourished less in Greece than in Rome. The Romans were remarkably versed in the knowledge of this useful branch of human pursuit. Their greatest citizens and warriors were, by turns, cultivators of the soil. The Israelites before them, and the Egyptians also, were devoted to this employment. The moderns, however, it is believed, have made the greatest proficiency in agriculture, as they have in most of the sciences and practical arts of life. This is the natural effect of time, of prolonged study, and multiplied experiments. In many of the fine arts, the ancients are still our masters.

Architecture was an elegant art, in which antiquity excelled. The necessary and useful were all that was first sought in buildings. Luxury aimed at ornament. Hence, arose the five beautiful orders of architecture, viz. the Tuscan, the Doric, the Ionic, the Corinthian, and the Composite. The Greeks perfected this art.

3. But we may properly notice a few of the minuter divisions of ancient art and contrivance. Among these were the following:

Embalming.—The ancients had an imperfect knowledge of the mode of preserving those bodies that were subject to decay. They relied principally on brine, honey, or a covering of wax; but each of these was defective, and far inferior to that by spirits of wine, which combines the advantage of preventing putrefaction, with that of perfect transparency. The more scientific modern process, employed in anatomical preparations, was wholly unknown. The Egyptians, however, were famous for embalming dead bodies.

§ The method of preventing corruption by means of brine, was the most ancient, as it was the most apparent, and the easiest of execution. It has been supposed to have originated in Persia, and Dion Cassius says, that when Pharnaces sent the body of his father, Mithridates, to Pompey, he had it placed in brine; but it seems pro bable, that in the East, nitre was more frequently employed for this purpose than common salt.

The custom of preserving dead bodies in honey, was also employed at a very early period. The remains of several Spartans, who died in foreign countries, were thus prepared for transmission to their native home. The body of Alexander the Great, is also said, by some authors, to have been thus deposited, although we are told by others, that it was embalmed in the manner of the Egyptians.

In the East, dead bodies were sometimes covered over with wax, and this practice, which was early introduced into Europe, gave rise to that of wrapping the remains of persons of distinction in waxed cloths, which has continued down even to the present day.

The Egyptian method of embalming, consisted in first extracting the brain through the nostrils, and injecting some viscous unguent in their stead; then opening the belly, and taking out the intestines, the cavity being washed with palm wine, impregnated with spices, and filled with myrrh and other aromatics; this done, the body was laid in nitre during seventy days, at the end of which, it was taken out, cleansed, and swathed in fine linen, which was gummed, and ornamented with various painted hieroglyphics, expressive of the deceased's character and rank. This was done only for persons of the highest distinction. Less expensive methods were used for others.

Roads and Street Pavements.—The public accommodations of the most splendid capitals of antiquity, were few in comparison with those of modern large towns. The streets of ancient Rome were only partially paved, during its most brilliant era, and are described by authors of that period as being filled with dirt. A few other cities are supposed to have been paved, but this is a matter of doubt.

Though the Greeks and Romans were indifferent to their streets, yet they paid particular attention to their great public roads. These, in some instances, were magnificent works. Travelling, however, was not generally rapid in those times.

§ There was no part of the Roman policy which so effectually promoted the good of mankind, or which has transmitted such exalted ideas of the imperial grandeur, as the number and magnificence of the roads. Though constructed principally for military purposes, they were of vast utility to the districts which they traversed, and proved the most efficacious means of promoting the comfort and civilization of the conquered people. Occasionally, there were instances of extraordinary celerity in travelling. We are informed by Pliny, that Tiberius travelled two hundred miles in a day and night, on being despatched by Augustus to console his sick brother, Germanicus. But the ordinary rate of travelling, even on their excellent roads, was slow in comparison of what it is at present. Cicero speaks of a messenger coming from Rome, to his government of Cilicia, in Asia Minor, in forty-seven days: *heu tam longe!* as the orator exclaims, on finding himself so far removed from the scene of his glory and exertions. To convey letters from Rome to the neighbourhood of Gibraltar, required, according to Pollio, forty days.

Mode of conveying Intelligence.—The oldest method of communicating the news, with which we are acquainted, was by means of public criers. Another mode was to post up a written advertisement against a column in some public place.

§ Public criers among the Greeks and Romans were under the superintendence of the police, and were generally employed by individuals, in the same manner as they still are in the country towns of England. The mode of posting was resorted to by the Roman government, to promulgate its edicts, and even, it is supposed, for imparting more trivial information of general import. Historians appear to have collected materials from them; nor is it improbable, that copies were taken by individuals and dispersed about the city, or sent to their friends in the provinces.

Glass.—The origin of the art of making glass, like that of many other valuable inventions, is probably due to chance. It is said to have been discovered in Syria. From ancient authors, it is supposed not to have been made in Rome, before the reign of Tiberius.

§ Pliny mentions that glass was first accidentally discovered by some travellers while dressing their food by the river Belus, in Syria. Being obliged to make a fire on the ground, where there was a great quantity of the herb *kali*, that plant burning to ashes, its salts incorporated with the sand, and thus became vitrified. The accident becoming known, the inhabitants of the neighbouring city of Sidon, availed themselves of it, and soon brought the art into use. It seems to be a corroboration of this account, that the most ancient glass-houses, with which we are acquainted, were erected in Tyre. Previously to the time of Tiberius, the Romans imported glass from the East, and vessels of glass were among their most costly pieces of household furniture.

Mirrors.—There is reason to believe, that artificial mirrors were made almost as soon as the ingenuity of man was exerted on mechanical objects, and as every solid body capable of receiving a fine polish, would suit this purpose, we find, that the oldest mirrors mentioned in history, were of metal. Silver, however, afterwards came into use, and the greatest number of ancient mirrors was made of that metal, as it is the most fit of the unmixed metals for this purpose. Inferior mirrors were also made, some of a mixture of copper and tin, and bset; some of obsidian stone, and others of other substances. Glass mirrors were most probably unknown to the ancients.

§ Metal mirrors are spoken of in the Bible, under the term looking-glass, as incorrectly translated.

At Rome, as the satirists declare, no young woman was without a silver mirror.

The date of the invention of glass mirrors is somewhat a matter of dispute. From Pliny, it is thought, that they were attempted in the glass-houses of Tyre, but it does not appear that the experiments he speaks of, whatever they were, met with success; and moreover, it is certain, that though glass was used by the Romans, their mirrors were alluded to among articles of plate.

Linen.—Linen, it is supposed, was first manufactured in Egypt. It is certain, that it was first obtained, and Europe was for a long time supplied, from that country; and that the invention was very ancient appears from the fact, that mummies are generally found swathed in linen. The Greeks, however, were unacquainted with it, and it was not until the second century of the Christian era, that it was first introduced into Rome. Before that period, the tunic or under garment of the Romans was made of wool.

Woollen.—The origin of the arts of spinning and weaving is lost in the obscurity of fable. The Egyptians ascribe the invention to their Isis, and the Hindoos trace it to the remotest period of their fabulous history; but this applies only to cotton and flax; for in those countries wool is not produced. Varro says, that the sheep was introduced into Greece by Hercules, and it is probable, that the first attempts to manufacture wool in Europe, were made by the Athenians. The chief seat of the Roman manufacture was at Padua, whose workmen are to this day highly celebrated.

§ Sheep came originally from Africa, but in that country, the animal bears hair instead of wool; and it is only in colder countries that its covering gradually acquires a woolly texture. It was long, most probably, before sheep became domesticated in the northern countries, whose inhabitants, living in immense woods, were contented, for ages, with their fine furs. It was only till a late period of ancient history, that the people of the north of Europe employed artificial means of clothing.

Among both the Greeks and Romans, spinning was the chief employment of the women. In weaving, the machinery, though perhaps rude in its construction, was, in principle, similar to that still in use. The process of fulling and preparing the cloth, seems to have resembled the modern practice in every essential point, except that of shearing the nap, with which the ancients do not appear to have been acquainted.

Dyeing.—Few arts can lay claim to greater antiquity than that of dyeing, and still fewer attained, in ancient times, so great a degree of perfection. It certainly preceded painting, and appears to have been known in the earliest ages of the Jews, Babylonians, and Egyptians, who selected and applied colours for stuffs, cotton, linen, and silk, with the greatest judgment and dexterity. These were extracted from the animal, vegetable, and mineral kingdom; and without confining themselves to cloth or silk, they dyed equally well, leather, ivory, tortoise-shell, the hair of animals, wood, earth, wax, and even imparted a permanent colour to marble.

Steel.—The invention of steel is of very great antiquity. Although we do not find any distinct mention of it in the Old Testament, still, it is clear, that it was known to the Greeks, in the time of Homer, and received from them several names, the most common of which was stomoma. Chalybs, was also a name given to steel, from the Chalybes, a people inhabiting the southern shore of the Euxine, between Cholcis and Paphlagonia, a country which was renowned for its works of iron and steel.

§ The steel of the ancients was capable of being hammered, and was not near so brittle as the hardest with which we are acquainted.

These, and many other inventions and discoveries, which cannot here be described, characterized ancient times; but modern ages have added greatly to the number, and improved many of those which were before known.

THE

WORLD DISPLAYED

IN ITS

HISTORY AND GEOGRAPHY;

EMBRACING A

HISTORY OF THE WORLD,

FROM THE

CREATION TO THE PRESENT DAY.

WITH GENERAL VIEWS OF THE POLITICS, RELIGION, MILITARY AND NAVAL AFFAIRS, ARTS, LITERATURE, MANNERS, CUSTOMS, AND SOCIETY, OF ANCIENT AS WELL AS MODERN NATIONS.

BY REV. ROYAL ROBBINS.

TO WHICH IS ADDED,

AN OUTLINE OF MODERN GEOGRAPHY.

TWO VOLUMES IN ONE.

VOL. II.

NEW YORK.
PUBLISHED BY H. SAVAGE.
1839.

PREFACE.

Modern History presents so wide and varied a field, that a volume of the ordinary size is scarcely adequate to the purpose, of pointing out all even of the more striking objects, which such a field contains. Indeed, comparatively little can be hoped to be achieved in a very condensed narrative of the events of modern ages, on the common plan. It would be apt to become a barren outline, or dry abstract, with little to interest or instruct the mind of the reader, and this, almost from the necessity of the case. The conciseness which is studied would preclude all minute relation, and with that the chief charm of history. The character of many publications of this class, otherwise very valuable, has suffered from such a cause. By the use of two sizes of type, this inconvenience is remedied in a degree, if there be sufficient skill in the execution; and a considerable space within a given compass, is thus allowed, for lively and entertaining matter not essentially connected with the leading facts or frame-work of history. The latter, necessarily dry in themselves, and having few attractions for common minds, but very important to every one who would obtain a correct idea of the course of events, may be all confined to the larger type: and thus, while a very brief epitome of history is presented in that part, the reader is at the same time, by means of the smaller type, made acquainted with details which will enliven the narrative, and the better impress the more material facts on his mind. This is one great advantage of reading history on the plan of the present work—a plan which has of late been adopted with much success;—though the work possesses other peculiarities, which, whether they are happy or not, the reader, it is believed, will not fail to perceive. The author would only add, that in preparing this outline of history, he has consulted a large number of valuable authors, from whom he has taken whatever was suited to his purposes, in many instances with little variation even in language, though he has generally endeavoured to maintain a homogeneous style and manner—that he has exercised much care in selecting the materials and topics, and in connecting and arranging them—that he has aimed at scrupulous fidelity in the statement of facts, and impartiality in estimating their value—and that he has occasionally interwoven in the narrative such moral remarks, and attempted throughout to exhibit such a spirit, as to render history not merely an agreeable exercise to the understanding, but an impressive lesson to the heart.

CONTENTS

INTRODUCTION.

GENERAL DIVISION.

Period I.

Period II.

Period III.

Period IV.

Period V.

Period VI.

Period VII.

Period VIII.

Period IX.

Period X.

GENERAL VIEWS.

MODERN HISTORY.

INTRODUCTION.

SEC. 1. Writers who have divided History into Ancient and Modern, are not agreed as to the most convenient separating line between them. Some have taken the subversion of the *Western Empire of the Romans* as the dividing period; and others the establishment of the *New Empire of the West*, under Charlemagne. We however agree with a third, and probably a more numerous class, who adopt the commencement of the *Christian Era* as the line of separation. In this there is an evident propriety.

2. It is the epoch from which civilized nations reckon time, both backwards to the beginning of creation, and forwards to the end of the world. Add to this, the event (the birth of Christ) that forms this era, is the most important of events It has had a commanding influence upon all subsequent history. It has altered the aspect of all human affairs, and it will alter them more and more, as Christianity becomes extended. The state of the civilized world was also singular. A change had taken place in the establishment of a mighty despotism, which was destined to oppress the nations, through many successive generations.

§ The period from which we commence Modern History, cannot be contemplated with too deep an interest. It was a remarkable era in Divine Providence. "The fullness of the time was come"—the ancient order of things was drawing to a close, and new scenes in the moral world, were henceforth to be presented to the view of mankind. It is therefore associated with our most solemn thoughts of the dispensations of the Supreme Being towards his creatures. It is the period whence we date the commencement of the spiritual renovation of the world.

The state of the world, in a political point of view, also deserves consideration. The principal nations were reduced under one head. Wars and dissentions, of long continuance and infinite ferocity, having terminated in one most formidable power, the whole earth enjoyed an unheard of calm. Mankind, for a short time, tasted the sweets of peace, though in servitude. One man was master of the lives and fortunes of all the rest, and therefore even the spirit of conquest could scarcely desire more.

3. The authenticity and the abundance of the materials of modern history, will be hailed with peculiar satisfaction by the inquirer after truth. A considerable portion of ancient history is plunged into darkness and uncertainty, from a variety of causes. And the scantiness, in some instances, of the materials from which it is drawn, is often perplexing But both the ecclesiastical and civil records of modern history, illustrate, with desirable fullness, the state of the times. It must be owned, however, that the rage of the barbarians who subverted the Roman Empire, has deprived us of some means of information which we should otherwise have possessed. But it is wonderful, after all, that so many monuments of the earlier periods of modern history, have come down to us.

§ The causes that have operated to render some portions of ancient history obscure, are such as the lapse of numerous ages; a series of great revolutions, in consequence of which the memory of many events was lost; the fury of barbarians, by which numerous monuments of early times have been destroyed; and more than all the rest, the designed or accidental destruction of libraries.

Some noble collections of books perished before the Christian era, particularly the celebrated library of Alexandria. This library was founded by Ptolemy Philadelphus, about 284 years B. C., and consisted of a vast collection of records, histories, poems, and other works. The number of volumes was reckoned at 400,000, and they might have been as many as were in all the world beside. Before the art of printing, books were comparatively scarce; and of some, there might have been no other copies than those contained in this library. It perished in the flames of Alexandria, when Julius Cæsar took that city.

In later ages, large libraries have been destroyed, particularly the same library at Alexandria after it was revived, and collections had been made during several centuries. In the latter instance 700,000 volumes perished. But books by this time had been much more multiplied, and though numerous destructions took place, many have survived the wrecks of ages.

GENERAL DIVISION.

Modern History may be divided into ten periods. They have each their peculiar characteristic, by which they may be always remembered, and by which distinct views of the subject are designed to be imparted to the mind.

Period I, will extend from the Nativity of Jesus Christ,

to the reign of Constantine the Great, 306 years A. C. This is the period of the *Ten Persecutions of Christians.*

PERIOD II, will extend from the reign of Constantine the Great, 306 years A. C., to the Extinction of the Western Empire, 476 years A. C. This is the period of the *Northern Invasions.*

PERIOD III, will extend from the Extinction of the Western Empire, 476 years A. C., to the Flight of Mahomet, 622 years A. C. This is the period of the *Justinian Code, and the Wars of Belisarius.*

PERIOD IV, will extend from the Flight of Mahomet, 622 years A. C., to the Crowning of Charlemagne at Rome, 800 years A. C. This is the period of the *Establishment of the Saracen Dominion.*

PERIOD V, will extend from the Crowning of Charlemagne at Rome, 800 years A. C., to the First Crusade, 1095 years A. C. This is the period of the *New Western Empire.*

PERIOD VI, will extend from the First Crusade, 1095 years A. C., to the Founding of the Turkish Empire, 1299 years A. C. This is the period of the *Crusades.*

PERIOD VII, will extend from the Founding of the Turkish Empire, 1299 years A. C., to the Taking of Constantinople, 1453 years A. C. This is the period of the *Papal Schism.*

PERIOD VIII, will extend from the Taking of Constantinople, 1453 years A. C., to the Edict of Nantes, (*Nantz*) 1598 years A. C. This is the period of the *Reformation.*

PERIOD IX, will extend from the Edict of Nantes, 1598 years A. C., to the Death of Charles XII, of Sweden, 1718 years A. C. This is the period of the *English Commonwealth.*

PERIOD X, will extend from the Death of Charles XII, of Sweden, 1718 years A. C., to the final Restoration of the Bourbons, 1815 years A. C. This is the period of the *American and French Revolutions.*

PERIOD I.

The period of the Ten Persecutions of Christians, extending from the Nativity of Jesus Christ, to the Reign of Constantine the Great, 306 *A. C.*

THE ROMAN EMPIRE.

Sec. 1. The great event with which this period properly commences, is the Birth of Jesus Christ. It belongs to the Roman History, only from the fact that Judea, the country of Our Saviour, was held in subjection to Rome. It is strictly an event of the Jewish History, and is hereafter to be more fully noticed under that head.

Here it may be mentioned only, that the Birth of Jesus occurred, according to the common reckoning, in the 31st year of the reign of Augustus, 752 years after the building of Rome, and in the 195th Olympiad, under the consulship of Caius Julius Cæsar. It is the general opinion of the learned, however, that our Saviour was born four years earlier than this date, viz. in the 27th of Augustus, and that the common reckoning or era is a mistake.

According to this opinion, Jesus, in the year 1, A. C., (the vulgar date) was really four years old.

§ It is a circumstance worthy of remark, that the temple of Janus, at Rome, which was always open in time of war, and shut only during peace, was shut at the period of our Saviour's birth, and that, for the third instance only, during the space of more than 700 years.

2. Rome had been an empire in the more proper sense of the word, from the beginning of the reign of Augustus. At the time of the nativity of Christ, the empire was at the meridian of its splendour, or perhaps a little past it. Most of the nations had bowed to the Roman yoke; and luxury and the arts poured in upon the queen of cities.

It had been for some years the most powerful dominion of the ancient world, and continued thus to be for several succeeding centuries. The times, however, were degenerate, and the real strength of the Roman empire, if it had not begun to diminish at this epoch, was certainly not greater than during the last days of the republic. A few nations afterwards were added to its sway, but these rather weakened than augmented the power of Rome. The wide extent of its dominions, we shall hereafter see, was one of the causes of its decline and downfall.

But the pomp and glory of so great a monarchy, continued long after the seeds of weakness and decay were sown. Distant nations admired and dreaded the splendid spectacle. Ambassadors from every region daily arrived at Rome, to do homage to her greatness, or to seek her friendship and assistance.

3. Augustus, who first established a despotism over the Roman people, died 14 years after the birth of Christ. The events which took place between the birth of Christ and the death of Augustus, pertaining to the Romans, were neither many nor important.

During this interval, Augustus adopted Tiberius, and finally associated him in the empire. Archelaus, king of Judea, was deposed, and that country became strictly a Roman province. Germanicus, grandson of Augustus, successfully commanded in Pannonia, and Q. Varus was signally defeated by the Germans, with the loss of three Roman legions.

4. Luxury and the arts having enervated the Roman people, and the former civil wars and the consequent calamities having paved the way for a different order of things, in the quiet establishment of despotism under Augustus, their fate from this time was fixed. He found no difficulty in riveting their chains, and for long ages, a series of despots, most of them monsters of vice and cruelty, ruled with a rod of iron, this once liberty-loving people, and mistress of nations.

§ Amidst the refinements and elegancies of modern times, connected with our ideas of the progressive improvement of society, we are perhaps inclined to overlook and undervalue the ages of antiquity. Many seem to forget what scenes of brightness and grandeur have illumined the nations before us, and how mournfully those scenes are departed.

The pensive, contemplative mind, however, does justice to such a subject; and no instance of human greatness of old, strikes such a mind more forcibly, than that of the proud empire of Rome, under her Cæsars. The memorial is both pleasant and mournful to the soul. The mixture of misery with its splendour, renders it, if any thing, more touching and impressive.

5. Tiberius, who had been named in the will of Augustus as his successor, immediately assumed the government, 14 years A. C. He was the son of Augustus's wife, Livia, by a former husband, and had distinguished himself in war.

During the first eight or nine years of his reign. he put on the appearance of justice and moderation, practising the most consummate dissimulation. His vicious and tyrannical disposition was indulged during this time in a very covert manner; but afterwards it was openly manifested, and carried to a most terrible extreme. His cruelties and debaucheries were enormous.

The first objects of his suspicions were Agrippa Posthumus, a grandson of Augustus, whom he ordered to be executed in compliance with the pretended will of that emperor; and the accomplished Germanicus, his nephew and distinguished general, whom he caused to be secretly poisoned. The Roman people indulged in unbounded sorrow, upon the death of Germanicus.

Afterwards, when he gave a loose to his passions, the best blood in Rome flowed. By means of Sejanus, a Roman knight whom he took into his confidence, and who exceeded even Tiberius in dissimulation, he exercised the most shocking cruelties towards his subjects. Sejanus first fell a victim to his crimes, in attempting to assume the government himself; and a few years after Tiberius was strangled or poisoned by one of his officers.

§ From the 12th year of his reign, Tiberius was persuaded by Sejanus to abandon Rome, and to retire to the island of Caprea, as a more convenient place for the indulgence of his indolence and debaucheries. His gloomy and cruel disposition also followed him there, and by means of this base minion, he perpetrated all manner of crimes.

At this time he was 67 years old, and the unpleasantness of his person comported with the deformity of his mind. He was quite bald in front; his face was disgustingly ulcerated, and covered over with plasters; his body was bent forward, while its unnatural tallness and leanness increased its ugliness. He now gave himself up to every excess. He spent whole nights in eating and drinking, and he appointed two of his table companions to the first posts of the empire, for no other merit, than that of having sat up with him two days and two nights, without interruption. These he called his friends of all hours.

His libidinous indulgences were still more detestable, and the most eminent women of Rome were obliged to sacrifice to him their virtue and honour.

His jealousy, which fastened on persons of the highest distinction, induced him to condemn them to death on the slightest pretences. Indeed to such an extent were legalized murders carried, that he began to grow weary of particular executions, and therefore gave orders that all the accused should be put to death together, without further examination. The whole city of Rome was filled with slaughter and mourning. The place of execution was a horrible scene dead bodies putrifying lay heaped on each other, while even the friends of the wretched convicts were denied the satisfaction of weeping.

In putting to death sixteen out of twenty senators whom he had chosen for his council, he uttered a sentiment never to be forgotten in the records of human cruelty. "Let them hate me, so long as they obey me." This monster often satisfied his eyes, with the tortures of the wretches who were put to death before him; and in the days of Suetonius, the rock was still shown from which he ordered such as displeased him to be thrown headlong.

He died in the seventy-eighth year of his age, and twenty-third of his reign. 37 A. C.

6. At this time the Romans were arrived at the highest pitch of effeminacy and vice. The wealth of almost every nation in the empire, having long circulated through the city, brought with it the luxuries peculiar to each country. Rome was one vast mass of pollution, and sensuality. It was thought a refinement upon pleasure to make it unnatural. Abating their genius, there never was a more detestable people, than the Romans at this epoch, and indeed, during the continuance of the empire. Cruelty and lust were essential ingredients in the Roman character.

§ It was a burst of joy, says Chateaubriand, which Tiberius was unable to repress, on finding the Roman people and senate sunk below even the baseness of his own heart.

Again, according to this writer, death formed an essential part of the festivities of the Romans. It was introduced as a contrast, and for the purpose of giving a zest to the pleasures of life. Gladiators, courtezans, and musicians, were procured to enliven entertainments. A Roman on quitting a haunt of infamous pleasure, went to enjoy the spectacle of a wild beast devouring human victims, and quaffing their blood.

7. Caligula had been adopted by Tiberius for his heir and successor in the empire. He was the son of Germanicus, and grand-nephew of Tiberius, and so called from Caliga, a short buskin which he wore, in imitation of the common sentinels. He commenced his reign immediately on the death of Tiberius, 37 years A. C. and at his accession, was popular from the virtues of his father.

He commenced his reign with a show of clemency and moderation. He restored some of the forms of the republic which his predecessor had entirely disregarded, and he abolished arbitrary prosecutions for crimes of state. But tyrannical by nature, in less than eight months he acted out his real disposition, in cruelties, extortions, and impieties, which surpassed even those of Tiberius.

Joining absurdity and extravagance to vice, he became supremely contemptible, as well as detestable. Indeed, his follies and absurdities were peculiar to himself, so that according to an idea of Seneca, he was one of those productions of nature, in which there was the greatest possible combination of vice and power. He died by assassination, in the fourth year of his reign and 29th of his age. A. C. 41.

§ Among the cruelties of this imperial monster, were his murder of Gemellus his kinsman, of Silenus his father-in-law, of Grecinus a senator of noted integrity, who refused to witness falsely against Silenus; afterwards, his killing many of the senate, and then citing them to appear as if they had killed themselves; indeed, the sacrifice of crowds of victims to his avarice, or suspicion.

He condemned many persons of the highest quality to dig in the mines, and to repair the high-ways, for ridiculing his profusion. He cast great numbers of old and infirm men, and poor decrepid housekeepers, to wild beasts, in order to free the state from such unserviceable citizens. He frequently had men racked before him while he sat at table, ironically pitying their misfortunes, and blaming their executioner. And as the height of insane cruelty, he once expressed the wish "that all the Roman people had but one neck, that he might dispatch them at a single blow."

His impieties, and the depravation of his appetites, made him still more a disgrace to human nature. He claimed divine honours, and caused temples to be built and sacrifices to be offered to himself, as a God. He caused the heads of the statues of Jupiter and some other gods to be struck off, and his own to be put in their places. He employed many inventions to imitate thunder, and would frequently defy Jupiter, crying out in a sentence of Homer "Do you conquer me or I will conquer you." Scarcely any lady of quality in Rome escaped his depraved solicitations. He committed incest with his three sisters, two of whom he prostituted to his vile companions, and then banished them, as adulteresses and conspirators against his person.

His follies and prodigality completed the infamy of his character. The luxuries of the former emperors were trifling, compared to his. He invented dishes of immense value, and had even jewels dissolved among his sauces. He sometimes had services of pure gold, instead of meat, presented before his guests; observing, "that a man should be an economist or an emperor."

For his favorite horse Incitatus, he built a stable of marble, and a manger of ivory; and appointed it a house, furniture, and a kitchen, in order to a respectful entertainment of its visitors. Sometimes indeed, the emperor invited Incitatus to his own table; and it is said that he would have appointed it to the consulship, had he not been prevented by death.

These and a thousand other follies, particularly the building of a bridge three miles and a half across an arm of the sea in a ridiculous manner, and which the first storm annihilated, constituted such a drain upon the public resources, as became exceedingly oppressive. Of a fortune of £18,000,000 sterling left by Tiberius, none remained in a space little beyond one year. He of course put in practice all kinds of rapine and extortion. Professor Heeren remarks, that "he was more pernicious to the state by his insane prodigality, than by his savage cruelty."

Against such a wretch, we naturally look for treason and conspiracies. After several attempts, his death was at length accomplished by Cassius Cherea, tribune of the prætorian bands, who was an ardent lover of freedom. Leagued with a number of conspirators, he met the emperor in a little vaulted gallery that led to one of his baths, and struck him to the ground, crying out, "tyrant, think upon this." He was immediately dispatched by the other conspirators, who rushed in and pierced him with thirty wounds.

8. A temporary confusion followed the death of Caligula, and in this crisis of affairs, the senate attempted to restore the republic. But the spirit of Roman liberty had fled; the populace, and in general the army, opposed the design. Claudius at this juncture, having been accidentally found in a lurking place, to which he had repaired through fear, some of the prætorian guards proclaimed him emperor, at the moment he expected nothing but death; 41 A. C. Claudius was the uncle of Caligula, and grand-son of Mark Antony and Octavia, the sister of Augustus.

Claudius was a man below mediocrity in understanding and education; and his capacity for business was even contemptible. He became almost of course infamous for his vices, and the dupe of his associates and even of his domestics. Many were the cruelties committed during his reign, though they seem to have been suggested principally by his wicked directors, among whom was the notorious Messalina, his wife.

§ The stupidity of Claudius was such, that he was alike indifferent, whatever was done, and often was he so operated upon by his fears, that he would consent to any act however unjust. His own family on one pretence or another was almost exterminated, and great numbers of others fell a sacrifice to the jealousy of Messalina and her minions, who ruled him at will. The historian, Suetonius, assures us, that there were no less than thirty-five Senators and above three hundred knights, executed in his reign.

One enterprise of importance marked his reign, and that was his expedition into Britain, 43 A. C. He undertook to reduce the island, and after visiting it in person, left his generals, Plautius and Vespasian, to prosecute a war, which was carried on for several years with various success. The Silures or inhabitants of South Wales, under their king, Caractacus, (Caradoc,) made a spirited resistance, though without avail in the end. Their king was led captive to Rome.

Messalina advanced in boldness as in profligacy, but her excesses became the occasion of her destruction. The emperor was persuaded to put her to death for her shameless infidelity to him. Afterwards he married Agrippina, the daughter of his brother Germanicus, who had poisoned her former husband, and who at length poisoned him.

Making every effort to secure the succession to the empire to her son Domitius Aenobarbus, (called Nero,) she prevailed on Claudius to adopt him, and then effecting the death of her husband, she opened the way to the throne for one, who was destined to exceed in wickedness, if that were possible, any that went before him. Claudius was put to death in the fifteenth year of his reign and sixty-third of his age.

§ Among the illustrious sufferers in the reign of Claudius, were Petus and his faithful Arria, whose story ought not to be passed over. Cecina Petus associated in the revolt of Camillus, had endeavoured to escape into Dalmatia. Being apprehended, he was conveyed in a ship to Rome. Arria, who had been long the partner of his affections and misfortunes, entreated his keepers, to be taken in the same vessel.

"It is usual," said she, "to grant a man of his quality a few slaves to dress, and undress, and attend him; but I will perform all these offices, and save you the trouble of a more numerous retinue." Her fidelity, however, could not prevail. She therefore hired a fisherman's bark, and thus kept company with the ship in which her husband was conveyed, through the voyage.

They had an only son, equally beautiful and virtuous. This youth died at the time his father was confined to his bed, by a dangerous disorder. However, the affectionate Arria concealed her son's death, and in her visits to her husband, manifested her usual cheerfulness. Being asked how her son did, she replied that he was calm, and only left her husband's chamber to give vent to her tears.

When Petus was condemned to die by his own hands, Arria used every art to inspire him with resolution; and at length finding him continue timid and wavering, she took the poinard, and stabbing herself in his presence, presented it to him saying, "it gives me no pain, my Petus."

9. Rome at this era contained nearly seven millions inhabi tants, a number so prodigious that nothing but the best evidence could prevent our doubt of its accuracy. Corruption and luxury were excessive. The Roman military spirit,

though much relaxed, still continued to awe mankind, by the terror of its name.

10. Nero Claudius, (the name he assumed,) the son of Agrippina, succeeded to the empire (54 A. C.) under favorable circumstances, and like his predecessors, for a short time, promised to govern with moderation and justice. So well did he conceal his innate depravity, that scarcely any suspected that his virtues were feigned.

The care of his education had been entrusted to Seneca, the famous philosopher, though he seemed not to have profited under his instructer any otherwise than to become affected and pedantic. While, however, he was controled by Seneca, and Burrhuss captain of the prætorian guards, a worthy and experienced officer, Nero appeared just and humane; but he could not long restrain the feelings of his base nature.

At the expiration of five years, he broke over all the bounds of decency and moderation, and pursued a course of conduct exceeding in puerility, levity, ferocity, and tyranny, whatever had been done before him. He became one of the most odious characters recorded in history. His flagitiousness was manifested in the murder of his mother, his wife Octavia, his tutor Seneca, and Lucan the poet, and Burrhuss his benefactor; in extirpating many of the principal families of Rome on suspicion of treason; in setting the city on fire, charging the crime on the christians, and then punishing them with unheard of tortures; and in unnumbered other acts in which he outraged reason, and nature itself.

His meanness and puerility almost surpass belief, and Rome contained not another so despicable a wretch in the character of an actor, musician or gladiator. At length having become an object of perfect hatred and contempt, a rebellion of his subjects headed by Vindex, an illustrious Gaul, and Galba who commanded in Spain, crushed this imperial monster, in the thirtieth year of his age, after a reign of fourteen years, A. C. 69. Too cowardly to kill himself, he died by the hand of a slave, just as he was on the point of being taken, and delivered up to public justice.

§ The burning of Rome by Nero was an act of mere wantonness. Some one happening to say in his presence, that the world might be burnt when he was dead, "Nay," replied Nero, "let it be burnt while I am living." Accordingly, as most historians report, he set it on fire, and standing upon a high tower, he indulged the pleasure of fancying it a representation of the burning of Troy. The conflagration continued nine days, and a great part of the city was consumed.

A conspiracy formed against him by Piso, but which was prematurely discovered, opened a train of suspicions, that almost turned Rome into a field of blood. All who were implicated or suspected of being so, he executed without mercy. It was at this time that Seneca and Lucan suffered.

No master was secure from the vengeance of his slaves, nor even parents from the baser attempts of their children. Not only throughout Rome, but the whole surrounding country, bodies of soldiers were seen in pursuit of the suspected and the guilty; whole crowds of wretches loaded with chains, were led every day to the gates of the palace, to wait their sentence from the tyrant's own lips, who always presided at the tortures in person, attended by Tigellinus, one of the most abandoned men in Rome, but now his principal minister.

"The principal reason why the despotism of Nero and his predecessors was so quietly borne by the nation, lay in the fact, that a great part of them were fed by the emperors. From the monthly distribution of corn of the times of the republic, there now sprang up the extraordinary *congiaria* (gifts in corn or money) and *viscerationes* (distributions of raw flesh.) The times of tyranny were generally the golden days of the rabble."

During the reign of Nero, the Britons, under their queen Boadicea revolted, and defeated the Romans with the loss of 70,000 men. The latter, however, avenged this loss at length by the slaughter of 80,000 Britons, which completely broke the British spirit and power.

A war was also carried on against the Parthians, under the conduct of Corbulo, who obtained many victories over them. About this time also, 67 A. C., the Jews, who had revolted under the tyranny of Florus the Roman governor, were massacred in great numbers.

11. Galba, who was associated with Vindex, in the insurrection which issued in the destruction of Nero, succeeded the latter in the empire 68 A. C. Vindex, at the commencement of his revolt, generously proclaimed Galba emperor, and after the death of Nero, both the senate and the legions under his command, sanctioned this measure.

Before his elevation mankind thought well of Galba. His descent was illustrious. His reputation as a commander stood high, and no stain was cast on his courage or virtue. Compared with his predecessors, he was certainly a respectable emperor. In seeking to accomplish two important objects, viz., the punishment of the enormous vices then prevalent, and the replenishing of the treasury, he was unduly severe; and as he was naturally parsimonious, he became an object of contempt and ridicule.

§ It was impolitic in Galba, to think of making the Roman people pass at once from the extreme of luxury to that of sobriety and economy. The state was too much corrupted to admit of such an immediate and total change. The emperor's intentions, however, should have shielded him from reproach; and had he not suffered his assistants to abuse his confidence, and had he been a little more equal, moderate, and conciliatory in his administration, he would have been as well thought of when an emperor, as he was when a private person.

It is mentioned as an instance of his severity, that upon some disrespectful treatment of him from a certain body of his subjects, he ordered a body of horse attending him to ride in among them, and thus killed 7000 of them, and afterwards decimated the survivors.

His parsimony is indicated by the following circumstances. He once groaned upon having an expensive soup served up for him at his table. To a steward for his fidelity he presented a plate of beans. And a famous player upon the flute, named Canus, having greatly delighted him, he drew out his purse and gave him fivepence, telling him it was private and not public money. His popularity sunk by such ill-timed parsimony. Through his love of money, some notorious villains purchased their safety.

Galba reigned only seven months. He perished in the seventy-third year of his age, in consequence of the attempt of Otho, one of his generals, to obtain the throne. Otho expected to be adopted by Galba for his successor; but the emperor, discarding all favouritism, sought the good of the empire by nominating the virtuous Piso. Otho consequently had recourse to arms, and thus accomplished the death both of Galba and Piso.

12. Otho was now raised to the throne, having received from the senate the titles usually given to the emperors, 69 A. C. He began his reign with several signal acts of mercy and of justice. The character of this prince, an unusual occurrence, was improved by advancement; in a private station he was all that was detestable; but as an emperor he appeared courageous, benevolent, and humane.

The good course, however, which he had marked out for himself, was soon terminated. He reigned only ninety-five days. Vitellius, who had been proclaimed emperor by his army in Germany, gave Otho battle at a place near Mantua, where the army of the latter was defeated, and he in a fit of despair ended his life by his own hand, 69 A. C.

§ Otho was descended from the ancient kings of Etruria.

It has been observed that the last moments of Otho's life were those of a philosopher. He comforted his soldiers who lamented his fortune, and he expressed his concern for their safety, when they earnestly solicited to pay him the last friendly offices before he stabbed himself; and he observed that it was better for one man to die, than that all should be involved in ruin for his obstinacy.

No circumstance, however, can excuse the crime of suicide, a vice which was awfully prevalent among the Romans.

13. Vitellius, upon his success, assumed the government 69 A. C., but he retained it only eight months. This wretch was not more given to cruelty, than to the infamous indulgence of his appetites. Like Nero, he abandoned himself to every species of flagitiousness and excess.

He perished justly. Vespasian, who at this time commanded the Roman army in Egypt, was proclaimed emperor by his legions. Entering Italy, a great part of the country submittted to his arms, and even Vitellius meanly capitulated to save his life, by a resignation of the empire. This act of cowardice rousing the indignation of the people, he was compelled to oppose Vespasian by force, but without effect. One of the generals of the conqueror took possession of Rome ; and Vitellius, falling into the hands of a party of the enemy, was ignominiously put to death.

§ Instances of the *cruel disposition* of this emperor are the following. Going to visit one of his associates who was in a violent fever, he mingled poison with his water, and delivered it to him with his own hands, in order to obtain his possessions. He never pardoned money-lenders who presumed to demand payment of his former debts; but taking away their lives he both cancelled their claims, and succeeded to their estate.

A Roman knight being dragged away to execution, and crying out that he had made the emperor his heir, Vitellius demanded to see the will, where finding himself joint inheritor with another, he ordered both to be executed, that he might enjoy the legacy alone.

Gluttony, however, was his predominant vice. In order to be able to renew his meals at pleasure, he brought himself to an habit of vomiting. His entertainments were prodigiously expensive; but oftener to others, than to himself. It has been remarked that had he reigned long, the whole empire would not have been sufficient to maintain his table.

In one particular dish, did this imperial glutton out-do all the former profusion of the most luxurious Romans. This was of such magnitude as to be called the shield of Minerva, and was filled with a medley, made from the air-bladders of the fish called scarri, the brains of pheasants and woodcocks, the tongues of the most costly birds, and the spawn of lampreys brought from the Carpathian sea.

14. Vespasian, having been declared emperor, by the unanimous consent of the senate and the army, 70 A. C. was received with the greatest joy on his arrival at Rome. Though of mean descent, he deserved the purple, and reigned during ten years, with great popularity. He was distinguished by clemency, affability, and a simple, frugal mode of life. His frugality, however, bordered upon avarice, which was the principal defect of his character.

In his administration of government, he acted under the forms of the republic, and even restored the senate to its deliberative rights. The famous war against the Jews, was terminated during the reign of Vespasian, by the arms of his son Titus. After this, the empire was in profound peace, and the emperor, having associated Titus in the government, soon departed this life, to the universal regret of the Roman people, in the 70th year of his age, 79 A. C.

§ It was some time before Vespasian could give security and peace to the empire. When this object was effected, he began to correct the abuses which had grown up under the tyranny of his predecessors. He restrained the licentiousness of the army—degraded such senators as were unworthy of their station—abridged the tedious processes in the courts of justice—re-edified such parts of the city as had suffered in the late commotions—and extended his paternal care over all parts of the empire.

Vespasian was liberal in the encouragement of learning and the arts. He was particularly kind to Josephus, the Jewish historian. Quintillian and Pliny, who flourished in his reign, were highly esteemed by him; and indeed the professors of every liberal art or science, were sure to experience his bounty.

He died by disease, a death quite unusual with the masters of Rome. Taken with an indisposition at Campania, which from the beginning he declared would be fatal, he cried out in the spirit of paganism, "Methinks I am going to be a god." When brought to the last extremity, and perceiving that he was about to expire, he declared that an emperor ought to die standing; and therefore raising himself upon his feet, he breathed his last in the arms of his supporters.

15. Titus succeeded to the empire upon the death of his father, 79 A. C. His character is celebrated as that of a highly humane, just and generous prince. He so devoted himself to acts of beneficence, that recollecting one evening that he nad done none during the day, he exclaimed, "O, my friends, I have lost a day!" His reign was a short, but pros

perous and happy one. He died in his 41st year, having reigned but little more than two years. His brother Domitian was suspected as being the author of his death.

§ Before he came to the throne, his character was thought not to be unexceptionable; but whatever vices he had indulged in, he seems to have abandoned upon that event. It is related as an instance of the government of his passions, that he relinquished the hand of his beloved Berenice, sister to king Agrippa, a woman of the greatest beauty, and the most refined allurements. Knowing that the connection with her was disagreeable to the Roman people, he conquered his affections, and sent her away, notwithstanding their mutual affection, and all her arts.

He was so tender of the lives of his subjects, that he took upon him the office of High Priest, in order to keep his hands undefiled with blood. He so little regarded such as censured or abused him, that he was heard to say, "When I do nothing worthy of censure, why should I be displeased at it?"

During his reign, Rome was three days on fire, without intermission; and this was followed by a plague, in which 10,000 persons were buried in a day. Titus, from his own resources, repaired the devastations of the city, and in all respects acted as a father to his people in their calamities. About this time the towns of Campania were destroyed by an eruption of Vesuvius. Upon this occasion Pliny, the naturalist, lost his life, by venturing too near the volcano.

When Titus was taken ill, he retired into the country of the Sabines, to his father's house. There his indisposition was increased by a burning fever. Modestly lifting his eyes to heaven, though with a spirit which christianity cannot approve, and without the hope it inspires, he complained of the severity of his fate, which was about to remove him from the world, where he had been employed in making a grateful people happy.

Domitian has incurred the suspicion of hastening his brother's end, by ordering him to be placed, during his agony, in a tub full of snow, where he expired.

15½ Domitian, upon the death of his brother, assumed the purple, 81 A. C. The beginning of his reign promised a continuance of their happiness to the Roman people. But the scene soon changed, and Domitian became a most execrable villain and tyrant. He condemned to death many of the most illustrious Romans, and witnessed, with the most ferocious pleasure, the agonies of his victims. He caused himself to be styled *God* and *Lord*, in all the papers that were presented to him. Though not destitute of learning himself, he banished the philosophers from Rome.

His reign was an era of prodigality and luxury, as well as of inhumanity and baseness. The people were loaded with insupportable taxes, to furnish spectacles and games for their amusement. His leisure was spent in the most degrading pursuits. One of the most constant occupations of his private hours, was the catching and killing of flies.

In his reign occurred the second great persecution of the christians, (that under Nero being the first) in which 40,000 of that profession were destroyed.

His general, Agricola, met with signal success in the expedition against Britain, though Domitian derived no renown, but rather disgrace from it, in consequence of his ungrateful treatment of Agricola. After a reign of 15 years, he was assassinated at the instigation of his wife.

§ To the senate and nobility, Domitian was particularly hostile, frequently threatening to extirpate them all. He delighted to expose them both to terror and ridicule. He once assembled the august body of the senate, to know in what vessel a turbot might be most conveniently dressed.

At another time, inviting them to a public entertainment, he received them all very formally at the entrance of his palace, and introduced them into a large gloomy hall, hung with black, and lighted with a few glimmering tapers. All around nothing was to be seen but coffins, with the name of each of the senators written upon them, and other frightful objects, and instruments of execution.

While the company beheld all these preparations with silent agony, on a sudden, a number of men burst into the room, clothed in black, with drawn swords and flaming torches, and after they had for some time terrified the guests, a message from the emperor, gave the company leave to retire.

His death had been predicted by the astrologers. This circumstance gave him the most tormenting inquietude. His jealousies increasing with a sense of his guilt, he was afraid by day and by night; and in proportion to his fears, he became more cruel. His stern air and fiery visage, directed and added poignancy to the tortures of his enemies. The gallery in which he was accustomed to walk, he ordered to be set round with a pellucid stone, which served as a mirror, to reflect the persons of all such as approached him from behind. But happily all his precautions were unavailing.

"The fall of Domitian," says Heeren, "confirms the result of universal experience, that a tyrant has little to fear from the people, but so much the more from individuals, whose throats are in danger."

His wife Domitia, having accidently discovered that her name was on the list of those whom he intended to put to death, at once concerted measures to secure her safety by the destruction of the emperor. Engaging some of the officers of his household, and others who were also on the proscribed list, to enter into her plan, she had the good fortune soon to learn, that he was dispatched at midnight in one of the most secret recesses of his palace, whither he had retired to rest.

The twelve Cæsars, as they have been denominated in history, ended with Domitian. In this number, however, Julius Cæsar is included, although Augustus was the first emperor strictly so called, and Nero was the last emperor of the Augustan family.

16. Nerva was elected emperor by the senate, upon the death of Domitian, 96 A. C. He was the first Roman emperor of foreign extraction, (being a native of Crete), and chosen on account of his virtues. His advanced age and the clemency of his disposition, with perhaps a want of energy, unfitted him to stem the torrent of corruption, and to cure the disorders of the empire. He however, adopted the excellent Trajan as his successor, and thus rendered a service to mankind which his administration otherwise could never have accomplished. He died 98 A. C. in the seventy-second year of his age, having reigned sixteen months.

§ During his short reign, Nerva made several good laws and regulations, and in every respect conducted himself like an indulgent father to his people. No statues would he permit to be erected to his memory, and he converted into money, such of Domitian's as had been spared by the senate. He sold many rich robes, and much of the splendid furniture of the palace, and retrenched several unreasonable expenses at court, yet he was not at all avaricious of money.

The following is a striking instance of his lenity. He had solemnly sworn that no senator of Rome should be put to death by his command, during his reign, from any cause whatever.

This oath he observed with such sanctity, that when two senators had conspired his death, he sent for them, and carried them with him to the public theatre. There presenting each a dagger, he desired them to strike, as he was determined not to ward off the blow.

17. Trajan, now in the possession of the throne, 98 A. C. was a native of Seville in Spain. He proved to be one of Rome's best sovereigns, splendid, warlike, munificent, courteous, and modest. The few vices he possessed were scarcely noticed amidst the blaze of his virtues, and the fame of his exploits. This, perhaps, is an instance of human infirmity in the estimation of character, since no vice should pass uncondemned. It is a matter of deep regret, that his equity, so visible in other respects, should be implicated by his conduct towards the Christians, whom he suffered to be mo-

lested. The third great persecution of them took place during his reign.

The boundaries of the empire were greatly enlarged by the victories of Trajan, in Dacia and the East. They never were so extensive, either before or after his time. The empire, however, was not improved by these conquests; it soon lost them, for the conquered countries immediately re-appeared in arms, and at length effected their independence.

Learning and learned men were signally encouraged by the emperor's liberality. His public works are also much celebrated. By his direction, the column still to be seen under the name of Trajan's column, was erected. It is one of the most remarkable monuments of ancient Rome. He died after a reign of nineteen years, at the age of sixty-three, 118 A. C.

§ It was a characteristic of Trajan, that he so little feared his enemies, that he could scarcely be induced to suppose he had any. Being once told that his favorite, Sura, was false to him; Trajan, to show how much he relied upon his fidelity, went in his ordinary manner to sup with him. There he commanded Sura's surgeon to be brought, whom he ordered to take off the hair about his eyebrows. He then made the barber shave his beard, after which, he went unconcerned into the bath as usual. The next day, when Sura's accusers were renewing their complaints; Trajan informed them how he had spent the night, remarking, that "if Sura, had any designs against his life, he had then the fairest opportunity."

The first war in which the emperor was engaged, was with the Dacians, who, in the reign of Domitian, had committed numerous ravages upon the provinces. Trajan, suddenly appearing in arms on the frontiers of their country, awed them at once into a treaty of peace. As, however, this was soon after violated, he entered the hostile territory, and obtained a complete victory, though with a prodigious slaughter of his troops; and Dacia became a Roman province. At his return to Rome he entered the city in triumph; and the rejoicings for his victories lasted for the space of one hundred and twenty days.

Trajan aferwards turned his arms eastward and speedily reduced Mesopotamia, Chaldea, and Assyria, and took Ctesiphon, the capital of the Parthian empire. At length, sailing down the Persian gulph, he entered the Indian ocean, conquering even the Indies, part of which he annexed to the Roman empire. This enterprise, which, at one time, he intended to pursue to the confines of the earth, he was obliged to relinquish on account of the inconveniences of increasing age.

Preparing to return to his capital in a style of unparalleled magnificence, he was unable from infirmity to reach home; and he died in the city of Seleucia, having refused to nominate a successor, lest he should adopt a person that was unworthy.

It may serve to show how highly Trajan was esteemed by his subjects, that it was the practice, during two hundred years in blessing his successors, to wish them "the fortune of Augustus, and the goodness of Trajan."

18. Adrian succeeded Trajan 118 years A. C. The wife of Trajan forged a will in the emperor's name, declaring Adrian his successor. This designation was supported by the army, and Adrian ventured to assume the government. This emperor was a nephew of Trajan, and in most respects worthy of being his successor. He chose to cultivate rather the arts of peace than war, and judging that the limits of the empire were too extensive, he abandoned all the conquests of Trajan, and bounded the eastern provinces by the river Euphrates. He was, however, remarkably expert in military discipline.

During an expedition of thirteen years, he visited in person all the provinces of his empire, and dispensed wherever he went the blessings of peace, justice, and order. In his capacity as a sovereign, he rendered important services to his subjects—in private life, however, it is said that his virtues were mingled with an alloy of vices, arising chiefly from irresolution. He indulged in vanity, envy, and detraction, in a degree which was too manifest to be palliated in a person of his exalted station. His virtues, however, were predominant, and Rome had few better emperors. His general knowledge, and his taste in the arts, were highly honourable in a sovereign. He died in the seventy-second year of his age, A. C. 138.

§ Among his exploits, it is known that when he came to Britain, he built a wall of wood and earth, between the modern towns of Carlisle and Newcastle, eighty miles in length, to protect the Britons from the incursions of the Caledonians. In a war with the Jews, he killed in battle five hundred and eighty thousand of that people who had become rebellious, and built a city on the ruins of Jerusalem which he called Aelia Capitolina. In performing his long marches with his army, Adrian generally travelled on foot, and went without any covering on his head.

His character was in many respects extraordinary, and none of the Roman emperors excelled him in variety of endowments. He was highly skilful in all the exercises both of body and mind. He was an author, orator, mathematician, musician and painter. His memory was so retentive, that he recollected every incident of his life, and he knew all the soldiers of his army by name.

He was the first emperor who wore a long beard, a fashion which he adopted to hide the warts on his face. His successor followed his example for the sake of ornament.

Though Adrian aimed at universal reputation, he strictly attended to the duties of his station. Through his cares he began to fail in health and strength, and adopting for his successor Titus Antoninus, he sought the repose which he needed. His bodily infirmities however, daily increased, and his pain becoming nearly insupportable, he vehemently desired death. Antoninus with difficulty persuaded him to sustain life, though the emperor frequently cried out in his agonies, "How miserable a thing is it to seek death, and not to find it." Alas! how pointed is the moral, that no station, however exalted, can exempt one from the infirmities of life and the sting of death. As he was expiring, the emperor repeated the following lines, as translated into English.

O fleeting spirit, wand'ring fire,
  That long has warmed my tender breast,
Wilt thou no more my frame inspire?
  No more a pleasing cheerful guest?
Whither, ah! whither art thou flying?
  To what dark, undiscovered shore?
Thou seemest all trembling, shivering, dying,
  And wit and humour are no more.

His reign was a prosperous one of twenty-two years. He died 139 A.C. aged seventy-two.

19. Titus Antoninus, surnamed Pius, having been adopted by Adrian, succeeded to the empire 138 A. C. His virtues were an ornament to human nature, and conferred innumerable blessings on mankind. He preferred peace to conquest, and yet whenever war became necessary, he carried it on with vigour and success. He was conspicuous for justice and clemency, and his love of the religion of his country.

His reign was marked by few events, as the reigns of peaceable monarchs usually are. The most remarkable foreign occurrences were the enlargement of the province of Britain by the conquests of Urbicus, and the suppression of some forminable rebellions in Germany, Dacia, and the East. He died at the age of seventy-four, having reigned twenty-two years. A. C. 161.

§ Such was the munificence of Antoninus, that in cases of famine or inundation, he supplied with his own money the wants of the sufferers. Such were his humanity and love of peace, that when told of conquering heroes, he said with Scipio, that "he preferred the life and preservation of one subject to the death of an hundred enemies!" His regard of the christians was extraordinary for a heathen emperor. He declared that "if any should proceed to disturb them on account of their religion, such should undergo the same punishment which was intended against the accused." A degree of persecution nevertheless took place, contrary to the princi ples of the emperor.

He was a distinguished rewarder of learned men, whom he invi ted from all parts of the world, and raised to wealth and honour. Among the rest, he sent for Apollonius the famous stoic philosopher, to instruct his adopted son, Marcus Aurelius, whom he had previous ly married to his daughter.

Apollonius being arrived at Rome, the emperor desired his atten dance: but the philosopher arrogantly answered that it was the scholar's duty to wait upon the master, and not the master's to wait upon the scholar. To this reply, Antoninus only returned with a smile, "that it was surprising how Apollonius, who made no difficulty in coming from Greece to Rome, should think it so hard to walk from one part of Rome to the other," and immediately sent Marcus Aurelius to him.

In the midst of his labours in rendering his subjects happy, he was seized with a lingering illness, which terminated in death in the seventy-fifth year of his age, and the twenty-third of his reign.

20. Marcus Aurelius Antoninus, the adopted son of Pius, now came to the throne, 161 A. C. His name before was Annius Verus, and he, together with Lucius Verus, his brother, had been designated by Adrian to succeed to the government, whenever Antoninus Pius should decease. Pius confirmed the adoption of Marcus, without once naming Lucius Verus. Marcus, however, upon assuming the empire, admitted his brother as a partner in the administration.

They were perfectly opposite in character; Marcus Aurelius being as much distinguished for his energy and virtue, as Verus was for imbecility, meanness, and vice. Aurelius was in every respect equal to his predecessor, and was even more conspicuous for his attachment to philosophy. This, as the stoics professed it, he has admirably taught and illustrated in his Meditations.

In the wars which were carried on during this joint reign, the worthless Verus brought disgrace upon the Roman name, wherever he commanded. The Parthians, however, were repulsed by the legions of the empire, and a rebellion of the Germans was subdued.

After the death of Verus, which happily soon took place, Aurelius directed all his energies for the improvement and happiness of his empire. For purposes of beneficence he visited the remotest corners of the Roman world. He died at length in Pannonia, in the fifty-ninth year of his age, and nineteenth of his reign, A. C. 180.

It was an infelicity of the otherwise admirable reign of Aurelius, that the christians at one time were violently persecuted. The fanatical Pagan priests were, however, the immediate instruments in this persecution, inasmuch as they ascribed to the christians the various calamities which the empire endured, under the excesses of Verus, the attacks of the barbarians, and the devastations occasioned by earthquakes, famines, pestilences, and inundations.

§ Aurelius loved retirement and philosophical contemplation, and improved for mental cultivation and enjoyment, all the leisure he could command. That, however, was far less than his wishes dictated. The disturbances in the empire called him frequently into the field, and until the death of his colleague, he suffered no small inquietude on his account. He was, however, successful in his military excursions.

One deliverance which he and his army experienced on a certain occasion, borders on the miraculous. In a contest with the barbarians beyond the Danube, the Roman legions unexpectedly, through the artifice of the enemy, found themselves inclosed in a place where they could neither fight, nor retreat. In this situation they became at length totally disheartened, from their long continued fatigue, the excessive heat of the place, and their violent thirst.

In these suffering circumstances, while sorrow and despair were depicted on every brow, Aurelius ran through the ranks, and used every effort to rekindle their hopes and courage. But all was in vain. At this crisis, and just as the barbarians were ready to follow them, we are told that the solemn prayers of a *christian legion*, then serving among them, produced such a shower of rain as instantly revived the fainting army. From the same clouds, was discharged such a terrible storm of hail with thunder against the enemy, as dismayed them, and made them an easy prey to the refreshed and inspirited Romans.

These circumstances are related by pagan as well as Christian writers, only with this difference, that the latter ascribe the victory to their own prayers, the former to the prayers of their emperor Aurelius, however, it seems, was favourably impressed in regard to the christians, since he immediately relaxed the persecution against them.

Some other particulars will be related respecting Aurelius, in our biographical sketches.

Upon the death of Aurelius the empire evidently declined. The emperors who succeeded were generally a weak or vicious race. The colossal size of the empire caused it to sink by its own weight. Enemies on its borders oppressed it from without, and tumults and factions paralized it within; patriotism and genius were becoming rare, and corruption pervaded all orders of the community.

At the period of Trajan's death, the empire comprehended the greater part of Britain, all Spain, France, the Netherlands, Italy, part of Germany, Egypt, Barbary, Biledulgerid, Turkey in Europe and in Asia, and Persia. At the demise of Aurelius, it was a little diminished in size, but still too large to be preserved entire, amidst the profligacy of he times.

21. Commodus, the son of Aurelius, had been nominated by his father to succeed him, and he accordingly now mounted the throne, 180 A. C. He had nothing but the merits of his father to commend him to the Roman people. He inherited the disposition of his infamous mother, Faustina, rather than of Aurelius. The change from the reign of the father to the son was indeed a most gloomy one. It is a singular fact, that the most detestable of all the emperors was the son of the best.

Commodus was given to low vices and mean pursuits—was fond of the sports of the circus and amphitheatre, the hunting of wild beasts, and the combats of boxers and gladiators. His administration of the government was entirely weak, contemptible, and tyrannical. He perished by assassination, in the thirty-second year of his age, and the thirteenth year of his reign, 193 A. C.

§ It had been happy for himself and mankind, had Commodus cultivated his mind, as he did his body, (for he was wonderfully expert in all corporeal exercises:) but he was averse to every rational and liberal pursuit. He spent the day in feasting, and the night in the vilest debaucheries.

His cruelty combined with avarice and levity, cannot be too strongly held up for the detestation of mankind. If any person desired to be revenged on an enemy, by bargaining with Commodus for a sum of money, he was permitted to destroy him in such a manner as he chose. He commanded a person to be thrown among wild beasts, for reading the life of Caligula in Suetonius. He would sometimes, in a frolic, cut off men's noses, under a pretence of shaving their beards; yet he was himself so jealous of mankind, that he was obliged to be his own barber; or as some have said, he used to burn his beard, after the example of Dionysius, the tyrant.

In imitating Hercules with his club and lion's skin, he would furiously fall upon a company of beggars in the streets, and beat them to death; having first dressed them up like giants and monsters, and giving them sponges to throw at him, instead of stones.

In such a manner did this wretch spend his time, while the troubles of his empire were daily increasing, and its strength and territories were diminishing by frequent warfares on the frontiers. He narrowly escaped destruction several times, from his personal exasperated foes. But he was destined at length justly to fall. His favourite concubine, Marcia, who accidentally discovered the emperor's determination to put her to death, with other conspirators, found the means of destroying him, partly by poison and partly by strangling.

22. Pertinax, who had been fixed upon by the conspirators as the successor of Commŏdus, was joyfully proclaimed by the prætorian guards, 193 A. C. Originally he was the son of an enfranchised slave, but rose to esteem by his virtues and military talents. Applying himself to the correction of abuses with too unsparing and rash a hand, he alienated the affections of a corrupted people, and was deposed and murdered by the same guards that had placed him on the throne, after a reign of only three months, aged sixty-eight years. The loss which the empire felt in the death of such a man is greater than can be well conceived.

23. Didius Julianus, next succeeded to the empire 193 A. C., having purchased it of the prætorian guards, who put it up to the highest bidder. At the same time, several commanders in the distant provinces, were each proclaimed by their respective forces. These, however, lost their lives except Septimius Severus, who marched to Rome and seized the government. Didius was hereupon deposed and put to death by the senate in the fifth month of his reign.

§ Didius presents a striking instance of the cupidity of the human mind for power, and of the infelicities that attend it. He was a man of consular rank, and the richest citizen of Rome. Hearing the singular proclamation of the prætorian guards, and charmed with the prospect of unbounded dominion, he hastened to the camp, and bid the largest price for the empire. He gave to each soldier (10,000 in number) the sum of 6250 drachmas, which amounts to nearly 9,000,000 dollars, in the whole.

From this period he was exposed to disappointment, mortification, insult, and danger. Indulging his ease and his avaricious disposition, he soon offended those who made him emperor. He was contemptuously treated at home, while two or more generals in the provinces abroad, disclaimed his authority. Upon the approach of Severus, he could raise no forces to meet him. He was nearly distracted by the multiplicity of counsels, and finally his perplexity and distress became extreme and overwhelming.

The senate, at this crisis, perceiving his timidity and irresolution, resolved to abandon him, and to proclaim Severus. His death then was no longer problematical; and though he persisted that he had a right to enjoy his purchase for the natural period of his life, as he had been guilty of no crime, all did not avail. The executioners, obliging him to stretch his neck forward according to custom, immediately struck off his head.

24. Septimius Severus was now at the head of the Roman world, 193 A. C. He was an African by birth, and possessed a restless activity with an unbounded share of ambition. He was endowed with a hardihood and decision of character, which fitted him for any enterprise. His military talents were conspicuous, and the credit of the Roman arms was sustained during his reign. In his administration of government he was generally wise and equitable, though highly despotic.

In his expedition into England, he built a stone wall extending from Solway Frith to the German Ocean, nearly on a parallel with that of Adrian. Severus died at York in England, in the sixty-sixth year of his age, after a reign of eighteen years, 211 A. C. He left the empire to his two sons Caracalla and Geta, whose dispositions gave the emperor the greatest inquietude.

§ The first act of Severus, even before he entered Rome, was to degrade the prætorian soldiers, whose irregularity had already become too conspicuous. These he stript of their title, and banished one hundred miles from the city. He soon after engaged in a terrible conflict with Niger, his competitor in the East, whom he finally conquered on the plains of Issus. Albinus also, his other competitor, who commanded in Britain, was soon after conquered in battle, in one of the severest engagements recorded in the Roman history. It was fought in Gaul, and lasted from morning till night, without any apparent advantage on either side. It was decided at length by a body of reserve, in favour of Severus.

His activity and love of conquest led him into the East, where he signalised his arms, and whence he returned in triumph to Rome. Having escaped a conspiracy formed by Plautian, to whom he had committed his domestic policy, he spent a considerable time in visiting the cities of Italy; and finally in affording protection to all parts of his empire, he made an expedition into Britain. The wall which he here built was eight feet broad and twelve feet high, planted with towers at a mile's distance from each other, and communicating by pipes of brass in the wall, which conveyed intelligence from one garrison to another with incredible dispatch.

Having given peace to the island, and secured it against the irruptions of the Caledonians, he began to feel the effects of age and fatigue; but he was more broken down by the irreclaimable life of Caracalla. Calling for the urn in which his ashes were to be enclosed, he moralized on his melancholy condition in the following remark. "Little urn," said he, "thou shalt now contain what the world could not contain." It is recorded that he hastened his death by purposely loading his stomach with food, in his weak state.

25. Caracalla and Geta were now established on the throne, 211 A. C. Their association in the empire created a mutual enmity, and indeed they were very unlike in native character. Caracalla was fierce and cruel to an extreme degree. Geta was mild and merciful. The former resolving to reign alone, seized an opportunity to murder Geta in the arms of his mother. During his reign of six years, he committed a continued series of atrocities. He was taken off by assassination, 217 A. C.

Within this short period the empire was every day declining; the soldiers were entirely masters of every election; and both discipline in the army, and subordination in the state, were almost destroyed.

§ The worst qualities of the worst emperors centered in this imperial wretch. He slew his friend Lætius, his own wife Plautina, and Papinian, the renowned civilian, for refusing to write in vindication of his cruelty—that upright man answering the emperor's request by observing, "that it was much easier to commit a parricide than to defend it."

He commanded all the governors to be slain, whom his brother had appointed, and destroyed not less than 2000 of his adherents. Upon a certain occasion, he ordered his soldiers to fall upon a crowded audience in the theatre, only for discountenancing a charioteer, whom he happened to favour.

As might be expected, he was harrassed with awful terrors. He feared the day of his death, and that day was fast approaching. One Martial, a centurion of the guards, was prevailed upon by a higher officer, Macrinus, to give the emperor his death-wound, on a convenient occasion, which was readily seized, and thus the world was freed from a monster, who was not only infinitely unfit to govern an empire, but was unworthy to live.

26. Macrinus, who instigated Caracalla's death, was proclaimed emperor, 217 A. C. Little is recorded respecting him. He was a person of obscure birth, and was deemed severe by the soldiery, who had now become so licentious, that they could scarcely bear the gentlest corrections. His attempts at discipline, together with the artifices of the grandmother of Heliogabalus, alienated from him the affections of the army, and he lost his life in the struggle to retain his power, after a reign of only fourteen months, 218 A. C.

27. Heliogabalus was, by the army, raised to the throne

when only fourteen years of age. The appointment of the army, as usual, influenced the decisions of the senate and citizens of Rome. This emperor proved to be another monster of wickedness of the same rank with Nero, Commodus, and Caracalla. He lived to be only eighteen years of age, and yet lived long enough to hasten the fall of the empire, and to cover his name with eternal infamy. He was murdered in the fourth year of his reign, 222 A. C.

§ Heliogabalus was a natural son of Caracalla, a beautiful youth, and loved by the army. Surrounded by flatterers, he soon yielded himself to their directions. His short life was but a tissue of effeminacy, lust, folly, and extravagance. Some parts of his conduct were too indecent here to be described.

In four years he married six wives, and divorced them all. He even assumed the dress and circumstances of a woman, and married one of his officers. After that he took for husband, one Hierocles, a slave, whom he suffered to beat him severely when guilty of any excess, all which he endured with great patience, saying, that it was the duty of a wife to submit to her husband.

His prodigality and epicurism were boundless. His supper generally cost six thousand crowns, and often sixty thousand. He always dressed in cloth of gold and purple, enriched with precious stones, and never twice put on the same habit. Whenever he took horse, all the way between his apartment and the place of mounting, was covered with gold and silver dust strewn at his approach.

His cruelties were equal to his licentiousness. He often invited the most common of the people to share in his feasts, and made them sit down on large bellows full of wind, which by sudden exhaustion, threw the guests on the ground, and left them a prey to wild beasts. It is even said he endeavored to foretel the secrets of futurity, by inspecting the entrails of young men sacrificed; and that he chose for this horrid purpose, the most beautiful youths throughout Italy.

These are a few of the thousand excesses, follies, and atrocities of a mad and vicious boy, who, with the possession of unlimited rule, could do as he pleased.

Being persuaded by his grandmother Mæsa, he adopted Alexander his cousin-german as his successor; but indignant that the affections of his army were bestowed upon the latter, he meditated revenge. His soldiers, however, perceiving his intention, took an opportunity to secure his person, and having dispatched him, treated his body with the greatest indignity, and consigned it at length to the Tyber.

28. Alexander Severus was declared emperor 222 A. C He was a prince of a kind, beneficent, and energetic character, and highly accomplished in learning and the arts. Every way calculated to make his subjects happy, he was greatly

honoured and esteemed by them. He was conspicuous also for his military talents, and for the defeat of the Persians and others during his reign. He thus restored the empire to its former limits: but this exertion of its remaining strength, rather hastened than delayed its decline.

He was cut off by a mutiny among his own soldiers in the fourteenth year of his reign, and the twenty-ninth of his age, at the instigation of Maximinus, his successor, 235 A. C.

§ As a specimen of his virtuous character we may mention, that he ever loved good men, and severely reproved the lewd and infamous. His remark is in point, when he decided a contest between the christians and a company of cooks and vinters, about a piece of ground, which the one claimed as a place of public worship, and the other for exercising their respective trades. "It is better that God be worshiped there in any manner, than that the place should be put to the uses of drunkenness or debauchery."

At the age of sixteen, when he ascended the throne, he had all the premature wisdom of age. His judgment was solid, and his talents were various. He was an excellent mathematician, geometrician, and musician. His taste in painting, sculpture and poetry was admirable.

The first part of his reign was spent in a reformation of the abuses of his predecessors; particularly in restoring the senators to their rank and influence. His first expedition, in the tenth year of his reign, was against the Parthians and Persians, whom he opposed with a powerful army. In one decisive engagement, he routed the Persians with great slaughter. About the same time, several of his generals obtained signal victories, over various nations then at war with the empire.

His manner of living was like that of the meanest sentinel; whenever he dined or supped, he sat with his tent open, that all men might be witnesses of his abstemiousness. He was at one time instructed by the famous Origen in the principles of Christianity; though it does not appear that he embraced that religion.

29. Maximinus, who was accessary to the murder of Severus, ascended the throne upon this event, 235 A. C. He was the son of a Thracian shepherd, and is represented by historians as a man of gigantic stature and Herculean strength. He was full eight feet in height, and perfectly symmetrical in form.

He rose by degrees into power; but though meritorious before his elevation, as a sovereign he was brutal and ferocious. He warred with the Germans, and wasted their country to the extent of four hundred and fifty miles, converting it almost into a desert. His cruelties soon aroused the Roman people against him, and he was finally assassinated by his own soldiers in his tent, after a reign of three years, 238 A. C.

During the period of his power, the two Gordians, father and son were proclaimed emperors, but these soon perished. The senate then proclaimed Pupienus and Balbinus, who survived Maximinus. These measures were dictated by the anxiety which the Romans felt, to free themselves from that tyrant.

§ Maximinus is said to have delighted in acts of the greatest barbarity, and no less than four hundred persons lost their lives, on the false suspicion of a conspiracy against his life. He caused to be removed from his sight or assassinated, many noble Romans, who, as he suspected, despised him, on account of his mean origin.

When he was apprised of the acts of the senate, appointing others to the supreme power, he raved and howled like a wild beast, and almost destroyed himself by beating his head against the walls of his palace. His fury, however, at length gave way to a spirit of revenge; but his bloody machinations were soon stopped. His guards having been corrupted, murdered him while sleeping in his tent, as he was too formidable an object to be attacked while awake.

Owing to his size, his strength was prodigious. He alone could draw a full loaded wagon. With a blow of his fist he could break the teeth in a horse's mouth, and with a kick of his foot could break its thigh. His voracity was proportioned to his size and strength. He generally ate forty pounds of flesh every day, and drank six gallons of wine.

The Prætorian soldiers who were enemies to Pupienus and Balbinus, soon embraced an opportunity of despatching them both, and accidentally meeting Gordian, grandson to one of the former Gordians, they proclaimed him emperor. The senate and people had been too long controlled by the army, on the subject of nominating the emperors, to withhold their consent in the present instance.

30. Gordian accordingly assumed the empire 238 years A. C. He was no more than sixteen years old at this time, and was a prince of very considerable merit. The Goths, and also the Persians, who had invaded the confines of the empire on different sides, were repulsed by his arms.

Towards the latter part of his reign, Philip, an Arabian, was chosen prætorian præfect, under whose administration the people began to be discontented. This state of things Philip fostered, till the odium against the emperor so far increased, that the præfect ventured to order his execution, with a view to his own preferment, an object which he accomplished. Gordian's reign was a period of nearly six years.

§ Gordian was a man so fond of learning, that he had collected 62,000 books in his private library.

31. Philip having acquired the empire 244 A. C., by the murder of his benefactor, reigned five years, and then was himself assassinated, while marching against Decius.

§ Philip was an Arabian by birth, and received, in the manner of his death, a righteous retribution, on account of his own nefarious conduct in gaining the sceptre.

32. Decius, whom Philip had appointed to command a revolted army, had been proclaimed before the emperor's death. Upon that event he began to assume the functions of government 249 A. C. His activity and wisdom would have stayed the progress of decay in the empire, if any human means could effect that object. But the tendency to this state of things was irretrievable and fatal.

The profligacy and luxury of the times, the disputes between the Pagans and Christians, and the beginning irruptions of the barbarous nations from without, were enfeebling the empire beyond remedy.

Decius reigned but two years and six months, having been cut off, in a war with the Goths, by the treachery of Gallus, his general.

33. Gallus, raised to the throne 251 A. C., by that part of the army which survived a defeat he had himself occasioned, reigned but two years and four months. He was a vicious sovereign, and during his reign the empire suffered incalculable misery. He perished in a civil war, in which Aemilianus, his general, opposed him, and was victorious.

§ It was in the time of Gallus, that a dreadful pestilence spread over the earth, threatening almost to depopulate it.

34. Valerian, a commander of one of the armies of the empire, succeeded to the throne 254 A. C., contrary to the expectations of Aemilianus. In a war with the Persians, having been taken prisoner, he suffered unheard of hardships and insult, and at length was put to death in the most cruel manner.

§ Sapor, the Persian king, happened to secure the person of Valerian. We are told that he always used the emperor as a footstool for mounting his horse, and that he often observed, "such an attitude was the best statue that could be erected in honour of his victory."

The manner of Valerian's death is almost too horrid to be mentioned. His eyes were first plucked out, and afterwards he was flayed alive, when his skin was dyed red, and exposed in a temple. He was seven years a prisoner.

35. Gallienus, son of Valerian, was chosen emperor 260

A. C. He promised to avenge the insults and death of his father; but after his elevation, he thought only of his own base pleasures, while the empire was attacked without, and distracted within. Thirty pretenders were at one time contending for the dominion of the state. Gallienus suffered a violent death.

36. Upon the death of Gallienus, Flavius Claudius was invested with the purple, 268 A. C., agreeably to the wishes of the army, and the whole Roman people. He was an active, wise, and good prince; but unhappily his reign was short, being less than two years. He died a natural death, which was more frequently the lot of the virtuous, than of the profligate emperors.

§ Claudius opposed with success the Goths, Heruli, &c. who had invaded the empire on the north, in one instance destroying an army of 300,000 men; and he likewise overthrew the Germans, who had reared the standard of revolt. His energy stayed, for a short time, the decline of the empire.

37. The army made choice of Aurelian as emperor, 270 A. C. His parentage was obscure, but he was esteemed the most valiant commander of his age. After his elevation, his time was passed in repressing the irruptions of the barbarians, and particularly in carrying on a war with Zenobia, a princess of Palmyra, commonly styled the Queen of the East, whom he conquered, and brought captive to Rome. With great courage and military talents, he was cruel. He fell in a conspiracy which was raised against him by some of his subjects.

§ His strength was said to be so great, that in one single engagement, he killed 40 of the enemy with his own hand, and above 900 at different times. The degeneracy of his people seemed almost to justify his severities, in punishing offenders; but it is said that when he was about to sign certain edicts against the christians, who were an inoffensive people, he was deterred from the act, by a thunder-bolt, which fell so near his person, that his escape was thought to be miraculous.

38. Several months elapsed before a new emperor was elected. At length Tacitus was prevailed upon to take the reins of government, 275 A. C. He was a man of great merit, but unfortunately to the empire, he died of a fever after a reign of only six months, at the age of 75.

39. His successor was Probus, though a minority in the

army chose Florian, a brother of Tacitus. Florian enjoyed this distinction but two months; for upon the establishment of Probus in the empire, he sought a voluntary death.

Probus possessed uncommon activity, courage, and integrity, and was constantly engaged in war with the barbarians, and in suppressing the numerous factions which arose in his dominions. Offending his soldiers by obliging them to drain an extensive fen in Sirmium, his native place, he was slain in a conspiracy which they had formed against him, 282 A. C.

§ Probus was born of noble parentage, and was early distinguished by his excellent qualities. He was frequently the first man that, in besieging towns, scaled the walls, or that burst into the enemy's camp.

His energy and virtue, great as they were, could scarcely present a sufficient barrier to the tide of calamities that rushed upon the empire. In a war, however, with the Germans in Gaul, he slew 400,000 men; and at various times repulsed many other enemies, particularly the Sarmatians, Goths and Blemii. The last were a people who had left the forests of Ethiopia, and possessed themselves of Arabia and Judea.

Among those of his subjects who had rebelled against him, was Bonosus, who was remarkable as given to intoxication. The rebel being overcome, hanged himself in despair. Probus seeing him immediately after this event, pointed to his body, and with great humour observed, "There hangs, not a man, but a bottle."

40. Carus, prætorian præfect to the deceased emperor, was chosen by the army to succeed him 282 A. C. He associated with him in command, his two sons, Carinus and Numerian. Carus, and his son Numerian, were worthy of the empire, but Carinus was given to vice. Their reign, however, was only of two years' continuance. Carus was smitten by a flash of lightning, in his tent, and his sons were killed soon after—Numerian by an act of treachery, Carinus in a contest with Diocletian, who had been chosen emperor.

§ Numerian was so affected by the death of his father, that through excess of weeping, he brought on a disorder in his eyes, in consequence of which he was obliged to be carried in a close litter. In this situation he was murdered by his ambitious father-in-law, Aper, who was soon cut off by the hand of Diocletian.

41. Diocletian began his reign in 284 A. C., and two years afterwards, associated with himself in the empire his general Maximian. Under their united auspices, the enemies of Rome were frequently repulsed. At the expiration of about

eight years from that time, they took two colleagues, Galerius and Constantius; and bestowed upon each the title of Cæsar.

This state of things was novel. There was a four fold division of the government, with two emperors and two Cæsars at its head, each having a nominal supremacy. Diocletian, however, was the master spirit that moved and controlled the whole. In this state, the government was administered a few years, when strange to relate the two emperors resigned their authority into the hands of the two Cæsars, and retired into private life 304 A. C.

Diocletian seems to have been sincere in his abdication, as he contentedly spent eight or nine years in rural privacy, and in cultivating his garden. Maximian soon began to be discontented, and made several attempts, but in vain, to resume his former powers. His intrigues in Britain, where Constantine and his son Constantine resided, cost him his life. Diocletian died about 312 A. C. Maximian perished 310 A. C.

§ Diocletian's parentage was mean. According to some he was the son of a scrivener; and according to others, of a slave. When elected to the empire he was forty years old, and owed his exaltation entirely to his merit, having passed through the various gradations of office, with sagacity, courage, and success. He chose Galerius for his associate, giving him the title of Cæsar, with a view to secure his aid in opposing Narses, the king of Persia and Parthia, who had invaded Mesopotamia. In this enterprise they met with signal success. Other enemies they subdued, except the northern nations, who, though repulsed and slaughtered in incredible numbers, were ever ready to embrace fresh opportunities of renewing hostilities.

Diocletian, after his abdication of the empire, retired to his native country, Dalmatia, where he built a magnificent palace for his accommodation, near the town of Salona. Here he led a secure and quiet life. When some of his friends attempted to persuade him to resume the empire, he replied, "that if they knew his present happiness, they would rather endeavour to imitate than disturb it."

Maximian was a native of Sirmium, in Pannonia, and was adopted by Diocletian as emperor, on account of his courage and fidelity. He defeated many enemies of his country, though his arms in Britain were unsuccessful. He adopted Constantius as Cæsar, with a view to oppose the claims of Carausius, a principal commander in Britain, who had proclaimed himself emperor.

42. When Diocletian and Maximian resigned their power, Constantius and Galerius were universally acknowledged 304 A. C. Constantius governed the western parts of the empire. Galerius the eastern. They took in with them two partners, so that the empire was again under the guidance of

four persons, all invested with supreme authority; each having his distinct department. Severus and Maximian were the persons who were created Cæsars.

Constantius was a worthy character, Galerius was the reverse. Constantius died at York, in Britain, 306 A. C., leaving his son Constantine as his successor. Galerius died four years afterwards of an extraordinary incurable disease. He had instigated Diocletian to persecute the christians.

§ The western parts of the empire, or the dominion of Constantius, consisted of Italy, Sicily, the greatest part of Africa, together with Spain, Gaul, Britain, and Germany. The eastern parts, or the dominion of Galerius, consisted of Illyricum, Pannonia, Thrace, Macedonia, all the provinces of Greece, and the lesser Asia, together with Egypt, Syria, Judea, and all other oriental countries.

An anecdote of the following kind is related of Constantius:—when he was persuaded to displace all the christian officers of his household; though he would not suffer the christians to be injured, he sent away in disgrace the few that complied, alleging, "that those who were not true to their God, would never be faithful to their prince."

43. From the commencement to the close of the present period, persecutions of the christians more or less prevailed in the empire. At times, this unoffending class of the Roman subjects suffered in an extreme degree, from the edicts of the emperors. Historians have usually reckoned ten general persecutions of the christians. The names of the emperors, under whom these persecutions were experienced, were the following:—Nero, Domitian, Trajan, Antoninus, Severus, Maximinus, Decius, Valerian, Aurelian, and Diocletian.

Most of these emperors persecuted the christians from malignity, and for the gratification of their cruel dispositions. Others did it, (though their conduct was indefensible,) from ignorance or prejudice, aided by the spirit of the age, and the common corruption of our nature.

§ As this period is named from the persecutions which the professors of Christianity endured under the Roman emperors, it might seem proper here, to enter into some details on this subject. But a few of these will be included in an article on ecclesiastical history, to be embodied in the present volume.

JUDEA.

44. JUDEA, already under the sway of Rome, became a province of the empire 6 A. C. upon the banishment of Ar-

chelaus, eldest son of Herod the Great. It was at the commencement of this period, that the birth of our blessed Saviour Jesus Christ, as before noticed in the Roman history, took place. Herod, in addition to all his other crimes shed the blood of the children of Bethlehem, in the hope that the infant Jesus would fall among them. He died miserably, soon after this transaction.

§ In the reign of Herod, the sceptre, agreeably to ancient prophecy, having departed from Judah, by the control which the Romans had over the government, Jesus Christ was born in the year of the world 4000. This has already been explained. We use, however, the vulgar era (4004) and assign the subsequent events according to that calculation. The mistake supposed to be made by the ancient chronologers has been too far sanctioned by Time, to be now remedied.

His birth, which was announced by angels to the shepherds of Bethlehem, and which brought the eastern magi to worship him, exceedingly troubled Herod and the principal Jews, who became apprehensive of new wars and commotions. After finding out the place of his nativity, (viz. Bethlehem,) Herod determined on his death, by destroying all the children of that place and of its vicinity, "from two years old and under."

The providence of God, however, had removed the holy child beyond his reach, inasmuch as his parents had fled with him, in the mean time, into Egypt. Herod's death soon occurring, they returned from Egypt, and dwelt in Nazareth, a city of Galilee.

It is not our design to detail events here, which more properly belong to ecclesiastical history. We would only say, that after a laborious and useful life, in the third year of his ministry, and in the thirty-third of his age, Jesus Christ expiated human transgression, by his death on the cross. He suffered under Pontius Pilate, the Roman governor, upon a false accusation brought against him by his own countrymen, the Jews.

This glorious personage, who was "God manifest in the flesh," came into the world to save his people from their sins. In his human nature he was lineally descended from David, though the family at the period of his birth, had become obscure and reduced to poverty. The effects of his appearance in the world were from the beginning, decisive. The holy system which he taught, considering the hostility of man to truth and piety, was diffused with great rapidity, under the ministry of the apostles. Reformation of moral character was its aim, object and result. Its effects have ever been great, and such they will be to the end of time.

The civil affairs of the Jews, from the commencement of this era to the destruction of Jerusalem by Titus Vespasian, are too unimportant to be particularly described. A brief summary of them follows.

§ Archelaus, under whom Judea became in form a Roman province, possessed only a tetrarchy, or the fourth part of the kingdom of Jewry. The rest of the country was divided into three more tetrarchies, which were those of Galilee and Petræa possessed by Herod Antipatas; that of Ituræa possessed by Philip, another son of Herod; and that of Abilene possessed by Eysanias, who being afterwards banished into Gaul, had his province governed by Pontius Pilate.

The successor of Archelaus was Herod II. named Antipas, who married his brother Philip's wife. This was the incestuous marriage on account of which John the Baptist reproved Herod, as mentioned in the New Testament. It was in the time of this Herod that our Saviour's crucifixion, resurrection, and ascension, occurred.

Herod II. was succeeded by his son Herod the Great. Caligula, the emperor of Rome, at that time invested him with the tetrarchy of his uncle Philip, and conferred on him the title of king. The other tetrarchies fell to his possession shortly afterwards. It was this Herod who caused the apostle James to be martyred, the apostle Peter to be imprisoned, and was himself smitten by an angel and devoured by worms.

His son Agrippa Minor, succeeded, and was the last king of Jewry. It was before him, that the apostle Paul pleaded in defence of the gospel.

45. During the reign of Agrippa Minor, Jerusalem was attacked by Titus (Vespasian) 70 A. D. The cause of this attack originated in the commotions and insurrections of the Jews, which were frequent about this time. This miserable people had suffered greatly, from the injustice and extortion practised upon them by the agents of the Roman government, and they consequently rose in rebellion.

A signal vengeance fell upon their heads. Jerusalem was beseiged, and one million of people are said to have perished on the occasion. To such distress were the Jews reduced by famine, that mothers murdered their children for food. The people suffered greatly in other parts of Judea; and though numbers remained in their native land, vast multitudes were dispersed over the face of the earth, on which they have ever since been wanderers.

The reader of the Bible will see in these events, a remarkable fulfilment of the predictions of the ancient prophets and of our Saviour; and he will also learn the evil and danger of despising divine admonitions, and abusing religious privileges. The Jews are to this day a witness of the truth of scripture.

§ Nero, who was emperor when the war with the Jews commenced, entrusted the management of it to his general, Vespasian, who, accompanied by his son Titus, and a powerful army, arrived in Syria, 67 A. C. Vespasian soon after being chosen emperor, left orders with his son Titus, to contiuue the war, while he himself set out for Rome.

Titus prosecuted the enterprise with diligence, and besieging Jerusalem, he took it within a few months, after an obstinate resistance on the part of its inhabitants. Twice, during the siege, Titus offered them very favourable terms, but so infatuated were they, that hey not only refused his offers, but insulted at length his messenger, Flavius Josephus, in the most wanton and virulent manner.

After this conduct, there remained no more mercy for the Jews. Titus caused the hands of those who had voluntarily sought shelter in the Roman camp, to be cut off, and sent them back to the city, and others he crucified in the sight of their countrymen. Famine, in the mean time, was performing its dreadful work within the walls. When Titus entered the city he gave it up to be plundered by the soldiers, and most of its inhabitants were put to the sword.

In pursuance of this general order, the city was destroyed to its foundations, and even the ruins of the temple were demolished. Josephus says that the number of prisoners taken during the whole time of the war was ninety-seven thousand; and the number killed in the city during the same period, amounted, as before stated, to one million. The Jews, who remained in the country, now paid tribute to the Romans, and were entirely subject to their laws.

46. After this event Jerusalem was partially rebuilt, and in 118 the inhabitants attempted again to rebel, but were speedily overcome. Adrian, the emperor, incensed at the conduct of this stubborn people, resolved to level their city with the earth, that is to say, those new buildings erected by the Jews, and to sow salt in the ground, on which the place had stood Thus was fulfilled a prophecy of our Saviour, who foretold, that neither in the city nor in the temple, should one stone be left upon another. This therefore may be called the final destruction of Jerusalem, which took place 47 years after that of Titus.

Adrian, however, soon built the city over anew, and called it Aelia Capitolina. It was a short lived change, for when the empress Helena, the mother of Constantine the Great, visited the city, she found it in a forlorn and ruinous state.

PARTHIA.

47. The PARTHIAN empire at the beginning of this period, continued under the sway of the first branch of the Arsacidæ. Phraates IV. then possessed the throne. Three sovereigns succeeded him, when after short reigns, the second branch of the Arsacidæ commenced.

Verones I. was the last of the three sovereigns of the first branch. He had been dispatched from Rome, where he was a hostage, to reign over the Parthians, who had invited him to be their king; but affecting the Roman dress and manners he incurred the dislike of his people, and was driven from the throne, to make room for Artabanus, of the royal family of Media.

48. The second branch of the Arsacidæ commenced 18 years A. C. under Artabanus III. It lasted nearly two hundred years under thirteen sovereigns. The Romans occasionally defeated the Parthians and made them tributary, but could never keep them long under the yoke. To the history of the Parthian kings, we attach very little importance. The empire was at length restored to the Persians after they had been subject to the princes of Parthia for the space of four hundred and seventy-five years.

§ Artabanus V, the last of this branch, having refused to give his daughter in marriage to the emperor Caracalla, the Romans entered Parthia and destroyed many cities; but Macrinus, the successor of Caracalla, after a hard fought battle, concluded a peace with the Parthians. Artabanus was killed in battle by Artaxares, a Persian, who, revolting from the Parthians, restored the empire to Persia. The subsequent details belong to the Persian history.

PERSIA.

49. After the Persians had been subject to the Parthians during four hundred and seventy-five years, from the time that they passed from under the Macedonian yoke, Artaxares, an ignoble but courageous Persian, excited a revolt among his countrymen, which terminated in the restoration of the Persian empire. 223 A. C.

Artaxares having accomplished his design, and ascended the throne, assumed the pompous title of king of kings, and asserted his right to all the provinces of the ancient empire, which were now under the authority of the Romans. War therefore ensued between these two powers, and the Persians were terribly defeated in a single battle by Alexander Severus. They soon however regained the ground they had lost.

Artaxares was followed by a series of princes, the most conspicuous of whom during this period was Sapores I. who was his immediate successor. The dynasty which Artaxares founded, is known in history under the name of Sassanidæ, from Sassan, his father.

§ Of Sapores, it is recorded that he conquered several cities in Syria and Mesopotamia, from the Romans, which however were recovered by the youngest Gordian; that in 258 he captured Antioch, penetrating into Cappadocia, and besieging Cæsara, which being taken through treachery, almost all the inhabitants were slain, and the city reduced to ashes. The next year the emperor Valerian having advanced into the east, was taken prisoner, and treated with the greatest cruelty, as has already been described. Sapores, after considerable reverse of fortune, having become odious to his subjects for his cruelties, was assassinated by the Satraps.

Hormisdas II. was the last prince of this period. He enjoyed a peaceful reign. After his death, the lords of the country seized his son and confined him in a tower, because he threatened to cause them all to be flayed alive, for not rising in token of obedience to him at a royal banquet, on a day when he returned from hunting. The queen being pregnant, the magi, by placing the crown upon her own person, affected to crown the prince, who, they persuaded themselves, would be born of her.

CHINA.

50. In the history of CHINA, the fifth dynasty which commenced about 200 years before the christian era, terminated during the present period, viz. in the year 221 A. C. It is called the dynasty of Han, and lasted four hundred and twenty-four years, under twenty-five emperors. The head of this dynasty was Lien-pang, a soldier, who, overcoming the last emperor, and ascending the throne, took the name of Kao-Tsou.

§ Kao-Tsou reigned with clemency and moderation. In his reign, paper, ink, and hair pencils, still used in China instead of pens, were invented. He was one of the few emperors who governed for themselves. Under the rest, the eunuchs obtained great authority.

Vuti, one of the princes of this family, was a great encourager of learning, and ordered the morality of Confucius to be taught in the public schools. He fell under the power of a strong delusion, in endeavouring to discover a liquor which would make him immortal.

The sixth dynasty began 221 A. C.; and ended 265 A. C. It is called the dynasty of Heou-Han, and lasted forty-four years. China at this time was divided into three empires, under three branches of the dynasty of Han. The various parts terminated at different periods, although the whole became reunited at length under the seventh dynasty in 265.

Distinguished Characters in Period I.

1. Livy, the prince of Roman historians.
2. Ovid, a distinguished Roman poet.
3. Tibullus, a famous elegiac poet of Rome.
4. Strabo, a celebrated geographer and historian.
5. Seneca, a Roman moralist and philosopher.
6. Lucan, a Roman epic poet.
7. Pliny, (the elder) the earliest writer on natural history whose works are extant.
8. Quintilian, an eminent Roman advocate and rhetorician.
9. Tacitus, an eminent philosophic historian.
10. Plutarch, the principal biographer of antiquity.
11. Juvenal, an eminent satirical poet.
12. M. Antoninus, a Roman emperor and philosophical writer.
13. Tertullian, } learned Christian writers, commonly called fathers.
14. Origen, }
15. Cyprian, }

§ 1. Livy was a native of Padua, but passed the greatest part of his life at Naples and Rome, particularly at the court of Augustus. Of his life not much is known, yet his fame was so universally spread, even in his life time, that an inhabitant of Gades, now Cadiz, travelled all the way to Rome, merely to see the man whose writings had given him so much pleasure. Livy died at Padua in his sixty-seventh year, A. C. 17.

This writer is principally known by his history of the Roman empire. It originally consisted of 140 books, of which only 35 are extant. In this work he is always great—clear, spirited, bold, and masterly in description. The high rank which he holds among historians will probably never be disputed. He often copied from his contemporaries and predecessors, and especially from Polybius.

2. Ovid was born at Sulmo, on the 20th of March, about 43 years B. C. His father intended him for the bar; but though his progress in the study of eloquence was great, yet nothing could divert him from paying his court to the muses. Every thing he wrote was expressed in poetical numbers. His name soon became known, and the great geniuses of the age honoured him with their notice, and some of them with their correspondence. Augustus also patronized him with the utmost liberality.

The days of his prosperity were not many. For some cause, which is not ascertained, the emperor banished him to a place named Tomos on the Euxine Sea. Here he spent the remainder of his life, and he spent it in unmanly repining and impatience. He offered the most abject flattery to Augustus, but both he and his successor

Tiberius were inexorable. Ovid died in the 7th or 8th year of his banishment.

The poems which he left behind him have, the most of them, survived to the present time. They are characterized by sweetness and elegance, though often debased by indelicacy of expression. Ovid every where paints nature with the hand of a master. His Fasti, a part of which is lost, are thought to be the best written of all his poems. It is known that the poems of Ovid were favourites with the great English bard, John Milton.

3. Tibullus was a Roman Knight. He at first engaged in the toils of war; but dissatisfied with such a life, he afterwards gave himself up to literary ease, and to the pleasures of an enervating Italian climate. His favorite study was the writing of love verses. In these elegant trifles he shewed himself an accomplished poet. Four books of elegies are all that remain of his compositions. They are so beautiful in language, and so pure in sentiment, that Tibullus is deservedly ranked as the prince of elegiac poets.

4. Strabo was a native of Amasia, and died 25 years A. C. His geographical work, divided into 17 books, is the only composition of his remaining. This is justly considered an elegant, classical, and learned work. It is written in Greek, and contains an account of the most celebrated places and countries of the world. Strabo travelled through most of the regions he has described, in quest of accurate information. Among his books which have been lost, are historical commentaries.

5. Seneca (Lucius Annæus) was born at Cordova, in Spain. He became early distinguished for uncommon abilities, and acquired at the bar, the reputation of an eloquent pleader; but he relinquished this road to fame, and became a candidate for public employments. He obtained the office of quæstor, but by a shameful indiscretion, having incurred the displeasure of Caligula, he was banished to the island of Corsica. In five years he was recalled by the empress Agrippina, to superintend the education of her son Nero, which office he discharged with honor.

Nero becoming impatient of the restraint, which his preceptor imposed upon his vicious inclinations, pretended that Seneca had conspired with Piso against his life, and sent a messenger to Seneca to acquaint him that he must die; permitting him to choose the manner of his death. The philosopher received the mandate with cheerfulness, and ordered the veins of his legs and arms to be opened. The blood however flowed slowly—poison and the warm bath were therefore resorted to: but being without effect, he was at last smothered in the vapour of a stove. His death took place in his seventy-second year, 65 A. C.

6. Lucan was a native of Corduba, and nephew of Seneca. He early went to Rome, where his rising talents procured him the favour of Nero. He had the imprudence, however, to enter into a poetical contest with his imperial patron, and obtaining an easy victory, as might have been expected, he ever afterwards was an object of the emperor's hatred. The insults to which the poet was continually

exposed, provoked his resentment to such a degree, that he joined Piso in his conspiracy against that monster. The discovery of the plot, of course, consigned him to death. He died a young man, being only in his 26th year.

Of his works, his Pharfalia only remains. This poem celebrates the wars of Cæsar and Pompey, and is unfinished. It has been variously estimated. The moral grandeur of its sentiments has been generally acknowledged, but some think him more of an orator than a poet.

7. Pliny (the elder) was born at Verona, of a noble family. He was distinguished in civil life, as well in scientific pursuits. To his public duties he attended through the day, but the night he devoted to study. He lost no time by idleness or dissipation. Every moment that could be spared from business was occupied in the cultivation of his mind. He turned his attention more particularly to Nature.

His work on Natural History, comprised in 37 books, is full of erudition. It takes in a wide range of topics, and is written in an interesting and sprightly manner, although the style possesses not the graces of the Augustan age. He wrote one hundred and sixty volumes of remarks and annotations on the various authors whom he had read, but these have not reached us.

His love of knowledge cost him his life. An eruption of Vesuvius happening at the time when he lay at Misenum, where he commanded a fleet, he was induced to approach the mountain, for the purpose of making his observations on the interesting phenomenon. While thus occupied, he was overtaken by the burning lava which poured from the volcano, and suffocated and scorched, he soon perished. This memorable event happened in the 79th year of the Christian era.

8. Quintilian was a native of Spain. After twenty years laborious employment in teaching rhetoric, and in pleading at the bar at Rome, he retired to enjoy the fruits of his labours and industry. Here he dedicated his time to the study of literature, and to composition. His success as an author, and the favours of the emperor Domitian, afforded him a high delight. But no situation is perfectly happy—the death of his wife and two sons, filled him with almost inconsolable grief. He died 95 A. C.

His Institutions, in 12 books, is the most perfect system of oratory extant. In this work, he delineates that which goes to constitute a perfect orator, together with all the preparation necessary. This work remained undiscovered until the fifteenth century.

9. Tacitus was the son of a Roman knight, and born in the reign of Nero. His genius and talents procured him the favour of several emperors in succession, and he was raised at last to the consular dignity. He was not destitute of distinction as an orator, but he is chiefly known to mankind as an historian. A peculiar friendship existed between him and Pliny, though the one was sternly partial to a republican government, and the other was a great admirer of imperial power.

The compositions of Tacitus were contained in thirty books, of which there now remain only twenty-one. Of these, his Annals include sixteen, and his History of the Roman Emperors five. Tacitus has many excellencies of style. Its most striking characteristic, perhaps, is conciseness. He has great force and depth of thought, and is candid and impartial in his statements. In his biographical sketches, he displays an uncommon knowledge of human nature. The History of the Reign of Tiberius, is his masterpiece. Some have complained of him as being obscure.

10. Plutarch was a native of Chæronea. He died at an advanced age, in his native place, about the 140th year A. C. Having travelled in quest of knowledge through Egypt and Greece, he retired to Rome, where he opened a school, with great reputation. Trajan, who admired his abilities, honoured him with the office of consul, and with the government of Illyricum.

After the death of his imperial patron, he removed from Rome to Chæronea; in which delightful retirement, he composed the greatest part of his works. His Lives of Illustrious Men, is the most esteemed of his productions. His precision and fidelity are remarkable. In his style, he is energetic and animated; though distinguished neither for purity nor elegance. Sometimes he is too circumstantial; yet, on the whole, he has been pronounced to be the most entertaining and instructive of all the writers of ancient history.

11. Juvenal was born at Aquinum, in Italy, and died in the reign of Trajan, 128 A. C., at an advanced age. He came early to Rome, where he applied himself at first to declamation, and afterwards to the writing of satires.

Sixteen of these pieces are extant. In them, he is an animated, severe, and bold reprover of vice, and displays also much humour. He, however, defeats his object, in a great measure, by the grossness and indecency of his manner. His correctness in delineation is the result of experience and age. He has been called, with some reason perhaps, the last of the Roman poets.

12. M. Antoninus, whose history has been given before, was born at Rome, in the 121st year of the christian era, and died on an expedition against the Marcomanni, in the nineteenth year of his reign. He was a prince of great talents and virtue. His death was regretted by mankind as a public loss, and the greatest honour was paid to his memory. According to the superstition of the times, he was ranked among the gods, and in almost every house his statue was found.

His book of Meditations has been much admired by scholars and philosophers.

13. Tertullian lived at Carthage, and flourished in the reigns of Severus and Caracalla. He was originally a pagan, but afterwards embraced christianity, and became one of its ablest defenders. His writings evince that he possessed a lively imagination, fervid eloquence, strength of reasoning, and a considerable acquaintance with style. His Apology for the Christians, and his Prescriptions, are the best esteemed of his numerous works. The historian Gibbon, calls him the "stern" Tertullian.

14. Origen was born at Alexandria, about the year 185, and died in 254, having been presbyter of that city. He wrote in Greek. He was much celebrated for his parts and learning. He was endowed with unaffected humility and modesty, and was extremely rigid in following the christian rules. In the sixty-ninth year of his age, he suffered martyrdom. His works are many, and include a number of homilies, commentaries on the Holy Scriptures, and different treatises, besides his Hexapla. This last work first gave the hint for the compilation of our polyglot Bibles. Mosheim calls him the luminary of the christian world, during the age in which he lived; but observes, that he failed in justness of judgment, and was given to the Platonic philosophy.

15. Cyprian was a native and a bishop of Carthage. He was born about the beginning of the third century, of heathen parents, but became a convert to christianity, and was a principal father of the church. To be more devoted to purity and study, he is said to have abandoned his wife; and, as a proof of his charity, he distributed his goods to the poor. He wrote eighty-one letters, besides several treatises, and rendered his works valuable, by the information he conveys respecting the discipline of the ancient church.

He was beheaded as a martyr, at Carthage, September 14, 258 A. C. Moshiem speaks of him as possessing the most eminent abilities and flowing eloquence, but rather too attentive to the ornaments of rhetoric.

PERIOD II.

The period of the Northern Invasions, extending from the Reign of Constantine the Great, 306 *years A. C. to the Extinction of the Western Empire,* 476 *years A. C.*

THE ROMAN EMPIRE.

Sec. 1. The empire of Rome, as has already appeared, had been for several years under the sway of a number of masters, on all of whom the burden of government equally devolved. At the time when Constantine was proclaimed in Britain 306 A. C. upon the death of his father Constantius, the two Cæsars, Severus and Maximin, had already been proclaimed 305 A. C.—Maxentius, son of Maximian, had about the same time, 306 A. C., declared himself. The next year Licinius was created emperor by Galerius, who had never willingly owned Constantine. These were Constantine's competitors, and in the course of a few years he lived to see them either destroyed in various ways, or overcome in battle, and himself remaining the sole master of the Roman world.

Constantine has been styled the first christian emperor. Whatever may have been his real character, as far as religion is concerned, it is certain that he stopped the persecutions of the christians—that he publicly favoured Christianity—defended it against its enemies, and tolerated the profession of it in the empire. Indeed, under his auspices it became the religion of the state, and that great change in the Roman government took place, which, from a persecuting, made it a protecting power. For the influence which Christianity exerted over the public conduct of this emperor, a cause has been assigned, possessing a miraculous character, viz.: his seeing a pillar of light in the heavens in the form of a cross, bearing the inscription—"By this conquer."

Whether this were a real sight, or a mere imagination, it is asserted in the records of the times, as an undoubted fact; and if it were such, we may readily account for the part which Constantine acted, even should we be forced to doubt the integrity of his religious principles.

§ The first exploits of Constantine were directed against the Franks, who had then overrun Gaul. It was in 311 or 312, when he was marching against Maxentius, and reflecting on the mutability of the world, and the opinions which then divided the attention of mankind, that he saw the pillar of light mentioned above. This was in the latter part of the day, and on the following night, Jesus Christ is said to have appeared to him with the same sign.

In consequence of these appearances, the emperor caused a royal standard to be made, bearing a figure similar to that he had seen, and commanded that it should be carried before him in his wars. Soon espousing the cause of Christianity, he entered Italy, and advancing towards the gates of Rome, he attacked and defeated Maxentius, who. in attempting an escape, was drowned in the Tiber. The next day Constantine was received into the city as a deliverer.

In 314, a war was kindled between Constantine and Licinius, but it soon ended in a peace. Nine years afterwards, hostilities broke out again, when Licinius after two defeats was obliged to abdicate, leaving the government to Constantine alone.

2. The administration of Constantine varied very much, in the different periods of his life. It was far more commendable at the beginning, than it at length became. His natural temper was severe and cruel, and the latter part of his reign was marked by several acts of intolerant zeal, and sanguinary rigour. In protecting and countenancing the Christian religion he deserves our approbation, although it must be acknowledged that he brought it into too close an al

liance with the civil power, to consist with its highest prosperity.

§ The character of Constantine has been the subject of extravagant eulogy, or violent censure, according as friends or foes have been concerned in drawing it. We shall do well perhaps to strike the balance between the different representations—the prejudices of the cotemporary pagans against it we should little regard, nor should we think too much of the panegyric which was resorted to for its vindication, by the professed Christians of his day. It was a highly mixed character which he possessed.

This emperor was the author of an essential change in the Roman affairs, in another respect besides that of religion. In transferring the seat of the empire from Rome to Constantinople, he affected its condition during the remainder of its existence. This step accelerated the destruction of the decaying fabric. His motives in this project cannot be accurately determined—whether they had reference to ideas of policy and advantage, or purely to resentment on account of affronts received at Rome Whatever they were, his own reputation and the public interests were injured.

The effect of this measure, though not immediately felt, was at length fatal. After the government was apportioned among the emperor's sons, there was such a division of the forces of the empire, that the northern barbarians, who fought with superior numbers, and had been hitherto repulsed, now began to prevail and to encroach on the provinces.

In an expedition against the Persians, Constantine died at Nicomedia, in the thirtieth year of his reign, and sixty-third of his age.

§ The new seat of empire is said to have been pointed out in the following manner:—Constantine had made choice of a situation at Chalcedon, in Asia Minor; but it seems, in laying out the ground-plot, an eagle caught up the line and flew with it over to Byzantium, a city which lay upon the opposite side of the Bosphorus.

Here, therefore, it was deemed expedient to fix the seat of empire; and Constantine, after having built a capitol, an amphitheatre, many churches and other public works, and many magnificent edifices, and after having dedicated the city to the God of martyrs, repaired thither, with his whole court.

From this period to the reigns of Honorius and Arcadius, when the empire was divided into two distinct sovereignties, the histories of Rome and Constantinople are necessarily blended.

3. The Roman world had long been composed of discordant parts, and the work of corruption and dissolution was at this time making a rapid progress. The immense mass was kept together for a period longer, only by the vigorous exertion of despotism. The fabric naturally tottered to its fall, when the Pagan principles of religion, which constituted an essential part of its foundation, were removed. The arm of power then supplied the props that upheld it, and this, more emphatically than was ever the case before.

§ The Roman armies at this era, were debased by the intermixture of Scythians, Goths, Germans, and other barbarous tribes; and Constantine, from a timid policy of guarding against mutinies of the troops, reduced the legion from its ancient complement of 5000 and upwards, to 1000 or 1500.

4. Before his death, Constantine had settled the empire on five princes—his three sons and two nephews. His sons were Constantine II., Constans, and Constantius II. The nephews, who were Cæsars, were named Dalmatius, and Annibalianus. Their sovereignty commmenced 337 A. C.

Immediately upon the accession of these princes, Constantius contrived to destroy the two Cæsars, with five others of his cousins and two of his uncles. Soon after this, Constantine entered into a contention with Constans, and was killed; and Constans in a few years perished in attempting to quell a revolt among his subjects. Constantius, therefore, remained in the possession of the whole empire. He reigned twenty-four years in misfortune and dishonour.

§ Domestic broils, and insurrections of the troops, had left the western frontiers of the empire exposed to the barbarians. The Franks, Saxons, Alemanni, and Sarmatians had devastated the fine countries on the Rhine, and the Persians had kept up a succession of wars in the eastern provinces. At first Constantius obliged the Persians to retire; but he was afterwards overcome in nine signal battles.

His cousin Julian, he created Cæsar, but afterwards regarding him with jealousy, and hearing that he was proclaimed emperor, Constantius marched against him, but died on the road. He had reached his 45th year. In person he was diminutive, but capable of exertion when occasion required; he was temperate, but extremely uxorious; and in a word, inherited the defects without the abilities of his father. He was much engaged in theological controversy, but his religious principles or character cannot inspire us with any great respect.

5. Julian, commonly called the apostate, on account of his relapsing into paganism from a Christian education, was

acknowledged by the senate, 361 A. C. His army had previously proclaimed him emperor, much against his will; but the insult he received from Constantius, who exacted submission to himself as the supreme head, determined him to assert his claims by force of arms. After due preparation and vigorous efforts, he was happily released from this necessity, by the death of Constantius.

Julian had already restored the glory of the Roman arms by repressing the invasions of the barbarians. He was not without several noble traits, and was fitted by knowledge and energy to govern a great people. His enmity against the holy religion of Jesus, was deservedly his greatest defect. To this he added bigotry in favour of paganism, superstition, and no small share of a foolish credulity. He was addicted to the studies of magic and astrology.

He immediately began the reformation of abuses of various kinds, but declared in favour of paganism, re-opened the temples, and without directly persecuting, did much to injure Christians and their cause. In 363, he attempted to rebuild the temple at Jerusalem; but certain miraculous appearances, it is said, prevented the execution of his design. During the same year, in a war with the Persians, while pursuing a victorious course, and in a successful engagement, he received a mortal wound. He had reigned but three years, and lived thirty-one.

§ The cunning and the malice of Julian, appeared, in treating the Christians with contempt. He removed them, as visionaries, from all employments of public trust. He refused them the benefit of the laws to decide their differences, because their religion forbade a contentious spirit; and they were debarred the studies of literature and philosophy, as this would subject them to the perusal of pagan authors.

Julian, like many others opposed to Christianity, employed wit and ridicule against this religion; for he was an author as well as a warrior. It is said in apology for him, that he used these weapon in self-defence—that he was first lampooned by the Christians. However that may be, religion is a subject too sacred to be treated in that manner. One of his works against the Christians, was *Misophogon*, or beard hater.

His Cæsars is the most famous of his compositions, being a satire upon all the Roman emperors, from Julius Cæsar to Constantine. This philosophical fable, according to Gibbon, is "one of the most agreeable and instructive productions of ancient wit."

His last moments were spent in conversation with a philosopher on the immortality of the soul—he expressed his expectation of being united with heaven, and with the stars,* which was one of his astrological vagaries, and he breathed his last without indicating the least sorrow for his fate, or the suddenness of his death.

His attempt to rebuild the temple at Jerusalem, was made with a view to furnish a specious argument against prophecy, and of course the truth of revelation. The prodigies on the occasion, which prevented the completion of the work, are attested by contemporary writers, such as Ammianus Marcellinus, and Gregory Nazianzen. This article of history has been the subject of much dispute. But whether we allow or not that the prodigies, such as earthquakes and balls of fire, happened, to the annoyance of the workmen and to the destruction of their commenced work, it is evident that something prevented the work, for the temple was never rebuilt, and thus our Saviour's prophecy remains as yet unsuspected. "Jerusalem is to be trodden down of the Gentiles till the time of the Gentiles is fulfilled."

6. On the death of Julian, the race of Constantius Clorus became extinct, and the Roman world was without a head, and without an heir. In this situation, the army finally fixed on Jovian, a Pannonian, and the emperor's first domestic, as his successor, 363 A. C. Jovian made peace with the Persians, by the cession of five provinces; for on Julian's death the army was brought to the brink of destruction, and by such a sacrifice only could he save it and himself.

This emperor applied himself to restore tranquillity to the Church. He displayed the banner of the cross, and reversed the edicts of Julian respecting Christianity. His reign, which continued only seven months, was mild and equitable. He died suddenly at the age of thirty-three years.

§ While Jovian was on his march to secure the palace of Constantinople, his wife with an imperial train hastened to meet him, carrying with her their infant son. The moment of embracing her husband seemed to be at hand: but the distressing news of his death which was immediately communicated to her, most cruelly disappointed her hopes. He had died the night before, as some report, by suffocation from the vapour of charcoal.

7. Valentinian I., after a delay of a few days was elected emperor by the army, 364 A. C. One month after, he associated his brother Valens, in the empire, and gave him the eastern provinces. From this period, the division of the empire into Eastern and Western, became fixed and permanent.

* This was in agreement with the doctrine of Pythagoras and Plato, which seems to exclude any personal or conscious immortality.

The empire, however, was still considered as one body. On the East, the Persians were making inroads. The West was continually invaded by the northern barbarians. The latter were repelled by the emperor in many successful battles. He favoured the Christian religion, and his domestic administration was equitable and wise. His temper, however, was violent. He died on an expedition against the Alemanni, 367 A. C.

§ It is said that the barbarians against whom he had last taken arms, had provoked him beyond all endurance, so that when their ambassadors came to sue for mercy, his anger was raised to such a height, and his tones and gestures were so violent, that he ruptured a blood vessel, and expired on the spot.

In the East, Valens held a weak and inefficient sceptre. Engaged in the Arian heresy which he favoured, he threw the provinces into confusion and contention, and at the same time exposed his dominions to the inroads of the barbarians, who came under the profession of friends and allies. He died in 378 A. C.

These were the Goths who emigrated from Scandinavia, and who, together with several other barbarous nations, will soon be described in this account of the Roman empire, since they are so intimately connected with its destiny.

§ In 376, Valens permitted vast hordes of the Goths, who had been driven out of their country by the Huns, to settle in Thrace Here, however, they soon plundered the very country conceded to them as an asylum. The emperor hastened to oppose them, but he was defeated in the famous battle of Adrianople, two thirds of his army having been cut to pieces.

Being himself wounded, he was carried into a cottage, where on the same day he was burnt alive by the barbarians, who set fire to the cottage, without knowing that it contained the emperor of the East.

8. Gratian, a son of Valentinian, succeeded his father, 367 A. C. He soon became possessor of the whole empire, by the death of Valens. Upon this event, he took Theodosius as his associate, on whom he conferred the eastern provinces. He began to reign in his 17th year, and died at the age of 24 years. He was a well disposed prince, but deficient in energy of character.

§ Gratian undertook to destroy the remains of paganism; but Rome, at the time, happening to be afflicted by a severe famine, the favourers of that superstition ascribed the calamity to the wrath of the gods. A general dissatisfaction ensued, and Maximus, who commanded in Britain, taking advantage of this state of things, caused himself to be proclaimed emperor. Gratian marching into Gaul to oppose him, was deserted by his soldiers, and killed at Lyons, 371 A. C.

9. Valentinian II. was the successor of his brother Gratian. Being dispossessed by Maximus, he took refuge with Theodosius, who was then reigning in the East, and who restored him to the throne. From that time he ruled with justice. After wearing the crown for several years, he was strangled by a Gaul named Arbogastus, who had assumed an authority over his sovereign, 392 A. C. The tyrant Eugenius, whom the Gaul caused to be proclaimed on this occasion, was defeated and put to death by Theodosius.

10. In the East, after the death of Valens, Theodosius succeeded to the throne, 379 A. C. He was deservedly surnamed the Great. The barbarians he repelled with success, and he secured the prosperity of his people by wise and salutary laws. It was during his reign, that Christianity obtained the entire ascendency over paganism, as the religion of the Roman people.

After the death of Valentinian II., the whole empire came into possession of Theodosius; and he was the last who reigned over both the East and West. Previously to his decease, he divided the empire between his two sons, assigning the West to Honorius, and the East to Arcadius. From this era they became two distinct empires, and will be treated of separately.

§ Theodosius the Great, was the son of Count Theodosius, a very able general, who had been beheaded by the order of Gratian. To atone for his injustice, Gratian chose the Count's son as his colleague, and gave him the East for his portion. A few days after his election, he gained a signal victory over the Goths, who immediately sued for peace.

In the year 390, Theodosius cruelly punished the inhabitants of Thessalonica, who had killed their governor on a certain occasion, by sending his soldiers against the place, and putting 7000 to the sword. Such, however, was the influence of St. Ambrose, that he obliged the emperor, by a public penance, to expiate his crime.

In religion, Theodosius espoused the orthodox party. His faith is said to have been confirmed by an argument adapted to the meanest capacity. He had conferred on Arcadius, his eldest son, the title of Augustus; and the two princes were seated on a throne to receive the homage of their subjects. Among others who offered their homage, was Amphilochius, bishop of Icenium. He, however, approached Theodosius alone with reverence, the son he accosted with familiarity.

The monarch, offended by the conduct of the bishop, gave orders that he should be thrust from his presence; but while the guards were engaged in this act, the good bishop exclaimed, "Such is the treatment, O emperor! which the king of heaven has prepared for those impious men who affect to worship the Father, but refuse to acknowledge the co-equal dignity of his divine Son."

This declaration had the effect of propitiating the emperor, and fixing his mind more strongly than before, in the faith.

11. The Roman empire had now become excessively weakened by its unwieldly extent, and had already suffered much from the incursions of its barbarous neighbours. It was, however, destined to suffer far more in the end, from the last named source. Its separation into two empires, favoured the projects of the barbarians, who, from this period, poured in like a torrent upon these cultivated regions. The Western empire in a few years was completely overwhelmed.

A short account of the barbarous nations, who acted so conspicuous a part in this tragedy, seems to be demanded in this place.

The Huns were a fierce and savage nation, at first inhabiting the vast deserts which border China on the north. A part of them, owing, it is said, to civil wars, retired to the westward, and settled to the north of the Caspian sea, near the source of the river Ural.

§ From thence, 376 A. C., advancing towards the Palus Mæotis (sea of Asof) under Balamir, their chief, they subdued the Alains, and forced such of them as were capable of bearing arms to join them; the remainder they put to death. With this accession of strength and numbers, they fell upon the Ostrogoths and Visogoths, and having driven them away from their country, took possession of it themselves. This was a region extending from the Tanais to the Danube. Their subsequent history, we shall find identified with the Roman affairs.

The Alains inhabited the north of Asiatic Sarmatia, and were known to the Romans in the time of Pompey. Under the first emperors, they several times invaded the frontier provinces.

§ Those of them who escaped the arms of the Huns, pushed their way towards Pannonia, whence advancing still further to the west, they united with the Suevi and the Vandals, and continuing their migrations, they finally settled in Lusitania, now Portugal, where in 477, they were conquered by the Visogoths.

The Vandals issued from Scandinavia, now Sweden, and crossing the Baltic, first settled in a part of Germany. On account of increasing numbers, they again emigrated, and taking their course eastward, possessed themselves of the country towards the Tanais, whence they made several incursions upon the Roman provinces.

§ They at length formed a junction with the Suevi and Alains, and marched into Spain, a part of which they settled, and called after their name, Vandalusia or Andalusia. Their history downward, is pursued in that of the Romans.

The Goths came originally from Scandinavia. They first settled in Pomerania, whence advancing towards the east, they took up their abode to the north of the lake Mæotis. Here they were divided into Visogoths, or Goths of the West, and Ostrogoths, or Goths of the East.

§ Being overcome by the Huns, they were forced to abandon their last settlement, and a part of them took refuge in Pannonia, where they remained till they formed the new kingdom of Italy, hereafter to be mentioned.

The Heruli also, originated in Scandinavia. They first emigrated towards the East, and settled on the borders of the lake Mæotis. They afterward returned towards the West.

§ It is said that coming to the ocean, they embarked for Thule, one of the Shetland islands, or, as others suppose, what is now called Iceland, where they finally settled. As we shall soon learn, the first sovereign of the new kingdom of Italy was a chief of the Heruli.

The Gepidæ were another Scandinavian tribe. They first planted themselves on the Vistula, whence they advanced east towards the Tanais.

§ Here being subdued by Attila, the Hun, they served under him in his expedition to Gaul. Upon his death, they shook off the yoke. They were finally destroyed by the Lombards.

The Suevi were a warlike nation of Germany, inhabiting that part of it in which Berlin is now situated. They were great wanderers, and often changed their habitations.

§ In 406, they entered Gaul with the Alains and Vandals, with whom they passed into Spain, in a part of which they established a monarchy. This was afterwards destroyed by the Visogoths.

The Burgundians first inhabited what now constitutes the kingdom of Prussia. From this country they were afterwards expelled by the Gepidæ. They frequently crossed the Rhine, and invaded Gaul, and brought trouble on the empire.

There were other minor tribes of barbarians, of which no particular account need be here given. They were such as the Bulgari, Alemanni, Venedi, &c. Other rude nations also, who followed in the train of these conquerors, will be noticed at the proper time.

12. In the Western Empire, Honorius, who held the sceptre by the appointment of his father, Theodosius, proved himself a degenerate son. Stilicho, a famous warrior, had been appointed guardian or minister to Honorius, during the minority of the latter; and it was owing to the vigour of the minister, and not at all to the merits of the emperor, that the barbarians of the north were repelled for such a length of time.

Alaric, king of the Goths, had penetrated into Italy, but was defeated by Stilicho near Pollentia, 403 A. C. But this able general, having, through the baseness of the emperor, been afterwards beheaded, 408 A. C., Alaric again advanced and beseiged Rome. The promise of a large sum of gold delayed his purposes of vengeance. As, however, it was never fulfilled, Alaric took the city, and committed some part of it to the flames, 410 A. C.

The pillage lasted six days, and multitudes of its inhabitants were massacred. During the space of more than six hundred years, Rome had not been violated by the presence of a foreign enemy; and even long before, as well as during that period, her power had been feared abroad.

§ The weakness of Honorius, among other causes, encouraged the attack of the barbarians upon the empire. From the wilds of Scandinavia, that *northern hive*, as it has been fitly called, as well as from the east, they issued in almost incredible numbers. Previously to their descent upon Italy, the Goths, under Alaric, had spread their devastations quite to the borders of the eastern capital, and through the classic fields of Greece.

Stilicho made a stand against the invaders. While they beseiged Asta, where the forces of Honorius had taken refuge, Stilicho cut his way through the Gothic camp under the walls of that place, and thus rescued the emperor. The Goths afterwards pitching their camp in the vicinity of Pollentia, were suddenly attacked by Stilicho, and several thousands of them were slain. Among the captives was the wife of Alaric, who was compelled to implore the clemency of the victor. The Goths, however, were but partially checked in consequence of this victory.

Stilicho might, perhaps, have delayed for some time the fall of the empire, but his plans were frustrated by the machinations of his rivals, and he fell a victim to the suspicions of the ungrateful emperor, 408 A. C.

Alaric had long stood in a menacing attitude, and now prepared to complete his designs upon Italy. About this time, vast numbers of Goths pouring down upon Germany, forced the nations whom they dispossessed, to fall upon Italy. These joined their arms to those of Alaric, who made an attack on Rome.

He met with success; and this great city, which had so long been the terror of the world, was sacked, plundered and partially burnt, 410 A. C., by the savage tribes of Germany and Scythia. The population of Rome, at this time, might amount to 1,200,000 men; but the nobles were wholly sunk in luxury and effeminacy, and the populace had become exceedingly debased, by the manumission of slaves or the influx of foreigners. They were nothing more than the shadow of their ancestors in bravery and spirit. Hence the success of the arms of the barbarian.

The catastrophe which Rome experienced, was hastened also by famine. War had prevented the cultivation of the lands, and the ports being blocked up, the citizens were reduced to the greatest extremities—human flesh was publicly sold.

Treachery completed the work. The Salarian gate was opened at midnight, by some of the Romans themselves, and the enemy rushed in. The scene was dreadful; for although the conqueror, in his magnanimity had given orders that none except the armed should be killed, great numbers of citizens were put to death, and larger numbers still, were reduced from affluence to want and captivity. Though the city was pillaged and set on fire, it is thought that few, comparatively, of its magnificent edifices were destroyed.

Alaric now prepared to invade Sicily and Africa, but death suddenly put an end to his ambitious projects. He died after a short illness. Honorius, instead of improving this opportunity to recover his lost provinces, entered into a treaty with Ataulfus, Alaric's successor, gave him in marriage his sister, Placidia, and ceded to him a portion of Spain. By these and other acts, Honorius suffered the empire, by degrees, to pass from the dominion of the Romans. Honorius continued to reign till the year 422.

13. Valentinian III. was crowned two years after the death of Honorius, 424 A. C. He was the son of Constantius, a general of Honorius, and during seven months, an associate with him in the government. In 439, the emperor lost his dominions in Africa, by the revolt of Count Boniface, who delivered that part of the empire to the Vandals.

§ Aetius, a general of Valentinian, being jealous of Boniface, by means of his artifices drew the latter into a revolt, and was employed on the part of the empire to punish him on this account. Boniface defeated the first army that was sent against him; but distrusting his strength to cope singly with his enemies, he was induced to call in the assistance of Genseric, king of the Vandals. The measure, however, was ruinous to his cause.

The Vandal having thus obtained a footing in Africa, which he greatly desired, could not be prevailed on afterwards, by the offer of large sums of money, to retreat. Although the compact between the two generals was, that they should divide Africa between them, Genseric occupied the whole country, except three cities, and these he soon took.

Shutting up Boniface in Carthage, he compelled him, at the ex piration of a year, to surrender; and the Roman general experienced the mortification of beholding all Africa, which he had once saved, ravaged in the most wanton manner by the barbarians whose assistance he had invited. The kingdcm which Genseric thus established, did not last quite a century.

The other provinces of the empire were protected against the invasion of the barbarians, by Aetius. The Huns, at this time, had begun to make their ravages in the empire. Under Attila, their leader, in 445, they first overran Illyricum, Thrace, Dacia, and Mæsia, and laid the Romans under tribute. Soon afterwards, with an army of 500,000 men, Attila invaded Gaul, and threatened the destruction of the empire. The forces of the Romans, under Aetius, met him in battle, on the plains of Chalons, and defeating him, with the loss of 160,000 men, checked his progress for a time.

Not long after, however, he invaded Italy, and Valentinian being shut up in Rome, by the arms of the barbarian, was compelled to purchase a peace. Attila dying suddenly, in the midst of his successes, the empire of the West was saved from immediate destruction.

§ The march of the Huns was extremely desolating. To their leader, Attila, the victims of his ambition have given the expressive appellation of "The Scourge of God." He first invaded the East, which he ravaged at pleasure; its emperor, Theodosius, being disposed rather to conciliate his favour by a tribute, than to attempt his expulsion by force of arms. Disdaining so mean spirited an enemy, he turned to the West; where his appearance has already been described. His body was secretly buried, enclosed in three coffins, the first of gold, the second of silver, and the third of iron. The men who dug his grave were put to death, lest they should reveal the place of his burial.

Aetius, whose military talents had been so serviceable to the empire, soon fell a victim to the jealousy of the eunuch Heraclius, and Valentinian stabbed him with his own hand. The next year the emperor himself was assassinated.

14. Maximus II. who had instigated the murder of Valentinian, was proclaimed, 455 A. C. He married Eudoxia

the widow of his predecessor, to whom he imprudently revealed his guilt in the assassination of the emperor. To revenge this deed, she called in the assistance of Genseric, king of the Vandals. Upon his arrival, Maximus fled, but he met the vengeance of his people, who stoned him to death, on account of his cowardice.

§ Maximus was a Roman senator of the Ancian family, and was incited to the destruction of Valentinian, by the dishonour which the latter had cast upon his wife. However respectable Maximus was in private life, his abilities were inadequate to stay the fall of the empire, had he been longer continued.

Eudoxia had reason to repent of her imprudence. The call upon Genseric for aid, well comported with his private, sinister aims. After he had landed in Italy, with an army of Moors and Vandals, he took Rome, delivered it up to pillage during several days, destroyed many of the monuments of ancient genius, and conveyed the empress and her two daughters back with him in triumph to Carthage.

15. From the death of Maximus, 455 A. C. there was a succession of eight emperors, during twenty years; at the expiration of which, as we shall soon learn, the empire terminated. Little more than their names can be mentioned below.

§ Avitus was acknowledged in Gaul by his troops. Having created Ricimer, a Roman senator, general of his armies, the latter soon entered into a conspiracy against his benefactor; and Avitus, at first arrested and deposed, at last died while on the road to Italy, 457 A. C. Ricimer, though an able commander, was a savage and turbulent demagogue.

Majorian was proclaimed after the deposition of Avitus. He made an unsuccessful attempt against the kingdom of the Vandals in Africa. This emperor published several wise laws for the reformation of abuses, but the reputation which he acquired for wisdom and virtue, excited the jealousy of Ricimer, who deposed and slew him, 461 A. C.

Severus III. was created emperor by Ricimer, who governed under his name. Ricimer, after the expiration of four years, found it convenient to poison the nominal master of himself and the empire.

Athemius was called to the empire by the united suffrages of the senate, the army, and the people, in 467. To attach Ricimer to his interest, who was become extremely formidable, he gave him, his daughter in marriage. Ricimer, however, soon having a difference with his father-in-law, besieged and pillaged Rome. During this transaction the emperor was murdered.

Olybrius, who was sent with an army by Leo, emperor of the

East, to protect Athemius against Ricimer, was seduced by the latter and proclaimed emperor, but died three months after, 472.

Glycerus, an obscure soldier, favoured by a Burgundian prince, assumed the title of emperor at Ravenna; but Leo had conferred it on Julius Nepos, who took Glycerus prisoner, and caused him to be consecrated bishop of Salona, 473.

Julius Nepos was proclaimed at Rome 474. The next year, Orestes, a Pannonian, whom he sent into Gaul, revolted, and besieged the emperor in Ravenna. Nepos escaped into Dalmatia, where at the end of five years he was assassinated.

Augustulus son of Orestes was made emperor by his father. After a reign of eleven months, he was taken prisoner by Odoacer king of the Heruli, and sent into Campania, where he lived in a private station.

16. In the Eastern Empire, after its final separation from the West, in the time of Theodosius, 395 A. C., there were transactions which deserve our notice. Theodosius, as we have seen, assigned the East to his son Arcadius. This prince was then eighteen years of age, and he proved to be both weak and dissolute. He suffered himself to be governed by favourites, and at length by Eudoxia, his empress, who made it her great object to plunder the revenues of the state.

17. Thedosius II. son of Arcadius, succeeded to the empire 408. He has the reputation of having been a prince of mild disposition, and piety of conduct, but otherwise destitute of those qualities that are essential to a sovereign. But his deficiencies were supplied by the genius and address of his sister, Pulcheria, who aided in the administration of the the government. The latter part of his life was greatly disturbed by the invasions of the Barbarians.

§ Pulcheria, whose talents for government were extraordinary, sought to strengthen her influence and power, by securing for her brother a companion in marriage, who, as she hoped, would ever be grateful to her benefactress. The person on whom her choice, as well as that of Theodosius, fell, was the beautiful and learned Athenais.

Chance had made her known to Pulcheria. She was the daughter of an Athenian philosopher, who had taken the greatest care of her education. Such was his conviction of her entire accomplishment in every respect, that in the disposition of his property, he left his two sons the whole of it, except one hundred pieces of gold, with the declaration that "her own good fortune would be sufficient for her."

With a view to obtain her just share of the inheritance from her brothers, after she had tried the forms of law in vain, the Athenian maiden came to claim the interference and protection of Pulcheria, at Constantinople. Her sense and merit highly pleased the princess, and in connection with her charms, won the heart of Theodosius. In 431 she embraced Christianity, and was baptised by the name of Eudocia, and the same year was united to the emperor in marriage.

She treated her brothers with singular magnanimity, raising them to the rank of consuls and præfects, and though she at length lost the affections of Theodosius on an imputation of infidelity, and chose to retire to Jerusalem, she ever protested that she was wholly innocent. She died about 460, ten years after the death of her husband.

18. Marcian, a native of Thrace, was called to the throne by Pulcheria 450, whose hand also he received in marriage. After a reign of seven years, he departed this life, while preparing for a war against Genseric, king of the Vandals.

§ Marcian possessed some eminent qualities, as is evinced by his reply to Attila when the latter claimed the annual tribute, consented to by Theodosius. "I have," said he, "gold for my friends, and iron for my enemies."

19. Leo I., also a native of Thrace, was called to the empire on the death of Marcian 457 A. C. He reigned till nearly the period of the destruction of the Western empire. He had some domestic enemies, who gave him trouble; though he finally crushed Asper, through whose influence he had been raised to the throne, and who at length revolted against his master. During the latter part of his reign, his dominions were much ravaged by the Goths. He died a natural death, at an advanced age, 474 A. C.

§ Leo Ist has been greatly praised by some historians, and censured by others. An instance of his temperate firmness in resisting the oppression of his patron Asper, is recorded as follows:—

Asper had presumed to reproach him with a breach of promise, in regard to a certain appointment. "It is not proper," said he, insolently shaking the purple, "that the man who is invested with this garment, should be guilty of a falsehood." "Nor is it proper," retorted Leo, "that a prince should be compelled to resign his own judgment and the public interest, to the pleasure of a subject."

PERSIA.

20. Of PERSIA, during this period, we have only to say in general, that it was governed successively by eight princes, of whom Sapores II. was the most distinguished; that at the beginning, and towards the conclusion of the period, the nation warred against the Romans; but that through the intermediate space, the most profound peace subsisted between the

two powers. A few particulars respecting some of the Persian sovereigns, will appear below.

§ Sapores, II., who was crowned before his birth, in the person of his mother, began to persecute the Christians of his dominions in 326. In a few years after, he endeavoured to recover the five provinces yielded by his grandfather, Narses, to the Romans, but was terribly defeated by Constantius. After this event, he gained a celebrated battle at Sirigate, in Mesopotamia, and took several cities.

In the war with Julian, in 363, he was pursued into the very heart of his dominions, but was delivered by the death of that emperor. He died in 380, after a reign of seventy years. His character was a compound of pride and ferocity. He cruelly persecuted the Christians, during forty years.

Sapores III., was a wise prince; he lived at peace with the Romans, and died lamented. Under Isdigartes I., a persecution of the Christians commenced, which continued fifty years, during his reign and that of some of his successors.

CHINA.

21. During this period, the seventh dynasty of the emperors of CHINA terminated; as also the eighth, a little after the conclusion of the period.

Under the first of these, the empire, which had been divided into three, became united. It continued one hundred and fifty-five years, under fifteen emperors. It is called the dinasty of Tcin-ou-ti. The eighth was the dynasty of Song. It began under a revolted general, 420 A. C., and lasted fifty-nine years, under eight emperors.

§ One of the sovereigns of the 8th dynasty, whose name was Venti, was killed by his own son, and the parricide fell by the hands of his brother. The latter made himself many enemies by the freedom of his speech, for which, in the end, he lost his life. One of his wives, whom he had offended by calling her old, stifled him in his bed.

Distinguished Characters in Period II.

1. Lactantius, an elegant writer, and an able defender of Christianity: sometimes called the Christian Cicero.
2. Ossian, a Caledonian bard.
3. Eusebius, an eminent ecclesiastical historian.
4. Eutropius, a Latin historian and sophist.
5. Julian, a Roman emperor, an acute, but malignant infidel philosopher.
6. Basil, the Great, an eminent father in the church.

7. Gregory Nazianzen, a theological and polemical writer.
8. Claudian, an elegant Latin poet.
9. St. Chrysostom, and } Learned and eloquent ministers
10. St. Augustine, } and writers.

§ 1. Lactantius proved the truth of the Christian religion, and exposed the absurdities of paganism. He was the most eloquent of the ecclesiastical Latin writers of his age. His principal works, are his treatises concerning the Divine Wrath, and the Works of God, and his Divine Institutions. The last, in seven books, is written with uncommon elegance and purity. As a theologian, he had some errors. He died in 325.

2. Ossian was a rude Caledonian. He is supposed to have flourished in the fourth century, and to have been the son of Fingal. He wrote in Gaelic; and the poems that go by his name, translated by Macpherson, are marked by a simple and sublime wildness. If they are really Ossian's, he must be considered as the first of the poets of this period. There is, however, strong ground of doubt, in respect to the authenticity of these poems, as a whole.

3. Eusebius died in 338 A. C. He was bishop of Cæsarea, and enjoyed the favour of Constantine. He opposed Arius, although he held to a certain disparity and subordination in the Godhead. He was a man of immense reading, and was greatly versed in ecclesiastical history and sacred erudition. He distinguished himself by his writings, which consisted of an ecclesiastical history, the life of Constantine, evangelical preparations, and many other treatises, most of which are now lost.

4. Eutropius lived in the age of Julian, under whom he was a soldier in the war against Persia. He is supposed to have been a Roman Senator. He wrote several works; but none of them remain except his Roman History. This was an epitome of the transactions of Rome, from the age of Romulus to the reign of Valens. It is characterised by conciseness and precision, but not by elegance.

5. Julian, as has been already narrated, was elevated to the throne, 361 A. C. He then, although he had been educated according to the principles of the Gospel, publicly disavowed its truths, and offered solemn sacrifices to all the Gods of Ancient Rome. This change of religious opinion, was attributed to the austere manner with which he was instructed in Christianity; though others ascribe it to his intercourse with the philosophers of Athens, and their influence over his mind. From this circumstance, the appellation of apostate, has been attached to him. Some of his writings have been preserved, in which he has shown great powers of ridicule in a bad cause. But we need not repeat the particulars that have already been given, respecting his character and writings.

6. Basil, surnamed the Great, was bishop of Cæsarea. He was persecuted by Valens, for refusing to embrace Arianism. According to Mosheim, "in point of genius, controversial skill, and a rich and flowing eloquence, he was surpassed by very few of his contemporaries." He died in 379.

7. Gregory Nazianzen, was surnamed the divine. He was patriarch of Constantinople, but the right to that station being disputed, he abandoned it. His birth occurred in 324, and his death in 389. He held an honourable place among the theological and political writers of the times. His writings compare well with those of the Grecian orators, in eloquence and variety. His sermons are better adapted to philosophers than common hearers, but are, nevertheless, not wanting in seriousness and devotion. He most ably defended the orthodox faith concerning the Trinity.

8. Claudian was a native of Alexandria, in Egypt, and flourished in the age of Honorius and Arcadius. His style is not corrupted by the false taste of the age. But although he wrote elegant verses, he depicted no powerful passions, and exhibited no commanding genius. His matter was meagre, but his language was pure, his expressions happy, and his numbers melodious. His best compositions are his poems on Rufinus and Eutropius.

9. St. Chrysostom, John, was so called on account of his extraordinary eloquence. He was born at Antioch, of a noble family, about 354, consecrated bishop of Constantinople in 398, and died in 407. His works are voluminous. He was an elegant preacher, and possessed a noble genius. On account of his severity in opposing the corruption of the times, he procured himself many enemies. He was so great a disciplinarian, that he even recommended to private believers, though very injudiciously, the use of outward violence, in resisting the wickedness of men.

10. St. Augustine was bishop of Hippo, in Africa. He led an austere life, and died in his seventy-sixth year, 430 A. C. He distinguished himself by his writings, and his reputation is great, even to this day. He was characterised by a sublime genius, an unintermitted pursuit of truth, an indefatigable application, an invincible patience, a sincere piety, and a subtle and lively wit. The solidity and accuracy of his judgment, were not, however, proportionable to his eminent talents in other respects.

Augustine's book concerning the City of God, has been pronounced to be "a work extremely rich and ample in point of matter, and filled with the most profound and diversified erudition." In all his writings, this father displayed an extensive acquaintance with Plato's philosophy.

PERIOD III.

The period of the Justinian Code, and of the Wars of Belisarius; extending from the Extinction of the Western Empire, 476 *years A. C., to the flight of Mahomet,* 622 *years A. C.*

THE ROMAN EMPIRE.

The dark ages, as they have been commonly called, commenced

with this period. The human intellect, and the state of society, had for some time previous, been retrograde. But upon the conquest of the Western Empire by the barbarians, the darkness became more especially obvious, and we shall find it prevailing over the nations, though with some intervals of light, nearly 1000 years. It is believed, however, that mankind have been apt to overrate, in some respects, the infelicities of the dark ages, and to forget, that after all, strong proofs were at times afforded, of intellectual vigour, and of the high enjoyment of life. A few men of distinguished abilities appeared during the present period, though, in general, the age is not to be compared with several that preceded it.

SEC. 1. We have now to record the melancholy extinction of the Western Empire of the Romans—an empire, the most powerful that has ever existed. This event occurred, 476 A. C. upon the taking of Rome by Odoacer, prince of the Heruli. Romulus, surnamed Augustulus, was at that time on the throne. Odoacer, having subdued Italy, and taken its capital, spared the life of Augustulus, upon condition of his resigning the empire.

§ The empire having been long beset on every side by barbarians, great numbers of them were admitted into the Roman legions, to protect it against the rest. These, in the reign of Augustulus, having revolted, demanded a third part of the lands of Italy, as a settlement for themselves and families. This being refused, they advanced to Rome, under Odoacer, and as conquerors, held the country.

Odoacer was an officer of the emperor's guards, at the head of the barbarians who had enlisted in the armies. When he had secured Rome, Augustulus, who was a feeble youth, was directed to express his resignation to the senate, while that body, in an epistle to Zeno, emperor of the East, disclaimed the necessity of continuing the imperial succession in Italy, since, in the submissive language of adulation, they observed, "the majesty of the monarch of Constantinople, was sufficient to defend both the East and the West:" at the same time they begged the favour, that the emperor would invest Odoacer with the title of patrician, and the administration of the diocese of Italy. Their request was granted, and to Augustulus, was assigned a splendid income, to support him in a private station.

Thus the Western Empire of Rome passed from the hands of its ancient masters, into the possession of the barbarians, who had so long harassed it by their invasions. As an empire, it had existed more than five hundred years, computing the time from the battle of Actium. The whole period of its duration, from the building of the city, was more than twelve hundred years.

The ruin of the Roman empire, was the result of its great extent, connected with its moral corruption. The perfections of God are concerned in accomplishing, by natural causes, the extinction of enormously guilty nations. Rome, having become a mass of luxury, weakness, and profligacy, fell, at last, an easy prey to the barbarous tribes that poured in upon its dominions.

§ The Northern invaders did not originate the catastrophe which Rome experienced; they scarcely hastened it. As much of crime and barbarism as they brought with them, they became, upon their settlement in the south of Europe, as reputable, at least, as the native citizens themselves. Without the agency of these invaders, darkness and barbarism would have visited the Roman world, from the operation of causes within its own bosom; especially from the extreme profligacy and irreligion which prevailed among all classes.

While the Roman empire in the West, thus fell into ruins, the sister empire in the East, which appeared to be in a similar situation, not only continued to stand, but even existed for the space of nearly one thousand years more, though in comparative imbecility and depression. It existed, notwithstanding it suffered all the internal evils which produce the ruin of a state, and was shaken by all the storms, which burst upon the nations, during the middle ages. This phenomenon, which has not a parallel in the history of the world, may, in some measure, be explained from the almost impregnable site of its capital alone, in connexion with the despotism, which sometimes remains the last support of fallen nations.

We shall continue the portion of its history belonging to this period, before we bring into view the new state of things, consequent on the occupation of Italy and the West by the barbarians. The recent kingdom which they founded, deserves a separate account.

2. The Eastern Empire of the Romans, sometimes called the Greek Empire, and the Empire of Constantinople, was at this time, (474 A. C.) under the sway of Zeno, son-in-law to Leo. He was odious, on account of his debauchery; and after having once fled from his throne, and been restored to it, and engaged in the suppression of several conspiracies, he met with a miserable end, being buried alive. He reigned about seventeen years.

§ Leo II., son of Zeno, and grandson to Leo I., was designed for the empire; but being of tender age when his grandfather died, Zeno was made regent. But the death of the child, the same year, left Zeno in the possession of the throne. The intrigues of the empress Verina, his mother-in-law, embittered his life, and distracted his reign. She aided one or two of the conspiracies that were carried on against him.

He came to his end by an awful act of Ariadne, his wife. She loved him not, and profiting by an epileptic fit, to which the emperor was subject, caused him to be precipitately interred. When the sepulchre was opened, a few days after, it was found that Zeno had devoured the flesh off his own arms.

3. Anastasius, an officer of the palace, marrying the widow of Zeno, was raised to the throne, 491 A. C. He was old at this time, but reigned about twenty-seven years. The beginning of his reign was auspicious, but it was otherwise in the end. He died a natural death, in his eightieth year.

4. Justin I., the Thracian, ascended the throne after the death of Anastasius. He governed with great prudence. In 526, he sent the celebrated Belisarius against the Persians, who had broken the truce subsisting between the two empires. The emperor, however, died before the conclusion of the war, having reigned about nine years.

§ Justin was the son of a ploughman, and rose by his talents to the first military dignities, before he was chosen emperor. He was so illiterate, however, as to be unable to write his own name, and secured respect, only by the good sense which he manifested in the choice of his counsellors.

5. Justinian I., nephew of Justin, assumed the reins of government, 527 A. C. His personal character was far from inspiring respect; but his reign was successful, and he was extremely fortunate in his generals and counsellors. The exploits of his generals, and the production of the code of laws that goes by his name, of which the learned Trebonian was the author, form an era in history.

Towards the brave and noble Belisarius, the warrior who at first fought his battles, the emperor was ungrateful in the extreme. This great general, by his arms and policy, preserved his master on his throne, when his expulsion from it was likely to be effected, by the civil factions which raged at Constantinople. He also defeated the Persians in three sanguinary battles, in different years; destroyed the kingdom of the Vandals in Africa, and recovered that province to the empire; and wrested Italy from its Gothic sovereign, restoring it for a short space of time, to the authority of its ancient masters.

Italy, however, was once more subdued by the Goths. From this time the fortunes of Belisarius began to change. He was compelled to evacuate Italy, having been more than once recalled, through the emperor's meanness and jealousy. On his final return to Constantinople, his long services were repaid with disgrace, and he was superseded in the command of the armies, by the eunuch Narses.

§ Belisarius, more than any other general during the later periods of the empire, revived the fainting glory of Rome. On the plains of Dara, he defeated the Persians, with great slaughter; and his conduct, in the sedition of Constantinople, secured the esteem of the emperor. When Justinian, by favouring a certain faction,* had nearly involved himself in destruction, and was about to seek his safety in flight, Belisarius, amidst the uproar and confusion which prevailed, came to the aid of his master. A corps of three thousand veteran troops he led against the populace of Constantinople, and it is computed that no less than thirty thousand persons perished in the carnage. So signal a chastisement had the effect of overawing the infuriated and divided citizens; and the games of the circus, out of which the contention arose, were, during several years, interdicted.

The war which Belisarius carried on against the Vandals, in Africa, was marked by signal success; but no particulars need to be related, except that Belisarius was recalled by the jealousy of Justinian, and that his victories and prompt obedience, secured him the honours of a triumph.

In the war against the Gothic power in Italy, 537 A. C. Justinian was equally fortunate through the exploits of his illustrious lieutenant, and equally mean in his conduct towards this hero. The Gothic forces were obliged to retire before the Roman army, upon its landing in Sicily and Italy. Resistance was made, but in vain. The fame of Belisarius, had inspired even the degenerate Romans with courage.

Long before this general reached Rome, the Gothic king had abandoned it; and though the policy was singular, the latter did it with a view to wrest the city from the hands of Belisarius, at some future time. In the course of a few months, Vitiges, the Gothic king, advanced towards Rome, at the head of one hundred thousand warriors. The inconsiderable army of Belisarius, however, performed prodigies of valour, and not only defended Rome, during a long siege, but, with the aid of some reinforcements from the East, obliged the Gothic king to retire, first to Ravenna, and at last to surrender all the towns and villages of Italy.

This was no sooner effected, than the jealousy of Justinian remanded his lieutenant to Constantinople; nor was the latter allowed the honour of a second triumph. But though the conduct of the emperor towards him was utterly despicable, the admiration of the people was an ample indemnity.

The valour of Belisarius, at this era, saved the East; but there is no time to recount his achievements. Suffice it to say, that the necessity of the emperor, induced him again to appoint Belisarius to the command of Italy, inasmuch as it had been nearly overrun,

* There were two factions in Constantinople, which were distinguished by a diversity of colour. The support of one or other of these, became necessary, to every candidate for civil or ecclesiastical honors. The greens were attached to the family or sect of Anastasius: the blues were devoted to orthodoxy, and Justinian. The latter, the emperor favoured during five years, though their tumults endangered equally his own safety, and the peace of the city.

during this interval, by the arms of the brave and virtuous Totila. No sooner, however, had he a prospect of driving the Gothic king from Italy, than he was called off to some less important warfare, which was intended as a disgrace to him.

The declining years of the life of this hero, were passed in Constantinople; but even at that late period, they were crowned by a victory, in which he saved the ungrateful Justinian and his capital from the ravages of the Bulgarians. The unnatural suspicions of the emperor followed him to the grave; for even in extreme old age, he suffered in his property and comforts, for a time, from the false imputation of conspiracy.

Narses, who was able in council, was also successful in war. He had the honour of completing the conquest of Italy, by defeating Totila, in a decisive engagement, in which the Gothic king was slain. Under the title of duke, Narses, gaining some other victories, governed Italy with ability for thirteen years.

Justinian died in his eighty-third year. He would be but little thought of by mankind, were it not for those illustrious men who fought his battles, and presided in his councils. He had the sagacity to perceive their merits, and happy would it have been, had he possessed the magnanimity to reward them. His vices were meanness, vanity, caprice, and tyranny: his virtues were chastity, temperance, vigilance, and studiousness. We pretend not to determine which preponderated.

Imposing as was his reign, he lived in a miserable age. His subjects were continually afflicted by war, pestilence, and famine. The empire shone out with a degree of brilliancy under his auspices, but after his death it shone no more. Its history, so far as it is necessary to notice it, is henceforth made up, more than ever, of disasters, miseries, and crimes.

6. Upon the death of Justinian, his nephew, Justin II. ascended the throne, 565 A. C. He was a man of weak intellect, and was governed by his consort, Sophia, though his intentions appear to have been good. The troubles and calamities which befel his family and empire, threw him into an incurable frenzy. In consequence of this event, Tiberius, his son-in-law, was associated in the empire. It was soon after his elevation, that the Lombards established themselves in Italy. In his reign, not only was Italy lost again to the empire, but Africa desolated, and the East ravaged by the Persians.

§ The advice which Justin gave to Tiberius, upon the introduction of the latter to the empire, was worthy of any prince. "Love.'

said he, "the people as yourself; cultivate the affections, and maintain the discipline of the army; protect the fortunes of the rich, and relieve the necessities of the poor." The last four years of his life were passed in tranquillity. He reigned nine years alone, and four in connexion with Tiberius.

7. Tiberius, who assumed the name of Constantine, was sole possessor of the throne in 578. His reign was short, but it was rendered glorious by his defeat of the Persians. He was accounted a just, humane, temperate, and brave prince.

§ On his death-bed, Tiberius bestowed his diadem on his son-in-law, Maurice, who had proved himself an excellent general.

8. Maurice, a native of Cappadocia, ascended the throne 582 A. C. He reigned twenty years, in almost continual turbulence. He chose his predecessors for his model, nor was he destitute of sense and courage, in whatever he undertook for the welfare of his subjects. Avarice is said to have been his great failing; but it is more probable, that his rigid virtue and economy were not duly appreciated in those corrupt times.

In 602, he obliged his army to take up their winter quarters beyond the Danube, upon which a revolt ensued, and Phocas, being proclaimed emperor, advanced to Constantinople. Maurice and his children were cruelly slain.

§ After Maurice fell into the hands of Phocas, the jealous and cruel rebel caused the emperor to be dragged from his sanctuary at Chalcedon, and his five sons to be murdered, one after the other, before his eyes. Maurice bore this agonizing sight with such firmness and resignation, that he repeated, with streaming tears, at every wound, the words of David, "Thou art just, O Lord! in all thy judgments."

When a nurse generously concealed a royal infant, and offered her own to the executioner, Maurice was too rigidly honest not to reveal the deception. The tragic scene was closed with the execution of the emperor himself, who fell on the dead bodies of his children. What sufferings have not princes and their families been often called to sustain—sufferings far surpassing the common lot of men!

9. Phocas seated himself on the throne 602 A. C. His character was despicable. His empire was ravaged by the Persians, and numerous seditions arose to disturb his peace. At last, Heraclius, governor of Africa, sent his son against him with a fleet, which quickly arrived at Constantinople. The emperor, forsaken by his people, on whom he had inflicted all manner of cruelties, was soon beheaded, and his body was treated with the greatest indignity.

§ The cruelty of Phocas towards the family of his predecessor knew no bounds. He finally caused the innocent empress, Constantina, and her three daughters, to be executed on the same spot where her husband and sons had suffered, three years before.

10. Heraclius I., was crowned 610 A. C. His reign extended several years into the next succeeding period. The Persians ravaged his empire; but terribly defeating them in six successive campaigns, he brought them to a peace. He reigned more than thirty years.

During the last part of his reign, the foundation was laid of the caliphate of the Saracens, under the impostor Mahomet, whose history will claim our attention at the beginning of the next period.

KINGDOM OF ITALY.

11. The kingdom which was established on the ruins of the Western Empire of the Romans, is sometimes called the KINGDOM OF ITALY. That country was held and governed, for the most part, by its northern conquerors, through the space of nearly three hundred years. During this time, however, there were several transfers of the sovereignty, from one of the barbarous tribes to another. The Heruli, who conquered the country in 476, held it till 493. It then passed from their hands into the possession of the Goths, or Ostrogoths, who held it till the year 568, when the Lombards seized and conquered the country. They were masters of the greatest portion of it, a little more than two centuries. The period of which we treat, will carry the history of Italy only through a part of the above named space of time.

12. The kingdom of the Heruli in Italy, was of short continuance. Odoacer, their king, reigned thirteen years without opposition; but at the conclusion of that period, Theodoric, king of the Ostrogoths, or Eastern Goths, invaded Italy, and after a struggle of four years, defeated and slew Odoacer, usurping his dominions, 493 A. C.

§ In the year 489, Theodoric twice overcame Odoacer in battle; but being betrayed by one of his general officers, he retired to Pavia, where he was besieged by Odoacer. In his distress, Theodoric called in the assistance of the Visogoths, and gained a third victory in 490. Odoacer, shutting himself up in Ravenna, vigorously defended the place for three years. He was at last forced to enter into a treaty with Theodoric, and obtained a stipulation that his life should be spared. The Gothic monarch, however, perfidiously caused him to be assassinated.

12½ The kingdom of the Ostrogoths (eastern Goths) began, 493. Theodoric, (commonly surnamed the great,) their king, was now acknowledged the sovereign of the country, and fixed his residence at Ravenna. He was an Arian in principle, but protected the Catholics. He reigned about thirty-three years. His administration of government showed him to be an able prince. The people were probably benefitted by a change of masters.

§ Theodoric, at the age of six years, was given as a hostage to Leo I. and remained thirteen years at Constantinople. He succeeded his father in Pannonia in 475. His success in his invasion of Italy, has already been mentioned. After a few years, his dominions consisted not only of Italy, and Sicily, but also of Dalmatia, Noricum, the two Rhœtias, Pannonia, and Provence. The latter part of his reign was tarnished by cruelty and suspicion. In the indulgence of these propensities, he put to death the celebrated Boethius.

13. The successors of Theodoric, in the Gothic kingdom of Italy, were seven in number. It was during the reign of several of these monarchs, that the events already related respecting the invasion and conquest of Italy by Belisarius and Narses, occurred. The best known of the Gothic kings of this country are Theodotus, Vitiges, and Totila. After the death of Theias, the last of them, the Goths endeavoured, under several leaders, to re-establish their dominions, but were subdued by the eunuch, Narses, who administered the government as duke, till 567 A. C.

14. The kingdom of the Lombards followed, in 568 A. C. Alboin, king of this people, was invited into Italy by Narses, to avenge the insult he received from the emperor, Justin II., in his recall. Alboin penetrated into Italy, and was proclaimed its king at the date above mentioned. He reigned but a short time.

§ His end was tragical, as it perhaps deserved to be. Having killed Cunimund, king of the Gepidæ, in a single combat, he married Rosemond, that king's beautiful daughter, and made a drinking cup of her father's skull, out of which he obliged his queen to drink. She dissembled her indignant feelings, but applied to two officers for revenge. One of them had been affronted by the king, and the other she knew was enamoured of her person. These she admitted into the chamber where the king slept, who was immediately murdered, while she contrived to effect her escape to Ravenna.

15. During the remainder of the present period, there were four kings, the successors of Alboin, but none of them

were distinguished. An anarchy, of ten year's continuance took place after the death of one of the kings, during which Italy was governed by thirty dukes.

§ Autharis, one of the kings, after his accession, in 584, confirmed the dukes in their authority, on condition of their paying him half of their revenues, and serving under his command in times of war, with troops levied within their respective jurisdictions. This is considered by some, as the origin of the feudal system.

PERSIA.

16. Seven kings in succession, swayed the sceptre of PERSIA during this period. Of these, Chosroes II., the great, was the most conspicuous. During much of the time, the Persians were at war with the Romans. Sanguinary battles were fought, and provinces were taken and retaken. The Romans at last penetrated into Persia.

§ Chosroes II. was a warrior. He repeatedly overcame the Roman generals, and was as often, perhaps, overcome. In one instance, however, he cut to pieces an army of 50,000. The Greek historians, who probably exaggerate the matter, represent him as a ferocious monster. He doubtless had the vices of his predecessors, but surpassed them in great qualities. He reigned nearly fifty years.

Chosroes III., son of Hormisdas, possessed the hateful character of a parricide. He caused his father to be beaten to death. He received, however, a terrible retribution, in the treatment he experienced from his own son. Siroes, the eldest of his sons, having revolted, and secured the kingdom, slew all his brothers in his father's presence, cast the latter into a prison, where he caused him to expire in insufferable torture, by being incessantly pricked with the points of arrows.

Soon after the expiration of the present period, Persia was invaded by the Saracens, and it was not long before it became a part of the empire of the Caliphs.

CHINA.

17. In the history of CHINA during this period, we find four dynasties of its emperors, from the 9th to the 12th inclusive. They were of short continuance, and included the reigns of seventeen sovereigns. Several of these appear to have been wise and virtuous men. In the reign of Yang-ti, in 605, many canals were cut through the empire, by which several rivers were united, and great facility given to commerce.

§ One of the sovereigns of the twelfth dynasty, is said to have had a very solid, penetrating mind. He loved his people, and did every thing in his power to promote their happiness. He built public granaries, which were every year filled with rice and corn, by the opulent, to be distributed among the poor in times of scarcity. He improved their music and eloquence. Against corrupt judges, he was always inexorable; and excluded from all public employments, those whose rank in life did not render them respectable.

SPAIN.

Before the Empire of the West was finally subverted by the Northern Barbarians, some of the nations which once constituted it, had been lost to the empire. This was the case, particularly, with Spain and Britain. Italy, the seat of the empire, and according to the best accounts, France, may date their separate existence, only from the annihilation of the Roman power. After that event, these several nations, and indeed all the rest of western Europe, were detached from one another, and held by the native inhabitants, or governed by different tribes of the barbarians of the north. We must therefore consider them in their separate sovereignties, according to the eras in which they began to exist independently. We begin with Spain.

18. Spain, while constituting a portion of the Roman empire, was invaded by the Suevi, the Alains, and the Vandals, about 406 years A.C., and mostly subdued by these barbarous tribes. Expelling the Romans, they divided the country, a part of which, viz. Vandalasia, or Andalusia, still bears the name of one of these tribes, (the Vandals.)

The Alains, in 418, were mostly exterminated by the Ostrogoths. The Suevi remained in the possession of the country, under a succession of their kings, till the year 585. The Vandals had early, viz. in 427, passed into Africa, and settled there, upon the invitation of Count Boniface.

The Visogoths, who entered Spain in 531, conquered the greatest part of the country by the year 585, and erected a monarchy, which existed till 712, when they were subdued by the Saracens, or Moors.

§ Spain was anciently called Hesperia or Western, on account of its situation, as being the extreme west known to the ancients. It was called also Iberia, from the river Iber, now the Ebro. The name Hispania, or Spain, is said to be derived from a Phœnician word, Sphavisa, which means, abounding with rabbits; these animals, according to Strabo, being very numerous in Spain.

Its original inhabitants were Celtes, of the same race with those of France, and who passed over from that country into Spain. The fertility of the soil, induced the Phœnicians, who were the earliest navigators, to open a trade with Spain, and they built the city of Gades. now Cadiz. This was about 900 years B. C.

This country has been often conquered, both in ancient and more modern times. About 500 years B. C., it was in part subjugated by the Carthaginians, who held their conquest three centuries. The Romans then succeeded as masters, in whose power it remained six hundred years. From the Romans, as we have already learned, it was wrested by the northern barbarians. These, as we shall see, in the next Period, are destined to be displaced by the followers of Mahomet.

It is deemed unnecessary to detail any events under the kings of the barbarous tribes who governed Spain, as they possess scarcely any interest. Euric may be considered as the founder of the Gothic monarchy of this country.

FRANCE.

19. France, anciently called Gaul, immediately previous to the dissolution of the Roman Empire of the West, was divided between the Romans, Visogoths, Franks, and Burgundians. A few years after that event, viz. 581 A. C., Clovis, king of the Franks, obtained, by degrees, possession of the country. He is therefore considered the true founder of the French monarchy, as before him, the Franks held only a few provinces on the right bank of the Rhine. From this people, ancient Gaul, obtained the name of France. The kings who have reigned in France, seem to be divided into four dynasties, viz. the Merovingian, the Carlovingian, the Capetian, and the Bourbon. The race of which we are now speaking, the first in order, derived its name from Merovœus, the grandfather of Clovis, who reigned over that portion of the Franks, who had obtained, in some former age, a settlement in the country. The Merovingian dynasty continued till 752.

§ The Franks were supposed to have been of German origin, and to have inhabited the country between the Rhine and the Weser, which now forms part of Holland and Westphalia. Some believe them to have consisted of a mixed multitude of various tribes, living beyond the Rhine, who, when Germany was invaded by the Romans, united in defence of their common liberty, and styled themselves Franks, i. e. free men. Of the clans into which they were divided, the Salii, and Ansuarii, were the most considerable. Between the years 234 and 254, they made an irruption into Gaul, but were signally overthrown by the Romans under Aurelian, then a military tribune. They finally obtained a footing in that country, about the year 264 A. C.

Succeeding this event, they had many contentions with the Romans, in which they often conquered, and were, oftener, perhaps, defeated. By the time, however, in which the emperor Constans reigned, they were generally at peace with the Romans, and several of them enjoyed places of distinction in the armies and at court. The petty sovereigns who preceded Clovis, were Pharamond, who made the last settlement of the Franks in Gaul, Clodio, Merovœus, and Childeric I.

Clovis made many conquests: first over the Romans in the battle of Soissons: then over the king of Thuringia, who had invaded his dominions; afterwards over the Germans in the battle of Tolbiac; and finally over the Visogoths under Alaric, when he subdued all the south of Gaul. In his contest with the Germans, 496 A. C., he invoked the God of Clotilda, a Christian princess, whom he had married three years before. In consequence of his victory, he became professedly a believer, and together with three thousand of his subjects, was baptised on Christmas-day, the same year.

About thirteen years afterwards, he cruelly murdered most of his relatives, which shewed how little influence Christianity had over him. Clovis made Paris the seat of his kingdom. He died, 511.

Clovis was followed by a series of obscure kings, through the remainder of this period. They need not, therefore, be mentioned particularly. They were, in general, weak and wicked, and plunged the nation into deeper barbarism than it was under during the Roman dominion.

ENGLAND.

20. ENGLAND, whose ancient name was Britain, had been abandoned by the Romans fifty years, when the Empire of the West was subverted. In the mean time, the inhabitants, who were left defenceless, suffered from the encroachments of their northern neighbours, the Picts and Scots, and in their distress, solicited several of the warlike tribes of the continent, for assistance. The Jutes first arrived for that purpose. These were soon followed by the Angles and Saxons, in 451, from the shores of the Baltic. The object was soon accomplished, for which the Britons had invited them into their country. Their enemy was repulsed; but they found a more formidable enemy in their protectors themselves.

The Saxons, procuring large reinforcements from Germany, turned their arms against the Britons, and took possession of the country. It was not, however, without a long and severe struggle, of nearly one hundred and fifty years, that this conquest was achieved. The result was, the establishment of seven distinct states, or sovereignties, which were governed, more than two hundred years, by their respective kings. These states are usually called the Heptarchy.

§ The island of Britain, before it was known to the Romans, was inhabited by a very rude and uncivilized people. They were either naked, or clothed only with the skins of beasts, having their bodies painted with various colours. Hence is supposed to be the origin of the name, Britain, which is derived from a British word, brit, signifying painted. The name England was given to the country, from the Angles, a tribe of those continental nations, who conquered it in the fifth and sixth centuries.

The island was originally settled, in all probability, by a colony from Gaul, who were called Celtes or Gaels, the remains of whom are chiefly in Wales, in the highlands of Scotland, and in the north of Ireland. The period of their settlement is quite uncertain. The Phœnicians, indeed, traded very early with the inhabitants of Cornwall, for copper and tin, but they were unacquainted with the interior of the country. The Romans have given us the earliest authentic information respecting it. This commences with the first invasion by Julius Cæsar, 55 B. C.

Cæsar began the dominion of the Romans in Britain; but the island was subdued, only by degrees, under the Roman leaders who succeeded him. Forty-three years A. C., it was again invaded by the emperor Claudius, whose general, Ostorius, defeated Caractacus, king of the Britons, took him prisoner, and sent him to Rome, in 51. In the reign of Nero, 61 A. C., Suetonius defeated Boadicea, queen of the Iceni, (inhabitants of Norfolk and Suffolk,) slaying 80,000 men in a single battle. Boadicea, however, had previously obtained several victories over the Romans, by her gallant conduct. She committed suicide, rather than fall into the hands of the conqueror.

Agricola, who governed Britain in the reigns of Titus, Vespasian, and Domitian, formed a regular plan for subduing the whole island, and rendering the acquisition advantageous to the conquerors. For this purpose he penetrated into Caledonia, (Scotland,) defeated the natives in various encounters, and established a chain of forts between the Friths of Clyde and Forth.

Subduing most of the island, he soon diffused among the Britons a knowledge of the arts of peace. He introduced among them, laws and government; taught them to value the conveniences of life, and reconciled them to the language and manners of their masters.

To protect the southern inhabitants against the Scots, Adrian, in 121, built a wall in the north part of Britain, between the river Tyne, and the Frith of Solway. This was afterwards strengthened with new fortifications, by Severus, in 208. From this period, till the abandonment of Britain by the Romans, in 426, the inhabitants enjoyed uninterrupted tranquillity.

As has been already mentioned, the Romanized Britons, when left by their masters, were thrown into a defenceless state. Their long peace had somewhat enervated them, and they were unable to resist the attacks of their barbarous neighbours on the north. It was Vortigern, one of their kings, who invited the German tribes to his protection. The latter gladly availed themselves of the opportunity to visit a country long known to them in their piratical voyages to its coasts. Hengist and Horsa, two brothers, were their leaders on this occasion, and with only 1600 warriors, in conjunction with the South Britons, they compelled the Scots to retire to their mountains.

After the Saxons, from being the protectors, had become the conquerors of Britain, and founded the Heptarchy, history records nothing that is very interesting respecting them, until the time of Egbert the Great, who became sole king of England, in 827. We may therefore pass over the English history, until that period, only remarking that the Saxons, who were partially acquainted with christianity before, were more fully converted to the faith, by the labours of the monk Augustin, in 597.

Distinguished Characters in Period III.

1. Proclus, a learned Platonist and unbeliever.
2. Boethius, a Roman poet, and Platonic philospher.
3. Procopius, a Roman historian—sometimes denominated the last of the classic writers.
4. Cassiodorus, the historian of Ravenna, and tutor to Theodoric, the Gothic king.
5. Belisarius, an heroic and successful general of Justinian.
6. Gildas, the most ancient British writer extant.

1. Proclus was born at Constantinople, in 410, and died in 485 A. C. He was a philospher among the later Platonists. In the chair of the academy, he taught philosophy with great reputation. Such was his industry, that frequently, in the same day, he pronounced five lessons, and composed seven hundred lines. "His sagacious mind," says Gibbon, "explored the deepest questions of morals and metaphysics, and he ventured to urge eighteen arguments against the Christian doctrine of the creation of the world." This, as might have been expected, proved to be labour in vain The foundations of truth can be overturned by no human sagacity, however great.

2. Boethius, who was distinguished both as a poetic and prose writer, was descended from one of the noblest families of Rome. In consequence of having remonstrated, with great spirit, against the tyranny of Theodoric, he was beheaded in prison, by the command of that king, in 524. Boethius wrote many philosophical works, the greater part according to the manner of the logicians; but his ethic composition, concerning the "Consolation of Philosophy," is his chief performance, and has always been justly admired, both in respect to the matter and the style. Mr. Harris, in his "Hermes," observes, that, "with Boethius, the last remains of Roman dignity may be said to have sunk in the western world:" and Mosheim testifies, that he "shone with the brightest lustre, as a philosopher, an orator, a poet, and a divine; and, both in elegance and subtilty of genius, had no equal in the sixth century."

3. Procopius belonged to Cæsarea, in Palestine, and flourished in 534. He was secretary to Belisarius, whom he greatly celebrated

in his History of the Reign of Justinian. This history is divided into eight books; two of which give an account of the Persian war, two of the Vandals, and four of the Goths, to the year 553; which was afterwards continued in five books, by Agalthias, till 559. The historian is thought to be too severe upon the emperor, though his performance, in other respects, has a high character. Some consider him as the last of the Roman classic authors.

4. Cassiodorus was a man of eminence, in many respects, and called, by way of distinction, "the senator." He united the statesman and author in his character. He was born in Italy, about 463, and died at near one hundred years of age. His writings relate chiefly to history, theology, and criticism. He was inferior in abilities to Boethius, but still was very respectable.

5. Belisarius was truly a Roman in spirit, and the greatest general of his age. His life and exploits have been already told us, as particularly as this work will admit. In a degenerate and effeminate age, he put forth an energy, and acquired a fame in war, which would bear a comparison with the first leaders of the most favoured days of the republic. He was, however, as distinguished by his misfortunes as he was by his victories, owing to the ingratitude of Justinian; and he spent his last days, it is said, under the frown of his master, and, as some report, in actual want.

6. Gildas was a native of Wales. He was surnamed, The Wise. As the most ancient of the British writers, he deserves a notice here. His famous "Epistle," was written A. C. 560, and is a most severe censure of the depravity of the Britons at that time. He has some things well calculated to invite the attention of the learned.

PERIOD IV.

The Period of the establishment of the Saracen Dominion; extending from the flight of Mahomet, 622 *years A. C. to the crowning of Charlemagne, at Rome,* 800 *years A. C.*

ARABS OR SARACENS.

During this period, the darkness in Europe very much increased, and the times exhibited a melancholy contrast to the former splendid eras of Grecian and Roman refinement and literature. But while the human mind sunk in Europe, it rose in the East, under the auspices of the Saracens, where it was for a short time displayed, not only in the energies of a warlike superstition, but, at length, in the cultivation of the arts and learning. The history of this people is connected with a remarkable change in the aspect of human affairs.

Sec. 1. The Arabs, in all ages, have lived as wanderers, in a state of independence, and have never been subdued by any of the great conquerors of the world, though almost always at war with their neighbours. They derive their origin from Ishmael, and, before the time of Mahomet, they professed a religion which was a mixture of idolatry and Judaism.

The name Saracen, which was at length applied to most of the Arabian nations, is derived from a tribe that occupied the north-western part of the country. This people, before the time already referred to, had forsaken their deserts, and made themselves useful or formidable (according as their services were purchased or neglected) to the respective empires of Rome and Persia.

Mecca, on the Red Sea, in 569, gave birth to Mahomet, (or Mohommed,) their pretended prophet. In 609, when he was about 40 years old, he began to concert a system of measures, the issue of which, was the establishment of a new religion in the world, and of an empire, which, spreading over many countries, lasted more than six centuries. The religion still remains.

His impostures were not, at first, well received. The citizens of Mecca, even, opposed them. Forsaking his native city, where his life was in jeopardy, he fled to Medina, at the epoch called by the Mahometans, the hegira, or flight, which was in the year 622, and the 54th year of Mahomet's age. By the aid of his disciples at Medina, he returned to Mecca as a conqueror, and making numerous proselytes, he soon became master of Arabia and Syria, was saluted king in 627, and, in the midst of his successes, died suddenly in 632. He left two branches of his family, who became powerful caliphs of Persia and Egypt.

§ As Mahomet will be spoken of again, as one of the distinguished characters of this period, it will be unnecessary to add many particulars here, respecting either his life, or the religion of which he was the founder. Some historians are of the opinion, that he attempted only an inconsiderable change in the creed of his countrymen, and that the mighty revolution which followed his efforts, was, in respect to Arabia, almost wholly political.

In his flight, this bold leader gained Medina with much difficulty, but being well received, he made it the place of his future residence. Besides those who fled with him, and shared his fate, he was soon followed and joined by many of the principal citizens of Mecca. Amongst his followers were Amrou, the future conqueror of Egypt; Saad, who afterwards overran Persia; Obeidah, whose fortune it was to subdue Syria and Palestine; and the very celebrated Kaled Eben al Walid.

Though Mahomet met with some reverses at first, he was no sooner aided by such men as Amrou and Kaled, than he overthrew whatever opposed him. After the submission of Arabia to his arms, the Arabs and Greeks were brought into contact; and the former were prepared to encroach on the remnant of the Roman empire.

Mahomet owed his success, in part, to several moral causes, originating in the state of society; such as the corruption of the true religion, the ignorance of mankind, and the prevailing licentiousness of the times—also to the nature of his doctrines, which, among other things, promising a sensual heaven, were suited to the depravity of the heart, and the taste of the voluptuous Asiatics; and, not least of all, to powerful political revolutions. It happened the same year in which Mahomet left Mecca, that a destructive war, as already mentioned, took place between the Eastern empire and Persia. Heraclius, the emperor, in six campaigns, penetrated to the heart of the Persian dominions, almost destroying that power, and greatly weakening his own. Neither of them, therefore, were in a condition to resist the torrent of Arabian fanaticism. Such was the prospect of Mahometanism, when its author met his fate.

The followers of this impostor, term their religion Islam, and themselves Musslemen, or Moslems, i. e. true believers. The book containing their creed, which was produced by Mahomet, in successive portions, and which he pretended to derive from the angel Gabriel, is called the Koran. Their priests are called moolahs or imans. Mahomet propagated his religion by the sword, and taught, that to profess any other religion, was a just cause of hatred, and even of murder.

2. The successors of Mahomet, in the dominion which he established, are called Caliphs, a word which means successors, or vicars. The first caliph was Abu-beker, the father of one of the wives of Mahomet. It is said that the impostor, on his death-bed, appointed Ali, his son-in-law, as his successor, but the influence of Abu-beker with the army was such, that he, by this means, secured the caliphate.

Thus the foundation was laid for a mighty contention, and over the body of Mahomet arose that schism, which, at this distant period, weakens the power of Mahometanism, and may eventually terminate its very existence. The sects are two, and the ground of dispute is the right of succession to Mahomet. Their names are Sheas or Shiites, and the Sonnites. The Sheas, who believe in Ali, as the true successor, are chiefly Persians. The Sonnites, who believe in Abubeker, consist of the inhabitants of East Persia, Arabia, Turkey, &c. The Sonnites receive the Koran only, whereas the Sheas adopt the traditions also.

In respect to conquest, Abu-beker pursued the course of Mahomet, and, with the aid of his general, Kaled, obtained an important victory over the emperor Heraclius, and enlarged the Saracen dominion. He died in the third year of his reign, having bequeathed the sceptre to Omar.

§ When the sceptre was offered to Omar, he modestly observed, "that he had no occasion for the place." "But the place has occasion for you," replied Abu-beker. He died; praying that the God of Mahomet would ratify his choice. It was so far regarded by Ali, his rival, that the latter treated him with the respect due to a constituted superior.

Omar commenced his reign in 633. In one campaign he wrested from the Greek empire, Syria, Phœnicia, Mesopotamia, and Chaldea. In the next campaign, the whole empire of Persia was brought under the Mahometan yoke. Egypt, Lybia, and Numidia, were at the same time conquered by the generals of Omar.

§ Amrou, one of his generals, by the order of Omar, destroyed the famous library at Alexandria, consisting of 700,000 volumes. The order of Omar betrayed the ignorance of a savage, and the illiberality of a fanatic. "If," said he to Amrou, "these writings agree with the Koran, they are useless, and need not be preserved; if they disagree, they are pernicious, and ought to be destroyed." Omar was finally assassinated.

Othman succeeded Omar, in 645. He added Bactriana, and a part of Tartary, to the Saracen empire. Upon the death of Othman, Ali, the son-in-law of Mahomet, was elected to the caliphate. His name is still revered in the east, and by none of the caliphs was he excelled, either in virtue or courage. After a short but glorious reign of five years, he was assassinated by a Mahometan enthusiast, or reformer. He had removed the seat of the caliphate from Mecca to Cuja, on the Euphrates.

§ Ali married Fatema, the daughter of Mahomet, but Ayesha, the widow of the prophet, and daughter of Abu-beker, bore an immortal hatred against the husband and posterity of Fatema. In a battle which Ali fought with a superior number of rebels, who were animated by the counsels of Ayesha, he was entirely victorious. Ayesha, it is said, had seventy men, who held the bridle of her camel, successively killed or wounded; and the cage or litter in which she sat, was stuck throughout with javelins and darts.

3. Within less than half a century, the Saracens reared a

powerful empire, and were formidable to all the nations around them. In 100 years, their dominion extended from India to the Atlantic, comprehending Persia, Syria, Asia Minor, Arabia, and other regions in the east, as also Egypt, North Africa, and Spain.

Of the race of Omar, already mentioned, there were nineteen caliphs who reigned in succession; after which, began the dynasty of the Abassidæ, descended from Abbas, the uncle of Mahomet. Almansor, second caliph of this race, built Bagdad, and made it the seat of the Saracen dominion, in 762 A. C. He introduced the culture of the arts and sciences among the Saracens.

§ It was during the reign of Almansor, that Abu Hanifa, the founder of the first of the four sects of the Sonnites, died in prison at Bagdad. He had been confined there for refusing to be made a judge, declaring that he had rather be punished by men than by God. Being asked why he declined the office, he replied, "If I speak the truth, I am unfit; but if I tell a lie, a liar is not fit to be a judge." It is said that he read over the Koran 7000 times, while he was in prison.

Haroun al Raschid, a caliph who ascended the throne in 785 A. C., and was contemporary with Charlemagne, was a famous prince, and celebrated patron of letters. His reign is regarded as the Augustan age of Saracen literature. Many of our proverbs and romances are to be referred to this period. Al Raschid was also a brave and victorious sovereign, and distinguished by equity and benevolence. He died in about 809 A. C.

The sciences to which the Arabians chiefly devoted their attention, were medicine, geometry, and astronomy. Poetry, and works of fiction, especially the One Thousand and One Nights, were the products of that period. Literature was cultivated also in Africa and Spain, under the auspices of the Saracens.

§ Soon after Al Raschid's accession to the Caliphate, he invaded and ravaged a part of the Greek empire, with an army of 135,000 men. Having taken the city of Heraclea, he reduced it to ashes; after which conquest he made himself master of several other places. He then attacked the Island of Cyprus, whose inhabitants suffered extremely from the invasion. The Greek emperor was so intimidated by this success, that he immediately made peace with the caliph, accompanied with a tribute.

Several interesting anecdotes are related of this caliph, two of which follow. Being once in Egypt, he said to his courtiers.

The king of this country formerly boasted himself to be God; in consequence, therefore, of such pride, I will confer the government of it on the meanest of my slaves."

As he was marching one day at the head of his troops, a woman came to him to complain that some of the soldiers had pillaged her house. He said, "woman, hast thou not read in the Koran, that princes, when they passed with their armies through places, destroyed them?" "True," replied she, "but then it is also written in the same book, that the houses of those princes shall be desolate on account of their acts of injustice." This fearless repartee, was so well liked by the caliph, that he forthwith ordered that restitution should be made.

EASTERN OR GREEK EMPIRE.

4. The Eastern Empire, which had alone survived the ruin of the Roman world, retained a portion of its ancient splendour. It was destined, however, soon to lose several valuable provinces, as has already appeared, in relating the victorious career of the Saracens. The conquests which Heraclius I. made in Persia, were wrested from him by that enthusiastic and warring people. They next deprived the empire of its Syrian and African dependencies.

During these events, several emperors successively filled the throne of Constantinople, after Heraclius. But very little need be said concerning any of them. It was in the reign of Constantine III., Pagonatus, that the Saracens, 672 A. C. besieged Constantinople for five months, but were obliged to retire. They returned for seven years in succession, but were every time defeated by Callinicus, who invented an inextinguishable fire, by which he destroyed their ships.

§ The Greek, or liquid fire, was made principally of naptha, or liquid bitumen, mixed with some sulphur and pitch, extracted from green firs. Water, instead of extinguishing, quickened this powerful agent of destruction. It could be damped only by sand, wine, or vinegar. It was a period of four hundred years, before the secret of its composition was obtained from the Greeks. The Mahometans at length discovered and stole it. It continued to be used in war, down to the middle of the fourteenth century, when gunpowder was introduced.

Justinian II., who succeeded Constantine in 685, was a second Nero, or Caligula. He ordered, at one time, a general slaughter of the inhabitants of Constantinople, but he was de throned the same day, and sent into exile with mutilated features. He recovered his throne by the assistance of the Bulgarians, and exacted a dreadful vengeance on his enemies. He was at last beheaded. Some of the emperors who followed during the remainder of this period, were, Leo III., Constantine IV., Leo IV., and Constantine V. The first three of these were strongly opposed to images, as used in churches.

§ The mother of the last Constantine, was regent during her son's minority. Her name was Irene, and she proved herself a monster of wickedness. She obliged the sons of Constantine IV. to receive the priesthood, and afterwards ordered them to be murdered. She was singularly cruel towards her own son, who, for attempting to govern by himself when of age, was, by her orders, scourged and confined in the interior of the palace. In 790, he was restored to liberty by the people, when he, in his turn, imprisoned his mother.

Two years after, she was apparently reconciled to Constantine, and by encouraging him in his vices, obtained an unhappy ascendency over him. Being rendered odious to his subjects, especially in consequence of repudiating his queen and marrying one of her women, by the advice of Irene, an insurrection took place. This was as she expected; and afforded a pretext for her cruel machinations. Being left with the army in Bythinia, she despatched several officers to depose her son.

Arriving at Constantinople without being suspected of such a design, they put out the emperor's eyes in so barbarous a manner, that he died, three days afterwards, in the most excruciating pain. Irene then remained in possession of the empire for five years; and in order to confirm her authority, she made overtures of marriage to Charlemagne, king of France. Her design, however, being divulged, a revolt ensued, in which Nicephorus, great treasurer of the empire, being leader, was proclaimed, and Irene deposed.

Having thus obtained the purple, and secured the riches of Irene, Nicephorus banished her to the isle of Lesbos, where the want of a decent provision obliged her to earn a scanty subsistence by the labours of the distaff. Here this miserable woman died of vexation, having enjoyed her ill-gotten power but six years after the murder of her son.

KINGDOM OF ITALY.

5. The Kingdom of Italy, which was formed as already related, continued until nearly the close of the present period, viz. 774 A. C. It had been fifty years under the sway of the Lombard kings. During the remainder of its existence, (viz. 150 years,) seventeen kings reigned over the country. The principal of these were Cunibert, Luitprand, Rachisius, Astolphus, and Desiderius or Didier. Luitprand possessed the greatest talents of all the Lombard

kings. Under Didier the kingdom of Italy came to an end. He was defeated by Charlemagne, his father-in-law, and Italy was afterwards incorporated into the new empire of the West.

§ A few particulars concerning these kings, are as follows. Under Cunibert, Italy was invaded by the duke of Brescia, and they met in battle on the banks of the Adda. Before the battle, a deacon of Pavia, named Zeno, who bore a great likeness to Cunibert, offered to take his armour and supply his place at the head of the army. Zeno was consequently killed, and Cunibert obtained a signal victory, and afterwards enjoyed a peaceable and happy reign.

Luitprand availed himself of an opportunity, soon after the commencement of his reign, to add to his dominions by conquest. His first efforts were directed against Ravenna, which was betrayed into his hands. He afterwards took several other cities. The next year, however, Eutychius, exarch of Ravenna, reconquered a great part of his dominions, with the help of the Venetians, whom Pope Gregory II. excited against Luitprand.

The king, resolving to avenge himself on the Pope, became reconciled to Eutychius, and they both advanced towards Rome. The Pope, however, met the king, and appeased him by his eloquence. In two successive instances, in his attempts upon the Pope and Rome, he was diverted from his design.

Rachisius, in 749, five years after the commencement of his reign, under the pretence of some infractions of a treaty with the people of Rome, besieged a city which belonged to the Pope. But the Pope had such influence with him when they met, that the king was persuaded to renounce the world, and retire to the abbey of Monte Cassino. His queen and daughter, at the same time, founded a monastery of nuns, near that abbey, whither they retired and took the veil.

Astolphus took Ravenna, and seized upon all the dependencies of that principality, not far from the year 750, but soon lost them, by the intervention of Pepin, king of France, who made war upon him. He died in 756, of a fall from his horse.

Didier, meditating the conquest of Ravenna, sought the protection of the French King, by marrying one of his daughters to Charlemagne, and the other to his brother Carloman. A difference, however, having arisen between Charlemagne and his father-in-law, the French monarch divorced his wife. Didier highly resented this act.

Applying to the Pope to favour his projects, and failing in the attempt, he attacked the papal territory, and endeavoured to seize on the person of the Roman pontiff. Charlemagne, however, coming seasonably to his assistance, met the Lombard king in battle, and taking possession of his sovereignty, sent the royal family to be confined in monasteries in France. The French king thus put an end to the Lombard dominion in Italy, and was himself declared, by the Pope, king of Italy, and patrician of Rome.

SPAIN.

6. SPAIN continued under the dominion of the Visogoths till the year 712. It was then conquered by the Saracens, who invaded the country from Mauritania, in Africa, whence they were called Moors. A small part of the north of Spain, never fell under the dominion of that people. Pelagius, the successor of the Gothic sovereigns, founded there the little kingdom of Asturias, in 718; and Garcias Ximenes, that of Navarre, in 758.

§ The Saracens, in their descent upon Spain, easily overran the country. They had lately founded, in Africa, the empire of Morocco, which was governed by Muza, viceroy of the caliph Waled Almansor. Muza sent his general, Tariff, into Spain, who attacking Don Rodrigo, or Roderic, the Gothic king, in a decisive battle, overcame and slew him. The conquerors succeeded to the sovereignty. Abdallah, son of Muza, married the widow of Roderic, and thus the two nations formed a perfect union.

7. Spain, in this manner conquered by the Saracens, was allotted to governors dependent on the viceroy of Africa, till Abdalrahman, the last heir of the family of the Omiades, formed it into an independent kingdom, and fixed his residence at Cordova. This was about the year 756 A. C.

It may be remarked here, that all that part of the kingdom of Spain which was under the dominion of the Moors, embraced the religion of their conquerors; but the two northern provinces above named, remained true to the Christian faith.

Abdalrahman, at Cordova, laid the foundation of a flourishing empire, which lasted for a considerable period. He greatly encouraged learning, and thus vied with Haroun Al Raschid at Bagdad, as a patron of letters. Cordova became renowned as one of the most enlightened spots in Europe, under several succeeding reigns.

§ The part of Spain which remained independent of the Moorish yoke, presents little that is important in its history. We may therefore pass it over with the remark, that its Christian sovereigns became rather strengthened than weakened in their power from time to time.

FRANCE.

8. In FRANCE, the weak race of the Merovingian kings continued to hold the sovereignty, till the year 751 A. C. On the death of one of them, viz. Dagobert II., (638) who left two infant sons, the government, during their minority, was assumed by their chief officers, termed Mayors of the

Palace. Under the management of these ambitious men, the kings of France enjoyed little more than the name.

In the time of Thierry, grandson of Dagobert II., the celebrated Pepin d'Heristel was mayor of the palace. He restricted Thierry, nominally the sovereign of the two great divisions of the Frank monarchy, (Austrasia and Neustria) to a small domain, and ruled France during thirty years with great wisdom.

The son of Pepin, whose name was Charles Martel, was still more celebrated than his father. Under three kings, he governed France with signal ability, having succeeded to the office of mayor of the Palace.

§ After his father Pepin's death, Charles was confined by his mother-in-law, in prison. But escaping thence, he was proclaimed duke of Austrasia, and took possession of the sovereign authority over all the kingdom. He made war several times on Childeric, his first nominal sovereign, and finally secured him as a prisoner.

9. Charles was victorious over all his domestic foes, and his arms kept in awe the neighbouring nations, whom he frequently defeated. But the most signal service which he rendered to France, to Europe, and to mankind at large, was his victory over the Saracens, in 732 A. C. These destroying fanatics threatened all Europe with subjugation to the Mahometan dominion and religion ; and, but for their providential defeat by Charles Martel, might have been, to this day, the masters of the civilized world.

§ The Saracens penetrated into France from Spain. They were led by Abderame, a consummate general, who commanded in the name of the caliph, and who soon defeated the duke of Aquitain. After this victory, his desperate bands were about to overrun the kingdom. Here, however, the genius and bravery of Charles rescued the nation from destruction. He brought them to a general action between Poictiers and Tours, and notwithstanding their bravery and numbers, he succeeded in defeating them with immense slaughter. They afterwards rallied in the vicinity of Narbonne, but were again defeated, and at last driven out of the French territory. By this event, the terror with which the Saracens had inspired Europe was greatly diminished, and Charles obtained for himself the surname of Martel, or the Hammer.

After the death of Thierry IV., Charles, without placing another king on the throne, continued to govern as before, with the title of duke of France. After several more victories over his enemies, Charles dying, bequeathed the government of France, as an undisputed inheritance, to his two sons

Pepin le Bref, and Carloman. As mayors of the palace, the one governed Austrasia, and the other Neustria and Burgundy. The nominal sovereign, at this time, was Childeric III., a weak and insignificant prince. The sole administration devolved at length on Pepin, as Carloman renounced the world and became a monk. Pepin, whose talents were powerful, and whose turn of mind was warlike, governed with great efficiency, and conquered several of the neighbouring tribes.

In the year 751, he assembled a parliament at Soissons. where he was proclaimed king of France, having first obtained the sanction of Pope Zachary. Childeric was confined in a convent, and thus ended the Merovingian race of kings. The Carlovingian now succeeded.

§ Pepin was called Le Bref, or the short, on account of the lowness of his stature, his height being only four and a half feet. Soon after he was crowned, he marched against the revolted Saxons, whom he defeated; and pursuing his brother Grippo into Aquitain, he united Septimia, now Languedoc, to the crown. His brother, who was a turbulent spirit, and gave him disquiet, at length perished. Pepin was thus left to pursue without molestation his useful designs.

10. Having been crowned the second time, by Pope Stephen II., in return for this service, Pepin marched against the Lombards, who had invaded the principality of Ravenna, and threatened Rome itself. The Lombards were spared, only by the surrender of Ravenna, which Pepin bestowed on the Holy See. Thus commenced the temporal authority of the popes.

The Saracens, who still possessed a part of the south of France, were forced by his arms from the country, and thus the limits of his dominions were extended in that quarter. After a splendid and successful reign, he died of a dropsy in the chest, at the age of fifty-three or fifty-four years, 768 A. C.

§ It is related of this monarch, that his diminutive size was compensated by an uncommon strength of body. Having been told that several of his courtiers had secretly ridiculed his personal appearance, he invited them, on the next day, to attend the spectacle of a fight between a lion and a bull. When the two combatants were let loose, the lion leaped on his adversary, and the bull was in danger of instant destruction. "Is there any among you," exclaimed the king to the courtiers that surrounded him, "who has sufficient resolution to oblige the lion to let go his hold?" No one spake. "Mine, then, shall be the task," said Pepin, elevating his voice; and leaping into the amphitheatre with a drawn sword, he approached the lion, and with a single blow separated the head from the body.

11. The dominions of Pepin were, at his death, divided

between his two sons Charles and Carloman. The latter dying two years afterwards, Charles came into possession of the whole kingdom. The exploits and policy of this prince, procured for him the title of Great, which was incorporated with his name, Charlemagne,* as he is known in history. He excelled all the sovereigns of his age, both as a warrior and statesman, although he is said to have been extremely illiterate. With a great reputation for talent, he has, however descended to us as being deficient in several moral qualities, particularly in humanity.

His cruelty was exercised chiefly upon the Saxons, with whom he was engaged in war during thirty years. Their bravery and love of freedom gave him infinite trouble. They revolted no less than six times, and were as often reduced by force of arms. As a means of subduing their bold and ferocious character, he attempted to convert them to Christianity; but their obstinacy induced him to resort to compulsory pro cesses for this end. Several thousands of them were butchered on their refusal to receive Christian baptism.

Besides his success against the Saxons, Charlemagne put an end to the kingdom of the Lombards in Italy, as has already been narrated; he successfully encountered the arms of the Saracens; defeated numerous barbarous tribes, and extended his empire beyond the Danube.

§ Notwithstanding the short stature of his father, Charlemagne is said to have been seven feet in height, and of a robust constitution. He was no less signalized for activity and vigour of mind. His supervision of his dominions was most strict and vigilant. He heard and saw every thing for himself. He discountenanced luxury, encouraged industry, and sought to elevate the social and intellectua. character of his subjects.

When he saw any of his courtiers sumptuously dressed, he would invite them to a hunting party, in the course of which he led them into the wilds and forests. On their return, he would not permit them to change their garments which the thorns had torn. Afte showing them his uninjured sheepskin cloak, as a contrast to their tattered vestments, he would say, by way of advice or reproach, "Leave silks and finery to women; the dress of a man is for use, not for show."

In his wars, Charlemagne met with scarcely a disaster. The only considerable reverse that he ever experienced, was when he was recrossing the Pyrenees, after conquering Navarre, and a part of Arragon. The rear of his army was then cut to pieces by the Gascons, in the plains of Roncevaux. On this occasion, his nephew, the cele-

* Charlemagne—Charles the Great.

brated champion Roland, lost his life—an event which laid the foundation of the "Orlando Furioso" of Ariosto.

As the reign of Charlemagne extends several years into the following period, we shall resume it, at the commencement of that period, with a sketch, in the biographical department, of his more private history and character.

Distinguished Characters in Period IV.

1. Mahomet, an Arabian impostor, and founder of the religion which is called by his name.

2. Adhelme, a British theological writer.

3. Bede, a venerable English historian.

4. Charles Martel, the father of a race of kings, and conqueror of the Saracens.

5. John Damascenus, a Christian writer, strongly tinctured with the Aristotleian philosophy.

§ From the paucity of great men during this period, genius and learning must have been at a low ebb indeed, and the human mind greatly debased and neglected.

1. Mahomet, as has already been stated, was born at Mecca, in 569 A. C. The tribe from which he descended, was that of the Korashites, the most noble in Arabia. His immediate ancestors, seem, however, to have been undistinguished; and though his natural talents were great, it is certain that his education was inconsiderable. He acquired knowledge, but not from books. Intercourse with mankind had sharpened his faculties, and given him an insight into the human heart.

The steps he took in propagating his religion have already been detailed in part. It may be added, that the main arguments which Mahomet employed to persuade men to embrace this imposture, were promises and threats, which he knew would work easiest on the minds of the multitude. His promises related chiefly to paradise, and to the sensual delights to be enjoyed in that region of pure waters, shady groves, and exquisite fruits. Such a heaven was very taking with the Arabians, whose bodily temperament, habits, and burning climate, led them to contemplate images of this sort with excessive pleasure.

On the other hand, his threats were peculiarly terrific to this people. The punishment attending a rejection of his religion, he made to consist of evils, that seemed most insufferable to their feelings. The reprobates would be permitted to drink nothing but putrid and boiling water, nor breathe any, save exceedingly hot winds; they would dwell forever in continual fire, intensely burning, and be surrounded with a black, hot, salt smoke, as with a coverlid, &c.; and to fill the measure of their fears, by joining the present with the future life, he threatened most grievous punishments in this world.

As it was one of the impostor's dogmas, that his religion might be defended and propagated by the sword, he invented the doctrine of a rigid fate, to reconcile the minds of the timid, and add ardour to the brave, under the exigencies of war. He taught that those who were slain in battle, though they had tarried at home in their houses, must, nevertheless, have died at that very moment,—the time of every man's life being before appointed by God, in that unqualified sense; that is, without reference to means.

Mahomet was distinguished for the beauty of his person. He had a commanding presence, a majestic aspect, piercing eyes, a flowing beard, and his whole countenance depicted the strong emotions of his mind. His memory was retentive, his wit easy, and his judgment clear and decisive. In his intercourse with society, he observed the forms of that grave and ceremonious politeness, so common to his country. His natural temper may not have been worse than that of many others; but the imposture which he forced upon mankind, was an instance of most daring impiety and wickedness.

Mahomet persisted in his religious fraud, or fanaticism, to the last. On his death bed he had asserted, that the angel of death was not allowed to take his soul, till he had respectfully asked the permission of the prophet. The request being granted, Mahomet fell into the agony of dissolution; he fainted with the violence of pain, but recovering his spirits in a degree, he raised his eyes upwards, and looking steadfastly, uttered with a faltering voice, the last broken, though articulate words, "O God!—pardon my sins.—Yes,—I come—among my fellow-citizens on high;" and in this manner expired.

2. Adhelme was the first bishop of Sherbourne, (England.) He is said to have been nephew to Ina, king of the West Saxons. The period of his death was 709. He composed several poems concerning the Christian life, but his fancy was quite indifferent. He wrote in Latin, and is reported to be the earliest Englishman who wrote in that tongue. A translator of his writings, speaks of him as profoundly versed in Greek, Latin, and Saxon.

3. Bede, who was surnamed the Venerable, was an English monk. His birth-place was Wearmouth, in the bishopric of Durham, where he was born in 672 or 673. He is celebrated as a writer on Ecclesiastical history. In his youth he studied with great diligence, and soon became eminent for learning. Such was his fame, that he was frequently consulted on various subjects, by scholars from different parts of the country.

He published his excellent Ecclesiastical history of England, in 731, when he was about fifty-nine years of age. He wrote other works, particularly an epistle to the bishop of York, which exhibits a more curious picture of the state of the church at that time, than is elsewhere to be found. That epistle was the last of Bede's writings. His last sickness, was a consumption, ending in an asthma, which he supported with great firmness. During his weakness, he never remitted the duties of his place, being employed the whole of the time in instructing the monks. He appears to have been a person of genuine piety. His death was in 735.

4. Charles Martel was the son of Pepin d'Heristel, and duke of

Austrasia. He succeeded his father as Mayor of the Palace, as has before been stated. That he was a man of great capacity, appears from the record of his exploits. As the progenitor of the Carlo vingian race of kings, and conqueror of the Saracens, when they were upon the point of overrunning all Europe, he is entitled to a very respectful notice in the page of history. Divine Providence seems to have raised him up for a great purpose, in checking the conquering career of the followers of the false prophet. The prodigious number of 375,000 Saracens, he is said to have defeated and slain. He died in 741.

5. John Damascenus flourished in the eighth century, dying about the year 750. His birth-place was Damascus. He was liberally educated, and early made great progress in literature. He succeeded his father, as counsellor of state to the Saracen Caliph of Damascus. Becoming zealous for the forms of religion, and warmly espousing the cause of images, he greatly offended Leo Isauricus, the Eastern emperor.

There is a wild legend of the times, that the emperor caused the hand of Damascenus to be cut off, and that it was miraculously replaced by the kind interposition of the Virgin Mary. After a while, he is said to have retired from public affairs, and spent the remainder of his life in solitude. In this situation he wrote books of divinity, of which he left many behind him. He is not generally thought to have been an evangelical writer. Mosheim says that he surpassed all his contemporaries among the Greeks and Orientals, but was superstitious, and absorbed in a vain philosophy.

PERIOD V.

The Period of the New Western Empire; extending from the Crowning of Charlemagne, 800 *A. C., to the First Crusade,* 1095 *years A. C.*

NEW WESTERN EMPIRE.

Sec. 1. The New Western Empire, so called, included the dominions of Charlemagne, or the countries of which he was acknowledged as the sovereign, in 800 A. C. It was at this period that the title of Emperor of the West, was conferred upon him. He was established in that august sovereignty, by being crowned at Rome, by Pope Leo III.

It is thought by some, that had he chosen Rome as the seat of his government, and at death transmitted an undivided dominion to his successor, the fallen empire of the Romans might have once more been restored to prosperity and greatness. But Charlemagne had no fixed capital, and divided, even in his life-time, his dominions among his children.

The countries, included under the title of the New Western Empire, were principally France, Burgundy, Germany, Italy, and a part of Spain. The Empire, as such, continued but a short time. One country after another separated from it under the successors of Charlemagne, and Germany, at last, became the sole seat or representative of the Empire. Before the expiration of the present Period, the structure reared by the French monarch, was dissolved. After pursuing the few details of the empire as a body, we shall resume our narrative of the individual countries, in their separate or independent state.

§ The occasion and the manner of the crowning of Charlemagne, were as follows:

He was wont to pass annually, from the Pyrenees into Germany, and thence into Italy. In approaching Rome for the last time, the Pope despatched a messenger to meet him with the keys of the Confession of St. Peter, and the standard of the city of Rome. From this union of religious and military attributes, it was evident that Charlemagne was on the eve of becoming emperor.

Accordingly, on Christmas day, which was then the day of the new year, being present at the service of the mass, and on his knees before the altar, the Pope came suddenly behind him, and placed on his head the Crown of the Cæsars. This act was followed by loud acclamations among the populace. An august title, which had lain dormant for several centuries, was thus revived, but it did not restore Rome to its ancient splendour, for reasons which were given above.

Charlemagne lived nearly 14 years after he became Emperor of the West. He died at Aix-la-Chapelle, in the 72d year of his age, and the 46th of his reign.

2. Charlemagne was succeeded, 814 A.C., by his son, Louis the Debonaire, or the Mild. Of the lawful children of Charlemagne, Louis alone survived his father, and all the imperial dominions came of course into his hands, except Italy, which the emperor had settled on Bernard, one of his grandsons.

The reign of Louis was highly calamitous. In 817, he associated his eldest son, Lothaire, in the empire, and gave Aquitain to Pepin, his second son, and Bavaria to Louis, his third.

A disagreement occurring between Louis and Bernard, king of Italy, the latter was subdued, and had his eyes put out, in consequence of which he died three days after. The murder of his nephew affected Louis with such a degree of remorse, that he performed public penance on account of the crime.

The children of Louis greatly embittered, and even shortened his life. First quarrelling among themselves, they then attacked their father; and as he was alternately subdued and restored, his spirits were at length broken, and he died after an inglorious and turbulent reign, 840 A. C.

§ Louis had a son by a second wife, named Charles, who, as will soon appear, became king of France upon the death of his father.—As a second partition of the empire was made, in order to give a share to this younger son, the other brothers were highly disaffected. This was one occasion of their contention.

When Louis found his end approaching, he set aside for Lothaire, a sword and a golden sceptre, the emblems of the empire he intended for him, on condition, however, that he should abide by the partition in favour of Charles. As he did not make any mention of his son, Louis of Bavaria, (Pepin had already deceased,) it was intimated to the old king, that as a christian, he ought not to leave the world, without bestowing upon Louis his pardon. The dying monarch shook his hoary locks, and pointing to them with emotion, replied, "I pardon him, but you may tell him, that it was he who has brought down my gray hairs with sorrow to the grave."

3. Charles, surnamed the Bald, succeeded Louis the mild, in a part of his original dominions, 840 A. C. Soon after his accession, followed the terrible battle of Fontenay, between the three brothers now left, viz. Lothaire, Louis and Charles, in which Charles and Louis were victorious. Lothaire, as the appointed emperor, had wished to obtain the possession of all his father's territories, and refused to allow the partition in favour of Charles. But being overcome in the battle of Fontenay, he was obliged to relinquish his pretensions, and to accede to such a division of the empire, as his brothers now made among themselves.

Lothaire, who preserved the title of emperor, had, assigned to him, Italy, and several of the southern provinces of France. Louis had the whole of Germany. France, including Neustria and Aquitain, fell to the lot of Charles. Thus the fine Empire of the West, founded by Charlemagne, was lost to the house of France, by the separation of Germany from that house. Instead of remaining hereditary, the crown became elective, after it had passed, as it did finally, into the hands of the Germans.

§ The battle of Fontenay was fought with the greatest obstinacy

Historians agree in stating that 100,000 men perished on that occasion. Lothaire fled to the Saxons, yet laid his plans in such a manner as to obtain from his brothers a portion of the empire.

In the reign of Charles, France was plundered by the Normans, who had begun their depredations even in the time of Charlemagne. But their progress was then inconsiderable. In 843, however, they sailed up the Seine, and plundered Rouen; while another fleet entered the Loire, and laid waste the country in its vicinity; the marauders not only securing great quantities of spoil, but carrying men, women and children into captivity. In 845, they entered the Seine again with a fleet, and advanced to Paris. Its inhabitants fled, and the city was burnt. With another fleet they approached to Bordeaux, and pillaged it. Charles, instead of repressing the incursions of these barbarians with his arms, purchased their forbearance with money.

(1.) Lothaire, the emperor, died in 855. Before his death, he divided his dominions among his three sons. Louis II. was the son who succeeded him with the title of emperor. He was a brave and virtuous sovereign, and died 875.

(2.) Louis, to whom Germany was assigned, was a powerful monarch, and rendered himself formidable to his neighbours. He died 876. Upon this event, Charles marched with a large army to seize his dominions, but he was soon defeated by his nephew Carloman, the son of Louis II., having been first crowned emperor by the Pope.

(3.) Charles, on the death of Louis II., son of Lothaire, (875) assumed the empire, or, as is said, purchased it from pope John VIII., on condition of holding it as a vassal to the Holy See. This prince, after contending for the space of two years, with the possessors of the other portions of the empire, with various success, died of poison, 877 A. C. His reign must be pronounced, on the whole, to have been a weak and inglorious one.

He was the first of the French monarchs, who made dignities and titles hereditary. Under the distracted reigns of the Carlovingian kings, the grandees obtained great power, and commanded a formidable vassalage. They chose to reside on their territorial possessions, and refused to take any interest in the general concerns of the country. Intrenched in their castles and fortresses, they defied the power of the government, while the country was disturbed and desolated by their feuds.

The Empire of the West being now effectually dismembered, though there were afterwards temporary junctions of its different parts, we may properly resume our narrative of the several countries in their separate state. As the power which formed this empire emanated from France, it is natural to speak of this first. Indeed, we have been under the neces sity of noticing it already more than the rest. Germany, not having had a political existence before the era of Charlemagne, will be new on the list of nations.

FRANCE.

4. LOUIS II., the Stammerer, succeeded Charles, as king of France, 877 A. C. Nothing of importance occurred during his reign, which was a short one, of only nineteen months. His two sons, Louis III., and Carloman, became joint possessors of the throne upon his death. Their reign was short, but it was characterized by union, vigour, and a degree of success against their enemies, the Normans. They died, the one in 882, and the other in 884.

§ Their deaths were each accidental. Louis, in pursuing a young female who fled from him, struck his head against the door, and was killed by the blow. Carloman, who survived him but a short time, in hunting a wild boar, was wounded by a spear which one of his attendants launched against the animal. To save the attendant from the blame that might be attached to the act, Carloman reported that he had been wounded by the wild boar. Though he lived several days, he persevered in keeping the cause of his death a secret.

5. Charles, surnamed the Fat, was chosen by the peers of France to fill the vacant throne, 885. He was brother and successor to Louis II., the German, and son of the Louis, to whom Germany was originally assigned. For a short time, France and Germany were again under the same sway. At the expiration of two years, however, Charles was deposed on account of his cowardice, and the imperial dignity was transferred to Germany.

The nobility then elected Eudes, count of Paris, to fill the throne, 887, till Charles, a younger brother of Louis III., and Carloman, should attain to the age of manhood. Upon the death of Eudes, Charles, who was surnamed the Simple, was introduced to the sovereignty, 898, but he was deposed by Robert, the brother of Eudes, in 922. Robert was succeeded by Ralpho, or Rodolph, duke of Burgundy, the year after.

§ Charles the Simple, died in prison, 929. He was a weak monarch, and despised by his nobles. It is said, however, that in battle, he killed the valiant Robert with his own hand. Upon the death of Charles, Rodolph was in quiet possession of the throne.

It was during the reign of Charles that the Normans invaded Neustria, which was ceded to them in 911. To Rollo, their chief, the king gave his daughter, Giselle, in marriage. From this peopl the country was called Normandy, and it is from this race of warriors, that we shall trace the future conquerors of England.

6. Louis IV., the son of Charles the Simple, was called to the throne of France, in 936. He was surnamed Outremer, or Transmarine, on account of having been brought up in England. During his reign, and that of his successor, Lothaire, Hugh the Great, the most powerful lord of France, directed, for the most part, the government. The same situation was held by his son, Hugh-Capet, under Louis V., the successor of Lothaire. When Louis died, Hugh, like another Pepin, placed himself on the throne of France.

§ The corruption of these times, and the peculiar uncertainty and infelicity attending the condition of kings, are manifest, from the fact, that both Lothaire and Louis were poisoned by their queens.

7. Hugh Capet, the head of the third dynasty of kings in France, called the Capetian, began to reign in 987 A. C. He was crowned at Rheims, on the third of July. His administration was marked with ability. He enacted several salutary laws and ordinances, and established his residence in Paris, which had been deserted by his predecessors during more than two hundred years. He delegated a portion of the supreme authority to his son Robert, near the beginning of his reign.

§ The true heir to the crown, was Charles of Lorrain, uncle to Louis V. Attempting to secure his rights by force, he was at last betrayed and confined in prison, where he soon died.

Hugh, either through modesty, or the fear of exciting the jealousy of his nobles, never assumed the insignia of royalty. He always, even on great and solemn occasions, appeared in a plain dress and simple style.

8. Robert, the son of Hugh Capet, succeeded his father in 996. Marrying a cousin in the fourth degree, Bertha, who was the daughter of the king of Burgundy, his marriage was annulled, himself excommunicated, and his kingdom put under an interdict by the pope. This was the first instance of such an exercise of the papal authority in France. The distress and confusion that ensued, obliged Robert, much

against his inclinations, to dismiss Bertha, and to expiate his offence by a solemn penance.

He soon after married Constantia of Toulouse, who proved to be a vexatious partner, and cruel queen.

§ The superstition of the times was seen in the affair of the Pope's interdict. The mass was no longer celebrated; the sacrament refused to the sick; and the dead left without burial. There were no longer any regulations of police; and, as all dreaded to approach an excommunicated person, the king was abandoned. He commanded, however, the services of two faithful domestics, who passed through the fire whatever he had touched, and threw to the dogs the refuse of the table.

The king, in his second marriage, was extremely unhappy. Constantia continually tormented him. She caused the king's favourite, grand master of the palace, to be assassinated. She sowed discord between the sons of Robert. And her intolerance in religion was such, that she ordered thousands of a certain sect of heretics to be burned at the stake.

It is a circumstance worthy of notice, that in the province of Languedoc, where these cruelties were particularly exercised, the protestant faith has since constantly predominated over catholicism.

Robert is said to have been the first of the French kings who, according to the superstitions of the vulgar, received the supernatural gift of curing scrofulous affections, thence denominated the king's evil, by touching the sick, and pronouncing these words, "The king touches thee, and may God cure thee."

9. On the death of the king, his two sons, Henry and Robert, both aspired to the throne. It belonged to Henry, but the infamous Constantia had contrived to create an interest in favour of Robert. After some bloodshed, Henry was invested with the sovereign authority, 1031 A. C. He was an active sovereign, who knew how to maintain, and even extend his dominion, but he was not always judicious in his enterprises.

§ He subdued several of his rebellious nobles, defeated an army of a younger brother who had claimed an inheritance in the monarchy, and espoused, for a time, the cause of William of Normandy, against the Norman grandees. He, however, soon attacked the latter—a rash step, which laid the foundation of long and disastrous wars.

About the commencement of Henry's reign, a dreadful famine desolated not only France, but the rest of Europe. The dead were disinterred to serve as food for the living. The passengers were intercepted on the high ways, and carried into the woods to be devoured by the famishing peasantry. In one place, human flesh was publicly exposed for sale; and in another, an innkeeper massacred the poor during the night, so as to furnish his table for guests on the following day. The season was such that corn could not be raised, and the want of pasture occasioned the death of cattle.

10. Henry left the crown to his son Philip I., then seven years old, 1060 A. C., under the regency of Baldwin, count of Flanders. Philip was rather a spectator than an actor in the political events of his reign. He lived beyond the commencement of the first crusade, having swayed the sceptre during forty-eight years. His principal war was with William of Normandy, now become king of England. From this date commenced a long hostility between the English and French monarchies.

ITALY.

11. In the division of the Western Empire among the sons of Louis the Debonaire, Italy, as we have seen, was assigned to Lothaire, with the title of emperor. His successor, as we have also seen, was Louis II., his son, who died in 875. The succeeding year, Charles the Bald, king of France, was proclaimed king of Italy by a diet at Pavia. But he retained this sovereignty only two years, his death occurring in 877.

Italy was afterwards ravaged by contending tyrants; but in 964, Otho, the Great, reunited it to the dominions of the German empire. A series of wars, however, continued during at least two centuries, occasioned by the invasions of the Normans, and the claims of the emperors, till Italy was divided into several independent states. These wars are too unimportant and uninteresting to be noticed in this, or the following period. Italy, therefore, once the mistress of the world, must, for a time, be left out of the records of nations, except as her affairs shall be incidentally noticed in the history of Germany. Her independent sovereignties, formed at different times, as Naples, the estates of the Church, Tuscany, Parma, Lombardy, the Genoese, and the Venetian territories, may, in some subsequent period, be duly noticed.

§ A transaction, in which Otho II., the second German emperor after Italy was re-united to the empire, was engaged, may be here related. Several cities of Italy took occasion to throw off their allegiance to the emperor. Otho, hearing of it, soon entered Italy with an army, and adopted the following most cruel method to punish the authors of the tumults.

He invited the nobles of Rome to a grand entertainment in the Vatican palace and when the guests had placed themselves at the table, he forbade them, under pain of death, to speak or move at what they should hear or see. Instantly they were surrounded by armed men, and while they sat trembling, the emperor composedly ordered the names of those concerned in the late disturbances to be read over, and the guilty to be put to death in the midst of the hall. After the bloody mandate was executed, he was all smiles and complaisance to the other guests, during the entertainment.

It may be recorded here, that it was during the present period, the foundation of the temporal power of the popes was laid. In 1080, Matilda, countess of Tuscany, bequeathed a large portion of her dominions to pope Gregory the VII. From that time the popes possessed great power in the states of Europe. Although the emperors (German) asserted their sovereignty over Italy and the popedom, and claimed the absolute right of electing the pope; yet it was with a constant resistance on the part of the Romans, and a general repugnance of the popes, when once established.

SPAIN.

12. The empire of Charlemagne, in Spain, comprised but a small part of that country. Indeed, all that the Christians, (including the native Spaniards and the French,) possessed, constituted only about a fourth of the kingdom, viz., Asturia, part of Castile and Catalonia, Navarre, and Arragon. Catalonia and Navarre were subdued by Charlemagne, but his successors seem to have taken no interest in the conquest; it probably soon reverted back to the Christians of Spain. All the remainder of the Peninsula, including Portugal, was occupied by the Moors.

Cordova, a luxurious and magnificent city, was the Moorish capital. It was a great school for the sciences, and the resort of the learned from all parts of the world. In the tenth century, their dominions were divided among a number of petty sovereigns, who were constantly at war with one another. Had the Christians availed themselves of this state of things, they might perhaps have then regained the whole kingdom; but they were unhappily contending among themselves, and it was sometimes the case, that the Christian princes formed alliances with the Moors against one another.

§ Taste and the sciences flourished in Cordova, and the south of Spain, when the rest of Europe had become involved in barbarism and ignorance. Cordova, as the seat of government, enjoyed a splendid period of two hundred years, reckoning from the middle of the eighth, to the middle of the tenth century. During that period, the Moorish portion of Spain boasted of a series of able princes, who gained the palm over all the nations of the West, both in arts and arms.

It was only after the Moorish princes became luxurious and effeminate, that the nation was divided into a number of petty states, the principal of which, were Toledo, Cordova, Valentia, and Seville.

To add to the divided state of Spain, both among the Moors and Christians, the country abounded with independent lords, who were warriors and champions by profession, making it their business to decide the quarrels of princes, or to volunteer their service and that of their vassals and attendants, on such occasions. Of this description of persons, termed knights-errant, the most distinguished was Rodrigo the Cid, who undertook to conquer the kingdom of New Castile, for his sovereign, Alphonso, king of Old Castile. Of the passion for knight errantry, however, it is proposed to speak in some other place.

The contentions among the petty kingdoms of Spain need not detain us here, nor will it be expedient to dwell on the subsequent history of Spain, until the expulsion of the Moors, and the union of the whole country under one head, towards the conclusion of the fifteenth century.

GERMANY.

13. Germany was known in ancient times, but it possessed no political importance till the era of Charlemagne. Previously, it was a rude and uncivilized country, and fluctuating in its government. Charlemagne may therefore be considered the reviver, if not the founder of the German empire. As a component part of his sovereignty, it has been already noticed so far down as the termination of the short reign, or rather usurpation, of Charles the Bald, of France, in 877. At that period, or perhaps a few years subsequent, it may be considered as having been effectually separated from France; and of all the dominions of Charlemagne, it has alone descended as an empire, and the representative of the sway which he once held over the nations of the West. The emperor of Germany is to this day, nominally at least, regarded as successor to the Emperors of Rome.

§ Germany, is said to be compounded of the Celtic word *ger*, brave, and *man*, signifying a warlike people. In ancient times, it comprehended all the country from the Baltic to Helvetia, and from the Rhine to the Vistula. The primitive inhabitants were most probably the Celts. But our information respecting Germany is scanty till the period of the Roman conquests in that country. Some ages before that time, the Goths, or Teutones, had migrated from the eastern part of Europe, along the Euxine, and established themselves on the shores of the Baltic, in Belgica, in the north of France, and the south of England; driving the original inhabitants into the northern and western regions.*

When Rome was in the zenith of its power, Germany seems to have been divided into a number of independent principalities; but the inhabitants frequently united in the defence of their common liberty, and many bloody battles established their reputation for bravery, before they sunk under the power and policy of their invaders. At length, however, their country was reduced to a state of provincial subjection to the masters of the world; and upon the decline of the Western Empire of Rome, Germany became a prey to the Franks, and a considerable part of it remained under the dominion of earls and marquisses, till Charlemagne extended his power, both military and civil, over the whole empire.

14. The successor of Charles the Bald, was Charles III, called the Fat, after an interregnum of three years, 881 A. C. France was also under his sway at the same time, but he was soon afterwards deposed, and reduced to the greatest extremities.

15. In 887, Arnold, a natural son of Carloman, and nephew of Charles III., was proclaimed emperor of Germany. In the course of his reign, he defeated the Normans, took Rome, and was crowned there by the pope. His son Louis III., became his successor in 899, when only seven years of age. He was the last emperor descended in the male line from Charlemagne.

§ The reign of Louis is said to have been so much agitated by divisions between the lords and the bishops, that the young emperor died of grief.

From the death of Louis, the empire became strictly elective, although, during the hereditary succession, the consent of the bishops and grandees had always been asked.

16. Conrad, duke of Franconia, was elected to fill the vacant throne in 912. He reigned seven years, during which time he quelled several revolts, and purchased peace of the barbarous Hungarians

§ The German grandees, who assembled at Worms, first offered the imperial diadem to Otho, duke of Saxony; but he declining it

* Webster's Elements, &c.

on account of his advanced age, persuaded them to apply the invitation to Conrad. The latter was of imperial descent by his mother, who was a daughter of Arnold. During his reign, the affairs of Germany were conducted with great prudence.

17. Upon the death of Conrad, the imperial dignity was bestowed on Henry I., surnamed the Fowler. This prince possessed great abilities, and introduced order and good government among his people. He built and embellished cities, reduced and conciliated many of the revolted lords, and conquered several tribes, as the Hungarians, Danes, Sclavonians, Bohemians, &c. He added Lorrain to his dominions.

§ Great as Henry was as a statesman, he manifested considerable zeal in propagating the Christian faith. A portion of the Vandals whom, he subdued, were, under his auspices, converted to this religion. He maintained no correspondence with the See of Rome, inasmuch as he had been consecrated by his own bishops.

18. His son Otho I., the great, was elected emperor, 936. He carried on the system of his father, in repressing the usurpations, of the lords. The conquest of Bohemia he began in 938, and finished in 950. In 961 he expelled Berenger II. and his son, Adalbert, from Italy, and caused himself to be crowned at Milan. The next year he was crowned by Pope John XII, and from that time he may be justly styled the emperor of the Romans. John afterwards revolted against him, but was soon deposed.

Otho was the greatest prince of his time. After an active and commendable reign of thirty years, he died of an apoplectic disorder, in 972. His remains were interred in the cathedral church of Magdebourg, where his tomb may be still distinguished by a Latin inscription.

§ Otho owed his ascendancy in Italy to the disorders and crimes of the Papacy. Being invited into that country by the Pope and the Italian states, while they were contending with Berenger, he defeated the latter, and in return for the honours which the Pope conferred upon him, he confirmed the donations made to the Holy See by Pepin, Charlemagne, and Louis the Debonaire.

§ The treachery of the Pope, (John XII.) obliged the emperor, in two or three successive instances, to visit Italy to compose the disorders that took place. The last time, he executed exemplary vengeance on his enemies, by hanging one half of the senate. Calling together the Lateran Council, he created a new Pope, and obtained from the assembled bishops, a solemn acknowledgment of the absolute right of the emperor to elect to the papacy, to give the investiture of the crown of Italy, and to nominate to all vacant bishoprics.

The power of parental affection is strikingly exhibited in the following incident of Otho's life. Ludolphus, his son, had engaged in an unnatural revolt, which produced some serious hostilities, and occasioned the destruction of the city of Ratisbon; but after some time, the prince was made sensible of his error, and seized an opportunity while the emperor was hunting, to throw himself at his feet, and implore his clemency. "Have pity," said he, "upon your misguided child, who returns, like the prodigal son, to his father. If you permit him to live after having deserved death, he will assuredly repent of his folly and ingratitude, and the residue of his life shall be spent in the faithful discharge of filial duty." To this affecting appeal, Otho could reply only by a flood of tears and a paternal embrace; but when his agitation subsided, he assured the penitent of his warmest favour, and generously pardoned all his adherents.

19. Otho II., surnamed the Sanguinary, succeeded his father in 973, during whose reign, and that of several others, nothing of importance occurred. The names of the sovereigns who followed, down to Henry IV., are Otho III., St. Henry, Conrad II., and Henry III. They occupied a period of about eighty-three years.

20. Henry IV., the Great, succeeded his father at the age of six years, in 1056. He maintained a perpetual struggle with the popes, who insisted, that only the cardinals should elect the bishop of Rome. It was the lot of this emperor to experience a large share of papal insolence and tyranny. After a spirited contest with Pope Gregory VII., during which, the pope was twice his prisoner, and the emperor as often excommunicated and deposed, Henry fell, at last, the victim of ecclesiastical vengeance. At the instigation of Pope Urban II., the two sons of the emperor, Conrad and Henry, rebelled against their father, and to such an extremity was he reduced, through their barbarity and the pope's act of excommunication, that he could scarcely obtain the means of subsistence.

His sufferings were terminated by death soon after the expiration of the present period, viz. in 1106, he having lived sixty-four years, and reigned forty-eight. Henry, in his youth, was vicious to an uncommon extent, and gave up himself freely to the indulgence of his passions. Misfortune, afterwards, abated his sensual excesses, if it did not thoroughly reform his character. He lived to acknowledge, that "the hand of the Lord had touched him." On the whole, he was endowed with many excellent qualities—courage, clemency, liberality, and, finally, with contrition and resignation.

§ The insolent treatment he received from the Pope, appears from the following. On one occasion, he set out for Italy, with his wife and infant, in order to humble himself at the foot of his holiness. On his arrival at the place where the Pope was, he was admitted within the outer gate, and informed that he must expect no favour until he should have fasted three days, standing from morning to evening, barefooted amid the snow, and then implored forgiveness for his offences. This penance was literally performed, notwithstanding the fatigue of the journey, and on the fourth day he received an absolution.

The liberality of Henry's disposition was such, that he is said to have entertained the sick, the lame, and the blind, at his own table, and even to have lodged them in his own apartment, that he might be at hand to minister to their necessities.

ENGLAND.

Saxon Kings.—Norman Family.

21. England, which had been divided into seven distinct sovereignties during more than two centuries, became one entire kingdom, in 827 A. C. This change was effected by the prudence and valour of Egbert, prince of the West Saxons, who inhabited that part of the heptarchy, which was called Wessex and Sussex.

The occasion which offered for the conquest and union of the heptarchy, arose from the fact, that Egbert alone remained of the descendants of the Saxon conquerors of Britain; he, therefore, naturally looked to the dominion of the several states, as a sort of right; nor did he hesitate to claim it, also, with his sword. Success attended his undertaking, and four hundred years after the arrival of the Saxons in Britain, were they united into one powerful kingdom.

22. The English, who were so happily united under Egbert, enjoyed their prosperity but a short period. The piratical Danes, or Normans, who had molested the English coasts for fifty years, now became still more troublesome. During the life of Egbert, they twice attempted an invasion, but were repulsed with much slaughter.

The death of Egbert, and the character of his successor, Ethelwolf, a prince of a very yielding disposition, encouraged the Danes to multiply their depredations. They were often defeated, but could not be expelled. By his will, Ethelwolf divided England between his two eldest sons—Ethelbald and Ethelbert. Alfred, afterwards so illustrious, was a younger son.

§ It was Ethelwolf who, through facility of disposition, not only granted to the priesthood a perpetual right to tithes, but exempted it from all services and imposts.

The reign of Ethelbald and Ethelbert was short,—commencing in 857, and ending in 866. To Ethelred, a third brother, the sceptre was bequeathed. He died bravely, in battle against the Danes, and then the immortal Alfred succeeded, in 872.

23. This prince, who was only twenty-two years of age, when he ascended the throne, found his kingdom in a most miserable condition. It was scourged and afflicted by anarchy, domestic barbarism, and foreign aggression. By his efforts, however, he succeeded in raising it to an eminence and happiness, surpassing what might have been expected at that period. His talents, virtues, and character, were of the highest order, and have justly endeared his name and memory to the bosom of every Englishman. The institutions which he founded are, to this day, the glory of the British realm.

He patronised learning and the arts—encouraged manufactures and commerce—appropriated a seventh of his revenue to restore the ruined cities, castles, palaces, monasteries—founded or revived the university of Oxford—divided England into counties and hundreds—took a survey of the country, and formed a code of laws, which, though now lost, is generally deemed the origin of the common law.

§ The wisdom of his civil institutions may be seen in his division of the country. This plan was resorted to with a view to restore the order which the violence and rapacity of the Danes had subverted. Besides a division into counties and hundreds, there were the smaller divisions of tithings. Ten householders formed a tithing, who were answerable for each other's conduct, and over whom a headborough was appointed to preside. Every man was registered in some tithing, and none could change his habitation, without a certificate from the headborough.

In the decision of differences, the headborough, also called tithing-man, summoned his tithing to assist him. In affairs of great moment, or in controversies between the members of different tithings, the cause was brought before the court of the hundred, which was assembled every four weeks. Here we may trace the origin of juries. Twelve freeholders, sworn to do impartial justice, tried the cause in this court. The county court, which met twice a year, and consisted of the freeholders of the county, was superior to that of the hundred, from which it received appeals. Here disputes between the inhabitants of different hundreds were settled. The ultimate appeal from these several courts, lay to the king in council.

The reign of Alfred was signalized by his contest with the Danes. Within the space of one year, he defeated them in eight battles; but a new irruption of their countrymen, forced him to solicit a peace, which these pirates frequently interrupted by fresh hostilities. At this juncture, Alfred was compelled to secure his person by retreating into an obscure part of the country. Here he continued, disguised in the habit of a peasant, for many months, until the disorders in the Danish army offered a fair opportunity for attacking them. This he embraced with great effect. Instead of cutting them off entirely, as he might have done, he incorporated many of them with his English subjects. It was after these exploits, that he turned his attention, as already mentioned, to the internal improvements of his kingdom. He died in the full vigour of his age and faculties, after a glorious reign of twenty-nine years, and was justly surnamed the Great.

§ Alfred having perceived the remissness of the enemy, from whose pursuit he had secreted himself, ventured at length to quit his retirement. With a few of his retainers, he had made some sudden and partial attacks on the Danes; but before he attempted to assemble his subjects generally in arms, he was determined to explore the state of the enemy. His skill as a harper procured him admission into their camp. Having been introduced to Guthrum, their prince, he played before him in his tent. Here he witnessed their supineness.

Encouraged by what he had seen, he sent private emissaries to the most considerable of his friends, and summoned them to meet him with their retainers, at a certain place. The English crowded around the standard of a monarch whom they so fondly loved, and before their ardour could cool, he led them victoriously against the enemies of their country.

24. Edward, surnamed the Elder, succeeded his father Alfred, in 901. He lived in a stormy period, being continually molested by the Northumbrian Danes; yet he was generally successful in his wars, and his administration of government was honourable to his character. He reigned twenty-four years.

§ Ethelwald, a younger son of Alfred, inherited his father's passion for letters, and lived a private life—a happy turn and destiny for the son of a prince.

25. Athelstan, a natural son of Edward, succeeded him, 925. He was an able and popular sovereign, and opposed with success the Northumbrian Danes, Welsh, Scots, &c. He encouraged navigation, by conferring the rank of thane, or gentleman, on every merchant who had made three voyages to the Mediterranean on his own account. His reign was of sixteen years continuance.

§ He effected the laudable design of translating the Scriptures into the Saxon tongue, which appears to have been the earliest version of that book into the language of Britain.

26. Edmund, a legitimate son of Edward, next ascended the throne, 941. He reigned about five years, having perished by the hand of Leolf, a notorious robber.

Edred, a brother of Edmund, became his successor, 946. In this prince, was the singular mixture of courage and superstition. His courage he manifested in reducing to obedience the Northumbrian Danes—his superstition, in becoming the dupe of the famous Dunstan, Abbot of Glastonbury. He abandoned his conscience to this deceiver.

§ Dunstan invented several marvellous legends of his conflicts with the devil—pretended piety, but possessed an inordinate ambition—and was at last canonized as a saint.

27. Edwy, a nephew of Edred, now filled the throne of the Saxon kings of England, 955. By marrying within the degrees of affinity prohibited by the canon law, he and his beautiful princess Elgiva, both became objects of monkish persecution.

§ Archbishop Odo, with a band of soldiers, seized Elgiva, burned her face with a hot iron, and forcibly carried her into Ireland. When afterwards she attempted to return to the arms of her husband, she was secured by this detestable ecclesiastic, and by his order so mutilated, that she died in a few days in the sharpest torment.

28. Edgar, the younger brother of Edwy, succeeded to the throne, 959. His reign lasted sixteen years. His private character was detestable, on account of his licentiousness; but energy and success distinguished his public administrations. He promoted the inhuman and fanatical Dunstan to the archbishopric of Canterbury, and paying that prelate a forced homage, he was able to carry into effect his various plans of government.

§ Edgar obtained his wife Elfrida, in the following manner. She was a daughter of the Earl of Devonshire, and the greatest beauty of the English court. Edgar designing to marry her if her charms were found answerable to report, sent his favourite, Athelwold, to visit her, and bring him an account of her person.

The courtier's fidelity was overcome by the beauty of Elfrida, and with a view to secure her for himself, he gave an unfavourable account to the king, at the same time intimating that she would on the whole be an advantageous match for himself, on account of her riches and birth. The king forwarded his favourite's views, and he obtained the hand of the fair damsel.

The truth, however, soon came to the ears of the king, and informing Atholwold that he would like to be introduced to Elfrida, and the courtier being afraid to decline the honour, he had an opportunity, of witnessing with his own eyes, the loveliness of her person. Atholwold, in the mean time, had been obliged, in the hope of saving his wife, to reveal the whole transaction to her, and besought her to disguise her beauty on the occasion.

She, however, resenting the artifice by which she had lost a crown, purposely sought to captivate the king by a display of her person, and easily succeeded. Edgar soon after embraced an opportunity in hunting, of stabbing Athelwold, and reaped the fruit of his crime in the possession of the enchanting fair one.

29. The reign of Edward, son of Edgar, by his first wife, was short and uninteresting. He perished by assassination, which was instigated by his step-mother Elfrida, 978.

Ethelred II., son of Edgar, by Elfrida, was placed on the throne at the age of eleven. His surname was Unready, the reproachful epithet of his weakness. His hatred of the Danes, who again molested England, was so great, that he ordered a massacre of all those of that people who had been retained as mercenaries in his army. This barbarous mandate was strictly executed.

The Danes at home, however, resolved on vengeance, and accordingly under Sweyn, their king, they invaded and ravaged the country. London was saved from destruction, only by the payment of a tribute. The weak Ethelred fleeing to Normandy, the English nobility were ashamed of their prince, and in despair of relief, offered the kingdom to Sweyn.

The Dane, however, died soon afterwards, and Ethelred was restored; but Canute, the son of Sweyn, asserted his claims to the crown by force of arms. He was opposed by Edmund, son of Ethelred, with various success.

In the mean time, Ethelred died, after a long and inglorious reign, and Edmund succeeded to the government, 1016. In the war which he carried on with Canute, he was obliged, at length, to divide his kingdom with the latter. But he survived this treaty only a month, having been cut off by the treachery of his brother-in-law, Edric.

§ Edmund was surnamed Ironside, from his strength and valour; but though he put forth every effort, he could not save his realm. He left two children, who, however, never succeeded to the throne.

Canute became sole monarch, upon the death of Edmund, in 1017, and proved to be the most powerful sovereign of his time. He was surnamed the Great, and possessed eminent abilities. He was terrible in his resentments, but an impartial dispenser of justice.

§ In the distribution of justice, he made no distinction between the Danes and English; he restored the Saxon customs, and gradually incorporated the victors with the vanquished. His mind was affected with religious considerations towards the close of life, and he became alarmed in view of the crimes he had committed, (for he had put many of his subjects to death without cause,) but his piety was of that superstitious kind, which displayed itself in building churches and endowing monasteries, the great virtues of those ages.

30. Of the three sons whom Canute left, two ruled in succession over England, viz.—Harold, surnamed Harefoot, from his speed in running, who reigned only four years, and Hardicanute, who reigned but a few months.

Upon the death of the latter, the English freed themselves from the Danish yoke, and restored the Saxon line in Edward, a younger son of Ethelred, 1041. He was entitled the Confessor, and reigned twenty-five years without merit of any kind, unless it were his ability to conciliate the esteem of the monks. Having no children, and wishing to defeat the views of Harold, the son of the Earl of Godwin, an aspirant to the throne, he appointed his kinsman, William, Duke of Normandy, his successor. Edward was the last of the Saxon kings of England.

§ Edward united all the laws of England in one body, called the Common Law. He was the first king of England, who pretended to cure the king's evil by his touch, a practice which was continued till the Hanover succession.

31. On the death of Edward, Harold actually took possession of the throne, but William determined to secure it as his rightful inheritance. His preparations were very formidable, and he was aided in this romantic age, by many sovereign

princes, and a vast body of nobility from the different kingdoms on the continent.

With an army of 60,000 men, he set sail for the English coast. Harold, with nearly the same number of soldiers, met him, and was defeated and slain in the field of Hastings. The English army was nearly destroyed, while the Normans lost about 15,000 men. William, from this time styled the Conqueror, soon assumed the prerogatives of sovereignty, 1066 A. C. The princes of the Norman family ruled till the time of Henry II.

William's administration of government was marked with ability, and in general, with success. In consequence of the discontent often manifested by his English subjects, he began to treat them too much as a conquered people, and the natural tyranny of his disposition increased by the commotions in which this policy involved him. Hence his measures were frequently arbitrary and cruel.

He alienated the minds of the conquered, by conferring on his Norman followers, all the important places in the government; by causing the Norman language to be the vehicle of the church service, and also of judicial proceedings; by reserving to himself the exclusive privilege of killing game throughout the kingdom, and by depopulating a tract of country about thirty miles round, in order to form a forest.

§ He was the author of several other regulations of an inauspicious nature, some of which were greatly vexatious to the people. He introduced the feudal system; substituted the murderous practice of single combat for the trial by jury; compelled the people to rake up their fires, and put out their lights at the sound of the curfew bell; and he made it a greater crime to destroy an animal, than to murder a man. One useful act of his reign, was a survey of all the lands and estates of the kingdom, with an estimate of their value, an enumeration of every class of inhabitants who lived on them, and other important specifications. This record is called the Doomsday-book, which is still in being.

The children of William brought on him no small share of trouble. His eldest son Robert, attempted to wrest from him the sovereignty of Maine, and his foreign subjects assisted the rebel. The king led against them an army of the English, and during the battle was on the point of being killed in a rencounter with his son. Soon after, while waging a war with Philip I. of France, who had aided in the rebellion, he was accidentally killed by a fall from his horse, 1087.

He reigned nearly twenty-one years over England, and bequeathed the sceptre to his second son William.

William was eminent as a statesman and warrior, and was at times capable of generous emotions; but the prominent traits of his character were very unamiable. His pride, ambition, austerity, and cruelty, both inflicted sufferings on his people, and robbed his own mind of peace. In his administration, though he was sometimes politic, he erred on the side of severity.

§ The person of William, was such as befitted a sovereign, especially in a rude and warlike age. He was tall, majestic, and well proportioned. His strength was so great that scarcely any other person could bend his bow, or wield his arms. He was, however, near being overcome by the prowess of his son Robert, on a certain occasion.

While contending with the forces of that rebel, he happened to engage with him in person. They were mutually unknown to each other, as they were concealed by their armour. Both being vigorous and resolute, a fierce combat ensued. Robert at length wounded and dismounted his father, nor did he discover who his antagonist was, till at that instant, in his cry for assistance, William's voice was recognized by his son.

Struck with remorse and horror, the young prince threw himself at his father's feet, and implored forgiveness, at the same time assisting him to mount his own horse. William was implacable at first, but reflecting on his son's generosity, he soon became reconciled to him, and invited him into England.

32. William II., surnamed Rufus, from his red hair, ascended the throne in 1087. He was destitute of the few virtues of his father, and inherited all his vices. Perfidy, tyranny, and cruelty, were the chief ingredients of his character. After the defeat of one conspiracy at the beginning, his reign was a series of despotic acts, which conferred neither peace nor honour on his country. After a reign of thirteen years, he was accidentally shot by Sir Walter Tyrrel, with an arrow, while hunting in the New Forest.

§ Tyrrel, from fear of the consequences, fled to France. The body of William, after several days, was found by the country people, and conveyed in a cart to Winchester, where it was interred. The person who carried the corpse of the king to interment, was named Purkis, and it is remarkable, that some of his decendants, are known, at this very day, to reside near the same spot.

The chief monuments that perpetuate the name of Rufus, are the Tower, Westminister Hall, and London Bridge.

EASTERN EMPIRE.

33. The EASTERN, or GREEK EMPIRE, during the present period, was ruled by thirty-nine emperors, most of them following in succession, though in a few instances, two or more ruled at the same time, and jointly. None of them were very distinguished, though a very few were respectable sovereigns. In general they were a weak or vicious race, yet scarcely too degraded to be rulers of the degenerate Romans. A few names will appear below.

This people, compared with what they had been, were low; yet still they were on an equality, at least, with the first nations of Europe, at that time. Their degeneracy was rather in moral and intellectual qualities, than in external show and consequence. There remained among them much of ancient wealth and splendour.

§ In the 10th century, the provinces that still acknowledged the authority of the successors of Constantine, had been cast into a new form by the institution of the themes, or military governments. Of these, there were twenty-nine, viz. twelve in Europe, and seventeen in Asia; but their origin is obscure. The victories of a few of the emperors had enlarged the boundaries of the Roman name; but in the eleventh century the prospect was darkened. The relics of Italy were swept away by the Norman adventurers, and the Turks had removed many of the Asiatic props of the empire. Still the spacious provinces of Thrace, Macedonia, and Greece, were obedient to their sceptre, and they possessed Cyprus, Rhodes, and Crete, with the fifty islands of the Ægean Sea.

The subjects of the Byzantine empire, were more dexterous than other nations, and in the support and restoration of the arts, their patient and peaceful temper, and refined taste, are highly to be commended. The first demand of the public revenue was the pomp and pleasure of the emperors. The coasts and islands of Asia and Europe, were covered with their magnificent villas. The great palace, the centre of imperial residence, was decorated and enlarged by the wealth of successive sovereigns; and the long series of apartments were adorned with a profusion of gold, silver, and precious stones.

Of the numerous emperors of this period, whose reigns in general must have been short, the following only can be noticed.

Basil I., who ascended in 867, was from an obscure family, but proved himself worthy of his elevation. He defeated the Saracens in the east, and in Italy, but could not prevent them from ravaging the Peloponnesus.

An incident of this emperor's reign is the following. His son, Leo, had been imprisoned on a false accusation of an attempt to assassinate the emperor. Frequent intercessions were made by those who believed in the son's innocence, to have him released, till the emperor in his impatience, forbade Leo's name to be mentioned in his hearing. It happened, however, one day, that a parrot which had often heard a regret expressed for the unhappy prince, on a sudden broke out with, "Alas, poor Leo!" in the emperor's presence. Basil, struck with the sounds, was so moved that he consented to his son's liberation.

Nicephorus Phocas possessed the reputation both of a hero and saint. His saintship, however, was only a pretence. He proved his claim to heroism in his wars with the Saracens. He invaded Asia, and overran Mesopotamia. His vices, especially his avarice, rendered him odious to his subjects. He was assassinated by John Zimesees, who succeeded him in the empire, and who afterwards met with the same fate.

Basil II. marched against the kingdom of Bavaria, and finally destroyed it. On this occasion, it is related of him, that having taken a great number of prisoners, he divided them into companies of an hundred each, caused all their eyes to be put out, and ordered them to be conducted to their king by a man who had one eye left. This horrible spectacle so affected the king of Bulgaria, that he fainted away, and died two days afterwards.

CHINA.

34. The thirteenth dynasty of the emperors of CHINA terminated during the present period, which included also five other dynasties. The number of emperors was thirty-three. Some of them were very wise men. In the reign of Tai-tsong, of the thirteenth dynasty, Christianity was introduced into a small part of China.

§ Tai-tsong was one of the greatest of the Chinese princes. He was wise, frugal, and affable. His ministers attempted to excite in him apprehensions from his too great familiarity with his subjects; but he replied, "I consider myself in the empire as a father in his family. I carry all my people in my bosom, as if they were my children. What then have I to fear?"

Chwang-tsong, of the fifteenth dynasty, from a general, stepped to the throne. As emperor, he preserved his martial habits, lived very frugally, and slept on the bare ground with a bell about his neck to prevent his sleeping too long. He was devout, and all his prayers were offered for the good of his subjects. Block printing was invented among the Chinese during his reign.

SARACENS.

35. At the commencement of the present period, the SARACENS were flourishing in science and the arts. Their military distinction was perhaps on the wane. Nearly forty

years had elapsed since the seat of their empire was transferred to Bagdad, and Arabia, in consequence, had lost much of its importance. Many of the chiefs of the interior provinces became independent, and withdrew themselves from the civil jurisdiction of the caliph.

§ It is supposed, that the Saracens, had they acknowledged only one head, might have established and perpetuated an immense empire. But after the extension of their conquests, they were broken up into separate states. Egypt, Morocco, Spain, and India, had, at an early period, their own sovereigns, who, though they paid a religious respect to the caliph of Bagdad, awarded him no temporal submission. Divided among themselves, they were destined ere long to fall.

36. The principal military expedition of the African Saracens in this period, was the invasion of Sicily, and the projected conquest of Italy. They actually laid siege to Rome, which was strenuously defended by Pope Leo IV. They were entirely repulsed, having their ships dispersed by a storm, and their army cut to pieces, 848.

37. The house of Abbas, which now enjoyed the caliphate, furnished twenty-two caliphs during this period. These reigned in succession, and Bagdad continued to be the seat of their power. In the year 1055, however, Bagdad was taken by the Turks, and the caliphs, from that time, instead of being temporal monarchs, became only the supreme pontiffs of the Mahometan faith.

At the time of the first crusade, in the beginning of the next period, Arabia was governed by a Turkish sultan, as were Persia, and the greater portion of lesser Asia.

§ We can notice only one or two of the caliphs of Bagdad. Adadodawla was deemed a great prince. He was magnanimous, liberal, prudent, and learned ; but he was also insatiably ambitious. A remark which he made when at the point of death, is a melancholy comment on human greatness. With a faultering tongue, he cried, " What have all my riches and prosperity availed me ? My power and authority are now at an end."

Mahmud Gazni, was a famous conqueror. He invaded and conquered a part of India. The following striking anecdote is related of him by historians. A poor man, who had complained to him that one of his soldiers had driven himself and family out of his house in the night, was told to inform the prince if that occurrence should take place again. The poor man had occasion to inform the prince, who went to the house, and causing the lights to be extinguished, cut the intruder in pieces. The prince then commanded the flambeaux to be lighted, and after closely inspecting the corpse, offered thanks to God, and asked for some refreshment. This being afforded, he ate heartily of the mean fare.

Being interrogated by his host respecting the reason of his conduct, he replied, "Ever since your complaint, my mind has been harassed with the thought, that none but one of my own sons would commit such an act of audacity. I had resolved to show him no lenity, and commanded the lights to be put out, that the sight of him might not affect me; but on seeing that the criminal was not my son, I returned thanks to the Almighty."

Distinguished Characters in Period V.

1. Charlemagne, a successful warrior and able sovereign
2. Photius, a learned Christian writer and philosopher.
3. Erigena, a Scotch philosopher and learned divine.
4. Alfred, a wise, learned, and virtuous prince.
5. Al Razi, an eminent Arabian scholar, and physician.
6. Avicenna, an Arabian philosopher and physician.
7. Suidas, a Greek lexicographer.

§ 1. Charlemagne, of whom some account has already been given, was king of France, by succession, and emperor of the west, by conquest, in 800. He laid the foundation of the dynasty of the Western Franks. Though his empire did not hold together, long after his death, his successors in the several states of which it had been composed, reigned several centuries, in the line of the Franks. Indeed, this was the case, till the house of Austria was founded.

Charlemagne was in many respects an admirable sovereign. He excelled in war; and although he was so illiterate that he could not spell his name, he was great in the cabinet, and patronised learning. He invited into France, literary and scientific men from Italy, and from the Britannic Isles. The latter, in those dark ages, preserved more of the light of learning, than any of the western kingdoms.

His private character has been much eulogized, though it is acknowledged that he was sometimes rigid and cruel. He was simple in his manners and dress, and opposed to parade and luxury. Economy, industry, and plainness, characterised him in a domestic state His daughters were assiduously employed in spinning and housewifery, and his sons were trained by himself in all manly exercises Except when he held his general assemblies, his dress, table and attendants were like those of a private person.

He was a man of almost incredible activity. Instead of confiding in the reports of others, he personally saw that his orders were executed. The condition of his subjects was constantly in his view. In one place, he ordered the repairs of a highway; in another, the construction of a bridge; and in another, he afforded the necessary aid to agriculture and commerce. Each of the provinces partook in its turn of his benefits.

Charlemagne founded several seminaries of learning; but the

darkness of the times could scarcely be alleviated by all his efforts. He suppressed mendicity, and established a fixed and invariable price for corn. The meanest of his subjects were thus enabled to provide against their wants, and all complaints on this head were banished. After rearing a splendid empire, he departed this life at the age of seventy-one years.

2. Photius was patriarch of Constantinople in the ninth century, and the greatest man of the age in which he lived. He possessed the patriarchate only ten years, during which, he was exposed to a most turbulent opposition and cabal. He was at last deposed, and died in a monastery. He deserves a high rank in point of erudition. He was the author of a commentary on the ancient writers, a collection of the canons of the church, epistles, &c. These are yet valuable on several accounts. In commenting on the scriptures, although he followed reason, rather than authority, he is not on the whole a model fit to be taken. He explained with ability the categories of Aristotle. He died in 886.

3. Erigena, John Scotus, was born at Ayr, in Scotland, according to some authorities, and was very learned, in a very barbarous age. He was employed by king Alfred to promote learning and the liberal arts. For this purpose he was appointed to preside at Oxford, over the studies of geometry and astronomy in particular. He spent three years in this situation; but some disputes and disturbances arising at Oxford, he left that place and retired to a monastery at Malmsbury. There he opened a school, but his harshness and severity to his scholars so provoked them, that they stabbed him with the iron bodkins they then wrote with, in such a manner, that he died, 883. Mosheim speaks of Erigena as an eminent philosopher and learned divine, and as manifesting uncommon sagacity and genius. He wrote a book on Predestination, and translated into Latin four pieces of Dionysius, the Areopagite, and was the author of some other works.

4. Alfred, so justly surnamed the Great, was born in 849, as is supposed, at Wantage, in Berkshire. He succeeded to the crown on the death of his brother Ethelred in 871; but he had scarcely time to attend to the funeral of his brother, before he was obliged to fight for his kingdom and life, with the piratical Danes. His military exploits, with several other things, have been above related. The particulars which may with propriety be added, are the following.

Alfred was both a wise and a pious prince. His qualities were most happily blended together, so that no one encroached on another. He reconciled a most diligent attention to business, with the purest and warmest devotion—the severest justice with the most exemplary lenity—the brightest capacity and inclination for science with the most shining talents for action. He was equally a warrior and a legislator. He united with rich mental endowments, every personal grace and accomplishment.

The darkness and superstitions of the age, were too powerful for his efforts and institutions. He could not expel them to any great extent. Yet he did considerable to elevate the character of his countrymen, and he aimed at much more. In addition to the schools and seminaries of learning which he founded, he afforded the attractive influence of his own example.

His time he usually divided into three equal portions—one was employed in exercise or the refection of the body—another in the despatch of business—and a third in study and devotion. He conveyed his instructions to the people in parables, stories, &c. couched in poetry; as he considered these best adapted to their capacity. He translated the Fables of Æsop, the histories of Orosius and Beda, and Boethius on the Consolation of Philosophy. In these various literary engagements, he sought the good of his people, as well as his own personal, intellectual improvement.

5. Al Razi, a name not perhaps well known in European literature, was famous in the Arabian annals; and the Arabians at this era were the most enlightened of the nations. This person is said to have been extremely well versed in all kinds of ancient learning; though he excelled most in physic, and is styled the Phœnix of the age. He applied himself to the study of philosophy with such success, that he made a wonderful progress in every branch of it, and composed a great number of books upon physical and philosophical subjects. He composed 12 books on alchemy, in which he asserted the possibility of a transmutation of metals, and was the first writer on the small-pox.

He is said to have contracted webs in his eyes by the immoderate eating of beans; and towards the close of his life, lost both of them by cataracts. He would not permit an occulist, who came to couch him, to perform the operation, because he could not tell of how many little coats the eye consisted; saying at the same time, that he was not very desirous of recovering his sight, as he had already seen enough of the world to make him abhor it. He died about the year 935.

6. Avicenna, who is much celebrated among his countrymen, the Mahometans, was born in the year 980, and died in 1036. The number of his books, including his smaller tracts, is computed at near one hundred, the majority of which are either lost, or unknown in Europe. At the age of ten years, he had made great progress in classical literature. It is said that he read over Aristotle's metaphysics 40 times, got it by heart, but could not understand it. Accidentally meeting with a book which treated of the objects of metaphysics, he perceived what Aristotle meant, and out of joy at the discovery, gave alms to the poor.

7. Suidas flourished between 975 and 1025. His native country is not known. He is the author of a very useful Greek Lexicon. The work contains much historical and geographical information. No particulars seem to have been recorded respecting his life, either by himself or by others. He is known only by his book.

PERIOD VI.

The period of the Crusades; extending from the First Crusade, 1095 years A. C., to the founding of the Turkish Empire, 1299 years A. C.

During this period, we have manifold proofs of the darkness o the times, with a singular mixture of a spirit of adventure, and lofty daring. The age was peculiarly characterised by the crusades, the passion for pilgrimages, the exploits of chivalry, and the production of romances. Barbarism and turbulence extensively prevailed, while the lights of science were few and dim. In England, however, there was the early dawn of literature.

THE CRUSADES.

SECT. 1. In giving an account of the CRUSADES, we include a portion of the history of the principal European nations. For this reason, less of the separate history of those nations will appear during this period, than would otherwise be introduced. The Crusades were common to all Christendom, and all felt a deep interest in them. The other peculiarities of the times, as pilgrimages, chivalry, the feudal system, &c. since they belonged to the established customs and institutions of Europe, will be unfolded in the General Views. In the Crusades, the political and military history of a great part of the world is carried on for a long time.

2. The Crusades were wars undertaken principally during the twelfth and thirteenth centuries, by the Christian nations of Europe, on account of religion. They were termed Crusades, from the cross which was the badge of the combatants. The object of these wars was the deliverance of Palestine, and particularly the tomb of Jesus Christ from the dominion of the Turks or Mahometans.

The Turks, or Turcomans, a race of Tartars, having, in 1055, taken Bagdad, and thus overturned the empire of the caliphs, came into the possession of the countries which these caliphs had governed, and the caliphs themselves, instead of temporal monarchs, became sovereign pontiffs of the Mahometan faith. Palestine, and particularly Jerusalem, were of course under the sway of the Turks, and the seat of their religion.

In this situation of things, the resort of pilgrims to the tomb of our Saviour was attended with much difficulty and danger. While the Saracens held possession of the country, the pilgrims were permitted to have free access to the holy city; but its new masters, the Turks, were a more wild and ferocious people. They insulted and robbed those fanatical devotees—a circumstance, in such an age, of sufficient importance to arouse all Europe for the deliverance of Jerusalem from the infidels. The Roman pontiffs were the principal instigators of these desperate adventures.

§ In an age of religious enthusiasm, and in an unenlightened state of society, it is not surprising that Judea should have been an object of veneration, or superstitious regard to the Christian world. Here the great events recorded in the sacred scriptures transpired—the chosen people of God subsisted through many generations—unnumbered miracles were performed—the Mosaic and Christian dispensations were set up—even God's own Son, the Messiah, lived, suffered, and died. Here prophets and apostles had preached, and written, and shed their blood in testimony of the truth, and every tenanted part, especially the Holy City, was marked by some divine interposition or manifestation, most dear to the lover of piety.

A country so hallowed, is capable, even now, of exciting the most delightful associations; and though we are in no danger of attempting any thing like a crusade, yet nothing relating to such a land can be contemplated without deep emotion. What sensations then must have been excited in a deeply enthusiastic and superstitious age! And much as we smile at their folly, how easily can we account for the ardour which was displayed by unlettered minds and fanatical tempers, on the subject of the crusades! Connected also, as was a pilgrimage to the holy land, with the idea of merit, and merit even sufficient to purchase salvation, nothing can be conceived more calculated to arouse every honourable and indignant feeling, than the obstructions in the way of such a devotion. It was a hardship not to be endured, that the Christian disciple should be prevented from approaching and musing over, with a sort of adoration, the sepulchre in which his blessed Redeemer was laid.

2½ There were five* expeditions of the kind here spoken of, which, during nearly two centuries, drained from Europe most of its life-blood and treasures. All western Europe became involved in these destructive wars, but the French entered upon them with more enthusiasm than any other nation.

The first crusade was preached by Peter, commonly styled

* Some reckon a larger number.

the hermit. After having sufficiently excited Christendom by his rude eloquence, he found vast multitudes ready to engage in the hazardous undertaking. The popes, however, had for some time contemplated the same design, and Urban II., the reigning pontiff, availed himself of this opportunity of executing his splendid project of arming the whole of Christendom against the Mahometans, through the instrumentality of Peter. Two general councils were called and held on the subject, one at Placentia and the other at Clermont, and were attended by many thousands. The pope himself harangued the multitude, and offered to all who would engage in the service, plenary indulgence, and full absolution of sins.

Peter, who possessed none of the necessary qualities of a military leader, was placed at the head of this motley crowd of all ages, conditions, and character, amounting to eighty thousand men. They commenced their march towards the East, in the spring of 1096, and were soon followed by an addition of two hundred thousand persons of the same promiscuous description. They were any thing rather than a regularly appointed army, or efficient military force. Their progress was marked by outrages; not more than one third of them reached the scene of action; and those who did, were nearly all cut off in battle on the plain of Nice.

§ Peter the Hermit, was a native of Amiens, in Picardy, (France.) He seems to have been the first effectual mover of this mighty, and it may be properly added, mad project. His own pilgrimage to the tomb of our Saviour, had made him acquainted with the dangers and vexations to which pilgrims were exposed in Asia, and became the occasion or cause of the enterprise in which he embarked. Fired with a sense of his own wrongs, and those of his fellow pilgrims, he sought the gratification of revenge, or at least, the means of preventing the recurrence of those evils, in future. For this purpose he travelled from city to city, and from kingdom to kingdom, representing with a rude but pathetic eloquence, the grievances of the pilgrims, and urging the necessity of making a common effort against the common enemy of Christians and their religion. On this subject he exhorted all whom he met, and hesitated not to call on nobles as well as their vassals—the rich as well as the poor.

His applications of this kind were aided by his personal appearance. He was a monk, and exhibited all the austerity of that character. He was an enthusiast, and displayed more than an enthusiast's madness. He travelled bare headed, and with naked arms and legs, having only a part of his body covered with a coarse garment. He seemed wasted with fasting, and exhausted with anxiety and toil. He bore aloft in his hand a ponderous crucifix, to which he pointed with the most animated gestures; nor did he restrain his prayers, whatever his situation might be, but poured his whole soul in loud and prolonged supplications in the streets and highways.

The body of enthusiasts who crowded around him was immense. Princes, noblemen, artisans, peasants, monks, and even women, manifested equal anxiety to bend their steps to the East, and expel the infidel hordes from the consecrated land. To the vicious and abandoned in character—to the ambitious and disorderly—to robbers, incendiaries, murderers, and other offenders, a fit opportunity was presented of procuring the pardon of their sins, and at the same time of indulging in unbounded lust and rapine.

As Malmsbury curiously observes, "the report of the council of Clermont, wafted a cheering gale over the minds of Christians. There was no nation so remote, no people so retired, as did not respond to the papal wishes. This ardent love not only inspired the continental provinces, but the most distant islands and savage countries. The Welshman left his hunting; the Scotch his fellowship with vermin; the Dane his drinking party; the Norwegian his raw fish." Robert of Normandy, after mentioning in general terms the contributions of men which France and England made to the holy war, thus singularly mixes other nations:

> "Of Normandy, of Denmark, of Norway, of Bretagne,
> Of Wales, and of Ireland, of Gascony, and of Spain,
> Of Provence, and of Saxony, and of Allemagne,
> Of Scotland, and of Greece, of Rome and Aquitain"

At this time, "every wonderful event in the natural world was regarded as an indication of the divine will. Meteors and stars pointed at and fell on the road to Jerusalem. The skies were involved in perpetual storms, and the blaze and terror of anxious and disordered nature showed the terrific harmony of heaven with the sanguinary fury of earth. Man fully responded to the supposed calls of God. The moral fabric of Europe was convulsed; the relations and charities of life were broken; society appeared to be dissolved. Persons of every age, rank, and degree, assumed the cross. The prohibition of women from undertaking this journey was passed over in contemptuous silence. They separated themselves from their husbands where men wanted faith, or resolved to follow them with their helpless infants. Monks, not waiting for the permission of their superiors, threw aside their black mourning gowns, and issued from their cloisters full of the spirit of holy warriors. They who had devoted themselves to a solitary life, mistook the impulses of passion for divine revelations, and thought that heaven had annulled their oaths of retirement. A stamp of virtue was fixed upon every one who embraced the cause; and many were urged to the semblance of religion, by shame, reproach, and fashion. When families divided, nature and fanaticism contended for the mastery. A wife consented to the departure of her husband, on his vowing to return at the end of three years. Another in whom fear was stronger than hope, was lost in violence of grief. The husband wore the semblance of indifference, unmoved by the tears of his wife and the kisses of his children, though his heart reproached him for the sternness of his countenance. On the other hand, fathers led their sons to the place of meeting—women blessed the moment of separation from their husbands, or if they lamented, it was from the cause they were not permitted to share the honours and perils of the expedition. In some instances, the poor rustic shod his oxen like horses, and placed his whole family in a cart, where it was amusing to hear the children, on the approach to any large town or castle, inquiring if the object before them was Jerusalem."

Such was the disordered rabble that attempted the conquest of Palestine, and such the circumstances under which the expedition commenced. Only a small part of the vast multitude ever reached Asia. From the beginning they were illy provided with necessaries, and therefore had recourse to acts of rapine. Their progress, so destructive to the countries through which they passed, was frequently arrested by collision with their inhabitants. The Jews of Germany were the first sufferers; but it was in Hungary and Bulgaria especially, that the outrages committed by the Crusaders were visited upon their own heads. When they arrived at Constantinople, the emperor, Alexius Commenus, to whom they behaved themselves with the utmost insolence and folly, was not slow to rid himself of his troublesome guests. For this purpose he furnihsed them with every aid which they required, and lent his ships to transport them across the Bosphorus.

They thence pursued their march, but the Sultan Solyman meeting them on the plains of Nice, their numbers were too much reduced to offer him any thing else than an easy victory. Of their bones, Solyman erected a pyramid near the city, as a monument of his own fortune, and of their headlong counsels.

3. A new host, which was the most valuable part of this expedition, arrived in the mean time, at Constantinople, as a general rendezvous. The commanders were experienced generals and men of renown. Among them, were Godfrey of Bouillon, by some called commander in chief; Baldwin his brother; Robert, duke of Normandy; Hugh, count of Vermandois; Raymond, count of Thoulouse; Bohemond, prince of Tarentum; and Tancred, his cousin. These and other warlike princes and captains, inspired by religious enthusiasm, or military ardour, pledged themselves to redeem the holy sepulchre from the infidels. The troops, when reviewed in the neighbourhood of Nice, amounted to 100,000 horse, and 600,000 foot, including women and servants.

Alexius, the eastern emperor, did not suffer them to remain long at Constantinople; but after seeking to obtain an ascendency over them as a superior ally, he had the address to accelerate their departure. They at length met the Saracens, whom they overpowered by numbers. Having twice defeated the enemy, they took, after immense difficulty, losses, and delay, the cities of Nice, Edessa, and Antioch.

§ Constantinople, at the period when the crusaders met there, was the largest and most beautiful city of Europe. The most that remained of ancient elegance in manners and in arts, was included in that emporium. It was the mart of the world, and the seat of empire. Though the Greeks were degenerate, yet such was the splendour of their capital.

The hardy warriors of the north, beheld with amazement, these scenes of magnificence and wealth, whilst they despised the effeminate manners and unwarlike character of the people. On the other hand, the accomplished inhabitants of Constantinople, looked upon the northern warriors as barbarians. They speak of them as illiterate, fierce, and savage, and as nearly resembling their ancestors, the Goths and Vandals, who overturned the Roman empire. They treated their guests sometimes with respect, but oftener with the most hateful duplicity.

The gold and artifices of the emperor were employed not without effect—most of the leaders of the Croises taking the oath of fealty to him as their liege lord. He was not averse to the destruction of his enemy, the Turk; but the numbers and bravery of the warriors of the north, filled his bosom with jealousy. On various pretences, many of them were cut off in his own territories, and they experienced several alternatives of peace and war in the country of the Greeks.

The characters of the celebrated leaders of the Croises, on this occasion, may require a passing notice. Godfrey was endowed by nature with her choicest gifts. He possessed all the knowledge of the times; and the gentlest manners were united with the firmest spirit. He was capable of the grandest enterprises; his deportment was moral, and his piety was fervent. To sum up his character, in arms he was a hero—in his closet a saint.

The qualities of Baldwin were not so conspicuous. He was brave indeed, but he was ambitious; and his courage was stained with selfishness, cruelty, and injustice. Hugh, who was brother of the French king, called to his side the armed pilgrims from Flanders, and England, and a part of France. He was a brave and accomplished cavalier, but undevout, and of a proud deportment. Robert, who was a son of William the Conqueror, entered upon the holy war with a furious and precipitate passion. He was eloquent and skilful, but imprudent, yielding, and voluptuous.

Bohemond posessed neither religion nor probity; yet to the eye of the vulgar, he was one of the most devoted soldiers of Christ. He was intriguing, rapacious and versatile. Tancred was a comparatively pure and brilliant spirit. He was bold and generous, and would have been humane to all mankind, had it not been for the spirit of the age. Raymond was inexorable in his hatred of the Musselmans; pride, selfishness, and avarice tarnished his character.

The soldier pilgrims all convened on the plains of Nice.

"There the wild Crusaders form,
There assembled Europe stands,
Heaven they deem awakes the storm,
Hell the paynims' blood demands."

The details of the siege and capture of Nice, and the subsequent operations against Edessa and Antioch, cannot be narrated. Suffice it to say, that Nice fell by means of the policy of Alexius, who had joined the Franks or crusaders. While the latter, who had with much difficulty and loss, effected some breaches in the wall, were about to storm anew the repairs, the emperor snatched the victory from their grasp, by secretly proposing more favourable terms to the besieged, than could be expected from an enemy that would enter the city sword in hand. The soldiers clamoured; while the Latin generals, thinking of greater objects, dissembled their disgust, and endeavoured by fair persuasions to stifle the anger of their troops.

The conquest of Edessa, beyond the Euphrates, was achieved by a few ambitious and courageous soldiers, who had separated for a time from the main body of the Franks, under the command of Baldwin and Tancred.

Before Antioch could be reached, some fighting was necessary, and the Christians triumphed—much fatigue was to be borne, and here many of them sunk. The horrors of the way, and the heat of a Phrygian summer, were fatal to multitudes. Five hundred perished in one day. Mothers, no longer able to afford sustenance to their infants, exposed their breasts to the swords of the soldiers. Many of the horses perished: the baggage was then placed on the backs of goats, hogs, and dogs. When the crusaders came to a country of streams, they threw themselves without caution into the first river that presented itself, and nature could not support the transition from want to satiety.

The siege of Antioch was protracted, nor was this wholly surprising, considering the state of defence in which the city was placed; as well as on the other hand, the unskilful operations of the Croises, the famine in their camp, the numerous desertions from among them, and the relaxation of their morals. The Latin chiefs put forth prodigious efforts of valour; but the city was finally taken by stratagem. A traitor delivered it into the hands of the Franks, and 10,000 Turks were massacred. When the thirst of blood was slaked, the assassins turned robbers, and became as mercenary as they had been merciless. They seized all the wealth of the place, and exchanged their fierceness for the more civilized vices of debauchery and hypocrisy. While they rioted in unbounded indulgence, they gave God thanks.

The taking of Antioch was very soon followed by a set battle with the Musselmans; for the hosts of the Moslem world pitched their tents round the fallen capital. The excesses of the crusaders were followed by famine in its every horrid form; and had not some superstitious frauds been practised, by which their zeal and courage were re-excited, they would have shrunk from a contest with the formidable army which now opposed them under the excitements of religion; however, they met it, and triumphed in the affray.

4. The Croises pursued their successes, and after various desertions and delays they penetrated to Jerusalem. This venerable city, which had been so often destroyed and rebuilt, was taken by storm after a siege of six weeks, and the whole of its inhabitants, both Mahometans and Jews, were barbarously put to the sword, 1099 A. C. The crusaders were by this time reduced to a very inconsiderable number. Of the 700,000 that appeared before Nice, 40,000 only encamped around Jerusalem. Of these, only 21,500 were soldiers. Including the rabble of Peter, the possession of Nice, Edessa, and Antioch, had cost the lives of more than 850,000 Europeans.

§ The victories of the Crusaders were gained with difficulty. After the capture of Antioch, their embarrassments were not a few. Alexius had acted a cowardly and perfidious part. Hugh, count of Vermandois, soon abandoned the holy cause, and returned to France. The march of the Christian forces was purposely delayed several months, by the commanders, although the soldiers were impatient to proceed to Jerusalem. This delay, however, was attended by the most serious evils. Discord prevailed among the princes—rapine and theft among the people. A pestilence spread throughout their hosts, which, in a few months, destroyed more than one hundred thousand persons. In the mean time, several wars of ambition were waged, in the neighbouring provinces. The forces which attacked the town of Marra, were so urged by famine, that many of the soldiers turned cannibals, and devoured the flesh of their enemies, whom they massacred with the utmost cruelty.

At length, the Christian warriors set their faces towards the holy city. When it came in view, every heart glowed with rapture—every eye was suffused with tears. The joy of a moment outweighed years of sorrow. In their heated imaginations, the sepulchre was redeemed, and the cross triumphed over the crescent. But the anticipation of success was much easier than the reality. The most strenuous exertions were necessary, and the enthusiasm and valour of the Christians were carried to the greatest height. After several alternations of partial victory and defeat, the walls of the sacred city were carried, and all Jerusalem was in possession of the champions of the cross. The blood of the Saracens attested the ferocity of the victory, and the price at which their conquest was obtained. Ten thousand of the vanquished were butchered in the mosque of Omar alone, to which they had fled as a sacred asylum. In this place, the croises are said to have ridden in the blood of the Saracens up to the knees of their horses. Ten thousand, or according to some, a much larger number, were massacred in the streets. The Christians committed these dreadful deeds from principle rather than from passion. It was a horrid principle indeed; but intolerance was unhappily the spirit of the age.

5. With considerable foresight, the conquerors of Jerusalem established a Christian kingdom in the heart of Palestine. An extension of territory was indispensable to the security of the city from the Mussulman hordes that surrounded it. At the head of this kingdom, Godfrey, the most worthy of the heroes of Christendom, was placed by the suffrages of the Christians. He reigned however but one year, during which time he defeated the sultan with an immense army at Ascalon. At the expiration of the year, he was compelled to give up his kingdom to the pope's legate. Several kings reigned after him, but their history need not be told.

An impolitic act of the crusaders, by which their power was weakened, was, at length, the division of Syria and Palestine into four separate states. Having accomplished their object, they began to return to Europe; but in proportion as they withdrew, the Turks recovered their strength. The crusaders, who remained in Asia, found themselves so surrounded by foes, that they were at last obliged to solicit aid from Christendom.

§ The fruits of this first crusade ill repaid its immense loss and expense, and were comprised within the small territory of Jerusalem, the dominion of which was bounded by the term of eighty years. The holy war, nevertheless, continued to be recommended by the pope and the clergy with unabated earnestness. It was still represented to be the cause of the Son of God, an engagement in which was the most meritorious of all acts, and insured salvation, whether in the success or defeat.

6. The aid which was needed in the East was soon afforded. Europe sent forth a second crusade in 1147. St. Bernard, who was the great oracle of the age, had the influence to excite Louis VII. of France, and Conrad III. of Germany, to undertake the defence of the kingdom of Jerusalem. Three hundred thousand of their subjects assumed the cross. The issue of this enterprise was disastrous in the extreme.

Manuel, the emperor of the Greeks, gave intelligence of their plans to the Turkish sultan, and provided them with treacherous guides. The army of Conrad, which took the lead, fell first into the snare. Those who did not perish by hunger in the deserts, fell into the jaws of the Musselmans. Only a tenth part secured their retreat to the army of Louis. Louis, also duped by the Grecian emperor, advanced through the same country to a similar fate. In the defile of a mountain near Laodicea, his army was totally defeated.

At Jerusalem, these unfortunate monarchs met to lament their sad reverses of fortune. The feeble remains of the mighty armies which they had led, were joined to the Christian powers of Syria, and a fruitless siege of Damascus was the final effort of the second crusade.

§ A few particulars may be given respecting the preacher of the second crusade. St. Bernard, by the superiority of his talents, and also of his consideration in the eyes of Europe, was far more capable than Peter the Hermit, of exciting enthusiastic emotions. His ardent and religious mind soon disdained the follies of youth; and casting off the desire of celebrity as a writer of poetry and songs, he wandered in the regions of spiritual reverie, or trod the rough and thorny paths of polemical theology.

At the age of 23, he embraced the monastic life, and soon afterwards founded the monastery of Clairvaux, in Champaigne. His miraculous eloquence separated sons from their fathers, and husbands from their wives. His earnestness and self-denial in religion, gained him the reverence of his contemporaries, and in disputes he was appealed to as an incorruptible judge. Such was his austerity, that happening once to fix his eyes on a female face, he immediately reflected that this was a temptation, and running to a pond he leaped up to his neck into the water, which was of an icy coldness, to punish himself and vanquish the enemy.

Such a man was the fit tool of the pope, Eugenius III., who ordered him to travel through France and Germany, and to preach a plenary indulgence to those who would, under the banners of their kings, bend their way towards the holy land. As Peter had represented the scandal of suffering the sacred places to remain in the hands of the infidels, the eloquent Bernard thundered from the pulpit the disgrace of allowing a land, which had been recovered from pollution, to sink into it again. This voice raised armies and depopulated cities. According to his own expression, "the towns were deserted, or, the only people that were in them were widows and orphans, whose husbands and fathers were yet living."

7. The state of the holy land between the second and third crusades deserves a passing notice. A feeble sway was held by most of the chiefs of the kingdom of Jerusalem. The death of Baldwin III., however, was lamented as a public calamity. His successors were Almeric, Baldwin IV., and

Guy de Lusignan. The miseries of war were often experienced from their Musselman enemies. It was during this period, that the celebrated Saladin, nephew of the Sultan of Egypt, attained the height of his glory, and became lord of that country. He formed the design of recovering Palestine from the Christians.

8. The occasion of the third crusade was, the success of Saladin against the Latins in Jerusalem. He had previously subdued Tiberias, and received the submission of Acre, Jaffa, and some other places. Jerusalem offered an obstinate resistance, but in vain. The city was taken after a siege of a few days, and Guy de Lusignan was made prisoner, 1187 A. C. The conqueror treated the inhabitants with singular clemency. The infidels were now once more established in the city of the prophets.

§ The conquered Latins, on being obliged to leave Jerusalem, consumed four days in weeping over and embracing the holy sepulchre. The women entreated the conqueror to release to them their fathers, husbands, and brothers. With courteous clemency Saladin released all the prisoners whom they requested, and loaded them with presents.

9. The conquests effected by the infidels, filled Europe with grief, and almost with despair. The losses occasioned by the former crusades, had rather dismayed the public mind. Small masses of men continued indeed to move towards the East, but it required a degree of management and much exhortation to wake up a general interest in favour of a third crusade. Pope Clement III. at length prevailed on three sovereigns to engage in the holy enterprise. These were Philip Augustus, of France, Richard I., surnamed the Lion-hearted, and Frederick Barbarossa, of Germany.

The forces of Philip and Richard are computed at one hundred thousand soldiers ; it does not appear how many followed the standard of Frederick. The latter, in passing through the Greek empire, was prudent and humane, although the haughtiness and duplicity of the emperor Isaac Angelus, subjected him to much inconvenience. The Germans defeated the Turks in a general engagement, and took Iconium. But unfortunately, their sovereign lost his life in consequence of bathing in the river Calycadnus. After the death of Barbarossa, his army dwindled to a small number.

The English and French, for a short time, proceeded harmoniously in the career of victory. They took Acre, a place of great strength. Soon, however, the bitter feelings of military envy and national hatred began to be excited, the consequence of which was, that the French monarch returned home, leaving a portion of his army under the command of Richard. Left alone to sustain the contest, Plantagenet displayed all the heroism of chivalry. He found himself at the head of nearly thirty thousand French, German, and English soldiers. With this force he defeated the illustrious Saladin, near the plains of Ascalon. Political disturbances in England, made Richard solicitous to return thither, especially, as his ranks were now thinned by disease and famine. With this object in view, he concluded a favourable treaty with his enemy, and attempted to return to his dominions. In passing through Germany, however, unaccompanied by his troops, he was seized by the order of the duke of Austria, and made prisoner. It was not until after a long captivity, and the payment of an immense ransom, that he was restored to his native land. Not long after the departure of Richard, Saladin paid the debt of nature.

§ In the treaty which was formed between Richard and Saladin, the Christian monarch, and the sultan of Egypt, interchanged expressions of esteem. The grasping of each other's hands, was the only and sufficient pledge of fidelity. A truce was agreed upon for three years and eight months; the fort of Ascalon was to be destroyed; but Jaffa and Tyre, with the country between them, were to be surrendered to the Christians.

In leaving Palestine, Richard, with his queen, embarked in a ship; but the violence of a tempest dispersed his fleet, and so shattered the vessel he was in, that it became impossible for him to reach England in that way. He then made for Germany; but his person was endangered as he travelled the country, since the fact of his being there became known to some of his enemies. After various escapes, he arrived at a town near Vienna. Two individuals only were with him, one of whom was a boy, who understood the German language.

The party were too harassed to proceed. The German boy was sent to the market-place to purchase provisions. Through the liberality of his master, he was so neatly and elegantly dressed, that the people could not but notice him. The consequence was that he was questioned, and giving unsatisfactory answers, he was seized and scourged. Being at length threatened with the cutting out of his tongue, if he did not tell the truth, he was obliged reluctantly to disclose the secret of the real quality of his master.

Richard was immediately secured, and though at first treated with respect, was soon confined in prison. Being sold at length to the emperor, Henry VI. removed him to a castle in the Tyrol. But the strongest walls are not sufficiently secure for the fears of a tyrant. Armed men were sent into his chamber, and commanded to watch him with the utmost strictness.

Here, sometimes, the royal captive calmed his angry soul, by singing the warlike deeds of the heroes of romance. At other times, he diverted melancholy by the composition of poems. Occasionally, he forgot his misfortunes, and the apparent negligence of his friends. His native hilarity conquered the bitterness of his spirit; he laughed at the frequent intoxication of his gaolers, he sported the keenness of his wit, and in the boisterousness of his merriment, displayed his personal strength and agility.

At the request of his mother, the queen Eleanora, the Pope interfered for his release; and, after a trial on some pretended crime, it was concluded to ransom the English monarch, as though he had been a prisoner of war, the English people paying about 150,000 marks of silver to the German emperor.

10. By the energy of Richard, Palestine was saved from becoming a Mussulman colony; and so much of the sea coast was in the hands of the Christians, and so enfeebled was the enemy, that it was safe to commence hostilities, whenever Europe should again pour forth her religious and military fanatics. This event was not long delayed, notwithstanding the infinite losses and sufferings, which had hitherto resulted from the crusades.

A fourth crusade was fitted out in 1202, by Baldwin, count of Flanders, who collected an army of the Flemish and French, professedly to attack the Mahometans, though it seems to have found another enemy. Like the other crusaders, he made the eastern Christians first feel the effect of European adventure and military enthusiasm. Indeed, his efforts ended here; for, arriving at Constantinople, at a time when there was a dispute for the succession, his interference afforded the occasion of plundering the city, and securing the possession of the imperial throne of the East. The Venetians lent their vessels for the enterprise, and participated in it.

§ Some historians reckon a crusade anterior to the war carried on by Baldwin, denominating his the fifth. There were expeditions from Germany in the intermediate time; but it may be doubtful whether they deserve the name of a distinct crusade. Indeed, there were so many different expeditions, some public and others private, that the designation of a certain number of separate crusades, seems somewhat arbitrary. According to the common accounts, we have assigned the name of the fourth crusade, to the expedition of which the count of Flanders was the leader.

The third crusade was created by the ordinary influence of papal power and royal authority; but the fourth sprang from genuine fanaticism. Fulk, who was worthy of companionship with Bernard, became a preacher distinguished by the vehemence with which he declaimed against certain vices of the age. With his celebrity, increased his desire to be generally useful to mankind. The natural consequence in that superstitious age, was, that he turned his eye towards the east, and assumed the cross. The copious matter of his sermons was the war with the infidels. Around the man of God, all classes thronged, and thousands were eager to assume the insignia of holy warriors. Nor was Pope Innocent III. inactive in the cause, having required the various temporal and spiritual chiefs of christendom to take up arms for the defence of Palestine, or at least to send him considerable succours of men and money.

Application having been made to the Venetians for the loan of their ships, and the Venetians themselves desiring to embark in the enterprise, the croises at length set sail for Constantinople. That proud city, once the sister and rival of Rome, was fallen so low, that the aid of the western barbarians was invoked by a claimant to the throne of the Cæsars. In his behalf, war against the Greek empire was resolved on, and Constantinople was made the point of attack. The particulars of the assault need not be given, but it is a striking account drawn up by an old writer, that when the invaders, at the distance of three leagues, beheld the city, "the magnitude and splendour of Constantinople awed the courage of the bravest; and not without reason, for never since the creation of the world, had so bold an enterprise been undertaken by so small a force." The Greeks made a display of numbers and strength, but the nerves and soul of war were not in them. The partisans of the usurper, Alexius, made only a feeble defence, and soon abandoned the city to its fate. The city was captured, and the young Alexius sat on the throne.

After one or two revolutions in the government, the allied army of French and Venetians, who had been paid the tribute which they required, and had been kept in the vicinity of Constantinople, determined to seize the city on their own account. This, after a severe struggle, was effected; and a severe struggle it ought to have been on the part of the invaders, when only 20,000 men captured the largest city in the world. There were 400,000 men capable of bearing arms in Constantinople. The excesses of the barbarians were enormous. To their eternal infamy, they destroyed most of the remains of the noble monuments of genius, in the sculpture and statuary of the Pagan world. In no conquered city, it is thought, was there ever obtained so much booty. One historian remarks, that the gold and silver, the silk, the gems, and precious stones, and all those things which are accounted riches, were found in more abundance than all the Latin world could furnish."

11. Baldwin, as the reward of his success against the capital of the East, was invested with the Roman purple, 1204. But he was dethroned and murdered, after a reign of a few months. The Imperial dominions were shared among the principal leaders; the Venetians obtained the Isle of Candia, as their portion. By the acquisition of Constantinople, the injuries of the crusaders were avenged; and, for the present they looked for no other conquest. The dominion of the Latins, however, lasted but fifty-seven years. Few events on the page of history have been equally curious and interesting, with the establishment of this people in the city of Constantine.

12. In the former part of the thirteenth century, succeeding the crusade against the Greek empire, several expeditions were fitted out against the Musselmans. In these, the Germans, Hungarians, French, English, and Italians, were principally concerned. Their object seems to have been, not so much Palestine, as Egypt. Success crowned their efforts at first, and one of the expeditions, under the duke of Austria, captured Damietta, an event which filled the Musselman empire with alarm; but the mortality of the country, and the return of many of the European soldiers, with other causes, finally rendered the acquisitions of the crusaders, in that country, of no avail, and the unbelievers still retained their power.

13. The fifth and last of these extraordinary expeditions against the infidel world, was led by Louis IX. of France. There had been previously a few smaller adventures, especially by the English, who had the good fortune to redeem the holy sepulchre. But it was soon lost, and the fears of the Christian world were in a degree aroused. It was, however, obvious that the crusading spirit in Europe had at length begun to languish, and it would at this crisis have entirely died away, had not Louis felt the strong stirrings of fanaticism and chivalry. He kept it alive a few years, after which, this folly of a dark and barbarous age was heard of no more.

The warlike heroism and religious devotion of the French monarch, commanded the reverence of mankind. Indeed, in many respects, he was an amiable and estimable prince, though deeply imbued with the unworthy superstition of the times. His efforts preserved to the Christians, for a time, the land of Palestine, which was in danger, not from the Saracens, but from the Tartars. This fierce people were then pouring over the face of Asia.

Louis spent three years in preparation, when he set out for Palestine, with his queen, three brothers, and a powerful train of French knights, 1248 A. C. He had greatly encouraged the fainting hearts of the Christians in Palestine, by the men and troops he had sent thither before his own departure. The invasion of Egypt was his first object. Here, he lost one half of his army by sickness, was defeated in battle, and fell a prisoner into the hands of his enemy.

After ransoming himself and his followers, he proceeded to the Holy Land, in which he continued a considerable time. On his return, to France, he devoted himself, wisely, to the regular cares of government, during thirteen years, and would probably have long continued useful and happy, had not the mad spirit of crusading seized him again. In obedience to its dictates, he embarked on a crusade against the Moors in Africa. In this adventure, he and the greater part of his army perished, in consequence of a pestilence. Louis has been honoured with the title of saint.

§ History records, that on the subject of crusading, the mind of Louis was influenced by the following circumstance. Agreeably to the temper of the times, he had vowed, whilst afflicted by a severe illness, that in case of recovery he would travel to the holy land. In the delirium of his fever he had beheld an engagement between the Christians and the Saracens; the infidels were victorious, and the brave king of a valiant nation fancied himself called upon to avenge the defeat.

The following incident indicated the king's zeal for a crusade. One night, during the Christmas festival, Louis caused magnificent crosses, fabricated by goldsmiths, to be sewn on the new dresses, which, as usual upon such occasions, had been bestowed upon the courtiers. The next day the cavaliers were surprised at the religious ornaments that had been affixed to their cloaks; piety and loyalty combined to prevent them from renouncing the honours which had been thrust upon them, and the good king obtained the title of the hunter for pilgrims and fisher of men.

Louis could have adopted the lines of a French rhymer of the thirteenth century.

"Lo, now the fruitful hour at hand!
To thee the precious boon is given,
For Paynims waste the holy land,
And spoil the heritage of heaven.
Shall we such faithless works behold,
With craven courage slack and cold?
How else, but to the Giver's praise,
May we devote our wealth and days.

The French, on landing in Egypt, captured Damietta; but the rashness of the Count d'Artois was the means of checking them in the career of victory. Sad reverses soon ensued, and though Louis defended himself with the greatest bravery, he was obliged to yield to the enemy. Being taken prisoner with his army, he offered for his own ransom the city of Damietta, and for the deliverance of his soldiers 500,000 livres. One fifth part of the latter was remitted through the generosity of the sultan.

In Louis' second expedition against the infidels, he was joined by the English; so that his force amounted to sixty thousand men. His fleet being driven into Sardinia, a change was made in the design of the pilgrim hero, and an attack upon the Musselman Moors of Africa was fixed upon. Pestilence, however, prevented the meditated blow, and the great stay of the crusades fell.

The English portion of the forces, which had not reached Africa, when the death of Louis took place, made their way to Palestine, under the conduct of Prince Edward. Feats of arms were performed; but the Turks were fast overunning the holy land, and with the capture of Acre, by that adventurous people, was connected the final loss of a country, on which the eyes of fanatical Europe had been fastened for more than two hundred years.

14. Among the causes of the decline and cessation of the fanatical military spirit of Europe, may be enumerated the following, viz. the decrease of the moral influence of the popes, and the increase of their tyranny, which the people were loth to bear—the avarice of the popes and priests, in converting to their own purposes the funds which were raised to support the holy wars—the consequent unwillingness of the people to be taxed—the scandal which was cast on the crusades, when many of the soldiers of the cross were diverted from their religious purpose, to promote the secular objects of the court of Rome—and most of all, the increasing conviction on the part of the people, that no lasting conquest of Palestine could be made by the sovereigns of Europe. These causes were too powerful even for the deep darkness and superstition of the age, ambition, love of military achievement, and desire of plunder.

15. Various opinions have been formed and maintained respecting the tendency and effects of the crusades. By some, they are thought to have benefitted Europe on the whole—by others, they are supposed to have been positively disadvantageous. We incline to the latter opinion. They who look upon the crusades in a favourable light in respect to their con sequences, nevertheless admit, that they were immediately

distressing and pernicious. It is in the final result that they imagine the crusades to have been beneficial on the whole. In the final result, it has been maintained that they improved the political condition, the manners and customs, the navigation and commerce, the literature, and the religion of Europe.

That there was a very gradual amelioration of the western nations in the above particulars, is admitted. But this was a state of things, which it is natural to believe, time might have produced, aided as it was by other causes. Indeed, from the nature of the convulsions which attended, or rather constituted the crusades, it is certain that they must have tended to retard the progress of society, learning, and religion, so far as they produced any effect. That they were not productive of any good, in any shape, it would be hazardous to assert. But providence can overrule the greatest evil, so that it shall be less evil than it would otherwise be; and our point is made out, if the evil flowing from the crusades overbalances the good, in quality or amount.

Let any one who doubts this, reflect that the crusades were the offspring of a dark and ignorant age—that they were kindled by the false fires of fanaticism and superstition, and moreover, were perverted, if so base a project could be perverted, by ambition, love of military renown, and a savage desire of plunder. They agitated, convulsed, and distressed Europe, and every family in Europe, for two centuries. They drained that portion of the globe of men and money, to an insupportable degree. The bones of two millions of Europeans were entombed in Asia, or whitened her plains. The treasures that were expended are past computation. Under the sacred name of religion, every crime and every folly was meditated and committed. The path of the fanatical warriors of the west was every where marked with blood. They were too stupid and too superstitious to regard with complacency or with a desire of imitation, those superior modes of life and specimens of genius which they met with in their excursions into the East. They even laid their sacrilegious hands on the monuments of ancient art, which chance or bravery put into their power, and in the repeated conflagrations of Constantinople, they rejoiced to see, in many instances, the destruction of those works, the remains of which the world has since been proud to own.

They *err*, who count it glorious to subdue
By conquest far and wide, to over-run
Large countries, and in field great battles win,
Great cities by assaults: what do these worthies,
But rob and spoil, burn, slaughter and enslave
Peaceable nations. * * * *

"A view of the heroic ages of christianity," says an interesting historian, "in regard to their grand and general results, is a useful and important, though a melancholy employment. The Crusades retarded the march of civilization, thickened the clouds of ignorance and superstition, and encouraged intolerance, cruelty and fierceness. Religion lost its mildness and charity; and war its mitigating qualities of honour and courtesy. Such were the bitter fruits of the Holy Wars. We can follow with sympathy, both the deluded fanatic, and the noble adventurer in arms, in their wanderings and marches through foreign regions, braving the most frightful dangers, patient in toil, invincible in military spirit. So visionary was the object, so apparently remote from selfish relations, that their fanaticism wears a character of generous virtue. The picture, however, becomes darkened, and nature recoils with horror from their cruelties, and with shame from their habitual folly and senselessness."

FRANCE.

16. In 1108 the throne of France was ascended by Louis VI., surnamed the fat, son of Philip I. He carried on a war with Henry I. of England, but was not successful. The English defeated his army at the battle of Brenneville, 1119 A. C. He was an accomplished and energetic sovereign.

§ In Louis' flight after the battle, an Englishman seized his horse's bridle, exclaiming, "the king is taken." "The king is never taken," said Louis, "not even in a game of chess," and then struck his enemy dead at his feet.

17. Louis VII., the young, succeeded his father in 1137. The extent of his reign was 46 years. He quarrelled with the Pope about the nomination of an archbishop, and had his kingdom put under an interdict. He was very unsuccessfully engaged in the holy wars, and in consequence of having divorced his queen, heiress of the great dutchy of Guienne, who soon married Henry Plantagenet, (afterwards Henry II. of England) he lost one fifth part of the French monarchy, including the provinces before held by the English.

§ Louis was educated in an Abbey, and the Abbeys at this period produced several distinguished men, among whom were Suger, his minister, a man of great political sagacity; St. Bernard, whose agency in the second crusade has already appeared; and Abelard, whose story remains to be told.

In conformity to the spirit of the age, and his own education, Louis made several pilgrimages, and among others visited the tomb of Thomas à Becket, at Canterbury. In one of these pilgrimages he died. His tomb, in the abbey of Barbeau, was opened in 1556, by Charles IX., and the body found in a high state of preservation. On the fingers were several gold rings, which, having been taken off, were worn by Charles, together with a gold chain, which was found in the tomb.

18. The son of Louis, Philip II., surnamed Augustus, ascended the throne in 1180. His reign was a long one also, being 43 years. Since the days of Charlemagne, France had seen no sovereign so ambitious and enterprising in war, as Philip. The most signal events of his reign, were his expulsion of the Jews from France; his engagement in the third crusade, with Richard Cœur de Lion; his invasion of Normandy during Richard's absence; his victory over Otho IV., emperor of Germany; and the offer of the crown of England to him for his son Louis, by the English barons

§ His engagement in the third crusade has already appeared. On the return of Richard to England, a disastrous war ensued between him and Philip, the English king determining to punish him for seizing Normandy. Richard, dying during the prosecution of this war, was succeeded by his brother John, whose pretensions to the crown of England were, however, disputed by his nephew, Arthur, aided by Philip. Arthur having been made prisoner, and put to death by his inhuman uncle, the latter was summoned by Philip, to appear in his quality as duke of Normandy, before a tribunal of his peers. On his refusal, Philip attacked and subdued several of the French provinces that were then held by the English, and united Normandy to the crown of France, 300 years after it had been detached from it by the incapacity of Charles the simple.

From the reign of Philip, may be dated the Inquisition, which was first established in France, whence it found its way into Italy, Spain, and Portugal.

19. Louis VIII., surnamed the Lion, mounted the throne of his father in 1223, and died in 1226. He was a man of valour, and hence his surname. He took all the possessions of the English on the continent, as far as the Garonne. His character was that of a persecutor.

§ Louis prosecuted a barbarous crusade against certain sectaries in Languedoc and Gascony, who presumed to attack the dogmas of the Church of Rome. At the siege of Avignon, he was poisoned by the count of Champaign.

20. Louis IX., styled Saint Louis, became king at the age of twelve years, in 1226, under the regency of his mother. Louis possessed many excellent qualities—was pious, upright, and benevolent. His single fault was fanaticism; though in every thing he did, the purity of his motive was conspicuous. He conferred a considerable benefit on his country, notwithstanding the errors into which his fanatical spirit led him. With Henry III. of England, he waged a successful war.

§ An account has been given of the two crusades in which he was so unfortunately engaged, and in the last of which he perished.

Henry III. demanded the provinces which, it seems, Louis' father had promised to restore. A tender was made of Poitou, and of the best part of Normandy; but this did not satisfy Henry, who resolved to try the issue of a battle, in which he was defeated.

21. Philip III., surnamed the Bold, succeeded his father in 1270. His surname, it is thought, was not well deserved. He was the dupe of the artifices of his courtiers, and had no predominant trait, except a passion for amassing wealth. He brought back from Africa the miserable remains of his father's army. He died on his return from an expedition against Peter III., of Arragon, who had usurped the kingdom of Sicily, and through whose instigation, eight thousand Frenchmen were massacred in that island.

§ Charles of Anjou, uncle of Philip, had lately become king of Sicily, and acted the tyrant towards its inhabitants. By a deed of cruelty towards a brother of the wife of Peter, he made the latter his enemy. Peter, in revenge, excited the Sicilians to revolt and murder. All the French of the island were, by a previous concert, butchered in cool blood, on the evening of Easterday. Philip undertook to avenge this massacre, but the general failure of the expedition, afflicted the French king so much, that he fell into a decay, of which he died.

22. Philip IV., the Fair, ascended the throne of his ancestors, in 1285. He was remarkable for his personal beauty and accomplishments. His disposition, however, was singularly contrasted with his features and form. He was ambitious, deceitful, perfidious and cruel. Refusing to obey the summons of the Roman pontiff, Boniface VIII., to march against the Saracens, he was excommunicated, and his kingdom laid under an interdict. A severe contest ensued, the result of which was the humiliation of the Pope, and eventually his death.

In 1314, Philip suppressed the order of the Knights Templars, from a desire, it was thought, to obtain their immense wealth.

§ The haughty Boniface, in a bull, had declared, that "the Vicar of Christ is vested with full authority over the kings and kingdoms of the earth." Philip, in return for the indignity put upon him, denounced Boniface as an impostor, heretic, and simoniac, and declared the see of Rome vacant. He contrived also, by means of a trusty agent, to seize the person of the pope. The persons concerned in the transaction, caused his holiness to ride on a horse without saddle or bridle, with his face turned towards his tail. He was, however, rescued at length; but the loss of his immense treasures, while he was detained from his palace, threw him into a frenzy that killed him.

ENGLAND.

23. *Norman family, Plantagenets.* The throne of England, on the death of Rufus, was secured by his younger brother, Henry I., surnamed Beauclerc, or the Scholar, 1100. The rightful heir was Robert, an older brother; but as he was absent on a crusade, Henry availed himself of so favourable an opportunity to fill the vacant throne.

Robert, who was duke of Normandy, soon arrived in England to claim his right; but he was prevailed upon to forego it, by the offer of a sum of money. Still, Henry was not satisfied, but ere long invaded Normandy; and at last defeated Robert, brought him prisoner to England, caused his eyes to be burned out, and confined him for life, in a castle in Wales.

The injustice with which he had treated Robert, seems to have been visited upon him by the hand of Providence, in the calamities of his after life; particularly in the death of his only son, who was drowned on his passage from Normandy to England.

Henry was one of the most accomplished of the English sovereigns—brave, affable, and learned; but his conduct in many instances, shewed that he was wanting in moderation, purity, and gratitude.

§ Henry married a Saxon princess, Matilda great grand-daughter of Edmund Ironside, and thus united the Saxon and Norman blood. This circumstance endeared him to the English, and procured their support.

The story of the death of Henry's son, whose name was William, is briefly the following. The captain and seamen of the vessel in which he set sail for England, becoming intoxicated, carelessly struck her upon a rock. She foundered immediately, but William was saved by being put into a long-boat. He had already got clear of the wreck, when hearing the cries of his natural sister, the countess of Perche, he ordered the seamen to row back, in hopes of saving her. But the numbers who then crowded in, soon sunk the boat; and the prince with all his retinue perished.

The effect of the news on Henry was melancholy indeed. He fainted away, and during the remainder of his life, was never known to smile.

24. Henry's cousin, Stephen, earl of Blois, was crowned king of England, 1135. His popularity enabled him to usurp the throne, when of right it belonged to the empress Matilda, or Maud, and her son Henry.

§ Matilda first married Henry V., emperor of Germany—afterwards Henry Plantagenet, earl of Anjou. By the latter she had several children, of whom Henry was the oldest.

In behalf of Matilda, the earl of Gloucester, natural brother of the empress, took up arms against Stephen, defeated him in the battle of Lincoln, and made him prisoner. But the fortune of war soon turned against Gloucester. He was defeated in the battle of Winchester, and taken prisoner, but was exchanged for the king.

Four years after this event, young prince Henry, son of Maud, invaded England; but the great men on both sides, fearing the consequences of a battle, compelled the rival princes to a negociation. The succession was secured to Henry, after the death of Stephen. This event taking place the next year, Henry became king.

Stephen was well calculated to be an efficient sovereign; but he reigned under unfavourable circumstances, and his elevation brought suffering on himself and his people. During his whole reign, England was rent with civil broils.

§ From the beginning, Stephen dreaded Robert, earl of Gloucester, a man of honour and abilities, and zealously attached to Maud. He took, indeed, the oath of fealty to Stephen; but he took it with the reserve, that the king should never invade any of his rights or dignities. This was an example for others; and many of the clergy and nobility, as the price of submission, required the right of fortifying their castles. England was soon filled with fortresses, and the power of the aristocracy rose to a formidable height.

25. Henry II. succeeded to the throne in 1154. He was the first of the Plantagenets who wielded the sceptre, till the time of Henry IV. In him was mingled the blood

of the Saxon kings of England, and of the Norman family He was the most powerful monarch of Christendom. His dominions were more extensive than those of any of his predecessors, as, in addition to England, he owned by inheritance and by marriage, nearly one half of France, and afterwards claimed Ireland by conquest.

Happy in the affections of his people, he had the prospect of a prosperous reign; but though England owed her first permanent improvements in arts, laws, government, and civil liberty, to his measures, he was personally subjected to many calamities. A most serious misfortune, was his contention with Thomas à Becket, archbishop of Canterbury. This arrogant ecclesiastic, a man of great talents and greater ambition, availed himself of the authority of his station, to exalt the spiritual power above the crown; and when the king undertook the reformation of the clergy, and to limit their prerogatives, he met with the most determined opposition from Becket. In the course of the contention, the ecclesiastic was killed. The horror excited in Henry's mind by this event, aided by the agitation into which England was thrown, led him to perform the most humiliating penance at the tomb of the saint.

§ Becket was first promoted by the king, to the dignity of chancellor of England, to which station his talents and learning entitled him. Henry afterwards appointed him to fill the high place of metropolitan, falsely supposing that from his gay and splendid turn, he would not be attached to ecclesiastical privileges. But no sooner was he in his new situation, than he affected personally the greatest austerity, and recited continually prayers and pious lectures, maintaining his ancient pomp only in his retinue and attendants. In all this, his determination to exalt the spiritual power, was visible to sagacious observers.

That power was already too great. The ecclesiastics of that age had renounced all immediate subjection to the magistrate; and as many of them were of low character, they committed the most detestable crimes with impunity. They were charged even with the foulest murders. The attempts of the king to put this order of men into a better state, resulted in what are called the Constitutions of Clarendon. These were the decisions of a general council of the nobility and prelates at Clarendon, in which, the limits between the civil and ecclesiastical jurisdictions, are distinctly marked, and which, by the king's influence, were framed so as to favour his prerogatives.

The clergy, generally, professed to submit to these decisions, but Becket stood aloof: and though at length he took oath to observe them, it was by no means in good faith. He repented of his temporary subjection, and endeavoured to influence the other bishops to follow his steps. Henry, however, made him feel the royal power, by the confiscation of his property on some pretence. This act, Becket resented, by excommunicating the king's chief ministers, and abrogating the constitutions of Clarendon. On some further instance of his arrogance, the king was so vehemently agitated, that he exclaimed, almost in reproaches, against his servants, whose "want of zeal," he said, "left him exposed to the machinations of that ungrateful and imperious prelate." Four knights of his household, taking these passionate expressions to be a hint for the primate' death, instantly agreed among themselves, to avenge their prince's quarrel; and pursuing Becket, found him, slenderly attended, in the cathedral of St. Benedict, and there, before the altar, clove his head with many blows.

Nothing could exceed the consternation of the king upon this event, and with a view to avert the resentment of the pope, he submitted to the most humiliating treatment, even to the scourging of his naked body, by the monks.

Endless were the panegyrics on the virtues of Becket; and the miracles wrought by his relics, were more numerous, more ridiculous, and more impudently attested, than those which ever filled the legend of any confessor or martyr. He was canonized; a jubilee was established for celebrating his merits; and innumerable pilgrimages were made to his tomb. In one year, 100,000 pilgrims are said to have resorted thither.

An important event in the reign of Henry, was the conquest of Ireland. He seized the opportunity of making war on the island, when one of its petty chiefs, expelled by his sovereign, sought his protection. Henry's arms were successful, and the island was formally annexed to the English crown, in 1172. From that time, however, for some centuries, there was little intercourse between the kingdoms; nor was the island ever considered as fully subdued, till the reign of Elizabeth, and of her successor, James I.

§ The Irish were an early civilized people, and among the first of the nations of the West, who embraced the Christian religion. But by the frequent invasions of the Danes, and their own domestic commotions, they were replunged into barbarism, for many ages. In the twelfth century, the kingdom was divided into five separate sovereignties, but these were subdivided among a vast number of petty chiefs.

Henry divided Ireland into counties, appointed sheriffs in each, and introduced the laws of England into a part of it; the rest of the kingdom being regulated by their ancient laws, till the reign of Edward I., when, at the request of the nation, the English laws were extended to the whole kingdom.

Henry, much as he accomplished for the welfare of his

realm, was seldom exempt from calamity for a long time together. His last years were particularly unhappy. The fault, however, was in a great measure his own. His illicit passion for Rosamond, whose extraordinary beauty made her the theme of many a ballad and romance, excited the resentment of his queen Eleanora, through whose means, three of his sons rebelled against him. Europe beheld with astonishment these sons, scarcely beyond the age of boyhood, engaged in a series of efforts to wrest the sceptre from so potent a prince as Henry. They were, however, aided by the king of France. The contest began in Henry's French territories. He soon crushed his enemies there; then returning to England, and obtaining a victory over the Scots, who had embraced the cause of the young princes, he immediately restored tranquillity to the country. He was not suffered long to rest; his unnatural sons, though leniently treated, revolted again, joined by John, his fourth and favourite son. Henry, distracted with care, and overcome with the ingratitude of his children, died of a broken heart, in the fifty-eighth year of his age, and the thirty-fifth of his reign.

§ Two of his sons, Henry and Geoffrey, died suddenly while engaged in their rebellion. The force of parental affection, is remarkably exemplified in Henry's death, and, to the honour of the king, deserves notice. When the son was seized with a fever, he was conscious of his approaching dissolution, and sent a message to his father, with a humble confession of his faults, and entreated the favour of a visit. The king was not very distant, but apprehensive that his sickness was feigned, durst not trust himself in his hands. But when he received intelligence of his death, he was overcome with grief; he fainted away, accused his own hard-heartedness, and lamented that he had deprived his son of the opportunity of pouring out his soul in the bosom of an affectionate and reconciled father. His son Richard associated his youngest brother, John, in the last insurrection. When the unhappy father heard this, already sinking in cares and sorrows, he broke out into expressions of the utmost despair; cursed the day of his birth, and loaded his ungrateful children with maledictions which he never would recall.

Henry II., was one of the ablest of the English kings. His reign was also highly beneficial to his subjects. He was endowed with a natural sensibility, which his long experience of the ingratitude of man never impaired. But his licentiousness was too apparent, and his enmities too durable. His person was of a middle stature, strong and well proportioned, his countenance engaging, and his elocution easy.

26. Richard I., the Lion-hearted, succeeded his father in 1189. He possessed a most heroic nature, and rivalled the heroes of Greece, in warlike enterprises. His disposition was open and generous, but at the same time, ambitious, haughty, and cruel. He spent most of his reign in the mad project of the crusades, which have already been described, and particularly the part which was acted by this chivalric king. After an absence of nine years, he reached England, but died within a few months, having first pardoned his traitorous brother John, and attempted to avenge the wrongs he had received from Philip of France. His foreign and distant wars exhausted the resources of his country.

27. John, surnamed Lackland, succeeded his brother upon the decease of the latter. His reign commenced in 1199, and continued to 1216 A. C. It was marked with the most disgusting tyranny and crime.

§ He received his surname from the loss of his territories in France, of which he was stripped by the French king. The latter supported the pretensions of Arthur, John's nephew, whom John finally murdered.

Early in his reign, he made the pope his enemy, by appropriating to his own purposes, some of the treasures of the church, and he met with the full extent of the papal vengeance. At first obstinate, he was finally intimidated into submission. His kingdom was put under an interdict, himself excommunicated, and after several personal concessions, he engaged to hold his kingdom tributary to the Holy See. By this conduct he incurred the deep hatred and contempt of his people.

§ So greatly did the court of Rome triumph over him, that John did homage to Pandulf, the pope's legate, in the most abject manner, and paid part of the tribute which he owed for his kingdom, while the legate, in the haughtiness of sacerdotal power, trampled on the money, as an earnest of the subjection of the kingdom.

The subjects of John, treated with such indignity, and even sold, felt it necessary to vindicate their rights. The barons, under the command of Langton, the primate, assembled, and binding themselves by an oath, to a concert of measures, demanded from the king a ratification of a charter of privileges, granted by Henry I. The king was highly exasperated, and refused the demand, till resort was had to the sword. Deserted by his people, he was obliged most reluctantly to yield a compliance. At Runnymede, where he met his barons, he signed, on the 19th of June, 1215, that famous deed called Magna Charta, (the Great Charter,) which has had so propitious an effect on the liberty of Englishmen. It secured important rights to all classes of his subjects, though some of its stipulations, from the change of manners and institutions, appear at this day trivial or ridiculous.

§ The charter consisted of fourteen specifications, of which, two or three, the most important, were—that no aids or subsidies should be allowed to be levied from the subjects, unless in a few special cases, without the consent of the great council—that no person shall be tried on suspicion alone, but on the evidence of lawful witnesses—and that no person shall be tried or punished, but by the judgment of his peers and the law of the land.

John granted at the same time, the Charter of the Forest, which abolished the royal privilege of killing game over all the kingdom, and restored to the lawful proprietors their woods, which they were allowed to enclose for their own private purposes.

The king, forced into these measures against his will, meditated a dreadful revenge against his barons, by the aid of foreign mercenaries, and began to lay his own realm waste with fire and sword. But, at a critical time, when Louis, the eldest son of Philip of France, had arrived in England, to assist the barons, with the expectation of receiving the crown himself, John suddenly died. Louis was obliged to return to France, and the succession was settled on Henry, the son of John, a boy of nine years of age.

§ In the person of John, the English were scourged with a tyrant, more odious and capricious than any other of their sovereigns, before or since. To tyranny, he added cowardice, levity, licentiousness, ingratitude, and treachery. His vices were, however, made, providentially, the occasion of great blessings to his subjects, in the enjoyment of a portion of liberty, which they wrested from his weakness.

28. Henry III. began his reign in 1216, the earl of Pembroke being appointed protector during the king's minority His disposition, which was easy and fickle, led him and his subjects into numerous difficulties and disasters. The weakness of his understanding scarcely preserved him from contempt, and joining profusion with oppressive exactions, and lavishing his favours on foreigners, he displeased both the nobility and the populace. His reign was as unhappy as it was protracted, being marked with many bloody contentions.

§ Henry, though in general a mild and merciful prince, yet violated the great charter in confiscating the estates of some of the obnoxious nobles, without a trial by their peers. When remonstrated with on the subject, he replied, "Why should I observe this charter, which is neglected by all my grandees, both prelates and nobility ?" to which it was justly returned, "You ought, sir, to set them the example."

Henry's imprudent measures encouraged Simon de Montfort, earl of Leicester, to attempt to wrest the sceptre from the feeble hand which held it. He succeeded in part ; and as the consequence of a battle, he took both the king and his son Edward, prisoners. But through the interference of the parliament, which Leicester summoned, he deemed it prudent to release the prince, who was no sooner set at liberty, than he took the field against the usurper, and gained over him the famous battle of Evesham. In this battle Leicester was killed, and the gallant Edward enjoyed the happiness of replacing his father on the throne.

§ Leicester had assumed the character of regent, after having compelled the king to resign the regal power. In the parliament which was called, he summoned two knights from each shire, and deputies from the principal boroughs. From this era, is dated the commencement of the House of Commons. Deputies representing the boroughs, had not before constituted a portion of the national council.

In the battle which took place between Prince Edward and Leicester, the rebels, who still retained the old king, had purposely placed him in the front of the battle. Being clad in armour, and thereby not known by his friends, he received a wound, and was in danger of his life ; but crying out "I am Henry of Winchester, your king," he was rescued from impending death.

Edward, afterwards, sought and revived the glory of the English name, in the land of Palestine; but the kingdom suffered most severely in the mean time, under the imbecile reign of the aged monarch; the barons oppressing the common people, and the populace of London returning to their accustomed licentiousness. The death of Henry, after a reign of more than 55 years, left the kingdom in more vigorous hands.

29. Edward I., (Longshanks) was crowned in 1272. His first object was to correct the disorders which the civil commotions had introduced. In this work, he let loose the whole rigour of his justice on the Jews, who had been accused of adulterating the public coin. Multitudes of them lost their lives, or their property and homes.

Edward's next project was the conquest of Wales. He invaded the country with a force too great to be resisted; and after killing Llewellyn, the Welsh prince, and the flower of his warriors, he received the submission of the Welsh nobility, 1283. From this period Wales has been united to England, and the English laws established throughout the principality.

§ It is said that Edward, in order to conciliate the Welsh, gave them for a prince, his own son, who was born in their country. The title of Prince of Wales, has ever since descended to the eldest sons of the English kings.

The Welsh, inhabiting the western part of the island of Great Britain, were the descendants of that portion of the ancient Britons, who had escaped the Roman and Saxon conquests, and preserved their liberty, laws, manners, and language. The occasion of Edward's attack upon this people, was their prince's refusal to perform the customary homage to the English crown.

The next project of Edward, was the conquest of Scotland. Great success attended his arms at different times, but he was never able to effect a total and final conquest of that part of the island. As the history of England and Scotland is so intimately connected, a brief account of the latter, to the time at which we are now arrived, will be in place below, and will supersede the necessity of a separate narrative.

§ The northern part of the island was anciently called Caledonia, from a word which is said to have signified a forest, or mountainous country. Subsequently, and at an early period, it received the name of Scotia, or Scotland; and then it derived it from the Scots, who originally lived in the north of Ireland. The name Scot, is probably the same as Scuth, or Scythian—the people being emigrants from the Baltic countries.

The history of Scotland, before the reign of Malcom III., is obscure, and in a degree uncertain. This prince, by the defeat of Macbeth, the murderer of his father Duncan, succeeded to the throne in 1057. A war which took place between him and William the Conqueror, was equally disastrous to both kingdoms. He prolonged the contest with Rufus, the son of William, with credit to his bravery; while to the virtues of his queen, Margaret, his kingdom, in its domestic policy, owed a degree of civilization scarcely known in those untutored ages.

Under his successors, Alexander I., a spirited prince, and David I., a most excellent sovereign, Scotland successfully defended itself against the English, and, under the latter king, onquered the whole earldom of Northumberland; but the defeat of William I., (the Lion) was disastrous to the kingdom, since he was taken prisoner by Henry II., and, as the price of his release, was compelled to do homage for his whole kingdom. This obligation, however, Richard I. generously discharged.

Alexander III., dying without male issue, in 1285, Bruce and Baliol, descendants of David I., by the female line, were competitors for the crown. Edward was chosen umpire of the contest, and on this ground, arrogated to himself the feudal sovereignty of the kingdom. He took possession of the country, and adjudged the crown to Baliol, on the condition of his doing homage to him, as liege lord. Baliol, however, soon renounced his allegiance, but was compelled at length by the English monarch, to abdicate the throne; the latter having defeated him with great slaughter, in the battle of Dunbar.

The war commenced by Edward against the Scots, did not terminate during his life time. It continued 70 years, and involved both countries in all the miseries of bloodshed. Edward twice defeated the Scots and took possession of their country, and twice they re-asserted their liberties; once under the heroic but unfortunate William Wallace, and once under the gallant and more fortunate Robert Bruce, the Scottish king. As Edward was preparing to invade Scotland the third time, with an immense army, he suddenly sickened and died, at Carlisle, in the 35th year of his reign, and the 69th of his age. He was removed for interment to Westminster Abbey.*

§ The conduct of Wallace was a remarkable instance of heroism. A few patriots, only, joined him at first, but his successes finally brought large numbers to his standard. While Edward was absent, and engaged in war on the continent, Wallace attacked his troops in a desperate engagement at Stirling, and obtained a complete victory.

The disaffection of the Scotch nobles, who envied Wallace his distinction as governor of the country, under Baliol, again exposed them to the attack of the English. Edward, in person, defeated them with an immense loss, in the battle of Falkirk. After a fruitless resistance, the Scots submitted to Edward; and the heroic Wallace, eventually betrayed, and carried in chains to London, was condemned as a rebel, and infamously executed on Tower-hill, to the lasting dishonour of the English king.

Robert Bruce, grandson of the Bruce who was the competitor of Baliol, redeemed the honour of his country. Resenting its humiliation, he set up the standard of war. The genius of the nation then roused itself. Bruce was solemnly crowned at Scone, 1306, and furiously attacking the English, who were dispersed in their quarters, he again expelled them the kingdom. It was immediately after, that Edward died, on his way to Scotland.

* The tomb of this king was opened in 1774, when his body was found unconsumed.

Edward was an able prince, and excelled both as a warrior and statesman. The wisdom of his political measures is especially conspicuous. In moral qualities, however, he was far from being an example fit for imitation. Ambition, a spirit of revenge, and an unfeeling heart, too plainly characterized him.

Under his reign, the Constitution of England gradually advanced. He passed a statute which declared that no tax or impost should be levied without the consent of lords and commons. He ratified magna-charta on several occasions; and henceforward this fundamental law began to be regarded as sacred and inviolable, while parliaments have been held in regular succession.

GERMANY.

30. Germany, during this period, enjoyed but little tranquillity. The contest between the Empire and the Papal See, continued under a succession of emperors and popes, but ended commonly in favour of the latter. The treatment which some of the emperors received from the popes, was extremely humiliating. Frederick I., (Barbarossa) a prince of high spirit, after indignantly denying the supremacy of Alexander III., and refusing the customary homage, was finally compelled to kiss the feet of his Holiness, and appease him by a large cession of territory. Henry VI., while doing homage on his knees, had his imperial crown kicked off by pope Celestinus, who, however, made some amends for this indignity, by the gift of Naples and Sicily. Henry had expelled the Normans from these places, and they now became appendages of the empire, 1194.

The claims of the popes upon the empire, rose to such a height, that in the begining of the thirteenth century, Innocent III., established the powers of the popedom on a settled basis, and obtained a positive acknowledgment of the papal supremacy, or the right irreversibly to confer the crown of the empire.

It was a consequence of the contentions between the imperial and papal powers, to divide the states of Italy, several of which belonged to the empire, into two violent factions, by which Italy was so long devastated. These were known by the name of the Guelphs,* and Ghibellines, the former maintaining the cause of the popes, the latter that of the emperors. Frederic II., carried on an opposition to four successive popes; but though he was excommunicated and deposed, he kept possession of his throne, and exercised his authority with a commendable firmness. On his death, 1250, the empire began to wane, and confusion and anarchy prevailed till the election of Rodolph of Hapsburgh, in 1273.

§ During the latter part of the period above referred to, there was a nominal sovereign, viz., Alphonso X., king of Castile, who was elected emperor, but who, detained at home, neglected the affairs of Germany.

No laws were then observed; no order was maintained; but murder, theft, and rapine, were committed with impunity, and the constitutions of the empire were totally neglected. Sanguinary wars resulted from the feuds of private noblemen; bishops and clergymen, forgetful of their sacred character, embrued their hands in blood, for the augmentation of their benefices; commerce was almost annihilated; and travelling could not be performed with any safety.

In the history of Germany, during the present period, few other occurrences are worthy of notice. The following anecdote may be worth recording. One of the favourites of Henry VI., observed to him that he fatigued himself too much with giving audience, which frequently interfered with his regular meals. Henry replied, "that although a private man was at liberty to eat when he pleased, a prince ought not to sit down to table, till he had discussed the affairs of his people."

The reign of Lotharius was rendered remarkable, by some excessive heats in Germany, which withered the corn and fruits of the earth, dried up the most considerable rivers, and occasioned a dreadful mortality among the cattle.

EASTERN EMPIRE.

31. The affairs of the Eastern Empire were, in part, narrated in the history of the crusades. Little, therefore, needs be added to this record, in respect to the present period. The outward splendour of the empire was yet considerable, but the progress of decay was obvious. The Greeks manifested their cunning, and sometimes their treachery, in their treatment of the crusaders. The emperors, though on many ac-

* The family now on the throne of Great Britain bear the surname of Guelph, and are descended from the Guelphs here spoken of.

counts they wished success to the crusaders, yet dreaded their power, and between these two passions, the soldiers of the cross became the dupes and the victims of their policy. The weakness of the empire was seen, when Constantinople, its capital, was taken by a handful of French and Venetian crusaders, and held in subjection nearly sixty years.

Within the limits of the present period, about nine emperors sat on the throne of the East, besides the five French or Latin emperors who reigned at Constantinople. During the reign of the latter, four Greek emperors reigned at Nice, over the remainder of the empire.

It was under Michael Palæologus, 1261, that Constantinople was recovered by the Greeks from its Latin conquerors. When the former and ancient sovereigns of the city determined to retake the seat of the empire, Palæologus was found possessed of the requisite ambition. Favoured by circumstances, and skilful in the application of means, he accomplished the object; and the second seat of the venerable Roman dominion was destined yet longer, to be held by the successors of the great Constantine.

§ The designs of Palæologus were promoted by the Genoese, the rivals of the Venetians. The Latins had been gradually driven from their last possessions in Thrace; and at a time when the bravest of the French and Venetians were absent from the city, a general of Palœologus advanced in the night to its gates. He succeeded in entering it, partly by a subterranean passage into the centre of the city. Baldwin, the Latin emperor, in dismay, escaping to the sea-shore, was conveyed to Italy, and spent the remainder of his life in vainly attempting to rouse the Catholic powers to join in his restoration.

No names besides Palœologus are much distinguished, except those of Alexis Comnenus, and his son John Alexis. The one was an able and politic sovereign, as his management of the crusaders abundantly evinced. The other, with talent, united moral worth, and seemed by his virtues to revive the age of Marcus Antoninus.

The lamentable end of a cruel usurper named Andronicus, is worth recording, as it shews how much the wicked, in death, sometimes feel that they need the divine mercy. The butcheries of Andronicus had wearied the patience of the citizens of Constantinople. They rose *en-masse* against him, headed by Isaac Angelus. In their rage the populace tore from him successively his teeth, his hair, an eye, and a hand; and being suspended for three days, every person who could reach the public enemy, inflicted on him some mark of ingenious or brutal cruelty, till at length two Italians, out of mercy or rage, plunging their swords into his body, released him from al human punishment. During this long and excruciating torture, "Lord have mercy on me," and "Why wilt thou break a bruised reed!" were the only words that escaped his mouth. Our pity for the man, seems almost to absorb our hatred of the tyrant

SARACENS.

32. The empire of the SARACENS, before the conclusion of this period, was destined to be no more. Their history is partly involved in the details of the crusades. The energies of fanatic Europe, were exerted against the followers of the prophet, with some intervals, nearly two centuries, and terrible was the destruction of life on both sides. The kingdom of Jerusalem, under christian sovereigns, which originated from the crusades, lasted not quite a century and a half. The Saracens, on recovering this domain, held it, however, but a short time. In a few years after, the Tartars from the east swept over the regions which the Saracens had conquered, and blotted out their name from the list of empires.

This event occurred 1258 years A. C. From the close of our last period to the termination of their dominion, ten caliphs of the house of Abbas, reigned at Bagdad. The last of the caliphs was Mostasem, who was put to death at the time the city was captured. The Tartars were led by Halaku, their general, who after a few assaults, took Bagdad, which contained immense riches, and gave it up seven days to be pillaged by his troops.

A few particulars may be noticed concerning some of the caliphs.

§ Of one, named Mohammed, it is said, that he quitted life with such extreme regret, that when about dying, he ordered his troops, his court, and all his treasures, to pass before him, as it were in a view; and after he had considered all these objects, observed, "how is it possible that a power so formidable as mine, is not able to diminish the weight of my disorder one single grain, nor to prolong my life only for a moment." He then concluded his reflection with the following remarkable words. "Unhappy is the person who spends his time in amassing those things which he must leave, and does not make the principal object of regard, that Being in whom all things are to be found."

The reign of Al Moktafi must have been remarkable for justice. This the following anecdote may prove. A man convicted of calumny, was sent by him to prison. One of his nobles offered to give him two thousand pieces of gold coin for his release, to which the caliph replied, "put another man, guilty of the same crime, in my power, and I will give you ten thousand; for I am extremely anxious to clear my dominions of these pests of society."

The later caliphs, in the decline of the Saracen empire, were not the warlike sovereigns that their predecessors had been. They thought only of securing their ease and pleasure. Mostasem, above spoken of, exceeded all the caliphs in ostentation and pride. When he appeared in public, he usually wore a veil, the more effectually to attract the respect of the people, whom he considered as unworthy to look at him. On those occasions, nothing could exceed the eagerness of the multitude to see him, by crowding the streets, and hiring the windows and balconies, at the most exorbitant prices. The manner of his death was degrading and distressing in the extreme, and Hulaki designed it as a punishment of his pride Through the same streets, and exposed to the view of the same populace, the cruel Tartar caused the wretched caliph to be dragged confined in a leather bag, till he expired.

CHINA.

33. In the history of CHINA, the present period includes a part both of the nineteenth and twentieth of the dynasties of her emperors. The whole of the nineteenth comprised seventeen emperors. It was during this period that the celebrated Genghis Khan, and his successors, established their dominion in China. Heading the Mogul Tartars, who inhabited a desert and inhospitable region, Genghis Khan, in 1209, entered China, poured over the northern provinces, and compelled them to submit to his authority. Kublay, his son, called by the Chinese, Houpilay, entered on his father's conquests in this country, and reigned for a time over the northern provinces.

Li-tsong, and his three sons and a nephew, in succession, were the last sovereigns of the nineteenth dynasty, and reigned over the southern part of the empire. It is said that Kublay (more probably a descendant of his) brought the whole of the country into subjection in 1280, and that with the nineteenth dynasty, ended, in fact, the Chinese dominion until the year 1357

Kublay had the wisdom and prudence to govern the Chinese according to their ancient laws and customs. This procedure, together with the general excellence of his character, entirely reconciled the people to the Tartar sway, so far as they were brought under it.

§ The Mogul Tartars, who conquered China. were a wandering

race, and given to arms. The extent and rapidity of their conquests have rarely been equalled in history. In the beginning of the thirteenth century, Genghis Khan overran, besides China, already mentioned, India, Persia, and Asiatic Russia. Batoucan, one of his sons, ravaged the western nations to the frontiers of Germany. But Genghis and his sons were not the only conquerors who arose from among this people. From the vast tract of country inhabited by the Tartars, have sprung the conquerors who produced all the great revolutions in Asia. Besides the personages just named, the Turks, who are a race of Tartars, overwhelmed the empire of the caliphs. Mahmoud, a Tartar, conquered Persia, and a great part of India, in the tenth century. After Genghis, as we shall hereafter see, Tamerlane, the scourge of the Turks, subdued a great part of Asia, and Baber, a remote descendant of Tamerlane, conquered all the region between Samarcand and Agra, in the empire of the Mogul. The descendants of those conquerors now reign in India, Persia, and China.

Distinguished characters in Period VI.

1. Abelard, a scholastic divine.
2. Walter de Mapes, a poet, the Anacreon of the twelfth century.
3. Averroes, an Arabian philosopher and physician.
4. Genghis Khan, a Mogul, conqueror of Asia.
5. Matthew Paris, an early English historian.
6. Th. Aquinas, a celebrated teacher of School Divinity.
7. Roger Bacon, an eminent English philosopher.

§ 1. Abelard, was born in Brittany, 1079, and became celebrated for his learning and misfortunes. He was one of the most eminent divines of the twelfth century, though his conduct ill agreed with his sacred profession. He was criminally vain of his personal and mental accomplishments, but his most notorious failings relate to his conduct towards Heloise. With the most consummate art, he gained the favours of that beautiful and accomplished female, to their mutual dishonour. They were soon afterwards married in private, to pacify her uncle and family, though she never would acknowledge the union, inasmuch as she preferred the name of a mistress, to that of a wife. Their subsequent conduct eventually excited the indignation of her friends to such a degree, that they hired certain ruffians to maim his person in the most shameful manner.

In the oratory of the Paraclete which Abelard built, the unfortunate Heloise finally found a refuge, where she spent her days with her sister nuns. She retained her affection for Abelard, though he returned it with a coldness and indifference, which cannot but excite our indignation. Whilst he languished during the decline of life, under the unmanly vengeance of the uncle of Heloise, he forgot that she, once virtuous, had sacrificed her name, honour, and happiness, to his passion. The poem of Pope, in which he celcbrates the loves of Abelard and Heloise, is a brilliant, but corrupting production, and not even the bard can soften the features of deformity, which mark the character of Abelard in this particular.

The writings of Abelard, are mostly on subjects of theology or logic.

2. Walter de Mapes, was chaplain to Henry II. Under king John he was made canon of Salisbury, precentor of Lincoln, and archdeacon of Oxford. He wrote in Latin, and in a satirical style. Some of his verses are still read and admired for their sprightliness. He imitated the gay humour of Anacreon. He was a facetious companion.

3. Averroes was born at Corduba, where his father was judge under the emperor of Morocco. His knowledge of law, divinity, mathematics, and astrology, was very extensive, and to this was added the theory, rather than the practice, of medicine. After being professor in the university of Morocco, he was called away to succeed his father in the office of Judge in Corduba, and soon after, he was invested with the same powers in Morocco and Mauritania.

His authority and talents procured him enemies, who envied and calumniated him, and through their efforts he was, for a time, suspended and degraded, on a charge of heresy. He was, however, restored at length to all his honours. He died at Morocco, 1206.

In his private life, Averroes was regular, and devoted much of his time to philosophical pursuits. He was particularly fond of Aristotle, on whose works he wrote commentaries. His medical works are scarce, and above mediocrity; and of his numerous verses on amorous and light subjects, very few remain.

4. Genghis Khan, was son of a khan of the Moguls, and born 1163. He began to reign at the age of 13, but on account of a revolt of his subjects, he fled for safety to Aventi-Khan, a Tartar prince, whom he supported on his throne, and whose daughter he married. But the jealousy of Aventi obliged him to escape a second time, and being pursued by Aventi and his son, he defeated them both, and their army revolting to him, he soon increased it.

From this occurrence, he became a renowned conqueror. In the space of 28 years he subdued the greater part of Asia, and rendered himself as famous for his skill in government, as for the valour of his arms. He died in 1227, leaving his vast dominions, which extended 1800 leagues in length, and 1000 in breadth, properly divided among his four sons.

5. Matthew Paris, a Benedictine monk, was a universal scholar, and in that dark age, confessedly possessed great and astonishing erudition. He is chiefly celebrated as a historian, though not unknown as an orator and poet. His abilities and well known integrity, fitted him for the work in which he so zealously engaged, of reforming the monasteries, and re-establishing the ancient purity of church discipline, even in opposition to the papal power. His great production was "Historia Major," in two parts, from the creation to William the Conqueror, and from the Conqueror to the year 1250.

With Henry III. he was familiarly acquainted; yet his account of the reign of that prince, seems not to be at all tinged with flattery, or sullied with any violation of historic truth.

6. Th. Aquinas, called the angelical doctor, was of a noble family, descended from the kings of Arragon and Sicily. His inclination to embrace an ecclesiastical life, was strongly opposed by his mother. She even confined him two years in her castle. But escaping from her custody, he found the means of improving himself by study, and it was not long before he appeared at Paris, reading public lectures to an applauding audience. On his return to Italy, he became divinity professor to several universities, and at last settled at Naples, where he led a chaste and devout life.

Gregory X. invited him to the Council of Lyons, to read the book which he had written against the Greeks, but he died on the way to join the pontiff, near Terraciña, 7th March, 1274, in his 50th year. Aquinas left a vast number of works, mostly upon theological subjects, which prove him to have been a man of extensive erudition. There is, however, in his writings, very little of sound, useful, or experimental views of religious truth.

7. Roger Bacon was born in 1214, near Ilchester, of a respectable family, and became a monk of the Franciscan order. A strong, inquisitive mind, soon raised him to consequence; and as he was liberally supported in his pursuits by his friends, he made a most rapid advancement in science and philosophy. His attainments becoming far above the comprehensions of his age, he was suspected and accused of magic. The monks of his order, actuated by jealousy and envy, contrived to have his works rejected from their library, and to prevent him from reading lectures to the students. He was finally imprisoned, and during 10 years was left to pursue his studies in solitary confinement. Within this period, he composed his "Opus Majus," or his Great Work. After being released from prisón by the interference of his friends, he spent the remainder of his life in academical repose, at Oxford. He died at the age of 80 years.

To the comprehensive mind of Roger Bacon, many of the discoveries, which have been made by the genius and toil of later ages, were known. His knowledge of mathematics and natural philosophy, was profound. He discovered the error in the calendar, and his plan for correcting it was adopted by Gregory XIII. He was acquainted with the structure of an air pump, with the laws of optics, and with the power of glasses. His acquaintance with chemistry was extensive. He gave such a description of gunpowder, that it is evident he was its inventor. In his writings, which amounted to above eighty treatises, some of which are published, and some preserved in manuscript, in the libraries of Europe, he uses an elegant and nervous style, and was always accurate in his observations on nature

PERIOD VII.

The period of the Papal Schism; extending from the founding of the Turkish Empire, 1299 *years A. C., to the taking of Constantinople,* 1453 *years A. C.*

TURKISH EMPIRE.

SECT. 1. The EMPIRE of the TURKS, claims the notice of history, from the important consequences connected with its eventual establishment, on the ruin of the Grecian sovereignty. The power of this people is felt on the soil of classical antiquity, and until lately, it extended itself over nearly the whole of it, in the south east of Europe. Their establishment as a separate empire, is an event which took place in 1299 A. C., under Ottoman or Othman, the first Sultan.

§ The Turks derive their origin from the Avares, a tribe of the Huns who dwelt in Great Tartary, till forced by the Huns of the south, to abandon their country, when they divided into several bodies, each of which taking a different direction, settled, some around the Caspian Sea, some in Pannonia, and others in Asia Minor.

The last colony, known under the name of the Seljukide Turks, founded an empire in Asia Minor, about the year 1070, and their chief took the title of Sultan of Iconium, a town of Lycaonia, where he fixed his residence. In 1294, this empire was destroyed by the Moguls, and the emirs or governors of most of the provinces became independent. The Turks embraced Mahometanism long before the time of Othman, as we gather from the history of the Crusades.

Othman was an emir under the last sultan of Iconium. Forming the scheme of raising a new empire from that which was just overthrown, he engaged the assistance of several other emirs, and seized Iconium. He soon fixed the seat of his government at Byrsa, the chief town of Bythinia, and assumed the title of Sultan. From this time the Turks were known as the Ottoman race and sovereignty.

By degrees, they encroached on the borders of the Greek empire, and were prevented from subverting it at an early stage, only by the necessity of defending themselves against the victorious Tamerlane. Their principal sovereigns, during this period, after Othman, were Orchan, Amurat I., Bajazet I., Mahomet I., and Amurat II.

§ In the reign of Orchan, the Turks crossed the Hellespont on rafts, took Gallipoli, the key of Europe, penetrated into Thrace. and laid the foundation of the Turkish power in Europe. Orchan created the order of Janizaries, though as they were more completely organized by his successor, Amurat, this institution is generally attributed to the latter.

Bajazet I., the successor of Amurat, purposed to besiege the capital of the Greek empire in form, but he was suddenly forced to defend himself against Tamerlane. Tamerlane, or Timer-bek, was a prince of the Usbec Tartars, and a descendant from Gengiskan. Having conquered Persia and most of the East. he was invited by the enemies of Bajazet, to protect them against the Ottoman power. He gladly accepted the invitation, and having met the Turk. he totally defeated him, and made him prisoner. The battle of Angoria, where the chieftains fought, is a famous one in history. Nearly 1,000,000 of men were engaged in this battle, and 300,000 were slain. The victorious career of the Turks was suspended by this event. Bajazet was shut up in an iron cage, in which he destroyed himself.

Under Amurat II., the Turks resumed the project of taking Constantinople, but did not succeed. This prince had devoted himself to retirement and study, but some violation of a treaty, led him into a war with the Poles, in which he was signally victorious. He left his dominions to his son Mahomet II., surnamed the Great, known in history as the final subverter of the Eastern empire.

ITALIAN STATES.

2. Italy, in the separate States of which it consisted during this period, and subsequently, appears again on the page of history. The principal states were Venice, Florence, Naples, Sicily, the possessions of the Church, Genoa, Parma; and a few others. Most of these sovereignties had been previously founded, but they existed in their most flourishing condition, during the present period.

3. Venice had become considerable in the ninth century. Afterward, in the year 1084, the eastern emperor, Alexius, confirmed to the Venetians, Istria, Dalmatia, and Croatia, which had been conquered by their arms. They subdued also Verano, Padua, and other Italian States, in 1405. On the death of the king of Epirus, they acquired that Island in addition. The Venetians, for a long time, were the principal merchants of the world, but their trade was greatly diminished by the discovery of the Cape of Good Hope, in 1497. During the latter part of this period, in consequence of their wars with the Turks, they lost many of their possessions.

§ The following incident in the Venetian history, deserves a particular notice. Ziani, the thirty-ninth doge, or chief magistrate of the republic, was involved in a war with Frederic Barbarossa, from whose persecution the Pope had retired to Venice. The Venetians dispatched embassadors to the emperor, who answered them in a rage, that if their doge did not instantly deliver up the Pope, bound hand and foot, he would be terribly revenged,—would bring his army before their city, and fix his victorious standard in their market place, which should float in the blood of its citizens.

The embassadors returned with this awful message, and it was agreed to equip a fleet with all expedition, and prepare for repelling the emperor's meditated vengeance. While the Venetians were thus employed, Otho, the Emperor's son, entered the gulf with seventy-five gallies, and was making sail to the city. The doge, with haste, met this fleet, with the few ships which were fit to put to sea, and in a dreadful battle took and destroyed forty-eight of the enemy's vessels, and returned in triumph to Venice. From this time was continued the ceremony of marrying the sea. The Pope going out to meet the victorious doge, presented him with a ring, saying, "Take, Ziani, this ring, and give it to the sea, as a testimony of your dominion. Let your successors annually perform the same ceremony, that posterity may know your valour has purchased the prerogative, and subjected this element, even as a husband subjecteth his wife."

4. Florence, which was the capital of Tuscany, early rose into notice. It became a republic in the thirteenth century, and maintained its independence during two or three centuries. It was distinguished, by the revival of Grecian literature, and the cultivation of the arts, in the fifteenth century. Before the close of this period, the family of the Medicis arose, and shed a splendour on the republic of letters.

5. Naples, just before the beginning of the present era, was entered by Charles, duke of Anjou, who became its king, as well as of Sicily. These countries were frequently united in one government, and as often separated from each other. They were the seat of long wars between the French and Germans on the one part, and the Spaniards on the other. But the latter at length obtained possession of the kingdoms.

6. The Estates of the Church, which include the middle portions of Italy, were, during the present period, greatly involved in controversies. The rival claims for superiority between the popes and emperors, still continued. Henry VII., the successor of Albert, triumphantly fought his way to Rome, where, in a solemn manner, he received the crown, and imposed a tribute on the states of the Church. He was suddenly destroyed, it was supposed, by papal vengeance.

It was in his time, that the remarkable event took place, by which the seat of the popedom was changed from Rome to

Avignon. This was done by pope Clement V., 1309, on account of being so much molested by the imperial faction. In the absence of this pope from Rome, Nicholas Rienzi, a man of mean parentage, but of great abilities, aspired to the supreme authority, in 1347. He retained the dominion of this portion of Italy, for a year; but was afterwards sacrificed to the fury of the people. In the year 1377, the holy see was removed back to Rome, by pope Gregory IX. After his death, the citizens of Avignon and Rome contended for the freedom of election. Three separate factions of the French and Italian cardinals, having elected three separate popes, the emperor Sigismund judged this division of the Church to be a fit occasion for his interference, to reconcile all differences, and establish his own supremacy.

In 1414, he summoned a general council at Constance, and ended the dispute by deposing all the three pontiffs, and naming a fourth, Martin Colonna. Historians call this division of the papacy, the great schism of the west.

7. Genoa, the ancient Liguria, became a republic in 953. The Genoese were afterwards involved in civil commotions, which so weakened them, that they were obliged to shelter themselves under the protection of the duke of Milan. They continually revolted to the French, and returned again to subjection to the Milanese, till, in the next succeeding period, Andrew Doria restored liberty to his native country.

§ The Genoese, next to the Venetians, were, for 200 years, the most commercial people in Europe. The city of Genoa, was afterwards celebrated as the birth place of the great Columbus.

FRANCE.

Capetian Race. Branch of Valois.

8. The successor of Philip the Fair, on the throne of France, was Louis X. surnamed Hutin, (the wrangler,) 1314. He was a prince of a weak and irresolute character, and reigned but a few months. A son, born after his death, was acknowledged, but lived only four days. Upon this event, Philip V. the Long, brother of Louis, succeeded to the throne. His was a short reign of five years.

§ Philip V. was notorious for his persecution of the Jews, and, in general, of all foreigners who resided within his dominion, and refused to embrace christianity. The Jews were accused of having poisoned the wells and springs of water.

9. Philip leaving no other than female issue, was succeeded, 1322, by his brother, Charles IV., the Fair. His reign was unfortunately short, for he was a wise and upright prince. He left no son behind him.

§ According to the Salic law, no female succeeds to the French throne.

10. The throne now devolved on Philip VI. of Valois, cousin to the late king, 1328. Edward III. of England, however, claimed it in right of his mother, Isabella, who was a daughter of Philip the Fair. He enforced his claim by arms; but Philip being acknowledged and supported by the French nation, retained the sceptre, notwithstanding the loss of the famous battle of Cressy, and the capture of Calais. In the celebrated wars which these rival pretensions created, the English were at first victorious.

Philip was vain, obstinate, and of a limited capacity, and died after a reign of twenty-two years.

§ In the midst of his losses, Philip was gratified with the cession of the province of Dauphine; the condition of which was, that the eldest son, the presumptive heir of the crown, should be styled Dauphin, and bear the arms of the province.

It was in the reign of this prince, that a general plague, surpassing in its horrors whatever besides the remotest history can furnish, ravaged, in the space of eighteen months, not only France, but every part of the known world. It broke out in the northern provinces of China, and swept over Asia, Africa, and Europe. In the places through which it passed, it cut down two thirds of the inhabitants. This calamity had been preceded by terrific earthquakes, which swallowed up whole cities.

11 John II., surnamed the Good, succeeded his father, 1350. He was a most unfortunate prince. Taking the field with 60,000 men, against the Black Prince, he was defeated by the latter with a far inferior number, in the signal battle of Poictiers, and made prisoner.

§ He was carried in triumph to London, and, after having been detained in captivity four years, was permitted to return to France upon ceding several important places to the English. He, however visited London again, on account, as is supposed, of a passion which he had conceived for the countess of Salisbury. He died very soon afterwards.

12. The Dauphin assumed the administration, during the captivity of the king; and, on the death of the latter, succeeded to the throne, under the name of Charles V. the Wise

Had it not been for this prince, France would most probably have fallen under the domination of England. During his reign, the French re-conquered almost all the places taken by the English. This prince possessed a vigourous mind, but a delicate constitution of body, and was suddenly carried off in his forty-seventh year. He was one of the best of the French sovereigns, a patron of literature, and a sagacious statesman. He possessed a library of several hundred volumes; which was extremely large for the age.

§ It was through Du Guesclin, a celebrated general, whom the king raised to be Constable of France, that the French, after having been beaten by the English during thirty years, began to beat the latter in turn.

13. Charles VI., styled the Well Beloved, succeeded to the kingdom, 1380. He first made war on the Flemings, whom he defeated in the battle of Rosebeck. A formidable invasion, of which the object was the British shore, failed, in consequence of a tempest that dispersed and wrecked his ships. During this reign, a civil war occurred between the houses of Orleans and Burgundy, the cause of which pertained to the regency. Charles had fallen into a state of insanity, which, of course, rendered a regency necessary. In the midst of the contention, and of the miseries which it inflicted on France, Henry V. of England, invaded the country, and gained the memorable battle of Agincourt. The consequence of this victory, and other advantages gained by Henry, was the acknowledgment of his right to the French throne, on the death of Charles. These sovereigns died soon after, and within two months of each other.

§ Charles was a weak prince, and his insanity reduced him almost to idiotism.

The fleet which was fitted out for the invasion of England, consisted of 1287 sail, of which, sixty were ships of the line. In the centre was a wooden city, having a diameter of 3000 paces, provided with towers and bastions, and constructed over boats fastened together. It was so contrived as to be put together, or taken to pieces, in a day; and was intended to furnish lodgings for the troops, when they should be landed. The wreck only, of this singular city, reached the British shore.

Cards were invented in the reign of Charles VI., to amuse that monarch, and to relieve him from the melancholy which followed his alienation of mind.

14. Charles VII., surnamed the Victorious, was crowned at Poictiers, 1422, while, at the same time, the infant Henry

VI., was crowned at Paris, through the agency of the duke of Bedford, the English regent of France. This competition issued in war. The first great military operation undertaken by the English, was the siege of Orleans, a place of the utmost importance. And here a transaction occurred, which is one of the most wonderful on record. This was the raising of the siege, and the consequent deliverance of France from the grasp of English power, by means of Joan of Arc, otherwise called the Maid of Orleans. The enthusiasm which she inspired at this juncture, by pretending to a divine commission, and by her singular and courageous appearance at the head of the French troops, rendered them invincible.

§ Joan was a young country girl, of twenty-seven years, a domestic of a tavernkeeper. Presenting herself to the council of Charles, who had fled in despair to Dauphine, she declared that God had, in a revelation, apprised her that the royal troops would force the enemy to retire from the siege. An assembly of divines pronounced her mission to be supernatural; and, at her own request, she was clothed like a man, and, in complete armour, headed the troops. A white palfrey bore her gaily to the scene of combat; while on her banner was displayed the image of our blessed Saviour. The English, raising the siege of Orleans, fled before her. The hopes of the nation were raised, as if by a miracle, and other conquests succeeded. The impulse which her heroism excited, enabled Charles to extend his triumphs to the banks of the Seine.

As a recompense for her important services, she was ennobled by Charles, together with the whole of her family, and their heirs and descendants. After she had effected the object of the mission, she requested leave to retire, but she was retained in the service, from the belief that it would be benefited by her presence. At the siege of Compeigne, not long after, she was made prisoner; and being tried by the English for sorcery, she was condemned to be burned. This sentence, which is an eternal disgrace to the judges who presided at the trial, was barbarously put into execution. When led to the stake, the heroic maid, overcome by her emotions, burst into tears. To prolong her tortures, a scaffolding of plaster had been contrived, with so great an elevation, that the flames required a considerable time to penetrate to her body, which was gradually consumed.

The tide of fortune turning against the English, they lost many of the French provinces; and, after the battle of Formigny, which was gained by Charles, they lost Paris itself. In the southern dominions, however, the French arms were paralized, for a time, by the brave Talbot, an illustrious English warrior. His death, and the fatal disputes between the houses of York and Lancaster, placed the whole of the French monarchy, with the exception of Calais and Greignes, under the dominion of Charles, 1450.

§ The death of this prince was hastened by the undutiful and unnatural conduct of his son, the Dauphin. The latter formed a plot to cut off his father by poison. This was discovered; but the king was so haunted by the idea of treachery and poison, that he could not be prevailed on to receive that degree of nourishment, which was necessary to support life.

The Pragmatic Sanction originated in his reign, in a general assembly of the clergy and nobility, representing the Gallican church. Its aim was, to check the despotism of the popes. The superiority of the assemblies of the clergy over the See of Rome, formed the basis of its regulations.

ENGLAND.

Family of Plantagenet.—Branch of Lancaster.

14½ Edward II., surnamed of Cærnarvon, from the place of his birth, ascended the throne in 1307. He was the opposite of his father in character and disposition, being weak, indolent, and destitute of penetration in selecting his advisers. Yet his inoffensive disposition, joined with his misfortunes, entitles him to respect, as well as commiseration. He made war on the Scots, but was terribly defeated by Robert Bruce, in the battle of Bannockburn. In consequence of this battle, the latter was established on the throne of Scotland, 1314. Edward was unfortunate in all his connexions. His queen, Isabella, sister of the French king, was an ambitious and worthless woman, and his favourites were equally detested by the people, and injurious to their sovereign. Edward, at last, fell a victim to his wife's cruelty and lust, and miserably perished.

§ It was in obedience to his father's dying request, that Edward invaded Scotland. He marched at the head of one hundred thousand men. Bruce met this immense force with only thirty thousand. The army of the latter was however advantageously situated. A hill covered his right flank, a morass his left, and to screen his front, he had dug deep pits, planted them with stakes, and covered them with turf. The English, confident in their superior numbers, rushed forward without precaution. Their cavalry was entangled in the pits, their ranks were broken, and the Scottish horse, pouring through the openings, scattered on every side slaughter and dismay. The English threw down their arms and fled, and were pursued to the gates of Berwick. The defeat of Edward sunk him in the estimation of his subjects.

The most famous of his favourites, were Gaveston, and the two Spencers, father and son. The queen, who persuaded the king to recal them after they had been banished by parliament, at length fixed her affections on Mortimer, a powerful baron. A breach soon followed between her and the Spencers, and going over to France with her paramour, she found the means to form such a party in England, that on her return with some French troops, she made her husband prisoner, and forced him to abdicate his crown in favour of his son, then fourteen years of age. While he was in prison, he was put to death by the keepers, who, with infinite barbarity, thrust a red hot iron into his bowels, until he was internally consumed. These wretches were instigated by Mortimer and the queen.

15. Edward III., succeeded his father, 1327, under the regency of Isabella and Mortimer. But to such a regency, he would not submit. At the age of eighteen, he assumed the reins of government, hanged Mortimer at Tyburn, and confined the queen, his mother, for life.

The conquest of Scotland soon became an object of ambition, and marching to the north with a large army, he vanquished the Scots at Halidown Hill, with little loss on the side of England.

On the death of Charles the Fair, in 1328, Edward, having a claim to the throne of France, as being the son of Isabella, the sister of the deceased king, and first in female succession, prepared to assert his claim (since the French rejected it) by the fortune of arms. For this purpose, he invaded France in 1339, and from that time to 1360, war raged furiously between the two countries, with only occasional suspensions.

During this long contention, were fought the famous battles of Cressy, in 1346, and Poictiers, in 1356. The battle of Cressy was fought between Philip, the French king, on the one side, and Edward and his son, the Black Prince, on the other. The army of Philip amounted to one hundred thousand men, that of the English, only to thirty thousand. The battle of Poictiers was fought between the Black Prince, and King John of France. The former commanded only sixteen thousand men, while the army of the latter amounted to sixty thousand. Notwithstanding the disparity of numbers, the English obtained a decided victory in both engagements. The heroism of the Black Prince has rendered his name ever famous in the annals of war.

§ In the battle of Cressy, there fell, by a moderate computation, twelve hundred French knights, fourteen hundred gentlemen, four thousand men-at-arms, besides about thirty thousand of an inferior rank. The action seems no less remarkable for the small loss sustained by the English, than for the prodigious slaughter of the French. Among the former, there only fell one esquire, and three knights, and an inconsiderable number of private men.

In the battle of Poictiers, the French king was taken prisoner, and afterwards was led by the Prince of Wales, in triumph, to London. He was treated with the greatest courtesy by his conqueror.

Edward, during his absence in France, left his queen, Philippa, with the care of the realm. Attacked by the Scots, who invaded England soon after the battle of Cressy, she entirely defeated them near Durham. David, their king, who had expelled Edward Baliol from the throne, was unable to effect his escape from the field, and thus he became a captive at the same time with king John in London.

16. The decline of Edward's life did not correspond with the early part of it. The tide of success turned against him in France, and besides the loss of his dominions abroad, he felt the decay of his authority at home. His age he unwisely devoted to pleasure; and to complete his disappointment, the Prince of Wales died, after a lingering illness, in his forty-sixth year. Never had king a more illustrious son, and never did a nation have greater cause to felicitate itself in the prospect of having such a model of heroism and virtue for its sovereign. The old king did not long survive this melancholy occurrence. He died in 1377, in the sixty-fifth year of his age, and the fifty-first of his reign.

The English nation has ever taken pride in its Edward III., and recurred to his reign, as one of the most glorious in its annals. The splendour of his foreign victories, and the tranquillity and efficiency of his domestic government, stamp the impression of greatness on his mind. But the moral purity of his character, and the justice of his wars with France and Scotland, are more than questionable.

17. Richard II., son of the Black Prince, succeeded to the throne, 1377, at the age of eleven years. He was unworthy of his great father. Indolence, prodigality, perfidiousness, and sensuality, marked his character. His kingdom suffered from the distractions attending a regal minority. The contests for power between his three uncles, the dukes of Lancaster, York, and Gloucester, who secretly directed the affairs of the realm, embroiled all the public measures. An insurrec-

tion, headed by Wat Tyler, put the government, for a time, in great jeopardy. While the kingdom was convulsed with domestic contests, it was also engaged in hostilities with France and Scotland. At length, during the king's absence in quelling an insurrection in Ireland, Henry of Lancaster rose in open rebellion, and compelled Richard, at his return, to resign the sceptre into his hands. The parliament confirmed the act, and the king was soon after privately assassinated or starved to death. Thus began the contention between the houses of York and Lancaster.

§ The finances of the kingdom were exhausted by the wars which were carried on with its foreign enemy. As nothing was obtained by conquest to repair the waste, parliament found it necessary to impose a poll tax of three groats on every person, male and female, above fifteen years of age. But the minds of the people were unfavourably disposed for this measure, and the principles of democracy gaining ground, this distich was frequently in the mouths of the multitude:

> "When Adam delv'd and Eve span,
> Where was then the gentleman."

Besides, the injustice of the tax, to which the poor were obliged to contribute as much as the rich, was apparent to every body. While the character of the measure was viewed in this light, the rigorous manner in which it was enforced, seemed insupportable.

An incident which occurred, respecting the wanton conduct of a tax-gatherer, in the family of a blacksmith, aroused the public mind, and became the occasion of a wide spread insurrection. The populace flew to arms. The spirit immediately pervaded Essex and the neighbouring counties. The leaders assuming the feigned names of Wat Tyler, Jack Straw, and Hob Carter, committed the most outrageous violence on such of the nobility and gentry as came in their way. At length, assembling their followers on Blackheath, to the amount of one hundred thousand, they broke into London, demanding certain immunities, which were granted, but in parties still continuing to insult and plunder the capital.

At this juncture, the king, slenderly guarded, met Tyler at the head of a large body of rioters, and entered into conference with him. Tyler ordered his companions to retire, till he should give the signal for attack, and then ventured alone into the midst of the royal retinue. Here he demeaned himself in so insolent a manner, that Walworth, the mayor of London, in a fit of indignation, drew his sword and brought him to the ground. He was instantly dispatched by the rest of the king's attendants. Richard's presence of mind saved himself and them from the meditated revenge of the mutineers. Accosting the enraged multitude with an affable and intrepid countenance, he asked them, "What is the meaning of your disorder? Are you angry, my good people, that you have lost your leader. I, your king, will be your leader."

The presence of majesty overawed the multitude, and they implicitly followed the king. Leading them into the fields, he peaceably dismissed them, with the same charters which had been granted to their fellows. These charters, however, were soon after annulled in parliament.

In regard to the death of Richard, after he was deposed and imprisoned, it was long the prevailing opinion, that his guards fell upon him in the castle of Pontefract, and dispatched him with their halberts. But it is more probable, that he was starved to death in prison, for after his body was exposed in public, no marks of violence were found upon it.

The particular ground of the controversy between the houses of York and Lancaster, was, that Edmund Mortimer was the true heir to the crown, being descended from Lionel, the second son of Edward III., whereas Henry, duke of Lancaster, who was placed on the throne, was the son of John of Gaunt, the third son of Edward III.

17½ Henry IV., was the title which the duke of Lancaster assumed, when he came into power. He was surnamed Bolingbroke, and the date of his reign is 1400. He was immediately oppressed by faction and discontent; and as a righteous retribution, he felt the uneasiness of "the head that wears a crown." A rebellion, raised by the earl of Northumberland, for placing Mortimer, of the house of York, the true heir, on the throne, first required his attention. The Scotch and the Welch took part with the malcontents, but their united forces were defeated at Shrewsbury, and their leader, young Percy, (Hotspur, so named on account of his fiery temper,) was killed on the field.

§ The armies on this occasion were nearly equal in numbers, consisting of about twelve thousand men, each; and rarely was there a battle in those times, where the shock was more terrible or more constant. Henry exposed his person to all the dangers of the field. His gallant son, the prince of Wales, who afterwards so signalized himself by his military exploits, urged on the fight with the utmost intrepidity, and even a wound which he received in the face with an arrow, could not oblige him to retire. On the other side, Percy and Douglas, terrible names, supported their ancient renown. But while the armies were contending in the most furious manner, the death of Percy, by an unknown hand, decided the victory, and the adherents of the king won the day.

18. A second rebellion, headed by the archbishop of York, was quelled by the capital punishment of its author. In the reign of this prince, the secular arm was unrighteously ex-

tended against the followers of Wickliffe; and history records the shameful fact, that Henry IV. was the first English monarch, that made the religion of his subjects, an offence to be expiated by the faggot and the scaffold.

The latter part of his life was embittered by the extreme profligacy of his son Henry, prince of Wales, who afterwards nobly discarded the vices and follies of his youth.

§ The following particular merits a recital. One of his abandoned companions having been indicted before Sir Wm. Gascoigne, the chief justice, the young prince was not ashamed to appear at the bar with the criminal, in order to give him countenance and protection. Finding that his presence did not over-awe the chief justice, he proceeded to insult him on his tribunal. But Gascoigne, mindful of his own dignity, and of the majesty of the laws, ordered the prince to be committed to prison. Henry, sensible of his error, quietly submitted to the order. When the affair was mentioned to his father, he is said to have exclaimed, "Happy is the king who has a magistrate sufficiently courageous to execute the laws upon such an offender; but still more happy, in having a son willing to submit to such chastisement."

Henry died, 1413, at the age of forty-six, in the fourteenth year of his reign. Notwithstanding distinguished military talents and political sagacity, he became a most unpopular sovereign. The illegality of his title, may have disaffected his subjects towards his person and his reign. He felt the miseries of guilt, and became suspicious and jealous. In religion, he was bigotted and intolerant.

19. His son, Henry V., ascended the throne in 1413. He laid aside his dissolute habits, as already intimated, and informed the companions of his pleasures, that they must enter on a similar reformation, if they would secure his favour. He also received the wise ministers of his father, who had checked his riots, with all the marks of esteem and confidence.

Henry early asserted by arms, the English claim to France. Taking advantage of disorders in that kingdom, he invaded it with an army of about thirty thousand men, and with half that number, defeated the French army, amounting to sixty thousand men, on the plains of Agincourt. His own loss did not exceed five hundred men, while that of the French amounted to twenty-two thousand in killed and prisoners.

§ Henry drew up his army on a narrow ground, between two woods, to cover each flank, and patiently expected an attack, having been surprised by the sudden appearance of the French, in great force, when his own army had been greatly reduced by sickness and fatigue. Had the French general declined a combat, the English must have relinquished the advantages of their situation; but the impetuous valour of the nobility, and a vain confidence in superior numbers, brought on an action, which proved to the English so glorious and successful.

After this battle, returning to England to recruit his forces, he landed again with an army of twenty-five thousand men, and fought his way to Paris. The war between Henry and the French king, was terminated by the treaty of Troyes, 1420. Henry then turned his arms with success against the dauphin, who assumed the style and authority of regent. Triumphing signally over his enemy, and realizing most of his wishes, he had nearly reached the summit of human glory. But his end was approaching, and one of the most heroic of the English monarchs, died at the early age of thirty-four years, and after a reign of nine years.

§ The treaty of Troyes was made with the Queen mother, and the duke of Burgundy—Charles, the French king, being insane. By this treaty it was agreed that he should marry the daughter of Charles, and receive the kingdom of France as her dowry, which, till the death of her father, he should govern as regent.

Henry was a true hero, and like all heroes, his views of conquest were pernicious in their tendency. Accordingly, England derived from his achievements, rather fame than solid advantage. He was able in the cabinet as well as in the field—was magnanimous, generous, and affable, but had more than the bigotry of his father in religion.

20. Henry VI., at the age of ten months, succeeded his father, in 1422, under the regency of the dukes of Gloucester and Bedford, the former for England, the latter for France. Henry was crowned king of France, at the age of eight years. At this era, in order to complete the conquest of that kingdom, it remained only to capture Orleans. The duke of Bedford, acting as regent of France, had laid siege to the place, but he was obliged to raise it by the valour and good conduct of Joan of Arc, the maid of Orleans. Thus was France saved, and England was afterwards stripped of almost every conquest it had made in that country.

When arrived at adult years, Henry proved himself to be mild and inoffensive, but deficient in the energy which becomes a sovereign. He had but a slender capacity. These defects in the king were supplied by his queen, the famous Margaret of Anjou, a woman of great talents, ambition, and heroism. She made a conspicuous figure in the wars which distracted his reign.

The insurrection of Jack Cade, was an event of some importance, and was quelled only after considerable bloodshed.

§ Jack Cade, a native of Ireland, whose crimes obliged him to retire into France, had assumed the name of Mortimer, and at the head of 20,000 Kentish men, encamped on Blackheath, in this way to London, in order to obtain a redress of grievances. The city opened its gates to Cade, who for some time maintained great order among his followers; but at length when he could not prevent them from committing depredations and outrages, the citizens, with the assistance of some soldiers, repulsed the rebels with great slaughter. Upon their submission, they received a general pardon, which was afterwards annulled, and both Cade, and many of his followers, were capitally punished for their rebellion.

The duke of Gloucester, who was heir to the crown in case the king should die without issue, was the favourite of the nation; but he had opposed the marriage of Henry with Margaret, and was therefore marked out by the latter for destruction. He was arrested and sent to prison, where he was found dead a few days afterwards. This event, in connection with the imbecility of the king, encouraged the Duke of York to assert his claim to the throne.

§ The duke of York, who was Richard, son of Lionel, second son of Edward III., was, however, averse to violent measures, and his forbearance, when appointed lieutenant of the kingdom, though amiable and unusual, proved the source of all those furious wars and commotions which ensued; for the queen at length persuaded Henry to annul the protectorship of Richard, and place the administration in the hands of the duke of Somerset. Richard then levied an army; but an account of the wars between the houses of York and Lancaster, properly belongs to the next period.

GERMANY.

21. In the history of the GERMAN EMPIRE, is to be noticed, the rise of the House of Austria, which constitutes an important portion of that empire. This event took place in the latter part of the former period, viz. 1274, when Rodolphus of Hapsbourg, a Swiss baron, was elected emperor of Germany. He owed his elevation to the jealousies of the electoral princes, who could not agree in the choice of any one of themselves. The king of Bohemia, to whom Rodolphus had been steward of the household, could not endure the supremacy of his former dependent; and refusing him

the customary homage for his Germanic possessions, Rodolphus stripped him of Austria, which has ever since remained in the family of its conqueror.

When Rodolphus ascended the throne, he found the empire distracted and almost ruined by anarchy and faction, but he restored order by his prudence and firmness. He was a prince generally esteemed for his virtues.

§ He demolished the retreats of the banditti, that every where infested the country, and executed great numbers of the marauders. The following anecdote, among others, is related of him.

A merchant complaining to him of an innkeeper at Nuremberg who refused to return a sum of money which he had deposited in the hands of the latter, Rodolphus, seeing the innkeeper soon afterwards, took an opportunity of praising his hat, and proposed an exchange. His proposal was naturally accepted, and he sent the hat as a token to the innkeeper's wife, desiring, in her husband's name, she would deliver to the bearer, the money which a merchant had left in his hands. By this stratagem, the plaintiff recovered his property, and the innkeeper was sentenced to pay a heavy fine.

Rodolphus had seven beautiful daughters, by means of whom, he contracted alliances, which proved highly advantageous to his posterity. He had also seven sons; but none of these survived him, except the duke of Austria. In Rodolphus began the good fortune of the house of Austria, of which he was the founder; a fortune which called forth the observation, "that Venus was even more favourable to them than Mars."

22. Adolphus of Nassau, was elected the next emperor of Germany, 1291, instead of the duke of Austria, the late emperor's son; but proving unworthy, he was deposed, and the duke, named Albert I., was duly raised to the empire, 1298. The pope claimed the empire, but finally acknowledged Albert.

This prince treated the Swiss with great rigour, contrary to the conduct of his father. Several of the Cantons were his by inheritance, but he formed the design of annexing the whole of the provinces to his dominion, and erecting them into a principality, for one of his sons. The Swiss revolted. The cantons of Schewitz, Uri, and Underwald, which always had resisted the authority of Austria, combined to assert their freedom; and a small army of four hundred or five hundred men, defeated an immense host of the Austrians, in the pass of Morgate, 1315. The rest of the Cantons, by degrees, joined the association, and with invincible perseverance, after sixty pitched battles with their enemies, they effected their freedom. It was the famous William Tell, who was instrumental in producing this revolution, and in laying the foundation of his country's liberty.

§ In so brief an outline of history as is attempted in this work, it will be impossible to include a separate account of every country. Several of the smaller ones must therefore be noticed in the account of others, or be grouped together. As this seems to be a fit place to touch on the affairs of Switzerland, a few particulars may be added. The story of William Tell, deserves a record. In this story is exemplified an instance of the lawless tyranny of the governor of Switzerland.

Geisler, governor of the Canton of Uri, had ordered his hat to be fixed upon a pole in a certain place, and commanded every passenger, on pain of death, to pay the same obeisance to it as to himself Tell, an inhabitant of Uri, indignant at this insulting mark of wanton tyranny, disdained to pay the homage required. Tell's death was determined, and he was condemned to be hanged, unless he should be able to strike with his arrow, an apple placed upon the head of his son. Being an excellent marksman, he accepted the alternative, and providentially cleft the apple without injuring the child. Geisler perceiving another arrow in his belt, asked him for what purpose that was intended. Tell heroically replied, "It was designed for you, if I had killed my son."

Condemned to perpetual imprisonment in a dungeon for this answer, he was bound and thrown into a boat, that Geisler himself might convey him across the lake of Altorf, to his castle. In the midst of the passage, a furious squall arose, and the cowardly governor was so intimidated by the danger he was in, that he unbound Tell, who was a most skilful boatman, and entreated him to row him safely across the lake. Tell soon effected his escape by swimming to the shore, and had an opportunity by the time Geisler arrived, to pierce the tyrant's heart with an arrow. This event paved the way for the conspiracy which followed.

23. Eight emperors succeeded Albert, during the remainder of this period; but a connected account of their reigns need not here be given. A few scattered particulars may be found below.

§ In the reign of Henry VIII., Germany groaned under all the miseries of plague and famine, by which whole towns were depopulated, and provinces brought to desolation. The rich sought an asylum in other countries, while the poor perished without pity or assistance; wolves, and other beasts of prey, compelled by hunger, quitted their dens, and rushing into the villages, satiated themselves with human blood; cataracts of water, bursting from the mountains, swept trees and houses before them with dreadful impetuosity; and the earth was convulsed by frequent shocks, which seemed to agitate it to its centre.

While Louis V. held the imperial sceptre, a spirit of fanaticism broke out in Alsace, and the lower class of people assembled under the banners of an innkeeper, who erected himself into a prophet, and persuaded his followers, that it was their indispensable duty to revenge the death of Christ, by an extirpation of the Jews. In obedience to this doctrine, they massacred great multitudes of that unhappy nation. In one place the carnage was so great, that the Jews themselves augmented the horror of the scene; for, being driven to despair, they butchered their own wives and children, and then murdered themselves, to elude the cruelty of their inhuman enemies. After some time, however, these frantic enthusiasts were driven out of the province; their sanguinary leader perished by the hands of the executioner, and the surviving Jews were permitted to live in peace.

In 1356, Charles IV., issued the celebrated Golden Bull, containing a declaration of the fundamental laws of the empire. The edict was so called from a golden seal termed Bulla.

The emperor Sigismund, became also king of Bohemia, in consequence of the death of his brother Winceslas. It was this emperor who betrayed the celebrated reformer, John Huss, to the Elector Palatine, who caused him to be burnt alive. The next year, Jerome of Prague suffered the same fate.

CHINA.

24. A part of the twentieth and twenty-first dynasties of the empire of China, is included in the present period. In the reign of Shistu of the twentieth dynasty, the famous canal was dug, which is nine hundred miles in length. Under some of the princes of this dynasty, the religion of Fo was established in the empire. Shunti was the last of the Tartar race, who held the sceptre in China.

The twenty-first dynasty was that of Ming, founded by Chu, who, ascending the throne, took the name of Fay-tsu. This dynasty, which commenced in 1368, lasted two hundred and eighty-one years, under seventeen emperors.

§ Chu had been a servant in the monastery of the bonzes. Heading a numerous company of revolters, he reduced many considerable cities and provinces, and defeated the imperial army in a battle. His successes were so great, that he assumed the title of emperor and fixed his court at Nankin. In a few months, however, he made himself master of Pekin, and erected that country into a sovereignty, which he gave to his fourth son. He proved to be a prince of great wisdom and penetration.

It is related of Ching-tsu, one of the emperors of this dynasty, that when specimens of precious stones were brought to him from a mine which had lately been discovered, he ordered it to be shut up, alleging, that it only harrassed his people with useless toil, as these stones could neither feed nor clothe them in times of scarcity.

Distinguished Characters in Period VII.

1. Dante, and } classic Italian poets.
2. Petrarch, }
3. Boccace, an Italian, one of the restorers of learning
4. Wickliffe, an English theologian and reformer.
5. Froissart, an entertaining French chronicler.
6. Gower, and } fathers of English poetry.
7. Chaucer, }

§ 1. Dante, (Alighieri,) who died at the age of fifty-seven years, early displayed poetical talents; but the ambition of being elevated among the ruling men of his native city, engaged him in continual discord and faction. He and his party were at length defeated, and with them he sought safety in banishment. While he was in this situation, he vented the bitterest reproaches against his enemies. The occasion of his death was, an affront which he received from the Venetians. The prince of Ravenna, (in which place he was in exile,) sent him to negociate with the Venetians, in order to avert a threatened war; but the magistrates of Venice treated the embassador with contempt, and refused to receive him within their walls. The irritable heart of Dante was so affected by this affront, that he could not survive it, and he died on his return to Ravenna.

His literary works owe their origin to his misfortunes and revengeful spirit. His great object seems to have been to pierce his enemies with the shafts of satire. The rancour of his feeling, mingled itself with the sweetness and graces of poetry. His poems are characterized by spirit, fire, and sublimity. His triple poem, of Paradise, Purgatory, and Hell, displays wonderful powers of genius.

2. Petrarch (Francis) is deservedly celebrated as one of the restorers of classical learning, and more, perhaps, than any other person, as the father of modern poetry. He displayed all the powers of genius and poetical inspiration, not only in his own native language, but in Latin. His sonnets are esteemed the sweetest, most elegant, and most highly finished verses, ever written in Italian; and his songs possess uncommon beauty and grace. Petrarch had a most charming fancy.

Some of the events of his life are rather singular; particularly his inextinguishable passion for his mistress Laura. He first saw this beautiful female in 1627, after he had fixed his residence at Vaucluse, near Avignon, and he was smitten with all the pangs of love. But though the soft passion was expressed in the softest language of poetry, the heart of the fair one was by no means moved To divert the melancholy which ensued, he travelled through various countries, and was at last persuaded to enter into the service of Pope John XXII. But, "amor vincit omnia," and Petrarch, abandoning the pleasures of curiosity and of greatness, fled to the shades of Vaucluse, to converse with his beloved Laura. He again devoted his hours to studious pursuits, and to the amatory effusions of his muse. But though the idolized fair one heeded not his poetry, the world did; and Rome, Paris, and Naples, at the same moment, invited him to come and receive the poetical crown. Rome prevailed, and in that famed seat of empire and of genius, the poet's brow was entwined with the resplendent honour. He was occasionally drawn from his favourite residence, on public business; and it was during an absence in 1348, that he was informed of Laura's death, which affected him with the deepest gloom.

The poet's purity in this affair, has been maintained by some, and denied by others; and some parts of his character certainly afford too much ground for the opinion of the latter. Petrarch was an ecclesiastic, though he never took priest's orders. He died at the age of seventy, 1374.

3. Boccace, (John,) born at Certaldo, in Tuscany, 1313, studied under Petrarch, who was his friend and patron. He lived abroad for a time, but afterwards returned to his native village, where he spent the remainder of his days, in literary pursuits. His constitution was weakened by his great application, and he died of a sickness in the stomach, 1375.

His works are both Latin and Italian. He possessed uncommon learning, and he shares with a few others the honour of contributing to the revival of learning in Europe. "Decameron," a licentious, though witty, satirical, and elegantly written romance, is his most celebrated composition. His poetry is not equal to that of Petrarch, but his prose is unrivalled, for its simplicity, grace, and varied elegance.

4. Wickliffe, (John de) was professor of divinity, in the University of Oxford, and deservedly considered as the forerunner of Luther, in the reformation. His elevation to the professorship of Oxford, exposed him to the jealousy of the monks, and he was soon displaced. He felt the indignity keenly, and it was not long before he boldly came out against the errors and encroachments of Rome The Romish clergy, with the pope at their head, took the alarm, and employed every effort to suppress the doctrines of Wickliffe. Most of his doctrines were pronounced as heretical, by the several councils that were called. He was seized as a heretic, by the emissaries of the Pope, and tried; but the judges, although they enjoined him silence, permitted him to depart in safety, as they feared the nobility and people. These, in general, favoured Wickliffe. Not at all intimidated, the reformer continued to preach his peculiar sentiments, and they became still more widely known. But the penal statutes were severe, and some who embraced the new heresy, were delivered over to punishment.

Wickliffe, in the mysterious providence of God, died at a time when nothing was wanting to emancipate the English nation from the tyranny of Rome, but the boldness, perseverance, and eloquence of a popular leader. Wickliffe's noble struggle proved almost abortive, and little was thought of it, till Luther arose to establish the same doctrines on an imperishable basis.

Trialogus, is almost the only work of Wickliffe's that was printed.

5. Froissart, (John,) as an historian, excelled all the writers of his time. His narrative of the events which took place in England, France, and Spain, from 1326 to 1400, is exceedingly lively and entertaining. He personally witnessed many transactions which he has described. He was a chronicler both of political events and of chivalric manners. He was bred to the church, but he was a greater reader of romances, than of his breviary. Of gayety, he was fond to an excessive degree. "Well loved I," as he said of his youth, in one of his poems, (for he wrote poetry as well as history,) "to see dances and carolling, and to hear the songs of minstrels, and tales of glee. It pleased me to attach myself to those who took delight in hounds and hawks." "My ears quickened at the sound of opening the wine flask; for I took great pleasure in drinking, and in fair array, and in fresh and delicate viands." He began his chronicle at the age of twenty, and continued it many years, travelling through England, Scotland, France, and other places. He was born at Valenciennes, in the year 1337, and died in 1397.

6. Gower (Sir John) was born in Yorkshire, 1320. He was eminent, both in law and poetry. He is, by some, associated with Chaucer, as a father of English poetry. He lived a little longer than Chaucer, though born eight years sooner, and was the successor of the latter in the laurel. His principal production in poetry, was "Confessio Amantis;" though he left behind, other poems of considerable spirit and energy. Though gentle in manner, he inveighed boldly against the debaucheries of the times, the immorality of the clergy, the wickedness of corrupt judges, and the vices of an abandoned court. He died at the age of eighty-two.

7. Chaucer (Geoffrey) was born in London, 1328. Compared with Chaucer, all who preceded him, not excepting Gower, were merely pioneers in English poetry: they were scarcely poets. He is, therefore, more commonly considered the father of English song. Though in the idiom of the fourteenth century, his poetry is not devoid of great smoothness and delicacy; the sentiments are bold, the characters are well supported, and the genius of the poet is every where brilliant, sprightly, and sublime. The Canterbury Tales, are his best production.

Chaucer enjoyed a signal share in the favours of royalty, and his honours and emoluments exceeded far the ordinary lot of poets. This circumstance may, perhaps, be partly owing to the fact, that he had a princely brother-in-law, John Gaunt, duke of Lancaster. At one period of his life, he suffered persecution, in consequence of embracing the tenets of Wickliffe. The latter part of his days was spent at a distance from the bustle and intrigues of public life, and in his retirement at Woodstock, and afterwards at Donnington, he devoted himself to the cultivation of his muse. He died 25th October, 1400.

PERIOD VIII.

The period of the Reformation; extending from the Taking of Constantinople, 1453 *years A. C., to the Edict of Nantes,* 1598 *years A. C.*

TURKISH EMPIRE.

SECT. 1. The history of the Turkish Empire, at this era, is signalized by the taking of Constantinople, and the consequent extinction of the Eastern Empire of the Romans, 1453. The Turks effected the object under Mahomet the Great, the Turkish Sultan.

Constantine was the name of the last emperor of the East, as it was also the name of the first. His dominions had become exceedingly circumscribed. The Turks had gradually encroached upon its borders, and Constantinople would soon have become the seat of the Ottoman power, had they not been obliged to defend themselves against the Tartars.

Mahomet II., after some delay, commenced the project which had long engaged the attention of the Turks. The indolent inhabitants of Constantinople, made but a feeble preparation for defence, and all Europe was supine and indifferent. The city was assailed both by sea and land—the walls were battered down with cannon, and all who opposed were massacred. The emperor was slain, and the city soon surrendered. The Turks forbore to destroy the imperial edifices, and the churches were converted into mosques. The exercise of their religion, however, was allowed to all the christians, and they have, till lately, chosen their own patriarch. The Eastern empire, from the building of its capital, had subsisted 1123 years.

After the fall of Constantinople, Greece and Epirus were subdued; and Italy might probably have shared a similar fate, but for the fleet of the Venetians, who opposed the arms of Mahomet with considerable success: but peace was soon concluded between the hostile powers. The death of Mahomet the Great, occurred 1481.

§ Mahomet was a youth of only about twenty-one years, when he undertook the project of extinguishing the empire of the East. The force with which he invested Constantinople, was fully adequate to the object, being nearly three hundred thousand men; while the whole population of that city, did not amount to more than one hundred thousand.

The Greeks, notwithstanding their degeneracy, displayed considerable bravery. Their all was at stake, and a small but faithful band adhered to Constantine, till they were nearly annihilated. Seeing his dearest friends fall by his side, and himself at last remaining, surrounded only by enemies, he exclaimed in the bitterness of grief, "Has death then made such havoc, that not one Christian is left to take my life?" As he spoke, a Turk to whom his person was unknown, for he had prudently laid aside the purple, struck him in the face; a second blow succeeded from another hand; and he fell, in the forty-ninth year of his age, a glorious example of honourable resolution, in expiring with his defenders, rather than surviving them.

Mahomet liberally patronized the arts and sciences; and to compensate for the migration of those learned Greeks, who, on the fall of the empire, spread themselves over the countries of Europe, invited both artists and men of letters to his capital from other kingdoms.

The successors of this sovereign during the remainder of the present period, were Bajazet II., Selim I., Solyman I., Selim II., Amurath III., and Mahomet III.

§ Bajazet II., prosecuted various wars against the Hungarians, Venetians, Persians, and Saracens, but having resigned the government to his son, who had revolted and was supported by the Janizaries, he was soon after poisoned by the order of the latter.

His son and successor, Selim I., was a prosperous, but tyrannical prince; who, in 1517, conquered Egypt, Aleppo, Antioch, Tripoli, Damascus, and Gaza.

Solyman I., surnamed the Magnificent, succeeded Selim in 1520; and was one of the most accomplished, enterprising, successful, and warlike of the Turkish princes. He took Buda, and besieged Vienna. From the latter place, however, he was obliged to retire with the loss of eighty thousand men.

Selim II., his son, besieged and took Cyprus and Tunis; but his fleet was defeated at Lepanto, with the capture or destruction of almost all his ships.

Amurath III. strangled his five brothers immediately upon his accession. This prince extended his dominions by the addition of Raab in Hungary, and of Tibris in Persia. In this reign, the Janizaries having lost their submission, and in great part, their discipline, began to kill their commanders, whenever they were dissatisfied with them.

His son, Mahomet III. was a monster of barbarity, having begun his reign by strangling his nineteen brothers, and drowning ten of his father's wives. He finally put to death his eldest son, a prince of estimable qualities, on an unfounded suspicion of ambitious views.

ITALIAN STATES.

2. We shall pursue the history of Italy, by giving an account of only two or three of the States of which it was composed. The events in the Italian history are not politically important at this era. It is chiefly in reference to the influence of Florence on the literature of the times, and the ecclesiastical influence of the Papal dominions, that these portions of Italy will be brought more particularly into view.

Florence, under the Medici, enjoyed a high degree of splendour, during this period. It was an era, in the cultivation of the sciences and elegant arts. The family of the Medici held sway in this country from the year 1428 to 1569, when Cosmo de Medici the Great was entitled Grand Duke of Tuscany. Under the title of the Republic of Florence, which they governed, were included not only Tuscany, of which Florence is the capital, but Modena, Mantua, and one or two other states.

§ Cosmo de Medici died in 1464, who, though the private subject of a republic, had more riches than any king in Europe, and laid out more money in works of taste, learning, and charity, than all the kings, princes, and states, of that or the subsequent age, the individuals of his own family excepted. His religious foundations were unrivalled. His private buildings were equally sumptuous. No palace in Europe at that time exceeded his in Florence. He had besides many others. With all this public magnificence and expenditure, he was in his private conversation, humble and unassuming; and in his person plain and modest. He was not celebrated for learning, though he was the greatest patron of learned men of his age.

Cosmo was succeeded in the government by his son Peter, and he by his sons Lorenzo and Giuliano. The latter was soon murdered, and Lorenzo died aged no more than fifty-four years, illustrious lik his predecessors, in every public and private virtue.

The tranquillity of the republic was much disturbed by wars with the Venetians and Genoese, for many years. In the course of these commotions, Florence assumed the popular government, but it was quickly reversed by the emperor Charles V., who, laying siege to the city, forced it to capitulate, and restored the family of the Medici.

Cosmo, the second of that name, now (1537) succeeded to the ducal crown, which he wore with honour, during thirty-eight years. The encouragement he gave to the practice and study of all the fine arts, proves him to have been one of the greatest patrons of human genius, since the days of Augustus. The names of his sons were John and Garcia. The latter was of a furious, vindictive disposition, and quarrelling one day with his brother, stabbed him to the heart with a dagger. The father charged him with the murder, but the youth denying it, was introduced into the room where the body lay, which is said to have bled, (doubtless by chance,) at his approach. He then threw himself at his father's feet, and confessed his guilt. The father, who had resolved on the part he was to act, solemnly desired his son to prepare for death, adding, that he ought to think himself happy in losing a life he was unworthy to enjoy, by the hands of him who gave it. He then unsheathed the dagger with which the cardinal had been murdered, and plunged it into the bosom of his son.

3. That part of Italy which constitutes the dominions of his holiness, became the scene of much crime and contention during this period. Both the temporal and spiritual power of the popes, was now at its height. In 1498, the papacy was enjoyed by Alexander VI., a monster of wickedness. Charles VIII., of France, had resolved on an expedition into Italy. The pope and the duke of Milan, who encouraged him in it, immediately betrayed him, and joined the interest of the king of Naples, who was the object of attack on the part of Charles. The latter, however, now first besieged the pope in Rome, and forced him to submission, but at length devoutly kissed his feet. He then marched against Naples, while its timid prince, Alphonso, fled to Sicily, after absolving his subjects from their allegiance. Charles entered Naples in triumph, but lost his new kingdom almost as soon as he had gained it. A league was formed against Charles, between the pope, the emperor Maximilian, Ferdinand of Arragon, Isabella of Castile, and the Venetians; and on his return to France, the troops he had left to guard his conquests, were all driven from Italy.

§ It has been remarked, that from the decisive effect of this confederacy, the sovereigns of Europe derived a useful lesson of policy, and first adopted the idea of preserving a balance of power, by that tacit league, which is understood to be always subsisting, for the prevention of the co-ordinate aggrandizement of any particular state.

History relates with horror, the crimes of Alexander VI., and his son Cæsar Borgia; their murders, robberies, profanations, and incests. They compassed their ends in attaining every object of their ambition, but with the universal abhorrence of mankind. Their death seems to have been a sort of retribution for their crimes, so far as retribution is known on earth.

If an author, Guicciardini, who was a mortal enemy to Alexander, may be believed, Borgia had sent a present of some flasks of poisoned wine to the cardinal of Corneto, in whose garden they proposed to sup, but ordered the servant to give none of it to any person. Alexander soon after coming into the garden, and calling for wine before supper, the servant gave him some from the poisoned flasks, thinking the prohibition could not extend to the Pope, however rare and valuable the wine might be; and Borgia, in the mean time appearing, unconsciously drank of the same wine with his father. They both immediately felt the symptoms of the poison, and Alexander died the next day; but Borgia, having drank his wine much diluted, survived with the loss of his skin and hair. He was afterwards stripped of all his possessions by Pope Julius II., and at last perished in miserable obscurity in Spain.

FRANCE.

Branch of Valois.—Branch of Orleans.

4. Louis XI., began to reign in 1461. He immediately removed all his late father's ministers, proceeded to humble the nobles, and in almost every respect acted the tyrant towards his subjects. Indeed, his character is that of a most deceitful, profligate and cruel prince; he followed too nearly the odious Tiberius in his measures. He left, however, some good regulations for the encouragement of commerce, and for the effectual administration of justice. Notwithstanding the odiousness of his character, he was the first of the French kings, on whom the title of His most Christian Majesty was conferred.

§ His severity occasioned a revolt of several of the first lords of the kingdom. The war which thence arose, they entitled "the war of the public good." His sanguinary disposition is evidenced by the following fact. When he pronounced sentence of death on a certain nobleman, he ordered that his infant children should be placed beneath the scaffold, to be sprinkled by the blood which gushed from the body of their parent. This was an almost incredible instance of refined cruelty, and cold barbarity. Louis died a victim of superstitious terror and remorse of conscience.

5. Charles VIII., surnamed the Affable, at the age of thirteen years, succeeded his father, under the regency of Anne of France, his sister, 1483. His marriage with Anne of Brittany, who was promised to Maximilian of Austria, occasioned a short war with the Germans. His expedition into Italy, and his conquest and subsequent loss of Naples have already been noticed in the Italian history. He reigned about fifteen years.

§ His surname is indicative of his disposition and manners but he led a life of intemperance, and was early cut off by this vice, in his twenty-eighth year. The direct line of Philip of Valois terminated with this monarch, as he left no issue.

6. Louis XII., who was duke of Orleans, and great grandson of Charles V., ascended the throne as the nearest heir, 1498. He was idolized by the French, and obtained and deserved the title of "The Father of his People," by his frugal policy, which eased them from taxes. Yet he was ambitious and imprudent in his military enterprises.

He conquered the Milanese and Genoa, but in prosecuting his claim to Naples, though he obtained some advantage at first, he was unsuccessful in the end. He was duped by his associates, Ferdinand of Spain, and pope Alexander VI. The whole of Naples finally fell into the treacherous hands of Ferdinand; nor did the French king long retain his other conquests in Italy, since they revolted from him on the first opportunity. Louis died suddenly, while preparing to recover, by arms, his lost Italian possessions.

§ In justifying himself for the pardon of his enemies, Louis made an observation worthy of royalty. "The king of France does not revenge the injuries done to the duke of Orleans." What this prince also said in vindication of his economy, will always be praised "I had rather see my courtiers laugh at my avarice, than my people weep on account of my expenses." It was an unhappiness, however, that he procured, in part, his supplies of money by the sale of offices, which was a very dangerous example.

7. Francis I., count of Angouleme, was called to the throne, 1515, Louis having died without male issue. He was a nephew of the late king, and began his reign at the age of twenty-one.

His real power, and the high opinion which he entertained of his own greatness, led him, in 1519, into competition with the celebrated Charles V., who had just ascended the throne of Spain. Charles, as grandson of the emperor Maximilian, upon the death of the latter, preferred his claim to the empire, but was opposed by Francis. Charles obtained the election, and these princes now became sworn enemies. Their mutual claims on each other's dominions, caused seas of blood to flow, in wars that lasted more than thirty-eight years.

§ Francis began hostilities by attacking Navarre. He first won and then lost that kingdom. The emperor attacked Picardy, and his troops at the same time wrested Milan out of the hands of the French

Henry VIII., of England, whose friendship had been assiduously courted by both parties, was brought over for a time to the side of Charles.

Just at this juncture, Francis, unfortunately, quarrelled with his best general, the constable of Bourbon, who revenged himself by deserting to the emperor. The constable was invested with command in the army of Charles, and thus greatly added to the superiority which was already apparent in the generals of the latter. The consequences were such as might have been expected. The French were defeated in the battle of Biagrassa. In this engagement, Bayard, the model of knights, perished. At his death, he replied to the marks of pity shown by the duke of Bourbon, with these words: "It is you who ought to be pitied, for fighting against your king, your country, and your oaths."

A temporary success attended the French arms in the capture of the capital of the Milanese; but a sad reverse soon followed in the battle of Pavia. That battle was fought on the 24th of February, 1525, and resembled in its catastrophe, those won by the English at Poictiers and Agincourt. Twenty-five thousand French were slain, and Francis himself made prisoner. He had the mortification to find himself the captive of that very man, the constable, whom he had treated with the greatest hauteur.

Europe being alarmed by the aggrandizement of Charles, a league of several states was formed against him, in favour of the captive monarch. In this league, England was included. The emperor was thus in a manner forced to liberate his prisoner, and he derived little benefit from his good fortune. The severity of the terms respecting his ransom was such, that the states general refused to fulfil them.

On the renewal of the war, Henry VIII. took part with France, but the powerful Charles was not intimidated. Resolving on an invasion of his enemy's country, he inundated Provence with fifty thousand men. But the defensive operations of the French were very successful, and Charles returned sorrowfully into Italy, having lost the one half of his army, cut off by diseases and famine.

In the interval of a truce, which was concluded at Nice, for ten years, Charles passed through France to the Netherlands, and on the part of Francis, was treated with the utmost courtesy and hospitality. He had previously stipulated to grant the French king the investiture of Milan. But though he was every where received with the utmost pomp, and staid seven days in Paris, where he was loaded with every mark of friendship and confidence, he left no authentic testimony of his promise.

The seeds of a renewed contest were thus sown, but though the French were victorious in the battle of Cerizoles, they derived from it little or no advantage. The Imperialists, on the whole, had a decided superiority, and France must have been ruined had not the disorders of Germany forced the emperor to conclude the treaty of Crepi, with Francis, 1544. The latter purchased a peace with Henry VIII., who had once more changed sides, and favoured Charles.

8. Francis died in 1547. He has the reputation of a great prince, and would have appeared greater, but for the manifest superiority of his illustrious rival. Notwithstanding the wars in which France was engaged during the reign of this monarch, he left his kingdom in a flourishing and prosperous state. Literature and the arts made great progress in France under his auspices, and the French court acquired that polish and refinement in taste and manners, for which it has since been so conspicuous throughout the world.

§ "The fine qualities of this prince," says Millot, "his open temper, beneficence, honour, generosity, and courage, have not been able to cover his faults, rashness in his enterprises, negligence in his affairs, fickleness in his conduct, prodigality in his expenses, and excess in his pleasures. Whatever merit he was possessed of, he would have met with fewer encomiums, had he not caressed and favoured men of letters, by whose suffrages the reputation of sovereigns is fixed. He founded the royal college and printing house. At the same time that he encouraged the culture of the learned languages, he had the prudence to command that the public acts should be written in French. In the same manner, he gave life to the fine arts, built Fontainbleau, and began the Louvre. In order to polish the manners of the court, he drew to it the most respectable women and distinguished prelates."

9. Henry II. succeeded his father in 1547. This prince, though brave and polite, was the slave of pleasure, and the dupe of favourites. He continued the war in which his father had been engaged with Charles V., and that emperor's son Philip II., of Spain. He obtained considerable advantage over Charles at the siege of Metz, but was terribly defeated by Philip, at St. Quentin. The event most glorious to his reign, was the recovery of Calais from the English, in 1557. The duke of Guise captured the place in eight days, to the surprise of all Europe.

The origin of those civil wars which distracted France during the three succeeding reigns, may be dated from this reign, or rather from that of Francis I., when the Huguenots, who were Calvinists, or Protestants, began to be persecuted. The spirit of persecution greatly increased during the reign of Henry.

§ The death of this monarch was owing to an accident which befel him at a tournament. Wishing to amuse the ladies with a tilt between himself and the count of Montgomery, who was esteemed the most dexterous justler of his time, he gaily entered the lists. In their rencounter both their lances were broken, and the count thrown from his horse. In his fall, the broken trunk of the spear, still, remaining in his hand, struck the king's right eye, and produced so violent a contusion as to terminate his life.

10. His son, Francis II., was raised to the throne in 1559. He was the husband of Mary, queen of Scots, and died the next year, having reigned about seventeen months. The only important event in this reign, was the conspiracy of the Protestants against the king, and the Guises, who were five brothers, at the head of the Catholics. Two of these, the duke of Guise and the cardinal of Lorraine, were conspicuous in the government. This conspiracy was detected, and 1200 of those engaged in it, were put to death.

§ The Protestants were wearied with the persecutions they had so long endured, and came to a resolution to devote their lives to the defence of their liberties. They were secretly abetted by the prince of Conde, brother to the king of Navarre. The prince, however, escaped punishment, having pleaded his cause before the king, in person.

11. Charles IX., a boy only ten years old, succeeded his brother, 1560, under the regency of Catharine de Medicis, who had been the wife of Henry, and was notorious for her profligacy and ambition. The difficulties between the Catholics and Protestants had arisen to a great height. Some of the first men of the French court, were included among the latter, particularly the prince of Conde and Admiral Coligny. Their influence was too great to be resisted; and after the conference held at Poissy, liberty was granted to the Protestants to exercise their worship without the walls of the towns. The violation, soon after, of the edict granting this liberty, occasioned the sanguinary civil war, which for a long time filled France with misery and blood.

§ The Protestant religion had spread greatly at court, as well as in the capital and the provinces, even under Francis I. The persecution of the Protestants under Henry II., only increased their number, and produced that exasperation of feeling, which ended in the conspiracy, already mentioned, under Francis II.

The celebrated conference at Poissy, was attended by the young king, the queen mother, and the whole court. Theodore Beza, an illustrious reformer, defended the Protestants, while the cardinal of Lorraine, undertook the cause of the Catholics. Both parties, as is usual on such occasions, claimed the victory. It was, however, difficult any longer to refuse certain concessions to the Protestants. Indeed, the queen mother found it politic to grant them liberty of worship, and to favour the prince of Conde, in order to counterbalance the power of the Guises.

The Protestants, in the war which ensued, were headed by Admiral Coligny, who was assisted by 10,000 Germans from the Palatinate. The command of the Catholics was assumed by Guise and Montmorency, who were aided by Philip of Spain. The latter were always victorious, though the Protestants were too powerful to be despised; and in the conditions of peace which they obtained, was included the toleration of their religion. Murders and assassinations aggravated the horrors of civil war. The duke of Guise fell by the hand of a religious enthusiast. And even the peace which was secured, was only a prelude to more awful scenes of atrocity and blood.

It became now the policy of the government to caress the Protestants, in order to destroy them. They received extraordinary marks of favour; even the prudence of Coligny was lulled asleep; and on the occasion of the marriage of the king of Navarre with the sister of Charles, these persecuted people were allured to court. By the order of the government, a dreadful massacre of the Protestants then took place, the horrid plan having been all previously arranged. On the night of the twenty-third of August, it being St. Bartholomew's, there perished in Paris and France, 60,000, some reckon 100,000 Protestants. The duke of Guise (Henry, son of Francis) went in person to Coligny's gate, and caused that great man to be murdered. The streets and houses in Paris floated in blood. The king barbarously fired upon his unhappy subjects, and afterwards beheld with pleasure Coligny's body insulted by the populace.

To crown this horrid act, the king declared that every thing was done by his command; the parliament ordered an annual procession to celebrate the deliverance of the kingdom; a medal was struck with this legend, *piety put the sword into the hands of justice*, and at Rome and in Spain, the massacre was made a subject of public rejoicings.

Calvinism was not at all crushed by this infernal plot, infernally executed. It only became more formidable through despair, and now both of the Bourbons,—the king of Navarre as well as the prince of Conde, were enlisted in the Protestant cause. It was found necessary again to grant them liberty of conscience. Charles died soon after the massacre of St. Bartholomew, at the age of twenty-four years.

12. The successor of Charles IX., was Henry III., duke f Anjou, who had just been elected king of Poland, 1574. He was a weak and worthless prince, joining to the utmost depravity of manners, the external observances of the lowest superstition. He became the scorn of his subjects, and the dupe of the contending factions. It was in his reign, that the Catholics, incensed on account of the privileges conferred on the Huguenots, formed the famous league for the purpose of extirpating them, having the duke of Guise at its head.

§ This league was nominally for the defence of the state and ..

religion, but in reality, besides the extirpation of the Protestant faith, it had in view the usurpation of all the powers of government. The king, with the weakest policy, united himself to this league, and thus became the avowed enemy of a large portion of his subjects. But in carrying on his military operations against the Protestants, he found himself thwarted at every step, by the duke of Guise and the Cardinal of Lorraine. To dispel the fears which he entertained from these men, he put them to death, by the hands of assassins. After a reign of fifteen years, the king himself was assassinated, 1589, by a fanatic monk.

13. On the death of Henry III., who died without children, the sceptre of France passed to the house of Bourbon, represented at this time by Henry III., of Navarre. As king of France, he is known by the name of Henry IV., afterwards surnamed the Great.

As his reign extends into the next period, the following particulars only, will be mentioned at present. He had been educated in the reformed religion by his mother, who avowed herself its protector. At the age of sixteen, he had been declared head of the party of the Huguenots. When invited to Paris at the peace of 1572, to marry the sister of Charles IX., he narrowly escaped from the massacre of St. Bartholomew, but remained three years a prisoner. Although his first military enterprises were unsuccessful, yet, when on the death of Charles, he again took the field against the army of the league, he defeated it in the battle of Coutras, 1587, and still more signally in that of Argues, 1589. After the death of Henry III., he won the celebrated battle of Ivry, against the army of the League, then commanded by the duke of Mayenne, who had proclaimed the cardinal of Bourbon, king, under the title of Charles X. As a protestant, however, he was environed with difficulties; a large portion of the people refused to submit to him; and influenced by the earnest entreaties of the duke of Sully, as well as by views of policy, he renounced protestantism, and became a catholic, 1594. In 1596, the duke of Mayenne submitted to Henry, and the whole kingdom acknowledged him as its sovereign.

ENGLAND.

Branch of York. House of Tudor.

14. Henry VI., had been on the throne of England since the year 1422; but the wars which now commenced between

his house and that of York, rendered his situation most insecure, and, at length, hurled him from his throne. Justice was on the side of Richard, duke of York, as he was a descendant from the second son of Edward III., while Henry was a descendant from Edward's third son. The whole nation took the side of one or the other, and each party was distinguished by a particular symbol. That of the Lancastrians was the red rose, and that of the Yorkites the white rose Hence, this contention was known by the name of the "quarrel of the two roses." Hostilities commenced in 1455.

§ The principal battles which were fought, previous to the accession of Edward IV., were, that of St. Albans, in which Henry was defeated and taken prisoner, and Richard assumed the title of Protector—that which was fought on Blòreheath, in Staffordshire, and which terminated in favour of Richard—that of Northampton, in which Henry was defeated and again taken prisoner, by the Earl of Warwick—and that of Wakefield, in which Henry's queen, Margaret of Anjou, gained a complete victory over Richard, who, together with his second son, was slain.

Upon the death of the duke of York, the earl of Warwick, known by the name of King Maker, from the conspicuous part he bore in the contentions of the times, took command of the forces belonging to that party.

15. Upon the death of Richard, the young duke of York, his son and successor, entered London at the head of a numerous army, amidst the greetings of the citizens, and assumed the powers of government. He did not, however, fully consider himself as king, until he had obtained, (1461.) at Towton, a signal victory over the adherents of Henry, of whom 36,000 were killed. His title was that of Edward IV. After various turns of fortune, in which he was once deposed, and Henry re-instated on the throne, he finally triumphed over the Lancastrians, in the desperate battle of Tewkesbury, in which Margaret, and her son, the Prince of Wales, were taken prisoners. The latter was assassinated, and king Henry, who had been confined in the tower, was found dead a few days afterwards. Margaret, whose ambition had kindled the desolating war, was punished only with imprisonment. She was afterwards ransomed by the king of France, and died in that country.

§ It is said that the young prince, when brought before the king, and asked in an insulting tone, by the latter, how he dared to invade his dominion, replied, with a spirit congenial to his high birth, that he came thither to claim his just inheritance. The ungenerous Edward, indignant at his answer, and insensible to pity, struck him on the face with his gauntlet; and the dukes of Clarence and Gloucester, with others, taking the blow as a signal for further violence, hurried the prince into the next apartment, and there dispatched him with their daggers.

It is said also, and generally believed, that Richard, duke of Gloucester, killed king Henry with his own hands.

When Edward was secured on the throne, his spirit sunk in indolence and pleasure. The energies of his reign seem to have terminated with the civil wars, unless we except his acts of detestable tyranny. He put to death, on the most frivolous pretence, his brother Clarence; and preparing to gratify his subjects, by a war with France, he died suddenly, in the forty-second year of his age, poisoned, as was suspected, by his brother Richard, duke of Gloucester.

§ The only favour which the king granted his brother, Clarence, after his condemnation, was, to leave him the choice of his death. The duke chose to be drowned in a butt of Malmsey—a whimsical choice, which implies that he had an extraordinary predilection for that liquor.

16. Edward V., a minor, succeeded his father, 1483, under the protection of his uncle, the duke of Gloucester. A few days afterwards, the duke of Gloucester caused himself to be proclaimed, under the title of Richard III. The young king and his brother having been removed to the tower by Richard's order, under pretence of guarding them, disappeared about that time. The diabolical Richard, had inhumanly deprived them of life.

§ Richard possessed a fierce and savage nature, and in making his way to the throne, had recourse to the most perfidious and cruel acts. Endeavouring to gain the assistance of lord Hastings, and finding that nobleman inflexibly favourable to the children of Edward, he accused him of treason, and ordered him to be decapitated, without even the appearance of legal forms.

The murder of the two young princes, was as deep a tragedy as any recorded in English history. Richard gave orders to Sir Robert Brakenbury, constable of the tower, to put his nephews to death; but this gentleman, who had sentiments of honour, refused to stain his hands with the infamous deed. The tyrant then engaged Sir James Tyrrel, who, choosing three associates, like himself, came in the night time to the door of the chamber, where the princes were lodged, and sending in the assassins, he bade them execute their commission, while he himself staid without. They found the unoffending young princes in bed, and fallen into a sweet and profound sleep. After suffocating them with the bolster and pillows, they showed their naked bodies to Tyrrel, who ordered them to be buried at the foot of the stairs, deep in the ground, under a heap of stones. These circumstances were all confessed by the bloody actors, in the following reign. In the reign of Charles II., the bones of two persons were found in the place indicated, which exactly corresponded, by their sizes, to Edward V., and his brother; and being judged the undoubted remains of these unhappy princes, were deposited in Westminster Abbey.

17. The earl of Richmond, the only surviving heir of the house of Lancaster, became the instrument, under divine Providence, of avenging the awful crimes of Richard. Assisted by the French king, he landed in England, and revived the spirits of a party almost extinguished in the kingdom. He gave battle to Richard, 1485, in the field of Bosworth, and entirely defeated the army of the usurper, who was slain while fighting with the most desperate courage. This battle terminated the terrible contest between the houses of York and Lancaster—a contest which lasted thirty years, and in which twelve sanguinary pitched battles were fought, and 100,000 brave men, including eighty princes of the blood. perished on the field, or by the hand of the executioner.

§ The person of Richard was as deformed as his character was detestable. He was small of stature, hump-backed, ugly in his features, and had his left arm withered. This infirmity, which had attended him from his birth, he pretended, on a certain occasion when he wished to confound lord Hastings, was the effect of Jane Shore's incantations, knowing that this nobleman had engaged in an intrigue with that lady.

18. The crown which Richard wore in the engagement that proved fatal to his life, was immediately placed on the head of the conqueror. The earl of Richmond assumed the title of Henry VII., Aug. 22, 1485. By marrying a daughter of Edward IV., he united the rights of the two houses of York and Lancaster. He was a descendant from Edmund Tudor, and first king of the house of Tudor.

Henry was a prudent and politic prince, but unhappily prejudiced against the adherents of the house of York. A degree of discontent was thus engendered, which tended to jeopardise his government. The general tranquillity of his reign was, on this account, occasionally disturbed by plots and conspiracies—two of which were rather singular, consisting in attempts to counterfeit the persons of the heirs of York, and to enforce their claims to the crown.

§ The name of one of these impostors was Lambert Simnel, the son of a baker, who counterfeited the person of the earl of Warwick, son of the late duke of Clarence. The name of the other was Perkin Warbeck, the son of a Flemish Jew, who personated the duke of York, who had been smothered in the tower. They were supported by men of distinction in the nation, and gave Henry great trouble, but were finally subdued and taken. Simnel was spared and made a scullion in the king's kitchen. Warbeck expiated his crime on the scaffold.

The aversion of Henry to the house of York, shewed itself even in his treatment of his wife. Though in the highest degree virtuous, amiable, and obsequious, she never met with a proper return of affection, or even of complaisance, from her husband; and the malignant ideas of faction, in his sullen mind, prevailed over all the sentiments of conjugal endearment.

Henry was by nature a despot; and indeed the principles of despotism were congenial to all the sovereigns of the Tudor race. Yet his sagacity led him generally to pacific counsels. Though he was by no means a popular prince, he was useful to the nation, having enacted many wise laws, promoted industry, encouraged commerce, patronized the arts of civilized life, and curbed and softened the spirit of a proud and rude aristocracy. His policy gave a death blow to the Feudal system. The greatest stain in this prince's character was his avarice, which, in the latter part of his reign, prompted to the most oppressive exactions.

§ He is said to have left at his death, in ready money, a sum equal to £10,000,000 at present.

19. Henry VIII. succeeded his father in the eighteenth year of his age, 1509. He came to the throne with flattering prospects, considered whether in respect to the improved and tranquil state of the kingdom, the affection and high expectation of his people, or his own supposed good qualities.

§ The succession was well established, the contending titles of York and Lancaster were fully united in him, the treasury was well filled, and peace and prosperity were universally enjoyed. The young prince's person was beautiful, his manners elegant, his disposition frank, his mind highly cultivated for the times, and his native talents commanding.

The nation, however, was greatly disappointed in its young prince. He soon shewed himself an unprincipled tyrant; and both friends and foes felt, at times, the effects of his caprice and cruelty. His ministers were talented men, but he took pleasure in abusing them. Only archbishop Cranmer continued to be an object of favour to the last. Cardinal

Wolsey, in whom he placed unbounded confidence for a time, was finally discarded. Wolsey, more than any one else, by ministering to the pleasures and ambition of the king, shaped his destiny and the fortunes of the people.

§ This celebrated man was the son of a butcher at Ipswich; but having received a learned education, and being endowed with an excellent capacity, he was taken into the service of the king, and by degrees rose into distinction, till he became the prime minister of his sovereign. Clergyman as he was, he countenanced the king in all his light sports, gaiety, and sensual indulgences, a quality in the companion, which contributed to the influence and elevation of the courtier.

20. In the early part of his reign, the counsels of Wolsey agreeing with the natural temper of Henry, prompted him to make wâr against Louis XII. of France. He invaded the country, and met with success so far as he went, having gained the Battle of the Spurs; (because the French on the occasion made more use of their spurs than their swords;) but he failed to improve his good fortune, and after taking Tournay, returned to England.

About the same time the Scots, who had made an incursion into England, were defeated by Henry's general, the earl of Surrey, at Flodden Field, where James IV., and a great part of his nobility, were slain. Henry, however, did not follow up his advantage, but generously granted a peace to Scotland.

Henry also took a part in the long and obstinate wars which were waged between Francis I. and Charles V., as before detailed. His foreign alliances cost him the expenditure of immense treasures to no purpose, as he was, by turns, the dupe of both parties.

The most important events in Henry's reign, are connected with his matrimonial alliances. Out of these, as a consequence, arose the ever-memorable Reformation in England. Henry was opposed by the pope in an affair so interesting to his passions, and therefore the pope was opposed by him, and at length lost his influence in the kingdom. In this great religious change, it is evident Henry had no good intentions, but sought the gratification of his own unhallowed appetites. He had previously declared himself the champion of the Romish church, and even written a book against

Luther. Hence was conferred on him, by the pope, the title of "Defender of the Faith."

§ Henry was married to Catharine of Arragon, his brother's widow, but having fallen in love with the beautiful Anne Boleyn, he applied to the pope for a divorce. This, however, was denied him. But Henry was not to be frustrated in his intentions. The opinion of the universities was favourable to him, and Anne was soon crowned queen.

The pope now was forced to pay the price of his conscientiousness or obstinacy. His authority, from that time, was abolished in England; the annual tribute was no longer paid to him; the dissolution of the monasteries was ordered; and the clergy, as well as all others, were obliged to acknowledge the king as head of the church; and the want of obedience, was punishable with banishment or death. On this account, Sir Thomas More, and the bishop of Rochester, among others, perished by the hand of the executioner. Cardinal Wolsey also, was conceived to be in the way of the king's wishes on the subject of his marriage, and after being deprived of his immense power and possessions, was arrested for high treason. He, however, died of a broken heart soon afterwards, uttering in the anguish of his soul, the never to be forgotten words, "Had I but served God as diligently as I have served the king, he would not have forsaken me in my gray hairs."

Anne Boleyn, in less than three years, was condemned and beheaded. After her, he married four wives in succession; the first dying in child-birth; the next having been divorced, because he found her not so beautiful as had been represented; and the third having been executed for adultery. The fourth survived him.

The tyrant died in the fifty-sixth year of his age, bequeathing his crown, first to Edward, then to Mary, and lastly to Elizabeth.

20½ Edward VI., Henry's son, by Jane Seymour, ascended the throne in 1547, in his tenth year. At first, the earl of Hertford was regent; afterwards, the duke of Somerset, who was decidedly friendly to the reformation. Edward was a prince of great promise and many virtues; but, to the deep regret of the English nation, he died in the sixteenth year of his age.

During his reign, the reformation made great progress, through the zeal of Cranmer; yet a large body of the people adhered to popery. The triumphs of the new religion were not, however, effected without public disturbances, and some sanguinary executions took place on account of religion.

A project was undertaken of uniting England and Scotland, by a marriage between Edward and Mary Stuart, the young queen of the Scots. It, however, failed, and a battle ensued, near Musselburgh, in which 10,000 of the Scots were slain.

§ So different in disposition was Edward from his father, that it is said he always wept, when he signed an order for an execution against any of his subjects. Edward's benevolent turn of mind is evidenced by his charitable endowments, as Bridewell, St. Thomas's Hospital, and several schools, which still exist and flourish.

21. Mary, Edward's sister, next ascended the throne, in 1553. History has assigned to her the unenviable title of "bloody," from the persecutions and martyrdoms suffered by the protestants, in her reign. Her disposition was morose, tyrannical, and cruel, in the highest degree. Bent upon the restoration of the catholic religion, she hesitated at no measures, however unjust, which were calculated to effect the object.

§ To force and violence, she naturally resorted. Some of the most eminent reformers, as Cranmer, Latimer, Ridley, Hooper, Ferrer, and Rogers, she consigned to the flames. In consequence, however, of these cruelties, a powerful prejudice was excited against the catholics. Their cause sunk, and that of the protestants rose; and the reformation was, in reality, extended, by the means employed for its extinction.

The beginning of Mary's reign, was stained with the blood of the celebrated Lady Jane Grey, grand daughter to a sister of Henry VIII. She more happily suppressed, soon after, an insurrection under Wyat.

Her husband was Philip II., of Spain; but, by the articles of marriage, she, or rather her parliament, has the merit of making provision for the independence and glory of the English crown. It was agreed that the administration should be solely in the queen, and, on certain conditions, her issue should inherit the dominions of Philip.

The loss of Calais, which the English possessed 210 years, together with the knowledge that she was hated, both by her husband and her subjects, caused her to die of grief and vexation of heart, in the forty-third year of her age.

§ Jane Grey, whose fate was so tragical, was designed by Edward to be his successor. Her title, however, was quite defective; and the law, assigning the crown to her, which Edward caused to be passed, was unconstitutional. Lord Guilford Dudley, son of the duke of Northumberland, had lately married her; and both the father and son strongly solicited her to accept of the perilous bequest of Edward. She reluctantly consented, and, by their intrigues, was proclaimed queen. Her youth and innocence might have excused her; but she was soon arrested, and, together with her husband, was condemned and executed.

On the day of her execution, her husband desired permission to see her; but she refused her consent, informing him by message, that the tenderness of their parting would overcome the fortitude of both, and too much unbend their minds from a greater concern. She adverted also to other topics of a consolatory kind. Her husband was first brought to the block, before her eyes; but, undaunted at such a sight, she addressed the spectators, in a most affecting speech, and, with a serene countenance, immediately submitted her own neck to the fatal axe.

Lady Jane Grey was an accomplished scholar, a devout christian, and the fairest ornament of her sex. Aschem tells us, that she wrote in Latin, with great strength of sentiment; and we are informed by her contemporary, Sir Thomas Chaloner, that she was well versed in Hebrew, Chaldee, Arabic, French, and Italian. Fuller adds, that she had "the innocency of childhood, the beauty of youth, the solidity of middle, the gravity of old age, and all at eighteen; the birth of a princess, the learning of a clerk, the life of a saint, yet the death of a malefactor, for her parent's offences."

22. Elizabeth succeeded to the throne, on the death of her sister Mary, 1558. This was a joyful event to the English people. The prudence which, as a subject, she had displayed during the sanguinary reign of her sister, gave promise of excellence in the sovereign.

§ It required all the sagacity and caution of Elizabeth, to elude the effects of the violent jealousy which the queen, her sister, entertained against her. When questioned respecting the real presence, the net for catching protestants, she replied:

"Christ was the word that spake it,
He took the bread and brake it,
And what the word did make it,
That I believe and take it."

That which was thus promised, was, in a great measure, fulfilled. By her wise counsels, the protestant religion was fostered; the church of England received its present form; and agriculture, commerce, arts, and literature, attained to an elevation unknown in England before. Her intrepid mind, and the measures of the government, so sagaciously and firmly pursued, rendered her the most respected and powerful sovereign in Europe. She colonized a large portion of North America, supported the infant republic of Holland against its tyrannical enemy, humbled the pride of Spain, in the defeat of its boasted armada, and assisted Henry IV. in the recovery of his kingdom. She sought the true interests and glory of her subjects, so far as concerned their temporal prosperity, or their external religious observances.

Yet it must be acknowledged, that she compassed her objects, often, by very questionable means. She was stern, unyielding, unrelenting, despotic, in her maxims of government, and was guilty, at times, of the basest acts of cruelty and hypocrisy. Her treatment of her cousin, Mary, queen of Scots, whom she caused to be beheaded, on the bare suspicion of a conspiracy, has loaded her memory with a degree of reproach, which the splendour of her reign, in other respects, can never obliterate. And her conduct towards her favourites, particularly the earl of Essex, is marked with singular caprice, if not injustice.

§ The invincible Armada, so called, was a fleet which Spain fitted out for the invasion of England, on account of the interference of the latter power in the affairs of the Netherlands. It consisted of 150 ships of war, carrying 27,000 men, and 3000 cannon—the largest naval armament which Europe had ever seen. The English fleet of 108 ships, commanded by Howard, Drake, and others, met the armada as it entered the English channel, attacked it in the night, and burnt and destroyed a great part of the squadron. A storm which drove the remainder of the Spanish ships on the coast of Zealand, completed their discomfiture, and only fifty shattered vessels, with 6000 men, returned to Spain.

The story of the beautiful and unfortunate Mary, will be briefly told in what follows. She was a daughter of James V., king of Scotland, and great-grand-daughter of Henry VII. of England, and next heir to the English crown. She succeeded her father, eight days after her birth. She was educated in France, as a catholic, and, in early life, married the Dauphin, afterwards Francis II. Influenced by her maternal uncles, the Guises, she consented to take the title of queen of England—an injudicious measure, equally calculated to wound her own peace, and excite Elizabeth's resentment.

After her return to Scotland, on the death of Francis, she gave her hand to her cousin Henry Stuart, (lord Darnley.) But the king, her husband, being excluded from any share in the government, by the advice (as he suspected) of Rizzio, an Italian musician, her secretary and favourite, he, by the assistance of some of the principal nobility, suddenly surprised them when at supper together, and effected the death of Rizzio, in the queen's presence.

The next year, the king was blown up with gunpowder, in a private house, to which he had retired with a few friends. The earl of Bothwell, the new favourite of Mary, is, not without reason, supposed to have been the contriver of this murder. He was, however, acquitted by the nobles of his and Mary's party; and, in about two months after, the imprudent princess condescended to marry him.

This shameful conduct, occasioned the revolt of the chief nobility and her best subjects, by whom she was taken prisoner, compelled her to resign the crown, and her son, James VI., was called to the sovereignty. The queen, soon after, escaped from prison, and raised an army to oppose the regent, Murray, who was determined on her destruction, and whom she had frequently condemned, and as frequently pardoned. She was, however, defeated, and fled to England, in 1568, where she expected, from the repeated declarations of Elizabeth, protection and security.

Elizabeth, secretly delighted to find a hated rival in her power proved unfaithful to her professions, and detained the unhappy fugitive a prisoner, for eighteen years. She first, however, under pretence of doing justice to Mary, had the cause of the latter enquired into, at a conference at York. But though nothing was proved against her, Elizabeth saw fit to detain her in close confinement.

The Scottish queen, during her tedious and merciless confinement, naturally desired, and her friends for her, a release. For a plot to effect this object, devised by her friends, and detected, she was held responsible; and though an independent sovereign, was tried by a foreign power. Presumed, only, to be guilty, she was condemned, and soon after barbarously beheaded, in Fotheringay castle, in the forty-fifth year of her age, and in the nineteenth of her captivity.

Historians tell us, that when Mary was informed of the order for her execution, she was surprised, but betrayed no symptoms of fear. The night before her execution, she called in all her servants, and bade them a solemn farewell. Next morning she dressed herself in a rich habit of silk and velvet, and declared her resolution to die in the faith in which she had been educated. It was on the 8th of Feb. 1587, when she was brought to the block, and in that awful conjuncture, displayed a fortitude and decency, which would have honoured a matron of Rome; and to the moment of her death, united the majesty of a queen with the meekness of a martyr.

The bishop of Lincoln, in a prayer on the occasion of her burial, used the following words—"It is a charitable saying of father Luther, 'Many one liveth a Papist and dieth a Protestant:' only this I have been informed, that she took her death patiently, and recommended herself wholly to Jesus Christ."

Mary, besides her eminent beauty, which was celebrated throughout Europe, possessed the highest mental accomplishments. She read and understood several languages, wrote poetry, and cultivated a knowledge of music. Her misfortunes were great; and though many of them were brought upon her by her indiscretions, if not crimes, the severity of her lot has called forth general commiseration.

In the early part of Elizabeth's reign, the earl of Leicester was her principal favourite; but after his death, she became attached to the earl of Essex, as her minister; and indeed there was, on the part of the queen, though quite advanced in life, much of the appearance of a more tender passion. She seems, however, unalterably to have kept her resolution "to live and die a maiden queen." She was pleased with courtship, but kept aloof from matrimony. Essex was a young nobleman of singular accomplishments, talents, and spirit.

The queen and Essex had many quarrels and reconciliations. In one instance, in consequence of some affront which he offered her, she angrily gave him a box on the ear; upon which Essex clapped his hand on his sword, swearing he would not bear such usage, were it from Henry VIII.; and immediately withdrew from court. His indiscretion, however, was soon pardoned. He was at length teased by her capricious humour into a crime, which she could not pardon. He had severely reflected on her person, (for though nearly in her seventieth year, she wished to be thought a beauty,) and connected this with some suspicious movements of a treasonable nature. He was soon arraigned, convicted, and brought to the block.

From this period her mind began to be depressed. The cause doubtless was, the revival of her tenderness for Essex. While under sentence of death, he sent by the countess of Nottingham, to Elizabeth, a ring which she had given him as a pledge of her affection, and of the confidence he might feel, in whatever disgrace he might be, that the sight of it would secure her favourable interposition. The countess, at the instigation of her husband, the mortal enemy of Essex, neglected to deliver it; and when on her beath-bed, sent for the queen, to inform her of the fact. Elizabeth, bursting into a frantic passion, shook the dying countess in her bed, and exclaimed, "God may pardon you, but I never can."

From that moment the queen fell into the profoundest melancholy, refused both food and medicine, and throwing herself on the floor, remained in that state several days and nights, till life became extinct.

Essex, it appears, was much thought of in his day. We find in an ancient account of him, the following quaint and hyperbolic epitaph:

> "Here sleeps great Essex, dearling of mankinde,
> Faire honour's lampe, foule envie's prey, Arte's fame
> Nature's pride, Virtue's bulwarke, lure of minde,
> Wisdome's flower, Valour's tower, Fortune's shame,
> England's sunne, Belgia's light, France's star, Spaine's thunder,
> Lysbone's lightning, Ireland's clowde, the whole world's wonder."

23. Little needs be added respecting the character of Elizabeth. In her private life, she was less commendable than in her public conduct. She possessed few qualities of the heart which we love to see in all, especially in woman. The rivalship of beauty, the desire of admiration, the jealousy of love, the meanness of insincerity, and the sallies of anger, sullied her character, and showed that she was still a woman, but without the amiability of her sex. The attributes of her intellect, however, merit the highest encomium, and her public conduct was that of a queen. We give her

full credit for vigour, firmness, penetration, and address—for heroism without rashness, for frugality without avarice, for activity without the turbulence of ambition. Her proficiency in learning was great, and she possessed extraordinary talents for government. The security and defence of the English people, were never placed in abler hands.

GERMANY.

24. At the commencement of the present period, Germany was under the sway of Frederick IV. He erected Austria into an Archduchy, and rendered his family the most powerful in Germany, by marrying his son Maximilian, to Mary, heiress of Burgundy and the Netherlands. He reigned fifty-three years.

25. Maximilian I., his son, succeeded him, 1493. He possessed most of the qualities that signalize a great prince. He freed Germany from the disorders of the feudal system, and established peace among its separate sovereignties.

§ He was wanting in decision of mind, which seemed to be his only failing as a prince; in consequence of which, some of his important projects miscarried. His memory was so tenacious, that he never forgot the names of persons he had once seen, or heard mentioned.

26. His grandson, Charles V., succeeded him in the empire, 1519, having carried the election in preference to Francis I., of France. Some particulars respecting this distinguished prince, were given in the history of that country. A few others will be added.

§ Charles was the eldest son of Philip, son of Maximilian, and of Jane, the daughter of Ferdinand and Isabella. He succeeded to the throne of Spain, in 1516.

The first act of his administration, was to appoint an imperial diet, with a view to check the progress of Luther's opinions, which were represented as inimical to the peace of Germany. About this time, also, Germany was divided into ten circles. In 1521, commenced the celebrated war between Charles and Francis, in which Charles obtained manifest advantage. In 1527, he took Rome, which was plundered by the Germans during nine months. A few years afterwards, Charles captured Tunis, and liberated twenty-two thousand Christian slaves.

But the most extraordinary event pertaining to this sovereign, was the voluntary relinquishment of his kingly and imperial authority. He resigned, first the Netherlands and the kingdom of Spain, to his son Philip, in 1556, and afterwards the empire, in favour of his brother Ferdinand. The remainder of his life he spent in a monastery. An occurence of this kind, is rare in the history of princes, who are generally more fond of authority, the longer they have enjoyed it.

§ Charles was the most powerful sovereign of Europe, his sway extending over Spain, Germany, the Netherlands, and a part of Italy. He was generally successful in war, though (if such was his aim) universal empire was beyond his reach. He never could bring his dominions into a well connected body. His enemies were numerous and powerful, and gave him perpetual annoyance. His cares and difficulties increased as he advanced in life, and finding his health also decline, he determined to relinquish the burdens of government.

Accordingly, he recalled his son Philip, on whom, at his recent marriage with Mary, queen of England, he had bestowed the kingdoms of Naples and Sicily, and also the duchy of Milan. Having assembled the states of the Low-Countries, at Brussels, he explained the reasons of his resignation, recapitulated the most important actions of his life, and transferred the sovereign authority to Philip, with such unaffected magnanimity and paternal affection, that the whole audience melted into tears. A few weeks after this solemnity, Charles conferred all his royalties and signiories, both in Europe and America, upon his son; reserving nothing to himself, but a pension of 100,000 crowns, to be deducted from the revenue of Spain.

After making some ineffectual attempts to secure the German princes in the interests of Philip, Charles made a formal resignation of the empire to his brother Ferdinand, and immediately set out for Spain, with a chosen retinue. Previously to his arrival in that country, a small building had been annexed to the monastery of St. Just, consisting of six rooms, four of them in the form of friar's cells, with naked walls, and the other two hung with brown cloth, and furnished in the most simple manner. Thither Charles retired, with only twelve domestics; and there, after a peaceful solitude of about two years, he resigned his breath, in the fifty-ninth year of his age.

27. The successors of Charles in the empire, during the remainder of this period, were, after Ferdinand I., his son Maximilian II., and Rhodolph II. These princes generally made use of pacific expedients, in the disputes carried on between the Protestants and the Catholics.

§ Ferdinand and Maximilian, are said to have been most excellent princes. From the latter, no one ever heard a harsh expression. So economical were his arrangements, that to every act of his life its appropriate hour was allotted. The empire flourished in a pecu iar manner under his administration. Rhodolph, though at war with the Turks, almost the whole of his reign, was more occupied with tournaments, and the study of mechanics, chemistry, and astronomy, than with the affairs of state. He frequently spent whole days at the shops of clockmakers, turners, &c., so eager was his desire for that species of knowledge.

28. The reformation in religion, by which the present period is so peculiarly distinguished, is the most important event in the history of Germany. It commenced in that country, whence it spread rapidly through several other European nations. It was connected with a new era in the religious history of the world. By it, Papacy received a wound, from which it can never recover. The date of this event, is 1517.

Martin Luther, an Augustine friar, was the first instrument employed by an overruling Providence, in accomplishing this great moral revolution. His attention was excited to the corruption and abuses of the Catholic religion, by the sale of indulgencies, at that time instituted throughout all the Christian kingdoms of Europe. Leo X., in order to raise money for the completion of his magnificent buildings at Rome, had published general indulgences; that is, remittances from the pains of purgatory: and the elector of Mentz, authorised the Dominicans to receive the money, and preach up the merits of such a contribution.

But the scandalous manner in which these pardons for all sins, past, present, and to come, were disposed of, gave great offence to many religious persons, and induced Luther, who was then a professor of divinity at Wittemberg, to expose the absurdity of such odious traffic. His indignation was aroused; and indeed, the enormity of these doings, opened his eyes to the iniquity of the whole system.

His anathemas found many willing hearers, particularly in the electorate of Saxony, though Tetzel, the papal agent, vigorously combatted him. Luther, however, by degrees acquired great popularity, and his influence brought other divines into the controversy. Persecution was now resorted to by the pope and his emissaries, but this only increased his zeal and indignation as a preacher. Luther was soon cited by the pope, to appear at Rome, within sixty days. Prince Frederick, elector of Saxony, however, requested that the reformer might plead his cause in Germany; and Luther repaired, under the protection of a safe conduct, to the imperial diet, convoked by Charles at Augsburg, before cardinal Cajetan; but instead of making any recantation, he boldly avowed his resolution of defending his doctrines, though all the terrors of the church should be denounced against him. As the pope's legate, however, proceeded to menaces, Luther retired privately from Augsburg, having first complained, by etter, to the pope, of the harsh treatment he had received from Cajetan.

Having arrived safely into Saxony, he found the mass there universally abolished, the images destroyed, and the convents shut up. The spirit which had been thus kindled, spread next into Switzerland, where it produced the most important changes. Sweden, Norway, and Denmark, soon embraced the Lutheran tenets; and the protestants, as they were all called who embraced the reformed religion, multiplied in the Netherlands, France, and England, as well as in Germany The quarrel which Henry VIII., who was no protestant himself, had with the pope, was the means of advancing the reformation in England, and of subverting the ancient faith The cruel persecutions of which the papists were guilty, greatly aided the good cause, in the end.

SPAIN.

29. SPAIN had, for several ages, been held by the Moors, or Mahometans. This people, however, had lost one province after another, till towards the close of the fifteenth century, only Granada remained subject to their authority. Upon the accession of Ferdinand and Isabella, in 1479, the crowns of Castile and Arragon were happily united, and thus all the Christian principalities in Spain, found themselves under one sceptre; and, with the conquest of Granada, which the king and queen effected in 1492, Spain became one entire monarchy. Ferdinand and Isabella were, in effect, two sovereign princes, though professedly united in marriage.

The Moors suffered terribly in the siege of Granada, and with the loss of their dominions, were, for the most part, obliged to retire into Africa.

§ To Ferdinand and Isabella, the establishment of the terrible Inquisition, in Spain, is owing. Two thousand persons are said to have suffered death under Torquemada, the first inquisitor general. This instance of intemperate and ferocious zeal, in the king and queen, may well be set off against the several good qualities, which it is allowed, they possessed. Their reign was signalized by the discoveries made by the great Columbus.

30. Jane, who became deranged, succeeded her mothe. Isabella, in Castile, with her husband, Philip of Austria. On the death of her father, Jane being unfit to reign, her son Charles I., afterwards Charles V., was acknowledged sovereign of all Spain, 1516. His history has already been related.

§ During Charles's reign, Mexico was conquered by Fernando Cortez, in 1519, and Peru by Pizarro in 1525. The Spanish dominions were thus greatly extended.

31. Philip II., succeeded his father upon the abdication of the latter, in 1556. In his time, the balance of power in Europe, was sustained by Spain, France, England and Germany, all, at this time, highly flourishing and respectable, either from the talents of their sovereigns, or their internal strength. Philip was an acute and able politician, though his policy partook somewhat of selfish cunning. He was sovereign of Spain, the two Sicilies, Milan, and the Netherlands. He had likewise, for a few years, the resources of England at command, by his marriage with Mary, the English queen. His power was great, but his ambition was greater; and though he met with occasional success, at the close of a long and busy reign, he had accomplished but few of his numerous projects.

§ Pope Paul IV., jealous of the power of Philip, formed an alliance with the king of France, to deprive the Spaniards of Milan and the Sicilies. Philip, with the aid of the English, defeated the French at St. Quintin, and hoped, from this signal victory, to force the allies into a peace. Another signal victory, however, was necessary. which Philip gained near Gravelines, the result of which was, that the French surrendered to Spain, no less than eighty-nine fortified towns, in the low countries, and in Italy.

Philip was an intolerant bigot in religion, and it was owing to his cruel attempts to enforce a uniformity of religious opinion in the Netherlands, that the latter broke away from his authority, as will be detailed below.

HOLLAND.

32. Holland became a republic by the union of Utrecht, in 1579. The states combined to defend their common liberties, on account of the tyranny of their sovereign, Philip II. Seven of the seventeen provinces, constituting the Neth-

erlands, came into the measure. The remaining ten provinces had their charter renewed by Philip, and did not become independent until in the beginning of the eighteenth century.

§ Holland, is another appellation for the Seven United Provinces, so called, from its chief province being of that name. The remaining ten are known by the name of Flanders. The duchy of Burgundy, composed of some of these provinces, was originally equal to any power in Europe. The whole of the Netherlands, except three states, were annexed to the German empire, by marriage, 1477 They were afterwards resigned to the king of Spain.

In the early periods of their history, the Hollanders became subject to the Franks, under whom, they were divided into small governments, the heads of which were despotic, in their own dominions. Holland and the Netherlands, were united to Germany, under one of the grandsons of Charlemagne, but became independent in the tenth century. At length, in 1443, they were subject to the dukes of Burgundy. The next transfer of these states, was to Germany, Charles V. being heir to the house of Burgundy.

They endured the rule of Charles, but the tyranny of his son Philip II., was not to be borne. The Reformation had made a considerable progress in the Netherlands. Philip, with a view to repress it, established the Inquisition, projected certain innovations, which created alarm and tumult, and sent an army under, the duke of Alva, to enforce implicit submission. The consequence of these measures was, that many thousands of persons, and some of the highest distinction, perished by the hands of the executioner. It is computed that 18,000 were the victims of the five years' administration of Alva.

William, the prince of Orange, on whom the government of several of the provinces had been conferred, and who was now, himself, under the sentence of the Inquisition, raised an army on this occasion, and undertook the deliverance of the states. Having reduced some of the most important garrisons, he was proclaimed Stadtholder of Holland and Zealand, in 1570.

The whole seventeen provinces had equally suffered from the tyranny of Philip; but only seven of them could agree to form a confederated republic. The influence of jealousy and competition, prevented the union of the whole. By the treaty which was formed, it was agreed that they should defend their liberties, as one united republic; that they should jointly decide in the concerns of peace and war, establish a general legislative authority, and maintain religious freedom. William was elected Stadtholder of the whole seven, a title which included the duties of a general, admiral, and magistrate.

The effusion of blood, which had been great prior to this union, was not hereby much diminished. The crown of Spain, strained every nerve to recover those provinces. Philip, venting his indignation, by a proscription of the prince of Orange, and offering 25,000 crowns for his head, compassed his revenge; for this illustrious man was cut off by an assassin, 1584. By persevering courage, however, and assisted by queen Elizabeth of England, and Henry IV. of France, the Hollanders, at length, completely established their independence, and brought the Spanish monarch to acknowledge them as a free people.

Maurice, the son of William, was elected Stadtholder, in the room of his father, and displayed the most consummate talents, as a statesman and warrior, having conducted the struggle to the issue already related.

AMERICA.

33. The immense portion of the earth called AMERICA, was unknown to Europe, Asia, and Africa, till the year 1492, when it was discovered by Christopher Columbus, a native of Genoa, in a voyage which he made from Spain, sailing west, for the purpose of finding a new continent, or at least of arriving at India, in this direction. He first met, not with the continent, but the islands in its vicinity.

§ The discovery of the new world, was one of the greatest and happiest results of genius, that mankind have ever witnessed. The importance of the discovery cannot be easily overrated. An event so unlooked for, so unthought of, expanded the views, and waked up the energy of the human mind. It excited a spirit of enterprise, unfelt before. Its influence on commerce, and consequently wealth, was, from the beginning, great and decisive, by immensely increasing the articles of traffic. The mines of America furnished, also, a great abundance of the precious metals; thus multiplying the amount of the circulating medium throughout the world. Colonization, and the arts of civilized life, have been advanced and extended, by means of this discovery; the sphere of human enjoyment enlarged, and especially the blessings of the true religion, communicated to greater numbers of mankind. America has also given to the world a new and bright example, both of civil and religious freedom; the effects of which, are destined to be felt through all time, and, perhaps, among all nations. Some evils have, indeed, been incident to the discovery, but they are exceedingly outweighed by its propitious results, and will continue to be so, judging from the known principles of human nature, and from the dealings of divine providence.

It has been believed by some, that America was not unknown to the ancients. The theory has gained advocates, from a few passages in the works of some of the writers of antiquity, and also from coincidences in the languages and customs of some of the nations of the old and new continent. But the theory has little ground for its support. Certainly, at the revival of letters in Europe, no traces of the knowledge of another continent existed; and it was generally supposed, that the Canaries formed the western boundaries of the world.

To Columbus, an account of whom will appear in a biographical sketch, about to follow, mankind are indebted for the correction of this error, and the discovery of a new continent. From a long and close application to the study of geography, this great man had obtained a knowledge of the true figure of the earth, far beyond what was common to the age in which he lived. Another continent, he conceived necessarily existed, to complete the balance of this terraqueous globe; but he erroneously supposed it to be connected with hat of India. The truth of his speculations, he now ardently desired to prove, by experiment. In this, however, he met with great difficulty, and it was not until the expiration of several years, that his project was patronized by any prince or court in Europe. Queen Isabella, of Spain, has immortalized her name, by rendering the first effectual assistance to Columbus.

One great motive which influenced Columbus and his patroness, aside from the hope of ascertaining the existence of a new continent, was to find a passage to China and the East Indies, by sea: or rather the latter, may have been the sole motive, connecting the supposed new regions with the east of Asia. It had been long an object of study, to find such a passage, and thus avoid the inconvenience and expense of transporting the merchandise of India, across the land, from the Red Sea, to Alexandria, in Egypt. The passage round the Cape of Good Hope, was not then known, and the shortest route was supposed, by Columbus, to be by the west. It is to be remembered, that the maps of that period, represented the oriental countries of Asia, as stretching vastly farther to the east, than has since been proved to be the fact. Columbus was fitted, in every point of view, for his mighty and perilous undertaking.

Never was success more complete, or a great idea more happily realized. With inconsiderable means, and an ill-appointed flotilla of three small vessels, victualled for twelve months, and having on board ninety men, he commenced his unpromising adventure. Leaving Palos, in Spain, on the 3d of August, he sailed directly for the Canaries, whence, having refitted his crazy ships, he kept a due western course, over an unknown ocean, not without a compass, but without a chart. His compass, however, occasioned perplexity. The variation of the magnetic needle from due north, was first observed, when he had sailed about 200 leagues from the Canaries, and so terrified his men, that they were scarcely restrained from mutiny. All his address and talents were now put in requisition. The phenomenon of the needle seemed portentous to himself, but his ingenuity devised a solution of it, which silenced the complaints of his crew.

After this, he pursued his voyage, yet not without the frequent manifestation of anxiety and impatience, on the part of his crew. Thirty days had transpired since they had left the Canaries, and no land appearing, both officers and men joined in a revolt. Columbus was forced partially to give way to their remonstrances, and proposed to return, after the expiration of three days, if they should find no land. Some indications of it had already begun to appear, and, on the 11th of October, the joyful sight was descried, first by Columbus himself. God was immediately praised, and the sailors were now as ardent in their expressions of repentance and admiration, as they had been, before, insolent and ungovernable.

34. St. Salvador, one of the Bahamas, was the island first discovered. Columbus afterwards touched at Cuba, and Hispaniola, (St. Domingo,) now Hayti. On the latter he left some of his men, to form a colony. His theory led him to call the regions he had discovered, by the name of West Indies; since he had reached India, or a portion of the globe which he supposed to be near it, by a western passage.

Columbus returned to Spain in the following May, and soon set out, with a much larger expedition, on a second voyage. In this he was so happy as to add many other islands to those already found. In a third voyage, he discovered Trinidad, and the continent at the mouth of the Oronoke, 1498.

The fame of his discoveries, drew adventurers from all parts of Europe; and, among others, Americus Vesputius, a Florentine, a man of science and genius, who, a few years afterwards, following the footsteps of Columbus, acquired the undeserved honour of giving his name to the new world.

In 1497, one year before the main land of South America had been discovered by Columbus, John Cabot, a Venetian by birth, but at that time an inhabitant of England, proceeded on a voyage of discovery, under a commission from the British king, and found the continent of North America. Touching at various parts of the coast, he took possession of the country, in behalf of the crown of England.

The Spaniards, after an interval of a few years, made settlements in the new world, and, impelled by a thirst of gold, committed horrible butcheries in several of the islands, and especially in Mexico and Peru, under Cortez, Pizarro, and Almagro. These brave adventurers, though base men, established the authority of Spain over countries which they depopulated by their avarice and cruelty. In the year 1500, the coast of Brazil was accidentally discovered by Alvarez de Cabral, the Portuguese admiral, in consequence of having been driven too far to the west, on a voyage round the Cape of Good Hope. Hence, the settlement and possession of that part of America, by the people of Portugal.

§ Columbus, as we have seen, entertained the idea that the region he had discovered, was India, or a part of the continent o.

Asia. This notion was generally received, until 1513, when the Pacific Ocean being descried from the mountains of the isthmus of Darien, the illusion began to be dispelled.

Fernando Cortez, was a successful, but execrable adventurer. It was on the occasion of being sent, in 1519, by the governor of Cuba, upon an expedition to the main, that he first heard of the existence of the rich and flourishing empire of Mexico. Stimulated by the love of power and gain, he resolved to make the conquest of that country. He had at his command only 617 men, and a very few fire-arms, (thirteen muskets and ten small field pieces,) these having not yet come into general use. His other instruments of death, were cross-bows, swords, and spears. But it was the former description of weapons, few as they were, that gained for this handful of Spaniards, a conquest over a numerous people. They looked upon fire-arms as the weapons of the gods.

Landing at Vera Cruz, Cortez advanced, though with a brave opposition from the natives, into the heart of the country. On the approach of the Spaniards to the capital, the terror of their name had paved the way for an easy conquest. The Mexican sovereign, Montezuma, received the invaders with great hospitality and kindness. Indeed, he regarded them with the reverence due to superior beings. An occasion, however, was not long wanting, on the part of Cortez, for putting his bold and hazardous project into execution.

Some difficulty between his soldiers and the natives, became the pretext for his seizure of Montezuma. Marching to the palace, with fifty men, he put the emperor in irons, and carried him off prisoner to his camp. This flagrant abuse of their hospitality, aroused the Mexicans, who fleeing to arms, expelled the Spaniards from the capital. Montezuma having, during the affray, offered to mediate between the Mexicans and their enemies, was indignantly put to death by one of his own subjects. Gautimozin, son of Montezuma, immediately succeeded him, and armed the whole empire against the perfidious Spaniards.

Cortez, by a fortunate concurrence of events, having induced a nation of the Indians to revolt, and having obtained a reinforcement of Spaniards, commenced the siege of the city, and soon took it, together with Gautimozin, and became master of the empire, in 1521. The emperor was treated by the Spaniards in a manner shocking to humanity. Refusing to discover the place where his treasures were hid, the miserable man was stretched naked, for some time, on burning coals. Soon after, on the discovery of a conspiracy against the Spaniards, he was executed on a gibbet, with all the princes of his blood. This was the last blow to the power of the Mexicans. The nefarious Cortez, and his few associates, enjoy the honour or the infamy, in the way now narrated, of having brought this simple and unsuspecting people, under the yoke of Spain.

While Cortez was employed in the reduction of Mexico, the Spaniards were informed of a still more rich and extensive empire, in the south. This was Peru, at that time governed by the inca, or king, Atabalipa. Francis Pizarro, in 1525, had sailed to and visited the coun ry. He afterwards undertook the conquest of it, in connection with Diego Almagro, and Ferdinand Lucques, two unprincipled adventurers like himself; and for this purpose, sailed in 1531, from Panama, with three small vessels and 300 men.

With this inconsiderable force, he invaded the country, and marching to the residence of the inca, he seized his person by stratagem, having employed friendship and religion as the cover of his villany. In this defenceless condition, the king was obliged to submit to the slaughter of his attendants, and to the exaction of an enormous quantity of gold and silver, as the price of his ransom. When, however, the treasure was committed into the hands of the Spaniard, with perfidious cruelty, he still retained the wretched monarch a prisoner, and finally, by a mock trial, condemned and executed him, as a usurper and idolator.

The vast booty which fell into the possession of the victors, became soon an occasion of dispute among themselves. War only could settle it; in the course of which, both Pizarro and Almagro perished. This contention lasted seventeen years, and Peru became the theatre of the most licentious rapine and cruelty.

In the year 1548, the celebrated Las Casas, was sent from Spain, as viceroy. Under his administration, the country obtained repose, as a province of Spain; and, notwithstanding the temporary success of their new inca, Huanca Capac, who rose against the Spaniards, the whole Peruvian people were effectually broken down and subdued.

The inhabitants of the American continent and its islands, were a race of men quite new to the Europeans. They were of a copper colour, and had no beard. In some parts of the continent, as Mexico and Peru, they had made considerable progress towards civilization. They were not wanting, in a degree, as to polish, and even luxury. Architecture, sculpture, mining, and working the precious metals, were understood. Their persons were clothed, their lands cultivated, and their state governed by fixed laws and regulations. In Peru there were some magnificent palaces and temples. In other parts of the new world, man was a naked savage, the member of a wandering tribe, whose sole occupation was hunting or war. The savages of the continent were characterized alike by their cruelty to their enemies, their contempt of death, and their generosity towards their friends. The islanders were a milder race, of gentle manners, and less robust constitutions.

The inhumanity with which the Spaniards treated these simple and unoffending people, is shocking to every reader of sensibility. To convert them to the holy and benevolent religion of the Saviour, the most violent means were employed, by men who were strangers to the spirit of that religion. The rack, the scourge, and the faggot, were the principal engines used for their conversion. They were hunted down like wild beasts, or burnt alive in their thickets and fastnesses. Some of the islands were nearly depopulated.

The conversion of the Indians, however, was less an object, than the desire of obtaining the precious metals which they possessed. So powerful was the passion for gold, that the first adventurers endured every fatigue, and encountered every danger, in search of it; and, by compelling the natives to dig in the mines, prematurely destroyed the lives of vast multitudes of this hapless race. It being the practice of the Europeans to take possession of the regions in America which they visited, by the pretended right of discovery, they seem to have made no account of the aboriginals, depriving them of liberty, or life, whenever occasion or passion demanded.

The Spanish acquisitions in America, before the late revolution among them, belonged to the crown, and not to the state: they were the absolute property of the sovereign, and regulated solely by his will. The pope, agreeably to principles which governed men in a dark and superstitious age, granted to the monarchs of Spain, the countries discovered by their subjects, in America. They were governed by viceroys, who exercised supreme civil and military authority over their provinces.

Distinguished Characters in Period VIII.

1. Columbus, an eminent navigator, and discoverer of America.
2. Raphael, } masters of painting among the moderns.
3. M. Angelo, }
4. Erasmus, a Dutchman, eminent in philology and general literature.
5. Copernicus, a Prussian astronomer, and discoverer of the true system of the universe.
6. Luther, } eminent theologians and reformers.
7. Calvin, }
8. Camoens, a distinguished Portuguese poet.
9. Buchanan, a Scotch historian and poet.
10. Montaigne, a celebrated French essayist.
11. Tasso, prince of Italian poets.
12. Spenser, one of the greatest of the English poets.

§ Columbus (Christopher) was born 1442, at Genoa, son of a woolcomber. He was early inured to the labours of the sea, and acquired great experience in navigation. With the sciences immediately connected with his profession, he was acquainted, beyond most men of his age. Indeed, this great man was far in advance of the rest of the world, and anticipated the illumination of a distant futurity. For the splendid discovery which he was destined to make, his temperament and his previous course of life, eminently fitted him. There was an enthusiasm in his character, a lofty expectation, and a religious fervour of soul, which spurned ordinary difficulties, and raised him immensely above ordinary men. By his knowledge of maritime affairs, as well as by reasoning, he became persuaded that a continent must exist in the western ocean. To ascertain the truth of his theory, was an object which soon engrossed all his time and faculties. And, after much effort and many trials and disappointments, in regard to assistance, he was permitted to realize the grand idea he had so happily conceived.

He made application to several courts, before he could obtain the requisite means and patronage, and it was only after much delay, that he was finally enabled to prosecute his discoveries under the auspices of Ferdinand and Isabella of Spain. He sailed on the third of August, 1492, in three small ships, and returned to Spain in May the following year. In the mean time he had discovered a new world, and had taken possession of a portion of it, in the name of his sovereign. This event filled Spain, and all Europe, with amazement, and the greatest honours were accorded to him in the country, whose annals he has so signally adorned. He made three subsequent voyages to the new world, in the second of which he reached the continent; but powerful enemies had now risen up, jealous of his ascendency, who impugned his motives or decried his services, and so much influence had they with the Spanish court, that Columbus, in his third voyage was sent back to Spain in irons. Though he suffered much in the latter part of life, he finally triumphed over his enemies, and peacefully left the world, on the twentieth of May, 1506.

The memory of Columbus will be cherished while the world stands; though in consequence of one of those untoward events that sometimes occur, he has been deprived of the honour of giving his name to the hemisphere which his genius brought to light. Signal must have been the satisfaction of his mind, notwithstanding the disasters through which he passed, in view of the transcendent benefits which Providence had made him the instrument of conferring on mankind.

2. Raphael (Sanzio) was born at Urbino, 1483. By studying the best masters in painting, he soon rose to eminence, and merited the appellation of the divine Raphael. He also excelled as an architect, and was employed in the building of St. Peter's, at Rome. He came to an untimely grave, in consequence of his addiction to licentious pleasures, dying at the age of thirty-seven years. By the general consent of mankind, he is acknowledged to have been the prince of painters. He excelled in beauty and grace.

3. Angelo Buonaroti (Michael) was not only a great painter, but sculptor, and architect. He was even an elegant poet. In architecture he surpassed all the moderns, and he was the greatest designer that ever lived. He is said to have sucked sculpture with his very milk, inasmuch as he was nursed by a woman whose husband was eminent in that art. The early displays of his genius, raised so great a jealousy among his youthful rivals; that one of them struck him with such violence on the nose, that he carried the mark to his grave. The most celebrated of his paintings, is the Last Judgment. His architectural abilities are best displayed on the church of St.

Peter's, at Rome, the building of which he completed. His style is that of grandeur and sublimity, united with the utmost simplicity and beauty. Sir Joshua Reynolds declared, that the last word which he wished to utter from the academic chair, was the name of Michael Angelo. Description can convey but a very imperfect image of

> "Buonaroti's car
> Midst epic glories flaming from afar."

Only the sight can give one an idea of his peculiar excellence. He lived ninety years.

4. Erasmus (Desiderius) was the most learned man of the age in which he lived, and contributed by his example and writings, to the restoration of learning in Europe. He was somewhat of a wanderer, having occasionally resided in Italy, Switzerland, Holland, France, and England. With the last of these countries he was best pleased, and there he met with the greatest encouragement from Henry VII., Sir Thomas More, and all the learned Englishmen of those days. He was the most correct and elegant Latin writer among the moderns. Rotterdam, is to this day proud of having given birth to Erasmus. The house in which he was born is still marked out to the admiration of the traveller by a suitable inscription, and a beautiful copper statue was long since erected to his memory in an open part of the city.

In the great question of Protestantism and Popery, he was claimed on both sides, though neither party was pleased with him. Here is a dark spot on his character. He was evidently temporising, timid, and undecided. He lashed the vices and follies of the Papists, while he seemed to be indifferent to the success, or jealous of the labours of the reformers. He died at Basil, July 12, 1536, aged sixty-nine.

5. Copernicus (Nicholas) was a native of Thorne in Prussia. In his twenty-third year he went to Italy in search of knowledge. After some years' absence, and having in the mean time acted as professor of mathematics at Rome, he returned home. Here he began to apply his vast knowledge, to an examination of the different theories respecting the universe. The simplicity of the Pythagorean system pleased him best; and after twenty years of profound investigation, he removed from the machine of the universe, the cycles and epicycles of former astronomers, and placed the sun in the centre to illuminate and control the whole. This great discovery he kept concealed for more than thirty years, for fear of exciting against himself the persecuting spirit of bigotry. When at last he consented, through the importunities of his friends, to have his work published, and a copy of it was brought to him, he was a few hours afterwards seized with a violent effusion of blood, which terminated his life, 24th May, 1543, in his seventieth year.

6. Luther (Martin) was born at Isleben, in Saxony, 1483. His parents designed him for a civilian, but by the following awful incident, his views were directed to the church. As he was walking in the fields with a fellow-student, they were struck by lightning

Luther to the ground, and his companion dead by his side. His mind was so much affected by the event, that without consulting his friends, he formed and executed the resolution of retiring from the world. He entered into the order of Augustine hermits, at Erfurth. From this place he removed to Wittemberg, being appointed by the elector of Saxony, professor of theology and philosophy in the university just founded there by that prince. It was in his retirement at Erfurth, that he providentially found a Latin Bible, the first he ever saw, and in perusing it he was astonished a the little knowledge of Scripture and Christianity, which the clergy then imparted to the people.

After he had been at Wittemberg three years, he was sent to Rome to plead the cause of some converts of his order, who had quarrelled with their vicar-general. While he was at the seat of the papal power, he became more than ever convinced of the ignorance and debauched lives of the dignitaries of the church. This probably gave him the first decided disgust to the Romish ecclesiastical government, especially as he had engaged in the monastic life, from motives of genuine piety. Upon his return to Wittemberg, he was created D. D. at the request of the elector of Saxony, and continued to act as professer of divinity in the university. Here he explained, with clearness and ease, the Psalms and the Epistle to the Romans, and supported his reputation by the most rigid morality, and the most exemplary conduct.

The minds of his auditors being thus prepared, a favourable occasion soon offered for carrying into execution his glorious plan of reformation. The completion of St. Peter's church, at Rome, at this time, required extraordinary sums, and pope Leo X. published, in 1517, general indulgences for the forgiveness of sin, to such as would contribute to the pious work. The Dominicans were intrusted with the selling of these indulgences in Germany; and in paying their money, the friar Tetzel informed the superstitious people, that they might release themselves, not only from past, but also future sins. Luther's holy indignation was roused by these vile practices, and he preached against them, with wonderful success. Persecution soon followed, and the reformer became the object of the papal vengeance. Luther, however, was undismayed, and, in an astonishing series of efforts, in which he was opposed by all the power and policy of the papal world, he achieved the object of his long cherished wishes.

In 1524, Luther threw aside the monastic habit. and the next year married a nun, who had escaped from a convent, and, though he was ridiculed and censured by his enemies, he confounded them all by his appeal to the Scriptures. By her, he had three sons, whose descendants are still respected in Germany. Luther died in the place of his nativity, 18th February, 1546.

Luther was singularly qualified for the service he performed. He was a man of high endowments of mind, and great uprightness—a friend of true religion, liberty, and human happiness. His understanding was vast, and his knowledge unequalled, almost, in the age in which he lived. Especially had he an admirable acquaintance with the Scriptures, which he expounded with equal eloquence and clearness. In courage, resolution, and decision, he was an example to all reformers.

7. Calvin, (John,) a coadjutor of Luther in the reformation, was born at Noyon, in Picardy, 10th July, 1509. His early piety marked him out for the church; but though he assumed the functions of the ministry, he was too much disgusted with the superstitions of the Romish church, to remain in her communion. His knowledge of the Bible had opened his eyes to the abominations of the "man of sin." He now applied himself to the study of the laws, in which he made great progress; at the same time, he extended his acquaintance with divinity. He soon entered most cordially into the reformation; and his zeal and labour as a writer and disputant, very essentially aided the work. With difficulty, however, he escaped from the vengeance of the catholics; but his confidence in God was not to be shaken, and having taken his position, he felt that it was to be maintained. He spent most of his active life at Geneva, where he undertook the ministry, and filled the chair of the professor of divinity. He was, however, once expelled the place on account of refusing to administer the sacrament indiscriminately, and again experienced trouble in the affair of Servetus.

Calvin, by his vast abilities, and by his clear views of religion, attracted the attention of the world, and it might almost be said, that "the care of all the churches" rested on him. Many of the reformed churches of Germany, France, England, and Poland, looked to him as their head, and he was in the habit of directing them by his letters. He died, 1564.

Calvin was a man of pre-eminent piety and talents, and, though not faultless, he has rendered such a service to the cause of evangelical truth, and of the reformation, as to deserve the gratitude of posterity. Scaliger says, that no commentator has better hit the sense of the prophets than he.

8. Camoens (Lewis) is known principally as the author of the Lusiad, an epic poem, which has been translated into the most important languages of Europe. Camoens is deservedly called the Virgil of his country, and in his work has displayed great powers of description, extensive learning, and a sublime imagination.

Misfortune marked his course in life. In the service of his country, he lost an eye. On his return from the Indies, whither he had gone to better his fortune, he was shipwrecked, and saved his life with difficulty, by swimming with his right arm, and holding up his poem, with his left.

After he had published his poem, and dedicated it to the king, he was cruelly disappointed, as to patronage; and feeling all the miseries of indigence and neglect, he expired in the midst of his ungrateful countrymen. He lived fifty-two years.

9. Buchanan (George) was born in the shire of Lenox, in Scot-

land, in 1506. He early embraced, from conviction, the tenets of Luther, and, as the consequence, suffered persecution from the catholics. He became tutor to James I. of England, and employed the last twelve or thirteen years of his life, in writing the history of his country. He occasionally resided in England and France, but died in his native country, at Edinburgh, 1582. His history is written in a nervous, elegant, and perspicuous style, but is occasionally deficient in fidelity and accuracy. He has the reputation of an able scholar, whose mind was stored with all the fire, the elegance, and the graces of ancient literature, and who, in a barbarous age, revived in his poetry, the beauty and grandeur of the Roman muses.

10. Montaigne was born of an ancient family at Perigord, in France, 1533. He was instructed to speak Latin first, as his mother tongue. Disdaining the drudgeries of law, for which he was intended, he travelled, with a view to make observations on men and manners. In the latter part of his life, he enjoyed learned ease and philosophical society. His essays have been repeatedly published. They are able and amusing productions, though unsafe to be put into the hands of youth, on account of their scepticism. Some persons have extravagantly praised them.

11. Tasso (Torquato) was born at Sorrento, in the kingdom of Naples, in 1544, and derives his celebrity from his "Jerusalem Delivered," an epic poem of great merit. Like the works of Homer and Virgil, it has gained the palm of immortality. Tasso passed a life of varied and great suffering. Among other calamities, he was confined by the duke of Ferrara, who had been his patron, in an hospital, for a long time, under the pretence that he was insane. Tasso had been guilty only of an imprudence. Unfortunately, he had fallen in love with the princess Eleonora, the duke's sister, and, on a certain occasion, he made bold to embrace her, in the midst of a crowded assembly. For this offence, the unfortunate lover was obliged to mourn his disappointment in a tedious solitude, rendered more tedious by a lingering disease, and occasional lunacy. He was at last released, and his merits as a poet began to be more known; but just as he was on the point of receiving the laurel crown from the pope, he suddenly expired, and that which was to have been, on the next day, his coronation, proved to be the melancholy procession of his funeral. He was fifty-one years of age.

12. Spenser (Edmund) is deservedly regarded as little inferior, either in invention or in judgment, and true fire of the muse, to any author, ancient or modern. But with all his beauties, he was fanciful and chimerical, and without uniformity, so that his poem is truly fairy land. His sublimity, variety, and fertile imagination, are unfortunately to be set off against his obsolete language, and heavy stanza. His Fairy Queen, is his most celebrated poem.

He was poet laureat to queen Elizabeth, and was employed somewhat in public life. At one period, he was possessed of wealth; but Desmond's revolt in Ireland, where his property lay, proved his ruin. He was plundered and robbed of his estate, one of his children was burned in the conflagration of his house, and broken in heart and fortune, he came to London, where he died, in 1598.

PERIOD IX.

The period of the English Commonwealth; extending from the Edict of Nantes, 1598 *years A. C., to the death of Charles XII. of Sweden,* 1718 *years A. C.*

FRANCE.

House of Bourbon.

SECT. 1. Henry IV., had now occupied the throne of FRANCE several years. He had changed his religion from political considerations, but did an act of justice to the Calvinists, by whose aid he had secured the sceptre, in granting the famous Edict of Nantes, by which he tolerated them, as well as all his subjects, in the unfettered exercise of their religion.

Henry's own great abilities and love of his subjects, aided by the talents and industry of his minister, the duke of Sully, enabled him to repair the desolations of a thirty years' civil war, and to place his kingdom in a state of financial prosperity and general happiness.

France never had a more popular sovereign. His talents, as a general and statesman, commanded respect, his person was prepossessing, his manners a model of good breeding, and his love of his subjects inspired a most enthusiastic attachment to him in return. His private and domestic life, was however very exceptionable, and infected, by the force of example, the manners of the court with no little dissoluteness.

§ A mistress of Henry, an artful, intriguing, ambitious woman, had, by consummate management, obtained from him a promise of marriage. This promise, the king showed to Sully, ready signed, and the minister, transported with indignation, tore it in pieces. "I believe you are mad," cried Henry in a rage. "It is true I am mad," replied Sully, "and I wish I was the only mad man in France." When, after so keen an altercation, Sully thought himself irrecoverably disgraced, he received the brevet of grand master of the ordnance.

Henry, who had lived through fifty conspiracies, fell by the hand of an assassin, named Ravillac, after a short reign of twenty years, too short for the glory of France, just as he was entering upon a splendid, but visionary project, of forming Europe into a Christian republic.

§ Ravillac was a desperate Catholic bigot, who had long formed a design to murder his sovereign. Henry was ready to join his army in prosecuting his singular scheme, but was detained against his will, on account of the coronation of the queen. In the midst of his impatience to depart, his mind was harrassed with sinister forebodings, and they were too truly realized by the event. Passing along a street in Paris, his coach became entangled, and his footmen quitting it for a moment, Ravillac, who had followed him secretly for a long time, took advantage of the opportunity, and stabbed him in the midst of seven courtiers. The crime of Ravillac was expiated by the most horrid tortures.

Henry's project was to divide Europe into fifteen settled powers, none of which should be suffered to make any new acquisitions, and should altogether form an association for the maintenance of a mutual balance, and the preservation of peace. There is little evidence, however, that he thought it practicable. He meant to effect it, if at all, by force, and it is certain that he strongly wished to set bounds to the house of Austria, both in Germany and Italy. The latter, therefore, may have been his only real design.

2. Louis XIII., in his ninth year, succeeded his father, 1610, under the regency of Mary of Medicis, his mother. During the early part of this prince's reign, France, which had arisen to splendour and prosperity, under Henry, evidently retrograded. Mary's partiality for her Italian courtiers, disgusted the nobility, and weakness, faction, and disorder, began to be experienced. But when cardinal Richelieu succeeded to the ministry, after the duke of Luynes, affairs wore a much more favourable aspect. He had vast abilities, and proportionable influence, which he successfully exerted in subduing the turbulence of the nobility, diminishing the power of the Protestants, and restraining the encroachments of Austria.

The principal events of the reign of Louis, were, the arrest of the prince of Conde, on account of his intrigues against the regent, and the subsequent temporary exile of the regent herself; the revolt of the Protestants at Rochelle, and the siege of that place, which lasted a year, and was attended with the loss of 15,000 lives; the junction of Louis with the Protestant princes of Germany, against the emperor Ferdinand II., and the revolt of the duke of Orleans, supported by the duke of Montmorency.

§ The Protestants were accused of a design to form France into an independent republic, to be divided into eight circles, on the model of those in Germany. Certain it is, that alienated by persecution, they attempted to throw off their allegiance, and Rochelle was the bulwark and head quarters of their party. Richelieu, having become master of the court, the armies, and the fleets, carried into execution, the plan he had long meditated, that of waging war against the Protestants, whom he was resolved to exterminate. He accordingly laid siege to Rochelle. On this occasion he acted as commander in chief; but chose to be accompanied by the king, for fear his enemies should take advantage of his absence.

The Protestants implored the aid of England, but were disappointed by the tardy measures of the duke of Buckingham. The garrison and inhabitants of Rochelle were resolved, however, to hold out until the last extremity. For twelve months they endured the miseries of a siege, but were at length obliged to yield to the active genius of the cardinal. He triumphed over the Calvinists, and deprived them of their most significant privileges. They never recovered from this blow.

The union of Louis with the Protestant princes of Germany, 1626, owed its origin to the influence of Richelieu, in his anxiety to humble the Austrian greatness. He forgot his hatred of Protestantism, for a time, and embarked most eagerly in the cause of the Protestant princes, who were alarmed at Ferdinand's avowed design of suppressing their religion, together with the liberties of the German empire.

Richelieu's plans were attended with complete success. The Protestants and Catholics, laying aside their theological disputes, conspired for the diminution of Ferdinand's power; the court of England embarked in the same cause; the Danes also took up arms, and Gustavus, king of Sweden, rushed like a torrent upon Germany. In the course of events, the emperor was effectually humbled, and a solid foundation was laid for the prosperity of the empire.

The haughty minister of Louis, amidst all the political intrigues and wars in which he was engaged, found leisure to patronize literature and science, and thus to extend the glory of the French nation, beyond the honour acquired by feats of arms. The French Academy owes its institution to the genius of Richelieu.

Louis died at the age of forty-three years. After he had been married twenty-three years, he had two sons, Louis XIV., and Philip, duke of Orleans. During his reign, the king was a less prominent object of attention, than his minister, and is not known to have been characterised by any particular talents or virtues.

3. Louis XIV., in the fifth year of his age, ascended the throne, in 1643, under the regency of Anne of Austria, his mother. The talents of this monarch, the vigour of his administration, the splendid events of his reign, his conquests and reverses, and the flourishing state of literature and the arts

under his patronage, have been themes of deep interest with historians. He is often styled the Great.

The most conspicuous events of his reign, were his war with the Spaniards, which commenced a few days after his accession, under the duke of Enghein; the civil commotions called la-Fronde, which grew out of Mazarine's ministry; the contention with Holland, in 1672, in which he was opposed by the German emperor and Spain, and in which Franche Comte was conquered and united to France; the revocation of the edict of Nantes; the league of Augsburg against France, by which war was waged against that country, by Germany, Spain, England, and Holland, and, in consequence of which, Louis acquired peculiar glory; and the war of the succession, in which he met with woful reverses, from the allied powers, under the duke of Marlborough, and prince Eugene.

§ In the early war with the Spaniards, the duke of Enghein gained the battle of Rocroi; that of Fribourg in 1644; that of Nordlingen in 1645; and that of Dunkirk in 1646. The Spaniards were the aggressors, having taken an advantage of the king's minority, and the popular discontents.

These discontents arose from the ministry of Cardinal Mazarine, the favourite of the regent, who was an Italian, and whose avarice was excessive. The burdens which he imposed on the people, and the consequent detestation in which he was held, terminated in the commotions of the fronde. Cardinal de Retz, had a principal agency in exciting this civil war. The parliament of Paris, and the chief nobility, took part with the rebels. The celebrated general, Turenne, also aided the rebels. A short pacification ensued, but the imprudent violence of Mazarine, soon renewed the disorders. At length, the parliament of Paris assumed the right of banishing this unpopular minister. When, however, the king became of age, Mazarine resumed his station as minister, while de Retz and Orleans, the chief promoters of the rebellion were banished in their turn.

On the death of Mazarine, in 1661, when Louis was twenty-two years of age, he took upon himself the entire control of affairs, and by the splendour of his projects, and the success with which many of them were crowned, established throughout the world, his reputation as an able monarch. His war with Holland soon commenced, in which Turenne, and Conde, another great general. gave signal proofs of the sagacity of Louis, in the leaders whom he had chosen to conduct his military operations. Although Spain and the emperor joined the Hollanders, yet Turenne defeated the Imperialists in the pitched battles of Ensheim, Mulhausen, and Turkheim. Sometime before, Conde had signalized his arms against Franche Comte which he subjugated in the space of seventeen days.

Several powers now became jealous of the ascendency of France, and the prince of Orange, whose dominions had been so wanton ly attacked by the French king, had sufficient influence with England, to obtain its alliance in aid of the republic. The arms of Louis, however, still continued to be successful, and the peace concluded at Nimeguen, in 1678, was much to the honour of France. Franche Comte was assured, as a part of the dominions of Louis, and Spain allowed his right by conquest to a great proportion of the Netherlands.

In the revocation of the Edict of Nantes, 1685, the French king manifested a complete dereliction both of wisdom and justice. The toleration which was granted to the Protestants by Henry IV., was taken away, their worship suppressed, their churches demolished, their ministers exiled, and an absolute renunciation of their religion, was made the condition with all who chose to continue in their native country. If they failed to comply with this requirement, death was the consequence, whenever they could be found. By this measure, the kingdom lost, according to some, 800,000 of her most industrious and useful citizens, who either perished, or driven into exile, carried the arts and manufactures of France, into various countries.

The League of Augsburg, in 1686, was brought about by William, prince of Orange, the sworn enemy of Louis. His attack on Holland had betrayed his ambition, and the splendour of his designs could not but excite the envy or jealousy of his neighbours. Victory however, attended his standard against all the forces of the leaguers. Though the valiant Turenne had perished in battle, the able Conde had retired, and Colbert, one of the greatest statesmen of any age, was no more, and their places could not be well supplied, yet the name of Louis was a host, and the successors of those renowned men, were by no means contemptible. Luxemburg defeated the prince of Orange, in the battles of Steenkirk and Norwinden; Noailles was victorious in Spain; and an army of one hundred thousand French, ravaged the Palatinate, and took many of the most important towns on the Rhine. This was the brightest period of his reign. Disasters were soon to follow him.

The extensive military enterprises of Louis, had been attended with enormous expenses. The pride of the monarch had been flattered by his victories, but no solid advantage had accrued to the nation. The finances had fallen into disorder, and the persevering efforts of his enemies, obliged him to conclude the peace of Ryswick, in 1697. The war, however, was soon renewed. That was the war of the succession. The nations engaged in it were England, Holland, and the empire, against France and Spain. The avowed object on the part of the former, was to put the house of Austria in possession of the throne of Spain, on the expected death of Charles II., without issue.

Louis had passed his prime, and lost his greatest generals and ministers; while the armies of his enemies were commanded by the ablest generals of the age, and supported by the treasures of the united powers. The war was carried on with manifest advantage on the part of the allies. The battle of Blenheim, in which the English Marlborough began his victorious career, cost the French twenty thousand men. He gained, besides, the battles of Ramilies, Oudenarde, and Malplaquet. One or two victories on the part of the French and Spanish, prevented Philip, king of Spain, from abandoning his possessions in Europe. Louis sued for peace, and even proposed very humiliating terms; but as they were rejected, and the hard condition of dethroning his grandson Philip, was insisted on, he made one more desperate effort in battle, in which he was so far successful as to preserve Philip on the throne. The change in queen Anne's cabinet, gave facility to propositions for peace, in which the English and Dutch secured many valuable acquisitions.

4. Louis died, aged seventy-seven years, having reigned more than seventy-two, one of the longest reigns on the page of history, and illustrated by many splendid achievements. His patronage of literature and the arts, constitutes, more than any other which he possessed, his claim to the admiration of posterity. No species of merit was suffered to go unrewarded, and the finest models of composition in the French language, were produced in his reign. All kinds of public works were extended and improved—the capital was enlarged and beautified, the splendid palace of Versailles erected, commerce and manufactures encouraged, and the fine canal of Languedoc constructed.

Louis was remarkable for his able administration of internal affairs. His sagacity was peculiarly displayed in the selection of his generals and ministers. Besides those that have been already mentioned, was the famous Vauban, whose great genius was successfully employed in fortifying towns. Colbert has been named. His skill in finances, has acquired him an immortal reputation. The latter was also a zealous patron of learning, thus seconding the designs of his royal master. At his suggestion, the celebrated astronomer, Cassini, quitted Italy, and placed himself under the protection of the king of France, who bestowed on him, and also on Huygens, a Dutch mathematician of equal celebrity, a very large pension.

Louis was reckoned the handsomest man in his dominions, and was celebrated for his politeness and urbanity. His intellect was vigorous, but indifferently cultivated. It was the great fault of Mazarine, to whom the childhood of Louis was entrusted, that he neglected his education. He sought for the young monarch, no other accomplishments than those

20

of dancing, fencing, and riding, so that when the latter was drawing on towards manhood, he scarcely knew how to pen an epistle.

The love of glory, was perhaps his ruling passion, though he was influenced unduly by other passions, to the indelible infamy of his private life. How often is it, that an admired public pageant, lamentably fails in that which constitutes rea· worth of character.

GREAT BRITAIN.

House of Stuart. Commonwealth. Restoration of Monarchy.

5. The throne of England, (called towards the close of the present period, GREAT BRITAIN,) was ascended by James I., 1603, who was the sixth king of Scotland of that name, and son of Mary Stuart, queen of Scots. Thus the sceptre passed with entire tranquillity from the house of Tudor, to that of the Stuarts—an event which was in exact accordance with the law of succession, and with the expressed wishes of Elizabeth, and which united the two crowns, and eventually made the two kingdoms one.

§ James I., was a great grandson of Henry VII. When Elizabeth was dying, upon being requested to make known her pleasure in regard to a successor, she replied "that she had held a royal sceptre, and required no other than a royal successor"—which she explained to be one who was then actually a king, viz. "her nearest kinsman, the king of Scots."

The history of Scotland, from the time of Wallace and Robert Bruce, to Mary, the mother of James, and rival of Elizabeth, is very summarily as follows:

The son of Robert, was David Bruce, who began to reign in 1329. During his minority, on account of the invasion of the kingdom by Edward Baliol, he was conveyed to France for security. He was a weak, but virtuous prince, and passed through many reverses of fortune. He was taken prisoner in the battle of Durham, by Edward III., and remained eleven years in captivity. He was ransomed by his subjects, and ended a turbulent reign, in 1370.

He was succeeded by Robert II., his nephew, and the grandson of the great Robert Bruce, whose reign of twenty years' continuance, was spent in a series of hostilities between the Scots and the English.

Robert III., then ascended the Scottish throne; but his infirmities and weakness, obliged him to resign the government into the hands of his brother, the duke of Albany

James I., a son of Robert, whom Albany had sought to murder, and whom the English had taken prisoner in his attempts to escape to France, next ascended the throne, 1424. He was a prince of great natural endowments, and profited by a captivity of eighteen years in England, adorning his mind with every valuable accomplishment. The kingdom had fallen into great disorders, during the regency of Albany; but James, on his return, soon placed affairs on a favourable footing. He bent all his attention to the improvement and civilization of his people. In restraining the power of the nobles, however, as necessary to this end, he incurred their enmity, and was accordingly assassinated.

James II., succeeded his father, 1437. He inherited a portion of his father's talents, but possessing an impetuous temper, he pursued the plan of humbling the nobles, with excessive rigour. Ruling with absolute authority, he was uncommonly successful in attaining the objects he had in view, and greatly improved his kingdom.

His son, James III., without the talents of his predecessors, affected to tread in the same steps. But he was impolitic in attaching himself to mean favourites; and quarreling with the barons, he was killed in an insurrection, 1488.

James IV., a great and most accomplished prince, succeeded to the throne. He was respected by his nobles, and beloved by his people. Invading England with a powerful army, he fell, with almost the whole of his nobility, in the rash and unfortunate battle of Flodden-Field, 1513.

James V., his son and successor, was a great, but uncultivated prince. His reign was long and turbulent, the aristocracy attempting to resume their power, and he being employed in defeating their projects. He died of a broken heart, in consequence of the infidelity of his troops, in a war with the English, 10,000 of the Scots having deliberately surrendered themselves to the enemy.

He was succeeded by Mary, whose eventful life and tragical death, have been already narrated.

6. Though the succession of James I. was tranquil, a few events soon occurred, which tended to disturb his reign. One event was, a conspiracy planned to subvert the government, by seating on the throne Arabella Stuart, the king's near relative, descended, like himself, from Henry VII.

§ Sir Walter Raleigh, was taken as one of the principals in this plot, and though he was convicted on incompetent evidence, he was only reprieved, not pardoned, and lay many years a prisoner in the tower.

A project of a much fouler kind followed. This was the gunpowder plot, which was ascribed to the catholics, who, disappointed in their expectations from James, were enraged beyond measure, and meditated the destruction of the royal family, lords and commons, at a meeting of parliament.

§ The plot was discovered, just as it was on the eve of execution It was intended, on the part of the conspirators, to blow up the house in which the parliament should assemble, by means of gunpowder, which had been secreted in the cellar of the building. Twenty conspirators had sacredly kept this dreadful secret, nearly a year and a half; but the same bigotry which had given rise to the plot, was directed as an engine by Providence, to reveal it. A few days before the meeting of parliament, a catholic member of it, received, from an unknown hand, a letter, advising him not to attend the meeting, and intimating to him, obscurely, what was about to take place.

* This, on the part of the member, was considered merely as a foolish attempt to frighten him. He, however, showing it to the king, the superior sagacity of the latter, led him to conceive, that allusion was made to danger from gunpowder. The following sentence in the letter, seems to have suggested the idea to the king. "Though there be no appearance of any stir, yet, I say, they will receive a terrible blow this parliament, and yet they shall not see who hurts them."

Search was now determined to be made in the vaults under the house of parliament. With the view, however, that they might detect not only the conspiracy, but the conspirators, they were quiet till the night before the commencement of the session. The plan of the king succeeded. A man by the name of Guy Fawkes, was found at the door, who was immediately seized, the faggots, and powder, to the amount of thirty-six barrels, discovered, and the very matches to set fire to the train, were detected in his pocket. He gave up the names of his accomplices, eighty in number, who, with himself, were all put to death.

7. The puritans, who had already become conspicuous, having first appeared in the reign of Mary, indulged the expectation at the accession of James, of meeting with special favour from the new monarch, because he had been educated a presbyterian. Their disappointment, but especially the restraints and persecutions which they endured, forced numbers of them to the new world, where they laid the foundations of a great nation.

Domestic events, such as have been recorded, chiefly distinguished the reign of James. He exerted, and wished to exert, no influence abroad. His disposition was altogether pacific. When, in the early part of his reign, he was solicited to join in a league with Henry IV., the United Provinces, and the northern crowns, to repress the exorbitant power of the house of Austria, he would have nothing to do with the scheme.

The Stuarts, as well as Tudors, were strenuous advocates

for the royal prerogative, in the widest exercise. This was especially the case with James. He was prejudiced against the Puritans, on account of their notions of liberty, and took part with the established church. It was a favourite maxim with him—"No bishop, no king." But the minds of Englishmen were undergoing a change. Light had increased, and juster notions of the people's rights began to obtain. The opposition of parliament to the royal prerogative, was carried to a great height, and laid the foundation of those fatal struggles which, in the next reign, subverted the monarchy.

James died after a reign of twenty-two years over England, and of nearly his whole life over Scotland. The private character of this prince, is not free from reproach. His disposition, however, was mild; and his reign, though not glorious, in the usual sense of that word, was yet, in many respects, happy and prosperous to his people. On them he bestowed the care of a parent.

§ James was ingenious and learned, and yet pedantic withal. Of flattery, he was excessively fond, and there were parasites to deal it out to him without measure. On a certain occasion, he publicly proposed the question, whether he might not take his subjects' money, when he wanted it, without the formality of parliaments. "God forbid," replied the obsequious Neile, bishop of Durham, "but that you should, for you are the very breath of our nostrils."

James is said to have been pusillanimous in life, but he shewed himself courageous in death, being so composed as to close his own eyes in his last struggle. Perhaps, a people who delighted in war, and valued blood and treasure less than the splendour of battles and conquests, were incapable of doing justice to the principles that guided the public conduct of this prince. Hence the contempt, which has sometimes been expressed against his benign and gentle policy. Saving his high notions of prerogative, and his attempt to sustain them, there was nothing, during this reign, to mar the happiness of a great people.

Two of the greatest names in the records of genius, Shakspeare and Bacon, besides others, adorned the times of James, and the latter part of the period of Elizabeth.

8. Charles I., ascended the throne in 1625. The kingdom, at this time, was in a prosperous condition; but the principles of liberty had expanded the minds of many of his subjects, and they demanded a more liberal system in the administration of the government, than was observed by his immediate predecessors. This demand, however, Charles

repelled, and he shewed that he possessed the same arbitrary principles with his father, without the prudence of the latter

The refusal of the parliament, to grant adequate supplies, for enabling the king to carry on a war, first in support of his brother-in-law, the Elector Palatine, and afterwards with France and Spain, led Charles to adopt the resolution of ruling without their aid, and of levying money in the most illegal forms.

§ The manifestation of a tyrannical disposition, on the part of Charles, first soured the minds of his parliament against him. Being engaged to his allies, the king could not brook the denial of supplies, and accordingly dissolved the parliament, and issued warrants for borrowing money of the subject. A new parliament was found equally uncomplying, and evinced its jealousy of the king, by the impeachment of his minister, Buckingham. Charles, however, avenged the insult, by imprisoning two members of the house of commons. A quarrel thus began, received continued additions from new causes of offence.

The king, in his wars with France, sent troops to assist the French calvinists; but, after an unsuccessful expedition under Buckingham, they were obliged to return to England. Rochelle was, in consequence, reduced to extremity, by which the protestant interest received an irrevocable blow in France. The blame of every public miscarriage was thrown upon Buckingham, who sheltered himself under the royal protection, till he was assassinated by one Felton, just as he was ready to embark for the relief of Rochelle.

The death of this worthless favourite, however, did not deter Charles from his arbitrary proceedings, which the English patriots, in that enlightened age, justly considered as so many acts of tyranny. His impositions upon trade, without the voice of parliament, many of the merchants, and some members of the house of commons, refused to pay.

A new parliament, which was now convoked, exhibited a spirit of determined reformation. A petition of right was passed by both houses, which declared the illegality of raising money without their sanction, or enforcing loans from the subject; annulled all taxes imposed without consent of parliament, and abolished the exercise of martial law; and Charles was obliged, with much reluctance, to give his assent to this great retrenchment of prerogatives. The taxes of tonnage and poundage had usually been continued from one reign to another. On this ground, the king conceived he was warranted to levy them without a new grant; and a member of the house of commons refusing to pay them, was imprisoned. A commotion being excited, parliament was dissolved.

9. About this time, a great number of Puritans, weary of the restraint they experienced in England, under the domineering spirit of Laud, archbishop of Canterbury, embarked for Ameri-

ca, where they spread the liberty of which they were deprived at home. But at length the enemies of that sect prevailed on the king to forbid these emigrations. This providentially proved a very unhappy affair for Charles, inasmuch as John Hampden, John Pym, and Oliver Cromwell, were prevented from going.

§ Hampden rendered himself illustrious, by his talents and virtue, and particularly by the firm stand he made against the illegal imposition called ship money. He refused to pay a small sum, that had been levied against him, and ventured to assert the liberty of Englishmen, by risking a legal prosecution. All England was deeply interested in the trial, and this was the favourable result which he realized, though the venal judge decided the cause against him. The people began to see their danger.

At a time when the public feeling was running strongly in favour of Puritanism, and a simpler form of worship, Laud, with a most intemperate and insulting zeal, was engaged in loading the church with new ceremonies. Things might have gone on in this train for some time; but attempting likewise to introduce the liturgy of the church of England among the Scots, the most violent commotions were produced. A bond, termed the National Covenant, containing an oath of resistance to all religious innovations, was subscribed in Scotland, by all ranks and conditions. To maintain this proceeding, the Scotch reformers took up arms, and soon marched into the heart of England.

At the same time, a catholic rebellion arose in Ireland, which the people imputed to the arts of the royalists; and to complete the misfortune of the king, the parliament, which had been necessarily convoked, proceeded to such extremities in its acts, that they were considered tantamount to a declaration of war against the king and his party.

10. Things had arrived at such a pass, that the sword was now to decide the contest. The two houses of parliament took into their hands the force constituted by the militia of the country, and at the same time the king erected his standard at Nottingham, 1642. Several battles were fought, during three or four consecutive years, with various success; but at length the royalists were overcome, and the king was thrown into the hands of his enemies. The cause of Charles was supported by a large proportion of the landed interest, all the friends of the established church, and all the adherents of the papacy; that of the parliament, by the city of London, and most of the great towns, and all the dissenters from the establishment. Cavaliers was the term applied to the supporters of the king—Round Heads to those of the parliament.

§ The parliament, in order to carry on hostilities with the greater prospect of success, had entered into a strict confederacy with the Scots, who were already in a menacing attitude. The new bond which they formed, was more specific in its objects than the former, and more determined in its spirit. It was called the "Solemn League and Covenant," and it brought an accession of 20,000 men to the forces of the parliament.

Oliver Cromwell, an officer under Fairfax, general of the parliament, in reality, directed all the measures of the army. This extraordinary man, as will presently appear, was destined to perform an extraordinary part in the transactions of this period. The two first battles, viz. those of Edgehill and Newbury, were favourable to the royalists; but those of Marston Moor and Naseby, terminated in their overthrow. Never were the morals and religion of an army more carefully watched, than those of the soldiers of Cromwell. Previously to each battle, it was customary with them, individually, to spend some time in prayer.

When the king was taken by a party of Cromwell's soldiers, after having been delivered up by the Scots, among whom he had sought protection, he was conveyed first to Hurst castle, and then to Windsor, and at last to London. The parliament at this time, influenced by Cromwell, having declared it treason in a king to levy war against his parliament, a court, consisting of 133 men, were appointed to try him as a tyrant, traitor, and murderer. Charles declined the jurisdiction of the court, and refused to plead. He was nevertheless condemned to suffer death, and was beheaded the third day afterwards, in the forty-ninth year of his age, and the twenty-fourth of his reign.

On the morning of the fatal day, which was the 30th of January, 1649, Charles rose earlier than usual, and calling one of his attendants, bade him employ more than usual care in adjusting his dress. As he was preparing for the block, he observed, in reply to some exhortations addressed to him by the bishop of London, "I go from a corruptible to an an incorruptible crown, where no disturbance can have place." He submitted to the stroke with entire resignation.

Charles had many virtues, and, in private life, was estimable and engaging, beyond most princes. As a sovereign, he had unfortunately imbibed, in his education, the arbitrary principles which distinguished his ancestors; but with the disadvantage of living in an age and country, in which a king could not be a tyrant with impunity. He deceived the parliament too often for them to trust him, and suffered himself to be guided by counsellors much inferior to him in knowledge and judgment, while he paid an unwise deference to the advice of his queen, who was a bigoted papist. Granger says, "He would have made a much better figure in private life, than he did upon a throne."

We may lament the fate of Charles, as severe, and perhaps unnecessary; and must condemn several of the acts of the republicans as passionate and oppressive; yet Providence seems to have overruled the events of the times, for the advancement of civil liberty, and for the general good of mankind. Had Charles lived, England might have been still governed by despots, instead of limited monarchs.

Charles was an author, both in prose and verse. The Icon Basilike, a work which appeared soon after the king's death, and excited much commiseration for his fate, has often been attributed to him. The authorship of that work, however, remains a matter of dispute. If Charles wrote it, his talents, in composition, must have been much superior to those of most contemporary scholars. Hume considers it the best prose composition which, at the time of its publication, was to be found in the English language: and D'Israeli remarks, that the political reflections it contains, will be found not unworthy of Tacitus.

In a poem of his, entitled "Majesty in Misery," the following stanzas will show his manner in poetry.

> "With my own power my majesty they wound,
> In the king's name, the king himself's uncrown'd;
> So doth the dust destroy the diamond.
>
> Felons attain more privilege than I,
> They are allow'd to answer ere they dié;
> 'Tis death to me to ask the reason why."

11. On the death of Charles I., monarchy in England was dissolved, and the house of lords was abolished as useless, by the commons. The forms of all public business were changed from the king's name, to that of the keepers of the liberties of England. Religion shared in the revolutions of the times.

§ Presbyterianism, which had succeeded episcopacy, now began to yield to the independent interest. Cromwell so managed, as to transfer to the army, the power which the parliament had not long before taken into their own hands. Presbyterians had been mostly excluded from parliament, and that part of the house which remained, termed, in derision, the Rump, was composed of Independents, under Cromwell's influence. As is often the case, the military power proved fatal to those Presbyterians who had employed it to effect their own purposes.

12. The confusions which overspread England, upon the dissolution of monarchy, could be settled only by the great influence, both civil and military, acquired by Oliver Cromwell, who was peculiarly fitted for the age in which he lived, and for the part which he was destined to act.

§ The situation of Ireland and Scotland, gave some inquietude to the new republic. The duke of Ormond, at the head of 16,000 men, had recovered many places in the former country, from the parliament; while in Scotland, Charles II., had been proclaimed king on the condition of his strict observance of the covenant. Cromwell, with his usual cunning, procured for himself the appointment of commander-in-chief in Ireland. He accordingly passed over to that country, and soon put an end to the successes and authority of Ormond. He next marched into Scotland, at the head of 16,000 men, and defeated the royalist covenanters, in the battle of Dunbar. Upon the retreat of their army into England, Cromwell pursued it thither, and overtaking it at Worcester, the whole was annihilated by him in one desperate battle. The king was obliged to flee.

It was with great difficulty, and after many adventures, that the latter effected his escape. He first retired to Boscobel, a lone house on the borders of Staffordshire, inhabited by one Penderell, a farmer, who, in conjunction with his four brothers, served him with unshaken fidelity. They clothed him in a garb like their own, and employed him, like themselves, in cutting faggots, and he partook of their homely fare. On one occasion, when his enemies were in search of him, he ascended an oak, where he was effectually concealed a whole day, among the leaves. In this situation, he saw several of his pursuers pass by, whom he overheard expressing their wish to be able to find him. This tree was afterwards known, and venerated, under the name of the royal oak. He succeeded, eventually, in reaching France.

The republic, at this era, acted with uncommon vigour. Admiral Blake, and other naval officers, now carried the terror of the English name, by sea, to all quarters of the globe. Under his command, a war with Holland was ably maintained against the celebrated Dutch commanders, Van Tromp and De Ruyter; but the advantage was greatly in favour of the English, who took 1600 of the Dutch ships. The famous Navigation act, which the parliament passed at this time had a most favourable effect on the commerce and naval superiority of Great Britain.

An attempt being made to reduce the land army, at this time, Cromwell remonstrated against it, and demanded a new parliament. But this meeting with no regard, he entered, in great rage, into the house, attended by 300 soldiers, and, loading the parliament with reproaches, bade them be gone, and give place to honester men. The republic of England, which had subsisted four years and three months, was thus, in a moment, annihilated, April 20th, 1653.

Cromwell, however, though he had seized the reins, could not well deny his subjects a parliament. He therefore summoned 144 persons in England, Scotland, and Ireland, to assemble as the representatives of the nation. They were his creatures; and though some of them possessed the quality and degree of gentlemen, they were generally, as Clarendon says, "a pack of weak, senseless fellows, fit only to bring the name and reputation of parliaments lower than it was yet." This body was called Praise God Barebones' parliament, from the name of a certain member, a leather seller, who distinguished himself by speaking. Incompetent to their duties, they re-delivered to Cromwell, at the expiration of five months, the instrument they nad received from him, calling them together, and besought him to take care of the commonwealth.

13. The supreme power of the nation, now passing into the hands of Cromwell and his Council of officers, he was declared, by the latter, Protector of the Commonwealth of England, with the title of Highness, 1654. In this capacity, he exercised greater power, than had ever been annexed to the regal dignity. He gave the command of all the forces in Scotland, to General Monk, and sent his own son, Henry, to govern Ireland. Administering the government with energy and ability, and granting religious toleration, the republic greatly flourished. Its rights were respected abroad. Success attended the usurper, both in negociation and battle. In an engagement which was fought with the Spaniards in Flanders, the latter were defeated; and Dunkirk being soon after surrendered, was by agreement, delivered to Cromwell.

Notwithstanding the general correctness of his administration, he was never popular, either with the royalists or republicans. He had subverted the freedom of his country, and his professions passed for nothing. He had reached a fearful elevation, and was consequently kept in perpetual inquietude. Neither society nor solitude could soothe his agitated mind. Fearing assassination, he was constantly attended by his guards, and changed the place of his sleeping, every few nights. Seized at length, with a slow fever, he died, A. C. 1658, in the sixtieth year of his age.

§ In regard to the character of Oliver Cromwell, what was said of Cinna, has been applied to him. "He attempted those things which no good man durst have ventured on; and achieved those in which none but a valiant and great man could have succeeded." This, however, is the judgment rather of an enemy than friend. Respecting his capacity, there can be but one opinion; but mankind have viewed his moral qualities in very different lights. He has in this respect been oftener condemned than approved. Indeed, he is no favourite of history, as no man of equal merit or fewer faults, has been so often held up to suspicion, derision, or hatred. There are, however, those who, while they promptly condemn his dissimulation and ambition, can see much to admire in the strict morality and devotions of a man, who, in private life, apparently reverenced the institutions of religion.

14. Richard Cromwell, by the father's dying request, succeeded the latter in the protectorate. He was acknowledged in all parts of the empire; but as he wanted resolution, and possessed none of those arts which take with the soldiery, he soon signed his own abdication. He retired to private life,

and his virtues secured to him, rare enjoyment to extreme old age.

15. After the abdication of Richard Cromwell, Charles II. was restored to the throne of his ancestors, 1660. The short interval that occurred, was a season of anarchy.

§ The restoration was effected by the wishes of the people, who seem to have thought, that neither peace nor protection could be obtained, unless the ancient order of things should be re-established Monk, a man of military abilities, had the sagacity to observe this change in the sentiments of the people; and after temporizing in various shapes, rendered himself master of the parliament, through which Charles was duly acknowledged.

16. Charles, who was thirty years of age when he began his reign, made a favourable impression on his subjects, by means of his personal appearance and accomplishments, and of the superior character of his intellect. He was easy in manners, unaffectedly polite, gay in his temper, lively, witty, and a great observer of men and things. It must be added, also, that he was base and unprincipled, and became at length immersed in pleasure and indolence. He was personally a favourite with his subjects, and continued so to be; although the government became unpopular, after the king was so immersed in private gratification, as to neglect the true interests of his realm. Still, in this case, he escaped the reproaches which he merited, and most of the odium of extravagance and unsuccessful public measures, fell on his advisers. The whole royal party were so elated at the return of their sovereign, that they were dissolved in thoughtless jollity, and many of the republicans, especially the younger part and the women, were glad to be released from the gloomy austerity of the commonwealth. During this reign, dissipation and infidelity became greatly prevalent.

Charles was distinguished by the same arbitrary notions which had prevailed with his ancestors; and though there were many struggles like those in the preceding reigns, a surprising change had taken place in the feeling of the people in general, in consequence of which, he escaped the fate of his father. The slavish doctrines of passive obedience and non-resistance, now came into repute, opposed indeed by the enemies of the crown. This was the origin of the distinguishing epithets of Whig and Tory—the former opposing the crown, the latter advocating it. This is a distinction of parties still existing. The Whigs have always favoured the rights of the people, the Tories, those of the monarch.

In consequence of high church, or tory principles, an act of uniformity in religion was passed, by which two thousand Presbyterian ministers, were deprived of their livings.

§ We may enumerate among the other events of this reign, the following—an act of indemnity, by which ten only, out of twenty eight who were tried and condemned for the murder of the king, were devoted to death—the sale of Dunkirk for £400,000, required by the prodigality of Charles, and which he soon squandered upon his pleasures—the war with the Dutch, which, after an immense expenditure, was attended with no material benefit—and finally, the measures excited by the influence of the duke of York, (afterwards James II.) consisting of numerous attacks upon the lives, liberties, and properties of the people, mingled with party intrigues, plots, and conspiracies.

Before the reign of Charles expired, the Whigs became predominant in parliament, and raging furiously against the Catholics, insisted on the king's assent to the bill for the exclusion of his brother, the duke of York. This affair induced the king to dissolve two parliaments in succession. The consequence was, that England was thrown into a flame. But the king took measures to crush or intimidate the opponents of the court. Lord Russel, who had been remarkable for his opposition to the popish succession, Algernon Sydney, and several other distinguished protestants, were tried, condemned, and executed. The ground of proceeding against them, was a pretended conspiracy in favour of reform, called the Rye-House Plot. A pretended Popish Plot had, previously to this, been disclosed by the unprincipled Titus Oates, by means of which Lord Stafford and some other Catholics were condemned and executed.

17. It was thought that Charles, having been guilty of arbitrary conduct, intended to take some measures for the future quiet of his reign, when he was seized with a sudden fit of illness, and after languishing a few days, expired, 1685, in the fifty-fifth year of his age, and the twenty-fifth of his reign.

§ In addition to what has already been said of the character of Charles, it may be observed, that though he was a genius, he acted in direct opposition to every principle of sound policy. He chose rather to be a pensioner of France, from whose king he received £200,000 a year, for the concealed purposes of establishing popery and despotic power, than the arbiter of Europe. Rochester's epigrammatic jest, that Charles "never said a foolish thing, and never did a wise one," forms a tolerable motto for his "picture in little."

Charles, it is said, had a constant maxim, which was, never to fall out with any, let the provocation be ever so great; by which he observed, he had found great benefit all his life, and the reason he gave for it was, that he did not know how soon it might be necessary for him to have them again for his best friends. It has likewise been said of this king, that had he loved business as well as he understood it, he would have been the greatest prince in Europe.

Dryden did not scruple to laud this prince, in a fulsome manner as in the lines,

"Truly good and truly great:
For glorious as he rose, benignly so he set."

18. On the death of Charles, the duke of York was immediately proclaimed king under the title of James II., 1685. The history of this reign consists of little more than the weak and irresolute efforts of a bigotted and tyrannical prince, to introduce popery; an attempt so absurd, that it did not meet with the least encouragement from the pope himself.

§ The capacity of James was by no means equal to the subversion of those deep and solid foundations, which supported the civil and religious liberties of his people. The share which he had in his father's sufferings had not sufficiently taught him, that the jealousy of the royal prerogative, was too strong in the hearts of his subjects, to be easily allayed. He was so violent and precipitate in his conduct, that he never failed to counteract his own purposes; and he established the protestant religion, on a firmer basis than ever, by his wild attempts to introduce those of the church of Rome. Though he ascended the throne with many advantages, he could never sit easy in it; and having taught even the advocates of non-resistance, to resist, he was forced to relinquish a crown, which he was absolutely unfit to wear.

19. One of the principal events of his reign, was the rebellion of the duke of Monmouth, a natural son of Charles II., who undertook to seize the crown. He was defeated at Bridgewater, by the king's forces, taken prisoner, and beheaded. Had this victory been managed with prudence by James, it would have tended much to increase his authority; but the cruelty with which the revolt was punished, and the rash confidence with which this success inspired the king, led to his ruin. That most profligate of all the judges that ever sat on the English bench, Jeffries, aided the king in the work of murder, to an extent that has called down on him the execrations of mankind. He was wont to boast of the numbers whom he had adjudged to the gallows.

The spirit of the nation was roused, by the offensive and tyrannical measures which James took to establish popery; and many great men in England and Scotland, applied for relief to William, prince of Orange, who had married Mary the eldest daughter of James. William accordingly embark ed for England, with an army, and determined, agreeably to request, to assume the government.

§ Upon the arrival of the prince, he was joined, not only by the whigs, but by many whom the king had considered his best friends. Even his daughter Anne, inspired with protestant zeal, deserted him, and, with her husband, prince George of Denmark, joined the invader.

Upon this, James, reasonably filled with distrust of his people, fled to France, where the palace of St. Germain was assigned him; but as one remarks, "the convent of La Trappe would have been a much more suitable retreat." In France, he spent the remainder of his life.

A convention-parliament declared the king's flight an abdication, and settled the crown upon William and Mary.

§ The duke of Buckingham gave this character of the two royal brothers, Charles and James; that "the elder could see things if he would, and the younger would see things if he could."

On the access of James, an address of the quakers to him, is highly characteristic of that shrewd sect. "We come to condole the death of our friend Charles; and we are glad that thou art come to be our ruler. We hear that thou art a dissenter from the church of England, and so are we. We beg that thou wouldst grant the same liberty that thou takest thyself, and so we wish thee well. Farewell."

20. William and Mary now ascended the throne. This event constitutes what the British writers are pleased to call the glorious revolution of 1688. In the settlement which was then made of the crown, the sole administration remained in the prince. The protestant succession was secured; religious toleration granted, and presbyterianism re-established in Scotland. A declaration of rights was also made, in which the chief subjects of dispute between the king and people, were finally determined. The powers of the royal prerogative were more narrowly circumscribed, and more exactly defined, than in any former period of the English government.

§ A revolution became indispensable, inasmuch as the principles of religious liberty were now generally established in Britain, and the princes of the house of Stuart, from their arbitrary notions, entertained a strong aversion to a large portion of their subjects. There was, however, a class, chiefly among the clergy, who held the doctrines of passive obedience, and the divine right of kings and bishops. Numbers of these, looking upon James as their lawful king, and refusing to take the oath of allegiance to William, were deprived of their stations. Hence, they were styled "non-jurors high-churchmen, and jacobites."

21. William experienced a degree of trouble from Ireland, as that country still adhered to James. The latter, being assisted by Louis XIV., landed with some French forces in Ireland, where he was joined by a large army of Irishmen. William, however, defeated them, in the memorable battle of Boyne, and the country submitted to the new king.

During most of the reign of this prince, the nation was involved in many active wars. Their principal cause was the ambition of Louis XIV. These wars were carried on with vigour and success, though without any distinguished actions, unless it be the sea-fight of La Hogue. The peace of Ryswick, in 1697, terminated hostilities, and it was apparent that the power of France was weakened. The principle on which William acted in his foreign wars, was, the balance of power, of which he was an ardent advocate.

§ Louis, who used James to promote his own interest, was determined, if possible, to restore him to the throne. With this object he furnished him with a powerful fleet, and the exiled prince repaired to La Hogue, whence he was ready to embark for England. The English admiral, Russel, put to sea with all possible expedition, and being reinforced by the Dutch squadron, he sailed for the coast of France, with ninety ships of the line, besides frigates and fire-ships. On the 19th of May, 1692, the hostile fleets met off La Hogue; and, after a bloody contest of ten hours, victory declared in favour of the English. The French, who had fifty-three ships of the line, lost a great part of their fleet, and could not be made to hazard another battle by sea. James returned in despair to St. Germains, where he died, in 1701, in the sixty-ninth year of his age, having, some time before his death, laid aside all thoughts of worldly grandeur, and subjected himself to uncommon penance and mortification. His body, brains, and heart, like those of Richard I., were deposited in different cemeteries.

22. After the death of James, notwithstanding the succession of the crown had been settled in the house of Hanover, his son was proclaimed king of England, at St. Germains, and treated as such at the court of Versailles. This act so exasperated the British nation, that both houses of parliament assured his majesty, that they would assist him to the utmost of their power, against all his enemies, and the whole kingdom joined in a cry for war with France. While William was making preparations for the approaching conflict, he was suddenly removed by death, in the fifty-second year

of his age, and fourteenth of his reign. His excellent consort, and partner in the throne, died seven years before him, of the small pox.

§ In person, William was small and slender. His complexion was brown, his nose Roman, and his eye piercing. His genius was penetrating, and his judgment sound; but in his manners he was distant, and better qualified to gain respect than love.

During this reign, the system of borrowing money on remote funds commenced, which laid the foundation of the present national debt. A standing army, too, was first sanctioned by parliament, in the time of this prince, a measure only to be defended by the relative situation of Europe.

23. The crown now, (1702,) devolved on Anne, the second daughter of James II., who was married to George, prince of Denmark. Her reign is one of the most illustrious in British history. The arms of England were every where triumphant, nor were the achievements of its scholars less conspicuous. The great names of Newton, Locke, Addison, Swift, and others, have immortalized the times of the "Good Queen Anne," as she has been familiarly called. Though not endowed with superior talents, she was respected for her virtues. The military and literary distinction of her reign, could not, in any great degree, be attributed to her personal conduct or councils.

The principal events of her reign were, her war against France, carried on by the duke of Marlborough, the greatest general of the age, who gained the splendid victories of Blenheim, Ramilies, Oudenarde, and Malplaquet, the constitutional union between England and Scotland, in 1706, and the confusions occasioned by the high party spirit which prevailed in the latter part of the queen's reign.

§ The war against France, continued from the commencement to the last year but one of her reign. Germany and Holland were in alliance with England. The commander, on the part of the empire, who was associated with Marlborough, was prince Eugene. In the famous battle of Blenheim, the French lost twenty thousand men. The duke, during the engagement, rode through the hottest of the fire, but neither in this, nor in any other conflict, did he receive a wound. This victory saved the house of Austria from ruin. In the battle of Ramilies, six thousand of the enemy lost their lives, and seven thousand were captured; and this success was soon followed by the general conquest of the Netherlands. In the course of a most successful war on the part of the allies, Louis was humbled to a degree, that obliged him to demand peace, which though at first refused, took place in 1713, when the change in Anne's ministry, gave a facility to negociations for that object.

In the treaty of peace which was signed at Utrecht, Spain yielded to England all right to Gibraltar, and the island of Minorca, while France resigned her pretensions to Hudson's Bay, Nova Scotia, St. Christopher's, and Newfoundland.

Of Marlborough, it may be said, that he never laid siege to a town which he did not take, or fought a battle which he did not win. His understanding was as injurious to France as his arms. At St. James', he was a perfect courtier, the head of a party in parliament, and in foreign countries, one of the ablest negociators that any age has produced.

In the constitutional union of England and Scotland, it was stipulated, that the united kingdoms of Great Britian, should be represented by one and the same parliament, that Scotland should be represented by sixteen peers and forty-five commoners, and that all peers of Scotland should be peers of Great Britain, and rank next after English peers, of the like orders and degrees.

The confusions occasioned by high party spirit, were aggravated after the occurrence of peace. The strife between the Whigs and Tories, was never higher than at this time. After the peace, the ministers, as leaders of the nation, no longer restrained by the tie of common danger, gave loose to their mutual animosity.

The great duke of Marlborough was sacrificed, in consequence of these dissentions; though every honour had been accorded to him, and the most munificent benefactions bestowed upon him, (£500,000 having been voted at one time, to build the castle of Blenheim,) when his enemies came into the ministry, the queen was induced to dismiss him from all his employments. The tories had now supplanted the whigs in her favour, an event brought about by the preaching of Dr. Sacheverell, who inculcated the tory principles of passive obedience, and who, on account of his trial, before the house of commons, excited a sympathy which he did not deserve.

24. Anne died in her fiftieth year, after a short reign of twelve years, in 1714. She became a victim to an apoplectic disorder, which was brought on, or hastened, by fatigue, and the agitation of her mind, in attending a prolonged cabinet council, in which, her ministers fell into violent altercations with one another.

§ Anne was of the middle size, majestic, and well proportioned; her face was round, her features regular, her complexion ruddy, and her hair a dark brown.

GERMANY.

25. Soon after the commencement of this period. 1612, Matthias was at the head of the German empire. He

attempted to reconcile the protestants to the catholics, but without success. The revolt of the Bohemians brought on a civil war, which lasted thirty years, in the course of which, Ferdinand, cousin to the emperor, was invested with the kingdom of Bohemia; and Hungary, also, was soon afterwards conceded. Matthias, overwhelmed with grief, died before the conclusion of the war.

§ An excellent rule of conduct for a prince, which the emperor delivered to his successor, was the following: "If you wish your subjects to be happy under your government, do not let them feel the full force of your authority."

26. Ferdinand II. became emperor in 1619. During his reign, the ambition of Austria appeared, in her attempts to extinguish the protestant religion, to abridge the liberties of the empire, and to render the imperial diadem hereditary in her own house. But these attempts, especially in regard to the first two objects, were frustrated by the agency of Gustavus Adolphus, king of Sweden, who, at the head of the Evangelical Union, made rapid progress in Germany, till death stopped his career, in 1632. Austria, however, has usually held the imperial sceptre, and has long had an ascendancy in the empire.

§ Ferdinand has been styled by the papists, the Apostolical Emperor, on account of his hatred to the protestants. He was an unfeeling bigot, and scourge of the empire.

27. Ferdinand III., son of the preceding, was elected king of the Romans, (so is the head of the Germanic body often called,) in 1637. The protestants in the empire, found the most active support during the former part of this reign, both from the Swedes and the French; and the emperor being forced to conclude the peace of Westphalia, 1648, these powers dictated its terms. By this celebrated treaty, all disputes were settled between the contending princes of the empire, and the contending religions.

§ The Swedes were indemnified for the charges of the war, and acquired Pomerania, Stettin, Wismar, &c., and their sovereign, the dignity of prince of the empire; the Palatine family was restored to its chief possessions; the king of France made landgrave of Alsace, and an equal establishment of the three religions, viz. the Catholic, Lutheran, and Calvinistic.

Ferdinand was a devoted Catholic. He experienced many calamities, but bore them with magnanimity.

28. Leopold I., king of Hungary and Bohemia, was elect-

ed emperor in 1657. His was a long reign, of nearly fifty years. Joseph I. succeeded him, 1705, and reigned till 1711 Both of these emperors were engaged in the war of the Spanish succession, which commenced in 1700, on account of the claim advanced by Leopold, to the crown of Spain. The house of Bourbon was his competitor. The war was carried on by Austria, (England and Holland being her allies,) with success. Joseph, after having conquered Naples and Sardinia, forced the pope to acknowledge the Archduke Charles, as king of Spain. But, at length, the Austrian claimant being elected emperor, the Spanish crown was relinquished to the house of Bourbon, in the peace of 1713. In 1683, Vienna was besieged by an immense army of the Turks, but the place was relieved by John Sobieski, king of Poland.

Charles VI. was elected in 1711. His reign extends many years into the next period, but before the conclusion of the present, occurred his memorable war with the sultan Achmet III., in which he obtained many victories over the Turks, by his general, the renowned prince Eugene.

SPAIN.

29. The successor of Philip II., on the throne of Spain, was his son, Philip III., 1598. From the commencement of this reign, Spain declined in power, and notwithstanding her great sources of wealth, the national finances were exceedingly embarrassed. He had lost the seven United Provinces, whose independence was solemnly acknowledged, 1609. A most ill judged measure of his reign, was the expulsion of all the Moors, from his kingdom, who were its most industrious inhabitants. This, added to the depopulation occasioned by her American colonies, rendered Spain a mass of weakness.

30. Under Philip IV., who succeeded his father, in 1621, the national weakness and disorders increased, rather than diminished. Philip was implicitly ruled by his minister, Olivarez, a man of an indiscreet and insolent turn, who, while he encouraged the licentiousness of his sovereign, himself wore the specious appearance of extraordinary piety.

The reign of Philip was indeed one continued series of miscarriages and defeats. The Dutch seized Brazil: the

French invaded Artois; Catalonia revolted to France; and Portugal, shaking off the yoke, recovered its independence.

31. The revolution of Portugal, was effected with unwonted ease and celerity. It took place, 1640, and Portugal, after having been an appendage of the kingdom of Spain for sixty years, asserted the rights of self government. The people, disgusted with the administration of Olivarez, were prepared for a change. The duke of Braganza, descended from the ancient kings of Portugal, having command of the army at this time, and instigated by the ambition of his dutchess, caused himself to be proclaimed king, at Lisbon. The Spanish guards were attacked and overcome, and the principal adherents of the government, were put to death by the populace. The whole was accomplished in two or three hours. The example of the capital was followed by all the considerable towns, and soon after, by all the foreign settlements. The duke of Braganza took the title of John IV.

§ The events which occurred in the history of Portugal, previously to the above revolution, are summarily as follows:

Portugal was the ancient Lusitania, and was successively subject to the Suevi, the Goths, and the Moors.

In the early part of the twelfth century, Henry of Burgundy grandson to Robert I., of France, rendered assistance to Alphonso. in his wars against the Moors, and having distinguished himself by great bravery, Alphonso bestowed on him his natural daughter Theresa, in marriage, and also created him count of that part of Portugal, where Oporto was situated, from which place, formerly called Portus Calle, the whole country took its name. By the valour of Henry, the country regained its liberty, and he governed it with the title of count.

His son, Alphonso Henriquez, having obtained a decisive victory over five Moorish kings, was proclaimed king, by the soldiers. Several princes succeeded him, whose reigns deserve no particular notice. On the death of Ferdinand I., in 1383, the states gave the crown to his natural brother, John I., surnamed the Bastard, who was equally politic and enterprising, and in whose reign, the Portuguese first projected discoveries in the western ocean.

In the reign of his great grandson, John II., who was a prince of profound sagacity and extensive views, the Portuguese made conquests in the interior of Africa, and discovered, under Diaz, the Cape of Good Hope. That cape was doubled in 1497, for the first time, by Vasco de Gama, who thence sailed for the East Indies.

Emanuel, cousin of John, ascending the Portuguese throne, in 1495, adopted the plan of his predecessors, and sent out a fleet. It was with this fleet, that Gama doubled the cape as above mentioned; others of the king's vessels discovered Brazil, in 1501.

These princes had the merit of exciting that spirit of discovery which led to many subsequent improvements of navigation and commerce. Their discoveries on the coast of Africa, led to the voyage of Columbus, and the discovery of America. They also established valuable colonies in Africa and America, and an extensive empire in India. The reign of Emanuel, was the most glorious in the annals of Portugal. He was a great and wise prince, and banished poverty and distress from his dominions.

John III., the son of Emanuel, admitted the new founded order of the Jesuits, which has since been a powerful engine of despotism and superstition. He encouraged, if he did not establish, the Inquisition in Portugal.

Sebastian, his grandson, fanatically led an army against the Moors, in Africa, where he and most of his army perished in battle. Sebastian, leaving no issue, was succeeded by his uncle, cardinal Henry, in 1578, who, also dying without children, Philip II., king of Spain, obtained the crown, in right of his mother, 1580. After sixty years of subjection to Spain, the Portuguese, as already related, threw off the Spanish yoke, and became independent, under the duke of Braganza, the legal heir of the throne.

32. Charles II., succeeded his father, Philip IV., on the throne of Spain, in 1665. In order to frustrate the schemes of the kings of England and France, and of the states of Holland, he left his dominions to Philip, duke of Anjou, second son of Louis, dauphin of France.

§ This prince is said to have been debilitated, both in body and in mind, by certain drugs which his mother administered to him in his chocolate. To so unnatural an act, she was led, in consequence of his refusal to accept of her assistance as regent. Certain it is, that active before, he lost, in the course of a few weeks, his wonted spirits; and his future imbecility, proved highly detrimental to the interests of his kingdom.

33. The duke of Anjou, under the title of Philip V., the first Spanish monarch of the house of Bourbon, ascended the throne in 1700. In 1701, nearly all Europe united against France and Spain, and a useless and bloody war was carried on till the peace of Utrecht, in 1713. Gibraltar was lost to Spain, in the course of this war.

TURKISH EMPIRE.

34. The most splendid period in the history of TURKEY, was that which immediately preceded the present. The spirit of military enterprise was now considerably abated; though the power of the empire continued undiminished, except in

a naval force. The latter never wholly recovered from the effects of the fatal battle of Lepanto.

The present period embraces the reigns of nine sultans, and a part of the reign of another. They were generally at war with the neighbouring powers; Persia on the one side Venice, Hungary, and Austria, on the other.

§ During the former period, the wars of the Turks with the Venetians, had been extremely frequent and bloody. That small, but enterprising and martial republic, had, during one hundred and fifty years, restrained the Ottoman power, and prevented it, most probably, from overspreading a great part of Europe. The spirit of hostility continued through the present period, and broke out occasionally into fierce fightings. The Turks were for a long time superior to the Christian powers of Europe in military tactics, on account of having an order of men exclusively devoted to the profession of arms, and also on account of their frequent use of artillery.

Achmet I., made war with Persia and Hungary, but with little success. During his reign, in 1611, Constantinople was afflicted with a dreadful plague, of which more than 200,000 persons died.

Othman II., invaded Poland, but was forced to make peace after having lost 80,000 men. In 1622, he was strangled by the Janizaries, whom he intended to disband.

Amurath IV., tarnished a victory which he had obtained in the capture of Bagdad, by the barbarous slaughter of 30,000 Persians, who had laid down their arms, as well as of all the inhabitants.

Mahomet IV. made a conspicuous figure in the annals of Europe, from the middle, till towards the close of the seventeenth century. Under him, the Turks again became formidable to Europe, and took Candia from the Venetians, and besieged the capital of Austria. The siege of Candia is one of the most remarkable of modern times. Candia was the ancient Crete, and an emporium for commerce. The Turks had long desired to take possession of it, and at length, in 1645, effected a landing on it, with 60,000 men. After several towns had surrendered, Candia, the capital, was invested. This siege continued twenty-five years. For the last two years, the Turks put forth every effort, inasmuch as the delay was mortifying to their pride, and disappointed their ambitious hopes. After the loss of 30,000 lives, on the part of the Venetians and their allies, and 118,000 on the part of the besiegers, in the space of two years and four months, the city surrendered on honourable terms, in 1670. It is said the besiegers made against it, fifty-six assaults and ninety-six sallies; and that the Venetians discharged 276,743 cannon balls, 48,119 bombs, and consumed 50,317 barrels of powder. The Turks have ever since held possession of the island.

In the siege of the capital of Austria, in 1683, John Sobieski, king of Poland, particularly distinguished himself. His assistance was requested by the emperor of Germany, and readily bestowed. Through his efforts, Austria seems to have been saved from destruction, and the Ottoman power prevented from effecting an establishment in the heart of Europe—a service which Austria has since ill requited. Sobieski, whose army, when joined by the Austrians, did not exceed 50,000 men, advanced to the environs of Vienna, and fought one of the most memorable battles of the age. An army of nearly 200,000 Turks, brave and well disciplined, was entirely defeated by the Pole, who lost only 600 men. The victors secured the great Ottoman standard, 180 pieces of cannon, and the immense treasures found in the camp of the enemy. The war continued after that defeat, in which the Turks were the greatest sufferers. The imperialists, however, were weary of it; but neither party could be speedily brought to an accommodation, on account of the intrigues of the French king, who wished to exhaust the resources of the house of Austria.

Under Solyman II., the Turks were almost constantly defeated by the imperialists. Mustapha II., was severely beaten in the famous battle of Zenta, in Hungary, by prince Eugene, in 1697; and, in 1699, concluded a peace at Carlowitz, by which he was forced to cede Transylvania, Kaminiek, the Morea, and Azof.

Under Achmet III., in 1715, the Ottoman court declared war against the Venetians, and recovered the Morea. At the same time, war was waged against Austria, but the most disastrous effects to the Turks, took place from this renewal of the contention. Prince Eugene defeated a powerful army, in the battle of Peterwaradin, and took Temeswar, in 1716. The next year, the strong town of Belgrade surrendered to his again victorious arms. The disadvantageous peace of Passarowitz, in 1718, followed these defeats. And the Ottoman, formerly so terrible in arms, was obliged to yield the palm of military skill, if not valour, to the disciplined legions of Christendom.

BRITISH COLONIES IN NORTH AMERICA.

35. Our own country, is intended by the British Colonies in America. During the present period, and part of the following, the people inhabiting, chiefly, the south-eastern portion of North America, were known by the above appellation.

These colonies were settlements made principally by the English, though some of them derived their origin from adventures set on foot by other European nations. They were all, however, included within the English patent, and claimed by the English crown.

36. It was more than a century, from the discovery of the northern portion of the American continent, by Cabot, before the English made any effectual attempts to colonize the

country. The first grant from the crown, under which settlements were actually made in North America, was dated April 10, 1606. James I., by his letters patent, granted an exclusive right or privilege to two companies, called the London and Plymouth companies, by which they were authorized to possess the lands in America, lying between the thirty-fourth and forty-fifth degrees of north latitude; the southern part, called South Virginia, to the London, and the northern, called North Virginia, to the Plymouth company. Before the present patents, however, a project to settle the country was undertaken by Sir Walter Raleigh, who, under a commission from Elizabeth, in 1584, had arrived in this portion of North America, which, upon his flattering account of it, was called Virginia, in compliment to the queen's virgin majesty. But this project, as well as two that followed it, wholly failed.

Under the king's patent, the London company sent Captain Christopher Newport to Virginia, December 20th, 1606, with a colony of one hundred and five persons, to commence a settlement on the island Roanoke, now in North Carolina. By stress of weather, however, they were driven north of their place of destination, and entered Chesapeake Bay. Here, up a river which they called James river, on a beautiful peninsula, they commenced, in May, 1607, the settlement of Jamestown. This was the first permanent settlement in the United States.

37. Seven years afterwards, 1614, a colony of Dutch commenced a settlement on the present island of New-York, which had been discovered in the year 1609, by Henry Hudson, an Englishman in the service of Holland. The English government claimed a prior right to the country, by virtue of Cabot's discovery; but the first settlers retained possession, until 1664, when it was surrendered to an armament fitted out by Charles II., and received its name from his brother, the duke of York. It had been previously called New-Amsterdam. The Dutch had built a fort here, and one also at Albany.

38. The same year in which the Dutch settled on the Hudson, Captain John Smith, ranged the coast, from Penobscot to Cape Cod. King Charles, to whom a map of the country was presented, named it New-England, instead of

North Virginia. Sixteen years from this, December 22, 1620, a colony of puritans landed at Plymouth, in Massachusetts, and began the first permanent settlement in New-England. These colonists were originally from England, but had resided several years in Holland, on account of the religious intolerance which prevailed in their native country. The colony of Plymouth was afterwards connected with another colony in New-England, called Massachusetts Bay, which was founded in 1628.

39. In 1623, a number of persons from England, arrived in the river Piscataqua, and began two settlements; one at the mouth, at a place called Little Harbour, the other at a place now called Dover. These were the first settlements in New-Hampshire.

40. The next settlement in the order of time, seems to be that which was made by some bodies of the Dutch and Danes, about the year 1625, in New-Jersey. This was followed by the colonization of Delaware, in 1627, by the Swedes.

41. In 1637, Charles I. granted a patent to Lord Baltimore, conveying to him a tract of country, on the Chesapeak Bay, which, in honour of Henrietta Maria, daughter of the French king, he named Maryland. The next year, Baltimore appointed his brother, Leonard Calvert, governor of the province, who, with about two hundred planters, chiefly Roman catholics, began a settlement, in 1634, near the mouth of the Potomac, on the northern side.

42. In 1633, the first house was erected in Connecticut. This was a trading house built by some Plymouth adventurers, who transported the materials up Connecticut river Two years from this, 1635, about sixty men, women and children, from Newtown and Watertown, in Massachusetts, commenced their journey through the wilderness to Connecticut river. By these people, Windsor, Wethersfield, and Hartford, were settled.

43. The settlement of Rhode Island, is dated from the year 1636, an event occasioned by the banishment of Roger Williams from Massachusetts, on account of his religious opinions. He removed with his family to Mooshawic, and began a plantation, which, on account of the Divine kindness, he called Providence.

44. The colony of New-Haven, was formed in 1638, in consequence of the English having occasion to visit the territory, in an expedition against the Pequots. This colony eventually united with that of Connecticut.

45. In 1663, some of the Virginia settlers laid the foundation of North Carolina, which was followed by the settlement of South Carolina, in 1670. The Carolinas were so called in honour of Charles IX., king of France, under whose patronage the coast had been discovered, in 1563.

46. In Pennsylvania, a small body of Swedes had plant ted themselves, at an early period. Their settlement in creased slowly, until the arrival of William Penn, in 1681, with a numerous company of Quakers, whom religious persecution drove across the Atlantic. Penn had acquired a grant of the territory now constituting the state, in consideration of the debts due from the crown, for services performed by his father, admiral Penn.

47. The last settled of the original thirteen states, was Georgia, founded in 1732, by General Oglethorpe. This comes within our next succeeding period. At first, Georgia, and even the Floridas, were covered by the Charter, as it was afterwards confirmed and enlarged, which conveyed Carolina to its proprietors.

48. The three eldest of the American states, it will be perceived above, are Virginia, New-York, and Massachusetts. These have hitherto been the most important and influential in the confederacy. Others, however, from their numbers, are beginning to acquire their just consideration.

49. The causes of the settlement of the American states, were various. Some were made on mercenary views, the usual principle of colonization, for the particular benefits of the proprietors. This was the case with Virginia. The immediate purpose of the settlement of New-York, was commerce. The Dutch were then particularly distinguished for their commercial and enterprising spirit. Massachusetts, and New-England generally, were planted principally to enjoy, in an unrestricted manner, the institutions of religion.

50. In the original foundation of three of the states, viz., Rhode Island, Maryland, and Pennsylvania, the free toleration of religion was recognized, and these were the first civil communities which acted on a principle that now seems to

be fast gaining the popular consent. In the other colonies, there was a degree of intolerance on the subject of religion, the fault of the age; and yet they laid the foundations of a civil community, the freest and best which the world had hitherto seen. In New-England, particularly, they wished to enjoy their religion in peace; and in shutting out others, whose religious opinions differed from their own, they seem to have justified themselves on the principle of self defence, with a view to be delivered, ever afterwards, from evils similar to those from which they had recently escaped. As, how ever, it must be impossible to prevent differences of opinion on the subject of religion, a civil community would be wise in providing for such a state of things, by suitable and tolerant regulations.

51. Many of the first settlers of the country, were men of talents and liberal culture; and a wilderness has never been planted by a body of people, who were more solicitous for the interests of learning, and general education. Next, after the establishment of the Gospel, their greatest object was to multiply schools and higher seminaries of learning. Indeed, the colonists possessed excellent traits. Their morality and piety, their spirit of enterprise and habits of industry, their love of liberty, and attention to education, were unparalleled in the history of similar efforts. They were not perfect men, but they were the best and the noblest that ever founded an empire. These remarks are intended particularly for New-England, though they have a degree of application to all the American states.

52. The colonists purchased their lands of the Indians; and notwithstanding what has been often asserted, respecting the frauds that were practised, there is little reason to question the purity of motive, and the good faith of those who were engaged in these transactions.

53. The settlers in some of the colonies, experienced at first but little trouble from the Indians, for many years. This was the case particularly with Massachusetts and Pennsylvania. In others, they were molested from this quarter, at a very early period. Connecticut, and particularly Virginia, were obliged, soon after their settlement, to make war against the savages, in self-defence. And all the colonies, sooner or later, suffered in various ways, and especially by contentions

with the natives. It is not to be denied, that in the end, wrong was sometimes done to these miserable tribes. Their ferocity and faithlessness were, occasionally, met with the sternest inflictions of vengeance on the part of the whites.

Respecting the colonists as a body, during the present period, it may be remarked, in a very general way, that they struggled long with all the hardships, difficulties, and privations incident to new establishments among savages; that they displayed a heroism and constancy, such as have rarely been witnessed among men, and though tempted to believe, in some instances, that their undertaking would never succeed, yet that their virtues finally overcame every obstacle, and they found themselves before the conclusion of this period, increasing in wealth and population.

It may be added, that the colonists were often involved in the wars of the mother country, with other powers; that a few of their wars with the Indians, affected several of the states at a time, and that a consideration of their common exposure, led to a general intercourse with one another, and particularly to the union which was formed between the New-England colonies, in 1643; a union which lasted more than forty years, or until their charters were revoked, and which furnished the example of that nobler confederacy which has since taken place, of all the American states. In general, however, it is with the individual colonies that we are mostly concerned in the history of this period, but the limits of our work will admit only of a very few details, in regard to one or two of the states.

§ Two years after the settlement of Connecticut, occurred the war with the Pequots, a tribe of Indians, whose principal residence was on a hill in the present town of Groton These savages had previously made depredations on the infant settlement, and killed several individuals, and carried others away captive. In this perilous state of affairs, a court, convened at Hartford, determined on war. Ninety men, nearly half the fencible men of the colony, were ordered to be raised. Forty-two from Hartford, thirty from Windsor, and eighteen from Wethersfield. These troops, together with seventy River and Mohegan Indians, were commanded by Captain Mason, who, sailing down the river, surprised Mystic, one of the principal forts of the enemy, in the present town of Stonington.

Before the savages could get themselves in readiness, the troops instantly pressed forward and fired. The destruction soon became terrible, but the Indians rallied at length, and made a desperate resistance. All, however, was in vain. Upon an order to burn them, the work of destruction was completed. Seventy wigwams were in ruins, and between 500 and 600 Indians, lay bleeding on the ground, or smouldering in ashes. With the assistance of a detachment of nearly two hundred men from Massachusetts and Plymouth, the whites pursued the rest of the tribe, who fled towards the Hudson, and, defeating them in another terrible battle, in a great swamp, in Fairfield, the power of the Pequot nation, was entirely prostrated.

In Virginia, the colonists were soon involved in contests with the Indians. In addition, they suffered severely by the scarcity and badness of provisions—the consequence of which was, that diseases swept off one half of their number, in a few months. In the latter part of the year 1609, Captain Smith, whose romantic story has been so often told, and whose name was a defence of the settlers, and a terror to the Indians, returned to England. Soon after his departure, the colonists were reduced to the greatest extremities, having had a company of thirty men slain by the Indians, and their provisions wasted on the occasion. A most distressing famine ensued, the effect of which was the reduction, in six months, of the colonists, from nearly five hundred to sixty. The remainder embarked for their native home; but being met by a new company of adventurers, with a large supply of provisions, they were induced to return, and try the fortunes of a wilderness once more. For a number of years, it was only by the arrival of new comers, that the colony was preserved from extinction. At last it began to prosper, from the date of Sir William Berkeley's administration, 1638, which lasted nearly forty years. Before the conclusion of this period, however, the colony experienced the evils of a terrible insurrection, known by the name of Bacon's rebellion, which terminated only with the death of its mover.

54. The principal events which relate to the colonies, as a body, or to the greater part of them, during the present period, were Philip's war, in 1675 and 1676, which was the most general and destructive war with the Indians, in which the colonies were ever involved—the oppressive measures relating to the colonies under the Stuart family, who attempted the destruction of their charters and liberties—and the wars occasioned by the hostilities into which the mother country entered with other European powers, usually called king William's war, and queen Anne's war; the former commencing in 1690, and continuing to 1697, and the latter commencing in 1702, and ending in 1713.

§ Philip's war was carried on by a king or sachem of that name, who was at the head of the Wampanoags, and whose residence was at Mount Hope, Rhode Island. This distinguished warrior, designing to exterminate the whites, formed a most extensive combination of the Indians. The greatest battle during this contest, is known by the name of the Swamp Fight, December, 1675, in the Narraganset country, at the Indian fortress, situated in a large swamp. The English, who were commanded by Josiah Winslow, governor of Plymouth, obtained a great victory, but dearly bought, with the loss of two hundred and thirty men, killed and wounded. The Indians lost more than four times this number, besides many women and children. Though their power was greatly broken by this defeat, they continued their depredations and massacres, until the death of their great warrior, in 1676, and in some parts of New-England, two years later. This was a melancholy period in the annals of the country, during which, six hundred men, the flower of its strength, had fallen; twelve or thirteen towns had been destroyed, and six hundred dwelling houses consumed—a terrible destruction, out of a population not exceeding 60,000.

The oppressive measures, under the Stuart family, were owing, in part, to the tyrannical disposition of the princes of that family, and, in part, to the sinister attempts of certain men, who, having visited the colonies, became hostile to them, and infused their prejudices into the king and his ministry. Under this baleful influence, the colonies were required to surrender their charters—a demand which was complied with, except in the case of Connecticut. The duration of this state of things, however, was short; the revolution occurring in England, in 1688, when William and Mary were placed on the throne.

From this time, the colonies, though unmolested by the mother country, in regard to their liberties, suffered by means of her wars with the French, who employed the savages as their auxiliaries. This was a long period of woe and desolation, lasting from 1688 to 1713, with an intermission of only four or five years.

RUSSIA.

55. The history of Russia is both obscure and unimportant, until the time of Peter I., surnamed the Great, who ascended the throne in 1689. Russia, then raised from barbarism and ignorance, was brought into notice with the civilized world; and, by successive advancements, has attained to a rank, in power and influence, second to no other state in Europe. To Peter, that country owes all its greatness.

§ In regard to the early history of Russia, it is only ascertained, that in the fourth century, the country was possessed by several different tribes. In the tenth century, it is said to have received the light of christianity. In the fifteenth century, John Basilowitz redeemed the empire from its subjection to the Tartars, and united the greater part of the country under one monarchy. The sovereigns of Russia, until Ivan Basilowitz IV., in the sixteenth century, bore the title Wenike Knez, "Great Prince," but he added that of czar, which, in the Sclavonican language, signifies king. Peter the Great assumed the title of emperor. It was not till the end of the six teenth century, that Siberia was added to the empire, which, to that time, was bounded by the limits of Europe.

The predecessors of Peter, maintained considerable splendour, as sovereigns; but their dominions were uncultivated, and their subjects barbarians. Alexis Michaelowitz, father of Peter, was the first who published a code of laws.

Peter became master of the empire, by setting aside a weak elder brother, and banishing a factious sister, who had seized the government. His youth was spent in ignorance and debauchery; but his new situation immediately displayed his talents, and gave birth tc the wisest plans for the improvement of a barbarous people.

56. The principal events of his reign, were, his war with the Turks, and taking of Azof, in 1696—his sending an embassy into Holland, which he accompanied in disguise, in order to learn the art of ship building—his destruction of the Strelitzes, a body of troops, much resembling the Janizaries of Turkey—his abolition of the patriarchate of Moscow, which rivalled the authority of the czars—the several defeats he experienced in a war with Charles XII. of Sweden—his signal victory over that monarch, in the battle of Pultowa—his building of Petersburgh—and, finally, his institution of a numerous infantry, and powerful army.

§ Having gained the little knowledge he possessed from foreigners, he resolved to travel in search of more. Appointing De Fort, an able Genevese, his ambassador, he travelled as a private person in his suite, through Germany to Holland, and when he arrived at Amsterdam, engaged himself as a workman in the dock yard, under the name of Peter Michaelof. Here was exhibited the astonishing spectacle of a mighty prince, at the age of twenty-five, quitting the luxury of a court, labouring with his own hands, at a toilsome mechanic art, fed and clad like the rest of his fellow-workmen, and obeying the orders of his temporary master! His occupation did not prevent him from attending the lectures on anatomy, surgery, mechanics, and other branches of practical philosophy, cultivated in Holland. From Holland he passed to England, where he was similarly employed, and where he gained still higher improvement. At the end of sixteen months, he returned to Moscow, laden with knowledge, and the fruits of experience, which he employed for the benefit of his own subjects.

Charles the XII. was, at this time, sweeping all before him. He had beaten the czar, in a number of engagements; and, suddenly breaking off a negociation, he entered Russia with 45,000 men, with the design of dictating peace at Moscow. He would probably have accomplished his object, had he not been induced, by a treacherous promise of aid from the Cossacs, to march through the Ukraine, in the midst of winter. Here Peter seized his opportunity, when the enemy's army was wasted by fatigue and famine, and meeting Charles, at Pultowa, he gave him battle, killing 9000 of the Swedes, and taking 14,000 prisoners.

Peter died in 1725. His usefulness, as a sovereign, is unquestioned; yet, as a man, he is justly obnoxious to the charge of being ferocious, impatient, passionate, and prodigal of the lives of his subjects.

SWEDEN.

57. The history of SWEDEN is unimportant, until the revolution of 1523, which placed Gustavus Vasa on the throne, who was followed by eight sovereigns to the time of Charles XII., in 1697. The crown was elective till 1544, when Gustavus persuaded the states to render it hereditary in his family. Sweden, Denmark, and Norway, had been united into one kingdom, from the time of Margaret of Denmark, in 1389, to the time of Gustavus. The last king (Christian II.) of the united countries, was so tyrannical, that Gustavus was induced to take up arms against him, and deliver his subjugated countrymen. He introduced Lutheranism into his states, administered the government with great firmness and wisdom; and, considering the age in which he lived, was one of the most extraordinary of men.

Two at least of his successors to the period of Charles XII., were eminent sovereigns, viz. Gustavus Adolphus, surnamed the Great, and Christiana. Gustavus was illustrious as a hero, and Christiana was enthusiastically devoted to literature, and distinguished for her patronage of learned men.

§ Sweden was the eastern part of the ancient Scandinavia, and, together with Denmark, was first inhabited by the Cimbri, a colony of the Gomerians. From this country came the Goths, the Gepidœ, the Heruli, and the Lombards. The Swedish monarchy is very ancient; but the history of its earlier sovereigns is too uncertain, to satisfy the sober enquirer. Eric IX., in the twelfth century, is the first monarch whose reign approximates to chronological truth. There appear to have been nine sovereigns between him and Gustavus Vasa.

During the oppressive reign of Christian II., Gustavus Vasa was sent as an hostage into Denmark, in 1518, whence he made his escape on hearing of the massacre at Stockhold of ninety-four senators, among whom his father perished. For a while he concealed himself in Dalecarlia; at length he entered into a small town on a day when a fair was held, harangued the country people, and with their assistance took possession of the fortress, and put the Danish commander to death.

From this moment his life became a scene of triumphs. Followed by his brave Dalecarlians, he besieged Stockholm; and it happening, when the Danes came to relieve that city, that a sudden frost detained their ships at a great distance from the port, Gustavus's soldiers advanced on the ice and set fire to them. This victory opened the gates of Stockholm, and he was proclaimed king.

Gustavus Adolphus began to reign in 1611. He became a hero in early life, having in his twelfth year been encircled with the laurels of victory. At the age of eighteen he was successfully prosecuting a war with Denmark, which he concluded in 1613 with an advantageous peace. He was equally successful in his wars with the Poles and Russians, from whom he took many towns. In his war with the Imperialists, he defeated their forces in the battle of Leipsic, in 1631, and afterwards in that of Lutzen; but in the latter he lost his life.

Christiana, in 1632, succeeded her father Adolphus when only seven years of age, and during her reign, Sweden preserved its ascendency in the affairs of Germany. She ruled the kingdom with great wisdom and prudence, till 1654, when she resigned her crown to her cousin, Charles Gustavus. She was so eager to quit Sweden, and to reach a land more congenial to the cultivation of science, that when she arrived at a small brook, which separates that country from Denmark, she alighted from her carriage, and leaped over the stream: "At length," said she, "I am free, and out of Sweden, whither I hope never to return." She visited Paris, where unbounded homage was paid to her genius, but where her manners gave offence to the court for want of decency and conformity to rules. Rome, however, became the place of her residence, where she embraced the Catholic religion, and where she died.

58. Charles XII. succeeded, in 1697, at the age of fifteen years. He was a competitor of Peter the Great, and divided with him the admiration of Europe. He has been ranked with the greatest conquerors of antiquity, on account of his heroism of character and, extraordinary achievements. But Charles was rather a singular, than a great man. His success as a warrior, for a time, alarmed and agitated Europe. Soon after his accession, his dominions were attacked on three sides, by Russia, Poland, and Denmark, and he, although then only a boy of seventeen years, successively took the field against these powers, and signally defeated them. Poland he humbled in the dust. A negociation having been begun by the czar, Charles abruptly terminated it, and declared that he would negociate only at Moscow. The rigour

of a Russian winter, prepared his army for the defeat, which it so signally experienced at Pultowa. After this battle, he fled into Turkey, where his conduct seemed to be that of a maniac, rather than of a man in his senses.

§ The war with Denmark he despatched in six weeks. The Danish king purchased the safety of his capital and kingdom, by making full indemnity to the duke of Holstein, whose territory he had attempted to wrest from him.

The Swedish monarch then hastened into Ingria, which the czar had attacked, and at the battle of Narva, with eight thousand men, he defeated an army of eighty thousand Russians, of whom he took thirty thousand prisoners.

In his chastisement of Poland, he satisfied the dictates of the amplest revenge. He reduced Courland and Lithuania, penetrated into the heart of the kingdom, and subdued the capitals of Warsaw and Cracow. He then, by means of the assembled states, declared the Polish Augustus deposed, and procured Stanislaus, his own dependent, to be elected sovereign of Poland.

When Charles fled into Turkey, he had only eighteen hundred men. He still hoped to dethrone the czar, by engaging the Ottoman power against him. After many efforts the Sultan was induced to send two hundred thousand soldiers against the Russians. But upon the capitulation of Peter's army, peace having been made, Charles was disappointed, and vented his rage against the Turk. He had been hospitably entertained more than three years, but his arrogance becoming insufferable, he was ordered to quit the Turkish dominions. This order he refused to obey, and proceeded immediately to fortify his camp. With only three hundred men, he defended himself for some time, against an army of twenty thousand Turks, and only yielded, when he was taken by the legs and arms, and dragged to the tent of the bashaw.

Distinguished Characters in Period IX.

1. Tycho Brahe, a Dane, celebrated as an astronomer.
2. Cervantes, a Spaniard, the celebrated author of Don Quixote.
3. Shakspeare, the greatest of dramatic poets.
4. Galileo, an Italian, distinguished for his discoveries in mathematics and astronomy.
5. Raleigh, an eminent navigator and man of letters.
6. Bacon, an English philosopher and universal genius.
7. Kepler, a German astronomer.
8. Grotius, a Dutch writer, of various and profound learning.
9 Des Cartes, a famous French philosopher

10. Gassendi, a Frenchman, distinguished as an astronomer.

11. Pascal, an eminent French philosopher and theologian.

12. Milton, the greatest of epic poets among the moderns.

13. Corneille, the prince of the French dramatic poets.

14. Boyle, an Englishman, distinguished in natural philosophy.

15. Dryden, an eminent English poet.

16. Locke, the greatest among the English metaphysicians.

17. Leibnitz, an acute German philosopher and mathematician.

§ 1. Tycho Brahe, descended from an illustrious Swedish family, was born in Denmark, 1546. He was sent by his father to Copenhagen, for the purpose of studying rhetoric and philosophy; but the great eclipse of the sun on the 21st of August, 1562, engaged him to study astronomy. With this science he was excessively delighted. He often spent whole nights with a small celestial globe in his hands, in learning the names of the stars, and in the acquisition of a science which he called divine. He was honoured by the noble and learned of his age, and patronized by his sovereign, for a time; but the malice of his enemies drove him from his country, and he found an asylum in Prague, where he died, in 1601.

It is said, that his learning made him superstitious, and his philosophy irritable, to such a degree, that in a philosophical dispute with some person, the argument rose to such a pitch of personal violence, that he lost his nose. This he supplied by a gold and silver one, admirably constructed.

The best of his works are, the Rodolphine Tables, and the Historia Cœlestis. He opposed the Copernican system, which is a sufficient proof of the unsoundness of his judgment.

2. Cervantes, who is better known by this name than by his surname, Saavedra, was born at Madrid, 1549. He led a life of hardship and poverty. Before he became an author, he engaged in the military profession, and five years and an half he endured all the horrors of an Algerine captivity. After his release and return to Spain, he began to write plays for his maintenance, but though his pieces were acted with universal applause, he pined in poverty, and at last, found himself in a prison. In his confinement, he began his immortal work Don Quixote, which was not finished till the expiration of several years. This work is read and admired in every known language; but though popular from the beginning, it produced him neither notice nor bread. He was, however, serene amidst his wretchedness.

In Don Quixote, Cervantes appears the purest of all humourists, gentle, genial, and kind.

3. Shakspeare, (William) was born of a respectable family, at Stratford-on-Avon, April, 1546. Few events of his life have been recorded, while scores of volumes have been written on his poetry and on the character of his genius. He was designed to carry on the trade of his father, which was that of a wool dealer, and with that view, he was early taken from school. He married at the age of seventeen, and soon became the father of a family. An unfortunate and criminal act, (deer stealing,) which he committed in connexion with some thoughtless companions, was the means of driving him to London.

Here, a new scene opened upon him, and he soon laid the foundation of a fame, which is unequalled in the history of human genius. He first enlisted among the players, and became an actor on the stage. It is not known that he excelled in the profession of an actor; the contrary is rather inferred. But from acting, he passed to the writing of plays, which, at first, he adapted to the lower classes; but when his performances had gained the favour of the queen and her court, he aimed at more elaborate compositions. Having by the productions of his pen, and by the management of the play-house, acquired a competent fortune, he retired to his native town, where he lived respected and beloved by his neighbours. Shakspeare died 23d April, 1516, in the fifty-third year of his age.

Several relics of the immortal bard, are still preserved in the house where he was born, the front of which is now occupied as a meat-shop. Among the articles are, his sitting-chair, a table on which he wrote, a Spanish card and dice-box, presented to the poet by the prince of Castile, part of a Spanish match-lock, the remains of the piece with which he shot the deer in Charlicote Park, a table-cover, a present from good Queen Bess, &c. &c. This is a place, which is visited by thousands, of all ranks, conditions, and countries, in homage to the genius which was there first brought to light.

Of Shakspeare, it has been said, almost in the language of adoration, "that he is the greatest of poets and of men—that he went beyond all men, and stands in the array of human intellect, like the sun in the system, single and unapproachable." But eulogy has been exhausted on him. After all, it is melancholy to reflect, that amidst his great and incomparable beauties, there are many moral blemishes and defects.

4. Galileo made discoveries in astronomy, that were too astonishing, and too opposite to the doctrines of Aristotle, to escape the censure of the philosophers of the age; and no sooner was it known, that he had embraced the Copernican system, than he was summoned before the Inquisition. Into its terrible dungeons was this illustrious man twice thrown, where, in the whole, he spent three or four miserable years, and this for embracing opinions then deemed so false in philosophy, and so heretical and contrary to the word of God.

Among the discoveries that have rendered the name of Galileo immortal, are his observation of the inequalities on the surface of the moon, and his knowledge of her vibration, his calculation of the longitude by the eclipses of Jupiter's satellites, which he first noticed, his invention of the cycloid, and his perception of the increasing celerity in the descent of bodies.

He lived seventy-eight years. Towards the close of his long life, he became blind. Milton has finely alluded to him in the lines

"Like the moon, whose orb
Through optic glass, the Tuscan artist views
At evening, from the top of Fesole,
Or in Valdarno, to descry new lands,
Rivers, or mountains, on her spotty globe."

5. Raleigh (Sir Walter) was one of the most brilliant and useful characters of the times in which he lived. His perseverance in making discoveries, first inspired the British nation with that ardour after maritime distinction, which has given both wealth and glory to the empire. He was also a valiant leader, an able negociator, and a man of letters. His works, composed in the obscurity of a dungeon, on history, politics, geography, and philosophy, as well as some good poetical pieces, will make him known to future time. It must be owned, nevertheless, that his genius was cramped by the fashions of the age.

His life, not indeed free from stain, was clouded by misfortune—he became the victim of royal persecution,—and his head was finally brought to the block. On the most frivolous and arbitrary charges, king James confined him in the tower thirteen years; and though he was afterwards released, it was not long before he fell again under the king's suspicion, the consequence of which was his tragical end, on the 29th Oct. 1618.

That at one time Sir Walter aspired to the hand of Elizabeth, would seem to be inferred from the following incident. On a window where the queen could see it, he wrote this line—

"Fain would I climb, yet fear I to fall."

Attracting Elizabeth's eye, she replied to it with her usual good sense.

"If thy heart fail thee, climb not at all."

6. Bacon (Sir Francis) was born 22d January, 1561, in Westminster. His astonishing faculties were early developed, and when only a child he was favourably noticed by Queen Elizabeth, who used to call him her "young lord keeper," alluding to the office held by his father. On the accession of James I., he rose into power—he was knighted, and successively made attorney-general and keeper of the seals, lord chancellor, and raised to the peerage. His elevation excited the envy of his enemies, and he was accused of bribery and corruption in the office of lord chancellor. The consequence was, that he was fined £40,000, and sentenced to be imprisoned in the tower. But his fine was remitted by the king, he was restored to the public opinion, and sat in the first parliament called by Charles. It is a matter of some doubt whether Bacon was guilty of

the crime alledged against him. The blame is with much reason supposed to attach to his servants, so that the eulogy of the poet, is more clearly due to him than the poet's censure—

"The wisest, brightest, meanest of mankind."

Bacon was indeed one of the greatest and most universal geniuses that any age or country has produced. As an author, his "Novum Organum Scientiarum," has, among his other performances, immortalized his name. He was the first who taught the proper method of studying the sciences: that is, he pointed out the way in which we should begin and carry on our pursuit of knowledge, in order to arrive at truth. In this view he has been very properly denominated "the miner and sapper of philosophy," "the pioneer of nature," "the priest of nature's mysteries." The great principles of the Baconian philosophy, are now universally established.

7. Kepler, (John,) though the contemporary of Bacon, and the worthy precursor of Newton, was by no means freed from the illusions of the old philosophy. The old or Aristotelian philosophy was the method of anticipating nature, or dictating to her as to what her operations are to be, instead of observing what they actually are, and inferring general truths from particular facts. Thus, Tycho Brahe anticipated nature, in taking it as a certain truth, that the earth must be at rest, though he admitted the reality of the planetary motions. Thus the great Kepler, imagined that the planets must be six in number, because of certain properties of numbers, and he maintained other puerile absurdities. He was, however, a man of high celebrity as an astronomer, and deservedly commended by most of the great astronomers who succeeded him. He first proved that the planets do not move in circles, but in ellipses; and that in their motions, they describe equal areas in equal times, &c.

His earliest years were not improved by education. When, however, he began to study, the turn of his intellect was abundantly manifest. He was born in 1571, and died in 1630.

8. Grotius (Hugo) was born at Delft, in 1583, and died, in 1645. A singular event of his life, showing the sufferings and dangers of literary men in those times, was the following. In consequence of the persecution of the Arminians, of whom Grotius was one, and an able defender, in 1618, he was doomed to perpetual imprisonment. His confinement was alleviated by his literary occupations, and the assiduities of his wife. The fond care of this worthy woman at last procured his deliverance, after a captivity of nearly two years. On pretence of removing books, which she declared proved injurious to her husband's health, she was permitted to send away a small chest of drawers, of the length of three feet and a half, in which he was confined. Thus, carried by two soldiers from the prison, the chest was then removed to a distance on horseback, and at the house of a friend the illustrious prisoner was set at liberty, pursuing his flight afterwards in the guise of a mason with a rule and a trowel.

His particular profession was the law, and he pleaded his first cause at the age of seventeen with great eclat. But polite literature engaged much of his attention, and he wrote many works on moral and religious subjects, together with histories, poetry, critical notes. epistles, &c. His learning was very various and profound.

9. Des Cartes, (Renedes,) though a man of genius and extensive attainments, was too much of a theorist. He, however, advanced far beyond his predecessors in many respects, and if he had done nothing besides introducing a spirit of inquiry, and a wish of examining the mysterious operations of nature, he would have effected much for mankind. He was well acquainted with mathematics and philosophy, and possessed a mind capable of profound meditation and patient inquiry, though highly imaginative. He wrote ingeniously on the laws of the universe, but his theory of vortices, accounting for the movements of the planetary worlds, is sufficiently visionary.

He was courted by the learned and the noble, and princes almost vied with one another in paying him their attentions. He died at the age of fifty-four, at Stockholm, but after he had been interred seventeen years, his body was removed to Paris, as his countrymen chose to claim it.

10. Gassendi, (Peter,) also a native of France, was born in Provence, 1592. He contributed somewhat to weaken the dominion of Aristotle over the human mind, though he was not himself altogether based on the true philosophy. He was nevertheless a great man and a great scholar; and to his genius and labours, the intellectual improvements of subsequent ages are not a little owing. His studious habits proved injurious to his constitution, but he was in some degree relieved by phlebotomy. He, however, at length sunk under his chronic complaint, and placing the hand of his faithful amanuensis on his heart, after perceiving that the motion of that spring of life was faint and fluttering, he exclaimed in these last words, "You see what is man's life," and immediately expired, 22d Oct., 1655.

11. Pascal, (Blaise) whose early extraordinary powers and attainments astonished the world, was born at Clermont in Auvergne, 19th June, 1623. From a child, he inquired into the reasons of every thing, and he could be satisfied with nothing but with such proof as the subject examined would admit. He always sought for demonstration and truth, if they could be attained.

The following circumstance evinces his wonderful aptitude for mathematical studies, and the superiority of his intellect. His father an eminent mathematician, had carefully secured him, as was supposed, from learning the mathematics, by denying the child the requisite books. The father's object was first to perfect Blaise in the languages; but the latter extorting from his father by entreaty, a definition of geometry, which was very vague and general, immediately entered on the study, without any other help. He was then but twelve years of age. He pursued his inquiries clandestinely, till his father happened to enter the room, where he was busy with his bars and rings, (used in place of geometrical lines and circles,) and to his infinite astonishment, found that the child was endeavouring to demonstrate what makes the thirty-second proposition of Euclid's first book. He had proceeded thus far in geometry, from axioms and principles which he had laid down, and which he had applied in a connected series, through the intervening propositions.

At the age of sixteen, he composed the ablest treatise on conic sections, that had appeared since the time of the ancients. At the age of nineteen, he contrived a mathematical machine, by which calculations of every kind could be made, without the help of a pen. And at the age of twenty-three, he demonstrated the phenomena o the gravity of the air, and soon after solved a problem, proposed by Mersennus, which had hitherto perplexed the ablest mathematicians of Europe.

All these mighty powers and attainments, he consecrated to religion, and christianity never received a more splendid offering than she did from the genius of Pascal. His religious views and feelings are embodied in his Provincial Letters, and his Thoughts on Religion, &c. works, whose celebrity has not surpassed their merits.

Voltaire, with his characteristic scorn of piety, calls Pascal, "a sublime madman, born a century too early."

12. Milton, (John,) was born in London, 1608. His political and controversial writings are justly celebrated, and contain many admirable passages. He was a strenuous asserter and defender of liberty, and, in many of his views on this and kindred subjects, was far in advance of his own age. But as a poet, he is still more justly celebrated, and is, at least, a compeer of Homer and Virgil. His Paradise Lost, is the greatest poem which modern ages have produced. In his life time, the poet never received the meed of praise which was his due; but ample justice has since been accorded to him, and all posterity will render homage to his transcendent genius.

The incidents of his life are interesting, but they are so well known, that we shall pass them over, except to say that he was thrice married; was subjected to much domestic infelicity, in his first marriage; became blind in writing his Defence of the English People, against the Attack of Salmasius; suffered not a little from personal and political enemies; and, finally, died comparatively poor and forsaken by the world.

It may be added, that he was uncommonly handsome, when young; was economical in his living, and rigidly abstemious; and, in religion, was a puritan, with some diversity, however, in his religious views, at the different periods of his life. He died of the gout, in 1674.

13. Corneille, (Peter,) whose poetical works are among the sublimest effusions of the French muse, was born at Rouen, 1606. He was brought to the bar, but he soon abandoned it for poetry, which was far more congenial to his taste. He wrote plays, the most celebrated of which was, the Cid, a tragedy, which drew against him the persecution and obloquy of rival wits and unsuccessful poets. He is said to have been a very meritorious man, in private life; liberal, humane, and devout, and rather inclined to melancholy. He died at the age of seventy-nine years.

14. Boyle, (Robert,) was the seventh son and fourteenth child of Richard, earl of Cork, and born in 1626. After having visited foreign countries, he retired, in 1646, to his estate at Stalbridge, and, amidst the confusion and tumults of the time, enjoyed there a peaceful solitude. He, however, laboured assiduously for the promotion of learning and religion, to both of which he was devoted in a most exemplary manner. He was eminent in natural philosophy and hemistry, in which, from adopting the Baconian method, he made many discoveries. "To him," says Boerhaave, "we owe the secrets of fire, air, water, animals, vegetables, fossils; so that, from his works may be deduced the whole system of natural knowledge." He invented the air-pump, and founded the Royal Society. His regard for religion, he showed in the purity of his life, the general tendency of his writings, his aversion to temporal honours, which were abundantly offered him, and his liberal benefactions in aid of benevolent and pious undertakings. His regular charities amounted to £1000 annually. He founded a public lecture for the defence of divine revelation against unbelievers, and particularly interested himself in the propagation of the Gospel among the nations, sending many hundred copies of parts of the New Testaments into the east. He died in his sixty-fifth year.

15. Dryden, (John,) early gave proof of his superior poetical abilities. He continued to write to old age, and improved to the very last, not only in judgment, but in fire, of which, his Ode on St. Cecilia's Day, and his Fables, are a proof. He wrote much, both in poetry and prose, and doubtless too much; for the rapidity with which he composed, prevented correctness. He produced no less than twenty-seven plays, besides a very large number of other works. He excelled less in dramatic composition, than in any other species of poetry. In his prose, he was equalled by few of his age, for judgment, criticism, and erudition. He professes himself to have derived, in regard to prose writing, more essential aid from Tillotson, than from any other writer.

Dr. Johnson's critique on Dryden, is very just and discriminating. The Edinburgh reviewers place him at the head of his line; they think him great as a satirist, but, in respect to genuine poetic power a step lower than the poets of Elizabeth and James. His writings are too much tinctured with the licentiousness of the age, and, in his religious views, the poet was too flexible and accommodating. The year of his birth was 1631—that of his death 1701.

16. Locke, (John,) so celebrated as a philosopher, and an ornament of English literature, was born in 1632. In the field of mental and political philosophy, he has won laurels that can never fade. He has been called, "the glory of theorists."

By the patronage of Lord Shaftsbury, he held a respectable situation under government, and wrote, at that time, several political tracts. The danger of prosecution for high treason, compelled his lordship, at length, to fly to Holland. Thither Mr. Locke followed him. After a time, the English demanded him of the States General, on suspicion of being concerned in Monmouth's rebellion

Thus persecuted, Locke concealed himself twelve months, devoting his time to literary labours; and, two years after, when he returned to England, in consequence of the revolution, he published his celebrated Essay on the Human Understanding, in the composition of which, he had been engaged nine years. The latter portion of his life was passed in religious retirement, and in the composition of theological treatises. He died at the seat of lady Masham, his friend, in 1704, giving emphatic testimony, in what he said, to the vanity of human life.

17. Leibnitz (William Godfrey) was not undistinguished as a statesman, lawyer, and poet, though he is most celebrated as a mathematician and philosopher. On the principle of the Baconian philosophy, he must be pronounced wanting, in some respects, yet he enjoyed the singular felicity of being esteemed the greatest and most learned man in Europe..

In civil life, he had considerable employment, and attained to some distinction. He spent thirteen years in studying the plan of an universal language, but he died before he had completed the extraordinary design. Leibnitz proposed characters which, like those in algebra, might not only be simple, but expressive, and enable men of all nations to converse familiarly together. He died in 1716, of those complicated disorders, the gout and the stone, aged seventy.

In temper, he was passionate; in character, avaricious. At his death, such a quantity of money was found in his house, hoarded in sacks, that the wife of his nephew, who possessed his property, died with excess of joy at the sight.

PERIOD X.

The period of the American and French Revolutions; extending from the death of Charles XII., of Sweden, 1718 A. C., to the final restoration of the Bourbons, 1815 A. C.

SWEDEN.

SECT. 1. In pursuing the history of SWEDEN, a country which at this time excited much attention, on account of the character of its sovereign, we have to record an event, which secured for Sweden a reformation of her government, and saved Europe from the ravages of a fatal ambition. This was the death of Charles XII., who, while besieging a Norwegian fortress, was killed by a cannon ball, on the 11th of December, 1718.

§ While Charles remained in Turkey, the czar and the king o Denmark ravaged Sweden on every side. At the same time, through the influence of the czar, Stanislaus had been driven from the throne of Poland, on which Augustus was replaced. This state of affairs made Charles desirous of returning to his own country, especially as he despaired of engaging the sultan in a war with Russia. Returning in disguise, he immediately conceived the design of wresting Norway from Denmark. This project, however, he soon abandoned, in consequenee of failing in the outset. Sweden was too much exhausted and distracted, and surrounded by too many powerful enemies, to sustain him at that time, in a war of conquest.

His able minister, Goertz, advised him to a different course, which was, to make peace with the czar, and with him, unite in the attempt to dethrone George I., and reinstate James, on the throne of Great Britain. These measures were agreed upon ; but in the interval of preparation, Charles, still wishing to wrest Norway from the Danes, made an attack on that country. It was in this expedition that he lost his life. A half pound ball, discharged from a cannon loaded with grape shot, struck his head, while he was exposing himself, with perfect temerity, to unnecessary danger. Though he expired without a groan, the moment he had received the blow, he instinctively grasped the hilt of his sword, and was found in that position, so characteristic of his temper.

No conqueror, either of ancient or modern times, ever had a more enthusiastic passion for glory, than Charles XII. This is the clue to all those eccentricities and acts of daring, which have justly entitled him to the epithet of "mad-man." His preceptor asked him, when a pupil, what he thought of Alexander. "I think," said he, "that I should choose to be like him." "Aye, but," said the tutor, "he lived only thirty-two years." "Oh," answered the prince, "that is long enough, when a man has conquered kingdoms."

After the death of Charles, Sweden, exhausted and impoverished, demanded repose and enjoyed it. She engaged in the pursuits of commerce, and cultivated the attendant arts. Her islands in the West Indies, were of great consequence to her foreign trade. The states took the opportunity to reform the government, and wisely restricted the prerogatives of the crown.

2. Charles XII. was succeeded by his sister, Ulrica Eleonora, by the election of the states, who permitted her husband, the prince of Hesse, to be associated with her in the government; but they greatly limited the power of the sovereign. Ulrica soon resigned the throne to her husband. On his death, in 1751, the states elected Adolphus Frederick, a prince of mild and pacific virtues, but whose reign was rendered most uneasy, by the factions of the senate. After his decease, the sceptre was given to his son, Gustavus III.' in 1771, who, notwithstanding his coronation oath, deprived

the senate of its privileges, and rendered himself absolute. The despotism, however, which he wrongfully procured, he moderately exercised, and the succeeding part of his reign was marked with peace and prosperity. In 1792, he was assassinated, at a masked ball.

§ Gustavus effected the change in the government, in the following manner. Having assembled the officers of his army, without making any communication of his design, he repaired to the senate house, where he read a decree, already prepared, for making the crown absolute, caused it to be signed by all the members of the senate, and then dismissed the assembly.

3. Gustavus IV., son of the former, now succeeded to the throne, under the regency of the duke of Sudermania. In 1800, he joined the Northern Confederacy against England, but made peace with that power the next year. In 1805, he united with Austria and Russia, in the war against France. He soon after, lost Pomerania and Rugen, and in 1808, Finland, which was conquered by Russia. He was dethroned in 1809, and the crown given to the duke of Sudermania.

§ The conduct of Gustavus, in the latter part of the period of these wars, was marked by so much extravagance, that he was considered mentally deranged; and to prevent the total ruin of the kingdom, it was determined to dethrone him. This plan was carried into effect, without difficulty or blood-shed.

4. The duke of Sudermania, under the title of Charles XIII., made peace with France; but the king having no children, Bernadotte, a favourite general of Napoleon, was, through his influence, declared crown prince, and successor to the throne, 1810. Bernadotte, however, has been faithful to the country which adopted him, and he never afforded any aid to his former master.

§ Upon the death of Charles, in 1818, the crown prince quietly succeeded to the throne. He rendered efficient aid in the wars which terminated in the overthrow of the French emperor. He proves to be a wise prince, and promotes the welfare of his subjects, by salutary improvements and reforms. A few years before the accession of Bernadotte, (1814,) Norway was taken from Denmark, and annexed to Sweden, in opposition to the wishes and efforts of the Norwegians.

PRUSSIA.

5. PRUSSIA was very little noticed, till some time within the present period, when Frederick II., the Great, raised the kingdom to a high degree of splendour. It had existed as a

kingdom, from the year 1700, when all the German states acknowledged it as such. It was before stlyed the Electorate of Brandenburgh.

§ This country was inhabited by the Borussi, who denominated it Borussia, which has been corrupted to Prussia. They were conquered by the knights of the Teutonic order, whom Cassimer IV., king of Poland, compelled to acknowledge themselves his vassals, and to allow Polish Prussia to continue under the protection of Poland.

Modern Prussia, is a kingdom formed of several states, united by alliances and conquests. The house of Brandenburgh, which now occupies the throne, is descended, in a direct line, from the ancient family of Hohenzollern, mentioned in history from the year 800. The more distinguished predecessors of the great Frederick, were Frederick William, surnamed the Great Elector, and Frederick William I., the father of the Great Frederick. Frederick William, the Elector, was a prudent and valiant prince. At the commencement of his reign, his electorate resembled a desert; the villages were burnt, the cities presented nothing but ruins, and a part of his inheritance was in the hands of the Swedes. He began by regulating the finances, and discharging his father's unworthy ministers, and by skilful negotiations, regained all the provinces guaranteed to him by the peace of Westphalia.

Frederick William I., would have been deemed an extraordinary man, had he not been eclipsed by his greater son. As the case is, his talents and management excite a degree of wonder. His father was profuse, and lavished treasures without an object. Frederick William was economical in the extreme, and expended nothing except on the soldiery. In his dress and diet, he was remarkably simple and plain. He even denied himself the common comforts of life, being wont to say, that a prince ought to spare not only the blood, but the property of his subjects. Voltaire describes this monarch thus. "He used to walk from his palace, clothed in an old blue coat with copper buttons, half way down his thighs; and when he bought a new one, these buttons were made to serve again. It was in this dress that his majesty, armed with a huge serjeant's cane, marched forth every day to review his regiment of giants. These giants were his greatest delight, and the things for which he went to the heaviest expense. The men who stood in the first rank of this regiment, were none of them less than seven feet high; and he sent to purchase them from the farthest parts of Europe, to the borders of Asia."

Frederick William was a man of vulgar habits, and coarse manners, and often treated his children with a rudeness and asperity, that would have disgraced a savage. According to an account given by his daughter, Wilhelmina, princess of Prussia, it would be difficult to count the canings and the fisticuffs with which he gratified his son, the great Frederick, who could never appear before the king without being beaten, or, at least, insulted. The princess, too, had her full share of the brutal liberality of her father, who often struck her.

She tells us, one day, "he seized her by the hand, gave her several blows on the face with his fist, one of which knocked her over." What added to their misfortunes was, the severe diet to which they were condemned, for they were almost literally famishing. There was often nothing at their father's table but garden-stuff, so badly cooked, that it disgusted them. Frequently, indeed, it was impossible to touch it, for, after serving the other guests, Frederic William would spit in the dish, that his children might not break their fast. What a specimen of a prince's court.

6. Frederick II., the Great, ascended the throne, 1740. His father had left him an efficient and well disciplined army, amounting to sixty-six thousand men. His views were bent on conquest, and on the enlargement of his small territory. With the best army in Europe, he was by no means backward in putting his ambitious projects into execution. The next year after his accession, he revived some obsolete claim to Silesia, and accordingly marched against the Austrians, whom he defeated at the battle of Molwitz. He effected the conquest of Silesia, in 1742. He next invaded Saxony, but the part he had already acted, was sufficient to alarm the neighbouring states. Accordingly, Russia, Austria, and France, concluded a treaty of defensive alliance against him. This confederacy took place in 1756, and constituted what is called, "the seven years' war," which proved to be an extremely sanguinary contest.

§ The success of this war was various. Frederick maintained his ground against his powerful enemies, sometimes conquering, and sometimes conquered. He lost, perhaps, as many battles as he gained; but so equal a contest was wonderful, considering the vast superiority of numbers on the side of his opponents. At last, however, his affairs became so critical, from his diminishing resources, and the increase of his enemies, that he began to act solely on the defensive. But the death of the Russian empress, at this time, afforded him the most essential relief. Her successor made peace with the Prussian king, and being joined by the Russian troops, with whose aid, Frederick obtained an important victory, he was enabled to secure an honourable peace with all the hostile powers.

In 1772, Frederick added New Prussia to his dominions, which, in conjunction with Russia and Austria, he dismembered from Poland. In 1786, he died, at the age of seventy-four years, with the reputation of being the greatest warrior of the time, and one of the most distinguished princes of whom history has preserved any memorial. This distinc tion, however, lies not in his moral, but in his intellectual endowments.

§ Frederick possessed a discernment, energy, activity, decision, and constancy of purpose, which fitted him to act the part of a hero; and, together with these qualities, as much moral perverseness as is required to make a *consummate* hero. He was not so distinguished for the conduct of a battle, or a campaign, as for resources in adversity, for celerity of operation, and, especially, for the discipline of his troops. An instance of his decision of character, and the severity of his discipline, appears in the following relation:

Intending to make, in the night, an important movement in his camp, which was in sight of the enemy, he gave orders, that by eight o'clock, all the lights in the camp should be put out, on pain of death. The moment that the time was past, he walked out himself to see whether all were dark. He found a light in the tent of a captain Zietern, which he entered, just as the officer was folding up a letter. Zietern knew him, and instantly fell on his knees, to intreat his mercy. The king asked, to whom he had been writing; he said it was a letter to his wife, which he had retained the candle these few minutes beyond the time, in order to finish. The king coolly ordered him to write one line more, which he should dictate. This line was to inform his wife, without any explanation, that by such an hour the next day, he should be a dead man. The letter was then sent as had been intended, and the next day the captain was executed.

Frederick was remarkably attentive to business, and every department of administration was under his own immediate inspection The most minute particulars of national and domestic policy, did not escape his observation. He extended the limits of his kingdom, and much increased its industry, population, and wealth.

His intellectual powers were great, and when we consider his situation, and the little care that had been taken of his education, we must acknowledge, that his literary acquisitions were considerable. He had much general knowledge of the sciences, and was well conversant with French writers on polite literature. He aimed at the reputation both of philosopher and poet, and was a voluminous author in prose and verse.

Nothing favourable can be said of his moral and religious character. He was sceptical, undevout, and addicted to various species of vice. Atheists and libertines were his bosom companions, particularly the corrupting and flagitious Voltaire.

7. He was succeeded, 1786, by Frederick William II., his nephew, an impolitic, pleasure-loving prince, who joined in the league against the French republic, and then deserted his allies. Dying in 1797, he was succeeded by his son Frederick William III., who unhappily revived some obsolete pretensions to Hanover, in 1805, and on Napoleon's proposing to restore that electorate to the king of England, in 1806, Fre-

derick took the field against him, and experienced an utter overthrow at the great battle of Jena, which was fought October 14, 1806.

§ A hereditary animosity against Austria, prevented a co-operation of strength, when their national existence was threatened. The whole of Germany well united and organized, would, probably, at any time, have resisted the power of Napoleon. But being divided, both Prussia and Austria, as well as the lesser states, were overrun and subjected by the fortunate conqueror. Prussia, after neglecting several opportunities of humbling the common enemy, with a strange inconsideration, risked her national existence on the issue of a single battle. She trusted too implicitly in her ancient military fame, and the beauty of her army, (for there was not a prouder army in Europe,) and, therefore, fell before her more sagacious and calculating enemy. Frederick was shorn of nearly half of his dominions.

8. In 1812, the Prussian monarch assisted the French in their Russian campaign; but on the failure of that enterprise, joined his forces with those of the emperor Alexander, and contributed to the subsequent overthrow of Napoleon. At the battle of Waterloo, his army, under the valiant Blucher, turned the fortune of the day, and thus essentially contributed to the restoration of the Bourbons. Prussia honourably acquitted herself in this great contention, and regained her former territory. Of late years, the Prussian king has been effectually engaged in promoting the intellectual improvement of his people. Perhaps, no monarch in Europe, has done more than he, to advance the true happiness and glory of his kingdom. He has declared, that a Bible shall be put into the hands of every peasant's family in his realm.

§ It has been conjectured by politicians, that Prussia cannot long preserve the rank that she has now attained, situated as her territory is, running out in different parcels of lands, of singular shape, and intersected by half of the secondary states of Germany. It is, therefore, further supposed, that Frederick only waits a favourable opportunity, to consolidate his territory; and they are little acquainted with the intelligence, energy, and ambition of the Prussian people, who imagine they will be backward in attempting any thing which promises to promote their national honour and security.

GERMANY.

9 In the history of GERMANY, during this period, we are principally concerned with Austria, its more important member, in which the imperial crown usually resides. From the

commencement of this period, there was no war of any con sequence, till that of the Pragmatic Sanction, which was an engagement of several powers, to secure the Austrian dominions to the female children of the emperor Charles VI., in case of the failure of male issue.

§ Charles VI. died without male issue, 1740. The house of Austria, in the male line, thus became extinct, after it had governed Austria for several centuries, and the whole of the Austrian dominions now belonged to Maria Theresa, the eldest daughter of the emperor. She was accordingly raised to the Austrian throne; but the neighbouring powers, regardless of their engagements, supported the duke of Bavaria, in his claim to the crown. After much opposition, the latter was invested with the imperial dignity, in 1742, under the name of Charles VII.; but this prince, worn out by a complication of bodily complaints, and by a long train of misfortunes, died two years afterwards. In the mean time, the queen, though nearly overwhelmed by her numerous adversaries, finally triumphed over them, and at the peace of 1748, was confirmed in the possession of her dominions, and her husband, duke of Lorrain, under the title of Francis I., was raised to the imperial throne.

10. Francis I., was crowned at Frankfort, in 1745. He continued the war till 1748, when the peace of Aix-la-Chapelle was concluded, and Maria Theresa obtained the succession of her father. She had all the time been sustained by the affection of her subjects, and had received important aid from Great Britain.

During the reign of Francis, the "seven years' war," the fiercest that had hitherto been waged in Germany, took place; but of this, an account has been given in the history of Prussia.

§ Maria Theresa, as heiress to the Austrian dominions, was queen of Hungary and Bohemia; and as the wife of Francis, was empress of Germany. She was a woman distinguished for her heroism, intelligence, felicity of temper, and captivating condescension. As a wife and parent, she was unrivalled; she was blessed with a numerous and amiable progeny, and left her possessions to a son, who was worthy of the empire. She built hospitals, encouraged commerce and science, and did every thing which humanity and munificence could devise to render her infirm soldiers comfortable.

11. Joseph II., the son of Francis and Maria, succeeded to the empire, in 1765. He seized Bavaria, on the death of Maximilian II., the elector, 1777; made war two years with Prussia; reformed the church of Germany, indulging the protestants with the imperial protection, and curtailing the authority of the court of Rome; dismantled the fortified towns in Brabant; restrained the excesses of the clergy in

that country, and carried on a disastrous war against the Turks. During that war, he died. He maintained the character of a most equitable and tolerant prince.

§ Joseph promulgated a decree in favour of the liberty of the press, which had been, hitherto, much circumscribed in the Austrian dominions. He even permitted, that all strictures upon the throne itself might be published, with full security, provided they did not descend to the character of libels and pasquinades. "If they be founded in justice," said he, "we shall profit by them; if not, we shall disregard them;" a remark well worthy of his character and dignity.

It was during the reign of Joseph, that a series of unfavourable seasons had occasioned a general dearth of corn, which was more or less felt in all the countries of Europe; but in parts of Germany, the scarcity was so great, that vast numbers of people actually perished, and the peasants, in many places, were compelled to unthatch their cottages, to supply the want of provender for their cattle. They themselves, in some instances, subsisted on the bark of beech and alder, mixed with a quantity of spice. A part of this time, terrible inundations overspread the country; several districts were totally ruined by a flood of the Elbe; Hamburgh was in a most critical situation; and the great suburb lying towards the Elbe, was so completely covered with water, that only the tops of the trees were discernible.

12. Leopold II., brother of Joseph, was invested with the empire, in 1790. Though powerfully solicited to arm against the revolutionists of France, his moderation and prudence kept him aloof from the vortex; but a speedy death cut short the promise of much excellence. At the time of his death, however, he was preparing to take the field against France.

§ After the "seven years' war," the Germanic body remained in comparative quiet, till the French Revolution. During that period, up to the time of the restoration of the Bourbons, Germany suffered more than most other nations. Its territory was the theatre of most of the wars that were waged during the great struggle. This country, however, had been eminently prepared to experience the evils which such an event was calculated to produce. The Germans embraced the fashionable prevailing system of anarchy and irreligion, with almost the same ardour which characterized the French themselves; and their country was early inundated with the deadly publications which proceeded from the school of atheistical disorganizers.

In nearly all the wars of the revolution, and of the subsequent period, Austria has had a share. She has generally been arrayed against France, and often been beaten. In the production of such a result, some have been disposed to ascribe more to French intrigue, than to the superiority of the French soldiers, or generals, over those of Austria. The archduke Charles, brother of the present emperor

Francis II., has often shown himself not inferior to any of the commanders of his time.

13. Francis II., son of Leopold, was crowned in 1792. He has proved to be a prince of mild virtues, and is much respected. He prosecuted the contemplated war with the French republic; but it proving unsuccessful, he concluded the treaty of Campo Formio, in 1797, by which, the Netherlands were ceded to France. This was the first in that series of hostilities, which distinguished that period of convulsion.

14. Hostilities were renewed in 1799, in Italy, on the part of Austria, assisted by Russia; for it was evident to the Austrian sovereign, that France was bent on aggrandizement. The Russian forces were commanded by Marshal Suwarrow. The war was carried on with great success, on the part of the Austrians and Russians, and the French were in a few months driven out of Italy. Much now might have been accomplished for the salvation of Europe, had it not been for the jealousy which the Austrian court felt towards their ally.

§ This jealousy was, without doubt, excited by the intrigues of France; and the consequence was, that Paul, the Russian emperor recalled his victorious troops.

Austria, left single-handed to sustain the contest, and meeting the enemy with scattered forces, suffered most severely in the great battles of Marengo and Hohenlinden. Peace was concluded at Luneville, in 1801. This was the second war, and more humiliating to Austria than the former.

§ During the peace, Francis formed a numerous army, and foreseeing the ruin of the German constitution, caused himself to be proclaimed hereditary emperor of Austria, in 1804.

15. The Austrian sovereign had been mortified too severely, to remain contented at peace. A third warlike coalition was formed between Austria and Russia, against France, in 1805. But the destruction of an Austrian army, under General Mack, and the fatal battle of Austerlitz, speedily terminated this war. The same year, the peace of Presburgh followed, in which the Austrian monarchy was far more humbled than ever, by the loss of some of its most important possessions.

§ A part only of the emperor of Russia's forces, had joined those of Francis, when the battle of Austerlitz took place. To this imprudence, was added the greater one, of risking an engagement without the assistance of the archduke Charles, who, at the distance of only a few days' march, was hastening with a victorious army of nearly one hundred thousand men.

In 1806, several of the states of Germany were united under the name of the "Confederacy of the Rhine," of which Napoleon was acknowledged the head; and in the course of the same year, Francis was compelled formally to resign the title of emperor of Germany, and to absolve the German states from their reciprocal duties towards the empire.

§ According to the terms of this confederacy, all those states of the ancient German empire, that did not accede to the act of federation, were excluded from common protection. By this means, the French emperor united Bavaria, Wirtemburg, Baden, Burg, Darmstadt, Nassau, Hohenzollern, &c., to the political interests of France, and, virtually, raised himself to the head of the German empire.

16. In 1809, Austria, for the fourth time, took the field against France. In this war, was fought the sanguinary battle of Essling, in which the French emperor, almost for the first time, was beaten in a regular field fight; but receiving a large reinforcement, he crossed the Danube, from which he had been driven back, and fought the long and obstinate battle of Wagram. This battle, lost by Austria, terminated the war, and the conditions of peace were soon after settled by the treaty of Vienna, according to which, Francis was obliged to relinquish a further portion of territory, and consented to bestow his eldest daughter and child, Maria Louisa, on the emperor of France.

§ In this war, the Austrians had taken wiser measures than before. Their best commanders were in the field; the archduke Charles, assisted by the archduke John, the prince of Lichtenstein, and the prince of Schwartzenburg. The whole strength and resources of the empire were held in requisition; but Austria had become essentially weakened, and really less a match for France than ever: and, besides, the French emperor was in advance of the Austrian. Anticipating the event of a declaration of war, he was soon prepared for action, and joining his army, marched at once into the heart of Germany. So expeditious was the French emperor, that forty-five days after the declaration of war by Austria, the battle of Essling was fought below Vienna.

17. In 1813, Austria engaged in a fifth war with France, having united its forces with those of Russia, Prussia, Great Britain, and almost all Europe, in the invasion of France, in obtaining possession of Paris, and in dethroning Napoleon. On this occasion, the emperor accompanied the army, which was commanded by the prince of Schwartzenburg. Then

was gained the celebrated battle of Leipsic, which produced the overthrow of Napoleon. The whole allied forces were, in this battle, principally commanded by Schwartzenburg.

§ When this junction of the greatest part of Europe was formed, Napoleon had just returned from Russia, having lost his great army, composed in part of troops of many European nations, then his tributaries. Austria, at first seemed reluctant to take the field, probably on account of its family alliance. A remembrance of former sufferings may also have had its effect. But, though late, the assistance of Austria was very efficient.

It was on hearing of the issue of the battle of Leipsic, which was announced by Schwartzenburg himself, to the emperors of Austria and Russia, and to the king of Prussia, that these three sovereigns, who were viewing the battle from a distant hill, on horseback, immediately dismounted, and, on their bended knees, offered a tribute of thanks to the God who had crowned their arms with victory.

18. On the return of Bonaparte from Elba, in 1815, Austria, for the last time, combined with the other powers of Europe, to dethrone him, and succeeded. At this time, a new union was formed by the states of Germany, designed to secure its future tranquillity, under the title of the Germanic Confederation. This was signed at Vienna, by its sovereigns and free cities; and it is to be hoped that, as it has done hitherto, so it will continue to prove, a powerful preservative against the renewal of those wars, domestic and foreign, of which Germany has so often been the cause and the victim.

§ In the new order of things, which succeeded the downfal of the French emperor, Austria manifested a due regard to the rights of the Germanic body, as appears from the nature of the confederation above noticed. The several states have been reinstated, as far as possible, in their former possessions, and Francis is now acknowledged, as formerly, the emperor of Germany.

Shortly after, another union, of a more doubtful character, was formed between the emperors of Austria and Russia, and the king of Prussia, to which they gave the name of the Holy Alliance. The object, in a great measure, seems to have been to confirm their own power, and to suppress any effort, on the part of their subjects, to obtain liberal constitutions.

The improper views of this confederacy, were openly displayed on the occasion of the Neapolitan revolution. A congress of the three sovereigns, in 1821, issued a manifesto against Naples, in which they plainly avow their hostility to every form of improvement. To enforce their views, an Austrian army marched towards the territories of Naples. This alliance may, at the present moment, be considered as virtually dissolved.

POLAND.

19. Poland, which existed in independence, during a part of the present period, was a nation of some importance, for several ages; but we feel little interest in its history, till nearly the memorable era when it was blotted out from the list of nations. Its fine situation, and rich natural resources, are strikingly contrasted with its wretched government and institutions; nor can we, perhaps, find a spot on the globe, where, with so many physical means of securing felicity, a civilized people are found, that have been involved in greater miseries. Its former government, which partook of all the different kinds, with a peculiarly strong infusion of aristocracy, and with a weak executive power, was wholly inadequate to the administration of justice, or the maintenance of peace. Weakness, anarchy and crime within, and injustice, treachery, and oppression on the part of others, without, constitute a great portion of the history of Poland. Yet its inhabitants were not without some striking and noble characteristics. They were a brave and martial people. Amidst their degradation, they cherished the love of liberty in an eminent degree.

Till the first division and plunder of Poland, in 1772, we find a long list of kings up to the year 842, A. C. But we can record the names of a very few only.

§ Poland is denominated by the natives, Poloka; which is a Sclavonian word, signifying a level or champain country. Such is the surface of Poland.

In the history of its sovereigns, we notice the name of Lech V., who is here introduced for the sake of a singular maxim, which he used to utter, and which must be very convenient to a king. "A sovereign is not bound to observe his oath, except when neither his safety nor his advantage requires that he should violate it." His reign, it is said, was the most inauspicious in the annals of the nation.

Cassimer III., the Great, formed a new code of laws, which he committed to writing; for, before his time, the Poles had only oral traditions. This was in the middle of the fourteenth century. Cassimer is said to have been a model of integrity, wisdom and prudence.

Sigismund I., whose reign began in 1506, was one of the most accomplished monarchs that ever sat on the throne of Poland. In his epitaph, which was not composed in the language of exaggeration, he was styled the "conqueror of the Russians, Wallachians, and Prussians," and obtained the still more honourable appellation of the "father of his country." He applied himself to the improvement of the manners of his subjects, by inspiring them with a taste for the arts and sciences, and fortified and embellished the cities

No Polish monarch was more distinguished, on the whole, than John Sobieski, who ascended the throne in 1674. Many of the rulers of Poland were foreigners, but Sobieski was a native, elected on account of his eminent virtues, and military talents. He was particularly distinguished by his wars with the Turks, and his victories over them. The assistance which he rendered to the house of Austria, when Vienna was besieged by an army of 200,000 men, has been mentioned in another place. He died in 1696, leaving his country in prosperity and peace.

Frederick Augustus, elector of Saxony, was chosen as the successor of Sobieski, after an interregnum of twelve months. The factious nobles, who had been kept in awe under Sobieski, were unwilling to place any one of his family on the throne, and thus showed themselves unworthy of such a sovereign. Augustus made war against Charles XII. of Sweden, mistaking utterly the character of his enemy. Being defeated and overcome, he was dethroned, and Stanislaus, through the influence of Charles in the diet of Warsaw, was elected to fill his place, in 1704. After the ruin of Charles, at Pultowa, Augustus was restored to the throne, and in 1773, was succeeded by his son Frederick Augustus II., after an interregnum of eight months. The reign of the latter was generally tranquil and peaceable, though both before and afterwards, the kingdom was in a very unquiet state, owing to political and religious controversies, as well as foreign wars.

Stanislaus Augustus Poniatowski, elected in 1763, was the last king of Poland. He was the creature of Catharine of Russia, placed on the throne, more by the influence of her armies and treasures, than by the free consent of the Polish nobles; and in the subsequent difficulties of his reign, was unable to manifest the independence of a sovereign. He was finally kept as an honourable prisoner, at Petersburgh, where he died, in 1798.

20. In 1772, the dismemberment of Poland, by Russia, Prussia, and Austria, which had, for some time, been secretly meditated, took place, to the utter astonishment of all Europe. This has been stigmatized as one of the most unprincipled acts recorded in history. The pretexts of the plunderers, as set forth in their manifestoes, were various; but they were doubtless encouraged to this act of violence, in consequence of the perpetual divisions in the Polish counsels, and the mutual animosities of the nobility. Indeed, they purposely increased the factions and difficulties in which the nation was involved.

§ Prussia laid the train of events, by flattering the Russians with the idea of giving a king to Poland; but not designing that Poland should sink into a Russian province, it was contrived on the part of Prussia, to make the Poles dissatisfied with their king. This was easily effected, and in the course of two or three years, nothing could exceed the disorder, dissensions, and weakness of the kingdom. In this situation of affairs, when the Poles were prevented from vindicating their sacred rights, the unholy deed of partition was perpetrated. Each party had previously agreed on its portion, the whole including nearly half of the Polish territory. The Diet was assembled, and surrounded by the partitioning powers, it could do no otherwise than sanction, by a legislative act, the crime which these powers had committed.

In the division which was made, Frederick seized Polish Prussia, and a part of Great Poland; the emperor of Austria, the kingdoms of Galicia and Ludomiria; and Catharine, Polish Livonia, with a part of Lithuania.

21. In 1791, a revolution took place in Poland; a new constitution was proclaimed, which opened to the middling classes, the avenue to every employment; and the crown, hitherto elective, was declared to be hereditary. This was done in an assembly of the people, with entire concord. But Poland, despoiled of half her territories, was weak; and though the change was approved by all Europe, except Russia, the Poles were suffered to become the victims of the Russian empress, and eventually again of the Prussian and Austrian sovereigns. A new division was agreed on, in 1793, which included a considerable portion of the remainder of Poland.

§ Catharine first resented the act of the Poles in framing a new constitution, as it was wholly opposed to her ambitious views in regard to the remainder of Poland. Frederick William, though he at first expressed his approbation of the measure, yet finally, with unblushing effrontery, consented, with the others, to act the royal plunderer.

22. Before, however, this second nefarious project could be executed, it became necessary to encounter the hazards of war. The spirit of the Poles was raised, and under the brave and patriotic Kosciusko, they resisted, for a time, the united force of their powerful enemies. But on the part of enfeebled Poland, numbers were wanting, which could not long be supplied by love of country and a desire of vengeance; and Kosciusko, after making every effort that man could be expected to make, was defeated and taken prisoner. Under the barbarous Suwarrow, Warsaw was captured and sacked.

In attempting to defend it, nine thousand gallant Poles perished.

§ But the carnage which succeeded the victory, was greater, and has forever tarnished the laurels of the Russian general. The houses were pillaged, women violated, children murdered, and thirty thousand victims fell a prey to a ferocity bordering on that of savages.

Kosciusko, who originated from a noble family, had been a distinguished officer in the United States of America, during the war of the Revolution. The Poles elected him their general, and he proved worthy of their choice. Under more propitious circumstances, he would have been hailed as the deliverer of his country. After his defeat, he was held as a prisoner at Petersburgh, till the death of the empress, in 1797. Upon the accession of Paul, he obtained his freedom, and was favoured with a pension—an act on the part of the Russian monarch, which received the applause of the civilized world. Kosciusko has since been in America.

23. A third and final dismemberment of Poland, took place in 1795, when the three powers appropriated it entirely to themselves. Both Stanislaus and Kosciusko, were secured; the spirit of the Poles was crushed, and the robbers had only quietly to divide all that remained of their bloody prey.

At the congress held at Vienna, in 1815, part of Poland was united to the Russian Empire, with the preservation of its own constitution; and on this event, Alexander, emperor of Russia, assumed the title of king of Poland.

RUSSIA.

24. In the history of Russia, we find Catharine I., the wife of Peter the Great, on the throne, near the commencement of this period. By his appointment, she succeeded him, in 1725. She reigned only two years, but with great ability, and pursued the plan begun by her husband, in civilizing her people.

§ Catharine was originally the wife of a Swedish soldier, but falling into the power of the Russians, she was employed in the general's kitchen, where Menzicoff, one of Peter's favourites, saw and obtained her. Peter having met her at Menzicoff's house, and being delighted with her understanding, at first made her his mistress, but afterwards married her. She obtained a complete control over the emperor, by her singularly gay and cheerful temper, as well as by her respectful and kind attentions.

25. Peter II., grandson of Peter the Great, succeeded her, in 1727. He reigned only three years, but his reign was a

scene of peace and prosperity. He was extremely beloved by his people.

§ The succession, during several reigns after Peter the Great, seems not to have been regular, or fixed by any certain rules; yet the princes came to their thrones with little difficulty, and pursued the general features of that wise policy which Peter adopted. The great object constantly kept in view, was the advancement of civilization and knowledge among the people.

26. Anne, duchess of Courland, next ascended the throne, in 1730, the male line of the house of Romanow, to which Peter the Great belonged, having become extinct. She was a niece of that monarch. Her reign was glorious and happy, and comprised the war against Turkey, in 1736; the conquest of the principal towns in Crim Tartary; and the victory of Choczim over the Turks, in 1739.

27. On the death of Anne, Ivan, or John, only about two month's old, was elected emperor, 1740; but the next year a sudden revolution took place, by which the young prince was deposed, and Elizabeth, daughter of Peter the Great, was proclaimed empress.

There were strong points of resemblance between her and her father, and like him, she seemed to possess an inherent capacity for reigning. She united benevolence with great political talents, and to her, Russia is indebted for much of its influence in the affairs of Europe and Asia. In 1757, her troops, in conjunction with those of Austria, entered upon "the seven years' war" against the great Frederick, and her part was so well acted, that had she lived, the Prussian monarchy would probably have been in jeopardy, as to its very existence.

§ Elizabeth founded the universities of Petersburgh and Moscow and decreed a new code of laws, called Elizabeth's code. It is reported that a few years preceding her death, this princess indulged in the most unbounded intemperance and sensuality.

28. She was succeeded, in 1762, by her nephew, Peter III., son of her elder sister Anne, and consequently grandson of the great Peter. He was at first somewhat popular with his subjects, but they soon became disaffected towards him. He was found to be deficient in talents and strength of character; and his wife, Catharine, becoming disgusted with him, and inspired with ambitious views, is supposed to have been

the mover of the conspiracy by which he was dethroned and murdered, in the first year of his reign.

§ Catharine of Anhalt, a princess of Germany, had been married to Peter several years before his accession; and as she began her political life with crime, she seems never afterwards to have been scrupulous as to the means with which she executed her plans. It was by the help of her paramour Orloff, that she arrested the emperor, and procured his deposition and death. Orloff first gave him poisoned brandy to drink, and then strangled him.

29. Catharine II., who was immediately proclaimed, combined with her singular depravation of principle, a powerful intellect. As a woman, she was a disgrace to her sex and to human nature, but as an empress she was great, and justly denominated "the Semiramis of the North." Her reign was brilliant and long, and at once the admiration and terror of all Europe. Notwithstanding the great extent of her empire, she sought continually to enlarge its boundaries. In her wars with Turkey, Persia, and Poland, she secured immense acquisitions of territory. Her transactions in regard to the dismemberment of Poland, have already been related. In regard to Turkey, her object appears to have been nothing less than the possession of the Ottoman throne in Europe—an object which Russia has ever since had at heart.

§ One of the victorious wars which Catharine carried on with Turkey, cost her two hundred thousand men, and 200,000,000 rubles; while it cost the latter three hundred and thirty thousand men, and 200,000,000 piastres—a war scarcely less ruinous than triumphant. In this war, Ismail was the last town that surrendered. Twice were the Russians under Suwarrow repulsed; but at the third attack, they scaled the ramparts, forced their way into the place, and put to the sword all who opposed them. Fifteen thousand Russians purchased with their lives the bloody laurels of their leader, who wrote to the empress with his usual brevity, "The haughty Ismail is at your feet."

30. Catharine was succeeded by her son, Paul Petrowitz, 1796, whose reign was the reverse of that of his mother, and who occupied himself with trifles. In 1799, he declared war against revolutionary France, and sent Suwarrow into Italy, who met with great success till he passed into Switzerland, whence he was recalled by his sovereign. In 1801, Paul declared war against England, and obliged Sweden and Denmark to join; but soon afterwards this unhappy monarch was strangled, by some conspirators, who were officers in his court.

31. Alexander I., the eldest son of Paul, was proclaimed in 1801, at the age of twenty-two. His name will descend with renown to after ages, as the deliverer of enthralled nations. His reign was at first pacific, nor did he make those efforts against France, which seemed desirable at that juncture. He, however, became alarmed at length by the ambition of Bonaparte, and in 1805, formed a coalition with Austria, against the conqueror.

He was able to effect a junction with only a remnant of the Austrian forces, which had previously been deserted, and being attacked unexpectedly at Austerlitz, he experienced a signal overthrow. He then withdrew his army into Russia, but designing to assist Prussia, the next year he hastened to the scene of war; but before his army could reach it, the battle of Jena had been fought, and the power of Prussia half annihilated. Russia left alone on the field, maintained the contest with the French emperor for a few months, during which several sanguinary battles were fought, without any decisive advantage on either side. At length the fatal battle of Friedland, obliged Alexander to sign the treaty of Tilsit.

In 1808, he engaged in a war with Sweden, in which Finland was conquered, and in 1811, he commenced hostilities against Turkey. At this critical time, a mighty contest was about to ensue, which was to decide the fate of a great part of the globe. The refusal of Alexander, in 1812, to concur in Bonaparte's scheme, of excluding British commerce from the whole European continent, highly displeased the latter. This circumstance, concurring with the French emperor's desire to establish an universal monarchy, induced him to march against Russia, with all the force of the territories under his dominion, and of every state rendered subservient to his views. "In that way," says Prof. Heeren, "a storm of nations arose, (about twenty were united under the standard of the conqueror,) unparalleled in history, since the expeditions of Xerxes and Attila." The Russians retreated steadily before the French, not without engaging in several bloody battles, in which the French were victorious, but by means of which they were continually weakened.

At Borodino, a few miles in advance of Moscow, the Russians made a stand, and here was fought one of the most terrible battles ever recorded. The loss on both sides was nearly equal; the Russians, however, retired, and the French entered Moscow. But they entered it to witness its conflagration; the Russians had set it on fire, and thus deprived the French army of its expected winter quarters. It was obliged to retreat; and the animosity of the Russians, aided by the terrible severity of the weather, contributed almost to annihilate the most efficient military force that ever invaded a nation.

§ Upon the invasion of his dominions, Alexander soon made peace with the Turks, and this on advantageous terms, as has always been the case in the wars between Russia and Turkey. Alexander might have met his foe with an equal number of nations, if he had had time to summon them from the mountains and deserts of Asia. All his troops, divided into three armies, by no means equalled, in number, those of the enemy, which amounted to more than half a million. But although the collection of the Russian force was only partially effected, yet there was a high moral preparation in the spirit, both of the prince and his people. After one conspiracy in the beginning of the contest was detected, and its authors summarily punished, all orders of the people manifested the most determined purpose to resist the enemy, submitting to sacrifices, which nothing but devoted patriotism and the deadliest hatred of the invader, could inspire. Alexander, in his manifesto, declared that he would never make peace, so long as the enemy remained within his empire. And to engage God and religion on the side of Russia, one entire consecration of the empire and of the church, was made to the God of armies.

The constant retiring of the Russians, without risking a great battle, greatly weakened the expectation indulged by Bonaparte, of speedily terminating the war, by penetrating into the heart of the empire. Fire and rapine, by friends and foes, marked the course of the invading army, and seemed to render return impossible. Wilna was occupied the 28th of June. The French advanced with many skirmishes by way of Witepsk to Smolensk, where two of the Russian armies formed a junction, August 6th, while the Prussian auxiliaries besieged Riga, and the Austrians were manœuvering in Volhynia. Smolenk was stormed and destroyed, August 18th; after which, Koutousoff was vested with the chief command. After the battle of Borodino, the solitary capital was entered, September 14th and 15th. In the Kremlin, the ancient residence of the Czars, the conqueror took up his head quarters, the limit of his expedition, and the grave of his greatness.

Moscow, fired by its own citizens, fell a victim for the empire; for such a drama demanded such a catastróphe; but in its pillars of fire the first dawn of freedom shone over shackled Europe in the farthest East. Instead of a Capua, the army suddenly stood in a waste. "The campaign may now end," was the proposal of Napoleon; "the campaign is now beginning," was the reply of Koutousoff. A specdy retreat, before the beginning of the winter's cold, might, perhaps, have saved the army; but the pride of the conqueror disdained this measure, till it was too late. When three-fourths of Moscow were consumed to the ground, just as the fatigued and debilitated army of the French entered it, needing repose and refreshment, and an unconquerable Russian army was before it, it was impossible for Napoleon to stay there. Never was a disappointment more sudden and more bitter. The retreat which he had declined, he was obliged to undertake, and such a retreat, so disastrous and terrific, history never before recorded.

32. Alexander pursued the enemy beyond the boundaries of his empire, and thus gave the signal for the emancipation of Europe. He first exhorted Prussia to war. She obeyed the call, and others, the late vassals of France, sooner or later, joined his standard. "From this time the storm of nations, which had gathered in the west, against the east, was to be turned from the east against the west." An immediate eruption was prevented, by the fortresses and countries which were occupied by the relations of the rulers, and the certainty that Napoleon had himself escaped. But in the nature of the case, it could not be long ere the subjugated nations should turn upon their falling master. Austria was the last to join the alliance; her weight in the scale was decisive.

The campaign of 1813, which thus began, is one of the most memorable in history. Never were more battles fought within a given space of time, and never were greater than some of them. In regard to the battle of Leipsic, which finished the campaign, Heeren says, "If the mass of combatants, almost half a million, met on the field, makes it the first battle of modern times, its consequences do so no less." The way was now opened to France itself, in the signal defeat of the French emperor. Accordingly, in the beginning of the year 1814, the respective sovereigns entered Paris, dethroned Napoleon, and replaced on the throne the house of Bourbon. The renown of Alexander was now complete, as the providential deliverer of Europe.

§ This prince deceased 1st December, 1825, and was succeeded by Nicholas I.

The character of Alexander, will appear with advantage on the page of history, and his success in saving Russia and Europe, from the grasp of military ambition, will consecrate his name as the most fortunate of sovereigns. The circumstances under which he entered upon his reign, were, indeed, calculated fully to bring into action all his faculties. Though inferior to his great antagonist in native intellectual power, he was, perhaps, of all the European sovereigns the most fit, by his indefatigable spirit, to contend with him. He appears to have been guided mainly by a principle of honesty; and if several private accounts are to be credited, there are pleasing indications, that he was one of the very few princes who can be called truly religious. The most inexplicable part of his character, in a moral view, was his suppression of the Russian Bible Society, which had, a few years before, commenced under his own auspices.

Since the event, which we have mentioned as the termination of the tenth period, the affairs of the Russians have been generally prosperous. Besides a successful conflict which they have maintained with Persia, they have rushed into war recently, with their old enemies, the Turks; and although the present is the second campaign, they have been met with so vigorous a spirit, on the part of the latter, under their warlike sultan, Mahmoud II., that the issue of the contest seems somewhat doubtful. Russia puts forth her whole power, and Turkey fights for her existence. Russian successes have, of late, been reported; but it is altogether probable, that other campaigns* will be necessary, in order to drive the Ottomans into Asia, should the other great powers of Europe suffer the contest to continue.

ENGLAND.

House of Brunswick.

33. George I., Elector of Hanover, had been proclaimed king, by the regency, on the death of Anne, 1714. At the commencement of the present period, he had, therefore, been on the throne about four years. Notwithstanding the divided state of the kingdom, the accession of George took place without the least opposition, tumult, or sign of popular discontent.

It was protestantism that gave the house of Brunswick the throne, and it was protestantism that was to preserve it to them. No new maxims, no new continental policy, could therefore become prevalent; it was the ancient policy of William III., modified according to the circumstances of the times. Thus harmony was established between the nation and the government; and fortunately for the new house, there was for a long time yet, a pretender, who did not permit these maxims to be forgotten.

* Since the above was penned, a series of splendid victories has attended the Russian arms, in consequence of which, a peace has been concluded between the contending powers, on terms exceedingly humiliating to the Turks.

The natural consequence of this policy was, the fall of the tory ministry, which had made itself more than suspected by its conduct towards the pretender, and the restoration of the superiority of the whigs.

§ George I., was the son of Ernest Augustus, elector of Hanover, and of Sophia, grand-daughter of James I., and was in the 55th year of his age, when he ascended the throne.

The Pretender, who was styled the Chevalier St. George, was the son of James II. His exclusion from the throne affected the public tranquillity, for a time. He had his partisans chiefly among the tories, and in Scotland; but the several attempts which they made in his behalf, were ineffectual; his intrigues were detected; his forces were overpowered in battle; many of the leaders among the rebels were captured and executed; but the chevalier had the good fortune to escape to France.

34. In 1720, the king having recommended to the commons the consideration of proper means for lessening the national debt, this proved a prelude to the famous South Sea act, which became so ruinous in its consequences. In this scheme, it was believed possible speedily to perform by art, what can be the result only of continued exertion—the liquidation of the public debt; but the projects of the South Sea company foundered, and thousands were involved in ruin. As the English government, however, allowed itself no despotic steps, its credit was preserved entire; and it found itself able, by a diminution of interest, to establish a sinking fund, which only needed a better administration, to effect its object.

§ The character of George I. was that of a wise and good monarch, but he was less popular than he might have been, had he staid more at home, and manifested less partiality for his German dominions.

He died suddenly, of a paralytic disorder, on the continent, in the 68th year of his age.

34½ George II., succeeded his father, 1727, and, like him, favoured the whigs, and was strongly attached to his German possessions. His character was that of an active, intelligent prince, possessing a violent temper, and a love of war. His administration of affairs was generally equitable, and satisfactory to the people. A period of peace, during ten years, in the former part of his reign, happily occurred through want of a plausible pretence for embarking in a war. At length, occasion was found for collision with Spain, and war was declared in 1739. It produced no important results. In 1744, England declared war against France, and assisted Maria

Theresa, of Austria, in the war of succession. In this public contest, the principal states of Europe were involved ; and among others, the battles of Dettingen and Fontenoy were fought ; the former terminating in favour of the allies, the latter in favour of the French. The British king commanded, in person, his army on the continent.

§ The minister who guided the destinies of England, during this part of the reign of George II., as also during the principal part of the former, was Sir Robert Walpole. Concerning him, the historic professor of Gottingen says, "that without the restless activity which is often called greatness, he was a statesman most worthy of respect. He introduced uprightness into politics, at a time, when they were disgraced by the profligate Dubois, and the false Alberoni. But his maxim, to be on good terms with all, entangled him in a web of negociations and relations; from which, only an island state, like England, could have disengaged itself." Others, however, speak of him as distinguished for the system of corruption and venality which he practised in his administration.

35. During the absence of the king on the continent, the rebellion in Scotland, 1745, took place, in consequence of an effort made by the son of the old pretender, for the British throne. The young Charles was assisted by Louis XV., and having landed in Scotland, led an army against the royal forces, which he defeated in the battles of Preston Pans, and Falkirk ; but in the subsequent battle of Culloden, he met with a decisive overthrow. The Stuart family made no more attempts to take possession of the sceptre which they had lost.

In 1755, war was renewed between France and England, on account of encroachments made on the British territories in North America. The war was not at first very fortunate to the British ; but, at length, they met with signal success, and the result of it was, the surrender of all Canada, on the part of the French. It was in this war, that the brave Wolfe perished, having distinguished himself by the capture of the city of Quebec.

§ In the expedition against Quebec, the courage and perseverance of General Wolfe, surmounted incredible difficulties. It was on the Heights of Abraham, which he succeeded in gaining, that he fought and defeated the French army. As he occupied a conspicuous station in the front of the line, he had been aimed at by the enemy's marksmen, and received a shot in the wrist. Wrapping a handkerchief round his hand, he gave his orders, as usual, without betraying the least emotion ; and while he was advancing, at the head of the grenadiers, another ball, unfortunately, pierced the breast of this young hero, who thus fell at the moment when victory was announced. His death was mourned as a national loss.

36. At this period, the arms of Great Britain were triumphant in every quarter of the globe; but in the midst of his successes, the old king suddenly expired, in the 77th year of his age, and in the 34th of his reign.

37. George III., grandson of the deceased, succeeded him in 1760. He was then in his eighteenth year, and swayed the sceptre during the long period of sixty years; the longest reign in the annals of Great Britain. It is distinguished as a period of important events, and of the nation's advancement in power, wealth, commerce, and the arts. The resources of the British, in their great contests, during this reign, appear to have been almost inexhaustible.

George III. commenced his reign at a favourable period, when the arms of the nation were triumphant, and when Chatham, the ablest and most popular of the British ministers, administered the government. His ministry, which began under the former reign, continued from the 20th of October, 1756, to the 5th of October, 1761.

§ "What five years!" says Heeren. "By the greatness of his own character, he elevated the spirit of his nation, for he was the first to breathe into it a confidence in itself." Upon the resignation of Mr. Pitt, violent political dissensions arose, which were afterwards increased, upon the retirement of the duke of Newcastle.

38. An ill-judged course of policy, pursued by the ministry towards the American colonies, gave rise to those animosities, which ended in the separation of the colonies from the mother country. This colonial war commenced in 1775. The eloquence of Chatham was arrayed against the unjust and oppressive measures of the British parliament. But his counsels were overruled, and after a long and distressing contention with the American states, Great Britain acknowledged their independence in 1783. Thus was laid the foundation of a great and rising empire in the new world, which bids fair, in time, to rival the most renowned nations of Europe, and of antiquity. Antecedently to this contention, party spirit had become general and violent in Great Britain, and produced frequent changes in public men and measures.

§ In the colonial war, France and Holland, after a time, formed an alliance with the American government, and took part in the contention. Though England thus lost important foreign possessions and increased her public debt, (from 146,000,000, to 257,000,000 sterling,) yet she lost nothing in her contest with other powers; her commerce and resources were constantly extending, and her spirit was equal to every effort.

39. Another important feature of this reign, was the extension of the British possessions in India. The British East India Company, before the year 1766, conquered, and took possession of the kingdom of Bengal, together with Bahar and part of Orissa, a large and flourishing country, containing above 10,000,000 of people, and producing an immense revenue. These territories, afterwards, received a very great addition, as the fruits of several wars, which the Company had with the natives. Hyder Ally, and afterwards Tippoo, his son, distinguished themselves by their opposition to the British encroachments, but they were obliged to submit to superior prowess.

§ Tippoo was vanquished by Lord Cornwallis, in 1792, and deprived of one half of his dominions. In 1799, Seringapatam, the capital of Mysore, was taken by Gen. Harris, and Tippoo was slain.

40. The Irish rebellion, in 1798, and the subsequent union, in 1800, of Ireland and Great Britain, were also important events during this reign. The rebels in Ireland were principally Romanists, the most numerous and least favoured part of the Irish population, whom the spirit of the French revolution had at this time affected. The Act of Union was the favourite object of Mr. Pitt, and made Ireland an integral part of the British empire. From the danger of the separation of Ireland from the British sovereignty, the ministry and the parliament, both had been urged to this project of a legislative incorporation; and in the anxiety which was felt, were less scrupulous as to the means of securing a majority in both houses, than became the dignity of the empire. For this object, the arts of corruption were employed. The effects of the union, however, have been mutually advantageous.

§ A spirit of discontent and revolution, had been working for a long time, in the minds of the Irish people. This was inflamed, by the countenance which the government of France had given to certain insurrectionary projects. With a view to effect a separation from England, and form a close connexion with France, several attempts were made on the part of the French, to land troops in Ireland; but these attempts proved abortive. The French fleets were either dispersed by storms, or defeated by the valour of the British admirals, Duncan and Warren.

In the summer of 1798, the spirit of revolution had arisen to such a height, that several counties were in a state of insurrection. Lord Cornwallis was now appointed lord lieutenant, and took command of the government's forces. He engaged the rebels, on several occasions, and many lives were lost. Pursued by the vigilance of the government, and despairing of foreign succour, they at last submitted. Some of them suffered punishment, others emigrated to America.

41. The reign of George III., was particularly distinguished, by the wars which grew out of the French revolution. This great event, which will be more particularly noticed in the history of France, commenced in 1789. It threatened in its consequences, the overthrow of all established governments, and deeply convulsed the whole civilized world. From the commencement of the revolution, to the restoration of the Bourbons, in 1815, Europe endured more, in the loss of lives and property, and suffered more misery, than in any other equal portion of time, since it has been known in history.

§ The government of Great Britain, early conceiving a just alarm for its own safety, zealously embarked in the European war, with a view to check the dissemination of disorganizing principles, both at home and abroad. All the Christian states in Europe, opposed in their turn, the tyranny and ambitious views of France; but Great Britain only pursued the object with undeviating constancy, and with a just conception of the character of the common enemy. William Pitt, one of the ablest ministers which it ever had, was then at its head. Under his auspices, after various vicissitudes of disappointment and success, victory crowned the efforts and sacrifices of the British nation; efforts and sacrifices, of which history does not, perhaps, record a second example. All Europe was arrayed against her at times; yet, so far was she from being intimidated, or disheartened, that she met the enemy, whether on the sea or land, wherever he was to be found. Her greatest efforts, particularly in the former part of the war, were made on the sea. Here Nelson, the first of naval captains, gained the battles of the Nile, Copenhagen, and Trafalgar, and almost annihilated the maritime power of the continent. In the latter part of the contention, Wellington conquered the armies of France, at Talavera, Salamanca, Vittoria, and Waterloo.

An interval of peace occurred between the years 1801 and 1803. But this short suspension of arms, was felt to be too long for the safety of the British government, while the emperor of France seemed to set no bounds to his ambition. The war was accordingly renewed; and though, on the part of the French, the invasion of England was threatened, and her commerce was designed to be excluded from the whole continent, yet one of the projects was abandoned, and the other proved fruitless.

In the battle of the Nile, which happened August 1, 1798, the maritime fame of Great Britain was established beyond all competition The French fleet had every advantage of situation, but Nelson captured nine ships of the line, and destroyed several others. In the battle of Trafalgar, which was fought on the 21st of October, 1805, the great English hero defeated a powerful fleet of the enemy, consisting of thirty-three ships of the line. His own force amounted to twenty-seven ships of the line. Nineteen of the French and Spanish ships were captured, though four of them only reached port, the rest having been purposely destroyed, as it was impossible to take care of them on account of tempestuous weather. Subsequently, the greater part of the enemy's ships which escaped, were either wrecked or captured. The day of this great triumph to the English admiral, was the day of his death. His person was much exposed in the battle, and being observed by the enemy, he was pointedly assailed by the musketry, and received a mortal wound.

42. While the resources of Great Britain were called forth in the great European contest, she found, or made an enemy in the United States of America. The long depending disputes between the two nations, respecting commercial rights, terminated in hostilities, which were commenced on the part of the United States, in the summer of 1812, by an attack on Canada. This war, though not very vigorously prosecuted, inasmuch as the affairs of Europe engrossed the attention of the British ministers, was, nevertheless, marked by uncommon acrimony. It continued until the last of the year 1814.

43. During the last ten years of the reign of George III., he was reduced to helplessness, by an inveterate insanity. In the meantime, his son, the prince of Wales, acted as regent. In regard to the great contest, the latter pursued the course which had been adopted by his royal father.

§ The old king died on the 29th of January, 1820. The subversion of his intellect, is supposed to have been brought on, by the sickness and death of his youngest daughter, Amelia, aided by the advance of age, and the toils and anxieties of state. Amelia, when sensible of her approaching dissolution, presented to him a ring, requesting him to wear it in remembrance of her affection. This tender incident, created a sympathy which soon mastered his faculties, and he gave way to an incurable despondency. He was a good monarch, seemed to be guided by religious principle, and was honoured and beloved, as the father of his people. His natural endowments were not great, though he possessed good sense, and a cultivated mind.

His successor, the present king, is George IV., who has, hitherto, generally reigned in peace and prosperity The only war of any consequence which has occurred during his reign, is that which was carried on a few years since in the East. By this, the British possessions have been immensely enlarged, particularly by a reduction of a considerable part of the Burman empire. To the above we may add, the single battle of Navarino, against the Turkish fleet, in connexion with the naval forces of France and Russia.

FRANCE.

House of Bourbon.—Revolution.—Napoleon.—Bourbons restored.

43½ The successor of Louis XIV. was a great grandson, who ascended the throne under the title of Louis XV., at the age of five years, 1715 A. C. Contrary to the will of the old king, his nephew, Philip of Orleans, obtained the regency.

§ Without morals, and without sense of shame, the duke of Orleans was regarded as more profligate than he actually was, and the long continued anxiety respecting the life of the young king, who was sickly, had a strong influence on the politics of the times. Corruption of manners was a natural consequence of such a regency, and the French court was never more dissolute than at this time.

It was during this regency, that France made an abortive attempt to pay off its debts by means of the paper bank law, and the Mississippi scheme, connected with it. These were of no small consequence for its future fate, and its whole influence in the European political system. The ruin of thousands of families might be repaired in time, but it was the arbitrary money operations of the government, that reduced its credit to irrevocable ruin. From this time, no paper money could be issued in France, under the old constitution. The French financial system was ever after in an unsettled state.

44. The minister whom Louis chose soon after he came of age, was cardinal Fleury, whose seventeen years' administration, if it was not free from faults in the interior, secured tranquillity to France, and was beneficial to Europe.

The reign of Louis, which was fifty-nine years, was too long for his reputation as a sovereign, and for the happiness of his people. He was at first styled well-beloved by them, but they had occasion eventually to lay aside that flattering epithet.

§ Louis pursued a long course of rapacity, profusion, and tyranny, and in the latter part of his reign, he became infamously licentious and debauched. He was the slave of his mistresses, and his government was a government of mistresses. The last epoch of his reign, may be compared to what has been mythologically denominated the iron age. He became insensible, not only to the disgrace and ruin of his state, but to the loss of his nearest and dearest relatives, many of whom deceased during the latter part of his life.

It is said, that the profusion of this monarch, led him, in the first instance, to undertake the scandalous traffic of a monopoly of corn, which, while it starved his subjects, enabled him to support the extravagant claims of his minions and mistresses. It is at least certain, that at his demise, 200,000,000 of livres, in specie, were found in his private treasury, and that their acquisition could be traced to no other source. It is no matter of surprise, that the vices and errors of Louis, particularly his extortions, should have produced difficulties between him and his people. These were manifested in the disputes which he carried on with his parliaments, and in the opposition which they expressed against his rapacious acts. He conducted the controversy, on his part, in so ill-judged and unjust a manner, that affairs grew worse and worse, and fast ripened for that dreadful state of things which followed under his unfortunate successor.

The aggregate of the reigns of Louis XIV. and Louis XV., is one hundred and thirty-one years, which is unparalleled in history. During so long a period, what treasures were drawn from the French people, in consequence of the ambitious wars of the one, and the profusion and fiscal mismanagement of the other! And is it to be wondered at, that they felt their burdens to be insupportable?

45. Louis XVI., who was grandson of the late king, ascended the throne in 1774, at the age of twenty years. His situation, from the first, was critical and dangerous, beyond the common lot of kings. With a temper fitted to make a people happy in ordinary circumstances, he was ill calculated for the evil days on which he was fallen, when his subjects were almost maddened by the oppression of their former master, and now unreasonably jealous of his successor.

§ Louis seemed to aim at a prudent and conciliatory course. He early made some removals from office, that were designed to be popular, and sought integrity and talents in his ministers. Turgot, Necker, and Calonne, were successively placed at the head of the finances.

After the efforts made by France in favour of American independence, and the consequent great increase of her debt, her financial situation became alarming, and demanded attention. The disclosures and discussions on this subject, led directly to the great convulsion which followed. There were other concurrent causes, such as the corruption of religion, and the abuses which existed in the church; the despotism and profligacy of the government; the inequality, and the enormous burden of taxation; the hauteur and odious privileges of the nobility and clergy; the notions respecting liberty and equal rights, generated by the revolution in America, and especially the progress of philosophy, freethinking, and atheism, which the writings of Voltaire, Rousseau, and others, so effectually aided. These, and perhaps other causes combined, threw a great nation into madness, and created a revolution which rocked the world.

A state of things arose not only in France, but among all civilized nations, very different from any which ever existed before. "The contemporary world, which lived in this period," says professor Heeren, "calls it the revolutionary; it is as yet, too early to decide with what name it shall be denoted by posterity, after the lapse of a century; probably, the constitutional; for the struggle after regular but free constitutions, is the thread that guides through the whole confusion."

46. Our limits preclude a minute account of the revolution which was now about to burst forth. Suffice it to say, that the operations of government being nearly suspended for want of supplies, the king was induced to convoke, first an assembly of the notables, next the parliament, and afterwards, the parliament and notables together; but nothing was effected by their measures. At last, the convocation of the states-general, May 5th, 1789, was resorted to; but difficulties arising between the branches of which it was composed, the popular branch soon declared themselves the representatives of the people, and constituted the National Assembly. Conciliatory as the language of the king had been, the measures of this body were dictated by a spirit of opposition to his prerogatives.

The revolution, properly speaking, began with the destruction of the ancient prison of the state, the Bastile, 14th July, 1789. This was followed by other excesses on the part of the populace, till Paris became a field of blood.

§ The States General consisted of three orders—nobility, clergy, and the "tiers etat" or commons. With the commons, a small portion of the nobility and clergy united in calling themselves a national assembly. When this measure was adopted, there actually remained of the monarchy only the name. The king and the royal family were obliged to yield to the popular feeling, which demanded their removal from Versailles to Paris. Here, however, the king was with difficulty preserved from violence, which the mob seemed inclined to offer to his person. He attempted to flee at one time, but his flight was intercepted.

The progress made by the National Assembly at its earlier sittings, in the work of reform, was manifested by several important acts, such as the abolition of titles of nobility, and feudal rights—the exclusion of the clergy from all judicial functions—the suppression of religious houses and vows—and the division of France into eighty-three departments.

In the year 1790, those political societies began to appear, particularly the Jacobin club, which controlled the measures of the Assembly in so remarkable a degree.

47. Although Louis accepted the new constitution of 1791, which established the equality of all ranks and was otherwise obsequious to the Assembly, yet the Jacobins were clamorous for the abolition of royalty; and accordingly, the regal government was abolished, and France declared to be a republic, on the 21st of September, 1792. This was done by a new body, called the National Convention, on the first day of its meeting. The views of the enemies of royalty, were not as yet, fully answered. For the king, nothing further was to remain, than in the language of Manuel the reporter of the commune, "the right of justifying himself before the sovereign people." He and the royal family were immediately imprisoned in the temple. Soon after, he was brought to the bar of the Convention, and being condemned on several charges brought against him, he was sentenced to suffer death, by the axe of the guillotine, which took place on the 21st January, 1793.

The fate of Louis has been widely commiserated. His character was that of an intelligent and inoffensive man, but he wanted firmness, to stem the torrent of faction. In death, he displayed a manly dignity and fortitude.

§ Among the charges alledged against the king, were, his having supplied the enemies of France with money; his being the author of the war waged on the French territory; his having conspired against the liberty of the country, &c. &c. He answered the accusations against him, in a self-possessed and dignified manner.

The man who was the most influential in procuring the destruction of the king, was the Duke of Orleans, one of the princes of the blood, and a monster of wickedness.

It was a sublime remark, made by the king's confessor to him, as he mounted the scaffold, on which he was executed, "Offspring of St. Louis," he said, "ascend to heaven."

48. After the death of the king, the "reign of terror," as it has been denominated, commenced in France, under the revolutionary tribunal erected by Robespierre and his associates. Factions soon arose in the Convention, and their mutual jealousy led to the most fearful consequences. The sanguinary excesses of monsters in human form, which France for a long time was doomed to suffer, are too shocking to be described. Besides the countless massacres of the rich and noble, and generally of those who opposed the revolutionary fury, the parties in the Convention sought the destruction of

one another. Each successive faction, as it triumphed, was at length put down, and made to answer with blood, the cruelties which it had committed. Thus these execrable wretches became the instruments of inflicting merited vengeance on one another. The Convention, in its acts, outraged decency, and rendered its infamy immortal, by renouncing the Christian religion. The queen of France, Maria Antoinette, perished by the axe, 16th October, 1793. Madame Elizabeth, sister of the late king, was beheaded 4th February, 1794.

§ The human monster who exercised the longest and most terrific sway, was Robespierre, with his villanous accomplices, at first Danton and Marat, and afterwards Collot d'Herbois, Billand-Varennes, Coulthon, and St. Just. The party which was opposed to Robespierre in the Convention, called the Girondin, fell under his ruthless domination. Among them was the infamous Orleans. He smiled at his condemnation, and made but one request, which was, that his punishment should not be delayed until the following day. On his way to execution, he braved the insults of the multitude, whose contemptible idol he had so long been; and perished without the smallest remorse of conscience.

Robespierre and his party, were at length put down, and of all the actors and victims of the revolution, he suffered the most in the circumstances of his death, and was the least pitied. In attempting to destroy himself with a pistol, he dreadfully mangled his jaw, and while overwhelmed with indescribable agony from the wound, he was conveyed to the place of execution, surrounded by a populace intoxicated with joy. With him perished eighty-three of his associates.

49. After the fall of Robespierre, the Jacobin clubs were suppressed, and in the course of the succeeding year, 1795, Oct. 26th, the Convention closed its sittings, having been the means, in all probability, of more human suffering than any other deliberative body that ever met. Two days after, the executive power was vested in a Directory of five, and the legislative power in two Councils.

50. While these transactions, which belong to the internal history of the revolution, were taking place, the external relations of France were seriously affected. The republic had waged a desperate war with the adjoining states, from nearly the commencement of the revolution. These states, particularly Austria and Prussia, took the part of Louis and his government, from natural sympathy, from a sense of danger, from resentment at the disorganizing principles which the revolutionists disseminated. and from the desire to restore

tranquillity, and reinstate the king on his throne. The numerous emigrants also, consisting of the nobility, clergy, and rich citizens, who had been enabled to escape from the scene of blood, offered encouragement and aid. Accordingly, several armies marched to the borders of France, but the republic, up to the time of the Directory, not only sustained itself against the efforts of its enemies, but made the conquest of the Netherlands, changed Holland, then perhaps the richest country in Europe, into a dependency of France, and invaded Germany. Such was the energy of the republic, that alone, without allies, it had at command, one million of fighting men, in the year 1794.

51. The government of the Directory, continued till 1799, when the executive power was vested in three consuls, of whom the first was Bonaparte, the second Cambaceres, and the third Le Brun. The Directory had been in several instances unfortunate in the field, and the consulate was designed to restore, and, as we shall soon see, did effectually restore, the energy of the government.

The series of hostile efforts, which the different states opposed to France directed against that country, are termed coalitions. Including both republican and imperial France, there were six of these coalitions with which she contended; two under the former character, and four under the latter. In these combined efforts, all the nations of Europe were, at one time or another, engaged.

The first of these coalitions, includes the wars already adverted to, and beginning in 1793, it continued till nearly the time of the consulate. In this coalition, England, Spain, and the Stadtholder, were included. France had declared war against these powers; and indeed Portugal, Naples, Tuscany, and the Pope, were involved.

§ William Pitt, was the founder and head of these combinations. "He was more correct than others in his estimate of the danger, and no less great in character than in talents, he never capitulated with political maxims. Whatever could be accomplished by gold and perseverance, he accomplished." This war was not merely a conflict of arms, but of clashing elements. An express decree of the Convention, announced the introduction of the sovereignty of the people, in every country which its armies should subdue.

The nature of the warfare carried on by the combined powers, aroused in France a resistance of despair. This called forth, as has already appeared, a reign of terror, with all its cruelties, and all its vigour, and sanctioned, at the same time, a maxim more momentous and fearful than a series of victories—that every citizen is a soldier.

The success of France in this war, was signal. At length, some of the powers, as Prussia, Spain, and the grand duke of Tuscany, withdrew from the coalition, and made peace with the republic. The coalition, however, was not entirely dissolved. It was held together by British gold. A foreign commerce, embracing every quarter of the globe, and aided by an oppressive maritime law, oppressive to neutrals, supplied Great Britain, at this critical time, with wealth, which no other nation, ancient or modern, possessed in an equal degree.

The war of the continent was carried on with the most vigour against Austria; but the fate of Austria was not to be decided in Germany; there, the archduke Charles repelled the armies of the republic. It was to be reached through Italy. This country, therefore, became the principal theatre of the war, in 1796, 1797. Here, Napoleon Bonaparte, in his 27th year, first entered on the splendid and bloody career he was destined to run. To him the command of the army of Italy was intrusted, February 23d, 1796. One campaign gave him Italy; the second, peace. This was the peace of Campo Formio. Out of the Austrian and Papal provinces in Italy, a new republic was formed, under the name of the Cisalpine Republic.

After the peace of Campo Formio, there was no suitable theatre in Europe, for the hero of the day. Egypt, the land of ancient wonders, was invaded and seized by the conqueror of Italy, 1798. Prepared under the mask of an expedition against England, the execution was yet more wonderful than the preparation. No undertaking ever created such immeasurable anxiety in England. Even the great naval victory at Aboukir, could not allay it, though that victory produced important results. England, therefore, was determined not to rest, till Egypt should be torn from France.

52. The second coalition was formed in 1799, by means of England and Russia. This was a consequence of the victory of Aboukir. Austria, and some other powers, soon engaged in it, making it a more extensive combination than the preceding. Prussia, however, maintained its neutrality. Under the mismanagement of the directorial government of France, one campaign gave the victorious allies, Italy, Switzerland, and Germany; but they were headed by the able archduke Charles, and the dreaded Suwarrow.

§ A brief account of the situation of Switzerland will now be given, as here a convenient place is found. That country, in the heart of Europe, had succeeded for three hundred years in avoiding all participation in those great disputes in which the world had been involved; but it was destined to come within the vortex of the French revolution. This country became agitated, and the revolution began in the Pays de Vaud, December, 1797. The evils of the federal constitution were disclosed; there was a want of unity. and the burden at last fell almost exclusively on Berne. The French advanced on two sides, with bloody fights; Berne was overpowered, March, 1798, and the other cantons were conquered, except the three smaller. These made an obstinate resistance, and an honourable capitulation. The consequence of the French military operations against Switzerland was, that the Helvetian Republic was proclaimed, April, 1798. Then followed five unhappy years of war and faction, till the French act of mediation, 1803, restored to the Swiss, their federal, but altered constitution.

It was at the critical period, when the success of the allies, and their approach towards the borders of France, excited such alarm for the fate of the republic, that Bonaparte returned from Egypt and Syria, to Paris, and overthrew the directorial constitution. The directory abdicated; the deputies of the people were driven asunder with clubs, and Bonaparte was appointed regent, as first consul. The most important results ensued. Factions were quelled; internal enemies were overawed; tranquillity was restored; and new energy and life were infused into every department of the government. From this time, the popular sovereignty was at an end. The military force of the nation was put in a better train, and a series of victories and conquests commenced, which have no parallel in modern history. Before Bonaparte put himself at the head of the French armies, Russia had seceded from the coalition, and it was necessary to conquer only Austria, on the continent, feebly aided by Naples, and the south of Germany. The great battles of Marengo and Hohenlinden, besides many smaller ones, brought Austria to terms, and led the way to the general peace of Amiens, 1802. This peace raised Bonaparte to the zenith of his renown. He was soon after elected first consul for life. At this epoch, he might have ruled Europe, without further contests, had he been able to rule himself. Absolute sovereignty only could suffice, and he was accordingly proclaimed emperor of France, in 1804, to which, the next year, he added the title of king of Italy. This elevation was brought about in consequence of a new war, which had commenced the preceding year, and which is soon to be spoken of.

§ The peace of Amiens was enjoyed throughout Europe; but it was enjoyed only for a short time. This was to have been expected, when the object for which the war had been waged by the coalitionists, viz. the freedom of Europe, was farther than ever from being secured. Ever England desired peace, inasmuch as she had effected the deliverance of Egypt. This was with her, after the failure of the general object, the turning point. She never could consent to see Egypt a colony of France. Egypt was restored to the Porte, in 1800, by means of the successes of Abercrombie, and others.

From the conflict which has been related, France had retired with its interior well ordered and tranquillized, with an increase of territory, and with the restoration of all its colonies. This seemed to be the work of Napoleon, together with the rebuilding of the altars, and the establishment of religious liberty. The project of an universal monarchy, was now in a fair way of being realized. Such a project, Napoleon doubtless had formed, but it was defeated by a concurrence of providential circumstances. No potentate in Europe ever had such resources at command. His sovereignty in the interior, was absolute. Abroad, France extended to the Rhine, and beyond the Alps, and the kingdom of Italy fell under Bonaparte's sceptre; the rest of Italy, Spain, Holland, Switzerland, and the German states on the Rhine, were kept in dependence by alliances, or by fear, and Hanover was occupied by a French army, in the heart of the Prussian monarchy.

53. The third coalition against France, was formed in 1805, by England, Austria, Russia, and Sweden. England was its centre. A general rising of Europe was, according to Pitt's plan, to reduce France to its ancient bounds, and the independence of the states was to be secured by judicious regulations and divisions. England had been at war with France nearly two years before this combination, the peace of Amiens having continued between these nations scarcely a year. The coalition was most unfortunate. The power of Austria was broken at Ulm, and at Austerlitz, and the peace of Presburg followed, 26th December, 1805. The expeditious movements of the French emperor, overthrew the whole plan of the allies.

§ The war between England and France alone, which commenced in 1803, was brought on by the refusal of England to give up the island of Malta, which is the bulwark of Egypt, and with that island, the dominion of the Mediterranean. France would not concede these points. Though these nations were professedly at war, there were found few points of contact, as the one, at that time, had no power, except on the sea, and the other none except on land. Great Britain swept from the ocean, all the enemy's forces that could be found on that element, and recovered the colonies that had been restored to France. Before the conclusion of this war, it was, that the famous naval battle of Trafalgar was fought.

The first instance of a royal family being dethroned, by a bare proclamation, occurred at Naples; and Bonaparte, by placing his elder brother, Joseph, on that throne, laid the foundation of the dominion of his family in Europe.

In this war, Prussia obstinately insisting on neutrality, was not to be gained. And yet, without the accession of this power, it was impossible to make an efficient attack on France; the northern half of which, was protected by Prussia's neutrality. The consequences, however, of the peace of Presburgh, revealed to Prussia, as well as to the rest of Europe, what was to be expected from the gigantic ambition of Napoleon. It was ascertained that neutrality could not be preserved, towards one who wished for none. Prussia stood directly in the conqueror's way, and its neutrality was violated without hesitation, by the march of French troops through one of its provinces. That power began to make preparations after the war had been actually decided at Ulm and Austerlitz. When, however, the Prussian monarch found that according to the treaty of peace, the quiet of northern Germany was to be purchased, on the condition that he was to cede to France several provinces, and occupy Hanover in return, thereby exposing himself to a war with England and Sweden, his embarrassment was extreme. But the scales turned in favour of a war with France, and thus arose a new combination, though the old one could hardly be said to have ceased, since Russia had not wholly retired from the field.

54. A fourth coalition, as it may perhaps be numbered, was soon matured, 1806, which included Prussia, Russia, Austria, Sweden and England. Prussia, which began the war, was utterly overthrown by one battle, that at Jena and Auerstadt. Its capital was entered, and here Bonaparte issued the Berlin Decree, announcing the blockade of the British islands. The conqueror's army passed into Poland, and the war was thus transferred from the banks of the Soal, to those of the Vistula, where Russia was under the necessity of defending its frontiers. In the course of this war, were fought the obstinate and bloody battles of Pultusk, Eylau, and Friedland, with the Russians. The last only was decisive, and led to a peace, which was concluded at Tilsit, 7th July, 1807. Peace was concluded two days after with Prussia, by which about one half of the monarchy was returned, as a gift of charity, and this once potent nation, was reduced to a state of second rank. Russia gained a small accession of territory, but both nations agreed to close their harbours and countries against British navigation and trade. All was now French law or influence throughout continental Europe, and all was made to bear against Britain.

§ By the peace of Tilsit, Russia had been made beforehand, not merely a spectator, but an active participator in the project of crushing Britain, by excluding it from all trade and communication with the continent. This was done by the secret articles of the peace.

England, however, anticipated the enemy's dependance on the fleet of Denmark, and effected its surrender, by the bombardment of Copenhagen. One consequence of this act was, a declaration of war by Russia against England, and another was an alliance of Denmark with France, which was to open to this latter power the road to Sweden.

The Berlin Decree was met by the British Orders in Council which prohibited every ship from entering any French port, or any port under French influence, under pain of confiscation. This was followed by the Decree of Warsaw, declaring that all British commodities, in the Hanseatic cities, were confiscated, without respect of owners. This decree was retaliated by a strict blockade of the Elbe and the Weser, and by the Order in Council, declaring in blockade, all ports from which the British flag was excluded, and that all ships proceeding thither, should be captured, unless they had touched at a British port, and paid a duty. This was answered by the Decree of Milan, by which every ship which should submit to these conditions, was declared denationalized, and a lawful prize. Thus, neutral powers could have no navigation. Afterwards, the mad Decree of Fontainebleau, consigned to the flames, all British manufactures from Naples to Holland, and from Spain to Germany. But Europe could not subsist under the operation of such measures. Industry was fatally paralized.

55. Napoleon, triumphant and powerful, now wished to enlarge the dominion of his family, by appropriating to his remaining brothers, the thrones of Portugal and Spain. Spain was destined to receive his brother Joseph, whom Murat, the emperor's brother-in-law, was to succeed in the kingdom of Naples. Louis Bonaparte had before been made king of Holland, and Jerome, king of Westphalia. His design on Portugal failed, though its throne was prostrated. A new and greater throne arose, on the other side of the ocean. Under a British convoy, the royal house of Portugal emigrated to Brazil. His design on Spain succeeded for a time, by his having artfully secured the person of the Spanish monarch, and compelling him to resign his crown, in favour of Joseph Bonaparte, 20th June, 1808.

This act, to say nothing of its moral character, was a political fault on the part of Napoleon; the first fatal step which he took, towards his subsequent downfal. He had already the control of Spain, by his influence. "It was done without a knowledge of the country and nation: an universal insurrection having ensued, it opened the abyss which devoured alike, the French armies, and the French finances; and it gave England a theatre for war. But it taught Europe that the people are more powerful than mercenary armies, and it was destined to give freedom to another quarter of the globe." The British, who were called to the aid of Spain, in connexion with the Spanish forces, carried on the war from 1808, to 1813. Many battles were fought, in which the English-Spanish troops were generally victorious. Here "the Marlborough of the nineteenth century," began his brilliant career. The French were eventually driven out of the country.

56. While the war in Spain, employed the best forces of the French empire, the insatiable conqueror meditated a new, greater, and more formidable war. That was the war with Russia, in 1812; a war which decided the destiny of Europe. It is unnecessary to repeat what has already been said concerning this terrible conflict, in the history of Russia.

57. After Napoleon's defeat, he fled to Paris, and raising another army, he hoped to regain the dominion which he had lost in the east. To oppose him, the Fifth Coalition was formed, consisting of Russia, Prussia, Austria, a part of the Confederation of the Rhine, and Sweden. Of this conflict also, no particular mention need be made here, since the details have been given elsewhere. It may only be said, that the allies carried the war into the heart of France--that after much and strenuous fighting, they entered Paris, which capitulated, 30th March, 1814—and that with the capital, France was conquered, because in France, the capital is every thing.

58. The results of these successes of the allied powers, were important, and great changes took place. The situation of Napoleon becoming extremely critical, he abdicated the throne of France, and was removed to the island of Elba. His mighty empire, reared by a military despotism, fell into ruins. And Louis XVIII., after an absence of twenty-three years from his kingdom, returned and took possession of his rightful throne.

§ Bonaparte had it in his power, while the allies held a congress at Chatillon, to preserve the throne and empire, had he been satisfied with ancient France. But it was fortunate that he demanded too much, and even this, as an intercepted letter of his minister, Maret, afterwards showed, was only a deception. After his defeats in defending France, the senate, lately his slave, openly proposed the deposition of Bonaparte, and he himself, not without many useless attempts in favour of his son, descended from the falling throne, having executed an unconditional abdication on the part of himself and his heirs, 1st April, 1814. He was soon after escorted to Elba, which he received with full sovereignty, with a pension of two and a half millions from the revenues of France, and with a body guard of four hundred men.

Louis XVIII. had spent his time in Italy, Germany, Russia, and finally England. The same month that restored to France her king, beheld three other princes, who had been driven from their thrones, ascend them again.—Pius VII., returned to Rome, Ferdinand VII. to Madrid, and Victor Emanuel to Turin.

59. To restore the political system of Europe, which had been so completely subverted, a General Congress was assembled at Vienna, 1st November, 1814. Six of the crowned heads of Europe were present, united in peace as in war, with a long and splendid list of princes, ambassadors, and ministers. While they were engaged in their difficult and important deliberations, an event occurred which was the cause of the sixth and last coalition of the European powers. "The man of destiny" again made his appearance on the bloody arena where he had lately acted so conspicuous a part, but whence, it was hoped, he had been excluded forever. Having escaped from Elba, Bonaparte, after an unparralleled adventure, reached Paris, and re-seated himself on the imperial throne. A temporary confusion ensued, but the result proved that the army, and not the nation, was the support of that throne. The great day of Waterloo, the 18th June, 1815, buried the hopes of Napoleon Bonaparte in the dust.

§ The French king, upon Bonaparte's return to Paris, withdrew to Lille, and afterwards to Ghent. He came back to his capital after an absence of one hundred days, and was the second time seated on his throne.

In the whole career of Bonaparte, nothing was more extraordinary than his progress through France, and re-occupancy of the throne. He landed at Cannes, March 1st, 1815, and in twenty days from that time, accompanied with about fifteen hundred men, he reached, though without opposition, the scene of his former triumphs. No blood was spilt. The previous conspiracy seems not to have been very extensive, because the emperor could, and of course did, rely on the assistance of the troops. They received him with enthusiastic shouts. The nation was held in mute astonishment for a time; but it soon became evident that he had lost in a measure his influence over it. Instead of ruling the parties as formerly, he seems to have been swayed by them. So much the more energetic were his warlike preparations—he could now indulge no hope of peace.

It was a happy circumstance that the news of Napoleon's return, reached the congress of Vienna, while still in session. The most prompt and decisive measures were adopted. By a special act, he was declared the enemy of the nations, and to have forfeited the protection of the laws. Almost every nation in Europe, small and great, combined against the usurper. The sum of all the contingents to be furnished, amounted to 1,057,400 fighting men. A British-German and a Prussian army were assembled with the utmost speed, under Wellington and Blucher. Napoleon was equally active, and pressed forward across the boundaries with 170,000 men, 15th June, 1815. He first met "the gray hero" (Blucher,) at Ligny, who, after a bold resistance was forced back to Wavre. Meanwhile the army of Wellington was drawn up at Waterloo. Napoleon commenced the attack at noon, of the 18th June, with a great superiority. After an awful conflict, the victory was fluctuating at evening, when Blucher appeared with his auxiliaries, at the right crisis, and decided the battle.

Bonaparte fled to Paris, abdicated anew in favour of his son, and after fruitless attempts to escape to America, he surrendered himself to a British ship of the line; but instead of being permitted to land in England, as he wished, he was transported to the island of St Helena, Oct. 16th, and was detained as a prisoner of war till his death, which happened 5th May, 1821.

Thus "on an island rock in the midst of the ocean, died, almost unnoticed, the man, whose name but a short space before, had filled the world. His plans were wrecked; from the thraldom, which he was preparing for the nations, there sprang liberty in more than one quarter of the globe. Unknown to himself, he was but the instrument of a higher power; for his objects were not its objects. Whatever judgement posterity may pass on him, universal history can view him only from this point." He was the author of several valuable institutions, and effected some propitious changes, not only in France, but in the rest of Europe; yet they were purchased at too dear a price—infinitely dearer than if he had taken Washington, and not Cæsar, as his model. Like other great conquerors, he sacrificed the repose, liberty, and happiness of millions, to his insatiable ambition.

France, having been conquered the second time, by the second taking of its capital, was required to indemnify the allies for their expenses and sacrifices. She was left a great and a powerful nation, little less diminished in territory than after the first pacification, which fixed her limits nearly as they were in 1789. The indemnity which the allies received, consisted chiefly in money, and in the occupancy of eighteen fortresses, by a portion of their troops, to be supported at the cost of France. These troops, however, were all withdrawn long before the term agreed on, which was five years.

Louis XVIII., whose reign was that of a prudent, though inefficient monarch, died in 1824, and was succeeded by his brother, the Count d' Artois, under the appellation of Charles X. The principal event of the reign of Louis, was the invasion of Spain, in 1823, by a French army under the Duke d' Angouleme, but without a declaration of war, in consequence of the decisions of the congress of Verona, in 1822. This unjustifiable act resulted in the overthrow of the Cortes; and the despotism of absolute royalty was immediately re-established.

ITALIAN STATES.

60. In the history of ITALY, during modern ages, nothing important occurred till the late convulsions, occasioned by the French revolution. The Italian states shared deeply in them, as has already appeared. It may be only added, that the Congress of Vienna, in 1815, decreed the subdivision of Italy, between the house of Austria, the king of Sardinia, the Pope, and the king of Naples. The free republics of Venice, Genoa, and Lucca, have, in consequence, been amalgamated with arbitrary sovereignties; and Austria is become the preponderating power of Italy.

SPAIN.

61. Philip V., the monarch of SPAIN, at the commencement of this period, reigned till the year 1746. During his long rule, the nation degenerated as before, from the operation of a despotic government, a superstitious and cruel religion, aided by the natural indolence of the people.

§ In 1717, the Spaniards took Sardinia; but the next year invaded Sicily, without success.

62. Philip was succeeded by his son, Ferdinand VI., 1746, who was a mild and pacific prince, but whose reign is barren of those events which usually furnish matter for history. The indolent and effeminate Charles III., brother of Ferdinand, succeeded him, in 1759, who reigned till the year 1788. The principal events of his reign were, the formation of the family compact, between France and Spain; the union of these nations against England, in the American war; and their unsuccessful siege of Gibraltar.

§ In the siege of Gibraltar, twelve thousand pieces of heavy ordinance were accumulated before the place, for the numerous intended attacks by sea and land; there were, also, in proportion, gun-boats, bomb-vessels, battering ships, military stores, and ammunition. Indeed, nearly all the frigates and smaller armed vessels of the kingdom, were assembled to afford requisite assistance, and the combined fleets of France and Spain, amounting to about fifty ships of the line, were to cover and support the attack. But all this formidable force was employed in vain, from the almost impregnable situation of the fort and the valour of its defenders. It seemed as if so many cannon and other means of destruction, playing upon the rock, would have annihilated it—all looked like a mass of fire in and around it, but the loss sustained by the besieged was much less than might have been expected, while that of the Spanish and French was immense. The mortification which the Spaniards always have felt, ever since this fortress fell into the hands of the English, was greatly increased by the unsuccessful issue of this celebrated siege.

63. Charles IV. possessed the crown upon the death of his father, 1788. He was an inefficient and unfortunate monarch. In 1792, he entered into a league against the French republic, but being defeated, he united with France against Great Britain. After the rupture of the treaty of Amiens, Spain professed to be neutral, till the capture of several of her treasure ships, by a British squadron, after which, the weakness of the government led to an insurrection, and Ferdinand VII. dethroned his father.

The father and son, under the influence of French intrigue, afterwards appealed to Napoleon, to whom the father formally surrendered his kingdom, at Bayonne, for the purpose of defeating the claims of his son; who, after being also obliged to sign a renunciation of the throne, was then treacherously detained a state prisoner, at Compeigne, in France. From this period, the situation of Spain, appears in the account already given concerning France.

§ Since the restoration of the general peace, Spain has been more unfortunate than any other of the European communities. Abroad, she has lost her colonies in South America; at home, the horrors of anarchy and internal war, and, at length, of despotism and the Inquisition, she has been doomed to bear.

Portugal has experienced scarcely a milder fate than Spain. Its situation since the emigration of the royal family to Brazil, has been singular, and at the present time, is deplorable. A monarch residing in a colony, and governing the parent state, is altogether a novelty in the history of the world; yet such has been the fact in regard to the emperor of Brazil. At this moment, the despotism of the usurper, Don Miguel, is producing consternation and distress among the adherents of the regular government.

The history of Portugal, from the time of its independence under John, duke of Braganza, in 1664, to the time of the French revolution, is of so little consequence, that it has been omitted altogether. Since the latter period, the incidental notices which have been given of its affairs, must suffice. It may be remarked, that the Portuguese are still rich in colonial possessions, notwithstanding they have lost most of what they used to hold in Asia.

THE NETHERLANDS.

64. The history of the Netherlands, under the name of Holland, was briefly sketched in the period preceding the last. Holland, as including seven united provinces, and as constituting an independent nation, was the most important portion of the Low Countries. The character of its inhabitants, as an eminently enterprising and industrious people, also placed them at the head of these countries. In the ages preceding the French revolution, their commerce was exceeded by that of no nation, and wealth from this source poured in upon them apace. Their maritime force was consequently extensive, and they had numerous collisions with their great rivals, the British, who were destined, at last, far to surpass them in riches and naval power.

Towards the latter part of the eighteenth century, it was apparent, that the Dutch were falling from their high elevation. Indolence, luxury, and avarice, the consequence of wealth, had, in a degree, affected this excellent people; and their spirit, which would otherwise have been invincible, yielded to French intrigue and military enthusiasm, at the era of the revolution.

The ten provinces, called Belgium, or Flanders, since they were freed from the Spanish yoke, have been usually divided into Austrian, French, and Dutch Netherlands. Prussia, also, has shared in them; and, indeed, they have often changed masters. They were swallowed up eventually in the great political vortex, to which reference has been so frequently made.

§ No space remains for an account of the stadtholders of Holland, since the time of Maurice, who was mentioned in the eighth period. Nor is their history very important, as the stadtholdership was several times abolished. During the separate times of its existence, it has been held by the princes of the house of Orange.

65. After the United Netherlands were overrun by the French, in 1795, and the stadtholder and his family were obliged to flee to England, the whole country was oppressed and plundered by the French, and the melancholy spectacle was presented, of ruined commerce and civil discord, with an

incredible mass of public and individual suffering. Besides misery at home, there was loss abroad; and Holland, rich in colonies, was stripped of most of them, by means of the revolutionary wars, in which she was involved.

In 1814, the prince of Orange was recalled, and Flanders being annexed to Holland, and forming one kingdom, he assumed the title of king of the Netherlands.

§ The restoration of the state of the Netherlands, was one of the principal points in the restoration of the political system of Europe, effected by the congress at Vienna. That its fate was connected with the fate of the Belgic, no less than the Batavian provinces, appeared from the fact, that Belgium, in the hands of France, first opened the avenue to universal dominion. It was felt to be necessary, to found there a powerful state, which, at least in alliance with Prussia, should be strong enough for its own defence; and the union of all the Netherlands into one kingdom, was resolved on by the Congress. The sovereign of the house of Orange adopted the royal title, and gave them a free constitution.

TURKISH EMPIRE.

66. In the history of TURKEY, we perceive the evidences of a rapid decline, from about the commencement of the present period. The people have been extremely depressed, and the nature of their institutions is such as to preclude, in a great measure, the improvements common to the rest of Europe. Some changes have very recently been effected. The discipline of the army has been improved, and the ancient body of the Janizaries, so formidable to the government and its master, has been broken up by the present energetic Sultan. Yet the empire, as it respects European dominions, is now on the brink of destruction,* from the victorious career of the Russians. From its conflicts with that people, it has generally retired, shorn of some portion of its territories, and with diminished strength and resources. With Persia, also, it has often fought, but on more equal terms.

At the commencement of this period, Achmet III. was the reigning Sultan. He was deposed in 1730, since which time,

* By the late treaty of peace, which the Sultan ratified, on the 20th September, 1829, European Turkey is nominally preserved in independence; but the terms of pacification were so favourable to Russia, that the latter enjoys almost every advantage which would accrue from the actual possession of the country.

there have been seven sultans, viz. Mahomet V., Osman III., Mustapha III., Achmet IV., Selim III., Mustapha IV., and Mahmoud II., the present sultan.

§ Under Mustapha III., Turkey and Russia engaged in a furious and bloody war, which lasted from 1769, to 1774. By means of a fleet which sailed to the Archipelago, the Russians seized a part of the Morea, whose inhabitants soon rose in a general revolt, and declared in favour of Russia. But the sultan sent an army to th Peninsula, and quelled the revolt, inflicting the severest punishment on many of the unhappy Greeks. This war was disastrous to the Turks.

The war was renewed by Achmet IV., in 1787, and concluded not until 1792, under Selim III. Important concessions were made to Russia. Koutousoff greatly distinguished himself in this war, as did also Suwarrow. It was during the reign of Selim, that Bonaparte invaded Egypt, and the transactions took place in regard to that country, which have been related in the history of France. Achmet, and also his successor, Mustapha IV., were deposed and murdered by the Janizaries.

The Porte had kept itself remote from the convulsions connected with the French revolution, with the exception of the war with Russia, from 1809 to 1812, which cost it Bessarabia, and a part of Moldavia. Assisted by the powerful Bashaw of Egypt, the Porte was more active in Arabia, against the Wechabites, than in Europe, the tranquillity of which it is not for its interest to disturb, if it be itself left in quiet. This, however, has not been suffered to be the case, since the year 1821. Since that time, it has had an almost incessant struggle with the Greeks, and lately it has been involved in a ruinous war with Russia.

The inhabitants of Greece, oppressed beyond endurance by the barbarous Turk, and recalling to remembrance their ancient freedom, and their ancient renown, have asserted their rights by arms. An insurrection broke out simultaneously, in almost every section of the territory, and has been pursued on both sides, on the mainland, and on the sea, with a furious rancour. After eight years of unprecedented suffering, Greece has become effectively free, by its own heroism, and the interference of Russia, France and England.

The insurrection, which has thus terminated in securing the liberties of Greece, broke out in the month of April, 1821, in Moldavia, and almost at the same time, in the Morea, as well as on most of the islands of the Archipelago. Of these islands, the naval force was generally superior to the Turkish. At the end of the year 1821, the Turks were driven from the Morea and the islands, with the exception of the garrisons of several strong fortresses. But these portions of Greece, have since been repeatedly harrassed by the vindictive Turks, till lately, their contest with Russia, for their own existence, has absorbed every other interest.

CHINA.

67. At the commencement of this period, Yong-Tching, of the twenty-second dynasty, occupied the throne of CHINA. Two emperors of this dynasty, which is that of the Tartars, had preceded him, viz. Chun-tsi, and Kang-hi. A revolution in China, which commenced in 1641, brought the Tartars a second time into power; but they were not considered as settled, till 1649, which is properly the date of the twenty-second, or the present dynasty. The successors of Yong-Tching, have been Kien-Long, and Kia-Khing. The name of the present emperor is not known to the author of this work.

§ In the reign of Yong-Tching, the Jesuits, who first penetrated into the empire, in 1683, were banished, and the christians were persecuted, not excepting those of the imperial family. In the reign of the same prince, also, an earthquake took place, at Pekin and its environs, such as had never before been felt in China. The first shocks were so sudden and violent, that in less than a minute, above 100,000 inhabitants were buried in the ruins of houses, and a still greater number in the surrounding country, where whole villages and towns were destroyed.

Kien-Long died in 1795, in the ninetieth year of his age, and in the sixty-second year of his reign. It is said to have been a peaceful and happy, as well as long reign. In 1793, the celebrated British embassy, under Lord Macartney, arrived in China, with a view to the establishment of a commercial intercourse between the two countries. An account of this embassy, has been written by Sir George Staunton. In the estimation of Europe, Kien-Long stood at the head of the sovereigns of half civilized nations.

Kia-Khing died in 1819, at the time when the famous Russian mission, under Timkowski, was approaching the celestial empire. He was the seventeenth son of Kien-Long, and reigned happily. The Russian mission, took notice that the buttons, which are so conspicuous in the Chinese official costume, disappeared from all the caps of the loyal Chinese and Mongul officers, and that they, as well as their countrymen, adopted a white dress. This, among them, is the mourning colour, for as good a reason, doubtless, as black among the Europeans, blue among the Persians, and violet among the Turks.

PERSIA.

68. Soon after the beginning of the present period, PERSIA, which was governed for a time by the posterity of Tamerlane, and afterwards by the Sophis, had the famous Kouli

Khan, or Nadir Shah, for its sovereign. He had been the general of Abbas III., his predecessor, whom it is supposed he poisoned, and thus supplanted the Sophia family. In 1739, he invaded India, and conquered the Mogul empire, taking Delhi, acquiring immense wealth, and committing the most horrible massacres. This monster then took the title of Emperor of the Indies, and returning into Persia, attempted to change the religion, and strangled all the priests, after which, in self defence, he was murdered in his tent, by his own officer.

After his death, Persia was desolated by civil wars, between various rivals for the throne; but the country, after being exhausted by these events, settled itself under Kerim Khan, an able prince, of obscure birth, who died in 1779. On his death, Persia again fell into confusion, till the last of his family was overthrown, and the sovereignty regained by Aga Mahomed Khan, in 1794. He delegated the government to his sons.

§ The origin of the Sophis, is connected with a revolution on account of religion, in the end of the fifteenth century. Hadar, or Sophi, a religious enthusiast, restored or established the sect of Ali in Persia, whom he considered to be the successor of Mahomet, rather than Omar. The Persians liking a doctrine that distinguished them from their enemies, the Turks, and being at the same time exempted from the obligation of performing pilgrimages to Mecca. embraced it in great numbers; and Ishmael, the son of Sophi, following the example of Mahomet, enforced his opinions by the sword. All Persia and Armenia submitted to his arms. His descendants ruled till the time of Kouli Khan.

Persia has been often conquered, yet the form of its government, and the state of society, have continued nearly the same through almost two thousand years. In a late war with Russia, it has lost considerable territory.

INDIA.

69. The vast and populous country under the name of INDIA, makes but an inconsiderable figure in history. Doubtless, many subjects of an interesting nature might be found, could the modern historian have a fair opportunity of research; but few have, as yet, appeared, and these in so detached a manner, that a regular account cannot easily be given of the events in Indian history. The mention of this country, separately from others, has accordingly been omitted till the pre-

sent period. Indeed, it has little claim on our attention, in an outline of general history, till very modern times. The few details that can be afforded, both of its earlier and later history, will appear below. Like most other Asiatic countries, it has been often and easily conquered, but without materially affecting the form of its government, or its manners and customs. Successive dynasties have ruled over most of the oriental nations, but they have left the latter where they found them. So far back as authentic records carry us, we find among the people, little or no advances made in civilization, refinement, or knowledge. They are the same in indolence, effeminacy, and luxury, that they were two thousand years ago; not ignorant, yet without a spirit of enterprise; accomplished in certain arts, yet incapable of learning others.

§ India was but little known to the ancients. Alexander the Great, first invaded, though he did not conquer it, except in part. The country was afterwards visited by Seleucus, to whose share it fell in the partition of Alexander's empire; and Antiochus the Great, two hundred years subsequently, made a short expedition thither.

The Arabians penetrated into Hindoostan, about 710, and founded an empire extending to the Ganges, which, in 1155, was usurped by the Persians. After this, followed the march of Genghis Khan, who is said to have given the name of Mogul, to India; and subsequently, the conquering career of Tamerlane, both of which have been elsewhere mentioned. The descendants of Tamerlane enjoyed no more than the northern parts, till after 1498, when sultan Baber subdued almost all the country, except the Deccan, Grezerat, and Bengal.

Aureng Zeeb, who reigned between 1660 and 1707, conquered Bengal, and the greater part of the Deccan. At his death, he left an empire of great extent, and producing a revenue of more than £35,000,000 sterling. But a succession of weak princes and wicked ministers reduced this vast empire, in the course of fifty years, to insignificance. In 1739, Hindoostan was invaded by Kouli-Khan, who annihilated the Mogul empire. It was, however, afterwards revived, for a time, but soon fell into decay, and can now be scarcely said to exist.

The British are now the principal possessors of India. Their dominions in India have been created, first, by the establishment of factories for trade; 2d, by wars made upon the natives by the residents of those factories; and lastly, by the capture of the Portuguese, Dutch, and French colonies in India.

The British Indian dominions, which were extensive before, and which began as early as 1757, have been greatly increased within the last thirty or thirty-five years. A statement, somewhat recent, makes the number of square miles of territory, under British jurisdiction or influence, 776,000, and the population not less than eighty six millions. To the above it must be added, that their Indian dominions have been lately increased by a portion of the Burman empire, in consequence of a war with the latter.

The government of this immense country, is vested in a Governor General, and a council of four, appointed by the British crown, who reside at Calcutta.

THE UNITED STATES.

70. THE UNITED STATES OF AMERICA, which, at the beginning of this period, were in a colonial condition, assumed before the conclusion of it, their separate and equal station among the nations of the earth. It was with them an era of great events, and the change from colonies to a state of independence, though it lay in the natural course of things, was equally unexpected and instructive to the world.

The colonies enjoyed a degree of tranquillity from the peace of Utrecht, to the year 1744. In that year, a war breaking out between Great Britain and France, America was involved in it, the result of which was the capture of Louisburgh, on the island of Cape Breton, a place of great strength. This conquest was effected principally by the troops of Massachusetts. A small proportion of the soldiers was furnished by the other New England states. The place, however, was restored to France, by the peace of Aix-la-Chapelle, in 1748.

After the peace of Utrecht, the French had built Louisburgh, as a security to their navigation and fishery, and had fortified it at a vast expense. Twenty-five years had been spent upon the fortifications, and though not entirely completed, they were considered the strongest in America. It was deemed indispensable to take this fortress, as it afforded a convenient resort to such privateers as disturbed the New England fisheries. Accordingly, efforts were made to engage the colonies in the enterprise, and circulars were addressed by the government of Massachusetts to the colonies as far south as Pennsylvania for their assistance. But New England alone undertook the expedition. Massachusetts furnished nearly three fourths of the troops, who were placed under the command of General Pepperell.

Their success was peculiar and almost unexpected. With some assistance from an English fleet, they brought the French to the necessity of surrendering the city of Louisburgh and the island of Cape Breton tc the British king, after a siege of forty-nine days.

71. In 1746, a powerful French armament was sent against America with a view to revenge the loss of Louisburgh; but by means of shipwrecks, sickness, and other disasters, it providentially failed of its object. The peace of Aix-la-Cha-

pelle now took place, which lasted eight years, or until 1756 For several succeeding years, powerful efforts were made on the part of the Americans and British, against the places and forts occupied by the French, particularly Louisburgh, Ticonderoga, Crown Point, Fort du Quesne, (Pittsburgh,) and Niagara. This war, which commenced in 1756, and ended in 1763, is commonly called the French and Indian war. Success eventually attended the Americans and British, and by the peace of Paris, in 1763, all the Canadas, together with Nova Scotia, and the island of Cape Breton, were confirmed to Great Britain. George Washington, the future deliverer of America, first came into public notice during these contests.

The French armament consisted of forty ships of war, fifty-six transports, with three thousand five hundred men, and forty thousand stands of arms, for the use of the French and Indians in Canada. The consternation of the colonies, as might be expected, was great; but Providence, by the means above mentioned, dispelled their fears, and blasted the hopes of their enemies.

The peace of Aix-la-Chapelle in 1748, which followed this attempt, left the respective parties, as to their rights and possessions, the same as they were at the commencement of the war. Great losses, however, had been sustained by the colonies in their commerce, and their pecuniary concerns were in a very embarrassed state. The return of this peace, and its continuance through eight short years, altered the aspect of the colonies much for the better. Commerce again flourished, population increased, settlements were extended, and public credit revived.

The French and Indian war was occasioned by the alleged encroachments of the French upon the frontiers of the colonies in America, belonging to the British crown. Besides the encroachments that were made on Nova Scotia, in the north and west they were settling and fortifying Crown Point, and in the west, were not only attempting to complete a line of forts from the head of St. Lawrence to the Mississippi, but were intrenching far on Virginia.

By an understanding between England and the colonies, hostilities were carried on between the latter and the French during two years, without any formal proclamation of war. The Virginians, who were particularly concerned in the beginning of these hostilities, entrusted to George Washington the difficult and dangerous service of going to the French commandant on the Ohio, a distance of several hundred miles, through a wilderness, to demand of him the reasons of his hostile conduct, and to summon the French to evacuate their forts at the west. He was then but twenty-one years of age, and at that early period stepped forth the champion of his country's rights. He executed his errand, but the result showed the necessity of force, which was accordingly resorted to under the command of Washington. He met with partial success, but the superior number of the enemy obliged him at length, after surrendering a fort he had taken, to retire to Virginia.

This was as early as 1754, but in the spring of 1755 more vigorous exertions were made by the colonies against the enemy. Four expeditions were planned—one against the French in Nova Scotia; a second against the French on the Ohio; a third against Crown Point; and a fourth against Niagara. The expedition against Nova Scotia, which consisted of three thousand men, chiefly from Massachusetts, met with entire success. The expedition against the French on the Ohio was disastrous in the extreme. It was led by Gen. Braddock, a British officer, at the head of two thousand men. His rashness, hauteur, and ignorance of the mode of Indian warfare, cost him his own life, and that of hundreds of his brave companions. Refusing to take counsel of Washington, he suffered himself to be ambuscaded by a body of French and Indians, who would have destroyed his whole army, had it not been saved by the skill and intrepidity of Washington, his aid on that occasion. The expedition against Crown Point, though it failed as to its main object, yet its results were cheering to the colonies after the gloom occasioned by Braddock's defeat. A body of the enemy which had landed at Southbay, now Whitehall, and which were marching towards Fort Edward to destroy the provisions and military stores there, were signally defeated by the Americans under the command of Gen. William Johnson. The expedition against Niagara was eventually abandoned, on account of the lateness of the season and other unfavorable circumstances.

After hostilities had been conducted in this manner for two years, war was declared in 1756 by Great Britain against France, and soon after by France against Great Britain, in turn. The operations of the British till the year 1758 were singularly unsuccessful, through the indecision of the commander-in-chief, the earl of Loudon; but a change in the English ministry that year, which placed Lord Chatham at the head of the administration, materially altered the aspect of affairs. Of three expeditions which were planned and carried into effect in the course of the year, two, viz. those against Louisburgh and Fort du Quesne, succeeded. That against Ticonderoga failed.

The campaign of 1759 had for its object, the entire conquest of Canada. Accordingly, it was determined on the part of the English and the colonists to attack all the strong holds of the French in that country—viz. Ticonderoga and Crown Point, Niagara and Quebec. These were taken in due time, three armies having entered Canada by different routes, nearly at once. The conquest of Quebec was the most important and difficult enterprise undertaken during this war, and has been greatly celebrated through the heroism and death of each of the opposing commanders-in-chief, Wolfe and Montcalm. Wolfe died in the field before the battle was ended, but he lived long enough to know that the victory was his. The words "they fly" caught his ear, as he was sinking in the agonies of death. "Who fly," the hero asked. "The French," was the reply. "Then," said he, "I die happy." Montcalm, in talents, in military skill, and in personal valour, was not inferior to Wolfe. He lived, after receiving a mortal wound, to be carried to the city, where his last moments were employed in writing, with his own hand, a letter to the English general, recommending the French prisoners to his care and humanity.

72. We come now to the most important period of the American history, that of the Revolution, when the colonies passed from a state of dependence on the British Crown, into free and independent communities. The long cherished democratic principles realized by the constitutions of most of the provinces, a consequent weaker political connexion with the mother country, and the feeling of growing strength, already tried in the seven years' war, were among the causes of the struggle after independence. Nothing was wanting but an occasion for a breach, and that could not long be wanting.

73. The origin of the dispute was not so much in any sensible oppression, as in a question of right. Had the British parliament a right to tax the colonies? Parliament maintained the affirmative; the colonies denied it, on the ground that they were not represented. Representation and taxation, according to their views, were inseparable. If their property could be taken without their consent, they had no safety.

74. The dispute arose as early as 1764, occasioned by an act, the avowed purpose of which was to raise a revenue in America without her consent. The famous stamp act followed, March 22d, 1765. This act was peculiarly obnoxious in its character, aside from the principle which it involved, as a revenue measure. The immediate consequence was a great commotion in all the colonies, especially in Massachusetts and Virginia, and a congress was convened at New York in October, which published a declaration of the people's rights. The stamp act was repealed March 19, 1766; but the principle was at the same time confirmed, by the bill, declaring the supremacy of the parliament in all cases whatever.

The stamp act came into operation on the first of November, 1765. In Boston and Portsmouth, the day was ushered in by a funeral tolling of the bells. In the latter place, in the course of the day, a coffin, with appropriate decorations, and inscribed with the word *Liberty*, was carried to the grave. During the movement of the mourning procession, minute guns were fired; and an oration was pronounced in favour of the deceased. Similar expressions of grief and indignation, occurred in many parts of the land. In some places, the stamp officers were obliged to resign, or to secrete themselves, to escape the vengeance of the people. Stamps were not permitted to be landed, and business in many places was conducted without them. At the same time, numerous associations were formed by merchants not to import goods until this odious act was repealed. In this measure they were sustained by the people, who submitted with the utmost cheerfulness to the necessary self-denial.

75. In agreement with the British doctrine, the ministry soon after attempted to effect its object by means of indirect duties. These were laid on tea, paper, glass, and colours, by the revenue act, June, 1767. The proceeds of these duties were to form a civil list for America, which should be wholly at the disposition of the ministers, for conferring remunerations, pensions, &c. The opposition to this form of taxation, and to every form, being renewed, especially in Boston, which was the centre of the resistance, Lord North abrogated these duties, except the one on tea, in 1770. By this reservation the right of taxation was explicitly asserted; but as the Americans, by voluntary agreement, would make use of no British commodities, the tea which was brought to this country could not be sold. The East India Company consequently became embarrassed; and after the repeal of the export tax in England, attempted to gain the Americans by a cheaper price. But, nevertheless, measures were adopted to prevent the importation of tea, and a cargo of it was forcibly seized and thrown into the harbour in Boston, Dec. 26, 1773.

76. The measures adopted by the Americans, impelled England to resort to severer acts. These consisted not only in shutting the harbour of Boston, but in regulations by which the charter of Massachusetts was annihilated. It was these regulations which created the general insurrection, since each colony now saw no security for its former constitution. The Boston port bill was passed, March 25th, 1774. The town was soon occupied by the British troops.

By the "Boston port bill," that town was precluded from the privilege of landing and discharging, or of loading and shipping goods, wares, and merchandise. The bill which destroyed the charter of Massachusetts, made the appointment of the council, justices, judges, &c. dependent on the crown, or its agent. Another bill was afterwards passed, authorizing and directing the governor to send any person indicted for murder, or any other capital offence, to another colony, or to Great Britain, for trial. The indignation occasioned by these acts was extreme. As an expression of their sympathy with the people of Boston in their distress, the house of burgesses in Virginia ordered, that the day on which the Boston port bill was to take effect, should be observed as a day of fasting and prayer.

77. Great harmony prevailed among the provinces, and a Congress, consisting of deputies from eleven of them, was opened at Philadelphia, Sept. 5th, 1774, which resolved to suspend all commercial intercourse with England, expressing at the same time all dutifulness to the crown. England was thus brought to the alternative of making concessions or a civil war. It chose the latter; and, notwithstanding the eloquence even of Chatham and Burke, parliament proclaimed the provincials rebels.

The name by which this congress is generally known, is "The Continental Congress." After the arrival of the delegates from North Carolina, twelve colonies were represented. Although the power of this congress was only advisory, their resolutions were approved, not only by the people, but also by the authorities, whether established or provincial; and exerted a commanding influence in consummating that union among the colonies, which had been increasing for a number of years. This congress finished their business, and dissolved themselves in less than eight weeks. It was recommended by them, that another congress should be assembled in case of necessity.

78. Hostilities began by the battle of Lexington, 19th April, 1775. New troops arrived from England in May. It was hoped that a few regiments would be sufficient to put down opposition—so profoundly ignorant was the British ministry of the spirit which had been aroused in America.

The battle of Lexington commenced by an unprovoked attack, from a detachment of British soldiers, who had been sent to destroy the American military stores at Concord, on a few militia who were assembled at Lexington, on account of the alarm occasioned by this movement. Eight of these were killed, and several wounded. The detachment after this went forward, and effected their object; but the news of the occurrence at Lexington, spreading with the utmost rapidity from place to place, brought together the militia in considerable numbers, who revenged the deaths of their countrymen, by firing upon the British, from behind walls, hedges, and buildings. The enemy, who lost nearly three hundred men, was astonished and mortified by the resistance it met with from the Americans, while the latter were greatly encouraged in their opposition to tyranny. The intelligence of this battle kindled the spirit of war through the length and breadth of the land.

79. The war, thus rapidly commenced on the part of the colonies, was soon signalized by the surrender of Ticonderoga and Crown Point, and by the memorable battle of Bunker's Hill An expedition led by Arnold and Montgomery

against Canada, in Oct. 1775, which was at first successful, at length proved fruitless, and the forts which had been taken in the progress of the invading army, were, one after another, given up and lost. The war, in general, necessarily became, from its nature, a defensive war; and who but the modern Fabius, was capable of waging it? "The greatness of Washington was not founded on splendid talents, but on laborious years—not on quick success, but on enduring perseverance."

The battle of Bunker's Hill, although the Americans were obliged to retire from the redoubt they had hastily thrown up, had all the effect of a victory. It showed that America was invincible. It taught the people the importance of stricter discipline, and greater preparations. This battle was fought the 17th of June, 1775, and cost the British, in killed and wounded, one thousand and fifty-four men. The Americans lost, in the whole, four hundred and fifty-three men.

As military opposition to Great Britain was resolved upon, it became necessary to select a leader. This was done by the second continental congress, which met at Philadelphia the 10th of May. The choice unanimously fell on George Washington, who was at that time a member of the body. Several major-generals and brigadier-generals, were then likewise appointed. The arrival of Washington at Cambridge, to take command of the American army, diffused through it universal joy. He soon introduced order and system into the army, and manifested, in all his military operations, that wisdom and that caution, which were more important to America, than his known personal bravery.

In the northern expedition, the attack on Quebec was unsuccessful; and, to the great loss and grief of the colonies, fatal to the brave Montgomery. Incredible hardships and difficulties had been previously encountered by the army which Washington had despatched, under the command of Arnold. In the same year, 1775, Lord Dunmore, the royal governor of Virginia, obliged to retire from the soil by fear of the provincials, proceeded with an armed naval force to reduce the town of Norfolk to ashes. The loss of property to the inhabitants was great. Royal government generally terminated this year throughout the country.

In consequence of Washington's operations, in taking possession of and fortifying Dorchester heights, which commanded the harbour of Boston and the British shipping, the enemy suddenly evacuated the place. This gratifying event happened on the 17th of March, 1776. Washington and his army entered Boston immediately, with every form of victory and triumph.

The same year, in the south, an unsuccessful attempt was made by Gen. Clinton, and Sir Peter Parker, to destroy the fort on Sullivan's Island, near Charleston, S. C. After an action of upwards of ten hours, the British were obliged to retire, having their ships greatly shattered, and with a loss of two hundred men killed and wounded.

80. It was not long before the idea of an entire separation from England, suggested by the vindictive measures which that country had employed, found every where a hearty reception in America. In that event only, was aid to be hoped for in Europe. Accordingly, the thirteen United States were declared independent, 4th July, 1776. After this decisive step, but one happy blow was wanting to give the colonies allies in Europe. That was realized by the capture of Burgoyne and his troops, on the 16th Oct. 1777. This joyful event had been preceded by a period of gloom and disaster in the middle states, while Washington, with the shadow of an army, enfeebled, dispirited, and destitute almost of clothing and necessaries, was closely pursued by a powerful British force through the Jerseys—while the enemy had come in possession of the city of New-York, Long Island, Staten Island, and Rhode Island—and while the inauspicious operations at Brandywine and Germantown, filled every American with terror. This sad picture, however, was relieved by the firmness of Congress—by the uniform, cautious valour, and steady perseverance, of the commander-in-chief—and by his successes at Trenton and Princeton. Upon the capture of Burgoyne, the French court acknowledged the independence of the United States, and declared war against England. France had Spain and Holland for its allies; and the war on their part became at first a contest for the dominion of the ocean. On this element the French contended with more glory than usual. But the fate of America, as the event has proved, was to be decided on the continent.

The idea of independence had not been long broached among the people before the way, in some degree, was prepared to bring the subject before Congress. Accordingly, on the 8th of June, 1776, Richard Henry Lee, of Virginia, made a motion before that body, to declare America free and independent. Some reasons existed for delaying the subject for a few weeks, at the expiration of which, viz. on the 4th of July, upon the report of a committee of which Thomas Jefferson was the head, the thirteen confederate colonies, by their delegates, dissolved their allegiance to the British Crown, and declared themselves *Free and Independent*, under the name of the *Thirteen United States of America.* This was a decisive and bold step, and constitutes an era in history. It has been the means, in connexion with the eventual success of the struggle, of giving to several other nations liberty and independence. Mexico, and most of the states of South America, have followed this example.

The period of disaster and gloom which followed in respect to American affairs, deserves a summary notice. Washington, in antisipation of the movements of the British, left Boston with his army, and proceeded to New-York, with a view to occupy the latter place. Here his army amounted to between seventeen thousand and eighteen thousand men, a part of whom were encamped near Brooklyn, on Long Island. The enemy soon after arrived by sea, with a superior force, and on the 27th of August attacked, with success, that part of the American army which was encamped near Brooklyn. The loss of a thousand of his best troops was most sensibly felt by the commander-in-chief. He soon after evacuated the city, upon which, on the 12th of October, the British army entered it. At White Plains, whither Washington had retired, he was attacked on the 28th of September, by Generals Clinton and Heister. The loss here was several hundreds, and about equal on both sides.

It is to be remarked, that previously to these recent battles, many of the Americans, in this region, deserted the cause of their country, in consequence of offers or threats held out by his majesty's government, in several proclamations which were issued at this period. These occurrences produced a disheartening effect on the people.

The strong places in the vicinity of New-York were now taken by or given up to the enemy, among which was Fort Washington, which surrendered with nearly three thousand men, after nearly a day's severe contest. The American army, now greatly reduced by the return of the militia, (for it was composed of the militia or troops enlisted for a year only,) by sickness, and other casualties of war, crossed the North River into New-Jersey. On the 22d November, the whole force under the command of Washington, did not exceed three thousand five hundred. With this small number, the American general fled before a superior force, under Lord Cornwallis; and even this remnant of an army was diminished on its march to the Delaware by the expiration of the term of enlistment of the Jersey and Maryland brigades. On crossing the Delaware in the early part of December, General Washington had only about seventeen hundred men.

Notwithstanding the general aspect of affairs, on the part of America, was thus forbidding and gloomy, the continental Congress, so far from betraying symptoms of despair, manifested more confidence than ever in the cause of their country; as a proof of which, we may notice the fact, that at this time they were calmly occupied in drawing up various *articles of confederation*, and perpetual union, among the states. These were adopted on the 4th of October. At the same time, also, the great mass of the American people remained firm and determined in the cause of independence. Congress having become sensible of the impolicy of short enlistments, and a reliance on the irregular services of the militia, determined by bounties of ready money, and promises of land, to raise eighty-eight battalions, to serve during the war.

Washington, now aware of the necessity of some immediate favourable turn in his military operations, not only to save Philadelphia, which the enemy evidently intended to possess, but to arouse the spirit of the nation, and to secure an army for the succeeding campaign, boldly resolved, even with his shadow of an army, to attempt a surprise of a body of Hessians, encamped at Trenton. This he completely effected on the morning of the 26th of December, after suffering great hardships in his march, and in crossing the Delaware, in a cold stormy winter night. Many of the Hessians were killed, and more than nine hundred taken prisoners. Having secured these prisoners on the Pennsylvania side of the Delaware, and re-crossed to Trenton, where he was met by a superior force under Cornwallis, he escaped by a wonderful stratagem, marched to Princeton, and attacked a party of the British, of whom he killed sixty, and took three hundred prisoners. These successes alleviated the gloom which had settled upon the public mind.

Notwithstanding all the exertions that had been made, the American army amounted to little more than seven thousand at the opening of the campaign of 1777. The British, after an indecisive course, some time in the month of August took up their march to Philadelphia, from the South, having sailed around into the Chesapeake. At Brandywine, on the 11th of September, the Americans met them, but were unsuccessful, having lost probably more than a thousand men in killed, wounded, and prisoners. On the 26th, the British entered Philadelphia without molestation. As, however, a part of their army was stationed at Germantown, six miles from that city, a battle occurred there on the 4th of October, but with defeat again on the part of the Americans. The plan of attack by Washington was judicious, and the commencement of the battle favourable, but failure finally ensued from the inexperience of a part of the troops, and the occurrence of a fog, which increased the darkness of the night.

The capture of Burgoyne's army had a most important effect on the destiny of America. A part of his force, in pursuance of the plan of operations, which was to invade the states from the north, having been detached to seize a magazine of stores at Bennington, Vermont, was gallantly met and totally defeated, by a party of Vermont troops and some New-Hampshire militia. This loss seriously embarrassed the British commander: he resolved, however, to proceed, and meeting the American army under the command of General Gates, at Saratoga, after a succession of contests, he was obliged to capitulate with his whole army, consisting of five thousand and seven effective men. This event increasing the probability that the American arms would finally triumph, decided France to espouse the cause of the United States, and to declare war against Great Britain, as already stated.

81. The countenance and aid which France offered to the cause of liberty, filled America with rejoicing; but Washington, however much assisted by the French auxiliaries under Rochambeau, and La Fayette's generous enthusiasm, has the glory of having struck the decisive blow. He surrounded Cornwallis at Yorktown, who was forced to capitulate, Oct. 19, 1781, with more than seven thousand prisoners of war. This event had been preceded by considerable fighting du

ring two or three years, though no very vigorous measures had been taken on the part of the Americans, and also by numerous depredations on the part of the enemy. The financial state of the country had also been, in the meantime, peculiarly distressing. After the capture of Burgoyne, England could entertain no more hope of reducing America, and it required only a change of ministers to produce a peace, which was accordingly done. The independence of the United States was acknowledged by Great Britain, and preliminaries of peace were signed Nov. 30, 1782, which were changed into a definitive peace, Sept. 3, 1783.

On the alliance of America with France, it was resolved in Great Britain immediately to evacuate Philadelphia, and to concentrate the royal force in the city of New York, which was accordingly executed. Washington, penetrating the enemy's design, marched in pursuit of the retreating army. On the 28th of June, the two armies engaged at Monmouth, and after a severe contest, in which the Americans, upon the whole, obtained the advantage, were separated only by the night. In the morning, it was found that the British general had left the field for New York.

Hitherto the conquest of the states had been attempted by proceeding from north to south; but before the close of the year 1778 that arrangement was changed, and the southern states became the principal theatre of the enemy's operations. Savannah, and with it the state of Georgia itself, soon fell into the power of the English under Col. Campbell, who was sent thither at the head of two thousand men. Nothing decisive occurred during the campaign of 1779, on either side. Actuated by motives of plunder, the British fitted out an expedition from New York to Virginia, which took possession of large naval stores, magazines of provisions, and great quantities of tobacco. A similar expedition, under the command of Gov. Tryon, was projected against several sea-port towns of Connecticut. New Haven suffered from pillage; and East Haven, Fairfield, Norwalk, and Green Farms, were wantonly burned.

During this campaign there was scarcely an important expedition attempted by the Americans against the English. Two only need be named, viz. one under Gen. Wayne, against Stony Point, on the Hudson, and the other under Gen. Sullivan, against the Six Nations, both of which were successful. The deficiency of exertion on the part of America during this campaign, was owing principally to two causes. One was, the failure of the French fleet in every scheme undertaken in behalf of the Americans. This operated by way of discouragement, since much had been expected from that quarter. Another cause, still more strongly operating, was the daily depreciation of American money, consisting of bills of credit. It has commonly been called "continental currency." From the state of public finances, Congress seemed to be under the necessity of adopting some such expedient, and accordingly emitted bills of credit, representing specie, under an engagement of the country ultimately to redeem them, by an exchange of gold and silver. These, in the course of five years, or up to the year 1780, amounted to the immense sum of two hundred millions. But long before they had reached that amount, they had begun to depreciate, till finally they became of little or no value. Under these circumstances, it was with the greatest difficulty that an army could be raised, and necessaries provided for its subsistence. This system produced many other evils, but they cannot here be enumerated.

In 1780, Charleston, the capital of South Carolina, after a gallant resistance, fell into the hands of the enemy. The state was, in a measure, overawed by the British force which was kept there in different garrisons, but the spirit of liberty often broke forth in attacks upon the enemy. After there was a sufficient concentration of force, by the arrival of Gen. Gates and his army at the south, the Americans ventured a general battle with the enemy, but were repulsed through the unpardonable failure of the militia. This occurred at Camden on the 16th of Aug. 1780.

While the campaign of 1780 was thus filled with important events in the southern department, it passed away in the north in a series of disappointments and distress. The treachery of Arnold had at one time nearly proved fatal to his country. He himself escaped, but the victim of his measures, Major Andre, a British spy, who was engaged in the negotiation between Arnold and the enemy, expiated his crime on the gallows.

General Greene having succeeded Gen. Gates in the southern army, soon after his appointment despatched Gen. Morgan against Tarleton, in South Carolina, between whom was fought the memorable battle of Cowpens, in which the Americans obtained a signal victory. This occurred on the 17th of Jan. 1781. On the 8th of March following, General Greene and Lord Cornwallis joined battle at Guilford Court House, in which the Americans were repulsed. Several othe battles took place in the south, in which, although the Americans were generally defeated, the force of the enemy was so weakened, that it retired to Charleston, leaving the rest of South Carolina in the hands of the Americans.

Lord Cornwallis had now directed his march towards Virginia, and having received considerable reinforcements, the expectation was indulged that this state would soon yield to his arms. The Marquis de la Fayette having been previously despatched to Virginia, to cooperate with a French fleet within the waters of that state, in the capture of Arnold, who was committing depredations there, was soon called to oppose Cornwallis. Prudence forbade him from risking an engagement with the superior force of the enemy, and Cornwallis, after having in vain sought to give him battle, retired to Yorktown, near the mouth of York river.

It was at Yorktown where the scene of the revolution was substantially closed. Washington, joined by Count de Rochambeau, drew off his forces from New York, where he had at first designed to attack Clinton, and marched towards Virginia. Here he was joined by the troops under La Fayette, and a French fleet commanded by Count de Grasse, and being in sufficient force to attempt the siege of Yorktown, on the 6th of October it was commenced in form. The French fleet had proceeded up to the mouth of York river, to prevent Cornwallis either from retreating or receiving assistance. Seldom, if ever, during the revolutionary struggle, did Washington or his troops appear before the enemy with more cool determination, or pursue him with more persevering ardour, than at the siege of this place. The result we have already mentioned. Upon this event the Americans indulged in the most enthusiastic joy, and the names of Washington Rochambeau, De Grasse, and La Fayette, rang through the land.

On the 3d of Nov. 1783, a little more than two years after the battle at Yorktown, the American army was disbanded, and the great Washington bid a final adieu to the partners of his toils and his victories. The gratitude of America to her providential deliverer knew no bounds.

82. The new republic at first languished under its liberty. The first constitution, which was formed during the war, created a federal government without strength and without credit. But the constitution of 1789, which is the present form of government, gave it a very desirable degree of solidity, and based the public credit on a system of finances for the union. Under this constitution Washington was chosen the first president, in which character he was no less essential to the welfare of the country, than in that of a general. "The Union can, perhaps, be preserved only by having great men in the first offices." This is the judgment of the liberal and learned historian, Heeren. Commerce felt the first great influence of the new republic, and almost all the maritime nations hastened to form treaties with it. The consequence was, that wealth and prosperity poured in upon the country apace. Seldom can a nation so increase, because it is seldom so favoured by circumstances. America, preserving its neutrality during most of the European maritime wars, had such a vast carrying trade, especially between the West Indies and Europe, that its commercial navigation was hardly surpassed by that of the British.

The evils existing under the early confederacy, after the termination of the revolutionary struggle, were so great, that there was imminent danger of losing all that had been gained. The powers of the government were in general small, and in respect to so vital a point as the payment of the public debt, contracted during the war, Congress could only recommend to the individual states to raise money for that purpose. In this and in other things there was by no means entire union among the states, and especially owing to mutual jealousies and the want of power, were they obliged to suffer from the regulations of foreign governments in respect to trade. This condition of things led to the consideration of a stronger bond of union, among these independent communities.

That bond was found in the Federal Constitution, which was presented to Congress on the 17th of September, 1787, who shortly after sent it to the several states for their consideration. It had been drawn up by commissioners from the states, who on the 19th of May assembled at the city of Philadelphia, with Washington at their head. By the terms of the instrument, it was to be carried into operation by Congress, as soon as nine states should have ratified it. Its fate was at length settled by the adoption of it, on the part of eleven states. From this time the attention of all classes of people, Federalists and anti-Federalists, (those in favour, and those against the new Constitution,) was directed to Washington, as their first president. He was accordingly elected to that office on March 3d, 1789.

The acts of his administration were, as it might be expected, eminently wise; though some of them were carried through, not without difficulty, owing to the spirit of party that had begun to arise. He was subjected at times to unjust censure, though the event proved, that the vast majority of his fellow citizens could not forget their obligations to so distinguished a benefactor of his country. After the first term of his office expired, he was unanimously elected president of the nation for a succeeding term, notwithstanding his wishes for retirement. Among the more important events that occurred during Washington's administration, we may summarily name the following, viz. the disturbances between the Indians and the whites on our frontiers—the difficulties growing out of the mission of Genet, the French envoy, who sought to entangle America into an alliance with the French republic—the suppression of the slave trade in American ports—the admission of three states into the union, Vermont, Kentucky, and Tennessee—the negotiation of Mr. Jay's treaty, by which the frontiers were secured against the remorseless savage—and the insurrection in Pennsylvania, occasioned by duties laid on home-made spirits.

83. John Adams, of Massachusetts, was chosen the successor of Washington in 1797. He retained the presidency during only one term. Some of the measures of his administration were peculiarly offensive to those who had been opposed to the policy of Washington, and the federal party; and the political strife which had been for some time begun, greatly increased, until Mr. Jefferson, the opponent of Mr. Adams, was placed at the head of the government. This took place in 1801. Under Adams's administration, the aggressions of the French republic were repelled with spirit—preparations were made for war—but, happily, at the very crisis, a treaty of peace was concluded at Paris, September 30th, 1800, under the auspices of Bonaparte. Mr. Jefferson,

after his first term of office had expired, was again elected for another term. The times of peace and prosperity, which, with few abatements, were enjoyed under the former administrations, continued till nearly the close of his.

It was perhaps impossible for the United States always to continue on terms of amity with the belligerent powers of Europe. Disputes arose both with France and England, especially with the latter, who saw in America a formidable rival. These disputes finally impelled the states to have recourse to the unexampled resolution of a voluntary suspension of their own commerce. On the 22d of December, 1807, Congress passed an act laying an embargo on all vessels within the jurisdiction of the United States. This was followed, March 1st, 1808, by an act interdicting commercial intercourse with France and Great Britain. This restrictive plan continued, in respect to France, until the 2d of November, 1810, and in respect to Great Britain, with one short suspension, until April 4th, 1812, when an embargo was laid on all American vessels, preparatory to a war with the latter power. It was hoped, on the part of the American government, that a suspension of all commercial relations with the belligerents, would induce them to rescind those edicts by which they had annihilated neutral rights on the ocean; but this failing ultimately in respect to Great Britain, war ensued between that power and the United States—a declaration of which was made by Congress on the 18th of June, 1812. In this contest, the young American navy gained a glorious distinction, the army did less, the capital itself became the spoils of the English, but New Orleans was defended with courage and success. The negotiations at Ghent led, in a happy hour, to a much needed peace, 14th December, 1814 The war took place during the presidency of Mr. Madison, who was inducted into the office in 1809. Mr. Madison, like Mr. Jefferson before him, served through two terms of the presidential office, retiring in 1817, when he was succeeded by James Monroe. The principal events that marked the administrations of Jefferson and Madison, besides those above noticed, were, under Mr. Jefferson—the admission of Ohio into the Union, the conclusion of the war with Tripoli, the revolutionary projects of Col. Burr, and the purchase of Louisiana; and, under Mr. Madison—the establishment of the Bank of the United States, and the admission of Louisiana and Indiana into the Union.

A few details only can be given respecting the war with Great Britain. The principal grounds of war, as set forth in the president's message, were—the impressment of American seamen by the British—the blockade of her enemy's ports, supported by no adequate force, in consequence of which the American commerce had been plundered in every sea, and the great staples of the country cut off from their legitimate markets—and the British orders in council. Both Congress and the country, during the whole period of the contention, were very much divided respecting both the justice and the expediency of it. The nation was not well prepared for the undertaking, and especially was the want of officers at first severely felt.

The commencement of the war, in the operations against Canada, was marked by disaster. General Hull, who had been sent at the head of two thousand and five hundred men to Detroit, with a view to putting an end to Indian hostilities in that country, surrendered his whole army to General Brock, without a battle, and with it the Fort at Detroit. This event occurred on the 16th of August. The battle of Queenstown, which soon followed, was bravely fought, and appeared at first to be successful, but by successive reinforcements the enemy at length gained the day. The brave British commander, General Brock, was, however, killed during the engagement. This battle was fought on the 13th of October, 1812.

But while disaster attended the operations of the Americans on land, victory crowned the efforts of their infant navy. The charm of British invincibility on the ocean, was almost, for the first time, broken. Capt. Isaac Hull, of the frigate Constitution, obtained the first triumph over the enemy on his own peculiar element, in the capture of the British frigate Guerriere. This occurred about the middle of August, 1812. On the 17th of October another victory was obtained by Capt. Jones, of the sloop of war Wasp over the Frolick. Before the expiration of the month, Commodore Decatur, of the frigate United States, captured the Macedonian, a frigate of the largest class, mounting forty-nine guns, and manned with three hundred men. And, finally, just at the close of the year, a second victory was achieved by the Constitution, then commanded by Com. Bainbridge, over the Java, a frigate of thirty-eight guns, but carrying forty-nine.

At the commencement of the year 1813, a battle was fought at the river Raisin, between a detachment of the north-western army under Gen. Winchester, and a superior force of British and Indians under Gen. Proctor, the result of which was fatal to the Americans, since, upon their surrender as prisoners of war, nearly all of them were inhumanly massacred by the Indians.

During the winter, another naval victory was obtained by the Americans, in the capture of the sloop of war Peacock, by the Hornet, under Capt. Lawrence. This, however, was followed on the 1st of June, by the loss of the Chesapeake, under the same officer, who had been promoted to the command of it, in an engagement with the

Shannon, off Boston harbour. The Argus, also, was soon after captured by a British ship of war. This, however, was but a temporary ill success of the American navy. No other considerable vessel, except the Essex, under the command of Com. Porter, after this, fell into the hands of the enemy; while on the part of the Americans, beside victories in single ships, two several fleet engagements ended in the complete triumph of the American navy. These occurred, the one on Lake Erie, under Com. Perry, and the other on Lake Champlain, under Com. Macdonough.

In the early part of the spring of 1813, a successful attack was made by the Americans upon York, the capital of Upper Canada, which fell into their hands. In this battle, the brave Gen. Pike perished. On the sea-board, during this year, the British shipping in our waters blockaded several important places, and made a number of predatory excursions, in which much property was plundered and destroyed. In the north-west, success attended the Americans under Gen. Harrison, and Detroit fell into his hands. This event gave security to the frontiers. A more extended plan of attack on Canada was now formed by the American army under Gen. Wilkinson; but, from various causes, very little was effected. During the remainder of the year, several events of importance occurred—as the capture of Washington, and the destruction of the public buildings of the place, and the defence of Baltimore. But we can give no more details respecting this war, except to add, that the battle of New Orleans, under Gen. Jackson, occurred on the 8th of Jan. the succeeding year, after negotiations for peace had been set on foot with the promise of success.

84. The war with England failed of its immediate object, but it showed us our strength and our weakness, and perhaps tended to consolidate our union. It caused us to feel the necessity of a navy, and, connected with the previous prohibitions of commerce, gave an impulse to our manufacturing industry. With the return of peace, our trade was diffused over every sea. The presidency of Monroe continued through two terms, and was an era of good feelings. Five states were added to the union during his administration. But the period of internal concord and good will soon came to a close. Party altercations arose in the choice of Mr. Monroe's successor, John Q. Adams, in 1825, and have continued with more or less violence, under the administration of President Jackson, who was elected to the high office in 1829. The measures, however, of these officers have been approved by respectable majorities of the American people. It may be remarked, generally, that amidst unexampled prosperity, party spirit has too often raged, not without danger to the republic, but love of country has in the end prevailed. Thus, we trust, it ever will

be, through the favoring providence of God. He has been better to us as a nation, than either our deserts or fears would have led us to expect.

Soon after the conclusion of the war, the attention of congress was turned towards the establishment of a national bank. The subject presented great difficulties at the time; but the measure was carried, and a bill, incorporating the "Bank of the United States," received the signature of President Madison on the 10th of April, 1816. The capital of the bank was fixed at thirty-five millions of dollars, and its duration, twenty years. Great efforts have lately been made to obtain a recharter of the institution, but they have all hitherto failed.

Soon after the accession of President Monroe, he made a tour through the northern and middle states, which, besides the great public objects he had in view, in respect to the defence of the Atlantic board, served very much to conciliate the affections of all classes of his fellow-citizens.

Early in the presidency of Monroe, an expedition, which had been set on foot by a number of adventurers from different countries, against East and West Florida, was terminated by the troops of the United States. These adventurers claimed to be acting under the authority of some of the South American colonies, and had formed an establishment at Amelia Island, a Spanish province, then the subject of negotiation between the United States and Spain. Their avowed object being an invasion of the Floridas, and of course an invasion of a part of the United States, the American government deemed itself authorized, without designing any hostility to Spain, to take possession of Amelia Island, their head quarters. Accordingly, a naval force, with the necessary troops, was despatched under the command of Captains Henley and Bunkhead, to whom Amelia Island was surrendered on the 24th of December, without the effusion of blood. The suppression of Galvezton, a similar establishment on an island off the coast of Texas, followed soon after.*

The states which were admitted into the union during the administration of Monroe, were Mississippi, Illinois, Alabama, Maine, and Missouri. *Mississippi* was received in Dec. 1817. Some parts of it had been early visited and settled by the French. They claimed the country until the treaty of 1763, when they ceded their possessions east of the river to the English. *Illinois* adopted a state constitution in 1818, and in the same year was admitted as a member of the union. The first settlements in Illinois were made by the French, and for a time, they were in a flourishing condition. Afterwards, however, they fell into decay. In 1762, all the country to the east of the Mississippi was ceded to the British; Illinois of course passed with the rest. After the war of the revolution, Virginia and some other states claimed the whole country north and west of the Ohio, but they saw fit at length to relinquish their claims to the general government. *Alabama* was admitted into the union in the latter part of the year 1819. This country continued the hunting ground of

* Goodrich's History of the United States

savages, until some time after the American revolution. In 1817 the eastern portion of the Mississippi territory, which included what are now the states of Mississippi and Alabama, was formed into a territorial government, and received the latter name. *Maine* was admitted as an independent state into the union, in the year 1820. It had been a part of Massachusetts, and after several ineffectual attempts to obtain a majority of its people in favor of a separation, the object was accomplished in the year 1819. The separation took place amicably. *Missouri* was declared by the president's proclamation, to be an independent state, and a member of the federal union, in the year 1821. Missouri with Louisiana remained in the possession of Spain through the war of the revolution, until the cession of the whole country to France in 1801, by which latter power it was ceded to the United States in 1803. The admission of Missouri into the union was attended with some difficulty, on account of a bill which was introduced into congress, providing for the interdiction of slavery in that state. Warm debates arose, and the matter was settled only through a compromise, by which slavery was tolerated in Missouri, and forbidden in all that part of original Louisiana lying north of 36° 30′ north latitude, and beyond the limits of the state.

An Indian war of some importance was carried on in 1818, under the presidency of Monroe. It is called the Seminole war, as a tribe of Indians of that name were principally concerned in it. It ended in their complete discomfiture. They consisted originally of fugitives from the northern tribes, resident within the southern states, and were then living partly on the borders of Florida, but mostly within the boundaries of that country. They had made aggressions on the white habitants of the United States, and had been guilty of repeated murders. This state of things determined the government of the country to inflict an exemplary chastisement on the barbarous offenders. An armed force was sent for this purpose, and after pursuing the enemy into Florida, and taking possession of several Spanish forts, the difficulty was terminated by their complete dispersion. Gen. Jackson was the leader in this war. He rendered a signal service to his country, but some parts of his conduct were deemed highly exceptionable, by a portion of the community. His appeal to the people of West Tennessee, calling for volunteers instead of applying to the governor for a draft of the militia—his course in relation to the trial and execution of Arbuthnot and Ambrister, two Englishmen, who were charged with giving encouragement and aid to the Indians—and his occupation of St. Marks and Pensacola—were subjects much commented upon in the public prints, and eloquently debated in the American congress. The general escaped the censure of that body, notwithstanding the efforts that were made to cast a stigma upon his conduct.

In the year 1819, a convention was concluded between Great Britain and the United States, some of the articles of which were, that the citizens of the United States have liberty, in common with the subjects of Great Britain, to take fish, on the southern, western, and northern coast of Newfoundland, &c.—that the northern boundaries of the United States should extend from the Lake of the Woods to the Stony Mountains—and that the commercial convention between the two countries concluded at London, in 1815, should be continued for the term of ten years.

In the year above named, (1819,) Spain, by its minister at Washington, ceded to the United States, East and West Florida, with all the islands adjacent. This country, which was discovered as early as 1497 by Cabot, was held first by the Spaniards, next by the English, and then by the Spaniards again. Its cession to the United States was accompanied not without vexatious delays on the part of the Spanish government. It was not until a forcible execution of the treaty which had been made, but not ratified, was about to be proposed by the United States, that the treaty was ratified by his Catholic Majesty. As an indemnity to the citizens of the United States, on account of Spanish spoliations and injuries, a sum not exceeding five millions of dollars was to be paid by the American government, out of the proceeds of sales of lands in Florida, or in stock, or money.

During the administration of President Monroe, a territorial government was formed for the Arkansas, and for Florida, the former in 1819 and the latter in 1822. The Arkansas was the southern part of what in 1812 constituted the Territory of Missouri. A division of the territory was made in 1819, the northern district being called Missouri, and the southern formed into a territorial government by the name of Arkansas.

In the second session of the seventeenth congress, President Monroe introduced to the notice of congress, the subject of the *piracy* practised in the West Indies upon American seamen, and recommended the immediate organization of an efficient force to suppress it. Measures were soon adopted by the government to put a stop to this infamous business, and the object was promptly effected under Commodore Porter, who sailed with a competent naval force to the scene of the depredations.

The year 1824 was signalized by the visit of the Marquis La Fayette to this country. He was accompanied by his son, and M. La Vasseur, his secretary. Landing at New York, he was received with the most enthusiastic feelings of admiration and gratitude. During his stay in this country, he visited almost every important part of it, and in every place he was welcomed, as emphatically the nation's guest. The important services which he rendered to the United States in the war of the revolution, were thus rewarded with the homage of a great people; while the American congress responded to the public demonstrations of respect, by voting him two hundred thousand dollars, and a township of land, as a compensation for his services and expenditures. In the autumn of 1825 he took passage in the ship Brandywine for France, where he has since figured in many interesting scenes.

The presidency of John Q. Adams, which commenced in 1825, and continued for one term only, encountered a bitter storm of opposition from the beginning. Party spirit too far gained the ascendancy to allow full justice to the measures of his administration. This may be sought partly from the circumstances under which he came into office. The choice of president not being settled by the electoral vote, devolved on the house of representatives. Mr. Adams was chosen by this body, but inasmuch as Gen. Jackson had a plurality of votes in the electoral college, many conceived that injustice was done to the general, and to the expectations of the country, and that the election of Mr. Adams was effected by bribery and corruption. Notwithstanding the difficulty of his situation, he secured a large share of respect, not only personally, but as an executive officer. The agitating subject of the tariff of duties on imports, was extensively discussed during the term of his administration, and some of its principles were settled, at least, for a time.

Andrew Jackson took the oath of office as president of the United States, on the fourth of March, 1829. The country was at that time in a flourishing condition, peace was enjoyed abroad, and the national debt had been greatly diminished. He entered upon the performance of his duties with energy and decision ; but the causes of collision and party alienation which had sprung up in connection with the election of his predecessor, have continued at work to the present time, and presented serious obstacles to the execution of his plans. The character of his administration hitherto has been strongly marked, and he seems destined to achieve most of the objects which he has had at heart.

President Jackson's cabinet consisted of Martin Van Buren as secretary of state, John D. Ingham as secretary of the treasury, John H. Eaton as secretary of war, John Branch as secretary of the navy, and John M'Pherson Berrien as attorney-general. This cabinet continued but a little more than two years, when it was dissolved in a manner that occasioned great surprise throughout the country.

A favorite measure with President Jackson, has been the removal of the Indians in the southern states, beyond the limits of the republic, to be congregated into a community by themselves, under the care of the general government. In the contests which the state of Georgia has had with the tribe of Cherokees within her borders, and with the United States, on the subject, Gen. Jackson has ever favored the pretensions of that state. On the 24th May, 1830, a bill for removing the Indians passed the house of representatives, by a vote of 102 to 97. Arising out of this controversy, history has to record the surprising fact, that three christian missionaries, Messrs. Butler, Trott, and Worcester, were sentenced by the superior court of Georgia at Lawrenceville, to four years imprisonment at hard labor, in the penitentiary, for residing in the territory occupied by the Cherokees, without taking an oath to support the constitution and laws of Georgia. It is consoling, however, to know, and it will appear on the page of history to the latest time, that the supreme court of the United States decided in the case of these missionaries, that the law of Georgia under which they were imprisoned, and by which the state assumed jurisdiction over the Indian territory, is contrary to the laws and treaties of the United States, and therefore null and void.

In the early part of the year 1831, a treaty was made between the

United States and the Creek Indians, by which the latter ceded to the United States, all their lands east of the Mississippi river. In the same year, the ratification of the treaties of commerce, navigation, and of the limits between the United States and Mexico, was exchanged at Washington. In June, of the same year, a bill for the further relief of the surviving offices and soldiers of the American revolution, having passed both houses of Congress, received the signature of the president. The same year was further signalized by the new tariff act, which passed the senate by a vote of thirty-two to sixteen, and also by the act which extended the charter of the Bank of the United States, but which, though passed by the senate, by a vote of 28 to 20, and the house of representatives, by a vote of 105 to 83, was returned by President Jackson to the senate with his objections to signing it; and less than two thirds voting for its passage, was rejected.

On account of the laws respecting the tariff, difficulties of a serious nature arose between the general government and some parts of the union, particularly South Carolina. In the month of October, 1832, an act passed in the legislature of that state, requiring "a convention of delegates of the people of that state to assemble at Columbia, on the 3d Monday of November, then and there to take into consideration the several acts of congress of the United States, imposing duties on foreign imports for the protection of domestic manufactures, or for other unauthorized objects; to determine on the character thereof, and to devise the means of redress; and further in like manner to take into consideration such of the acts of said congress, laying duties on imports, as may be passed in amendment of, or substitution for, the act or acts aforesaid, and all other laws and acts of the government of the United States, which shall be passed or done for the purpose of more effectually executing and enforcing the same."

The convention of delegates of the state of South Carolina thus assembled at Columbia, passed an *Ordinance*, (unless the acts of congress imposing duties on imports should be repealed,) declaring and ordaining "that the several acts and parts of acts of the congress of the United States, purporting to be laws for the imposing of duties and imposts on the importation of foreign commodities, and now having actual operation and effect within the United States, and more especially, 'An act entitled an act, in alteration of the several acts imposing duties on imports, approved on the 19th of May, 1828, and also an act entitled an act, to alter and amend the several acts imposing duties on imports, approved on the 14th of July, 1832,' are unauthorized by the constitution of the United States, and violate the true meaning and intent thereof, and are null and void, and no law, nor binding upon this state, its officers or citizens; and all promises, contracts, and obligations, made and entered into, or to be made and entered into, with the purpose to secure the duties imposed by the said acts, and all judicial proceedings which shall be hereafter had in affirmance thereof, are and shall be held utterly null and void."

Soon after the meeting of congress on that year, President Jackson issued his proclamation, stating his views of the constitution and laws applicable to the measures adopted by the convention of South Carolina, and to the reasons put forth to sustain them, declaring the course which duty would require him to pursue, and warning the people of South Carolina of the consequences which must result from the observance of the dictates of the convention.

This document was well received in most parts of the United States, as it addressed itself to the patriotism of the people, and gave a correct exposition of the principles of the constitution. The president soon after communicated a message to congress, laying before it the acts and proceedings of South Carolina, giving information respecting the measures which he had already taken for the collection of the revenue, and suggesting such further measures as he deemed necessary. Following this communication, a bill for collecting the revenue, called the "enforcing bill," passed in the house of representatives, after an animated debate of several weeks. This occurred on the first of March, 1833, and on the eleventh of the same month, the state convention of South Carolina assembled, and in the course of a few days passed two ordinances. The first repealed the nullification ordinance of the preceding year, and most of the laws passed by the legislature, in pursuance thereof. The other was an ordinance to nullify the late act of congress, further providing for the collection of the national revenue.

SOUTH AMERICA.

85. The provinces of South America, which were colonized by Europeans, continued, with little variations in their circumstances, from the time of their settlement, to the convulsions attending the French revolution. Those convulsions, inasmuch as they affected the parent countries, also reached them. Within the present century they have become independent sovereign states, generally with republican governments, resembling that of North America. Brazil, belonging to the Portuguese, having ceased to be a colony, is styled by its ruler, an empire. The Spanish provinces had a long struggle for liberty and independence, which they have attained, so far as concerns the interference of the mother country. If our information be correct, all of them have not yet agreed on permanent forms of government. Seven states are already enumerated among the free governments of the South, viz., 1. Colombia; 2. La Plata; 3. Chili; 4. Mexico; 5. Peru; 6. The Capitania of Guatimala; 7. Bolivia, formed out of the provinces of Upper Peru.

§ The struggle for freedom in the Spanish provinces, did not origi nate in the intention of an entire separation from the Spanish throne, but from resistance to the usurpation of Napoleon and his brother. The insurgents were, therefore, no more rebels, than the Spaniards themselves. But they were as unwilling to be ruled by Spanish Juntas, as by their viceroys, in whom they could not confide. Like the Spanish, they established Juntas of their own, during the imprisonment of their lawful king. Meanwhile, after the erection of the regency in the mother country, and after its refusal to comply with their just demands, they would not recognize its authority, nor that of the Cortez assembled by it; upon this they were declared rebels. After the accession of Ferdinand VII., they had gone too far to retreat. His violence and insincerity finished the rest.

Distinguished Characters in Period X.

1. Addison, an elegant English essayist and poet.
2. Newton, a most profound mathematician and philosopher.
3. Boerhaave, a skilful and learned Dutch physician.
4. Pope, an eminent English poet.
5. Swift, distinguished as a wit, poet, and prose writer.
6. Montesquieu, a Frenchman, a great political philosopher.
7. Edwards, an illustrious American metaphysician and divine.
8. Hume, a Scotchman, an able historian, and an acute and skeptical writer.
9. Voltaire, a French poet and writer of great celebrity.
10. Linnæus, a Swede, the father of botany.
11. Rousseau, a renowned Swiss philosopher, and fine writer.
12. Pitt, a distinguished statesman and orator.
13. Metastasio, the most illustrious poet of modern Italy.
14. Euler, a renowned Swiss mathematician.
15. Johnson, an eminent lexicographer, critic, and essayist
16. Franklin, an American, a distinguished philosopher and discoverer of electricity.
17. Gibbon, an eminent English historian.
18. Burns, a Scotch poet, a great untaught genius.
19. Burke, an Irishman distinguished for eloquence and political knowledge.
20. Washington, an eminent statesman and warrior, and father of the American republic.
21. Cowper, a celebrated English poet.
22. Klopstock, a German poet of great repute.
23. Heyne, an eminent German critic and scholar.

24. M. de Stael, a learned and accomplished French female writer.

25. Dwight, a celebrated American divine and belles-lettres scholar.

26. Buonaparte, a renowned warrior, conqueror, and statesman.

1. Addison, (Joseph,) "so great in prose, so little in poetry,"* was the son of a clergyman, and born in 1672. He was educated at Oxford, where he so cultivated and improved his mind, by the composition of Latin verses, that he acquired an uncommon correctness of style, and elegance of diction. His merits, as a writer, procured for him public employment, and he even became, in 1717, secretary of state; a place, however, to which he was unequal, as he possessed neither boldness nor eloquence. He was unable to defend the measures of government in the House of Commons, and only wasted away his time in his office, in quest of fine expressions.

Late in life, he married the countess dowager of Warwick and Holland; but if this event added to his elevation, it diminished his happiness, for she ever remembered her rank, and treated him with very little ceremony; an emphatic warning against ambitious love. He died at the age of fifty-seven.

The Spectator, of which the most admired pieces came from the pen of Addison, has immortalized his name. In that work, and in most of his other prose productions, he is remarkable for a delicate and gentle humour, and an entertaining seriousness. His style is admirable, for purity and ease; and the idiomatic excellence of the English language, is seen in his pages, to the greatest advantage. Some have thought well of his poetry; and his tragedy of Cato, according to the French notions, would be pronounced one of the best in the English drama. But others have a very different opinion of Addison's poetry, and at the present day, it certainly does not stand very high in public esteem.

2. Newton, (Sir Isaac,) the most illustrious philosopher and mathematician that ever lived, was born in 1642, and died in 1727. The place of his nativity, was Woolstrope, in Lincolnshire. Particular care was bestowed on his education by his mother, for he early lost his father. At the age of eighteen, he entered Trinity College, Cambridge, and there he began to show the astonishing strength of his mind in the mathematics. At the age of twenty-two, he discovered the method of fluxions, which he afterwards greatly improved. His next pursuit was the grinding of optical glasses, for the improvement of telescopes, and soon after, connected with his investigation of the prism, followed his new theory of light and colours. His greatest discovery, and the greatest that the world ever saw, viz., the principle of gravitation, next succeeded. His immortal work, the Principia, was published in 1687. The friendship of the earl of Halifax,

* Edin. Review

now procured for him a very lucrative employment, in being made master of the mint. His reputation extended with every effort of his genius, and he enjoyed numerous honours, and the favour of princes.

He began to be affected with disease, about the age of eighty. An incontinence of urine, and the excruciating pains of a stone in the bladder, were the melancholy presages of approaching dissolution. He, however, lived about five years from this time. For a few weeks before his death, the agonies which he suffered were very great yet he bore them with exemplary patience, and though, from the severe paroxysms which he endured, large drops of sweat ran down his cheeks, he preserved his usual smile of cheerfulness and serenity.

The character of Newton, is represented as being amiable, and adorned with the virtues of a christian. Irreverence towards the Deity, or the holy scriptures, always drew from him the severest censure. The bible he made his favourite study. His person was of a middle stature, and his countenance, though venerable and pleasant, did not indicate that transcendant sagacity, which he is known to have possessed.

It is superfluous to comment on his intellectual superiority. A celebrated writer has observed, that if the literati of all ages and nations could meet in one assembly, they would choose Sir Isaac Newton for their president. In his researches, he proceeded on the method laid down by Bacon, but with a clearness and strength of comprehension in abstruse studies, even exceeding the father of experimental philosophy.

3. Boerhaave, (Herman,) was born near Leyden, in 1668. He was intended for the ministry by his father, but the circumstance, that in his twelfth year only, he cured a distressing complaint with which he was afflicted, and which baffled all the powers of his surgeon, turned his thoughts to the medical profession. Still, however, he studied theology in connection with it. He stood at the head of his profession, and as a lecturer on physic and botany, he became renowned, not only in his own country, but throughout Europe, so that students resorted to him from all quarters. His powers of mind were vast, and his learning extended to almost every subject of human investigation. He was a great and good man. His valuable works are in Latin, and all on medical, botanical, and chemical subjects. His death occurred in 1738.

4. Pope, (Alexander,) who died in 1774, aged fifty-six years, was a native of London. After having been at school a few years, he went, at the age of twelve, to live with his parents at Binfield, in Windsor forest, and first discovered, or rather improved his taste for poetry, by reading the translated works of Virgil and Ovid; but especially the poems of Spenser, Waller and Dryden. He early began to try his strength in poetry, and so early, that to use his own expression, he "lisped in numbers." His first regular composition seems, however, to have been his Ode on Solitude, written when he was about twelve years old. Four years after this, when he began his pastorals, his merit introduced him into the society of the wits of the

age; and he became the wonder of the literary world, when, at less than the age of twenty, he published his Essay on Criticism. This is, perhaps, as faultless a piece of composition, as the history of youthful genius has ever recorded. It evinces all the mature reflection, and developed capacities of age. But the fame of the Essay was soon surpassed by the Rape of the Lock, which he produced at the age of twenty-four. The Temple of Fame, next engaged the public attention. His next great effort, was the translation of Homer's Iliad, from which he realized a fortune, receiving £6000. from his subscribers, and £12,000, from his bookseller. After this, he wrote several other works, particularly the Dunciad, a work of the keenest satire, and the Essay on Man, which, though beautiful in language, and elaborate in disquisition, shews the writer to have been skeptical, as to religion.

Pope was bred a Roman catholic, but, in the latter part of his life, he attended the service of the English church. In his person, he was diminutive, and somewhat crooked—when tauntingly reminded of it, he would say, "God mend me." In disposition, he was fretful and easily displeased, and, to his no small reproach. it must be said, that he was capricious in his friendships. His manners were easy, and his wit fascinating. Many of the great and noble were his admirers, but he made them feel, that he did not servilely adore superiority of rank.

Puny and delicate as the constitution of this poet was, his life was prolonged to his fifty-sixth year, by means of peculiar care and temperance.

5. Swift, (Jonathan,) was born in Ireland, in 1667. He was descended, however, from an ancient English family. In early life, he was poor, but his relatives furnished him with the means of procuring his education. So indifferent a scholar was he at the university, that he obtained his first degree only by special favour. This mortification of his feelings, had a most propitious effect on his literary progress, for it stimulated him to a methodical and diligent application to his books, during several succeeding years. Swift, under the auspices of Sir William Temple, with whom he had formed an intimacy, might have risen in civil or military life, as the king, in one instance, offered to make him captain of horse; but his thoughts were directed to the church. A little after the year 1694, he took orders, and engaged in the duties of a parish priest. His hopes of preferment were, from time to time, disappointed. He had expected some fat benefice in the English church, and even looked to a bishoprick; but he attained only the deanery of St. Patrick, Dublin. After the accession of queen Anne, he became deeply engaged in political controversy, and wrote some able political works. He died in a state of alienation and weakness, in 1745.

The works of Swift are numerous, and highly respectable for the ability they display. He wrote in a pure and plain style, and had, as Johnson says, "an equable tenor of easy language, which rather trickles than flows." The effects of his writings were very decisive, at the time, and some of them are still read with great pleasure. His

Gulliver's Travels, and his Tale of a Tub, have lost nothing of their popularity.

Swift was an eccentric being, and little better than a madman. He delighted to differ from all other men, on those subjects, or in regard to those interests, in which all other men are agreed. Though married, he was never known to be in company with his wife, except in the presence of a third person. He was strongly attached to her, and yet his strange cruelty broke her heart. Like some men, however, he was avaricious. "He made a rule to himself, to give but one piece at a time, and therefore always stored his pocket with coins of different value." But what he did give, was graced neither with tenderness nor civility. "When his friends, of either sex, came to him, in expectation of a dinner, his custom was to give every one a shilling, that they might please themselves with provision. At last, his avarice grew too powerful for his kindness; he would refuse a bottle of wine; and, in Ireland, no man visits where he cannot drink." Whether he really believed in the truth of christianity, is, to say the least, doubtful. His professed dread of hypocrisy, might rather be termed the fear of man, or indifference to religion, when it induced him to read prayers to his servant, every morning, with such dexterous secresy, that Dr. Delany was six months in his house before he knew it.

6. Montesquieu (Charles de Secondat) was born at Brede, near Bordeaux, 1689, of a noble family. He devoted himself early to literature, and first displayed strong powers of mind in his Persian Letters. His great work, that which has conferred on him an immortal name, is, his Spirit of Laws. In this production, he displays astonishing depth of thought, vigour of imagination, and solidity of judgment, and deserves the honourable appellation of the Legislator of the Human Race. While he was engaged in that work, he visited several countries for information, as Germany, Hungary, Italy, Switzerland, Holland, and England. In the last he resided two years, where he was greatly honoured. It was an observation of his, "that England was the country where to think, and France where to live."

7. Edwards, (Jonathan,) so advantageously known at home and abroad, for the power of his intellect, and the usefulness of his writings, was a native of Windsor, Connecticut. He was born in 1703, graduated at Yale College, in 1720, where he spent two years, as a tutor; settled in the ministry at Northampton, 1727, whence he was removed; appointed missionary to the Indians, at Stockbridge, in 1751; and called to the presidency of Nassau Hall, in 1758. He had scarcely entered on the duties of that station, when he fell a victim to the small pox, in the fifty-sixth year of his age.

President Edwards was one of the greatest and best men of modern times. He possessed an acute metaphysical turn of mind, which he most usefully employed in the investigation of divine truth. His treatise on the Will, is deservedly ranked as one of the ablest productions of the human mind. This work did that for the moral nature of man, which Locke's Essay on the Understanding did for man's intellectual nature. It settled several controverted subjects, which had perplexed the divines and philosophers, who went before him. Edwards, as a metaphysician, stands by the side of Locke, Bacon, and Aristotle; while, as a christian, he was pre-eminent in conscientiousness, humility, fear of God, and faithfulness to the spiritual interests of men. There is an awful power in his sermons. His Treatise on the Affections, is an invaluable book, which no christian, probably, ever read without profit.

8. Hume (David) was designed, by his family, for the law, but the turn of his mind led him to literary pursuits. For this purpose, he retired to France, and, though he possessed slender means, he was able, by the most rigid economy, to pursue his studies in that country. Here he wrote his treatise of Human Nature. In 1742, the first part of his Essays appeared. His Political Discourses, and his Inquiries concerning the Principles of Morals, followed, in 1752. At different periods afterwards, the several portions of his English History were given to the public. These works were little noticed at first, unless his History be excepted, but some of them gradually grew into reputation, and he realized, from the latter works particularly, a handsome reward. This, together with the avails of other employments, made him, in his own view, very opulent, as he possessed a revenue of £1000 a year. He was born at Edinburgh, 1711, and died at the same place, 1776.

Hume, doubtless, is an able writer, ingenious, subtile, and acute; but the sophistry of his arguments, on the subject of morals and religion, is unworthy of a man of his penetration. He knew better than to use the fallacious language with which he has often clothed his thoughts, and by means of which he has confounded truth with error, and right with wrong.

9. Voltaire (Marie Francis Arouet de) was a Parisian by birth. He died in 1778, at the age of eighty-four. For a long period, he was a sort of dictator in the republic of letters on the continent. By his free remarks on government and religion, he contributed, perhaps more than any other man, to lay the foundation of that state of things which afterwards existed in France, known under the name of the Revolution.

In early life, he evinced superior powers of mind, and especially a sprightly imagination. He wrote verses, he says, before he left his cradle. His fondness for satire, directed against the government, procured his imprisonment in the bastile, till he was liberated by the interference of the duke of Orleans. After this event, he devoted himself more entirely to the composition of poetry. His principal efforts were directed towards the drama; and his Alzire, Mahomet, and Merope, placed him at the head of the dramatic poets of France. His Henriade, an epic poem, he had previously published in England. Encouraged by the Prussian monarch, he spent some time at the court of Berlin; but he at last fixed his residence in a village on the borders of France, named Ferney. The boldness and effrontery of his muse, had rendered a residence in the French capital vexatious, and even dangerous to him, and hence he willingly left his country at different times, and at last retired to a remote corner of it, so that he might pursue his studies in quiet. Here he continued long to direct the taste and literature of the age. He died at Paris, while visiting that city; and according to some accounts, he departed in great horror, from reflections on the irreligious tendency of his writings. The blasphemous atheist often, indeed, appeared in his works.

The following particulars respecting Voltaire, are given from a contemporaneous account. Many others might be added. "The most piercing eyes I ever beheld," says Dr. Moore, "are those of Voltaire, now in his eightieth year. His whole countenance is expressive of genius, observation, and extreme sensibility. In the morning, he has a look of anxiety and discontent, which gradually wears off, and after dinner, he seems cheerful; yet, an air of irony never entirely forsakes his face, but may always be observed lurking in his features, whether he frowns or smiles. By far the greater part of his time is spent in his study, and whether he reads himself, or listens to another, he always has a pen in his hands to take notes, or make remarks."

10. Linnæus (Charles Von) was the son of a Swedish clergyman, born in the province of Smaland, 1707. He practised physic with such popularity and success, that at the age of thirty-four, he was nominated professor of physic and botany in the university of Upsal, where he had been educated. His sovereign duly noticed his services, and besides other favours, conferred on him the honour of nobility. With an unparalleled ardour after knowledge, Linnæus undertook to explore the inhospitable deserts of Lapland, and through ten degrees of latitude, he exposed himself, generally on foot, to every sort of fatigue. He afterwards visited other countries. He died in 1778, having been seized with an apoplexy two years before.

To his sagacity and discernment, science is indebted for the useful and familiar division of plants, of animals, &c. into classes. To the most extensive knowledge, he united the most indefatigable industry, and before his publication of his Genera Plantarum, he most minutely examined the characters of more than eight hundred plants.

11. Rousseau (John James) was born in Geneva, in 1712. He was of a weakly constitution, but his mind was strong and active, and the early reading of Plutarch and Tacitus expanded his ideas, and inspired him with courage. His life was somewhat eventful, though we cannot dwell on the particulars. The strangeness and inconstancy of his character, subjected him to no inconsiderable calamities; and, while by nature he was formed to enjoy the pleasures of the world in perfection, he endured self-inflicted tortures to such an extent, as to leave the balance of pleasure very little, if at all, in his favour. He had a perpetual hankering after some unattainable state of voluptuous virtue. Though equally skeptical with Hume and Voltaire, he quarrelled with the one, who was his protector in England, and he incurred the persecution of the other, for maintaining the immoral tendency of the stage. (Strange to tell, he had written for the stage himself; but he was a creature of inconsistency.)

Some of his opinions were so obnoxious, that the popular indignation was aroused against him, and he was obliged to flee from place to place on the continent, and, in fact, he found no asylum till he reached England. At length, however, he returned to Geneva, and spent the last years of his life in the company of a few friends, and resigned himself to peaceful studies. He died of an apoplexy, in 1778, aged sixty-six years.

His works show him to have been a man of transcendent genius, but convict him of the utmost eccentricity, joined with licentiousness and skepticism. He may be called the Diogenes of modern times. His literary career commenced at the age of thirty-eight, by a prize essay, in which he maintained the superiority of savage nature to the comforts of domestic and social life. This opinion he defended, for a long time, against all Europe. His New Heloise, and his Emilius, moral romances, attained to a great celebrity. His Confessions, a work published after his death, is one of the most singular productions of the human mind.

12. Pitt (William) was earl of Chatham, and is commonly known by that name. He was born in 1708. At the age of twenty-seven, he was elected a member of parliament, and soon began to distinguish himself as an eloquent and well-informed speaker. He enlisted early in the ranks of opposition, and in his speeches displayed such acuteness, vehemence, and depth of argumentation, as astonished the house, and marked him as worthy of the highest offices of the state. Wealth now poured in upon him, from private benefactions, and from his public employments. In 1756, he received the seals of secretary of state for the southern department; but his continuance in office was of short duration. His popularity, however, with the mass of the nation, recalled him to the secretaryship in 1757. This restoration was the beginning of a new era of splendid conquests, and of national glory. At the accession of George III., his resignation took place, accompanied not only by a nation's regrets, but by the most substantial testimonials of his worth, on the part of the government. He deprecated, with all his eloquence, the measures relating to the American war, in the house of lords. His constitution, however, was, at this time, so enfeebled, that on one of these occasions, as he arose to speak, he fell into a fit, and died in a few days.

As a statesman and orator, he stands, perhaps, at the head of the men of his profession, in modern times. It is said, that Walpole, the minister, surrounded with power, and the unshaken support of a decided majority, never heard his voice, in the house of commons, without being alarmed and thunder-struck.

13. Metastasio (Pietro Bonaventura) early began the exercise of the poetic art. At the age of ten, he often collected little audiences, who listened with attention and admiration to the sweetness of his extemporary verses. He found a patron in the celebrated Gravina; and without neglecting the muses, he first studied the law; but at last assumed the clerical habit. Gravina, at his death, left the poet his whole fortune, worth 15,000 crowns, which the latter dissipated

in two years by his convivial and hospitable habits. He now wrote for the stage, at the solicitation of Bulgarella, the celebrated singer, and soon found himself the object of general admiration. A very large portion of his life, he spent at Vienna, enjoying the patronage of the sovereigns of Austria. He died at the age of eighty-four. Rome was the place of his birth, Vienna of his death.

His works consist of twenty-six operas, eight sacred dramas, besides masques, sonnets, and other poetical miscellanies. They have been translated into various languages, and possess a high reputation. The sweetest pictures of virtue and morality are delineated in his writings; nor is he wanting in flights of sublimity. It is said, that Metastasio believed in no poetic inspiration, or propitious seasons for the composition of poetry, and that he trusted to no such thing in himself, but always set himself down calmly to his prescribed task, and completed it as he would any other piece of business.

14. Euler (Leonard) was born at Basil, 1707. His father intended him for the ministry, but the genius of his son was bent to philosophical pursuits. In 1727, he went with the Bernouillis to Petersburg. Here his publications ranked him among the greatest of philosophers. In 1740, he gained, with Maclaurin and D. Bernouilli, the prize of the academy of Paris, on the nature of tides. In 1741, he removed to Berlin, at the invitation of the king of Prussia, and assisted that monarch in the establishment of an academy of sciences. Here he produced his theory of the motions of the planets and comets, that of magnetism, &c. He died suddenly, while conversing with a friend, on the new planet, and as he was playing with one of his grand-children, at tea time. He was attacked by a fit of apoplexy. "I am dying," were his last words, and in a few hours after, he expired, aged 76 years.

His mental powers were astonishing. While his fellow academicians asked four months to complete an important calculation, he finished it in three days, but so intense had been his application that it produced a fever, by which he lost the sight of one of his eyes. In one night, he calculated in his head, the six first powers of all the numbers above twenty, which he repeated the next day most correctly to his astonished friends. His erudition was immense. He read all the Latin classics, and had the history of all ages and nations, even to the minutest facts, ever present to his mind. Indeed, so retentive was his memory, that he could repeat the whole of the Æneid.

In society he was never absent like Newton or Adam Smith; but like Hutton and Hume, he was thoughtless and playful in his hours of relaxation, and entered into all the trifles and frivolous anecdotes with which many choose to kill time while in company.

15. Johnson, (Samuel,) surpassed by no one in literature, was born at Litchfield, 1709. He was educated at Oxford in part, the insolvency of his father obliging him to leave the university prematurely. Involved in poverty, and with unpromising prospects before

him, he tried various expedients to obtain a livelihood, but abandoned them successively, till in company with his pupil Garrick, he went to London in quest of employment, in 1737. From this period till 1762, he was engaged in literary labours, under the pressure of poverty and disappointment. A part of the fruit of these labours were his immortal works, the English Dictionary and the Rambler. He completed his Dictionary, in the space of seven years, and received for it £1575; but owing to the urgency of his wants, the money had been advanced during the composition of the work. During this period he was once arrested for a debt of five guineas, from which he was relieved by the kindness of Richardson. His services to literature were not, however, to pass unrewarded; for, in 1762, he was presented by the king with a pension of £300 per annum, as the grant expresses it, for the moral tendency of his writings. The Lives of the Poets, he began in 1777, and completed in 1781. This is a noble model of that description of writing, and embodies some of the choicest criticism in the English language.

The inflictions of disease now began to be felt, and Johnson contemplated, not without gloomy apprehensions, the end of his earthly being. His fear of this event was excessive, for his temperament was deeply melancholic, and he did not at first perceive the true ground of confidence for sinful men. At least, his mind was not satisfied on this subject. But as he approached the tomb, darkness fled from his soul. He was soothed and cheered, he saw the proper ground of confidence, and departed with the faith and consolation of a christian.

Johnson's works are numerous; none are indifferent, and some are of the highest order of literary excellence. His powers of conversation were admirable. The particulars of his life, character, opinions, connexions, &c. have been minutely recorded by Strahan, Mrs. Piozzi, Boswell, and others.

16. Franklin (Benjamin) was born at Boston, Mass., 1706. In his youth he was apprenticed to an uncle in the business of printing; and eager after knowledge, he read attentively, in the night, the works which he had printed in the day. In this way he early amassed a valuable stock of information, and as he possessed a reflecting and philosophizing, and withal a practical sort of mind, he turned his knowledge to the best account. After he commenced business for himself in Philadelphia, he soon rose in public esteem, so that he was called to offices of trust in the commonwealth, and finally, in the contention of the colonies with the mother country, he acted a most conspicuous and useful part. He was a member of the American congress during that eventful period. Several times in the course of his life, he went to Europe, where he was received with the distinction due to his pre-eminent worth as a statesman and philosopher. As a public negociator, he effectually secured the honour and the interests of his country. He died governor of Pennsylvania, full of years and glory, 1790, aged eighty-four years. His discoveries in science have associated his name with that of Newton.

He is the father of that branch of philosophy which explains the laws of the electric fluid; and the utility of the lightning rod, will forever point him out as a temporal benefactor of the human race. His political reflections have placed him by the side of the greatest legislators of antiquity

17. Gibbon (Edward) was born at Putney, 1737, of a respectable and ancient family. He acquitted himself poorly at the university, and it would seem, from his own account, that he was not much in the fault. "The fellows," he says, "were easy decent men, who supinely enjoyed the gifts of their founder; their days were filled by a series of uniform employments; the chapel and the hall, the coffee-house, and the common room, till they retired weary and well satisfied, to a long slumber. From the toil of reading, or thinking, or writing, they had absolved their consciences." The student with such examples before him, might well be excused for indolence. Gibbon afterwards, when at Lausanne, paid much attention to classical literature, and acquired such a perfect knowledge of the French language, that he could both speak and write it with as much facility as his own. A portion of his printed works is in French.

The great work which has immortalized Gibbon, is his Decline and Fall of the Roman Empire. It was in the midst of the ruins of Rome, that he conceived the idea of this magnificent topic. This history cost him twenty years of labour. His resources for it he derived, in a considerable degree, from his own library, which consisted of ten thousand volumes. It is an elaborate and splendid production, and generally accurate. But his account of the causes of the progress of Christianity, is highly exceptionable, and he appears throughout the work, a thoroughgoing skeptic and unbeliever. His sneers at the holy religion of the Saviour, very much detract from the value of the work. He received from his booksellers, eight thousand pounds for his history.

Among his miscellaneous works, are a volume or two of letters, highly spirited and entertaining, and rich with the stores of an elegant, cultivated, and playful mind. These, however, are also tinctured with infidelity. He wrote memoirs of himself. He acknowledges that from the Provincial Letters of Pascal, he "learned to manage the weapon of grave and temperate irony, even on subjects of ecclesiastical solemnity." In describing the characteristics of his intellect, he says, "Wit I have none; my imagination is rather strong than pleasing; my memory both capacious and retentive. The shining qualities of my understanding are extensiveness and penetration, but I want both quickness and exactness." He died of a dropsy, in 1794.

18. Burns (Robert) was born, 1759, at Ayr, in Scotland. Though a ploughman originally, he rose to high poetical fame. He has been called the greatest untaught poet since Shakspeare. His poems, which are in the Scotch dialect, possess uncommon beauty, and an elegant simplicity. He no sooner appeared in print, than he was noticed and drawn from the plough, to associate with men of letters and opulence. By the exertions of his friends, a handsome sub-

scription of nearly one thousand one hundred pounds was raised for him, and a place in the excise was obtained, and a farm rented, where he might exercise his genius, and live in comfortable affluence. But the change ruined him. He became a sot, and indulged in licentious pleasures, till his constitution gave way, and the tomb received him. His age was thirty-nine.

19. Burke (Edmund) was the son of a respectable attorney, at Carlow, in Ireland, where he was born, 1730. He took his bachelor's degree at Trinity College, Dublin, where, it is said, he was not much distinguished. In 1753, he came to London, and entered at the Middle Temple. With all his powers of elocution, he paid no serious attention to the law, but devoted his time principally to literature and politics. His style and arguments as a writer, soon attracted notice, and his Essay on the Sublime, procured for him distinction. He therefore became a public man, and in 1765, was introduced into parliament. He then joined to the character of a most elegant writer, that of a most eloquent speaker. The American war, he denounced with great vehemence and justice, and was so happy at length as to witness its termination. When the French revolution broke out, he became alarmed at the progress of licentious principles, and with a view to counteract them in England, he published his celebrated Reflections. His Anti-Gallican zeal brought on a rupture between him and his former associates—Mr. Fox and others. From this time, though he affected to be as fond of liberty as ever, he favoured the administration of Mr. Pitt, and the court rewarded him with a large pension for his able services. By many, in his high-wrought enthusiasm in favour of the war against France, he was considered as the oracle and bulwark of the country. Some time before his death, Mr. Burke retired from public life, but though loaded with honours, he sunk, three years after, a melancholy victim to the recent loss of his only and dearly beloved son. His death occured in 1797.

As an author, his merits are universally acknowledged. He was copious, elegant, and forcible. His pieces are numerous. His Reflections were so interesting in the public opinion, that 18,000 copies were sold in a few weeks.

20. Washington, (George,) who has filled the world with his own, and his country's glory, was born 1732, in the county of Fairfax, in Virginia, where his father was possessed of large landed property. Washington was educated under the care of a private tutor, and after making rapid progress in mathematics and engineering, he embraced the military profession. Here he displayed his great talents, particularly his wisdom and caution, and showed himself master of the knowledge of military stratagems. Eminent also was his personal valour, and he proved he could fight, whenever he calculated upon the prospect of decisive advantage, or certain victory. He had greatly distinguished himself in several expeditions in his native state, before he was called to the command of the American army, in the war of the Revolution. How ably he sustained his country's cause, and to what a successful termination he brought the great

struggle, our readers need not be informed. As a military captain, he ranks among the greatest, whether of ancient or modern times. But in some respects, he is beyond a comparison with the most celebrated heroes. He had no stain of an unhallowed ambition. At the close of the war, America was in his power, but instead of a dictator, he became one of her most obedient sons. Military command he assumed as a duty, and whenever an opportunity offered, he hastened to resign it, that he might retire to the shades and peace of private life.

Washington was the first president of the United States, and was inaugurated into that high office, in 1789. Having served during two presidential terms, he declined the honour which his countrymen would doubtless have again conferred upon him, and sought the gratifications of his farm at Mount Vernon. The All-wise Disposer did not suffer him to enjoy many years in his peaceful retirement. He was called away from life, rather unexpectedly, after a few days illness, 14th December, 1799. "He was buried with due national honours. America, in a public mourning, deplored in him the loss of her father, and of her friend, and a new city was erected on the borders of the Potomac, which, in becoming the capital of the United States, records to distant times, in bearing his name, the services, the patriotism, and the glories of her great and illustrious founder."

Besides the qualities which distinguish the warrior and statesman, Washington was endowed with every virtue of humanity. His passions were naturally strong, but he attained to a wonderful command of them. He was modest, condescending, and affable, and excellent in all the relations of private and domestic life. His punctuality and method in managing his multifarious concerns, are a model to every one. And his exemplary conduct, as a Christian, and his calmness in death inspire the belief that his memorial is on high.

21. Cowper, (William,) who died in 1800, was son of Dr. Cowper, chaplain to George II., and rector of Berkhampstead, Herts. He was in his eighteenth year, when he left Westminster school, and as he was destined for the law, he entered at the Inner Temple, and at the age of thirty-one, was apprenticed clerk in the house of lords. But weakness of nerves, and the most distressing diffidence, unfitted him for public employment of any kind. He soon fell into a religious melancholy, which arose to such a height, that in a fit of desperation, he attempted his own life, but was providentially saved from so awful an end. He, however, attained at length the cheering and serene hope of religion. He became an author, not until he was fifty years of age. His first volume of poems, appeared in 1782, and in 1785, his second volume, which raised towards him the general voice of approbation. He afterwards executed a valuable translation of Homer's Iliad and Odyssey, in blank verse.

About this time, (1787,) a similarity of literary undertakings, brought Cowper and Hayley the poet, into an intercourse of friendship, which continued to the last period of life. Hayley has commemorated the genius and virtues of his friend, in an interesting and elegant account of his life and poetic labours. In this account, many of Cowper's letters are embodied, which, together with a volume or two, since published, place him at the head of English epistolary writing. In 1794, the king, as became the sovereign of an enlightened nation, honourably bestowed upon the poet a pension of three hundred pounds per annum. But the bounty came too late to be much enjoyed. Cowper was again sunk into dejection and religious melancholy, which continued, with few intervals of reason and hope, till he ceased to be an inhabitant of this world. He died at the age of seventy.

The Task, is Cowper's most celebrated work, and abounds in beauties of every kind. It exhibits religion, particularly, in a most engaging form.

22. Klopstock (Frederick Theophilus) was born at Quedlinburg, in 1724. He studied theology at Jena, where he wrote a great part of his Messiah, which he published in 1747. His name is immortalized chiefly by this poem. Though at the time of its publication, it was censured by some, it was admired by more, and Bodmer, and the Swiss in general, were loud in its praises. Klopstock was invited into their country, whence he was called to Copenhagen, by the most flattering promises, which were amply fulfilled. He died in 1803. His funeral was conducted with extraordinary pomp. It was attended by the senate of Hamburgh, where, at the time of his decease, he was residing as Danish legate. The diplomatic body, also the clergy, men of letters, and merchants, honoured his remains by their presence. The whole constituted a procession of seventy-six coaches. At Altona, it was joined by fifty more carriages, to the village of Ottensen, where he was buried, with every ceremony expressive of profound regard.

As a writer, he is characterized by a fervid imagination; but though rich in imagery, and lofty in sentiment, he is frquently obscure and turgid. Besides the Messiah, he was the author of three tragedies, called the Death of Adam, Solomon, and David.

23. Heyne (Christian Gottlieb) was born in Silesia, 1729. He succeeded Gesner, in 1763, in the professorship of Rhetoric, at Gottingen, where also he became secretary to the society of Sciences. He drew up a catalogue of the library at Gottingen, which made 150 folio volumes. King George III. placed his three younger sons under his care, and they all treated him with the greatest respect. He died suddenly, in 1812. As an editor of the classics, he is justly celebrated, and his critical skill has been the admiration of the learned world. He is the first of his class. From poverty and obscurity, he arose to comfort and fame, and he is an encouraging instance of the rewards which often attend diligent and well-directed mental efforts.

24. Stael, (Anne Louisa Germaine Necker,) a baroness, was the daughter of the celebrated M. Necker, and born at Paris, 1766. She received a liberal education, and early displayed extraordinary talents. Her understanding was of a masculine character. Perhaps no female of ancient or modern times, has equalled her in native strength

of intellect, especially as manifested in an elegant and profound philosophy. In 1786, she married baron de Stael, a Swede, by whom she had four children, two of whom only survived her. She began her literary career, 1789, in Letters on the Writings and Character of Rousseau, and soon afterwards took an active part in the French Revolution. At Paris, she engaged in political intrigues, to which she had a great propensity. The consequence was, that she offended Buonaparte, who banished her from the capital. From this, she went to Germany, next to Italy, and twice visited England. She died in 1817. Her works are highly finished productions, among which may be particularly noticed, her Corinne, or Italy, a novel, and her book on The Influence of Literature upon Society. She seems to have been a votary of the new philosophy, so called.

25. Dwight (Timothy) was born at Northampton, Mass., on the 14th of May, 1752. He was a grandson, on the mother's side, of the illustrious Edwards. His great capacity was early displayed, and to his excellent mother he was peculiarly indebted, by her precepts and example, for the moral and intellectual qualities with which he was so richly gifted. At the age of seventeen he took the bachelor's degree at Yale College, and two years afterwards, he was elected a tutor of that institution. In the tutorship he continued six years, after which he was variously employed for several years, residing for the most part of the time in his native place. In 1783, he was settled in the Christian ministry, over the parish of Greenfield, in the town of Fairfield, Con. Here he continued twelve years, and acquired a high reputation as an eloquent preacher, and faithful pastor. His fame also, as a teacher of youth, (for he had previously been much engaged in that business,) was greatly extended, by the academy which he established and superintended in that place. During this period he published his Conquest of Canaan, and his Greenfield Hill; the one an epic, in eleven books, which was completed in his twenty-fourth year, the other a descriptive and didactic poem, in seven books.

In 1795, he was elected to the presidency of Yale College, which station he retained till his death, in 1817. Under his auspices, that institution flourished in a most remarkable degree; every department was improved; the standard of literary attainments was greatly raised; extensive religious reformations took place; and the number of students, by the time of his death, had increased nearly three-fold.

His death, which, under the visitation of a protracted and most severe disease, took place before he had reached the ordinary bounds of human life, gave a shock alike to the republic of letters and to the church of God. It was lamented as the fall of one of the greatest, best, and most useful men that have adorned the annals of this country.

Since his death, his theological lectures, under the title of Theology, have been published in five octavo volumes, and have passed through several large editions, both in the United States and Great Britain. No American work, it is believed, has ever been more popular in the latter country, than this. His Travels also, have been extensively circulated at home and abroad.

26. Buonaparte (Napoleon) was a native of Corsica, where he was born, in 1769. His education was chiefly military, though the wonderful powers of his mind, enabled him to appear with advantage on almost every subject which engages human attention. The times in which he entered on the stage of action, were big with events, and afforded him rare occasions for the display of his talents, and for the gratification of that inordinate ambition which was so natural to him. The revolution in France was beginning to bear down all the land marks of former ages, and Buonaparte embraced the opportunity of playing his part on that imposing theatre. By a masterly management, and by a series of successes, he rose in the military profession, till he was placed at the head of it, and till he eventually placed himself at the head, not only of France, but of almost all the nations of continental Europe. From the time he was appointed to the command of the army of Italy, in 1796, to near the termination of the campaign against Russia, he met with an almost uninterrupted series of brilliant successes and victories, dictating peace to one nation after another, till the idea of an universal empire seemed likely to be realized. From that period, though he gained two or three important victories, he met in general with sad reverses; but it was not until nearly the whole of Europe was allied against him, that he was crushed. Twice he abdicated the throne: in the former instance, retaining the sovereignty of the island of Elba, whither he retired for a time, only again to seize on his dominion: in the latter instance, after his defeat in the battle of Waterloo, fleeing to a British fleet with a view to protection. He was, however, exiled to St. Helena, and continued there, guarded by a body of British troops, till his death, which occurred on the 6th May, 1821; having been kept in confinement between five and six years.

Buonaparte has received, and will continue to receive the applauses or execrations of mankind, according as they view his mighty achievements, connected with the good which has incidently grown out of them, or with the evil which they directly produced, and which the author did not care to avert from the world.

GENERAL VIEWS:

OR A BRIEF ACCOUNT OF THE PECULIAR INSTITUTIONS OF THE MIDDLE AGES, AS THE FEUDAL SYSTEM, CHIVALRY, &c.; ALSO OF THE MANNERS AND CHARACTER OF THE GOTHIC NATIONS; LEARNING AND THE ARTS; DISCOVERIES AND INVENTIONS; INCIDENTS AND CURIOUS PARTICULARS; AND THE PRESENT STATE OF SEVERAL NATIONS IN RESPECT TO AGRICULTURE, ROADS, CONVEYANCES, INTERCOURSE, EDUCATION, MANUFACTURES, &c.; AND FINALLY, OF THE CHRISTIAN CHURCH.

The Feudal System.

SECT. 1. A peculiar system of policy prevailed among all the nations of Europe, at an early period. Singular as it seems, and different from the establishments of the present times, it was the general state of society, among the ancestors of modern Europe. This was the Feudal System.

The Feudal System, means that tenure on which the owners of land held their possessions, viz., an obligation to perform military service, whenever required by the chief to whom they owed allegiance. Such is its nature; its origin and history, its principle and its effects will be soon pointed out.

§ It was on the following plan, that the feudal policy was arranged:—every freeman or soldier, upon receiving an allotment of conquered lands, bound himself to appear in arms against the common enemy, whenever his leader should call upon him for this purpose. This military service was the condition upon which every one received, and the tenure by which he continued to hold his lands. It was not at first considered either a degradation or hardship. The same service which a vassal owed to his lord, was due from the lord to his king. The king required those among whom the conquered lands were distributed, to repair to his standard, with a number of followers, in proportion to the extent of their respective estates, and to assist him in his expeditions. This service was due to the king; but when obedience was refused, it could be enforced, not by civil regulations, but only by war Under such a system, the nobles or barons, enjoyed a subordinate sovereignty, in their own dominions; while their vassals or dependants, were in complete subjection to their will.

2. The origin of this institution lies in a remote antiquity Some writers have attributed it to the kings of the Franks, who, after the conquest of Gaul, are supposed to have divided their lands among their followers, on the condition of military service. But we must look for it to a remoter source. It is consonant with the usages of all warlike, barbarous nations, among whom we remark a strict subordination of the members of a tribe, to their chief or leader. This subordination affords the clue to the general policy, and so far as the history of it can be traced, it is a fact, that Julius Cæsar noticed it among the Gaulish nations, before the Christian era.

§ With the Gauls, this subordination was peculiarly strong, and subsisted not only between the soldiers and their commander, but between the inferior towns or villages, and the canton or province to which they belonged.

When in peace, every man cultivated his land, free of all taxation, and subject to no other burden, than that of military service, required by his chief. When the province was at war, each village, though taxed to furnish only a certain number of soldiers, was bound to send, on the day appointed for a general muster, all the males capable of bearing arms, from whom the rated number was selected by the chief of the province.

This relation between soldiers and their commander, subsisted among the Franks, as well as among the Gauls. It subsisted among the Romans also, who, to check the inroads of the barbarian nations, and to secure their distant conquests, were obliged to maintain fixed garrisons on their frontiers. To each officer in those garrisons, it was customary to assign a portion of land, as the pledge and pay of his service. These gifts were named benficia or fiefs.

§ When the Franks overran Gaul, a great part of the land was found in the hands of the Romans, held by this tenure, as the rest was found so held by the Gauls. The conquerors, accustomed to the same policy, would naturally adopt it, in the partition of their new conquests, each man being bound to service, on receiving his share of the land.

The fiefs were at first revocable by the sovereign, and reverted to him on the death of the vassal. But the possession of fiefs, under the imbecile Merovingian kings, at length obtained independency and security of property.

It was a consequence of a fief becoming hereditary, that it should be capable of being given out in portions, and that the vassal himself, holding his lands of the sovereign, by the tenure of military service, should be able to create a train of inferior vassals, by giving to them parts of his estate, to be held on the same condition, of following his standard in battle, rendering him homage as their lord, and paying, as a symbol of their subjection, a small annual present.

3. The principle of policy upon which this singular establishment was founded, was self-protection. The new settlers in a country, wished to secure themselves, not only against the attacks of the inhabitants whom they had expelled from their possessions, but especially against the inroads of fresh invaders. ' But unfortunately for the peace of society, it was attended with many evils, especially after the land had become unalienable property.

The effects, therefore, of the feudal system, demand some notice in this place. It was natural, in those disorderly times, when the authority of government, and the obligation of general laws, were extremely weak, that the superior or over-lord should acquire both a civil and criminal jurisdiction over his vassals. Such power, in their hands, must have been an engine of oppression. They moreover exercised the privilege of coining money, and carried on wars against their private enemies. So situated, they disdained to consider themselves as subjects; and the consequence was, that a kingdom was broken into as many separate principalities, as it contained powerful nobles; and the occasions of war thus became innumerable.

§ Every country in Europe was wasted, or kept in continual alarm, by the feuds of the barons, and in every country, vast multitudes of castles and places of strength, were erected for the security of despotic chieftains, against domestic invasions.

In the reign of Stephen of England, when the feudal system was at its height, not less than one thousand castles, with their dependencies, had been erected in the southern part of the Island. Private retaliation and revenge were the only law in the minds of proud and ferocious chieftains. The edicts of kings and magistrates were trampled on. A baron who was provoked by injury, met his adversary at the head of his vassals, in hostile array, and sought redress only by his sword. The most numerous and useful part of the community, the common people, were no better than slaves, and though not chained by the leg, as was the fact with slaves among the Romans, yet they were transferred from one lord to another, like cattle, and the implements of husbandry. They were styled serfs or villeins, a name implying their servitude and degradation.

In this state of things, neither the innocent could be protected, nor the guilty punished, by the regal authority. A general anarchy prevailed; the feelings of the people became familiarized to violence and blood, to despotism and injustice; intellectual and moral improvement was suspended, the arts and sciences were banished, the light of Christianity was obscured, and only the stern and rough virtues were nourished. Never was there a period in the annals of Europe so filled with atrocious actions, as that which intervened from the seventh to the eleventh century, the era of the prevalence of the feudal system.

At the commencement of the twelfth century, this unhappy state of things began to abate, and government, laws and manners, exerted a degree of influence on the minds of men. Chivalry produced a propitious effect, and a variety of other causes, operated to check the licentiousness of the barons, and to soften their ferocity. Perhaps no one cause was more efficacious, than the establishment of standing armies, in the fifteenth century. This engine, wielded by kings, crushed the power of the nobles, and reduced them to order and obedience.

The first monarch who adopted this measure, was Charles VII. of France, in the year 1445; but so opposed was it to the genius of feudalism, that it required the greatest boldness to carry it into execution. Charles, however, did not shrink from the attempt. He retained a large body of forces in his service, and appointed funds for their regular payment. The principal nobility soon repaired to his standard; and as the feudal militia were only occasionally called out, they were in time regarded with contempt by regular soldiers. This example was followed by the politic Henry VII., of England.

Chivalry.

SECT. 1. *Nature, Origin, and First Appearance.*— Chivalry, or knighthood, was an institution common to Europe, during the middle ages, having principally for its object, the correction of those evils that were peculiar to the state of society which then existed. The feudal system at that time prevailed, the disorders flowing from which, connected with the ignorance and barbarism of the people, rendered some such institution as chivalry, necessary, provided a better could not be found. Considered in this aspect, chivalry was co-existent with feudalism. It was designed as a corrective of feudal despotism, injustice, and licentiousness. It sought to support the weak, to protect the oppressed, to restrain the lawless, to refine the rude, to avenge wrongs, and, especially, to maintain the rights, and defend the purity of the female sex. In its elements, it combined bravery, honour, courtesy, love, and religion.

§ In the origin of the term chivalry, or knighthood, reference was had to the nature of its duties, which were performed on horseback. Hence, the languages which were formed on a Latin basis, derived their phrases descriptive of military duties on horseback, from caballus, a horse; cabillarius, a horseman; and cabillare, to ride—the letter b, being pronounced like v, in the south of Europe. In all languages of Teutonic origin, the same circumstance was expressed by words literally signifying service. The German knight, the Saxon cniht, are synonymous with the French cavalier, the Italian cavaliere, &c. The word, rider, also designated the same person.

Chivalry was, in many respects, a beautiful and beneficial form of manners, though in others, it was highly objectionable, as will appear in the sequel. We must not, however, confound the extravagant knight-errantry of the old romances, or even the natural chivalry common to most nations, with the gallant and Christian chivalry of Europe, which constituted a military barrier against oppression. That was, in some degree, a moral institution, which sought to make travelling safe, and the intercourse of society refined and liberal, though it would have been more moral, had it not itself employed violence.

Chivalry had its origin in that state of society in which the feudal system arose; and regarded particularly in a military light, we find it a part of the earliest condition of most of the European world. Its foundation, in fact, was the ancient character of Europe, and it grew into the form and consistency which it at length assumed, from the following practices common among the early Europeans, particularly the Germans, viz. from receiving their weapons in an assembly of the nations associating in clans, protecting and revering women, and performing acts of service when affection and duty commanded them.

The exact time when these elements were framed into that system of thought and action, which we call chivalry, it is impossible to tell. Knighthood was certainly a distinction of society before the days of Charlemagne. But it wanted religion. When it began to be marked by religious rites, it formed a regular institution. Its union with religion, took place somewhere between the ninth and eleventh centuries. Its character was raised and perfected by the crusades.

§ Religious rites were not used in the days of Charlemagne, for he girt the military sword on his son, Louis the Good, according to the rude principles of ancient Germanic chivalry; and a century afterwards, we read of the English Edward the Elder, clothing Athelstan, in a soldier's dress of scarlet, and fastening around him a girdle, ornamented with precious stones, in which a Saxon sword, in a sheath of gold, was inserted. In the century following, however, during the reign of Edward the Confessor, we meet with the story of Hereward, a very noble Anglo-Saxon youth, being knighted by the abbot of Peterborough. He made confession of his sins, and after he had received absolution, he earnestly prayed to be made a legitimate knight.

Knighthood was always, and essentially, a personal distinction, and in this respect, different from nobility. The nobility of Europe were the lords of particular districts of a country, and although originally they held their dignities only for life, yet their title soon became hereditary.

Every person of noble birth, was required, when twelve years old to take a solemn oath, before the bishop of his diocese, to defend the oppressed, &c. This was ordained at the Council of Clermont, in the eleventh century; thus giving a public and sacred sanction to the humanities of chivalry. But besides the nobility, others might be promoted into the order, by meritorious valour.

Almost the whole of Europe was affected with the chivalric spirit. It flourished most, however, in France, Spain, and Germany, and more early developed itself as a fixed principle of action, in these countries than in others. England, at length, was not undistinguished for its chivalry.

2. *Degrees of Chivalry.*—There were three degrees in the chivalry of Europe:—knights bannarets, knights, and esquires.

A soldier must have passed through the ranks of esquire, and knight, before he could be classed with the knights bannarets. That high dignity could be possessed only by a knight, who had served for a length of years in the wars, and with distinction, and who had a considerable retinue of men-at-arms, and other soldiers.

§ The privileges of a knight bannaret, were considerable. He did not fight under the standard of any baron; but he formed his soldiers under his own. The baron and bannaret, as soldiers, were of equal authority.

The second and most numerous class of chivalric heroes, consisted of knights. A general qualification for knighthood, was noble or gentle birth, which, in its widest signification, expressed a state of independence.

§ There was no fixed amount of estate necessary for knighthood. It was, however, a costly dignity, and many were obliged to forego it, on account of its expenses.

Though it was often bestowed as an ornament of custom on the nobility and gentry of a state, it never altogether lost its character of being a reward of merit. Men-at-arms, and other soldiers, were often exalted to the class of knights.

The last class of chivalry, the squirehood, was composed of a body of efficient soldiers, inferior in rank to the knight, and superior to the men-at-arms. Many of them, on various accounts, remained in this station, during all their military career.

§ It was a maxim in chivalry, that a man had better be a good esquire, than a bad knight. Military honours could be reached by the squirehood, as well as by the knighthood of a country.

3. *Education of a Knight.* The education of a knight in the family of a feudal lord, generally commenced at the age of seven or eight years. The place of education was sometimes a school appointed by the nobles of the country, but most frequently the nobleman's own castle, or that of some brother nobleman, served.

§ The duties of the boy, for the first seven years of his service, were chiefly personal. He learned the dignity and beauty of obedience, being made to feel it a privilege to attend the lord and his lady in the hall, and follow them in their exercises of war and pastime. The intellectual and moral education of the boy was given by the ladies of the court.

From the lips of the ladies, the gentle youth learned both his catechism and the art of love. He was directed to regard some one lady of the court as the type of the future mistress of his heart; she was the object of all his hopes and wishes; to her he was dutiful, faithful, and courteous.

The ingredients of religion, love, and war, were strangely combined in chivalry. Surrounded by noble females and valorous cavaliers, the first impressions of the future knight were on these subjects; and he was taught to regard chivalry and its honours, as the most noble object of ambition.

The military exercises of the youth were not many; and they were important only as they were the earliest ideas of his life. During the first seven years, he was called a valet damoiseau, or a page—in the old English ballads a child.

§ During this period, he was taught to leap over trenches, to launch or cast spears and darts, to sustain the shield, in his walk to imitate the measured tread of the soldier, and in mock battle to fight against stakes or his youthful companions.

At the age of fourteen, he received the title of armiger, or esquire; and though he was then authorized to carry arms, yet his personal domestic service continued for some time. His education was not completed, till the age of twenty-one.

§ The esquire prepared the refection in the morning; and at dinner, he, as well as the pages, attended at the table, and presented to the lord and his guests the water used for washing. The knight and the squire never sat before the same table, not even in the case of father and son—so strict was the principle of chivalric subordination. The squires often made the beds of their lords. Each one had his respective duties—one was the squire of the chamber, or the chamberlain, and another the carrying squire. But their many duties cannot here be described. Spenser, in the following stanza, beautifully paints the domestic squire discharging some of his duties.

> "There fairly them receives a gentle squire,
> Of mild demeanor and rare courtesy
> Right cleanly clad in comely sad attire;
> In word and deed that show'd great modesty,
> And knew his good to all of each degree,
> Hight reverence. He them with speeches meet
> Does faire entreat, no courting nicety,
> But simple, true, and eke unfained sweet,
> As might become a squire so great persons to greet."

In the life of a squire, the anxieties of love, and military exercises, were commingled. Chaucer delightfully paints the softer employment.

> "Singing he was or floyting all the day,
> He was as fresh as is the month of May,
> He could songs make, and well endite,
> Just and eke dance, and well pourtraie and write;
> So hotè he loved, that by nighterdale*
> He slept no more than doth the nightingale."

He practised every mode by which strength and activity could be given to the body. He learned to endure hunger and thirst, heat and cold, in their extremes, and to plunge all covered with dust into the running stream. He accustomed himself to wield the sword, to thrust the lance, to strike with the axe, and to wear armour. But no exercise was more important than that of horsemanship. Of the true knight, it could be said,

> "Wel could he sit on horse and fair ride."

4. *Inauguration of a Knight.* The full dignity of knighthood, was seldom conferred on a squire before the age of twenty-one. The ceremonies of inauguration were solemn. The preparation consisted in prayer, confession, and fasting—was accompanied by clothing him with a white dress, which was considered symbolical of the purity of his new character; and by throwing over him a red garment, which was to mark his resolution to shed his blood in the cause of heaven. These and other rites were a necessary preliminary.

* Night-time.

A church, or hall of a castle, was generally the place of inauguration. The candidate first offered his sword to the priest, who blessed it. Before it was returned to him, he took his oaths of chivalry.

§ He solemnly swore to defend the church, to attack the wicked, to respect the priesthood, to protect women and the poor, to preserve the country in tranquillity, and to shed his blood, even to the last drop, in behalf of his brethren.

The young warrior having kneeled with clasped hands before the supreme lord in the assembly, (a purely feudal ceremony,) and having declared that his only object is to maintain religion and chivalry, was now invested with all the exterior marks of the order. The knights and ladies of the court attended on him, and delivered to him the various pieces of his harness.

§ The armour varied at different periods and in different countries, but some matters were of permanent usage. The spurs were always put on first, and the sword was belted on last.

The concluding sign of being dubbed or adopted into the order of knighthood, was a slight blow given by the lord to the cavalier, and called the accolade, from the part of the body, the neck, whereon it was struck. The lord then proclaimed him a knight, in the name of God and the saints.

§ The ceremonies of inauguration, which have been concisely described, were gone through when knighthood was conferred on great and public occasions of festivity, but they often gave place to the power of rank, and the necessity of circumstances. Princes were exempted from the laborious offices of page and squire. Men who were distinguished soldiers were often adopted into chivalry on the eve of a battle, as it was considered that a sense of their new honours would inspire their highest gallantry.

5. *Equipment of a knight.* The horse of the cavalier was his peculiar pride, and skill in the management of the animal was a distinction deemed worthy of every effort. The knight bore about with him a variety of the instruments of death. His chief offensive weapon was the lance. His other offensive weapons were a sword, (a favourite weapon,) dagger, battle-axe, and maces. His defensive armour was also various. He had his shield, helmet with its visor and beaver, and body harness made of plates of steel, to which different names were given according to the different parts of the body which it covered. A long flowing robe, reaching down to the heels, constituted the dress of the knight.

Some of the defensive armour was so constructed, that it could be rolled up, and carried by the squire on horseback. It was too rigid, heavy, and cumbersome to be worn for a long time together, though the knights were often subjected to that inconvenience. When they were completely armed, no weapon could reach the body. It was not often that a knight could be killed, except by being unhorsed. In that event, a thin dagger, which was worn by each assailant, was employed. This could be thrust into the body between the plates.

It is only in romance, that we read of swords cutting through that solid front of iron, by which a knight was protected. The only way in which death could be inflicted, when he was mounted, was, by thrusting a lance through the small hole in the visor. Such a mode of death was not very common, for the cavalier always bent his face almost to the saddle-bow, when he charged. He might, however, be unhorsed, in the shock of meeting. In that case, he was at the mercy of the foe, who was in the better condition.

The horse of the knight was defended by mail, or plate, agreeably to the fashion of the age. His head, chest, and flanks, were either wholly or partially protected, and sometimes, on occasions of pomp, he was clad in complete steel.

6. *The Chivalric Character.*—In the character of a true knight, were combined many virtues and noble endowments. It necessarily included, also, some prominent defects. *Companionship in Arms,* was a sacred principle, and a knight would fly to the relief of his companion in arms, even were his services demanded by a female, at the time. His valour was connected with modesty, and both were, in the highest degree, conspicuous. In chivalric war, much humanity was displayed, though in contentions of a different kind, it was unhappily suppressed. As a knight fought for the church, he was intolerant, and towards infidels and heretics he ceased to exhibit his wonted forbearance. His sense of honour was keen, and his independence was consistent with discipline and submission. His whole course was dictated by a regard to religion. His devotions were frequent. Religion entered into all the observances of chivalry, but it was only the religion of the times—a form rather than spirit—too corrupt to be a safe guide. The knight, finally, was characterized by a very remarkable fidelity to obligations, by generosity, and by courtesy.

§ Companionship in arms, was the strongest tie in chivalry:

> "From this day forward ever mo,
> Neither fail, either for weal or wo,
> To help other at need.
> Brother, be now true to me,
> And I shall be as true to thee.

Such a thirst for renown in arms, for the display of valiancy, had a knight, that he would sometimes attempt the very height of heroism, and engage in the execution of impossibilities. It was this passion, which dictated many of his vows. Certain young knights of England, during the French wars of Edward III., each bound up one of his eyes with a silk ribbon, and swore before the ladies and the peacock, that he would not see with both eyes, until he had accomplished certain deeds of arms in France.

The valiancy of chivalry was finely chastened by humility:

"And of his port, as meek as is a maid.'

Every hero, as well as Chaucer's knight, demeaned himself in all things, as if God solely had controlled; and in the divine name, used his arms, without vaunting or praising himself; for praise was regarded as blame, in the mouth of him who commended his own actions.

The clemency of chivalry was often shown, especially in sparing inferior people. As a knight could gain no honour in slaying an unarmed peasantry, so he seldom attacked one of this class; and even an enemy of his own order, if prostrate and supplicating, was not often despatched.

Still, he was ruthless towards the infidel and heretic. He knew no other argument than the sword, to gainsay the infidel, and he was ready, at all times, to "thrust it into the belly of a heretic as far as it would go."

Of his moral virtues, perfect fidelity to a promise was very conspicuous; for his nobleness disdained any compromise with convenience or circumstances. However absurd the vow, still he was compelled to perform it, in all the strictness of the letter.

Knights were renowned for their courtesy; and this principle, like every other blessing of modern times, had its origin in the Christian religion. The world thought, that courtesy and chivalry accorded together, and that villanous and foul words, were contrary to an order which was founded on piety. A knight was always spoken of as gentle. The following anecdote curiously marks this quality of chivalric manners. The wife and sister of Du Gueselin, were once living in a castle, which was attacked by a force of Normans and Englishmen. The success was great and important; but public indignation was excited against the invaders, because they had transgressed the license of war, in being guilty of the uncourteous action of surprising and disturbing ladies while they were asleep.

7. *Every day life of the Knight.*—The military and moral qualities of knighthood, were fostered by all the circumstances of chivalric life, even those of a peaceful nature. Their common life was one of amusement and revelry, in which the images of their favourite pursuits were easily recalled to their minds. They passed most of their hours of peace, in the diversions of falconry and chess-playing, in listening to the minstrels, who sung the feats of chivalry, in read

ing romances, and in conversation, which turned almost wholly on love and war. Entertainments, also, at each other's castles, were frequent; in these, the utmost merriment prevailed.

§ The minstrel's lay, the poetry of the troubadour, the romance of the learned clerk—all spoke of arms and amours—of the duties and sports of chivalry. Every baronial knight had his gay troop of minstrels, that accompanied him to the field, and afterwards chanted in his hall the martial deeds which had renowned his family.

At their entertainments, the knights were wont to repose on couches, or sit on benches. The guests were placed two by two, and only one plate was allotted to each pair; for to eat on the same trencher or plate with any one, was considered the strongest mark of friendship or love. Peacocks and pheasants were the peculiar food of knights, on great and festival occasions.

8. *The Chivalric lady-love.* The females of chivalry, possessed a distinct and peculiar character. The lady, like the knight, was regularly trained up to become, at length, the mistress of his affections. She was commonly educated in the castle of some knight or baron, her father's friend. One of the first duties or accomplishments which she learned, was that of courtesy, and condescension to her inferiors. In those days, her mental education was not of a high polish. Some knowledge of medicine was deemed desirable, as chivalry required her to take care of her wounded knight. Her dress was required to be plain, except on festive occasions.

§ The only tasks on her intellect, were to repeat the prayers of the church, to sing a brief piece of poetry, or the longer romaunt. She could also play on the harp. Sometimes the graver sciences were introduced into female education. There were solitary instances, in which might be applied what was sung of Felice, the daughter of the earl of Warwick.

> "Busy they (her masters) were that maiden to leer,
> And they lered her of astronomy
> Of armsmetrick, and of geometry;
> Of sophistry she was also witty,
> Of rhetorick and of other clergy;
> Learned she was in musick,
> Of clergy was her none like."

In that singular system of manners which we call chivalric, love, next to religion, was the most influential principle. In many instances, it was doubtless the most influential. The true knight was a more perfect personification of love, than poets and romancers ever dreamed. The fair object of his passion, reigned in his heart, with absolute dominion.

Every gallant spirit of "gentle" Gower's days, the reign of Edward III., said of his mistress,

"What thing she bid me do, I do,
And where she bid me go, I go."

Chivalric love, had both its absurdities and impieties. Knights were not satisfied to fight in defence of the ladies, and to joust ir their honour, but from the extravagance of their love, each knight maintained at the point of his lance, that his mistress surpassed all other ladies in beauty.

Chivalric love, became a foe to the distictions of wealth and rank, and many a knight, whose whole fortune lay in his prowess, gained the hand of high born beauty.

In chivalry there was always a generous consideration for woman. Hence proceeded the honorable maxim, that it was not just or courteous to take ladies in war.

§ In the wars of the Guelphs and the Ghibellines, the emperor Conrad, as an offended sovereign, had refused all terms of capitulation to the garrison of Winnisberg; but as a courteous knight, he permitted the women to depart with such of their precious effects as they themselves could transport. The gates of the town were thrown open, and a long procession of matrons, each bearing a husband or a father, or brother, on her shoulders, passed in safety through the applauding camp.

9. *Tournaments and Jousts.* Tournaments and jousts, were both the offspring and the cherisher of chivalry. No amusement or exercise was so delighted in by gallant knights and beauteous ladies, by kings, the nobility, and the gentry, as these images of war. They were often splendid beyond description, especially at coronations, the marriage of princes, and important victories.

Tournaments were military exercises, performed by two parties of cavaliers, with hurtless weapons.

§ If the occasion was high and solemn, it was announced at the courts of different sovereigns, by heralds, sent by the king who proposed to hold the martial exercise; and all those who valued their knighthood, together with respected dames and maidens, were invited to repair to the appointed city, and prove their chivalry. Not knights alone, but kings and princes, pricked over the plain in gallant and graceful array; for though they were not expected to stoop to many knightly observances, they were eager to prove their chivalric character, by deeds of valour. For this they overlooked the pride of station

Not every knight might tourney. He must have been guilty of no unchivalric deportment. He must never have blasphemed God, or offended the ladies; must never have been false, ungrateful, or deserted a brother-in-arms in battle. The rules of tourneying, however, were sometimes evaded. Young knights, particularly, often concealed their names, and came in disguise.

The place of combat was, the lists, a large space, surrounded by ropes or railing, in single or double rows. Sometimes there was a wooden division in the lists or area, to prevent the horses of the adverse knights from careering against one another.

The ladies were the supreme judges of tournaments; but they generally deputed their power to a knight, who was called on this account, the Knight of Honour. They sometimes proposed the rewards, such as a diamond, ruby, &c. But the meed of renown was oftener military.

§ When the knights reached the lists, their arms were examined by the constable, in order that only hurtless ones might be used. But, notwithstanding this regulation, there existed a strong disposition, in many instances, to convert tournaments into real battles. Victory at a tournament was scarcely less glorious than victory in the field. The ladies, the minstrels, and the whole assembled multitude, acclaimed the conqueror. The practice of converting the elegant tournament into a deadly fray, occasioned an oath to be imposed on all knights. that they would frequent tournaments, solely, to learn military exercises.

The chivalric bands were so well poised, that one encounter seldom terminated the sport. The lances were broken, horses and knights overthrown, and the tide of victory flowed to either end of the lists. The air was rent with names of ladies. Each knight called upon his mistress to assist him, thinking that there was a magic in beauty, to sustain his strength and courage. Death sometimes, though not often, ensued. It was on the whole a hazardous and dissolute amusement. The revelry which followed, lasted often two or three days. The court of Rome was justly hostile to tournaments, and thundered its denial of christian sepulture to those who fell in a tilting ground; but still the practice went on.

Of jousts, there were two sorts; the joust to the utterance, and the joust of peace. The former expressed a single combat between two knights, who were generally of different nations. In strictness of speech, the judicial combat was a joust to the utterance; and so was every duel, whether lawful or unlawful; but with such jousts, chivalry has no direct concern, though the absurd and iniquitous practice of modern duelling, grew out of its principles.

§ The joust was not so favourite an amusement as the tournament, for baronial pomp was not necessary to its display; often was it held without a store of bright ladies distributing the prize.

The joust of peace often took place at the conclusion of a tournament. A knight who had acquired honour, would ride about the lists, and call on the surrounding cavaliers, by their valiancy, and for the love of the ladies, to encounter him in three strokes of the lance. The joust was more frequently held at a place expressly appointed for the occasion. The mode of combat was always specifically described.

Jousts possessed a more martial character than tournaments. Such usually was the dexterity of the combatants, that the encounter of the lance was seldom fatal.

§ Through the long period of the middle ages, tournaments and jousts were the elegant pastimes of Europe and Greece. Knighthood had its triumph over classical institutions, when the games of chivalry were played in the circus of Constantinople. In the West they survived chivalry itself, whose image they had reflected and brightened, for changes in the military art, did not immediately affect manners; and the world long clung with fondness to those splendid and graceful, though dissipating shows which had thrown light and elegance over the warriors and dames of yore.

10. *Orders of Knighthood.* Chivalry had its various orders, or associations of cavaliers, formed for specific purposes, generally of a benevolent character. Ten of them remain to the present time. Most of the present orders are otherwise than of a chivalric origin. The orders of chivalry were of two general descriptions, viz. religious and military. They extended over various countries, particularly the Holy Land, England, Spain, France, and Italy. Some of the religious orders were those of the Templars, St. James, Calatrava, Alcantara, the Lady of Mercy, and St. Michael. In the religious orders, the cavaliers were bound by the three great monastic vows, of chastity, poverty, and obedience.

The military orders, were imitations of the religious. Those of the Garter, the Golden Fleece, and St. Michael, in France, were clearly of chivalric origin. Many others that now exist, cannot boast of such a descent. All these institutions had particular rules by which they professed to be governed, but they varied with the spirit of the times. They need not here be recited.

§ Our limits will not permit us to describe the character and progress of chivalry in the several countries in which it flourished, or to detail the exploits of renowned individuals. It belongs to this work to sketch only the general features of the system, which has been done. It remains now to notice the merits and effects of chivalry.

11. *Merits and Effects of Chivalry.* Chivalry was, in many respects, a whimsical institution; but it well suited the period in which it rose and flourished, and seems to have

been needed in those ages. It was probably the best system that could have been adopted to aid the improvement of society, at a time when Christianity was so deeply corrupted. The principles of this religion, as it was then understood and practised, were incorporated in it; and much of the good which it included, was the fruit of the Gospel. Its theory, however, was in several respects indefensible, and its practice was rarely ever so good as its theory. Still we find much to admire in chivalry, considering the character of the nations among whom it prevailed.

§ "The patriarchal system of manners, shaped and sanctioned by Christianity, formed the fabric of chivalry; and romance, with its many coloured hues, gave it light and beauty. The early ages of Europe gaily moved in all the wildness and vigour of youth; imagination freshened and heightened every pleasure; the world was a vision, and life a dream. The common and palpable value of an object, was never looked at, but every thing was viewed in its connection with fancy and sentiment. Prudence and calculation were not suffered to check noble aspirations; duties were not cautiously regarded with a view to limit the performance of them; for every principle was not only practised with zeal, but the same fervid wish to do well, lent it new obligations. From these feelings proceeded all the graceful refinements, all the romance of chivalry."

This institution fostered civilization, and was therefore needed in a barbarous age. It refined the manners, and added harmony to social intercourse, where otherwise little but rudeness and misrule would have prevailed. It contributed to the safety and order of society, inasmuch as it thinned the ranks of robbers and ruffians. It infused kind and beneficent feelings into the bosom, and enjoined external propriety of conduct, and courtesy of behaviour. It cultivated a humanity which was not limited by kindred or country. As chivalry was spread over Europe, it formed mankind into one band, one order of men. The features of war were softened by its influence. It taught the warrior gentleness and clemency. A nice sense of honour and a scrupulous regard of truth were fostered by its maxims. It was a principle, as well as a feeling and a love in chivalry, to guard and cherish woman, and many of its amenities proceeded from her mild influence. In fine, it corrected the peculiar evils of the feudal system, haughtiness, tyranny, oppression, and misrule.

Notwithstanding these beneficial effects of chivalry, it must be acknowledged that other effects attended it, which may well qualify the language of praise. Still we are willing to believe, that it did more good than mischief, in a secular view. It has, however, been more condemned than lauded, and every one knows the exquisite ridicule which has been thrown upon it, or rather upon its extravagancies, by the inimitable author of Don Quixote. It resulted in some degree in looseness of morals, in respect even to the intercourse of the sexes; the purity of which it so highly professed to regard and defend. Instances of gross violence and injustice in the conduct of knights, too often appeared; and it nourished feelings of resentment and the love of war. While it stript war of many features of savageness by the civilities and courtesies with which it surrounded it, it at the same time nourished that proud and sensitive spirit, falsely called honour, which suffers no wound, without seeking redress in the private duel.

These, it is thought, are mostly exceptions to its general spirit and tendency; and as to individual persons, it is doubtless too true, that recreant knights may be found, on the same principle, that false professors may be found of the only true religion on earth, viz., the imperfection of human nature.

A witty old English author says, that "errant knights were arrant knaves." And another remarks, that "their horses groan under the burden, not of weapons, but of wine; not with lances, but cheeses; not with swords, but with bottles; not with spears, but with spits." This is spleen.

It is difficult to define the precise period of the duration of chivalry. It was a light which was kindled in a dark age, and it went out when that age was beginning to be brightened with superior luminaries. Viewing the subject in its great and leading bearings, chivalry may be said to be coeval with the middle ages of Europe, and all its power ceased when new systems of warfare were matured, when the revival of letters was complete and general, and the reformation of religion gave a new subject for the feelings and thoughts of men.

Romances.

A peculiarity of the middle ages, connected with chivalry and subservient to it, was the production of Romances. These were books which describe an extravagant kind of chivalry, and were then read with singular avidity, and indeed constituted the principal reading of the people. They were so called, from the language in which they were written; Romance, a mixture of the Gallic and Latin. They first appeared about the middle of the twelfth century, and their origin is to be traced to the Provençal Troubadours, a sort of story tellers and bards in Provence. In these productions, it has been observed, appeared the first dawnings of modern literature.

§ The more ancient romances did not record contemporary events, since fiction or exaggeration here would have been detected. Their subjects were an ideal chivalry. They depicted not only knights, setting forth to redress all manner of wrongs, but magicians, dragons and giants, invulnerable men, winged horses, enchanted armour, and enchanted castles; adventures which nobody could really believe, but the possibility of which, owing to the ignorance and superstition of the times, might have been admitted by the readers.

Among others of the early romances, the following were celebrated, viz:—the Seven Champions of Christendom, Sir Launcelot, Amadis de Gaul, Charlemagne and his Twelve Peers, King Arthur and the noble knights of the Round Table. From these sprung a progeny no less wild and extravagant, till in a subsequent era, at a considerable distance, a revolution occurred in this species of writing. Romances of a new order, appeared in the Astræa of Durfé, the Grand Cyrus, the Clelia and Cleopatra, of Mad. Scuderi, and others, which, though leaving out the dragons and necromancers, were still unnatural, and too marvellous for belief. Both classes of these productions, partook of a moral and virtuous turn, and highly extolled heroism, generosity, and piety. The familiar novel of modern ages, was the last form of the Romance.

These books, as an author has observed, "composed upon the striking subjects of gallantry, war, satire, and history, first awakened Europe from its ignorance and lethargy, amused the minds of men with grotesque and lively images and descriptions, and first taught them to think, reflect, and judge upon subjects of imagination." Much of the popular literature of Italy, consisted of romances; and the chief topics of them were the exploits, both in arms and amours, of Charlemagne and his Paladins. In England, so much was thought of romances, that Caxton, the father of English printing, could exhort, "Read the noble volumes of St. Graal, of Launcelot, of Perceforest, of Gawayn, of Tristem, of Galaod, of Perceval, and many more. Then shall you see manhood, courtesy, and gentilness."

Pilgrimages.

The pilgrimages so common to the people of Europe, before and at the time of the crusades, were journeys undertaken to some holy place, in order to adore the relics of some deceased saint. They were considered meritorious acts, a religious discipline of great importance. It was about the middle ages of the church, that pilgrimages began to be made, but their reputation was highest after the end of the eleventh century, when almost every one was inclined to visit places of devotion, not excepting kings and princes, and even bishops did not hesitate to absent themselves from their churches, on the same account. The places most visited, were Jerusalem, Rome, Tours, and Compostella.

§ Jerusalem, as the resort of pilgrims, was far the most famous and all the wars of the crusades were occasioned on account of that place. As to Compostella, we find that in 1428, abundances of licenses were granted by the crown of England, to captains of English ships, for carrying numbers of devout persons thither, to the shrine of St. James, provided, however, that those pilgrims should first bind themselves by an oath, not to take any thing prejudicial to England, nor to reveal any of its secrets, nor to carry out with them any more gold or silver, than what would be sufficient for their reasonable expenses.

In almost every country where popery has been established, pilgrimages have been common. In England, the shrine of St. Thomas-à-Becket, was the chief resort of the pious, and in Scotland, St. Andrew's, where, as tradition informs us, was deposited a leg of the holy apostle! In Ireland, pilgrimages have been continued, even down to modern times.

Manners and Character of the Gothic, or Scandinavian Nations.

The brevity of the plan of this work, will not admit a separate account of the manners and character of the various nations, whose history it narrates. The genius and national character of the Romans, during the long period in which they were masters of the world, have been exhibited to some extent in the political history of that people. The manners and character of the present nations of Europe, and of nations decended from them, in other parts of the globe, except the particulars included in the account of chivalry, the feudal system, &c. already given, must be learned from more extended works. But in regard to those barbarous nations of the north, who conquered the Roman empire, and from whom many of the present European communities are descended, it is proper that something should be said in these General Views. The manners and institutions of these tribes, are curious objects of inquiry, from their influence on the constitutions and national character of most of the modern kingdoms of Europe. The inhabitants of these kingdoms are a mixed race, compounded of the Goths and of the nations whom they subdued, and consequently the manners, laws, and institutions of the conquerors and the conquered, would naturally affect and modify those of one another.

The Gothic, or Scandinavian nations, were the Goths, properly so called, the Gepidæ, the Lombards, the Heruli, and the Vandals. Other barbarous tribes from the north of Asia or Europe, were the Huns, Alains, Bulgari, Suevi, Burgundians, Franks, Alemani, Normans, Saxons, &c. The parts which these various nations acted, in the political history of the world, have been described in the proper place. Their manners, character, &c. particularly those of the Scandinavian tribes, may be learned, in part, from the following brief account.

(1.) Some characteristics were common to them all. Whatever difference of manners and customs there may have been among the various tribes of Scandinavian origin, the prominent features of their character, appear to have been the same. They were formed by all their habits and education for a brave and conquering race. The corrupted Roman world could not but fall before a people, whose bodily frame was invigorated by the climate which they inhabited, and inured to danger and fatigue, whose habitual occupation was war, and whose religion taught them that the loss of life in battle, was a certain passport to the halls of Odin.

§ The Scandinavian and Scythian nations, probably had the same origin, inasmuch as they agreed in manners and institutions. The characteristics of the Scythians, as given by Herodotus, may be applied to the Scandinavians. Their life was spent in hunting, pasturage, and predatory war. They entertained a high respect for their women, despised learning, and for many ages had no other records than the songs of their bards.

The theology of the Scandinavians, was a proper index of their manners. One of their leading articles in religion, was to be intrepid in fight. As, moreover, they believed the world to be the work of some superior intelligences, so they held that it was regulated and fixed by an unalterable destiny. These notions had a wonderful effect on the national manners, and on the conduct of individuals. The Scandinavian had no other delight, than what war afforded; he entertained an absolute contempt of danger and of death: and the larger the number of his enemies slain in battle, the more highly was he esteemed by others, and himself. The solace of his departing spirit, was a recital of his acts of carnage.

His God was Odin, a God clothed with every terror, and delighting in war, revenge and slaughter. From him and Frea, the heavenly mother, sprung various lesser divinities; as Thor, who perpetually wars against Loke and his evil giants; and the virgins of the Valhalla, whose office it is to minister to the departed heroes. The joys of paradise are fighting, perpetual carnage, and drinking beer out of the skulls of their enemies. Of these joys, the cowardly are never suffered to partake.

There was a great similarity between the manners of the Scandinavians, and those of the ancient Germans. The latter, however, seem to have sprung from a different origin. The Germans as well as the Gauls, were branches of the Celtæ, a great original nation, who inhabited most of the countries of Europe, south of the Baltic, before they were invaded by the Scandinavian tribes. The religion of the Celtæ, differed in some respects from that of their northern neighbours, though it was founded on the same principles. It was the Druidical system. They usually performed their devotions in sacred groves, woods or forests. Of their sacrifices, horses were accounted the most acceptable, but their altars, like those of most barbarous nations, were sometimes sprinkled with human blood.

The warriors of Scandinavia, upon their settlement in the provinces of the Roman empire, soon lost much of their native ferocity and barbarism. Sometime previously to this change in their condition, they had nominally embraced christianity, and their morality had become respectable. The Gothic conquerors of Rome, generally spared the noble works of art, and Theodoric the Great, at the head of the Gothic monarchy in Italy, was an excellent sovereign, mild, indulgent, prudent, and enlightened. Under this monarch, and even under Alaric, Amalasonte, and Totila, the Romans were treated with an indulgence which they could scarcely have expected. Their government was monarchical; at first elective, afterwards hereditary, in the sense that the sovereign on his death bed appointed his successor.

(2.) A few things may be noticed as applicable to particular tribes. There were some diversities of character and institutions, that throw additional light on the genius and manners of modern civilized nations.

§ The Goths, properly so called, appear to have been famed, even in the earliest ages, for their hospitality and kindness to strangers. They encouraged the study of philosophy, above all other barbarous nations: and Horace has bestowed some warm encomiums on the virtue of their women. Poligamy, however, was universally countenanced among them; and their martial disposition, induced them to commit many unwarrantable depredations on the territories of their neighbours. Their principal weapons consisted of bearded lances, and missile hatchets. Their government was monarchical.

After the Goths, upon their conquest of the Roman empire, became divided into Ostrogoths and Visogoths, their policy somewhat varied. The former enforced, in their new dominions, the observance of the Roman laws. The latter adhered to a code compiled by their own sovereigns, and founded on their ancient manners and usages. From this code may be gathered much information respecting their national character and genius.

The following are a few particulars, imparting this information. "It is enacted by laws of the Visogoths, that no judge shall decide in any law suit, unless he finds in that book, a law applicable to the case. All causes that fall not under this description, are reserved for the decision of the sovereign. The penal laws are severe, but tempered with equity. No punishment can affect the heirs of the criminal. Death was the punishment of the murder of a freeman, and perpetual infamy of the murder of a slave. Pecuniary fines were enacted for various subordinate offences, according to their measures of criminality. An adulterer was delivered in bondage to the injured husband; and the free woman who had committed adultery with a married man, became the slave of his wife. No physi cian was allowed to visit a female patient, but in the presence of her nearest kindred. The *lex taliationis* was in great observance for such injuries as admitted of it."

The Heruli appear to have had some laws peculiar to themselves; for among them, when persons had attained to a certain age, they were placed on a pile of wood, put to death, and their bodies reduced to ashes. When a man died, his wife was obliged either to strangle herself on his tomb, or become an object of universal contempt; and human sacrifices were frequently offered to appease the gods of the country. The generality of the people were distinguished for courage, swiftness, and activity; but their manners were greatly corrupt, and every kind of impurity was practised without shame or control. Their government is said to have been monarchical; but it appears that their kings possessed a very small share of authority, and differed but little, in any respect, from their subjects.

The Huns, though not of Scandinavian origin, but from the vast deserts bordering on the north of China, were a hardy, warlike, and ferocious people, who at first subsisted entirely on roots or raw meat; lived constantly exposed to the air in the woods, or among the excavations of the mountains; were accustomed even to eat and sleep on horseback; and professed the utmost contempt for raiment, houses, and other conveniences of life. They were destitute equally of religious and civil institutions, and abandoned themselves without restraint to the gratification of their unruly passions. Hence we find them making frequent incursions into the Roman empire, in defiance of the most solemn oaths, and even occasionally turning their arms against their own countrymen for a pecuniary reward. Their distinctive character and institutions were lost, after they were subdued by Charlemagne, and dispersed among other nations.

Learning and the Arts.

Sect. 1. The interesting topics embraced in this article may be treated synchronically, or according to certain eras. Including literature, science, philosophy, and the fine arts, such as painting, sculpture, and architecture, they are too numerous and extensive to be treated particularly according to the different states or nations, in so compendious a work as the present. The mere sketch here to be presented, will include three eras. 1. From the close of the Augustan age to the destruction of the Western Roman empire, or the commencement of the dark ages. 2. From the commencement of the dark ages to the revival of learning in the 15th century. 3. From the revival of learning to the present time.

§ The Augustan age of literature may be considered as extending a few years into the period assigned as the commencement of modern history; for Livy, Ovid, and Phædrus lived and wrote till after the Christian era.

2. In the FIRST ERA, we have to notice the gradual and very perceptible decay of literature, and polite learning. Immediately succeeding the Augustan age, there were many persons of superior erudition and intellectual powers, but whatever pertains to taste and elegant literature, began visibly to decline. A pompous, affected, and false style of writing, soon prevailed in the room of the classic beauties of the age of Cicero, Virgil, Horace, and Tibullus. No works so finished as those of these masters, were produced after the Augustan age; and though there were writers whose endowments and genius were quite equal to those of the above named, yet their deficiency in taste, is too certainly indicated by luxuriance of ornament, and by continual efforts after brilliancy of thought and expression. In science and philosophy, the decline is not so perceptible at first, as it was towards the middle or conclusion of the era. Perhaps at first, if there was any difference, science and philosophy were more indebted to some of the writers succeeding the Augustan age, than to any who flourished during that age.

§ In poetry, Lucan, Juvenal, and even Martial, have a native power, but little, if at all inferior to that of Virgil, Horace, or Ovid, however they may fail as to purity of style compared with the latter. Yet in general, it must be allowed that the writers who figured in polite literature, during this era, were deficient both in art and genius, as is evident from the works of Statius, Silius Italicus, and Valerius Flaccus. Affected obscurity, bombast, and new-coined words, are too heavy a tax for the few occasional felicities of representation found in these authors.

In physical science, Pliny the Elder, was a great name; in moral philosophy, Seneca and Marcus Antoninus, shine with a superior lustre. These writers, with Plutarch the biographer, and Tacitus the historian, and a few others, were men of great power, though the faults of their style are to be regretted. The Natural History of Pliny, is a most valuable repository of the knowledge at that time possessed, in physics, œconomics, and the arts and sciences.

3. The princes who succeeded Augustus, were no enemies to literature, and some of them were not only patrons of learning, but were learned themselves. They were, however, despots, and despots of a different stamp from Augustus.

Generally, they favored a literature which harmonized with despotism; and genius being indulged at the risk of life, was cramped within narrow bounds. Eloquence was abandoned to pedants. Sophists at length occupied the chair of philosophy.

§ Towards the conclusion of this era, learning, taste, and genius, greatly declined. Very few of the later writers observed, or seemed to comprehend, the perfect models of the Augustan age. A small number of poets, as Ausonius, Prudentius, and Claudian, wrote elegant and harmonious verses, but they exhibited no commanding genius, and depicted no powerful passions. We look in vain in them for the happy invention and artificial conduct of an interesting fable, or a just and lively representation of the characters and situations of real life. Seldom do they contain any thing sublime or pathetic. A few philosophers, philologists, and historians, appeared between the age of Constantine and the destruction of the empire, but no names are peculiarly distinguished. We read of some great names as connected with the defence of Christianity, though the style of writing prevalent at that time, and especially among that class of authors, was very faulty. There were hardly any vestiges of the ancient classic taste, towards the close of the empire.

4. Seminaries of learning, at Rome and in Italy, were first endowed from the public treasury by Vespasian. The principal school next to that of Rome, was at Milan. In Greece, the schools of Athens continued to flourish for a considerable time, and when the seat of the Roman empire was transferred to Constantinople, that city included, for more than a thousand years, most of the literature and books that existed. Previously to that time, and during the decline of the empire, the destruction of books was extended and increased, in the midst of the turbulence and rapine of the civil contests for the imperial throne.

Until the destruction of Jerusalem by Titus, the Jews had schools in Judea, particularly at Bethhoron Jerunia, and Tiberias. In the schools of Egypt, the chief of which was Alexandria, were taught the Greek philosophy, mathematics, jurisprudence, medicine, magic, and astrology.

§ The despotism, disorders, civil commotions, and unparalleled sufferings of the Roman people in the latter stages of their political existence, together with the destruction of libraries and books, could not but prepare the way for the melancholy era which followed in regard to the debasement of the human intellect.

It may be remarked, that the arts declined with literature and science—the cultivation of them being neglected amidst the troubles of the times. The Romans, as they were never eminent in any of the arts dependant on design, employed Greek artists, for the most part. But little encouragement was given to architecture, or to the labours of the chisel and pencil, in the latter periods of the empire. All things were tending towards a state of ignorance and barbarism among the nations.

5. In the SECOND ERA, which begins and ends with the dark ages, as they have been commonly called, we have to remark an extraordinary depression of the human mind during a long period. The time that intervened between the fall of the Western empire of Rome, and the era of the revival of learning, was nearly one thousand years, during which, the world presented a sad scene of ignorance, barbarism, and misrule. There were, however, some intervals of light, as in the times of Al Raschid, when Arabian literature flourished, and of Henry II., when in England, Henry of Huntingdon, and some others, studied and wrote. At Constantinople, there was throughout the whole period, a degree of refinement and knowledge. The central portion of the era was the darkest, including the ninth, tenth and eleventh centuries. The classic authors ended with the former part of the era, as also the spoken Latin tongue.

The civilized nations bound up together in one mighty and unwieldy community, had been prepared by a variety of causes, for the catastrophe which awaited them. The northern invaders did not originate; at most, they only hastened this catastrophe. As much of ignorance and ferocity as they brought with them, they became, upon their settlement in the south of Europe, as reputable, at least, as the native citizens themselves. Considering their previous habits and temper, they did more than could have been expected, to preserve learning and the arts for a time, in the dominions which they conquered. Without the agency of the northern invaders, darkness and barbarism would have covered the world, so long as such abuses of human rights, and especially of the divine system of the Gospel, were suffered to exist. Still the conflict of arms, and the overturning of the empire, could not but have given a shock to learning and the arts.

§ "In the revolution of ten centuries," says Gibbon, "not a single discovery was made to exalt the dignity, or promote the happiness of mankind. Not a single idea has been added to the speculative systems of antiquity. Not a single composition of history, philosophy or literature, has been saved from oblivion by the intrinsic beauties of style or sentiment, of original fancy, or even of successful imitation." "Of the writings of antiquity," says the same author, "many that existed in the twelfth century are now lost: the literature of the Greeks had almost centered in the metropolis; and without computing the extent of our loss, we may drop a tear over the libraries that have perished in the triple fires of Constantinople."

The ignorance and infelicities of the dark ages, cannot perhaps be easily overrated. Those times, compared with our own, enjoying as we do the meridian light of knowledge and religion, must have been indeed undesirable. But there is a side to the picture, which is not altogether cheerless. There were some bright and joyous scenes; and the relish of life in certain portions of the community, must have been strong, if we may judge from the noble works of gothic architecture which were then erected—from the convivialities of baronial halls—from the gayeties of chivalry—and from the inspiring strains of the troubadours. The love of a sort of intellectual display, was indeed mingled with grosser propensities. But this is the most favourable aspect of the dark ages.

Christianity, properly understood, and exercising its due influence on the understanding and character, must be a warm friend of knowledge and literature; but the spurious christianity believed and acted upon in the dark ages, was hostile to some of the noblest productions of the human mind. The temples of the heathens, with the public libraries they contained, were the objects of vengeance and destruction. The classics were regarded as sinful books. In addition to these causes, the devastations of the northern conquerors, notwithstanding the commendable moderation which characterized them generally—and the plunder of Milan, which, next to Rome, was the chief repository for books in Italy—necessarily reduced the number of manuscripts, and so far injured the interests of learning.

After the commencement of the sixth century, scarcely any writers or men of genius worthy of notice appeared. The sciences suffered great decay. Taste was fast extinguishing. A sort of attention was paid to learning during these times, but with little or no effect. The common course of studies in all the schools was grammar, logic, rhetoric, music, arithmetic, geometry, and astronomy. The first three were called Trivium, or trifling studies: the last four Quadrivium or high studies. A vain and ideal philosophy had begun universally to infect the minds of men.

When we come to the more palpable darkness of the present era, we find that literature, science, and taste, were words but little known and used. Many of the clergy, whose profession should have secured to them a competent degree of knowledge, did not understand the breviary, which they were obliged daily to recite; some of them could scarcely read it. The human mind, in general, neglected, uncultivated, and depressed, sank in the most profound ignorance. Charlemagne, and after him Alfred the Great, by their superior genius, endeavoured to dispel this darkness, and to give their subjects a short glimpse of light. But the ignorance of their respective times was too powerful for their efforts and institutions. The darkness returned and prevailed throughout Europe more or less, till about the middle of the fifteenth century.

The scarcity of books in those times, and the nature of their subjects, as legends, lives of the saints, &c. evince the singular dearth of learning. What of learning was cultivated, was confined to a few ecclesiastics. The monks of those religious houses whose rules did not prohibit the reading of the classics, turned their attention to procuring and copying manuscripts. Most of these indeed were worthless; but truth obliges the historian to add, that some of the abbots, and even the monks, employed themselves in procuring or copying the choicest works of Greece and Rome. Cassiodorus, to use the words of Gibbon, "after passing thirty years in the honours of the world, was blessed with an equal term of repose in the devout and studious solitude of Squillace." To this place, the monastery of Monte Cassio, in Calabria, he carried his own extensive library, which he greatly enlarged by manuscripts bought in various parts of Italy. His fondness for literature spread among the monks; and he encouraged them to copy manuscripts. What he did there seems to have been imitated in the other monasteries of that part of Italy; for fifty religious houses there are mentioned, which afterwards principally supplied the libraries of Rome, Venice, Florence, and Milan, with books.

The only national exception to the profound ignorance of the middle portion of the dark ages, were the Arabians. That part of Europe which they held, viz. Spain, was much more enlightened than any of the other states. The caliph Al Raschid rendered Bagdad illustrious, by the successful cultivation of the arts and sciences. At the same time the Moors of Cordova emulated their brethren of the East in pursuing a similar course. The sciences to which the Arabians were devoted, were principally medicine, geometry, and astronomy. In the end of the 10th century, they introduced into Europe the use of figures instead of letters.

The arts, like literature and science, were low in this era of ignorance. This was the case even with the mechanic arts during much of the time. The fine arts, particularly sculpture and painting, were preserved from absolute extinction, only by the existing remains of ancient art. Charlemagne, in his time, seems to have been solicitous for the improvement of music, and the Italians are said to have instructed his French performers in the art of playing on the organ. The musical gamut was invented in the 11th century. Architecture was cultivated in a style termed the Gothic, which, notwithstanding its barbarous proportions, possesses a beauty peculiar to itself.

In the 12th century there was the dawn of literature in England under William of Malmsbury, Geoffrey of Monmouth, Henry of Huntingdon, Giraldus Cambrensis and others. It was, however, a transient dawn, and darkness again succeeded. The barbarism and subtleties of the schools triumphed over the better principles and the more correct taste which had begun to prevail. The great teachers and patterns of logic and scholastic divinity, were characterized by the high-sounding epithets of divine, angelical, irrefragable, &c. The most eminent among these teachers, otherwise called schoolmen, were Lanfranc, Abelard, Petrus Lombardus, Thomas Aquinas, and Duns Scotus. Their great business seems to have been to make innumerable nice and metaphysical distinctions, founded neither in nature nor good sense, and to draw conclusions which had no moral end whatever. Their speculations were founded on the philosophy of Aristotle, and the folly lasted long after the light had shone on other departments of human investigation.

6. In passing to the THIRD ERA, which commences with the revival of learning during the 15th century, we notice a favourable change, though not at first strongly marked. It is difficult to fix upon the exact point where the darkness ended, and the light began. The transition was too gradual to admit of nice discrimination. Occasionally, a distinguished individual appeared towards the conclusion of the era of darkness, and some nations were in advance of others as to the cultivation of learning. In the middle of the 13th century, Roger Bacon arose; and as Wickliffe at the distance of a century and a half from the Reformation has been called its "morning star," so may Bacon, preceding the revival of learning by nearly the same distance, be entitled to a similar distinction. He was the morning star of the restoration of letters in Europe. To his original genius and vast scholarship, the advancement of science in subsequent times is singularly indebted. His own age was too unenlightened to appreciate his merits or to profit by his discoveries. In the 14th century also, men of genius arose in Italy, who were devoted to classical learning and the cultivation of their native tongue. The works of Dante, Petrarch, and Boccacio have fixed the standard of the Italian language. In the same age also, flourished the English Chaucer and Gower, and the accomplished James I. of Scotland, all of whom, by their learning, genius, and taste, were fitted to give a character to the time in which they lived. Spain also at this period began to emerge from ignorance and barbarism. Although on some accounts we might be tempted to fix on the 14th century as the era of the revival of learning, we are on other accounts led rather to fix on the period commonly assigned, viz. the 15th century.

A few nations only felt at this time the spirit which has

been described, and that to a very small extent. It was, moreover, poetry only that then attained a degree of splendour. There was but little advancement in general literature and science. Miracles and fables were woven too much into the texture of history, though we find much curious information in the writings of Walsingham, Everard, Duysburg, and particularly Froissart. France and England, though they contained a few learned men, were in general extremely barbarous. Few books, and scarcely any classics, were found in either of these countries. During nearly a hundred years from the time of Petrarch, little advance was made; but a concurrence of circumstances, favourable to the development of the human intellect, took place, which eventually altered the whole aspect of affairs. Every subsequent age has felt the effects which in the middle of the 15th century proceeded from a taste for classical learning, from the dispersion of the Greeks on the fall of Constantinople, and especially from the noble invention of the art of printing. These were the principal causes which renovated the intellect of Europe. General literature and the fine arts first felt their influence; and after the dominion of Aristotle was broken by the great Sir Francis Bacon, in the beginning of the 17th century, discovery succeeded discovery, and the most astonishing efforts of genius were put forth in science and philosophy. Improvements in knowledge have been making ever since, till, at the present time, both Europe and America enjoy the clear and full light of an intellectual sun.

A volume would scarcely suffice for a satisfactory account of the particulars, by which the above might be profitably illustrated and expanded. The few notices that follow are all that the design of this work can admit, and can furnish only a very slight sketch of the revival of learning, of the intellectual advancement since made, and of the present state of literature, science, philosophy, and the fine arts.

Long before the fall of Constantinople, the love of classical literature had been gradually reviving;—that event increased it by compelling a great number of learned Greeks to seek a shelter in Italy. But it could not be gratified, till the manuscripts, which lay buried and neglected, were brought to light. The discovery of manuscripts, therefore, was a most important step in the restoration of learning. In some former centuries classical manuscripts had been looked up, and particularly by Pope Silvester II., in the tenth century. Petrarch and Boccacio, in the fourteenth century, were zealous and successful labourers in this field. But no man, during the first half of the fifteenth century, devoted himself with so much industry to the search of manuscripts, or made so good a use of them, as Poggio

His youth was spent in travelling, to attain what seemed to be the sole object of his life. To these names may be added those of the Medici family; also Emanuel Chrysoloras, who was one of the first that introduced a knowledge of the Greek language into Italy; and Theodore Gaza. At this important era there arose also a succession of enlightened and munificent popes, who gave every encouragement to learning and the sciences. Among these Leo X., soon after the beginning of the sixteenth century, was the most conspicuous. It was during his pontificate, that a perpetual indulgence was granted for rebuilding the church of a monastery, because it possessed a manuscript of Tacitus.

As a neglect of the standard works of Greece and Rome was one great cause of the decline of learning, and of the bad taste and barbarism of the middle ages; so a renewed attention to those works was one great cause of the restoration of learning, taste, and refinement. From an accurate knowledge of the masterpieces of antiquity, two great advantages resulted, viz. the scholar acquired the rich stores of ancient thought and eloquence, and he learned the art, by imitating such perfect models, of expressing his own ideas with perspicuity and elegance. In the exercise of the new studies, the Italians were the first, and the most numerous; and there soon shone among them an illustrious constellation, having Ariosto and Tasso foremost in the train. It was not long before these improvements were received in other countries, and spread their influence over France, England, Spain, and Hungary. In France, Amyot and Marot, the one in prose, the other in verse, wrote with a sweetness and simplicity unknown before; and the poetry of Malherbe glowed with all the fire of genius. The last writer is more commonly considered as the father of French poetry. In England, Henry VIII., and his minister, Wolsey, gave considerable countenance to letters, and the English writers and scholars who had the greatest influence in restoring elegant learning, were, Sir Thomas More, Linacre, Lily, and Hector Boece.

In the former part of the present era, criticism, poetry, and history, as well as classical studies, made a rapid progress in most of the kingdoms of Europe. Criticism and general learning were advanced by the researches of Scaliger, Erasmus, and others on the continent. Poetry attained to considerable distinction. Dramatic composition began to be regular towards the conclusion of the 16th century. Some finished epics were produced in Italy, particularly the Orlando Furioso of Ariosto, and the Jerusalem Delivered of Tasso. Lyric poetry was cultivated in Italy, France, and England, but not with so much success. In history, Machiavel particularly excelled, though, like Tacitus, he was fond of those ambiguous expressions, dry phrases, and abrupt turns, which, under the appearance of brevity, border on obscurity and bad taste. The French De Thou wrote accurate history in the purest latinity Science and philosophy, however, did not keep pace with literature. Aristotle, whose works were the great text-book of knowledge, and whose logic was the only weapon of truth in the middle ages, reigned over the schools till the 17th century. A few, nevertheless, arose in the 15th and 16th centuries to dispute his authority, among whom were Copernicus, Luther, Ramus, Bruno, Campanella, and others. But legislatures and inquisitions were against them. In regard to Ramus, it may be remarked that in an edict of the French parliament, he was gravely pronounced to be "insolent, impudent, and a liar, and he was solemnly prohibited from copying, or even reading his own works!"

Soon after the commencement of the present era, the fine arts passed suddenly from obscurity to splendour. Statuary and painting were at their lowest ebb in the middle ages. They had revived a little in the 13th and 14th centuries. A few painters in those ages imitated nature with some fidelity, but they were altogether destitute of grace or elegance. Bouchet, a Greek by birth, was the first architect, Nicolas the first sculptor, and Cimabue the first painter, that recovered the antique style from the ruins of Rome and Greece. But these attained only to mediocrity. Towards the end of the 15th century, however, in the great age of Leo. X., Raphael and M. Angelo carried the art of painting to perfection. The masterpieces of antiquity were their models. And Angelo and others at the same time carried also statuary and architecture to perfection. In painting, these artists were followed by names of great distinction, as those of Titian, Giorgione, Corregio, and others. Italy most excelled in the production of painters, but Germany, Flanders, and Switzerland, were not undistinguished. The most eminent of the schools were those of Rome, Florence, Lombardy, and Flanders. These several schools were characterized by peculiar attributes, which it is here unnecessary to describe.

In that which may be considered the middle portion of the present era, viz. the 17th century, the human mind put forth its mightiest efforts, and the most profound researches were made in science, philosophy, and literature. The foundation was then laid for the improvements that have since been realized, in every department of study and intellectual effort. That period was distinguished throughout for inventive genius, originality of thought, depth of investigation, and solid acquisitions. Philosophy had been trammelled by the schools till the beginning of the 17th century, when Bacon, Lord Verulam, disenthralled the human mind, and taught the sure method of advancing knowledge, by experiment and the observation of nature. He sketched the outline of one grand and comprehensive plan, that should include in it the endless varieties of our knowledge, and guide our inquiries in every branch. The progress of philosophy was not, however, rapid at first. Much of theorizing remained even in Gassendi and Des Cartes, the latter of whom, according to Le Grand, found out more truths than all the philosophers who went before him. But Newton at length arose, who, imbibing most deeply the spirit of the Baconian philosophy, completely dispelled the illusions which Bacon before him had detected and exposed. Before the light of his investigating intellect the dreams of more than 2000 years utterly vanished. Locke, the contemporary of Newton, applied the same mode of inquiry to the study of the mind, and overthrowing the sys tems of the old philosophers, met with nearly the same success as his compeer in physics.

On the continent, a century anterior to the time of Bacon, Copernicus published his system of the planets, (the true system,) which the Romish church, in the plenitude of its wisdom, condemned. Galileo, nearly a century before the time of Newton, constructed telescopes, and discovered the satellites of the larger planets. But the same church saw fit to imprison the illustrious astronomer. Kepler, about the same time, and contemporaneous with Bacon, discovered the laws of the planetary motions. But Kepler, as well as Tycho Brahe before, and Huygens after him, by not observing the method of science fell into error. Instead of following, Tycho Brahe anticipated nature, in taking it as a certain fact that the earth *must* be at *rest.* Kepler imagined that the planets *must* be *six* in number, because of certain properties of numbers. Huygens suffered himself to be imposed on in a similar way. The discoveries in astronomy in that age led to improvements in navigation, and a great advancement in geometry in all its branches. In Scotland, logarithms were invented by Napier, in 1614, by which calculation was abridged and the acquisition of science facilitated. Many instruments, besides the telescope already mentioned, connected with the advancement of knowledge, were invented in the middle portion of the present era. In Italy, Torricelli invented the barometer, by which the weight of the atmosphere is determined. The same instrument was invented also in France, by Pascal. Before this time (1610,) the thermometer was invented in Holland, as also the miscroscope in 1619. England claims the invention of the micrometer in 1640, and the air-pump was invented by Guericke, at Magdeburg, in 1654. In the 17th century also, several learned societies were instituted, as the Royal Society in England, and the Royal Academy of Sciences in France, which have greatly contributed to the advancement of learning and the useful arts. Indeed, the useful and mechanic arts were very much multiplied during the century spoken of. Hundreds of conveniences and luxuries, which were unknown to antiquity, sprung into use; though many others which distinguish modern times, owe their origin to an earlier period. A spirit of adventure and settlement in distant regions eminently prevailed, and the globe was circumnavigated by English, Dutch, and Spanish sailors. The sphere of knowledge by these means was immensely enlarged.

The progress of literature, in the middle portion of the present era, was no less remarkable than that of science and philosophy. Numerous were the productions of taste and genius, and many of them sustained the highest reputation. Minuteness of detail is precluded here; it can only be remarked in general, that Shakspeare, Milton, Dryden, and Addison, in England, and Corneille, Pascal, Moliere, Racine, and La Fontaine, during the Augustan age, in France, produced works which will be as lasting as the languages in which they are written.

In this part of the present era the fine arts continued to be cultivated with success. It cannot be expected that the old school of painting, with Raphael and Angelo at its head, will ever be surpassed in the essential perfections of the art. The second Roman school flourished at this time, which included the Caraccis—three brothers Guercino, Albano, Lanfranc, Domenichino, and Guido.

The last portion of the present era, comprising the eighteenth century, and the nineteenth thus far, is perhaps less distinguished than the portion of it just reviewed, for profound attainments and original works in science and literature. This seems to arise rather from the force of circumstances, than from any other cause. Many subjects of investigation had been forestalled, yet great improvements have been made in every department of knowledge, nor have discoveries been wanting; and where the genius of former ages has not exhausted research, research has been made. Within this period some sciences have been created, and others have been greatly advanced. By a course of observation agreeably to the Baconian philosophy, the great principles of chemistry, botany, electricity, galvanism, mineralogy, geology, statistics, in many respects geography, and perhaps one or two other sciences, have been fixed on a new and firm basis. Both the science and the practice of astronomy have been carried to a very high pitch, by the talents and ingenuity of many eminent persons in France, Britain, Germany, Italy, &c. Five planets have been added to those formerly known as belonging to our solar system. But it would be endless to specify particulars in respect to the advancement of knowledge.

In polite learning, the eighteenth and nineteenth centuries have been greatly distinguished. The Augustan age of English literature is said by some to have begun with the eighteenth century under Queen Anne, and to have continued, without any visible decline, till the accession of George III., a period rendered glorious by the names of Addison, Swift, Congreve, Rowe, Steele, Prior, Pope, Young, Watts, Thomson, and many others. But ever since the accession of George III., though the period has been more particularly fruitful in scientific and philosophic research, there has been an illustrious train of fine writers, with Johnson and Burke at their head; and though poetry declined in the latter part of the eighteenth century, a new school has arisen since the commencement of the present century, including several names, both in Great Britain and in the United States, destined to immortality. In our own country literature has made a rapid progress during the last twenty or thirty years, as is also the case with every branch of learning. In lexicography we can boast a standard work, (Webster's Dictionary,) which, it is believed, for extent of learning, and accuracy of thought, is superior to any other publication of the kind in the English language. In periodical literature, both countries, Great Britain for a long time, America more recently, have made the most laudable efforts; and indeed this is a form in which the mind of all intellectual nations now chooses to exhibit much of its wealth. It is needless to speak of continental Europe in respect to polite learning, since it is impossible to particularize. France and Germany have more especially excelled in works of taste and imagination, as well as in the departments of science and philosophy. Other nations on the continent, however, have a share in the glory of these noble pursuits.

During the eighteenth and nineteenth centuries the fine arts have been cultivated with much success. Architects, painters, and sculptors, have generally received a patronage worthy of their merits. Hogarth, Reynolds, Mengs, Cipriani, West, and David, in painting, and Canova, Flaxman, and Chantrey, in sculpture, are great names. American talent has been conspicuous in the former art. Within the period here spoken of, there have been numerous inventions and discoveries, many of which are exceedingly important. By means of them, the conveniences and comforts of life have been almost indefinitely extended and multiplied. On these objects the human intellect has been most vigorously and happily employed. The numerous inventions which are designed to aid the various branches of manufactures, and the application of steam to the same and to many other purposes, are the glory of the age. A very few of the more important discoveries and inventions are the following, viz.: inoculation, and much more recently vaccination, spinning machines, stereotype printing, lightning rods, life-boats, and life-preservers, the cotton-gin, engraving on steel plates, steam engines, steam-boats, and locomotive engines.

To concentrate and give effect to individual labors, societies, in more modern times, have been formed in all parts of the world; and on these now depends, in a great degree, the further improvement of mankind in knowledge. Thus in England there is the Royal Society which has been already mentioned, the Antiquarian Society, the Royal Academy, the Society of Arts, and the Board of Agriculture. In France there is what is now called the Imperial or Royal Institute; and at Berlin, Madrid, Vienna, and Petersburg, there exist royal societies like those of London. America also has its literary associations, and there are others in India, and even Turkey—all laboring for the promotion and propagation of knowledge.

The power of association for such a purpose, as well as for its great collateral object, viz. religion, was scarcely realized until comparatively of late years. It is a distinguishing feature of the age, and will doubtless be increasingly relied upon in future time. Multitudes of students and readers have been brought into being by these means, especially in connection with the periodical press. The extent to which newspapers have been published in the United States, and Great Britain, particularly the former, show how much may be calculated upon for the diffusion of knowledge, on that means alone. More probably than two millions of prints of that kind are put into circulation every week in these two countries. With every deduction on account of the light character of many of these vehicles of intelligence the amount of information which they diffuse cannot but be considerable. That information, it is to be noted, operates, particularly in the United States, on the great mass of the people. It cannot be denied, however, that these papers, in many instances, have produced a degree of political animosity, that endangers the stability of free institutions. It becomes important, therefore, that they should be controlled in their character, by the good sense of the community, as enlightened by early moral and religious instruction. The periodical press, as it might and ought to be conducted, would be of incalculable advantage, in respect both to the intelligence and morals of the community.

On the whole, as we have now the advantage of looking over the entire history of human genius, we arrive at the following result. "In several of the fine arts, in which chiefly the taste and imagination are concerned, such as poetry, rhetoric, statuary, and architecture, the ancients, according to the general opinion, have equalled, if not surpassed, any of the moderns. The ancients nobly distinguished themselves also in those more vigorous exercises of the understanding which are demanded by pure mathematics; in proof of which it is sufficient to quote the name of Euclid and of Archimedes. But it was reserved for the moderns to invent a calculus—a new and more profound arithmetic, which was called for by a more exact acquaintance with nature herself, and was to be applied to that more improved state of natural science which is peculiar to later times; we allude to the doctrine of *fluxions*, or to the *differential* method of Newton and Leibnitz, since cultivated and applied to physical astronomy with great success by the French, and especially by La Place. In most of those branches of knowledge, however, which rest on the basis of experiment and observation, the ancients almost entirely failed. The case is, that to form theories, or systems of science and philosophy, from a hasty view of facts and appearances, is an easy task, since this can be done without the labour of close and patient thinking: and if antiquity be in truth, as Bacon represents it, but the childhood and youth of the world, it is nothing more than we might expect, that, at that period of its existence, imagination should prevail over reason; and that the calmer and more successful exercises of the latter should not unfold themselves till a maturer age."

Discoveries and Inventions.

1. A passing notice only can be taken of the discoveries and inventions which have characterized modern ages, as a full and adequate account of them would require volumes. Many of them are altogether new and original; others are essential improvements of the works of antiquity. Those of a mechanical character, will claim principal attention in this place, since some that pertain to science and philosophy, are naturally included in the consideration of those subjects. Somewhat of a chronological order will be observed. The following are a few of the many inventions and discoveries that are presented in modern history.

2. *Corn Mills.* In remote antiquity, corn was rather pounded than ground; and the hand-mills of which we read in scripture, were probably not unlike the pestle and mortar still in use. Im-

provements were made in these machines. till, in process of time, shafts were added to them, and they were driven by cattle. The first mention of public water-mills which occurs in the Roman laws, dates in the year 398, A. C., when some enactments were made, which shew they were then considered as a new establishment. These mills were situated on the aqueducts which supplied Rome with water and as these were cut off when the city was besieged by the Goths, 536, Belisarius, who commanded the garrison, caused boats to be moored in the Tyber, on which he erected mills, which were driven by the current. Hence the origin of tide mills. Wind-mills, which for a long time were so constructed, that they could work only when the wind was in one quarter, are not spoken of till the time of the first crusade.

3. *Clocks and Watches.*—The art of constructing mechanical clocks was unknown to the ancients. It was not until late in the fifth century of the Roman era (293 B. C.) that the first sun-dial was introduced into Rome. At a later period, a machine was invented at Alexandria, termed a water-clock, which was simply a conical glass, with the scale marked on the sides; and which, being perforated at the base, denoted the hour, as the liquid, with which it was filled, subsided. To this may be traced the origin of the hour glass, still in use.

The inventor of clocks moved by machinery, is not certainly known. Several names of the ninth century have been mentioned, but there is reason to believe that the origin of the present invention is not older than the eleventh century. About that time, clocks moved by weights and wheels, certainly began to be used in the monasteries of Europe. The writers of the thirteenth century, speak of them as being well known; still they were for a long time confined to monasteries. It was not till towards the close of the fifteenth century, that they began to be used in private houses; and about the same time, mention is first made of watches. These were originally formed in the shape of an egg, or at least of an oval, and catgut supplied the place of a metal chain. The first watch is said to have been made in Germany. In England, watches appear not to have been in general use, until about the time of Queen Elizabeth.

The invention of pendulum clocks, is due to the ingenuity of the seventeenth century, and the honour of the discovery is disputed between Galileo and Huygens. The most ancient, now existing in England, is that of Hampton Court palace, the date of which is 1540.

4. *Linen used as clothing.*—Although linen was known in ancient times in the East, and was introduced into Rome in the second century, it was not used in Europe, in the form of a garment, till sometime in the third century. It was earlier adopted for the table than for the person. The emperor Alexander Severus, is said to have been the first European, who wore a linen shirt. But inasmuch as the web was usually interwoven with threads of gold, it was too rough to be much of a luxury. The manufacture of this article made but little progress in Europe, during the middle ages. It was confined both then, and for a long period afterwards. to private families,

among whom it was made for domestic use; and its scarcity as an article of apparel, has been considered as one chief cause of that cutaneous disorder, formerly called leprosy. About the middle of the twelfth century, linen was so little known, that woollen shirts were generally worn in Milan; and flannel, or rather linseywolsey, formed the usual underclothing of ladies. Linen was first imported into England from Flanders.

5. *Glass Windows.*—The venerable Bede tells us, that artificers, skilled in making glass for windows, were first brought into England from the continent, in 674, and were employed in glazing the church of the monastery at Wearmouth. But the art was not generally practiced, and the luxury of such windows was slowly adopted, for it was not until a century after the Norman conquest (1160, or 1170) that they began to be used in private houses, and even then, few could support such a style of magnificence. The manufacture of glass was not commenced in England, until the middle of the sixteenth century.

6. *Glass Mirrors.*—There is no positive evidence that glass mirrors were known before the year 1279. At that time, an English Franciscan monk speaks of them, in a work on optics, but also mentions that they were covered on the back with lead. It may be inferred that this invention cannot be much older, from the circumstance that glass mirrors were scarce in France, even in the fourteenth century. Various methods were adopted to perfect the art, before that which is now in use.

7. *Mariner's Compass.*—The date of the invention of the mariner's compass, is near the commencement of the fourteenth century. Gioia, of Amalfi, in Naples, a celebrated mathematician, from his knowledge of the magnetic powers, was the author or improver of this important contrivance. The polarity of the magnet had been known in Europe, as early as the thirteenth century, but the compass was not used in sailing, till the time of Gioia. It is said that the Chinese, as in several other inventions or discoveries, lay claim to a knowledge of the compass long before; but we may well be incredulous in regard to most of their pretensions of this sort, since they are so much in accordance with that vanity, which derives their national existence from ages long preceding the scriptural account of the creation. By this discovery, the dominion of the sea has been opened to man, and he is also put in full possession of the terrestrial globe, by being enabled to visit every part of it. The art of steering by this instrument, was gradually acquired. Sailors unaccustomed to quit sight of land, durst not launch out and commit themselves to unknown seas. The first appearance of a bolder spirit may be dated from the voyages of the Spaniards to the Canary Islands.

8. *Gunpowder.*—It is said that the Chinese claim acquaintance with gunpowder from the remotest era of their history; but however that may be, it is certain, that several centuries of the Christian era had passed away before it was known in Europe. Some have thought that the knowledge of it was obtained in Europe through

the Saracens, as early as the latter part of the seventh century; but it has more generally been supposed, that Friar Bacon was the first European who possessed the secret of the composition of gunpowder, and that he was the inventor. He certainly so far alludes to it as to say, that from saltpetre and other ingredients, a fire may be made that shall burn at any distance. Bacon died in 1294.

9. *Fire-arms.*—It is generally admitted that artillery was used by Edward III., at the battle of Crecy, 1346; and though Froissart does not mention the circumstance, we have the decisive testimony of Petrarch, that these guns were common before the year 1344. The invention of portable fire-arms would appear to have originated in Germany, from the old names by which the different kinds were distinguished. These names were either German, or immediately derived from that language. They were, however, too long and heavy at first to be conveniently fired from the hand alone. When used, they were placed on a prop, with a fork at the upper part, between which the piece was fixed, by means of a hoop projecting from the stock. They were first used at the siege of Parma, in 1521.

The first muskets were discharged by means of a match applied with the hand; but this was afterwards adjusted to a cock for greater security and precision in shooting. There were other improvements, but flint-locks do not seem to have entirely superseded the match-lock in the continental armies, until towards the close of the seventeenth century. The first gun-lock was invented in 1517. The term fire-lock, was given to the invention, which is still in use, and it was applied to the gun itself, in order to distinguish it from that which was fired by a match-lock.

10. *Paper made of cotton or linen rags.*—Letters were written, or ideas transmitted, on a variety of substances, previously to the time when the art of making paper from cotton or linen rags was discovered. Sometimes a hard and solid substance was used, as stone, metal, or wood. Of these, wood was the most generally used. in various forms and modes, which cannot be here described. The leaves of trees also were employed; hence the meaning of leaf, as applied to a book. This mode of writing was superseded by the use of the bark of trees, liber, hence the Latin name for a book. Linen cloth also was employed by the Egyptians and Romans. Leather, or skins prepared in the present manner, seems to have been often used by the Jews, on which to write portions of the Bible. Skins of animals rudely prepared, was another material, which originated with the Ionians. A more common material was parchment, which was a certain preparation of the skins of animals. Most of the ancient manuscripts now extant, are written on parchment. Papyrus was also celebrated as a substance for writing upon; hence the word paper is derived. This was a species of rush which the ancients procured exclusively on the banks of the Nile. The paper manufactured from the papyrus, was of an inferior quality, until the time of the conquest of Egypt by the Romans.

The time when the manufacture of this paper was lost or superseded, is not known. It is generally supposed that few, if any, manuscripts on papyrus are of a later date than the 8th or 9th century. About this period cotton paper was first made: according to some in Bucharia, according to others it had been known long before in China and Persia. There is no doubt, however, that the Arabs, having gained a knowledge of the process, established a manufactory in Ceuta, and afterwards in Spain, and thus introduced it into Europe about the 12th century. At first it was made of raw cotton; then of old worn out cotton cloth. The use of cotton paper became general only in the 13th century; and about the middle of the 14th it was almost entirely superseded by paper from linen, such as is at present made.

11. *The Art of Printing.*—No evidence exists that moveable wooden types were ever used, except in the capital letters of some early printed books. It has indeed been contended that Lewis Coster of Haarlem, invented and used them; that he therefore was the original inventor of the art of printing. But it is now proved that this opinion is without foundation; that wooden types were never used; and that the art of printing as at present practised, with moveable metal types, was discovered by John Guthenberg of Mayence, about the year 1438.

Three years before this, Guthenberg entered into a partnership with three citizens of Strasburg, binding himself to disclose a secret which would enrich them all. One of the partners dying, and some of the most important implements having been stolen from the work-shop, a lawsuit took place. In the course of this lawsuit, five witnesses, among whom was Guthenberg's confidential servant, proved that Guthenberg was the first who practised the art of printing with moveable types. The result was a dissolution of partnership. The whole proceedings on this trial are in existence, and have been published in the original German.

Misfortune and pecuniary loss attended his efforts for a time. In 1450 he entered into partnership at Mayence, with John Fust: this also was a failure. The art was so little perfected that in their early efforts, neither the printing was fair, nor the expense supportable. It is not certain whether during their partnership, they found out the art of casting characters in metal, which they had previously been obliged to cut with a knife; or whether this great improvement was made by Schœffer, who assisted them at this time. The general opinion is, that Schœffer is entitled to this honour. Guthenberg and Fust at length separated; and in consequence of a lawsuit, the former was obliged to give up his apparatus to Fust.

Guthenburg, however, was not discouraged, but established a new printing office, until 1465, when he obtained a situation, with a good salary, under the Elector Adolphus. In the mean time Fust, in conjunction with Schœffer, continued printing. Upon the taking of Mayence in 1457, the partners suffered much, and their workmen dispersing themselves, this most wonderful art was thus spread over Europe.

In regard to stereotype printing, Holland has a far more substantial claim to the merit of inventing that, than to the glory, through

Coster, of originating the art of typography. Besides a quarto Bible, published in 1711, there exists a Dutch Bible stereotpyed in folio at the commencement of the 18th century. These are satisfactory proofs that stereotype printing was employed in Holland long before it was even known in France. In a note to No. 1316 of Barbier's catalogue, it is also recorded, that Johann Mueller, pastor of the German church at Leyden, had devised in 1701, a novel method of printing, which much resembles the process of stereotyping as now practised. This method consisted in composing the page in the usual manner, correcting it accurately, securing the type with iron ties, turning it over on its face, and then cementing it into a solid mass by means of a metallic composition, or preferably, of mastic.

12. *Steam Engine.*—This grand machine, which has done so much for the human race, and is destined to do much more, was unknown to the ancients. Its powerful effects are the result of the scientific combinations by which the immense expansive force exerted by water, when converted into steam, is rendered available to the most important purposes.

The original projector of the Steam Engine is generally believed to have been the marquis of Worcester in 1655; but his apparatus was intended to raise water by the expansive force of steam only. His project was neglected in his own age, nor does the subject appear to have excited the attention of scientific persons, till the year 1698, when Captain Savary obtained a patent for a new invention for raising water, and occasioning motion to all sorts of mill-work, by the impellent force of fire. Other improvements were attempted on the steam engine by Amonton, Papin, Blakey, Newcomen, and others; but nothing essential was achieved except by the philosophical genius of Mr. Watt. Being accidentally employed to repair a model of the then imperfect steam engine, Mr. Watt observed that a great quantity of heat was lost by the unnecessary and improper mode of condensing the steam: he completely obviated the defect, and by the introduction of a condenser apart from the cylinder, and an alternate action of the steam against each side of the piston, he effected the most essential improvement in the above particular. Under his hands, however, the machine received other improvements, particularly in the mechanical arrangement throughout. Since the expiration of Watt's patent, a variety of other improvements have been made by several mechanical gentlemen, but details must be omitted.

Steam engines are now common all over the world. Their application to the purposes of navigation forms an era in their history. The Americans first made this application, as the genius of Fulton, a native of Pennsylvania, was successfully employed on this subject, as early as the commencement of the present century. He first made the experiment of propelling boats by steam at Paris in 1803; after which he returned to America, and exhibited a boat in successful operation, on the waters of New-York. Vessels propelled by his machinery are now in common use, throughout the United States and in Europe. They are known also in India, and their number is continually on the increase. In 1827, American steamboat tonnage alone amounted to 40,197 tons. It is now much greater.

Incidents and Curious Particulars.

1. Miscellaneous matter which cannot be conveniently arranged under any other head, is here designed to be presented. A few only of the vast mass of facts appropriate to this article, will be selected from the annals of different nations. From the present sample may be learned, among other things, the state of the useful arts, the modes of living, and the progress of society and improvement, at different periods.

2. The most extensive and splendid of the libraries at Rome was the Ulpian, founded by Trajan. It is believed that at the suggestion of Pliny the younger, this emperor commanded all the books that were found in the conquered cities to be placed in this library. Most of the principal cities throughout the empire, at this time, had public libraries. The desolation of the western empire destroyed or dispersed most of the books in them, so that in this part of the world, after this period, and during the dark ages, monasteries almost exclusively possessed libraries. In the eastern empire it was different: both Constantinople and Alexandria preserved theirs, till the Turks obtained possession of these cities.

3. From the origin of monasteries till the close of the 10th century, it is said there were no schools in Europe, except those belonging to monasteries, or episcopal churches. At the beginning of the 11th century, they were opened in most of the cities of Italy and France, by qualified persons among both the laity and clergy. But though their general introduction and establishment, must be assigned to this period, yet it is certain that Charlemagne founded several in his dominion. Afterwards, or in the middle ages, there were distinct schools for clerks, for laymen, and for girls. But the education of the highest ranks seldom went beyond reading, writing, and a little arithmetic.

4. We learn from Seneca three curious circumstances relating to the journeys of the Romans. 1. They were preceded by a troop of Numidian light horse, who announced by a cloud of dust, the approach of a great man. 2. Their baggage-mules transported not only their precious vases, but even the fragile vessels of crystal and murra, which last has been almost proved by the learned, to mean the porcelain of China and Japan. 3. The beautiful faces of the young slaves were covered by a medicate crust or ointment, which secured them against the effect of the sun and frost.

5. The use of braccæ, breeches or trowsers, was considered in Italy in the 3d century as a Gallic and barbarian fashion. The Romans, however, had made great advances towards it. To encircle the legs and thighs with fasciæ or bands, was understood in the time of Pompey and Horace to be a proof of ill health and effeminacy. In the time of Trajan the custom was confined to the rich

and luxurious. It was gradually adopted by the meanest of the people.

6. After the age of Tiberius, the decay of agriculture was felt in Italy, and it was a just subject of complaint that the life of the Roman people depended on the accidents of the winds and waves.

7. In regard to habitations, our English ancestors in early times had few luxuries or even conveniences. Down to the reign of Elizabeth, the greater part of the houses in considerable towns had no chimneys: the fire was kindled against the wall, and the smoke found its way out as well as it could, by the roof, the door, or the windows. The houses were mostly built of watling, plastered over with clay; the floors were of earth, strewed, in families of distinction, with rushes; and the beds were only straw pallets, with a log of wood for a pillow. In this respect, even the king fared no better than his subjects, for in Henry the Eighth's time, we find directions, "to examine every night the straw of the king's bed, that no daggers might be concealed therein." A writer in 1577, speaking of the progress of luxury, mentions three things especially, that were "marvellously altered for the worse in England;" the multitude of chimneys lately erected, the increase of lodgings, and the exchange of treene platters into pewter, and wooden spoons into silver and tin, and he complains bitterly that oak instead of willow was employed for the building of houses.

In the middle ages the fires in the houses were made in a cavity in the centre of the floor, over which there generally was an opening in the roof for the escape of the smoke; and when the fire was out, or the family retired to rest, the place in which it was made was closed by a cover. In those days a law was almost universally established on the continent, that fires should be extinguished, and the family be all at home, at a certain hour in the evening, which was notified by the ringing of a bell; that, in England, was called the corfeu, curfew.

8. In 1100, an inundation of the sea happened which overflowed the lands of Godwin, earl of Kent, called Godwin's Sands, to this day. Of these shoals the following account was given not many years since. "Upon our journey to Ramsgate," says Mr. Smeaton, civil engineer, "having visited the Godwin Sands, in order to examine their nature, we found that though, like quicksand, they were clean and unconnected, yet they lay so close that it was difficult to work a pointed iron bar into them more than to the depth of six or seven feet.

9. The spirit of the middle ages is shown in the following instances of wild magnificence or barbarity. On a certain occasion, when the nobility of Languedoc met in 1174, the countess of Urgel sent to the meeting a diadem, worth 2000*l*., to be placed on the head of a wretched buffoon. The count of Thoulouse sent a diadem also of twice that value, to a favourite knight, who distributed the same amount in money among the poorer knights. Other acts of mad prodigality were performed, particularly the sowing of a piece of plowed ground with small coin to the amount of 1500 English

guineas, by count Bertrand Rimbault. But the barbarous wasteful ness of lord Raymond was the most remarkable feat on the occasion. Having ordered thirty of his most beautiful and valuable horses to be tied to stakes, and surrounded with dry wood, he wantonly set it on fire, and suffered his favourites to perish in the flames.

10. Among the Romans the interest of money was not fixed by law. It is on this account that we find in the Roman satirists so many loud complaints of extortion, and of the severity with which pecuniary claims were enforced. Horace describes a rich old miser, who

> "Dooms the wretches, on the appointed day,
> His interest or principal to pay."

Many of the bankers acquired large fortunes, and arrived at the highest dignities of the state. Their establishments were of a private nature, and such banking houses are known to have existed in the chief cities of Italy in the 13th and 14th centuries; and about the some period the first public banks appear to have been established by some of the Italian states, for the purposes of contracting loans and managing the collection of the revenue. The most ancient general bank for the deposit of cash and the issue of its own paper in return, appears to have been formed in the city of Barcelona, in 1401.

11. The specious miracles of Arabian magic were introduced into Europe, by means of pilgrimages and the holy wars. Fairies and giants, flying dragons and enchanted palaces, were blended with the more simple fictions of the West; and the fate of Britain depended on the art or predictions of Merlin.

12. The magnificent castle of Windsor, was built by Edward III., in the fourteenth century, and his method of conducting the work, may serve as a specimen of the condition of the people in that age. No contracts were made with workmen as in the present times, but every county in England was assessed to send the king a certain number of masons, tilers, and carpenters, who were to perform their quota of labour.

13. In the year 1414, the citizens of London were ordered to hang out lanterns to light the streets, and one of its mayors, in 1417, renewing the order, "ordained lanthornes with lights to be hanged out on the winter evenings between hallontide and candlemasse." In this particular, London must have set the example to the other cities of Europe. During three centuries afterwards, the citizens were occasionally reminded of this regulation, under pains and penalties for its non-observance; but the frequency of the repetition only proves, how ill it was obeyed. In 1716, it was directed that each house should have a lamp hung out on every night between the 2d after full-moon until the 7th after new moon, from the hour of six in the evening until eleven. In 1736 and 1739, the present mode of lighting was partially adopted, but it was not till 1744, that an act of parliament was passed for completely lighting the cities of London and Westminster.

14. During the periods of feudal strife, when neighbouring chieftains often made sudden inroads on each other, every baronial castle was provided with its warders, i. e. men that were posted on the tops of towers to watch the approach of an enemy. In Wales, these persons were furnished with horns to sound an alarm; and those in the castles of the German princes, in the sixteenth century, blew a horn every morning and evening, on the relieving and setting of the guard.

15 Between the years, 1312 and 1315, Germany groaned under all the miseries of plague and famine, by which whole towns were depopulated, and provinces brought to desolation. The rich sought an asylum in other countries, while the poor, unpitied and unassisted, miserably perished. Hunger so preyed upon wolves and other ravenous beasts, that overcoming their fear of man, they rushed into the villages, and gorged themselves with human blood. Trees and houses were swept away by cataracts bursting from the mountains; and the earth was dreadfully convulsed by earthquakes.

16. It was not until towards the close of the sixteenth century, that potatoes made their appearance in Europe. They were first brought by Sir Walter Raleigh, from America to Ireland. From thence they passed by slow degrees over to Scotland, and the northern counties of England, and have since become general throughout Great Britain. The lapse, however, of two centuries has not sufficed to introduce so important a vegetable into common consumption, in the south of Europe.

17. In the year 1500, there happened so great a plague in England, that it obliged the king and court to remove to Calais, and carried off upwards of 30,000 people in London.

18. The progress of improvement has been slow in many respects. Many centuries of the christian era had passed away, before any thing better than splinters of wood, was used by our English ancestors for lighting their houses by night. It was not until towards the close of the thirteenth century, that tallow candles were employed for this purpose. It was not until this period that cups and saucers were used, and then they were considered as luxuries. A few centuries only have gone by since knives and forks were used in eating; since hats were worn in lieu of cloth hoods and knit caps; since the ladies were accommodated with pins instead of skewers; and since knit stockings were introduced in the room of cloth hose.

19. In 1546, a law was made in England for fixing the interest of money at 10 per cent. This was the first legal interest known in that country. Strange as it may seem to us, all acts of that nature were formerly considered as usurious.

20. Between the years 1660 and 1670, two awful calamities befel London—a plague which carried off 68,000 persons—and a fire, which, breaking out near London bridge, and continuing several days, destroyed eighty-nine churches and thirteen thousand two hundred dwelling houses

21. A few years before the landing of the puritans at Plymouth, a remarkable pestilence destroyed most of the Indians from Naraganset to Penobscot, which seems to have been a providential occurrence to facilitate the settlement of New-England.

22. The waste lands in the united kingdom of Great Britain and Ireland, amount even at this time to 15,301,994 acres.

23. In the year 1828, American shipping in foreign trade amounted to 824,781 tons, and foreign shipping employed in American trade was 149,435 tons—the whole being 974,216 tons. The enrolled coasting tonnage of the country is nearly or quite equal to that in foreign trade.

24. In the year 1829, the public libraries in Europe were computed to contain 19,847,100 volumes.

25. The expenses of Great Britain in war, since 1688 amount, as appears from a statement lately made, to £2,023,500,000, viz.—

	Years.	*Expense.*
The war of the Revolution,	9	£36,000,000
Spanish Succession,	11	62,500,000
Spanish war, 1739, and Austrian Succession,	1 9	54,000,000
The "Seven years war" with the French, Spanish, Austrians and Russians, of 1756,	7	112,000,000
The American war, of 1775,	8	136,000,000
French Revolution war,	9	464,000,000
The war against Bonaparte, the three last years of which with the United States,	12	1159,000,000

There were about sixty-five years of war, and seventy-five of peace, in a period of one hundred and forty years.

Present state of several Nations in respect to Agriculture, Roads, Conveyances, Intercourse, Education, Trade. Manufactures, &c.

1. The history of culture, in respect to many characteristics, were they to be traced from their origin, and described as they have existed in past ages, would be interesting and instructive. Some subjects of this kind have been thus traced and described. It may answer the purpose of so succinct an outline, to present others to the reader, as we now find them, with little reference to the past. The articles above enumerated, may therefore come under review, in respect chiefly to the present times. They are properly characteristics of the age, or the history of it, so far as such particulars are concerned.

2. *Agriculture.*—Agriculture, as the foundation of the means of living, and as connected with the state of society, and with the civil and intellectual character of a people, deserves a high degree of attention. Accordingly, it has been a commanding object of pursuit, with all civilized communities, from the beginning. But it is only to be remarked here, that in modern times it has received more consideration than formerly. The ancient Romans, perhaps, were as much devoted to it as any modern nation; and their agricultural wealth, as individuals, when, in some instances, several thousand yokes of oxen were the property of a single farmer, exceeds probably any thing known at present. But with the exception of the Romans, if they were on the whole an exception, modern nations manifestly excel antiquity. Especially do they excel the middle ages, for then this great interest suffered, with every thing else, a lamentable decay. In very recent times, peculiar attention has been bestowed on the subject, both in Europe and America, by means of numerous agricultural societies. Indeed, science has been of late most successfully applied to the purposes of advancing the agricultural art. The business in the hands of scientific practical farmers, has assumed a systematic arrangement, unknown in former days.

3. *Roads.*—In Europe, as the Roman empire declined, the roads gradually fell into neglect; and during the dark ages, their ruinous condition, rendered communication difficult, beyond what we can now find it easy to conceive. It is not readily ascertained what the state of the roads was, but they must have improved as trade increased. We know that the amelioration of them was slow; that the arts of constructing and directing them, were for a long time understood very imperfectly; and that the first kingdom in which the condition of the great roads, at all approached the present standard of excellence, was Sweden, where from its want of wealth, and its remote situation, no such occurrence could reasonably have been looked for.

In England, the change in regard to the arrival and departure of the mails, which took place in 1793, greatly forwarded that improvement of the principal roads, which had been going on through the eighteenth century; and from 1793 to the present moment, the highways, cross-roads, bridges, and ferries, throughout the whole extent of that country, are decidedly superior to those which are to be seen any where else.

A remarkable improvement, however, has recently taken place in roads and bridges, all over Europe. Materials for road making have been found where formerly they were not believed to exist, and the skill with which they are employed is surprising. Neither clay, sand, morasses, torrents, precipices, nor any other obstacles, are deemed insurmountable. A terrace has been conducted along the whole face of the Appennines, from Nice, to the gulf of Spezzia. The finest carriage roads cross the Alps, over mount Cenis, St. Bernard, the Simplon, St. Gothard, the Splugen, from the lake of Como to the source of the Inn from Trent to Brixen, and where the road from Vienna to Venice crosses them at Ponteba. An entirely new road has been formed in the kingdom of Netherlands, from Namur to Luxembourg; another runs along the banks of the Rhine from Mentz to Nimeguen; another from Hamburg to Hanover, and from Hanover to Deventer. Others have been formed, and particularly the whole way between Berlin and Petersburgh, probably presents by this time an admirable line of communication between these two capitals. Other roads are said to be under consideration, and particularly one from Berlin to Hamburg, through sands which appear almost impassable. Indeed, the traveller in Europe, since the cessation of wars, every where witnesses the utmost zeal in building bridges, in opening, widening, levelling, and repairing roads.

Nor has less been done, or is less doing in the United States. Probably no people in the same time, ever made so many improvements in roads and bridges. Where two hundred years ago, all was a wide wilderness, traversed only by the foot-paths of the Indians, there are now thousands of good roads. The extent only of post-roads in this country, now considerably exceeds 100,000 miles. In some parts of Europe and of the United States, rail-roads have been made, or are in progress, which promise the greatest advantages to commerce and inland transportation. The recent construction of carriages moved by steam, which are designed to pass over roads of this description, will form an era in the history of travelling. Moving with the velocity of thirty miles or more by the hour, these vehicles will seem to annihilate space.

4. *Water Conveyance.*—The progress lately made in water conveyance, is also very remarkable. The first canals known in Europe, were those which were formed in Italy and the Low Countries, and served in several cases both to drain the ground, and for the conveyance of merchandize. France followed their example, and by means of the canal of Languedoc, joined the channel and the Mediterranean. Several others have since been completed, and others are begun; but that country is never likely to place much dependence on its canal communications. About the middle of the last century, the commercial prosperity of Great Britain, induced it to turn its attention to canals, and from its abundance of water, and the moderate elevation of its surface, it has now pushed canal navigation, beyond every other country. The total length of canals in Great Britain at the present time, is 2,600 miles. Austria, Prussia, and Sweden, now possess canals; and Russia, both within her old limits and in Poland, is zealously encouraging canals, to connect her rivers, and transport the produce of her soil. Next to Great Britain, the United States have displayed the most enterprise in the business of canals. In the several states, twenty-two canals are finished, in progress, or in immediate contemplation, whose aggregate length is about 2,500 miles. The greater part of them are either finished or in progress. Two of them, viz. the Hudson and Erie, and the Chesapeake and Ohio canals, are each 360 miles, the Ohio state canal is 306, and the Pennsylvania canal is 296 miles. The Hudson and Erie canal, which is in operation, is the boast of the new world.

The application of steam to shipping, which deserves to be ranked among the greatest discoveries, theoretical or practical, that were ever made, has done more within the last twenty years, to facilitate the communication between different places, by water, than all the contrivances that went before it. Steam vessels are now found permanently or occasionally plying from the bottom of the Mediterranean, all round to the top of the Baltic. No place in the eastern part of the world has derived so great advantage from the discovery of steam vessels, as England. Its situation, coal, and commerce, enables it to shoot forth these vessels in every direction, and by means of the certainty and celerity of their passage, they have diminished its distance, and multiplied its means of access to every part of the European continent. In the United States, where the application of steam to the purposes of navigation was first made, these vessels are most extensively employed. They abound, with all their facility of conveyance, on our coasts, and in our rivers; hundreds of them are owned on the Mississippi alone. The combination of the above discoveries and improved arrangements, has produced an ease, certainty, and rapidity of intercourse, exceeding all past experience or imagination.

5. *Travelling.* The increase of the number of travellers which these facilities have caused, is a characteristic of the times worth noticing. Travelling for improvement or gratification, has increased fifty or an hundred fold, and it is continually augmenting. In peace, Europe is now one great family, and certainly many advantages attend this state of things. Such a degree of travelling and intercourse tends very much to bind nations together, and to promote liberal views, and a charitable feeling, one towards another. Some good things, however, are sacrificed to it. Simplicity of heart, and the earnestness of kindness in domestic life, are diminishing. The love of home, the warm gush of affection, is checked. The bonds of society now set loosely on a man. Attachment to country ceases to operate as it once did.

6. *Increase of Education.* Another characteristic of the present times, is the extraordinary increase of education. A much larger portion of the people of civilized countries read than formerly. Protestants have always been more devoted to reading than the Catholics. Except in Spain and Portugal, reading has increased every where. Both the means and the habits of reading are increased. The multiplication of newspapers and periodical publications—the number of booksellers' shops—the profusion of literary institutions and circulating libraries, are infallible indications of the extraordinary spread of education and reading. There is evidently, therefore, the more need of moral discipline. The Bible should by all means be made a study, and its heavenly truths should be more than ever enforced upon the heart. The cheapness of books, the number of teachers, the spare time created by the extension of machinery, and the fashion for reading, have operated very considerably on the common people in Europe. In the United States, the same causes have operated on the same portion of the community, though here

the common people have always been distinguished, above those of other nations, for a love of reading and a competent education.

Among the higher orders of European society, there are so many books, and so much to learn, that few are profound. The stream of knowledge flows wider, but has not become deeper. To master all the branches of science and knowledge, is impossible. Daily and periodical publications abound, but perhaps too much so for a sound and permanent literature. They include the principal stock of reading, except novels, books of travels, and memoirs. The mind of the public cannot be more effectually abused and unsettled, than by the systematic conversion of history, private life, religion and morality, into themes for works of fiction; and the full extent of the mischief will be seen only when it is too late. A similar change to that which has taken place among readers, has affected authors. Most of this class are so impatient to reap the rewards of their labours, or so apprehensive of being supplanted by competitors for the public favour, that few are willing to bestow the time and trouble which are necessary for the composition of a standard work.

7. *Improvement in external condition.*—In the present state of most civilized nations, a surprising improvement has taken place in the outward condition of all ranks of society. Many shocking and painful disorders have almost wholly disappeared, and others, which flesh must still be heir to, have by superior treatment, been rendered less violent and dangerous. The small pox, the ravages of which were once so terrible, has now ceased to alarm the community. The discovery of vaccination, in 1798, by Dr. Jenner, was the instrumental cause of so propitious a change. This is one of the diseases referred to; others might be named. The plague, except in Turkey, and some other countries bordering on the Mediterranean, is almost unknown. Famines, arising either from cold or heat, are now of much less frequent occurrence than they formerly were, and the cruelties and calamities of war, have been mitigated. While these scourges of mankind have been removed or diminished, the length of human life has been extended, as a consequence. A greater proportion live to old age than was the fact a century ago. Other causes, however, may have operated here, as greater temperance, better food and clothing, less exposure, &c. Connected with the above, inventions of every sort, conducing to personal enjoyment, have been multiplied or brought to perfection. In houses, furniture, horses, conveyances, and every thing which can minister to the ease and gratification of mind or body; in the number and refinement of the sources of amusement, and in all articles of domestic luxury and convenience, the progress that has lately been made, is unprecedented either for extent or rapidity. There is not a district to be found in any European state, in which the traveller is not struck with the taste and magnificence displayed in the architecture of public and private buildings, the multiplication and commodiousness of bathing and watering places, hotels, coffee houses, and reading rooms, the exquisite arrangement of gardens, grounds and villas, and the neatness of cottages, shops and manufactories.

This alteration is very conspicuous in England. The comforts of life appear in great profusion; no native or foreigner can travel fifty or sixty miles, along a public road, without being lost in wonder and astonishment. Towns, villages, hamlets, mansions, farm houses, and cottages, are every where scattered about in the most pleasing and romantic situations. It were to be desired that the reality in every respect, corresponded with the appearances, but it is not to be concealed that the present stagnation in business, has thrown many o the English operatives into distress. In the United States, however these improvements not only abound, but the favourable appearances are generally connected with a more delightful reality.

8. *Increase of population.*—In consequence of the improvement in the physical circumstances of the people in christian countries, the population has increased in an unexampled manner. Some places, owing to political revolutions, or change of trade, may have decreased in population, as Rome, Venice, Bologna, Genoa, Verona, Seville, Barcelona, Cadiz, Lubec, Bremen, Ghent, Bruges, Cologne, Strasburg, Nuremburg, and Augsburg. These, however, are exceptions to the general rule. Petersburg, Berlin, Vienna, Brussels, Paris, Hamburgh, Frankfort, Milan, Munich, Stuttgard, Stockholm, and the territories to which they belong, are swelling in extent and population. England has outstripped the continent within these last thirty or forty years. London, Glasgow, Liverpool, Manchester, Birmingham, and many other cities and towns in Great Britain, have experienced a great increase. According to statistics, which have lately appeared,* it is found that the inhabitants of Europe have, within the period that has elapsed since the general peace, in 1815, been augmented by the number of 28 or 29,000,000. Every country has had a share in this increase. Europe, however, can hardly be compared with the United States, in this particular. Within the time above mentioned, the population of this country has increased to the amount of at least one third of the whole number. History probably does not furnish another instance of the rapid rise of cities, equal to that of New-York, Philadelphia, Baltimore, New-Orleans, and several others.

9. *The approximation of the lower classes to the higher.*—This is a characteristic of the age more particularly observable in the old world. In America, owing to its institutions, and the abundance of the means of living, the difference in the classes of the people has never been so wide as it is in Europe. The approximation spoken of is very perceptible in European society. It is obvious in dress, manners, and acquirements. It is encouraged by the improvement which has taken place in manufactures, and by the substitution of machinery for manual labour. Dress is scarcely a test of rank. In language and address, the middling classes have advanced. There are few above the lowest rank, if possessed of good sense, who do not speak and act, in these days, with ease and propriety. Much taste and elegance, are in many instances displayed. In mental ac-

* The American Almanac for 1830, a most valuable production.

quirements, particularly, the assimilation is visible. Children of the nobility, from the greater pains taken with them, excel at first, but are outstripped afterwards, by those who feel the necessity of excelling. The procession in society, has extended to attainments of every kind, especially in matters of legislation.. The numerous papers and documents which are published, and which are accessible to most readers, have contributed to this result. In regard to Great Britain, an American gentleman long resident in that country, at this moment writes, "A spirit is silently at work, which is gradually undermining the power of the Aristocracy, and will one day (and that not far distant) show itself in a form too powerful to be resisted."

10. *Trades and Manufactures.*—The spring of late years given to trade and manufactures, is quite characteristic of the times. Our remarks have reference more especially to the continental portion of Europe, where, since the general peace, the products of manufacturing industry have been wonderfully multiplied.

Sugar refineries have within a recent period been established to a great extent, at Trieste, Petersburg, Hamburg, and Gothenburg. At Motala, near Orebro, in Sweden, there is perhaps the largest establishment in existence for all sorts of implements in steel and iron. The manufacture of muskets and fowling-pieces has lately been greatly improved in Germany, and particularly at Herschfeld, in Hanover. Admirable travelling carriages of all sorts, both in point of elegance and durability, are built at Brussels, Berlin, and Vienna. The glass manufactories in France, at St. Quentin, St. Gabin, Comenty, and Premontre, in the department of Aisne, are all in the most flourishing condition, and glass is made at Munich, of a most superior quality, so that the Bavarians have deprived even the British of the manufacture of telescopes. The elegant iron and steel ornaments, made at Berlin, have now become a valuable and extending branch of commerce. The utmost attention is paid to the improvement of wool throughout France, Austria, Saxony, Holstein, and some other parts of Denmark. The woollen manufactures established in Moravia, Saxony, and Silesia, and in the Low Countries, are increasing, and in addition to those which have been long seated at Sedan, Elboeuf, and Louviers, in France, they have now been introduced at Carcassone, Castres, and Lodeve, in the south, and at Bourges, and Chatevuroux, in the centre. A determined and successful degree of anxiety to improve the breed of horses, has manifested itself in Prussia, Russia, and France. England no longer supplies nearly the whole of Europe with lead; a great quantity is now raised near Almeria, in Spain. The manufactories of iron, and steel, which are flourishing in France, are prospering still more at Liege, which has become the Birmingham of the Low Countries, as Ghent is their Manchester and Glasgow. The cotton manufactures of France and Belgium, have increased tenfold in ten years. They are now firmly fixed at Elberfeld, near Dusseldorf, and rapidly extending themselves in the Prussian Rhenish provinces. The silk trade of France, which used to be confined to Lyons, has now spread its ramifications to Avignon, Nismes, and Tours, and its annual value amounts to £6,000,000. The silk trade is carried on in Switzerland, a fact which is little known abroad. There is in Zurich and its neighbourhood alone between 12 and 13,000 looms. It is also established at Arau, Basle, and several other places. In the Prussian Rhenish provinces, it is spreading from Mentz through all the towns and villages along the Rhine, and is carried on to a great extent at Dusseldorf and Elberfelt, but particularly at Creveld, where it is conducted with great capital and great spirit. All sorts of household furniture are now made extremely beautiful in most large towns throughout the continent. Exhibitions of works of genius and industry are every where encouraged, especially at Petersburg, Berlin, Brussels, Paris, Munich, Stuttgard, and Vienna.

The manufacturing industry and talent of Great Britain, and the trade therewith connected, have been long celebrated, and have grown with her growth, till she has filled the world with the choicest works of mechanic art. But particulars will not be needed in regard to a country so well known. In the United States, also, trade and manufactures have of late risen in a remarkable degree, considering the comparative newness of the country. Many new branches have been established, and many old ones enlarged, so that although we are essentially an agricultural people, and must remain so for a long time to come, we already produce a great variety of important articles of mechanical skill. The ingenuity and enterprise of our citizens are here, as in every other department of human effort, alike conspicuous and successful.

11. *Reform in Government.*—A desire among many nations to free themselves from their oppressions, or to new model their governments, is a prominent characteristic of the age. It has been observed in the course of this work, that the present period, though by the contemporary world which lived in it called the revolutionary, will probably be denominated the constitutional period by posterity. The nations for some time have been struggling to obtain free and regular constitutions. The spirit began with the United States, more than fifty years ago. France afterwards made a misguided, abortive attempt, and some other despotisms have been considerably agitated. The strict despotic principles have hitherto prevailed, except in the colonial establishments; yet even in countries governed on those principles, such has been the influence of popular feeling, there has been a degree of amelioration. The attempts of the Spaniards, Portuguese, and Neapolitans, to change their forms of government, have been frustrated chiefly by the despotic sword from abroad; but it is evident, that knowledge is increasing, and that the minds of men are turning with fond desire towards their long lost rights and liberties, and that a spirit is at work, which promises eventually the destruction of all despotic thrones. The colonial struggles, however, have been successful, and the various republics of South America, and that of Mexico, in North America, attest the energy of that feeling which resolves on independence. Greece, too, favoured by circumstances, and by the sympathies of nations, but more by her own he-

roism and self-denial, is an arm broken off from the Turkish power, and with the lingering remains of genius found in her, and quickened into life by the principles and systems of American education, is destined, we may hope, to be twice immortal.

12. *Religious Enterprises.*—The present era is greatly distinguished by a spirit of enterprise in religion. Many, in protestant countries, are especially waked up in regard to the precious interests of the Christian church—its prosperity at home, and its extension abroad. Great reformations have taken place, and signal revivals of piety have abounded, especially in the United States; and both here, and in Great Britain, the work of Christian missions has been vigorously prosecuted. Vast numbers of associations are formed in various parts of Protestant Christendom, to give the Bible to the destitute—to educate pious, indigent youth for the ministry—to imbue the minds of children with scriptural knowledge by means of sabbath school instruction—to promote religion and morality among sailors—to enlighten the inmates of dungeons—and in this country, especially, to secure the observation of the sabbath—to do away the abominations of intemperance; and to benefit the descendants of Africa, by colonizing them in the land of their fathers. The establishment and support of missionary seminaries, and theological seminaries, are also among the important religious enterprises of the day. Indeed, there is scarcely a conceivable form of benevolent and pious movement which does not receive a portion of regard from the Christian public.

The Christian Church.

We shall attempt a very brief history of the Church of Jesus Christ, or of Christianity as a divine establishment common to most of the nations, whose affairs have been narrated in a different portion of this work. This is the only religious system that claims much of our attention, in modern annals. A sufficient notice has been taken of the religion promulgated by Mahomet, in the history of the Saracens. As to the religion of paganism, we have had so little occasion to bring into view the nations, who, in modern times, possess the pagan creed, that we need not trace its distinctive features. A few, however, of the religious notions of the barbarous heathen tribes, whence sprang the modern European states, have appeared in a description of the manners, institutions, &c. of those tribes. The religion of the Greeks, Romans, and other early nations, all of whom, except the Jews, were pagans, is a topic of Ancient History.

1. It will suffice for the object here contemplated, to sketch the affairs of the Christian Church under three distinct heads. 1. In its primitive and pure state, extending from the birth of Jesus Christ, to the year 325 A. C., when Christianity became the religion of the Roman empire. 2. In its cor

rupted state, extending from 325 A. C. to the commencement of the Reformation, 1517 A. C. 3. In its reformed state, extending from 1517 A. C. to the present time.

2. In the first era, as it might be expected, we behold the Christian church in its best condition. Compared with the subsequent era, it was distinguished for the simplicity of its order, purity of practice, and attachment to the doctrines of the Gospel. Among the many events of the present period, we can notice only the following leading ones, viz., the appearance of Jesus Christ on earth; the general success of the Gospel under the preaching of the apostles and others; and the ten great persecutions of the Church, so enumerated and called, beginning with Nero, and ending with Diocletian.

§ The *appearance of Jesus Christ on earth* was the most remarkable event that ever occurred. Its date, as commonly given, is four years later than the real time. The prophets had pointed out the period, and the world was in an unusual degree prepared for the coming of the Son of God. But though the nations were expecting the appearance of some extraordinary personage, and the Jews particularly were waiting for their Messiah; yet Jesus was almost universally rejected, both by the Jew and Gentile. In the circumstances of his birth and life, and in the doctrines which he taught, the expectations of his countrymen were disappointed, and upon a frivolous pretence, they put him to the cruel death of the cross. By this procedure, so unjust on the part of the Jews, the divine plan, which sought the redemption of the nations, was accomplished, for on the third day, Jesus rose from the dead, and forty days after, having given his disciples suitable instructions respecting their duty as preachers of his religion, he ascended to heaven, a cloud receiving him out of their sight.

The *general success of the Gospel under the preaching of the apostles and others*, was also a remarkable circumstance, and strongly confirmed the truth of Christianity. Many reasons might be given for this opinion, but our limits forbid. In regard to the fact of the early and general extension of the Gospel, we are left to no doubt, from the nature of the case, and from historic records. The apostles and evangelists were early spread abroad among the nations; and even before the destruction of Jerusalem, the Gospel had been preached to multitudes in several parts of the known world. Within thirty years of the death of Christ, says Paley, the institution had spread itself through Judea, Galilee, and Samaria, almost all the numerous districts of Lesser Asia, through Greece and the islands of the Ægean Sea, the sea coast of Africa, and had extended itself to Rome, and into Italy. At Antioch in Syria, at Joppa, Ephesus, Corinth, and many other places, the converts were spoken of as numerous. The first epistle of Peter, accosts the Christians dispersed throughout Pontus, Galatia, Cappadocia, Asia, and Bythinia. In a short time, nations and cities more remote, heard of the Gospel. The Gauls received the knowledge of Christianity from the immediate successors of the apostles; and during the second century, the Germans, the Spaniards, and probably the Britons, were converted to the true religion.

The *ten great persecutions of the Church* have given a character to the whole era. They were not, however, in every instance, general through the Roman empire. Persecutions indeed existed from the beginning, and there were not many periods of entire tranquillity to the Church, during three hundred years. But those of a more marked character, are included within the above expressed number. Their order is as follows:

1. The persecution under Nero occurred thirty-one years after our Lord's ascension. When the emperor set fire to the city of Rome, he threw the odium of that execrable action on the Christians, and made it the pretext of persecuting them. Accordingly, they were hunted like wild beasts, and torn to pieces by devouring dogs, and in innumerable other ways, were vexed, tortured, and put to death.

2. The persecution which Domitian instigated, took place in the year 95. It is computed that 40,000 persons suffered martyrdom at that time.

3. The persecution which existed in the reign of Trajan, began in the year 100, and was carried on with great violence for several years.

4. The persecution which was permitted by Antoninus, commenced in the year 177. Many indignities, deprivations and sufferings were inflicted on the Christians in this persecution.

5. The persecution under Severus, began in the year 197. Great cruelties were committed at this time against the patient followers of Christ.

6. The persecution which Maximinus ordered, began in 235. It was the more severe to the sufferers from the indulgence they had enjoyed under the reign of his predecessor, Alexander Severus.

7. The persecution under Decius, began in 250. It was the most dreadful hitherto known. The Christians were in all places driven from their habitations, stripped of their estates, tormented with racks, &c.

8. The date of the persecution under Valerian, is 257. Both men and women suffered death, some by scourging, some by the sword, and some by fire.

9. The persecution by Aurelian, was in 274. But this was inconsiderable compared with the others before mentioned.

10. The persecution in which Diocletian was concerned, commenced in 295. This was a terrible persecution. It is related that 17,000 were slain in one month's time. The enemies of Christianity had the presumption to think "that the name and superstition of the Christians" had been effaced from the empire. The period, however, was just at hand, (a salutary lesson to persecutors,) when this holy

faith was to rise on the ruins of all the former religions of the Roman people.

During these persecutions, Christians multiplied, and Christianity became a principle of life and power to the hearts of its votaries. So long as their profession of religion was attended with danger—so long as they had the prospect of the dungeon, the rack, or the faggot, their lives were pure and heavenly. The gospel was their only source of consolation, and they found it in every respect sufficient for all their wants. Affected with mutual sufferings, they sympathised most tenderly with each other, and their Lord's new command of brotherly love, was never fulfilled in a more exemplary manner.

3. The Church, at the commencement of the second era, was externally prosperous and flourishing. The storm of pagan persecution had ceased, and Christianity was supported by the Roman government. Under Constantine the Great, that government (which had long included the limits of the civilized world) changed from a persecuting to a protecting power. But its love was more fatal to the real interests of the Church than its hate. Evils soon began to arise within, produced or aided by the aggrandizement it received without, which eventually reduced the Church to the lowest state of spiritual weakness and degradation. Worldly prosperity produced pride, ambition, emulation, luxury, and many other vices equally opposed to the spirit of the gospel. The mixture of pagan philosophy and superstition exceedingly debased the purity of religion, and the general ignorance which prevailed during the dark ages, rendered ineffectual its heavenly truths.

Among the more important particulars constituting this state of things, or affording proof of the disorders of the church and the consequent degeneracy of the people through this long period, may be named the Arian and Pelagian heresies, the institution of monkery, image worship, the establishment of the papal supremacy, the passion for relics and pilgrimages, the separation between the eastern and western churches, the crusades, sale of absolution and indulgences, the persecution of the Albigenses and Waldenses, the inquisition, the great western schism, the bulls and interdicts of the popes, and the contention of scholastic divines.

§ These and several others are interesting objects of attention in this portion of the church's history; but except so far as a few of them have been already treated of separately, recourse for information must be had to more extended accounts

4. Towards the commencement of the third era, the religious state of the world was deplorable. All Christendom was held in bondage to the papal power. Corruption, both in doctrine and practice, prevailed to an extent before unknown. The Reformation of religion, which is the distinction of the present era, was therefore greatly needed; and we have the satisfaction of exhibiting the christian church under the influence of so propitious a change. The greater part of this body adhered to the papacy, and perhaps still adheres to it; but though the whole of Christendom did not participate in the reformation, the whole may have derived benefit from it indirectly. The reformed, which is also called the protestant* faith, spread rapidly at the beginning, and even now, from the increase of the population in nations embracing this faith, as well as from efforts made to diffuse it abroad, it is favourably extending its influence.

The date of the great event of which we speak, is 1517, and the instrumental agent whom Providence employed in bringing it to pass, was Martin Luther. The immediate occasion of the reformation was the sale of indulgences, which had been authorized by Leo X., in order to furnish the means of gratifying his taste or extravagances. This traffic having been intrusted to the care of one John Tetzel, an insolent and dishonest wretch, attracted the notice of Martin Luther. His indignation was first excited by the base manner in which it was carried on; but from noticing the mode, he was led to inquire into the thing itself, and his eyes were soon opened to the enormity of the principle which it involved, and the nefarious character of the whole system. From this period his opinions were openly and boldly expressed, on the various errors which he found prevailing in the Church, and many were convinced on the subject by his preaching and writings. Hence the memorable rupture and revolution which took place—the blessed effects of which have been more and more felt from that age to the present.

§ During his life time the benevolent labours of Luther were blessed in no small degree, and around him gathered a host of able and

* So called from the protest which the elector of Saxony and other princes, entered against a decree of the diet at Spires, in 1529, by which every departure from the Catholic faith and discipline was forbidden, till a general council should be assembled.

godly men, who proved to be, in many instances, the most efficient coadjutors. Among these were Carolstadt, Melancthon, Zuinglius, Bucer, Oecolampadius, Martyr, Calvin, and Beza. Several of the princes of Germany were his patrons, and afforded him the most essential aid, among whom especially were Frederick the Wise, and John his brother, electors of Saxony.

The new opinions were not long confined to Germany. Through the oppressive measures of the papacy, as much as by any other cause, they were diffused abroad among the neighbouring nations Sweden, Denmark, and Switzerland, participated in the reformation, and it found many friends in France, the Netherlands, Spain, Hungary, and Bohemia. In England, also, it was firmly established, though by an instrumentality at first very different from friendship to the cause. The passions and obstinacy of Henry VIII., as has elsewhere appeared, were, by the providence of God, concerned in effecting the religious revolution in that country. In Scotland the denunciations of Knox demolished the papal hierarchy.

The opposition of the Catholic power to the reformation, produced in Germany much bloodshed, desolation, and discord. These scenes continued till the year 1555, when a treaty was formed at Augsburg, called the Peace of Religion, which established the Reformation, inasmuch as it secured to all the inhabitants of Germany the free exercise of their religion. The protestant princes of that country never at any time ceased their exertions, till this desirable result was brought to pass.

5. A few years after the establishment of the reformation, the countries of Europe which favoured it and became protestant, were Denmark, Norway, Sweden, Prussia, England, Scotland, Ireland, and Holland. One half of Germany, and a small majority in Switzerland, embraced the reformation. The countries which adhered to Rome were Italy, Spain, Portugal, the Belgic Provinces under the Spanish yoke. France became decidedly papal, though at first the hope was entertained that she would favour the protestant cause. A goodly number, however, of the French population were protestants.

That portion of the professed Christian body which constituted the Eastern or Greek church, was not affected by the revolution in the West. Though religion in this church was then at a very low ebb, and the church had experienced many external calamities, corruption and error had not made so fatal a progress in the East, as among the Latins. Russia and a part of European Turkey were the seat of the Greek religion. Many of its professors, however, were found in various countries of Asia and Africa. In 1589, the Russian church separated from the government, though not from the communion, of the Greek church—a circumstance which has reduced the latter to an inconsiderable body.

§ As the Russian and Greek branches of the Christian church need not be referred to again, it may be added, that they have undergone but few changes in more modern times—perhaps some improvement is visible. Still they seem to be little acquainted with evangelical piety, are in general destitute of the Bible, and consequently involved in ignorance. Their numbers are variously estimated. Hassel makes them seventy-four millions, which is the highest calculation. Members of the Greek church are at present found scattered over a considerable part of Greece, the Ionian isles, Wallachia, Moldavia, Egypt, Abyssinia, Nubia, Lybia, Arabia, Mesopotamia, Syria, Cilicia, and Palestine.

It must suffice for a rapid survey of the Roman and Protestant churches, from the time that their separation was consummated to the present era, to notice the following particulars.

First, the Roman church.—Desperate efforts were made by the popes to regain their lost power, but on the whole with little effect. The means which they used, as enumerated in a recent interesting publication,* were principally these four. 1. The employment of the order of Jesuits, formed in the year 1540, by Ignatius Loyola, whose object was to go forth, as advocates of the papal power. 2. An attempt to christianize the heathen, in several parts of Asia and South America. 3. The better regulation of the internal concerns of their church. 4. The persecution of the protestants. In regard to the last, it may be observed, that scarcely a country, in which protestants were to be found, but was the scene of awful sufferings. Our blood boils with indignation at the thought, that cruelties which would have disgraced Domitian, were inflicted by the minions of the papacy, under the sanction of the mild religion of the Saviour, upon his own followers. In these persecutions, fifty millions of protestants are computed to have perished, principally in Italy, the Netherlands, Spain, France, parts of Germany, and England.

But all the efforts of the Roman church were in vain, except as by propagating her religion in heathen countries, she was for a time nominally mistress of greater numbers of mankind than before. Several causes have contributed to weaken, essentially, her power, wealth and splendour. These, as enumerated in the work above referred to, are, 1. The loss of foreign conquests. 2. Unsuccessful contests with several European governments. 3. The suppression of the order of the Jesuits. 4. The revolution in France. 5. The abolition of the inquisition.

The *statistics* of the Roman church, as it exists at the present day, are as follows:

The *temporal dominions* of the pope, are a small territory in

* Outlines of Ecclesiastical History, by Rev. Charles A. Goodrich.

Italy, south of the Po, containing 15,000 square miles, and 2,500,000 inhabitants.

Its *ecclesiastical subjects* are supposed to amount to 80 or 100,000,000, in all parts of the world. Malte Brun put them down at 116,000,000.

The *countries* where they most abound, are the pope's dominions in Italy, Spain, Portugal, and South America. These are considered entirely papal. France, Austria, Poland, Belgium, Ireland, and Canada, are chiefly papal. Switzerland has 700,000; England half a million, and the United States about that number. Others are found in Russia, Sweden, Denmark, and the West Indies. The pope is at present making great efforts to extend his influence in the United States; but it is believed either that the system cannot widely prevail here, or if from any temporary causes, it is destined to meet with some successes, that it will be in a degree modified by the genius of our institutions, and not be the dark, intolerant, cruel, and licentious system that it has been in other countries.

Second, the Protestants.—A diversity soon took place among those who separated from the fellowship of Rome. A general division of the protestants is into the Lutheran church, and the Reformed churches.

1. *Lutheran Church.*—The Lutherans, as the name imports, were the immediate followers of Luther, who consider their church as having been established at the time of the pacification at Passau, 1552. Their standard of faith is the Augsburg confession. They suffered far less from the persecutions of the times than the other portions of the reformed church, though they were unhappily engaged in a controversy among themselves, relating to various points of faith and practice.

These controversies were followed by a low state of religion; and this by efforts which many of the better sort made to bring about a happier state of things. Some good was done by the Pietists, (so this class of people were called,) but far less than might have been, had not their views and principles been misconceived or opposed. The Pietists flourished about the middle of the seventeenth century, but they degenerated after a time, and were succeeded by a set of wild religionists, who did much mischief to the cause of godliness. To counteract this evil, the system of the Neologists was introduced, which consisted in the application of human philosophy to the interpretation of the Bible. The remedy was as bad as the disease, and the Gospel, stripped of its peculiarities, has become a dead letter very extensively in Germany. It is believed, however, that a better spirit is now commencing in some parts of the Lutheran church, while it is a happiness to know that, in other parts of it, both in Germany and the neighbouring churches, there are those who have all along maintained their integrity.

In regard to the *statistics* of the Lutheran church, it may be observed, that portions of it are found chiefly in Denmark, Norway, and Sweden, in a great part of Germany, particularly in the north, and in Saxony and Prussia, where Lutheranism is the established religion. Churches of this denomination also exist in Holland, France, Russia, North America, and in the Danish West-Indies. The number of Lutherans is probably between fifteen and twenty millions.

2. *Reformed Churches.*—These are numerous, and little more than their names can be here mentioned. The term "Reformed" was a title originally assumed by those Helvetic or Swiss churches, which adhered to certain tenets of Zuinglius, in relation to the Sacrament. But in latter times it has a wider signification, and under it may be included all those sects in Protestant Christendom, that dissent from the tenets of the Lutheran church. These are

principally the Calvinists, the Church of England, the Presbyterian Church of Scotland, the Moravians, the Congregationalists of New-England, the Presbyterian Church in the United States, the Episcopal Church in the United States, the Baptists, Methodists, and Quakers.

1. *Calvinists.*—The Christians so called, taken loosely for those who explain the Bible as Calvin explained it, constituted at first the whole body of the Protestants as distinguished from the Lutherans. Protestant Christendom even now owns this distinction on the continent of Europe. They were called Huguenots in France, and suffered terrible persecutions. They are not known as one particular denomination, but constitute a portion of several bodies of Christians. They exist in France, Holland, Prussia, Great Britain, and other countries in Europe, and extensively in the United States. The sect of Arminians is, as to sentiment, directly opposed to the Calvinists, though persons of both persuasions are often found together in the same churches. The Arminian doctrines began to be propagated at the beginning of the seventeenth century.

2. *Church of England.*—By this name is known the reformed church as established in England and Ireland. Its history is deeply interesting, as it passed a bloody ordeal, but there is no space for particulars. The rise of puritanism is connected with the history of the church of England, than which few events in the records of religion are more important; but this also must be passed over. Dissenters from the church of England are tolerated in the United Kingdom. The establishment embraces 5,000,000 of the inhabitants: its livings are 10,500. The dissenters, or independents, in England and Wales, have more than 1000 congregations.

3. *Presbyterian Church of Scotland.*—The date of the establishment of the Reformation in Scotland, is about the year 1560. At this time the Presbyterian church in that country began to assume a regular form. This church passed through various vicissitudes, and has in general been distinguished for the piety of its members. It includes nearly the whole population of Scotland.

4. *Moravians.*—The Moravians, or United Brethren, date their modern history in 1722. They are an exemplary people, and devoted to missionary enterprises. They have settlements in Germany, Denmark, Holland, England, Scotland, Ireland, Russia, and the United States. Their converts among the heathen, amount to 30,000.

5. *Congregationalists of New-England.*—Under this name are known the descendants of a class of the English puritans, who fled from persecution to the wilds of America. They began the settlement of New-England, on the 22d December, 1620. The sufferings, piety, and success of the fathers of New-England Congregationalism, are rich topics in religious history. The Congregationalists have about 1000 churches in New-England, and about 200 in other parts of the United States.

6. *Presbyterian Church in the United States.*—This body of Christians was originally composed of a few Presbyterians from Scotland and Ireland, united to a like number of Congregationalists, chiefly from New-England. They have greatly prospered and increased, and are found throughout the middle, southern and western states. The number of their churches is nearly 1900.

Our limits preclude an account of other reformed churches, several of which are respectable for their character and numbers.

A

SYSTEM

OF

MODERN GEOGRAPHY,

EXHIBITING THE PRESENT STATE OF THE VARIOUS NATIONS ON THE GLOBE.

THE EARTH IN GENERAL.—The earth is a large globe, the diameter of which is nearly eight thousand miles, its equatorial circumference is about 24,970 miles, and its surface contains nearly two hundred millions of square miles.

More than two thirds of the globe are covered with water.

The land is occupied by at least a thousand millions of human beings, and is divided into four great nominal parts, sometimes called quarters: Europe, Asia, Africa, and America.

There are only two Continents; one contains Europe, Asia, and Africa;—the other consists of North and South America.

There are five *oceans:* the Pacific Ocean, the Atlantic Ocean, the Indian Ocean, the Northern Ocean, and the Southern Ocean.

The earth is ninety-six millions of miles from the Sun. It moves round the Sun in a year, which causes the changes of the seasons; and turns on its own axis every twenty-four hours, which occasions night and day.

EUROPE.

EUROPE is the smallest of the grand divisions or quarters of the world, but is inhabited by an active and intelligent race of people.

Europe is bounded north by the Frozen Ocean, east by Asia, south by the Mediterranean Sea, and west by the Atlantic ocean.

Europe comprehends Lapland, Norway, Sweden, Russia, Denmark, Prussia, Batavia, the German States, Austria, Turkey, France, Switzerland, Italy, Portugal, Spain, and the United Kingdom of Great Britain and Ireland.

Its three grand inland seas are the Mediterranean, the Baltic, and the White Sea.

Its principal rivers are the Wolga, the Danube, the Nieper, the Rhine, and the Elbe.

Its most elevated mountains are, the Alps, which separate Italy from Germany, Switzerland, and France.

The Pyrenees, between France and Spain:

The Dofrafield mountains, between Norway and Sweden:

The Carpathian mountains, which bound Hungary to the north and east.

LAPLAND is divided into Danish or North Lapland; Swedish or South Lapland; and Russian or East Lapland.

It is covered with immense forests, chiefly of fir, and with pastures full of rain-deer.

The Laplanders are hospitable, generous, and courageous.

They make long excursions upon the snow, and will, without much fatigue travel fifty miles a day; and in their sledges, drawn by rein-deer, they pass over hill and dale, with far greater speed.

In some parts of Lapland, the sun is absent for about seven weeks; but from ten in the forenoon till between one and two in the afternoon, the twilight is sufficient for persons to read without a candle. The stars are visible at noon, and the moon shines without intermission. In the summer, on the contrary, the sun never sets for seven weeks together.

NORWAY is bounded north and west by the Northern Ocean, east by Swedish Lapland and Sweden, and south by the Categat.

Norway formerly belonged to Denmark, but has recently become a dependency of Sweden.

The chief town of Norway is Bergen.

Norway is the most mountainous country in the world, and the rivers and cataracts which intersect the mountains, render travelling exceedingly dangerous.

On the coast of Norway is the famous vortex of the sea called the Maelstroom; it is heard at a great distance, and forms a whirlpool of vast depth and extent, and so violent, that if a ship come near it, it is drawn in and shattered to pieces.

The chief wealth of Norway lies in its fir timber, with which foreign nations are supplied.

DENMARK Proper is an exceedingly small kingdom, containing only the peninsula of Jutland, and the islands of Zealand, Funen, &c. at the entrance of the Baltic.

Its chief town is Copenhagen.

Iceland, which is subject to Denmark, abounds in sulphur, subterraneous fires, and volcanoes. Mount Hecla is a volcano one mile high, and is always covered with snow; while the boiling springs and craters on the summit continually propel fire and smoke.

SWEDEN is divided into Sweden Proper, Gothland, Finland, Swedish Lapland, and the Swedish islands.

The chief towns are Stockholm, the capital, which stands on seven rocky islands; Upsal, famous for its University; Gottenberg, in Gothland; and Torneo, in Lapland.

The chief wealth of Sweden arises from its mines of silver, copper, lead, and iron.

The mines are very spacious, afford commodious habitations for numerous families, and seem to form a subterraneous world.

Sweden is a mountainous country, and is celebrated for the number and extent of its lakes.

In the Baltic Sea there are no tides, and a current is always running into the German Ocean.

RUSSIA is bounded north by the Frozen Ocean, east by Asia, south by Turkey and the Black Sea, west by Sweden, the Baltic, Prussia and Austria.

The Russian Empire, the largest in extent in the world, comprehends most of the northern parts of Europe and Asia, but only a small part of its inhabitants are in a state of civilization.

In some parts of this country the climate is so severe, that icicles are frequently seen hanging to the eye-lashes, and the drivers of carriages are often found frozen to death on their seats.

The principal towns are Petersburgh, the capital; Moscow; Archangel, on the borders of the White Sea; Cherson, on the Black Sea; Astracan, near the Caspian; and Tobolsk, the capital of Siberia.

Russia is mostly a level country: from Petersburgh to Pekin in China there is scarcely a hill: the same may be said of the road from Petersburgh to the north of France.

The inland navigation of Russia is very extensive; goods may be conveyed by water from Petersburgh to China, with an interruption of only 60 miles.

Russia is celebrated for its timber and flax trade, its iron and copper mines in the Uralian mountains, and its fisheries.

PRUSSIA is bounded north by the Baltic, east by Russia, south by Austria, and west by Germany.

The Prussian dominions were formerly very small, but the acquisition of Silesia, and a third part of Poland, has rendered it a considerable empire.

Before the partition of Poland, the Prussian subjects amounted to about five millions and a half; with that addition they count nearly eight millions.

HOLLAND OR BATAVIA, *now Kingdom of the Netherlands*, is bounded north and west by the North Sea, east by Germany, south by France.

The kingdom of Holland consists of seven provinces, viz. Groningen, Griesland, Over-yssel, Holland, Utrecht, Guelderland, and Zealand.

The chief towns are Amsterdam, Leyden, Rotterdam, Haarlem.

Amsterdam, the capital, is curiously built upon wooden piles.

The principal rivers are the Rhine, the Maese and the Scheldt.

The canals are very numerous, and serve for the same purposes as roads in other countries.

GERMANY is bounded north by the German Sea, Denmark, and the Baltic, east by Prussia and Austria, south by Switzerland, and west by France and the Netherlands.

Germany was formerly divided into nine great divisions, called circles; latterly a new political association has been formed of many considerable states, under the title of the Germanic confederation; the principal of these states are the kingdoms of Saxony, Bavaria, Wertemberg, Baden, and Hanover. The principal rivers are the Danube, Rhine, Elbe, and Maine. The chief town is Vienna, the residence of the Emperor.

THE AUSTRIAN DOMINIONS are bounded north by Prussia, south by Turkey and the gulf of Venice, west by Switzerland and Germany.

The Austrian dominions comprehend Austria, Bohemia, Hungary, part of Poland, and the Venetian states.

The chief towns are, Venice, Prague, Presburg, Buda, Cracow, and Trieste.

The principal mountains are the Tyrolese, the Alps, and the Carpathian mountains.

TURKEY IN EUROPE includes ancient Greece and other countries, formerly the finest in the world, but owing to the despotism and wretched policy of the Turks, is now the most desolate and miserable.

It is bounded north by the Austrian dominions and Russia, east by the Black Sea, the Sea of Marmora, and the Archipelago, south and west by the Mediterranean.

The metropolis of Turkey is Constantinople, finely situated between the Sea of Marmora and the Black Sea, and one of the most considerable cities in Europe.

The principal rivers are the Danube, the Saave, and the Neister.

The chief mountains are Pindus and Olympus, which separate Thessaly from Epirus; Parnassus in Livadio; Athos, and Haemus. Athos is celebrated for its loftiness, and is inhabited by thousands of monks and hermits.

France is bounded north by the British Channel, and the German Ocean, east by Germany, Switzerland, and Italy, south by the Mediterranean and Spain, and west by the Bay of Biscay.

Paris, the capital of France, is, next to London, the largest and most considerable city in Europe. It contains at this time immense collections of works of art, ancient and modern. The other principal towns of France are Lyons, Marseilles, Bordeaux, and Lisle.

The principal mountains in France are, the Alps, which divide it from Italy; and the Pyrennees, which divide it from Spain.

The principal rivers are the Rhone, the Garonne, the Loire, the Seine, and the Somme. The Rhine forms the boundary between France and Germany.

The canals in France are numerous; the chief work of this kind is the canal of Languedoc, about 180 miles in length, connecting the Atlantic with the Mediterranean.

Switzerland is bounded north by Germany and France, east by Austria, south by Italy, and west by France.

Switzerland, remarkable for its mountains, is divided into thirteen cantons Zurich, Berne, Underwalden, Zug, Schweitz, Basil, Glasis, Soleure, Uri, Appenzel, Lucerne, Friburg, and Schaffhausen.

The principal towns are Basil, Berne, Zurich, and Geneva.

The sources of the Rhine and the Rhone, two of the grandest rivers in Europe, are to be found in the mountains of Switzerland.

The lakes of Constance and Geneva have been long celebrated for their beauty.

The Alps, which divide Switzerland from Italy; the mountain of St. Gothard, in the canton of Uri; and Mount Blanc, on the borders of Savoy, are the highest in Europe.

Italy is bounded north by the Alps, east by the Gulf of Venice, and south and west by the Mediterranean.

Italy, the garden of Europe, the parent of the arts, and of civilization, and once the mistress of the world, is still a fine, populous, and interesting country, but inhabited by a race of people, who have become degenerated by superstition and political slavery.

The Appenines form a grand chain of mountains, which runs through almost the whole extent of Italy.

Mount Vesuvius, near Naples, is a celebrated volcanic mountain. But Vesuvius, compared with Mount Etna in Sicily, is but a small hill; the circuit of Vesuvius is only thirty miles, that of Etna is one hundred and eighty. The lava of Vesuvius is sometimes thrown seven miles, that of Etna is frequently thrown thirty miles.

Rome is the principal seat of the Pope's dominion.

Spain is bounded north by the Pyrennees and the Bay of Biscay, east by the Mediterranean, south by the Atlantic, the Straits of Gibraltar, and the Mediterranean, and west by Portugal and the Atlantic.

Its chief towns are Madrid, the capital; Barcelona, Seville, Corunna, and Cadiz.

The principal rivers are, the Ebro, the Tagus, and the Douro.

On a promontory in the south of Spain stands Gibraltar, which has been in possession of the English for a century, and is so defended by nature and art as to be considered impregnable.

PORTUGAL, like Spain, has been enervated by its foreign possessions, and is now one of the most abject powers in Europe. The people are debased by indolence and superstition.

It lies between Spain and the Atlantic, and is the most westerly kingdom in Europe.

The chief towns are Lisbon, the capital; and Oporto, famous for its exports of wine.

THE UNITED KINGDOM OF GREAT BRITAIN AND IRELAND.—ENGLAND is bounded north by Scotland, east by the German Sea, south by the British Channel, and west by St. George's Channel.

The Island of Great Britain is divided into England, Wales, and Scotland. It is six hundred miles long and three hundred broad; and contains about twelve millions of inhabitants.

Her wealth, the value of her manufactures, and the extent of her commerce, are unequalled. The intelligence and industry of her inhabitants, the excellent form of her political constitution, the just administration of her laws, and the independence arising from her insular situation, combine to render her an object of admiration to all other nations.

London contains upwards of a million of inhabitants, is thirty miles in circumference, and is the largest and most opulent city in Europe.

The principal towns, famous for their respective manufactures, are Birmingham and Sheffield, for cutlery and hardware; Manchester for cotton goods; and Leeds and Wakefield for woollen cloth. The great commercial sea-ports, besides London, are Liverpool, Bristol, Hull, Newcastle, Whitehaven, Yarmouth, and Poole. The dock-yards for the marine are Portsmouth, Plymouth, and Chatham. The universities are those of Oxford and Cambridge.

The principal rivers in England are, the Severn, the Thames, the Humber, the Mersey, the Trent, and the Medway.

The principal lakes are those in Cumberland, and Winander Mere in Westmoreland.

The Isle of Wight, on the south, is famous for its cultivation; Jersey and Guernsey are near the coast of France. The Isle of Man is in the Irish Sea.

SCOTLAND, the northern division of Great Britain, is inhabited by a valiant, hardy, industrious, well informed, and temperate race of people.

The most considerable towns in Scotland, are Edinburgh, Glasgow, and Aberdeen, famous for their universities; and Glasgow no less for its extensive commerce.

IRELAND, lies west of England; the chief towns are Dublin, the capital, Cork, Londonderry, and Belfast.

ASIA.

ASIA is bounded north by the Frozen Ocean, east by the Pacific Ocean and Bhering's Straits, south by the Indian Ocean, and west by Europe and the Red Sea.

The southern Asiatics are in general effeminate, luxurious, indolent, and servile; but they evince considerable genius in various arts and sciences.

The great inland seas, peculiar to Asia, are, the Red Sea or Arabian Gulf, the Persian Gulf, and the Caspian Sea.

The chief rivers of Asia are, the Kian Ku, the Koan Ho, the Lena, Yenisci, and the Ob, the Amur, the Burrampooter, the Ganges, the Euphrates, and the Indus.

The Himmaleh mountains, said to be the highest on the globe, form the boundary between Hindoostan and Thibet; the height of one of their peaks has been estimated at 27,550 feet above the level of the ocean.

Asiatic Turkey.—Turkey in Asia is bounded north by the Black Sea, east by Persia, south by Arabia and the Mediterranean, and west by the Archipelago and the Sea of Marmora.

The climate of Turkey in Asia is delightful and salubrious; but that dreadful scourge to mankind, the plague, is rendered doubly destructive from the native indolence of the Turks, and from their superstitious belief in predestination.

It is divided into several provinces, as Natolia, Kaarman, Armenia, Mingrelia, &c.

Armenia is also styled Turkomania, to the south of which are Kurdistan and Irak Arabi, in which is the celebrated Bagdad.

The ancient Mesopotamia, between the Tigris and Euphrates, corresponds with Diarbeck or Algezira. Syria, or the ancient Canaan, is situated on the eastern extremities of the Mediterranean.

These provinces are subdivided into different governments under Pachas.

The prevailing language is the Turkish, next to which is the Greek, but the Arabic, Syrian, Persian, and Armenian, are used in different parts.

The principal cities are Smyrna, Aleppo, and Bagdad

Balbec and Palmyra are famous for their extensive ruins.

The principal river in Asiatic Turkey is the Euphrates. Next to this is the Tigris.

The mountains in Asiatic Turkey have long been celebrated; these are Taurus, Ararat, and Libanus.

The chief islands are, Mytelene, Scio, Samos, Cos, Rhodes, and Cyprus.

Russia in Asia is bounded north by the Northern Ocean, east by the Pacific, south by Tartary, the Caspian Sea, and Persia, and west by Russia in Europe.

This vast extent of northern Asia was first known by the name of Siberia.

It is divided into two great governments, that of Tobolsk in the west, and Ikurtsk in the east.

The principal city in Asiatic Russia is Astracan.

The Kurilian islands belong to Asiatic Russia; they extend from Kamschatka to the land of Jesso.

The Chinese Empire.—China is celebrated for its immense and industrious population, for the variety of its manufactures and peculiar productions, for the excellence of its inland navigation, and for the jealous policy of its government towards other nations.

This empire, the most ancient and populous in the world, consists of three principal divisions, viz. China Proper; the territory of the Manshurs and Moguls, on the north and west and the region of Thibet.

China Proper extends from the great wall in the north to the China Sea in the south; and from the shores of the Pacific Ocean to Thibet.

The chief cities are Pekin, Nankin, and Canton.

The imperial canal intersects China from north to south, and employed 30,000 men forty-three years for its construction.

The largest of the Chinese islands, which are very numerous, and scattered along the southern and eastern coast, are, Formosa and Hainan.

The isles of Leoo-Keoo, between Formosa and Japan, constitute a small civilized kingdom subject to China.

Chinese Tartary is included between the great wall of China and Siberia, and between the cloudy mountains and the Pacific Ocean.

Chinese Tartary is inhabited chiefly by the Eastern and Western Moguls; the former conquered China in 1644, under whose government the empire still continues.

The Island of Segalien, on Tchoka, belongs to Chinese Tartary.

Thibet is included between China and Hindoostan. The chief town is Lasca.

The islands contiguous to the Chinese Empire, besides those already noticed, are,

1. Those of Japan, forming an extensive, rich, populous, and remarkable empire. The largest island is Niphon, and the chief town Jeddo; Miaco, the spiritual capital, and Nagaski. These islands trade only with the Dutch and Chinese.

2. The Jesso Islands, to which the Danes trade for furs.

3. Macao lies in the Bay of Canton, and belongs to the Portuguese.

There are many small isles dependent upon Japan, among which is Fatfisio, the place of exile for the disgraced grandees.

The Birman Empire.—(*Malacca, Siam, Laos, Cambodia, Siampa, and Cochin-China.*)—The Birmans are separated from the Hindoos by a very narrow range of mountains, but the dispositions of the two people are extremely different. The Birmans are a lively inquisitive race, irascible and impatient.

The Birman empire is divided from Asam on the north; on the west a range of mountains separate it from the British dominions in Bengal.

The capital city is Ava. Pegu, south of Ava, is supposed to be the Golden Chersonese of the ancients.

This empire extends its dominions over Laos and Cambodia, and is divided by deserts and mountains from Cochin-China and Tonquin.

Ava, the present capital, and Pegu, the former, are both going to decay.

The Birmans, like the Chinese, have no coin; but silver in bullion, and lead, are current.

The forests in this empire are large and numerous; the teak-tree is lord of them, and superior to the European oak.

Malaya, or Malacca, is a large peninsula, containing several kingdoms and provinces.

The inhabitants are called Malays or Malayans.

This country is celebrated for its numerous wild elephants.

Opposite to the coast of Malacca are the islands of Andaman and Nicobar.

On the barren isle to the east of the Amandans is a volcano which emits showers of red hot stones.

The kingdom of Siam is situated in a large vale between two ridges of mountains.

The River Meinam, which signifies the *mother of waters*, is celebrated among oriental rivers.

The elephants of Siam are distinguished for sagacity and beauty.

Cambodia is celebrated for the camboge-gum.

The chief river in Tonquin-China is Hole-Kian, which passes by Kesho. the capital.

HINDOOSTAN.—The population of Hindoostan, subject to Great Britain, amounts to fourteen millions; and the revenue derived from them is computed at four millions sterling. So great a power and revenue, main tained in so distant a country, is unexampled in ancient or modern times.

BRITISH INDIA consists of certain immense territories on the banks of the Ganges. of which Calcutta is the capital; of other territories on the coast of Coromandel, of which Madras is the capital; of the newly acquired island of Ceylon; and of the island of Bombay.

PERSIA is bounded north by the Caspian Sea and Tartary, east by Hindoostan, south by the Arabian Sea and Persian Gulf, and west by Arabia and Turkey.

Persia is divided into the eastern and western; and the provinces near the Caspian Sea, which have asserted a sort of independence.

The principal towns and cities are Ispahan the capital, Teffliz, and Gomron.

In Persia rivers and trees are very uncommon: hence the respect paid by the Persian monarchs to *planes* and other trees that diffuse their shade.

The singular features of Persia are mountains and deserts. On the western coast of the Caspian Sea, near Baku, are foundations of naptha, or pure rock oil. The earth when dug two or three inches deep will easily take fire.

INDEPENDENT TARTARY is bounded north by Asiatic Russia, east by eastern Tartary, south by Persia and Hindoostan, west by the Caspian Sea.

This extensive region is celebrated as the seat of the most ancient Persian kingdom. It was afterwards distinguished by the wide empire of Jenghiz and Timur. It gave birth to many ancient men of letters, among whom were Zoroaster and Abulguazi. Such is the hospitality of the Tartars, that all the families in the country seem to belong as but to one house.

1. The chief divisions of Independent Tartary are the barren plains in the north.

2. To the south of the Argun mountains is Great Bulcharia.

3. On the south of the Ak-Tau mountains are the provinces of Sogd, (the capital of which is Samarcand,) Balk, and Gaur.

The chief rivers are the Jihon and the Sirr or Sihon, and the most considerable lake, or inland sea, is that of Aral.

ARABIA is bounded on the north by Turkey, east by the Gulf of Persia and Ormus, south by the Indian Ocean, and west by the Red Sea.

The Arabians in general are such robbers, that travellers and pilgrims are struck with terror on their approaches towards this country. The climate is very various: in some parts it is excessively hot and dry, and subject to poisonous winds. In other parts the soil is fertile, and the air is highly salubrious. In the desert, travellers are guided by the stars and compass, as mariners are at sea.

Arabia is divided into three parts; Arabia Stony, Arabia the Desert, and Arabia Happy.

Stony Arabia is a small province north of the Red Sea, between Egypt and Palestine. The chief town is Suez.

Between the narrow branches of the northern extremity of the Red Sea, are, Mount Sinai, and Mount Horeb: on which are several cells or chapels possessed by monks.

Arabia the Desert is the middle part of the country, the inhabited parts of which lie on the borders of the Red Sea.

The chief towns are Mecca and Medina: the former the birth place of Mahomet, and the latter that at which he was buried. The famous temple at Mecca is called the Kaba or Caaba.

Arabia Happy comprises the south-west part of the country.

The Eastern Archipelago is divided into:

1. The islands of Sunda, or the Sumatran chain, which comprise Sumatra, Java, Balli, Lomboek, Florez, and Timor, with several other of less importance.
2. Borneo, and some smaller islands surrounding Borneo, is, excepting New-Holland, the largest island in the world.
3. The Minilias or Phillipine islands, including Luzon, Mindonao, Palawa, Mindora, Pany, Negros, Zebu, Leyta and Samar, and several hundred smaller islands.
4. The Celebezian isles, viz. Celebes, Boutan, and the surrounding small islands. Boutan is governed by a Mahometan Sultan.
5. The spice islands, including the Moluccas: these are Gilola, Ceram, Bouro, Oby, Amboyna, Banda, Tidore, Ternate, &c. These famous islands produce nutmegs, cloves, and other valuable spices.

Australasia contains the following islands:

1. New-Holland or Notasia, and all the islands between twenty degrees west, and between twenty or thirty degrees east of it. New-Holland is about three fourths as large as Europe.
2. Papua or New-Guinea, and the Papuan isles.
3. New Britain, New-Ireland, and the Solomon isles.
4. New-Caledonia and the New-Hebrides.
5. New-Zealand.
6. Van Dieman's Land, which is separated from New-Holland by Basse's strait or channel, which is about thirty leagues wide.

Polynesia consists,

1. Of the Pelew Islands.
2. Of the Ladrone or Marian Islands, the principal of which are Guan and Tinian.
3. The Carolines, the largest of which are Hogolen and Yap.
4. The Sandwich Islands, discovered by Captain Cook, at one of which he lost his life.
5. The Marquesas, which are very numerous, but the largest island in Polynesia is Owyhee, about 100 hundred miles in length.
6. The Society Islands are about sixty or seventy in number; the Otaheite is the largest.
7. The Friendly Islands, and the Feejee Islands.
8. The Navigator's Islands, the principal of which is Maouna.

AMERICA.

America was unknown to the inhabitants of the other continent, till a little more than three hundred years ago, when it was discovered by Christopher Columbus; and hence it is called the New World, in contradistinction to the eastern continent, first known, and hence called the Old World.

It extends from Cape Horn, lat. 56° south, to the Frozen Ocean north, being upwards of 7,000 miles in length. Its breadth varies from 37 to 5,000 miles. It lies between the Atlantic on the east, and the Pacific on the west; and is supposed to contain about 35 millions of inhabitants.

It is divided into North and South America, which are connected by the Isthmus of Darien.

North America includes the United States, Spanish America, British America, and the independent Indian nations.

The inland seas of North America are the Gulfs of Mexico, California, and St. Lawrence, with Hudson's Bay, and Davis's Straits.

The Gulf of St. Lawrence is closed by the island of Newfoundland, and the great sand bank, about four hundred miles in length, celebrated for the cod-fishery.

The Lakes Superior, Michigan, Huron, Erie, Ontario, Winnipeg, and Slave Lake, are the grandest in the world, and might with propriety be denominated seas.

The rivers are also grand features of North America. Of these the principal are the Missouri and Mississippi, the Ohio and St. Lawrence.

The most celebrated mountains are the Apalachian, passing through the territory of the United States.

The United States are bounded north by the River St. Lawrence and the Lakes, from the Lake of the Woods to the Rocky Mountains its northern boundary is in lat. 49°—from the Rocky Mountains to the Pacific, its northern boundary is in lat. 50°;—On the east they are bounded by the Atlantic—on the south by the Gulf of Mexico—on the southwest by the River Sabine and Mexico—on the west by the Pacific; extending from east to west, nearly 60° of longitude, about 2,700 miles.

The United States are celebrated for the excellence of their constitution, which secures political liberty, and individual security.

There are 24 independent States, which are divided into the New-England or Eastern, the Middle, Southern and Western States:—the inhabitants at this day (1830) amount to about 12,000,000.

New-England comprises Maine, Vermont, New-Hampshire, Massachusetts, Rhode Island, and Connecticut.

The Middle Division comprises New-York, New-Jersey, Pennsylvania, and Delaware.

The Southern Division comprises Maryland, Virginia, North Carolina, South Carolina, Georgia, and Alabama. In this division is also included the Territory of Florida.

The Western Division comprises Ohio, Indiana, Illinois, Kentucky, Tennessee, Mississippi, Louisiana and Missouri. In this division are included the Territories of Michigan, Arkansaw, and Missouri; and also the North West Territory.

MEXICO, AND GUATAMALA—IN NORTH AMERICA.—The most unfertile of these dominions is said to produce two crops of corn in a year; the valleys are extremely rich, and produce spontaneously the fruits and vegetables common to the most fruitful parts of the United States.

The largest city in this country is Mexico, and the principal river and lake in these regions is the Rio Bravo del Norte, in Mexico; and the lake known as the Nicaragua, in Guatamala.

BRITISH POSSESSIONS IN NORTH AMERICA.—This part of North America is mountainous and barren, abounding, however, with lakes, rivers, and bays, that afford plenty of fish. The fur trade and fisheries render this colony exceedingly valuable.

The British dominions are extensive, and include Upper and Lower Canada, Nova Scotia, New-Brunswick, the island of Cape Breton, Newfoundland, the Bermudas, or Summer Islands.

NATIVE TRIBES AND INDEPENDENT COUNTRIES.—These are, Greenland, Labrador, the regions around Hudson's Bay, those nations lately discovered by Sir A. Mackenzie, and those on the western coast.

THE WEST INDIES.—The most important of these islands are Cuba, and Porto-Rico, Spanish; St. Domingo, Free Blacks; and Jamaica, English.

North of St. Domingo and Cuba, are the Bahamas, the principal of which is Providence island.

The Caribbee islands extend from Tobago, in the south, to the Virgin islands in the north.

Those belonging to Britain are, Barbadoes, Antigua, St. Christopher's, St. Vincent, Dominica, Granada, Trinidad, Montserrat, Nevis, and the Virgin isles.

The French Carribbee islands are, Martinique, Guadaloupe, St. Lucie, and Tobago.

The Danes possess St. Croix and St. Thomas.

St. Bartholomew belongs to the Swedes, and Eustatia to the Dutch.

SOUTH AMERICA comprehends, New Granada and Venezuela, now known as Colombia; Guiana; Peru; Bolivia, or Upper Peru; Amazonia; Brazil; La Plata, or Buenos Ayres; Chili, and Patagonia.

South America has no inland sea; but the River Amazon, and that of La Plata, are celebrated as the largest in the world.

The mountains of South America (excepting Himmaleh, in Asia,) are the loftiest on the whole face of the globe, and are intermixed with volcanoes of the most sublime and terrific description. The Andes follow the windings of the coast, and extend 4,600 miles. The highest are near the equator.

In Chili it never rains, the sky is seldom cloudy, but the dews of the night supply the want of rain.

The Portuguese territory of Brazil is, perhaps, equal in extent to what formerly was the Spanish, compensating by its breadth for its deficiency in length.

The southern extremity of South America is Patagonia, a desolate country, inhabited by savage Indians, some of whom are of colossal stature.

The islands contiguous to South America are, Trinidad, the Falkland Islands, and Terra del Fuego.

The Galliapago Islands are near the equator, and the Pearl Islands lie in the bay of Panama.

AFRICA.

In Africa there are no inland seas, and but one lake of any great extent, viz. that of Maravi.

The principal rivers are the Nile, the Niger, and the Senegal.

The Atlas mountains have long been celebrated, and the mountains of the Moon are a lofty range.

The most striking feature of Africa consists in its immense deserts, which, perhaps, comprise one half of the continent; of these, Zaara is the chief.

Africa may be considered in the following order: first, Abyssinia, then Egypt, the Mahometan States in the north, the western coast, and the Cape of Good Hope: from thence proceeding along the eastern shores.

The chief cities are, Grand Cairo, the capital, Alexandria, Rosetta, and Damietta. Rain is a very uncommon phenomenon in Egypt.

The northern Mahometan states are, Tripoli, Tunis, Algiers, and Morocco They are chiefly remarkable for their piracies.

Benin, Loango, and Congo, present the most interesting objects in this wide extent of country.

Zaara, or the Great Desert, extends from the Atlantic to the Nile.

Caffraria, or the land of Hottentots, extends to the Cape of Good Hope, the most southerly part of Africa. The Cape of Good Hope is a free port for all nations.

The coasts of Mozambico and Zanguebar are succeeded by the desert regions of Ajan and Adel, which complete the circuit of Africa.

The island of Madagascar is one of the largest in the world.

On the west of Africa is St. Helena, an English colony, and a desirable port.

The Cape de Verd Islands are ten in number, the two largest are St. Jago and St. Anthony.

More northerly are the Canary or Fortunate Islands. Among these is the famous peak of Teneriffe.

The island of Madeira, the last that is reckoned contiguous to Africa, is famous for its wine.

vol. i. *Founding of Ancient Rome.* p. 57.

vol. i. *Cincinnatus at his Plough.* p. 85

vol. i. *Roman Agriculture.* p. 224.

vol. i. *Olympic Games—Boxing.* p. 51.

vol. i. *Regulus Defeats the Carthagenians.* p. 104.

vol. i. *Olympic Games—Boxing.* p. 51.

vol. i. *Olympic Games—Discus.* p. 51.

vol. i. *Pompilius Crowned King of Rome.* p. 58.

vol. i. *Leading to Sacrifice.* p. 187.

vol. i. *Roman War Galley.* p. 205.

vol. i. *Roman Aqueduct.* p. 211

vol. i. *Roman Coasting Vessel.* p. 215.

vol. i. *Chariot Race.* p. 207.

vol. i. *Sabine women carried away by the Romans.* p. 58.

vol i. *Battering Ram.* p. 204.

Roman Emperor.

Roman Senator.

Roman General.

Roman Soldier.

vol. i. *Death of Alexander.* p. 96.

vol. i. *Spartans returning from the Messenian War.* 66.

vol. i. *Royalty Abolished at Rome.* p. 62.

vol. i *Defeat of the Persians by Alexander.* p. 96.

vol. i. *Grecian Temple and Ruins.* p. 191.

vol. i. *Front of a Grecian Temple.* p. 191.

vol. i. *Grecian War Galley.* p. 181.

vol. i. *Trojans Deceived by the Greeks.* p. 42.

vol. i *Ancient Grecian Building* p. 191.

vol. i. *Cecrops colonizing Greece.* p. 31.

vol. i. *Grecian Court—Areopagus.* p. 179

vol. i. *Grecian Sacrifices.* p. 181.

vol. i. *Ancient Athens.* p. 174.

vol. i. *Grecian Gymnasium.* p. 175

vol. i. *Achæan League.*

vol. ii. *Conversion of Constantine.* p. 52.

vol. ii. *Peter Preaching to the Crusaders.* p. 127.

vol. ii. *Taking of Constantinople by Mahomet.* p. 185.

Tower of London.

vol. ii. *Edward IV. and Queen Margaret.* p. 196.

vol. ii. *King Alfred in Disguise.* p. 113.

vol. ii. *Queen Elizabeth and her Army.* p. 203.

vol. ii. *Penn's Treaty.* p. 255

vol ii. *Convention at Philadelphia*, 1787. Per. X.

vol. ii. *Massacre at Fort Griswold.* Per. X.

vol. ii. *Death of Montgomery.* Per. X.

Cape Town—Cape of Good Hope.

Siberian mode of Travelling.

Lapland Traveller.

Ladies and Gentlemen of South America.

South American Indians

Hottentots.

North American Indians.

Scots.

Danes.

South American Gentleman.

Cossacks.

Austrians.

Swedes.

Swiss.

Asiatics.

Italians.

Egyptian Peasants.

Circassians.

Ancient Greeks.

Dutch.

French.

Japanese.

Greeks.

Turks.

Tartars.

Arabians.

Gypsies.

Nootkaians.

Society Islanders.

Sandwich Islanders.

vol. i. *Jupiter*. p. 182.

vol. i. *Apollo*. p. 182.

vol. i. *Mars*. p. 182.

vol. i. *Mercury*. p. 182.

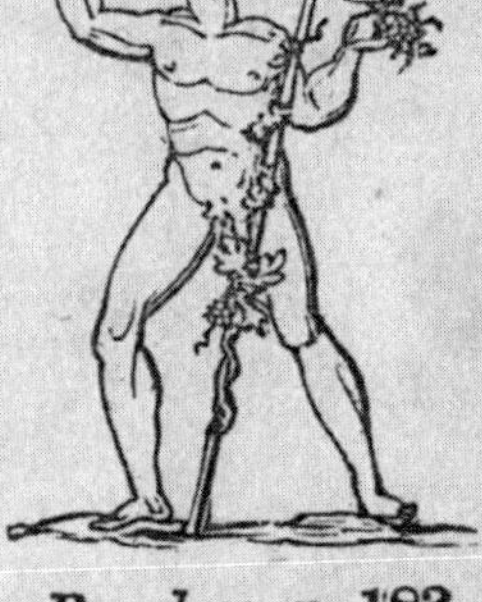

vol. i. *Bacchus*. p. 183.

ILLUSTRATIONS OF THE WORLD DISPLAYED.

vol. i. *Vulcan.* p. 183.

vol. i. *Minerva.* p. 183.

vol. i. *Juno.* p. 183.

vol. i. *Venus.* p. 183.

vol. i. *Diana.* p. 184.

ILLUSTRATIONS OF THE WORLD DISPLAYED

vol. i. *Ceres.* p. 184.

vol. i. *Vesta.* p. 184.

vol. i. *Neptune.* p. 184.

vol. i. *Oceanus.* p. 184.

vol. i. *Triton.* p. 184,

vol. i. *Pluto*. p. 185.

vol. i. *Furies*. p. 185.

vol. i. *Charon*. p. 185.

vol. i. *Fates*. p. 185.

vol. i. *Cupid*. p. 185.

v. i. *Graces* 186

ILLUSTRATIONS OF THE WORLD DISPLAYED.

*Caliope.**

*Clio.**

*Erato.**

*Euterpe.**

*Melpomene.**

*Polyhymnia.**

*Terpsichore.**

*Urania.**

*Thalia.**

* See Vol. i. p. 186.

ILLUSTRATIONS OF THE WORLD DISPLAYED.

vol. i. *Cæsar Passing the Rubicon.* p. 135.

vol. ii. *Crowning of Charlemagne.* p. 99

vol. i. *Combat between Horatii and Curiatii.* p. 59.